Using OS/2® 2.1

Special Edition

BARRY NANCE

with

GREG CHICARES
CAROLINE M. HALLIDAY
SUE PLUMLEY

Screen reproductions in this book were created with Collage Plus from Inner Media, Inc., Hollis, NH.

Publisher: Lloyd J. Short

Associate Publisher: Rick Ranucci

Operations Manager: Sheila Cunningham

Publishing Plan Manager: Thomas H. Bennett

Acquisitions Editor: Chris Katsaropoulos

Marketing Manager: Ray Robinson

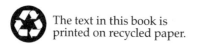

The text in this book is printed on recycled paper.

We dedicate this book to the talented, hard-working team of people who make OS/2 2.1 a better DOS than DOS, a better Windows than Windows, and a better OS/2 than ever before.

CREDITS

Title Manager
Walter R. Bruce, III

Product Development Specialist
Timothy S. Stanley

Production Editor
Colleen Totz

Editors
Tracy Barr
Elsa M. Bell
Barb Colter
Jane A. Cramer
Susan M. Dunn
Lorna Gentry
Lori A. Lyons
J. Christopher Nelson
Heather Northrup

Technical Editors
Todd Brown
Russ Jacobs
David M. Medinets

Book Designer
Scott Cook

Production Team
Claudia Bell
Julie Brown
Paula Carroll
Laurie Casey
Brook Farling
Heather Kaufman
Bob LaRoche
Jay Lesandrini
Caroline Roop
Linda Seifert
Johnna VanHoose
Phil Worthington

Composed in *Cheltenham* and *MCPdigital* by Que Corporation

ABOUT THE AUTHORS

Barry Nance, a columnist for *BYTE* Magazine and a programmer for the past 20 years, is the author of *Network Programming In C* and *Introduction to Networking*. Barry is the Exchange Editor for the IBM Exchange on BIX, where you can reach him as "barryn."

Greg Chicares is a Fellow of the Society of Actuaries and an avid user of personal computers. Greg is an officer of a major insurance company, where he manages a group of people who develop new life insurance products. You can reach Greg on BIX as "gchicares."

Caroline M. Halliday is an electrical engineer with High Tech Aid, a Pittsburgh-area company specializing in technical documentation and training for the PC environment. She is also the author of *The First Book of AutoCAD*.

Sue Plumley, an account representative for ComputerLand of Beckley, is the author of Que's *Look Your Best with Word for Windows*, *Look Your Best with Ami Pro*, and contributing author to *Using Ami Pro*, Special Edition. She specializes in desktop publishing.

We thank the people at IBM who helped make the writing of this book possible. In particular, we thank John Tiede, Irv Spalten, Jeff Cohen, Dave Reich, Steve Mastrianni, and John O'Hara for their assistance. We also thank Glen Horton for his timely and excellent technical editing and for his assistance in capturing screen shots in Collage Plus.

Trademarks

All terms mentioned in this book that are known to be trademarks or service marks have been appropriately capitalized. Que cannot attest to the accuracy of this information. Use of a term in this book should not be regarded as affecting the validity of any trademark or service mark.

CONTENTS AT A GLANCE

VI Using the Command Reference

TABLE OF CONTENTS

I Introducing OS/2

II Installing and Configuring OS/2

III Using the Graphical Interface

IV Learning the Basic Features of OS/2

14 Using the OS/2 Text Editors 335

V Exploring OS/2's Advanced Features

Introduction

Not long ago, Lee Reiswig of IBM said that OS/2 2.0 is "a better DOS than DOS, a better Windows than Windows, and a better version than Version 1.3." He described OS/2 2.0 with these words at the June 1991 PC Expo trade show at the Jacob Javits Convention Center in New York. Demonstrating some of OS/2's capabilities, Reiswig showed DOS, DOS with Windows, and OS/2 1.3 in side-by-side comparisons. He impressed the audience with the speed and versatility of OS/2 2.0 by using it to run several different DOS, Windows, and OS/2 applications simultaneously. Although the operating system was still being developed and tested during the summer of 1991, IBM had finished enough of the product to excite people with its capabilities.

Reiswig pointed out that OS/2 2.0 is the highest quality operating system that IBM has ever produced. He defined quality not only in terms of zero defects, but also in terms of the degree to which OS/2 2.0 reacts to user commands by doing what the user wants, even though the user may have given OS/2 a command that, technically, is invalid within a given OS/2 mode or context. If you inadvertently run a DOS application at an OS/2 command line prompt, for example, OS/2 starts a new DOS session for you, automatically.

That was then...this is now. OS/2 2.1 gives you even more as an operating system—for example, Windows 3.1 compatibility. You can run a Windows 3.1 application from OS/2 2.1 just as though you were running Windows 3.1. Additionally, OS/2 2.1 adds increased hardware compatibility, including support for high-resolution video displays.

OS/2 is an outgrowth of IBM's PC DOS and Microsoft's MS-DOS operating systems, that frees you from most of the constraints that DOS imposes. The most significant of these constraints is the amount of computer memory (RAM) available to the applications you run on your computer. OS/2 2.1 gives you more memory to run DOS applications, Windows applications, and OS/2 applications.

OS/2 is not an extension of DOS; however, OS/2 is a completely new operating system. From version 1.0 through version 2.1, OS/2 has been designed to support sophisticated business applications with its high performance features and its consistent, easy-to-use interface. Version 2.1 exploits your PC's hardware to give you multiple simultaneous DOS sessions, Windows sessions, and OS/2 sessions.

As you work your way through this book, you will see that OS/2 2.1 offers you a wide array of features, including the following:

- System Integrity for Applications

- Virtual memory

- Preemptive multitasking and task scheduling

- Fast, 32-bit architecture

- Overlapped, fast disk file access

- DOS compatibility

- More available memory for DOS applications (typically about 620K of conventional memory)

- Capability to run OS/2, DOS, and Windows software concurrently and seamlessly

- Multiple concurrent DOS sessions

- High Performance File System (HPFS)

- Presentation Manager (PM) graphical user interface

- The object-oriented Workplace Shell (WPS)

- National Language Support (NLS)

- Boot Manager

- Small, easy-to-use applications (*applets*) bundled with OS/2, such as notepad, diary, spreadsheet, presentation graphics software, and other productivity tools

- Interactive on-line documentation and help screens

- Capability to run OS/2 on both IBM and IBM-compatible hardware

The Purpose of This Book

If some of the terms in the preceding list confuse you or seem foreign, take heart. *Using OS/2 2.1*, Special Edition will quickly bring you up to speed with OS/2 and help you get the most from the program. This book will help you understand OS/2, guide you in learning to use OS/2, and serve as a reference when you need to look up commands or intricate procedures.

Who Should Read This Book

This book assumes little or nothing about your previous computer experience and knowledge. You will find the book useful whether you are new to OS/2 or just want a handy OS/2 reference. If you have DOS experience, you will be interested in Chapter 3, "Learning OS/2 If You Know DOS," which compares OS/2 with DOS and shows you the relationship between the two operating system environments. If you're not a DOS veteran, Chapter 2, "Learning OS/2 If You Don't Know DOS," is a friendly introduction that will help you learn how your computer can be a useful, productive tool in your work.

What You Need To Use This Book

The first few chapters use illustrations to help you visualize and understand OS/2 and your computer. Chapters 4 and 5, "Deciding How You Want To Use OS/2" and "Using Non-IBM Computers and OS/2," get you involved with your computer system, but don't assume that you have installed OS/2. From Chapter 6, "Installing OS/2," through Chapter 24, "Networking with OS/2," you should have both your computer system and your OS/2 Version 2.1 system disks handy so that you can give yourself on-the-job experience with OS/2 2.1.

The Details of This Book

The first five parts of this book explain how to use OS/2 2.1 effectively. Part VI is a Command Reference you can turn to when you need to know the exact usage of an OS/2 command. The appendixes contain infrequently used but still important information about OS/2.

Part I: Introducing OS/2

Part I is an introductory tutorial that helps you clearly understand what your computer and OS/2 can do for you. As you learn IBM's latest operating system, you will begin to think of your computer as a more useful tool. And you will quickly gain self-confidence as you discover exactly how to use that tool.

Chapter 1, "Taking a Quick Tour of OS/2 and Your Computer," starts you on the road to OS/2 expertise by examining your computer and its components and showing you how they work together. The chapter also shows you what OS/2 looks like and what it can do for you.

Chapter 2, "Learning OS/2 If You Don't Know DOS," introduces you to your personal computer. If you're a first-time computer user, Chapter 2 gently but thoroughly acquaints you with the fundamentals of both DOS and OS/2.

Chapter 3, "Learning OS/2 If You Know DOS," describes the differences between DOS and OS/2. If you're one of the 60 million DOS users in the world, you will quickly see the relationship between OS/2 and its predecessor. You will discover the extra things you can do with OS/2 that you cannot do with DOS, such as running several large applications at one time and easily copying data from one application to another.

Part II: Installing and Configuring OS/2

Part II helps you install OS/2 on your computer so that you can begin using the program immediately. In Part II, you learn how to consider carefully the many configuration settings and options you need to select, how to install OS/2 on your computer, how to change your configuration, and—should it become necessary—how to make corrections to your OS/2 configuration when errors occur.

Chapter 4, "Deciding How You Want To Use OS/2," describes the options available under OS/2 so that you can decide which ones to choose during installation. For example, the chapter explains the pros and cons of installing the games, tools, and utilities that accompany OS/2.

Chapter 5, "Using Non-IBM Computers and OS/2," is for you if you use IBM-compatible hardware. If your computer system is non-IBM, or if you have a non-IBM mouse device or monitor, Chapter 5 shows you how to make OS/2 work on your hardware.

Chapter 6, "Installing OS/2," quickly gets you up and running with OS/2 by leading you carefully through the installation process.

Chapter 7, "Modifying Your OS/2 Configuration," tells you how to modify your computer's configuration safely, should it become necessary.

Chapter 8, "Troubleshooting OS/2," helps you identify and quickly fix OS/2 configuration problems.

Part III: Using the Graphical Interface

Part III helps you through the new language of icons, action bars, and dialog boxes. In this chapter, you learn how the mouse, keyboard, and screen work together. You learn about the object-oriented nature of the Workplace Shell and how to make Presentation Manager and the Workplace Shell work for you. In addition to the chapters in Part III, you will find a quick reference guide for Workplace Shell operations on the inside front cover of this book.

Chapter 9, "Using Your Computer Screen as a Desktop," brings you the latest terminology of graphical user interfaces (GUIs). Icons, action bars, pushbuttons, and dialog boxes will become second nature to you.

Chapter 10, "Managing the Workplace Shell," gives you an understanding of the techniques you need to customize the Workplace Shell.

Part IV: Learning the Basic Features of OS/2

You earn your OS/2 wings in Part IV as you explore the full utility of the operating system. You gain practical experience with useful commands, the OS/2 on-line help facility, the OS/2 Enhanced Editor, printing, and DOS/Windows sessions.

Chapter 11, "Using the Drives Object," shows you how you can manage disk drives by using the Drives object. You learn about how the Drives object displays information and how to change the way that you view files. You also learn to manage files, format disks, and associate files with application programs.

Chapter 12, "Learning the Commands You Use Most Often," explains the OS/2 commands that you will use every day to accomplish your work. You will not always be able to use Presentation Manager's graphical interface to give directions to OS/2. When you're faced with OS/2's command line prompt, however, you will know what to do.

Chapter 13, "Using the Built-In Help Facility," helps you access, manage, and understand the wealth of on-line help that OS/2 offers. From how to ask for help at a command line prompt to how to get instant help for a menu option, Chapter 13 reveals the many sources of help you have at your fingertips.

Chapter 14, "Using the OS/2 Text Editors," describes the text editing tools supplied with OS/2 2.1—the System Editor and the Enhanced Editor. You first master the basics of creating and changing text files. Next you learn how to perform operations such as cutting, copying, and pasting. Chapter 14 also leads you through setting tab stops, setting margins and text fonts, and editing multiple files at the same time.

Chapter 15, "Printing with OS/2," ensures that your printed reports, documents, letters, memos, and charts come out looking the way you want, when you want. You learn when to tell OS/2 to recover from printer problems (such as paper jams) and how to set up your computer to print several different kinds of forms.

Chapter 16, "Running DOS and Windows under OS/2," helps you run your DOS applications easily and productively under OS/2. You will gain insight into the OS/2 options that control your DOS sessions and learn what you can and cannot do in an OS/2-controlled DOS session.

Chapter 17, "Configuring Your DOS and Windows Sessions," shows you how to change global DOS settings by using CONFIG.SYS commands to get more memory and more speed and how to fix common problems. You also learn how to modify the global settings to effect individual DOS sessions.

Chapter 18, "Batch File Programming with OS/2," discusses the power and flexibility you can gain by using batch files. The chapter discusses the difference between OS/2 and DOS batch files and lists the batch commands that you can use. Chapter 18 also describes how you can use the batch commands to automate many tasks that you would otherwise perform manually.

Part V: Exploring OS/2's Advanced Features

OS/2 is more that just an operating system that controls a single computer. The system comes with several applications that you can use to increase your work productivity immediately. In addition, you can use your OS/2 computer and connect to other computers to share and use information not found on your computer. Part V walks you through using OS/2's productivity applets and shows you how to access information on other computers.

Chapter 19, "Using OS/2 Utilities," provides you with information for using advanced OS/2 utility programs. These utilities help you customize, manage, and maneuver when you're working in the operating system. Some of these utilities aid in gathering information; others help correct system problems.

Chapter 20, "Using the OS/2 Time Management Applets," teaches you to use the personal information applets that come with OS/2. Specifically, you learn about the Activities List, Alarms, the Calendar, the Daily and Monthly Planners, and the To-Do List.

Chapter 21, "Using the OS/2 General Purpose Applets," introduces you to nine of the OS/2 applets that give you varied capabilities. These applets are the Calculator, the Clipboard Viewer, the Icon Editor, the Notepad, Pulse, Seek and Scan Files, Sticky Pad, Time, and Tune Editor.

Chapter 22, "Using the OS/2 Data Management Applets," shows you how to use four useful productivity applications. You learn how to manage information using Database, create charts with PM Chart, connect to other computers using a modem with PM Terminal, and create ledger sheets (including calculations) with Spreadsheet.

Chapter 23, "Understanding Extended Services," introduces you to the powerful capability of accessing information on larger mainframe computers. You learn to connect to these computers by using the Communications Manager and to access database information with the Database Manager.

Chapter 24, "Networking with OS/2," describes how to use OS/2 on a local area network. Specifically addressed are NetWare networks and Microsoft LAN Manager networks. Mentioned also in this chapter are LANtastic, POWERLan and Banyan VINES networks.

Part VI: Using the Command Reference

Part VI is a comprehensive Command Reference you can use to look up specific OS/2 commands. OS/2 has three categories of commands: commands you give at a command-line prompt, commands you put into batch files, and commands you use to configure the system. Part VI groups the OS/2 commands by category and shows them alphabetically within each group. You will also find an alphabetical listing of all the commands on the inside back cover of this book, as well as a Workplace Shell Quick Reference on the inside front cover.

Each reference entry describes the command in detail and shows its exact syntax. (*Syntax* means the precise form that the wording of a command must be given so that the computer can recognize and process the command correctly.) You will find practical examples of each command in Part VI, along with notes that tell you when to use the command, cautions you should observe, and advice on how best to use the command. Each entry prominently identifies the command as belonging to OS/2, DOS, or both environments.

Appendixes

The Appendixes provide less frequently needed but still essential information about OS/2. Most notably, Appendix G, "Programming with REXX," includes information for using the powerful REXX programming language. Of additional interest are two keyboard guides, information about games that come with OS/2, and a listing of OS/2 files by function.

Conventions

To make the information as clear to you as possible, this book follows certain conventions. File names and OS/2 commands appear in capital letters, for example, (you can type them in either capital or lowercase letters). When a keyboard key has a special name, such as PgUp or F1, the name appears exactly that way in the text. When you are instructed to choose a menu command, the shortcut key is underscored (for example, File).

Words or phrases defined for the first time appear in *italics*. Words or phrases you are to type appear in **boldface** or indented on a separate line. All on-screen messages use a special typeface.

To understand an OS/2 command fully, you need to know what to type verbatim from the book (fixed, constant words and phrases) and what to type based on your knowledge of what you intend the command to accomplish (variable, fill-in words and phrases). This book shows commands in the following manner (syntax):

> **CHKDSK filename.ext** */switches*

In this example, the variable, fill-in items (filename.ext) appear in boldface, the command itself (CHKDSK) appears in bold uppercase letters, and the optional switch appears in italics. To use the CHKDSK command, you type **CHKDSK** and follow it with information you supply, such as the name of a file or so-called command switches to tell CHKDSK exactly what you want it to do. Not all parts of a syntax entry are essential; optional elements appear in italics.

The new world of OS/2 2.1 awaits your pleasure. To get started, just turn the page.

Introducing OS/2

Taking a Quick Tour of OS/2 and Your Computer

I n the office today, personal computers are as common as telephones, fax machines, and copy machines. You can now begin to treat a personal computer just about the same way you treat your automobile. You start it up, navigate your way to your destination, and shut it off when you are done. Of course, a computer can do quite a bit more than a car. A computer is a multipurpose tool, with each application helping you to do a different kind of job.

You take for granted that cars have steering wheels, brake pedals, turn signals, and speedometers, usually located in the same place in all cars. Until OS/2 came along, personal computers didn't have this sort of consistency. The keyboard may have looked the same, but the information presented to you on-screen was nearly always different for each job you wanted to do. You had to learn how to use a spreadsheet application all over again or start learning over again how to use a word processor. If you needed to use a communications program, you had to return to square one.

OS/2 Presentation Manager brings consistency to your personal computer. Figuratively speaking, when you learn where the steering wheel, brake pedal, turn signals, and speedometer are located for one type of OS/2 application, you learn them for all OS/2 applications. OS/2 Presentation Manager's interface is easy to learn; Part III of this book, "Using the Graphical Interface," helps you become an expert.

Examining Presentation Manager

New versions of computer applications do not appear overnight, so there will be a transition period while non-Presentation Manager (inconsistent-interface) applications coexist on your computer with the newer, consistent-interface PM applications. (You will often see the abbreviation PM for Presentation Manager in this book and in other OS/2-related documentation.) OS/2 2.1 supports these non-PM applications at the same time it supports PM applications. In fact, OS/2 2.1 enables you to run several kinds of applications at the same time, on the same personal computer.

PM is a part of OS/2. Along with a set of standards and guidelines that IBM developed, called *System Applications Architecture (SAA)*, PM is the foundation for the kind of consistent interface in your personal computer that you expect from the car you drive. For you, the computer user, PM is the most important part of the operating system. OS/2 has other features in addition to PM, however.

If you have used Microsoft Windows before, you have experienced the *Common User Access (CUA)* interface, which complies with SAA. PM and Windows look very much alike and you manipulate them in much the same ways. Versions 3.0 and 3.1 of Windows have been around for well over a year, which means that software companies have had time to develop several applications for Windows. OS/2 supports Windows applications as well as PM applications.

During the transition period mentioned earlier, you still need to run non-PM, non-Windows applications. These software tools are the ones you would have run under plain DOS. For a while, you may even find that the majority of the applications you use are DOS applications.

OS/2 supports these applications the same way DOS does, but OS/2 gives DOS applications more memory in which to run than DOS does. This feature is why you will want to use OS/2 2.1 now, even if you don't have any PM applications yet.

In this chapter, you take a guided tour of OS/2 2.1 and your computer. If you have used a computer before, some of the material may be familiar to you. If so, skim through the hardware descriptions until you get to the section on software, where the discussion turns to OS/2.

You don't have to turn your computer on to take the tour; you can see the sights just by studying the illustrations.

For Related Information

▶▶ "Understanding CUA Principles," p. 216.

▶▶ "Introducing Presentation Manager," p. 221.

FROM HERE...

Understanding Hardware and Software

Hardware is easy to define. If you can touch it, it's hardware. Software is trickier; it exists as magnetic recordings on disks or other media. Like an audio recording on a cassette tape that you play back with your tape deck, or a video recording on a videocassette that you play back with your VCR, software comes alive when you "play it back" with your personal computer.

> **WARNING:** Software is subject to accidental erasure, just like other types of magnetic recordings.

Unlike these recordings, however, software is interactive. You give information to the software application, tell the software to store the information for later use, and instruct the software to collate, process, select, calculate, and print the information. With the computer hardware and software, you can do your work more quickly and accurately than you could by hand.

Examining Hardware Components

Figure 1.1 shows the hardware components of a typical computer system. The computer in the illustration may be a little different from yours, but you can easily spot the essential components (the keyboard, the monitor, and the system unit) and relate them to your own computer's appearance. With many computer systems sold today, the mouse also has become an essential component.

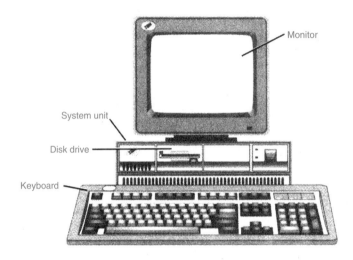

Monitor

System unit

Disk drive

Keyboard

Fig. 1.1

Typical computer hardware components.

Using the Keyboard, Mouse, and Monitor

The keyboard and the mouse enable you to enter information into the computer and tell the computer what to do with that information. The monitor (the screen display) shows the results.

Using the Keyboard

Figure 1.2 shows the common 101-key IBM keyboard, sometimes called the Enhanced Keyboard. The original IBM AT computer came with an 83-key keyboard that had the function keys on the left of the keyboard instead of at the top. For several years, however, IBM and makers of compatible keyboards have offered the 101-key keyboard as standard equipment for desktop computers. Laptop computers use a smaller keyboard with fewer keys, which means that you sometimes have to press two keys together to get the effect of a single key on the larger keyboard. The principles are the same for all keyboards, however.

You use the center section just like a typewriter. The numeric keypad has two modes, which can be switched with the Num Lock key. The keypad behaves like the buttons on an adding machine when Num Lock is on, and like cursor control keys when Num Lock is off.

Besides those keys in the typewriter and adding machine sections, special computer keys tell the computer what actions you want it to take. For example, you often use the PgUp and PgDn (page up and page down) keys to tell the computer to show you the previous or the next screen. If the application software has no previous or next screen to show you, the PgUp and PgDn keys do nothing.

PgUp and PgDn are not difficult to decipher, but what about the keys labeled F1 through F12? Or the Home and End keys? Table 1.1 lists these keys and their usual meanings.

Table 1.1 Special Keys on the Computer Keyboard

Key	Usual meaning
Enter	Tells the computer to perform the command you have typed, presses the highlighted button on-screen, or ends a line of text that you have entered into a word processor (similar to the function of the carriage return key on the electric typewriter).
Cursor keys	The up-, down-, left-, and right-arrow keys move the text cursor on-screen, but do not move the mouse cursor (the section on computer screens explains cursors).
PgUp/PgDn	Shows the previous screen or the next screen.
Home/End	Moves the cursor in one big jump to the left side of the screen or to the right.
Backspace	Moves the cursor to the left one character and deletes that character.

continues

Table 1.1 Continued

Key	Usual meaning
Ins/Del	Inserts characters at the current text cursor location, or deletes characters.
Ctrl	A modifier key, like Shift, Control changes the meaning of another key pressed in combination with Ctrl.
Alt	Another modifier key; also used to activate menus in Presentation Manager applications.
Esc	Escapes from (abandons) the current operation and returns to a prior level.
Num Lock	Toggles the numeric keypad from adding-machine mode to cursor-control mode.
PrtSc	In non-PM applications, sends the current screen to the printer. Sometimes labeled Print Screen.
Scroll Lock	Tells the cursor control arrows to scroll the on-screen information instead of just moving the cursor.
Pause	Suspends display output until another key is pressed; the 83-key keyboard assigns this function to Ctrl-Scroll Lock.
Ctrl-Break	Stops the currently running program.
F1-F12	Function keys whose meaning depends on the currently running application. The 83-key keyboard lacks the last two function keys, F11 and F12.

Using the Mouse

Figure 1.3 shows two of the many types of mice available to PC users. A computer mouse is a pointing device. Some mice are optical, some are mechanical; some have one button (the Macintosh mouse); others have two or three buttons. Some kinds of pointing devices are called trackballs. Basically, all pointing devices enable you to move the cursor and manipulate items on-screen. To interact with many of the items shown on your computer screen, you roll the mouse on your desk or table, or you roll the ball in a trackball. Mice are generally optional. Except for applications that allow you to draw pictures on-screen, for example, most software products and Presentation Manager applications recognize certain keystroke combinations as equivalent to the common, standard mouse operations.

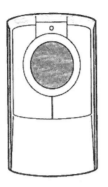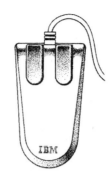

Fig. 1.3

The two-button mouse and the trackball are two types of mice available to PC users.

Using the Monitor

Your computer monitor, sometimes called the screen display, shows your work. More accurately and specifically, the screen shows the computer's response to your work. Many times, the screen also shows you options from which you can choose. Because the screen can sometimes look cluttered, you may find it difficult to understand what the screen is telling you. Later in this book, you learn to recognize the on-screen landmarks by which you can navigate.

What you see on the computer screen is placed there by OS/2, Presentation Manager, your application software, or a combination of all three. The distinction is important because when you want to look something up you need to know whether to refer to this book (for OS/2 and PM), or to the manuals that came with your application. Chapter 10, "Managing the Workplace Shell," explains how to distinguish between on-screen elements.

Figure 1.4 shows OS/2's Workplace Shell on a computer screen. This example may differ from the appearance of the Shell on your own screen. OS/2 offers many ways for you to customize the Workplace Shell to suit your personal preferences.

Most computer screens have two *modes*: text and graphics. In graphics mode, the mouse cursor typically is an arrow pointing to the left and upward, although the mouse cursor sometimes turns into a picture of a clock or perhaps an I-beam. You see *icons* (small pictures) that represent applications and other OS/2 tasks. The thin, blinking underline (sometimes a solid one-character-wide block) is the *text cursor*.

Text mode also shows the text cursor as a thin blinking underline or as a solid block. The mouse cursor in this mode, however, is optional and appears as a solid block (if you move the mouse, the mouse cursor moves). The software application determines whether the text mode mouse cursor shows. The text mode screen is 80 columns wide, usually 25 lines high, and takes up the entire display.

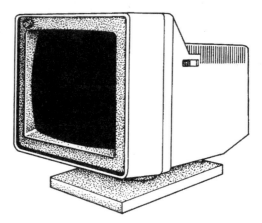

Fig. 1.4

A typical
computer
monitor.

OS/2 supports both modes, text and graphics, and can even display a text mode screen inside a graphics window. A *window* is a subsection of the display. A window has a rectangular border and functions like an entire screen, with the added benefit that you can move and resize the window to suit your own preferences.

Understanding Disks, Disk Files, and Disk Directories

The data you enter, the results, and the applications reside on disks, either *floppy disks* (removable) or *hard disks* (nonremovable). Figure 1.5 shows the two types of floppy disks, 5 1/4-inch and 3 1/2-inch. The *hard disk* is a sealed unit, usually hidden inside your computer, although some hard disks are removable. When you turn the power off or if you suffer a power failure, the data you have stored on a hard disk remains on that disk for future use. If you entered data into the computer but have not yet saved the data on disk at the time the power fails, the data is lost and you must reenter it later.

Using Disks

Floppy disks are sometimes called floppies or microfloppy disks. Hard disks are sometimes called fixed disks. Hard disks rotate whenever the computer is on; floppy disks rotate only when they are being accessed. In either case, a red (or perhaps orange) light on the front of your computer indicates when the disks are in use. The light on the disk drive indicates when the drive is busy; the light on the main computer indicates when the hard disk is busy. When one of these lights comes on, the computer is reading or writing data.

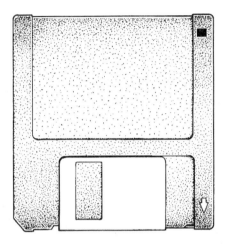

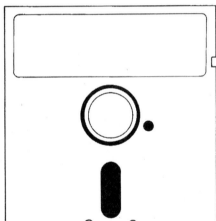

Fig. 1.5

The 3 1/2-inch and 5 1/4-inch floppy disks.

WARNING: Do not remove a floppy disk from the disk drive when the disk drive light is on. You may damage the data on the floppy disk because OS/2 must also make a record of where the data can be found. Imagine adding a book to a library's collection but not making an entry in the card catalog. When you need the book (or your data) later, you cannot locate it.

Using Disk Files

To put the application software and data on disks, you copy files or you instruct an application to store (or save) your data into a file. A *file* is a single stream of data that you refer to by name; it is a named collection of information. One file might contain a single memo, letter, or spreadsheet. Figure 1.6 shows the magnetic tracks and sectors on the disk that store saved files. If you are familiar with audio cassette tapes that have songs on both sides, think of a file as one song; the number of songs the tape can hold depends on the length of the songs and the space of the tape. Like cassette tapes, disks have varying capacities.

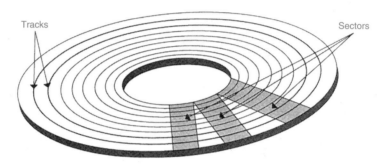

Fig. 1.6

The magnetic tracks and sectors on the disk that store saved files.

5 1/4-inch disks come in 360K (kilobyte) and 1.2M (megabyte) capacities. 3 1/2-inch disks come in 720K, 1.44M, and the relatively new 2.8M capacities. A *kilobyte* is equal to 1,024 characters; a megabyte is equal to 1,024 kilobytes. OS/2 provides tools you can use to monitor disk usage so that you know how much room you have left on your hard disk, for example, or how many files you can fit on a 40M hard disk. Make sure that you use disks of the proper size and capacity in your computer. Check your computer manual to find out the specifications of your disk drive(s).

Using Disk Directories

How do you organize files if you have hundreds (or thousands) of them? Chapter 2, "Learning OS/2 If You Don't Know DOS," explains *disk directories* in detail. Basically, you use directories to organize a disk into an outline structure. A directory can contain other directories as well as files. The structure of the directories (the outline) is up to you, so plan your organization thoughtfully. Directories are a wonderful convenience but can sometimes cause confusion. OS/2 provides tools for finding misplaced files.

Using Printers

Printers seem simple—blank paper goes in one side and the printed result comes out the other side. Printers are almost as complicated internally as the computer to which you connect them, however. A laser printer, for example, works much like a photocopy machine and contains a variety of fonts (typefaces) you can use to make your print-outs look their best. Figure 1.7 shows a typical laser printer connected to its computer. Dot-matrix printers, which work by striking an inked ribbon with tiny pins, are also common.

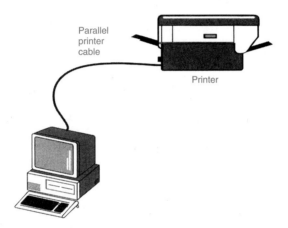

Parallel printer cable

Printer

Fig. 1.7

A typical laser printer connected to its computer.

Laser, dot-matrix, and other types of printers connect to your computer through a serial interface (requiring a serial cable), a parallel interface (requiring a parallel cable), or perhaps through a local area network (LAN) cable. In this last case, several people share the same printer. Each type of interface has a device name and number. Serial cables connect to COM1, COM2, COM3, or COM4 (your computer may not have all four of these devices). Parallel cables connect to LPT1, LPT2, or LPT3. When you tell an application to print something, you specify the device name and number for your printer. On a network, for example, you still print to LPT1, but the LAN redirects your print material to the shared printer. The parallel interface is the most common type.

The care and feeding of a printer requires some work on your part. You need to buy the correct size and weight paper for your printer. You need to regularly change the ribbon or toner cartridge, and you need to clean the printer periodically. You also may need to purchase fonts and memory cards (printed circuit boards). Study the owner's manual to learn the sophisticated things your printer can do.

Using Fonts

Several companies sell add-in fonts for laser printers. These fonts come as cartridges you insert into the printer, or as disk files. You store the fonts on the disk files in your computer and download the contents into the printer. If you need numerous fonts, you may have to buy extra memory for your printer (each font is a different size and takes up space inside the printer). In general, whether the font is built into the printer, on a cartridge, or downloaded, you select fonts with instructions you give your application software.

Learning More about Printing Text and Graphics

The following table lists some other characteristics of printers you should know about. Check your printer manual to see whether your printer supports or uses any of the features described in the table.

Feature	Function
Graphics	Makes charts, pictures, digitized photographs, and other images.
Landscape	Sometimes called sideways printing, prints the page with the long edge at the bottom, instead of upright.
Duplexing	Prints on both sides of the page.
Postscript	A special language of page layout and drawing commands, developed by Adobe Systems, Inc.
PCL	Another printer control language. PCL is used mainly in Hewlett-Packard printers.

So far in this chapter, you have absorbed a considerable amount of information about your computer hardware. Next, the tour of your computer and OS/2 turns to the topic of software.

Understanding Software Components

As mentioned earlier, software is more intangible than hardware, but you cannot use your computer system without it. (Some people colorfully describe a computer without software as a big, expensive paperweight.) Software exists as disk files. Sophisticated software products comprise many disk files—sometimes several disks' worth. Some of the disk files that make up a software product contain computer programs that give the computer instructions on what to place on-screen, what data to accept, and how to process the data. Other files contain information to which the computer programs need to refer when you interact with the programs and process your data.

You usually install software on your system by running a special computer program that copies the product's disk files to your hard disk. Simple software products may just ask you to use OS/2 commands copy the disk files, however. These commands are explained later in this book.

Running a computer program is easy. If you (or the installation program) added a program to the Workplace Shell desktop, you double-click the program's icon with your mouse. If you are using the keyboard, you use the cursor control keys to highlight the item and press Enter. If you have not added the program item to the Workplace Shell desktop, you run the program by typing its name at a command line prompt. (More on Workplace Shell and command line prompts in a moment.)

OS/2 is a type of software product known as an operating system. Utilities and applications are the other two types of software.

Learning Operating Systems

An *operating system* is the first software to run on your computer when you turn it on. An operating system loads itself into your computer "by its bootstraps" (hence the term "booting" to describe the power-on sequence). An operating system can display a set of icons from which you can choose applications or utilities that you want to run, or the system can display a command line prompt (such as C:\>) and await your commands. OS/2 provides both icons and command line prompts.

Any operating system, OS/2 included, provides services to utilities and applications while they run. The best example is file access. When a computer program needs the contents of a particular disk file, it asks OS/2 to open the file, read the data, and close the file. The computer program does not need to know where on the disk the file is physically located; OS/2 manages the disk at that level of detail.

OS/2 is full-featured; it provides an easy-to-use *graphical user interface*, command line prompts, and a rich set of services to utility and application software as well as some utilities and small applications. You sometimes see the latter identified as *applets*.

Examining Presentation Manager and the Workplace Shell

Presentation Manager is the component of OS/2 that manages the computer display and provides screen-related services to utilities and applications. The Workplace Shell uses PM to enable you to select icons to run programs.

Figure 1.8 shows a Workplace Shell screen. Notice the icons at the top of the screen; they represent OS/2 programs and folders. The DOS Window is active and appears in the middle of the screen. If you use either the mouse or the keyboard to select one of the icons, the Workplace Shell uses OS/2's internal services to run the computer program represented by that menu item. In fact, figure 1.8 shows the result of choosing DOS Window.

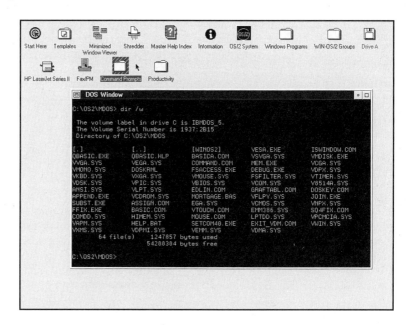

Fig. 1.8

A Presentation Manager screen, showing the Workplace Shell, several icons, and an active DOS session.

Using DOS and OS/2 Sessions

Figure 1.9 goes beyond the previous screen in several ways. First, two DOS Windows have been started and appear on-screen. One of them contains Lotus 1-2-3 and the other shows a C:\> prompt. The desktop icons remain on-screen in the background.

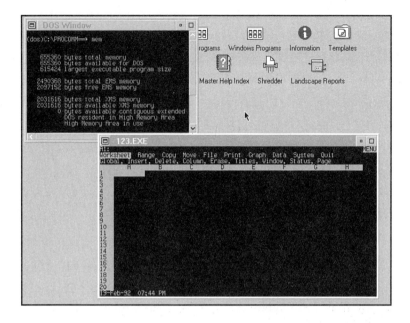

Fig. 1.9

Two DOS
Windows open
simultaneously
under OS/2 2.1.

When you tell the Workplace Shell to open a DOS Window, OS/2 creates
a Virtual DOS Machine (VDM) in your computer and shows the new
DOS session to you in a window on your computer screen. You can do
anything inside this window that you could have done with DOS 5.0
before OS/2 2.1. In addition, VDM has the following features, which DOS
did not support:

- You can open multiple DOS Windows on-screen at the same time.

- You can copy and paste from one screen to another.

- You can run graphics-mode programs inside the window.

- You get considerably more memory for your programs in DOS
  sessions.

- You can choose the font in which text appears in the window (this
  also determines the size of the window on-screen).

- You can run different versions of DOS in different windows.

When you choose DOS Full Screen in the Command Prompts folder,
which appears when you double-click the OS/2 System icon, OS/2 creates a new VDM for you. Rather than putting the DOS session in a window, however, OS/2 gives the session the entire screen with which to
work. You might choose DOS Full Screen for applications that do on-
screen graphics so that they work a bit faster, or you might prefer to
have the entire screen dedicated to a particular application.

You also can choose OS/2 Window and OS/2 Full Screen from the Command Prompts folder. These selections create special sessions inside your computer system, but the sessions are not VDMs and they are not running DOS. These sessions are for the OS/2 applications you run. You might run Microsoft Word in an OS/2 Window, for example, while you are running Borland's Paradox in a DOS Window. And yes, you can perform copy-and-paste operations between DOS and OS/2 Windows.

Figure 1.10 shows a Microsoft Windows application, Word for Windows, running under Microsoft Windows, which is running under OS/2. You probably will run Microsoft Windows full-screen to enhance performance, but the figure illustrates that OS/2 is capable of running Windows on the OS/2 desktop. Microsoft Windows becomes just another DOS task for OS/2 to manage.

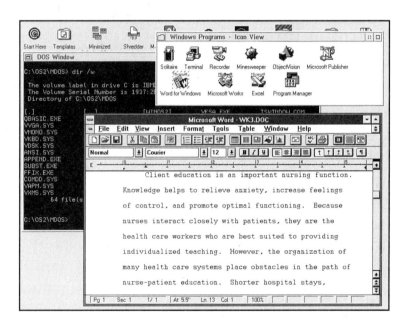

Fig. 1.10

Word for Windows running under Microsoft Windows, which in turn is running under OS/2.

Learning Utility Programs

OS/2 includes several utility programs to make your life easier. Figure 1.11 shows the OS/2 Enhanced Editor (a text editor for changing the contents of text files) in the upper right window of the screen. The folder at the top of that window is the Productivity folder, from which the Enhanced Editor was started, and you can see that the editor's icon is highlighted to show that it is in use. Chapter 14, "Using the OS/2 Text Editors," discusses the Enhanced Editor and the System Editor.

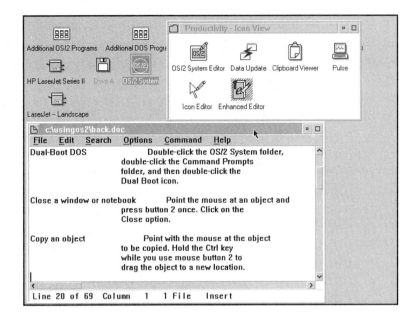

Fig. 1.11

The OS/2
Enhanced Editor.

Examining the Drives Object

The screen in figure 1.11 is cluttered. You can click the mouse to close some of those windows, and double-click the Drives icon in the OS/2 System folder to bring up the OS/2 Drives object. Clicking the Drive D icon gives you a screen similar to the one shown in figure 1.12.

As mentioned earlier in this chapter, disk directories are a method of organizing your files into an outline structure. The Drive object shows the tree structure of your directories in graphic detail. Files can be shown by name or represented as icons (refer to fig. 1.12). You can use the Drives object to create or remove directories as well as to copy files from one disk to another.

Learning the System Setup Utility

Figure 1.13 shows the result of closing the Drive D window and then starting the System Setup utility in the OS/2 System folder. System Setup is your tool for changing many of your OS/2 configuration options. You can adjust the cursor blink rate and the mouse double-click rate here (not everyone presses the mouse buttons in exactly the same way). You also can use System Setup to install fonts (recall the discussion of downloadable printer fonts earlier in this chapter) or to tell OS/2 you added a printer to your system.

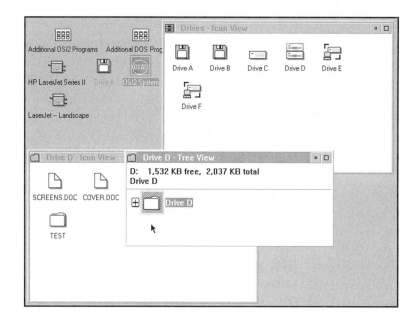

Fig. 1.12

Using the
OS/2 2.1
Drives Object to
examine Drive D.

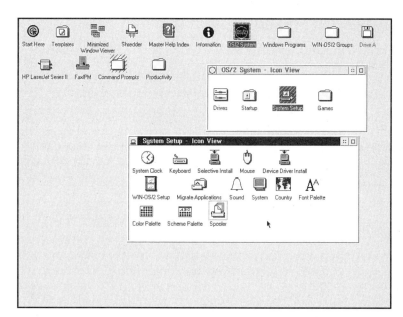

Fig. 1.13

The OS/2 2.1
System Setup
utility.

Using the Printer Object

If you can run multiple applications at the same time under OS/2, what happens if all those applications try to use the printer at once? The Printer object solves this problem by putting each printout (a print job, in Printer object terms) into a queue and printing each assignment one after the other. In figure 1.14, the Printer object window, in the lower half of the screen, shows the print queues and any pending print jobs. The details for one print job appear across the window. Chapter 15, "Printing with OS/2," gives you the information you need to use Printer objects effectively.

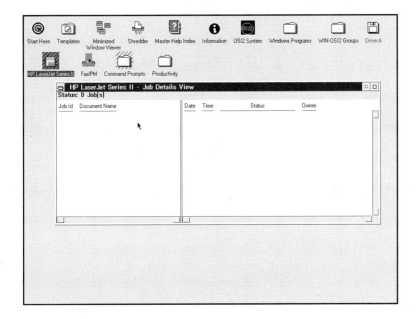

Fig. 1.14

Using the OS/2 2.1 Printer Object.

Using the Help Facility

OS/2 has basically two types of on-line help. At a command line prompt, you can type **HELP command name** to get a brief display of information about a particular command (but you will not get help if you type **HELP ME**). You access the other type of help by choosing the Master Help Index or Information icons on the desktop. Figure 1.15 shows a screen of information you can obtain from the OS/2 Command Reference, which is inside the Information folder. Notice that the mouse cursor points to a highlighted box (containing OS/2*) on-screen. The box is a *hot link*; clicking it provides more information on the highlighted subject. Chapter 13, "Using the Built-In Help Facility," discusses OS/2's on-line help, including concepts such as hot links.

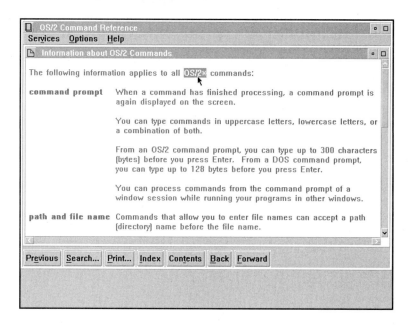

Fig. 1.15

The OS/2
Command
Reference.

Learning the Workplace Shell

With its consistent, graphics-based user interface, Presentation Manager makes your computer much easier to use than DOS did. OS/2 goes a step beyond PM, though, by offering the Workplace Shell. The Workplace Shell carries the desktop metaphor farther than PM, enabling you to organize your documents, reports, memos, spreadsheets, charts, lists, and tables as objects that you file in folders. When you double-click a folder, you see the folder open on-screen. If you click a memo in the folder, for example, OS/2 runs whatever application you use to edit your memos, and your memo appears on-screen, ready for editing. If you want to print your memo, you can use the mouse to drag the memo object to a picture of a printer on-screen. When you drop the memo onto the printer icon, OS/2 prints the memo. Chapter 10, "Managing the Workplace Shell," describes this object-oriented interface in more detail.

Examining Application Software

Your tour of OS/2 and your computer ends with a look at a popular
personal computer application—1-2-3 for OS/2, from Lotus Development Corporation. Formerly called 1-2-3/G, this Presentation Manager
application uses several features of OS/2 to transcend the limitations of
earlier DOS-based versions of 1-2-3. In particular, you can create much
larger worksheets with the OS/2 version of 1-2-3. Figure 1.16 shows
what 1-2-3 for OS/2 looks like. Notice the CUA-compliant pull-down
menu interface, the different fonts, and the other PM characteristics.
Above the application's window, you see the normal Workplace Shell
desktop icons.

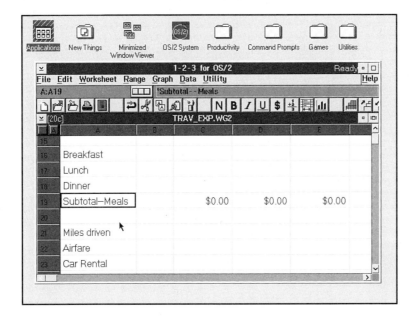

Fig. 1.16

A typical OS/2
application: Lotus
1-2-3 for OS/2.

For Related Information

▶▶ "Working with IBM-Compatible Computers," p. 102.

▶▶ "Using the Workplace Shell," p. 218.

▶▶ "Introducing Presentation Manager," p. 221.

▶▶ "Working with Program Objects," p. 232.

FROM HERE...

Chapter Summary

You have just ended your tour of OS/2 and your computer. Later chapters of this book go into detail to explain the features and operations of OS/2 2.1 that you saw briefly in this chapter. Your tour covered hardware such as the computer keyboard, mouse, and monitor. The chapter also covered software, including disks, files, and directories. Printers, printer fonts, and printer connections were briefly explained as well. Finally, the chapter introduced OS/2 basics, such as the definition of an operating system, Presentation Manager, Microsoft Windows, full-screen and windowed OS/2 sessions and DOS sessions; OS/2 utilities such as File Manager, Control Panel, Print Manager, and the Help facility; the Workplace Shell; and a typical OS/2 application software product.

OS/2 and DOS are somewhat alike. Especially at a command line prompt, many OS/2 commands function much the same way as their DOS counterparts. If you have not used DOS before, however, you need to become familiar with it.

In Chapter 2, you learn about DOS—what it is, how to start it, and how to use it. If you already feel comfortable using DOS, you can move on to Chapter 3, which explains the differences between DOS and OS/2.

Learning OS/2 If You Don't Know DOS

C hapter 1 was a whirlwind tour of OS/2 and your computer. If you have used DOS before, you should feel free to move on to Chapter 3, "Learning OS/2 If You Know DOS." If you're new to computers and want a little hand-holding to help you get your bearings, however, this chapter is for you.

The first thing you learn in this chapter is what makes up an operating system. Next, you learn how to start (and restart) your operating system. After you know how to get your computer system up and running, you find out why it's difficult for you to hurt the computer. You learn how to prevent your work from being lost, as well as techniques that make the computer a compliant and useful tool.

You then move on to practical topics, including how the operating system manages hard disks, hard disk partitions, and floppy disks. After exploring files, file names, and directories, you learn how to format disks and copy files.

Understanding Operating Systems

OS/2 is an operating system, like DOS, UNIX, and MVS. An operating system consists of one or more computer programs. These programs are the first software to run inside your computer when you turn it on, and they display a set of icons or a command line prompt so that you can run applications (programs) and type commands. You saw some OS/2 icons illustrated in Chapter 1, "Taking a Quick Tour of OS/2 and Your Computer." A command line prompt looks like the following:

```
C:\>
```

An application performs the work that you tell it to do. The application also uses the operating system to read and write information from and to disks, display information on-screen, find out what you are doing with the mouse, and obtain directions and information from you when you use the keyboard.

The following sections describe OS/2 and operating systems in general, but some operating systems don't have all the features discussed. DOS cannot support many new applications and cannot run more than one application at a time, for example.

Supporting Your Applications

When you choose a menu item or type the name of a computer program at a command line prompt, the operating system starts the software (which might very well be an application you want to use). The computer program is a stream of recorded data that rotates on your disk. The stream of data has a name; you typed this name to tell the operating system which computer program to launch.

The operating system copies the computer program into internal memory from the disk and allows the program to have control of the computer. (Internal memory, which also records information like a disk does, is made of silicon chips and does not rotate; its recorded information disappears when the computer is turned off.) Every few thousandths of a second, the operating system regains control of the computer to see if other applications, previously preempted, want to have control of the computer. This round-robin scheduling of multiple computer programs is called *multitasking*.

Not only does the operating system decide which application controls the computer next, but it also offers services to those applications. If this seems contradictory, consider this example: your telephone can ring and interrupt you as you work, but at another time it can be used to make a phone call. An operating system that features preemptive multitasking is like a smart telephone—the system can call applications to wake them up, putting others on hold for a moment, and it can answer calls from applications that need its services.

Your applications use operating system services to perform the following functions:

- Open, read, write, and close files

- Create, remove, and use directories

- Use the computer's internal calendar and clock

- Display information on-screen

- Read the keyboard

- Send information to a printer

- Send and receive information to and from a modem

- Locate the mouse and detect which mouse buttons you have pressed

If the operating system did not provide these services to the applications, they would have to provide their own services. This situation would lead to inconsistency and perhaps incompatibility among the applications.

Supporting Your Work

An operating system supports you at the same time that it supports the applications you run. To manage your computer system, you must do several tasks. Most of these tasks cannot be handled by your applications. The most important of these tasks is making backup copies of your data. Other tasks you need to do include the following:

- Occasionally restoring your data from your backup copies

- Formatting disks

- Copying files that you need to share with others (or that others want to share with you)

- Editing system configuration text files

- Viewing system help files

■ Removing old files and directories

■ Customizing your computer system

■ Finding misplaced files and directories

■ Installing new applications

■ Installing a new printer or new fonts

An operating system may help you do these jobs by enabling you to choose icons on-screen and pick tasks from menus, or it may expect you to type commands. (OS/2 has all these kinds of interfaces.) Step by step, this book helps you do all these tasks.

For Related Information

▶▶ "Understanding Application and General System Options," p. 84.

FROM HERE...

Starting the Operating System

You can start or restart the operating system in one of three ways: using the power switch, pressing the Ctrl-Alt-Del keys simultaneously (called a *warm boot*), or running a utility program called BOOT.COM.

Understanding the Power-On Sequence

When you apply power to your computer by turning on the power switch, the computer checks itself in a process known as the *Power-On Self Test* (POST). The POST makes sure that the CPU is okay; that the internal memory chips are in good health; and that the keyboard, mouse, hard disk, and other components are responding. After the computer system passes these tests, it checks your hard disk for an operating system to load and run.

The operating system ensures that it is the first software to run on your computer by inserting, at installation time, special computer instructions onto the *boot sector*, a special location of your hard disk. The computer instructions in the boot sector load the remainder of the operating system and give control to the just-loaded operating system. The operating system then displays a menu of available tasks or a command line prompt at which you type commands.

If the computer is already running, you can reload the operating system from the keyboard or run a utility that reboots (restarts) the computer.

Before you reboot the computer, make sure that you save the information you're working on. Otherwise, you have to redo your work. Also, you might want to close and exit from all your applications before performing a reboot. Using the power switch to reboot the computer is a bad idea, as you see later in this section.

If you have installed OS/2's Boot Manager, you see an optional screen display at boot time. This screen allows you to choose which operating system you want to use next. You probably will not use Boot Manager, which is covered in detail in Chapter 7, "Modifying Your OS/2 Configuration." Boot Manager is intended for use on computers that have both OS/2 and UNIX.

Dual-Boot is another OS/2 option for starting your computer system with a different operating system. You can alternate between booting DOS and booting OS/2 with the Dual-Boot option. Chapter 16, "Running DOS and Windows under OS/2," discusses Dual-Boot in detail.

Don't worry about Boot Manager or Dual-Boot yet. You now know these options exist, and that is enough for now.

Stopping the Computer

Incidentally, OS/2 provides a menu option for shutting down (stopping) your computer system. You should form the habit of using the menu option before you turn off your computer. You learn more about OS/2's menu options in Chapter 10, "Managing the Workplace Shell." If you need to use this feature before you get to Chapter 10, however, the procedure is as follows: click the right mouse button on any vacant part of the Workplace Shell desktop. From the pop-up menu, choose the Shutdown option and wait for the message that tells you it is safe to turn the power off.

Restarting from the Keyboard

To reboot your computer system, simultaneously press the following three keys on the keyboard: Ctrl, Alt, and Del. Your computer system restarts.

If pressing these keys doesn't work the first time, try them again—you may have a sticky keyboard. After a few tries, however, you may discover that your computer has locked up. When that happens, you may want to reach for the power switch. Before you do, though, use this hint to tell whether the computer is responding to the keyboard: press the Caps Lock key (located above the numeric keypad on the enhanced keyboard). Check to see whether the green light on the keyboard labeled Caps Lock goes on or off. If pressing Caps Lock has no effect on the green light, your computer has locked up and you must use the power switch.

Restarting Using the Power Switch

Using the power switch is the most obvious way to restart your computer, but it is also the worst way for the following reasons:

- Any work you have in progress is not saved when you turn the power off.

- Even if you do not have any work in progress, the computer may not have finished storing (recording) the information on the surface of the disk.

- The electrical surges during power-on and power-off strain your computer; the hardware lasts longer if you infrequently use the power switch.

Use the system shutdown option mentioned earlier ensure that the computer has finished storing information on the surface of the disk.

Some experienced computer users would have you believe that understanding hard disks, floppy disks, files, directories, formatting, and copying is all you need to know about DOS or OS/2. This is not the whole truth. If you have watched an expert use a computer, you probably had the feeling that the person had more skills and knowledge than you would find in an encyclopedia of operating system commands and concepts. You were right, and you are about to acquire those skills and that knowledge in the following sections.

FROM HERE...

For Related Information

▶▶ "Using the Workplace Shell's System Menu," p. 247.

Hurting the Computer or Losing Your Work

The previous discussion on starting and stopping your computer system may have given you the idea that your computer system is fragile and that you should give up before you begin. Not so. You *do* need to observe some cautions when shutting down your system, but shutting down is an action you probably take only once a day. You can form good habits for doing it properly.

You cannot physically hurt your computer system with software or by giving wrong directions to your application software. The worst things that can happen are as follows:

Problem	Likely cause(s)
Frozen system	The programmer made a mistake, or perhaps your computer needs repair.
Wrong results	The programmer made a mistake, or perhaps you entered the wrong data.
Acts funny	The programmer made a mistake, the keyboard/mouse/monitor connections are loose, or perhaps your computer needs repair.

The most common cause for computer error is programmer error (a *bug*). You learn to identify and solve computer system problems in more detail in Chapter 8, "Troubleshooting OS/2." In this chapter, however, the usual solutions to computer problems are to reenter the data, close and restart the application, or reboot the computer; which action you take depends on the nature of the problem.

Unfortunately, you can lose data. You might accidentally erase data, for example. You might save data and give it a name that is the same name you used for other data (thus replacing the old data with the new), or you might experience a computer failure and not have a copy of your work. In each case, the process of periodically and regularly making backup copies of your work would have saved you much grief.

Experimenting and Exploring

Power users is a term that describes computer experts. These people have two characteristics in common. They experiment and explore until they understand their computer systems thoroughly, and they use their computers a lot. You can do the same.

First, you need to set aside time to experiment with your computer. If you're naturally curious, you probaby tend to use spare moments to try out new techniques and methods. Encourage yourself to spend time with your computer.

Next, you need to find things to try, and you need to have data with which you can safely experiment. This book gives you many things to try; you can attempt these operations on data that you make up. In fact, you might want to set up "test cases" of data with which you can experiment. You may even want to have a disk directory titled TEST that contains files with pretend data on which you can try things out.

Knowing What Hurts the Computer

Compared with most electronic equipment, computers are fairly rugged—especially considering that computers contain mechanical parts such as rotating hard disks. You can find information in your computer's user manual on how to take care of your computer. In general, avoid moving your computer while it is on. Don't drop it. Don't spill things on it (particularly on the keyboard). If you plan to up-end your computer (relocating it from a horizontal desktop position to a desk-side, upright position or vice versa), you may need technical assistance in doing what is called a reformatting of your hard disk. Also, watch out for power surges (during thunderstorms, for example)—they can cause damage to your computer's electronic circuitry. You can buy surge protectors, or you can turn off your computer during a thunderstorm.

Note that many of these precautions are the same as the ones that apply to other electronic components you own.

Saving Your Data and Making Backups

As mentioned earlier, you should make frequent copies of your data in case something happens to your computer or the data on it. You can purchase several software utilities that help you back up and restore data—OS/2 supplies BACKUP and RESTORE utilities that do the job nicely if you don't mind working with floppy disks. If you have a lot of data, you may want to purchase a tape drive. If your computer is part of a local area network, however, you can copy your files to a file server and have your network administrator make backups.

If you make your own backup copies, you can choose one of three approaches depending on how often your data changes, how important your data is, and how much work you would have to do if you had to reenter it. The approaches are *occasional, serious,* and *professional* and are defined as follows:

■ *Occasional.* You may get by with occasionally copying individual files to one or more floppy disks. This approach is the least secure, but it is better than nothing. If you adopt this method, make sure you label your disks. Disorganization is your enemy with this approach. Another caution is this: If you have to restore a file, you may find that your backup copy is not as recent as you would like. When this happens, you have to redo any work you have done since the backup copy was made. You may even find that the disk containing the backup copy is damaged, and you have to re-create *all* of the data.

■ *Serious.* If you make backup copies regularly (perhaps more than once a day), if you use a backup utility such as OS/2's BACKUP.EXE, and if you use two sets of disks (or two tapes) to do your backups, you are in this category. You know exactly how much time has elapsed since your last backup copy was made, and you know exactly which disks to use if you need to restore a file.

■ *Professional.* Data centers with multimillion dollar mainframe computers use this method. You can, too. Essentially, you always have three copies of your data on three sets of disks (or tapes). To make your backup copies, you first identify each set of disks as A, B, and C. (For safety's sake, you should actually have two Asets, two B sets, and two C sets.) Rotate your use of the three sets of disks. If today's backup is labeled C, you should have yesterday's backup copies on B and the previous day's on A. Then, tomorrow, you use the A set to make your backup copies. You might even extend this approach to a fourth set of disks and make sure that the oldest copy is taken to a different location just in case something happens to the building in which your computer is located. (This backup method is sometimes known as the grandfather/father/son scheme.)

For Related Information

▶▶ "Preparing for Trouble," p. 192.

▶▶ "Learning the Commands To Back Up Your Hard Disk," p. 313.

FROM HERE...

Making the Computer Work for You

Make the computer work for you, not against you. This strategy is the key to getting your time and money's worth from your computer system. In this section—before the discussion turns to more practical topics such as disks, directories, and formatting disks—you investigate ways to think of the computer as a tool, similar to the way a carpenter thinks of his saw or hammer as a tool. You learn ways of being methodical in your work and methods for developing attitudes and work habits that make using your computer fun and productive.

Treating the Computer as a Tool

Longtime DOS users are familiar with their applications and know how to use those applications to get work done. They have a good idea of what software products are available and what products work with what; if they need application software to solve a problem or accomplish a task, DOS users know the cost of the software and can quickly determine whether getting the application software will save time and money. A carpenter or an auto mechanic treats his tools (and the hardware store) the same way. Armed with a little knowledge and the right attitude, you can treat your computer as a tool.

The first thing you need to learn is how to use your new operating system, and that is why you bought this book. Even after you read the narrative portions, keep this book handy so that you can refer to the "Command Reference," in Part VI, or perhaps reread the explanations of how the parts of OS/2 work. Similarly, keep the manuals that came with your computer, printer, and other equipment in a certain place so that you can refer to them occasionally.

Talk with other people to learn more about computers and application software. Almost everyone has a personal computer these days, and discussing them is fun. Computer-related topics are good conversation-starters, and your knowledge of computers increases when you hear how other people use them.

The best way to learn more about an application software product is to try it out. If you know someone who uses a product in which you are interested, ask the person to show you how it works. Computer people invariably like to show what they have done with their applications.

The weekly and monthly trade magazines are useful for keeping up-to-date on what hardware and software products are available, how good a product is, and how much it costs. Some of the more popular magazines are *PC Magazine*, *PC Week*, *InfoWorld*, *Computer Shopper*, and *BYTE Magazine*.

The best attitude to have toward computers is curiosity. You must take the time to understand how to make your computer do what you want. If you use a cookbook approach to run through a series of steps without understanding what each step does, you probably cannot put those steps into a different sequence to do a different job. On the other hand, if you use your natural curiosity to understand the steps, you can use those steps as building blocks to do many different things.

The next best attitude is patience—with yourself and your computer system. You can avoid a great deal of frustration by patiently analyzing your interactions with the computer. By having patience, you also obtain the best results.

Being Methodical

Computers are incredibly predictable (unless they need repair, which is rare). If you use the same sequence of steps to enter exactly the same information into two equivalent computers, using the same application software, both computers function the same and produce the same results.

By methodically analyzing how the computer responds to each step in the sequence, you can use this predictability to your advantage. The key is knowing and understanding the steps you use to reach a desired result and knowing that those steps always have a predictable outcome. The next time you need to do a similar task, you can use your prior experience with those steps to figure out what your computer system is telling you and how to make it do what you want. This approach is the opposite of the cookbook approach.

Being methodical can pay big dividends. The first time you try something new, pay careful attention to the effect of each step you take. Examine the text and the on-screen prompts closely. Try to avoid making assumptions.

You know what an operating system is, you know how to start and restart your computer, you understand the necessity of making backup copies, and you have set yourself on the road to becoming a computer expert—possibly even a power user. The preceding sections covered topics (and ingrained habits) that everyday computer users take for granted. Soon you will, too. Next, you explore the more practical side of operating systems and OS/2 in particular. You learn about disks, disk files, directories, formatting disks, and copying files.

FROM HERE...

For Related Information

▶▶ "Reflecting Personal Preferences," p. 94.

▶▶ "Knowing What Steps To Take," p. 203.

▶▶ "Manipulating Icons," p. 241.

▶▶ "Learning the Commands To Back Up Your Hard Disk," p. 313.

Understanding Disk Partitions and Disks

You learned about hard disks and floppy disks in Chapter 1, "Taking a Quick Tour of OS/2 and Your Computer." You know that both the information you enter and the calculated, processed results become streams of recorded data identified by name. Each single stream of named data—a memo, letter, or spreadsheet—is a *file*.

In the following sections, you learn what a disk partition is, how OS/2 and DOS organize disk partitions, how OS/2 and DOS store files in disk partitions, and how hard disks and floppy disks differ.

Allocating Disk Partitions

A hard disk in an IBM or IBM-compatible computer contains up to four disk partitions. DOS and OS/2 organize one or more of these partitions in a method that enables them to store files you save (*write*) and retrieve files you load (*read*). DOS and OS/2 organize by subdividing the partition into many small, numbered data blocks of fixed size. For each file, DOS or OS/2 maintains a table of which data blocks belong to which file. The operating system also keeps track of unoccupied blocks (disk free space).

You (or whoever sets up your computer) allocate the partitions of your hard disk to one or more operating systems you want to use. Most people give all their hard disk space to a single operating system, such as OS/2, in one partition. The OS/2 utility program for allocating these partitions is called FDISK; the DOS utility is also called FDISK. OS/2 supplies a Presentation Manager version of this utility called FDISKPM. You learn about FDISK later in this book.

After you allocate (or re-allocate) disk partitions, you then *format* the partition. You learn more about formatting later in this chapter. Periodically, in the ongoing maintenance of your system, you run the OS/2 utility CHKDSK (Check Disk) to ensure that OS/2 (or DOS) has fully allocated all the data blocks to files or has marked them as unoccupied.

In general, an operating system in one partition cannot see data stored in other partitions. The same operating system can use more than one partition, however, and may be able to use data in the partitions (if you allocate it that way). Because its compatibility with DOS, OS/2 can use the data on any DOS partition.

If you use multiple operating systems on your computer (UNIX and OS/2, for example), you might allocate partition 1 to the Multiple Operating System Tool utility mentioned earlier, Boot Manager. You then could allocate partition 2 to OS/2 and partition 3 to UNIX. At boot time, Boot Manager runs first and enables you to choose which of the other operating systems you want to run.

Even if you use only OS/2 (and the DOS sessions that OS/2 provides), you still must choose between two different file systems. DOS understands only a single kind of partition, called the *File Allocation Table* (FAT) file system. OS/2 understands FAT partitions and *High Performance File System* (HPFS) partitions. HPFS is faster than FAT.

Table 2.1 simplifies these rules.

Table 2.1 Partition Compatibilities

Operating system	Partition
DOS	Can use only FAT partitions
OS/2	Can use FAT or HPFS partitions
DOS under OS/2	Can use FAT or HPFS partitions
Boot Manager	Needs a small partition itself and can boot any one of the other partitions

Chapter 6, "Installing OS/2," provides more detail about disk partitions. If you use only OS/2 and the DOS sessions it provides, you don't have to worry a great deal about allocating your hard disk partitions; you should probably choose HPFS in this case. After you get your hard disk set up the way you want, you may never have to think about disk partitions again.

Working with Floppy Disks and Hard Disks

Floppy disks, which you learned about in Chapter 1, do not have disk partitions. Floppy disks *do* need to be formatted, however, before you can put files on them.

Each hard disk partition you allocate to OS/2 and each floppy disk drive installed in your computer has a *drive letter*. You use drive letters to identify on which disk a file is located. Your first floppy disk drive is drive A. Your second drive is B; but if you do not have a second floppy disk drive, drive B refers to the same drive as drive A. Your hard disk is drive C, and you can use other drive letters with your computer system, depending on the number of additional floppy disk drives and hard disk partitions you have.

FROM HERE...

For Related Information

▶▶ "Understanding the Drives Object Display," p. 259.

▶▶ "Learning the Commands for Managing Directories," p. 295.

Storing Files and File Names

When you save data on a hard disk or floppy disk, your application software (or the command you type) gives the data and the name of the data to OS/2 to store on the disk's surface. OS/2 records the data in one or more of the small data blocks mentioned previously, puts the name into a directory (a table of file names), and does the bookkeeping necessary to associate those particular data blocks with that named file. OS/2 also stores in the directory the date and time the file was modified and the file's exact size. OS/2 and DOS show a file's size as the number of characters (sometimes called *bytes*) in the file.

The process is analogous to filing documents in a folder and putting the folder into a file cabinet. Your disk is a file cabinet; a directory is a file folder in the file cabinet; and a file is one of the documents in the folder. The small, fixed-size data blocks are like the pages in a document: the larger the document, the more data blocks it needs.

In fact, the Workplace Shell, a part of OS/2, uses this analogy and displays file folders on-screen.

Identifying Your Files

A few applications assign file names, but most allow you to name your files the way you prefer. DOS and OS/2 impose a few restrictions on how you name your files.

Files in a FAT partition have two parts to their file names. The first part is called the *name* and the second part is called the *extension*. The name can be from one to eight characters long, and the extension, which is optional, can be up to three characters long. If an extension is used, a period separates the name and the extension, as shown in the following example:

MAY5MEMO.DOC

DOS and OS/2 consider the following characters legal in a file name or extension:

- The letters *A* through *Z* (DOS and OS/2 do not distinguish between upper- and lowercase letters, so you can use either.)

- The numbers *0* through *9*

- Special characters and punctuation marks, such as the following:

    $ # & @ ! ( ) - { } ' _ ~ ^ `

If you try to name a file by typing characters other than these, OS/2 displays an error message, and you have to retype the name.

In addition, certain names denote devices and cannot be used to identify disk files. If you try to use names that begin with COM1, COM2, COM3, COM4, LPT1, LPT2, LPT3, PRN, CON, or NUL to name disk files, you generally cause an error or obtain unexpected results. If you try to copy LISA_PT1.DOC to a file named LPT1.DOC, for example, the operating system sends the file to the printer (which is named LPT1).

To specify a particular file on a particular disk drive (floppy or hard), you type the drive letter, a colon, and the name of the file, as shown in the following example:

C:\MYFILE.DOC

Using File Names and Wild Cards

You also can specify which directory a file is in; a later section covers directories and directory names. Also, some commands and utilities can operate on more than one file at a time. To indicate a group of files, you can use the wild-card characters * (for any number of characters) and ? (for any single character). When you specify which files are in the group, you put one or both wild-card characters in the name. OS/2 finds the files that match the name you have typed. An asterisk matches any number of characters, and the question mark matches any single character. If you want to refer to the group of all files with the extension DOC, for example, type ***.DOC**.

Listing Your Files with DIR

The DIR command displays a list of files and, if you use command line prompts, is the command you are likely to use most frequently. DIR shows each file's name, extension, size, last-modified date, and last-modified time. You can use wild cards with DIR to list only certain files.

File names in an HPFS partition are less restrictive than in a FAT partition. The maximum number of characters in an HPFS name is 255, and the name can contain spaces (blanks) and multiple periods. Also, you can use upper- and lowercase letters in your HPFS file names. OS/2 displays the name exactly as you typed it, but otherwise does not distinguish between upper- and lowercase. The two file names in the following example specify the same file:

Memo.of.December 1st

memo.of.December 1ST

Working with Files

Two types of files exist on your hard disk after you install OS/2 and have used OS/2 for a while. The first type is executable computer software and has a file extension of EXE, COM, BAT, or CMD. Any other file extension denotes a nonexecutable data file. Some of these data files are part of OS/2, some are part of application software products you install, and others are files you create.

You can name your files anything you like, within the restrictions mentioned previously, but you probably want to use meaningful names that suggest the contents of the file. This practice helps jog your memory later when you need to remember the file name. (OS/2 supplies utilities you can use to locate a file if you do happen to forget its name.)

You certainly want to follow a file-naming convention that DOS users have found advantageous over the years. In essence, this convention uses the file extension to identify the type of the file. Table 2.2 lists commonly used file extensions and their customary uses.

Table 2.2 Common File Name Extensions

Extension	Common use
ARC	Archive (compressed file)
ASC	ASCII text file
ASM	Assembler source file
BAK	Backup file
BAS	BASIC program file
BAT	Batch file
BIN	Binary program file
BIO	System file
BMP	Font and picture file
C	C source file
CBL	COBOL source file
CFG, CNF	Program configuration information
CHP	Chapter file (Ventura Publisher)
CMD	Executable program file
COM	Executable program file
CPI	Code page information file (DOS)
DAT	Data file
DBF	Database file (dBASE)
DCP	System file
DCT	Dictionary file
DEV	Program device driver file
DIF	Data Interchange Format file
DLL	System file
DOC	Document (text) file
DRV	Program device driver file
DTA	Data file
EXE	Executable program file
FON	Font and picture file
FNT	Font file

continues

Table 2.2 Continued

Extension	Common use
IDX	Index file (Q&A)
IFS	System file
IMG	GEM image (graphics) file
INF	Help file
INI	System file
HLP	Help file
KEY	Keyboard macro file (ProKey)
LET	Letter
LST	Listing of a program (in a file)
LIB	Program library file
LOG	System file
MAC	Keyboard macro file (Superkey)
MAP	Linker map file
MSG	Program message file
NDX	Index file (dBASE)
OBJ	Intermediate object code (program) file
OLD	Backup file
OVL, OVR	Program overlay file
PAK	Packed (archive) file
PAS	Pascal source file
PCX	Picture file for PC Paintbrush
PIF	Program Information File (TopView/Windows)
PRO	Profile (configuration file)
PRN	Program listing for printing
PS, PSF	PostScript program file
RC	System file
RFT	Revisable Form Text (Document Content Architecture)

Extension	Common use
SAV	Backup file
SYS	System or device driver file
STY	Style sheet (Ventura Publisher; Microsoft Word)
TIF	Picture file in tag image format
TMP	Temporary file
TST	Test file
TXT	Text file
WK1	Worksheet file (1-2-3 Release 2)
WK3	Worksheet file (1-2-3 Release 3)
WQ1	Quattro spreadsheet file
WKS	Worksheet file (1-2-3 Release 1 and 1A)
ZIP	Compressed file (PKZIP)

For Related Information

▶▶ "Manipulating Files," p. 273.

▶▶ "Learning the Commands for Managing Files," p. 295.

FROM HERE...

Organizing Directories

As mentioned in Chapter 1, "Taking a Quick Tour of OS/2 and Your Computer," a disk directory can contain files, as well as other directories, in an overall outline structure. This structure helps you organize your files and your work. OS/2 creates a basic directory structure during the installation process; Figure 2.1 shows this initial structure for your hard disk. You see directories named SPOOL, OS2, and DESKTOP. The DESKTOP directory contains directories for the icons INFORMATION, TEMPLATES, and OS/2 SYSTEM. In this last directory, you see the icon representations for PRODUCTIVITY, GAMES, and COMMAND PROMPTS.

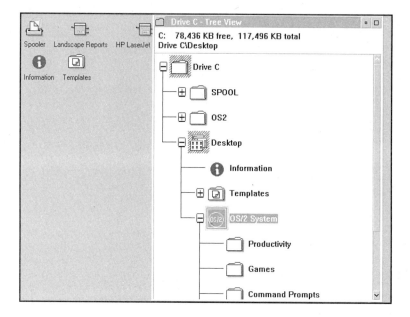

The directory structure created during the installation of OS/2, displayed by the Drives object.

You have at least one directory on every formatted disk, the *root directory*. A few operating system files exist in the root directory of your hard disk. You should create other named directories on your hard disk to hold your files (instead of putting them all in the root directory) so that you have little or no clutter in your root directory.

Organizing Files into an Outline

OS/2 creates an initial directory structure on your hard disk. Each application you later install may create one or more directories to hold its files. You create any other directories you need later by using either OS/2 commands or the icons in the Drives folder. Should you create only a few directories or several that are many layers deep? How should you name your directories?

You need to decide how to structure and name your directories. In general, you should think of the work you do in terms of an outline and create directories accordingly.

If you are a commercial loan officer at a bank, for example, you might create the following structure:

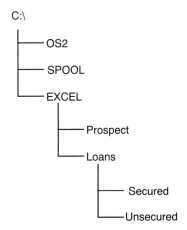

The first two directories—OS2 and SPOOL—were created by OS/2; The application Excel created the EXCEL directory during its installation.

Creating and Using Directories

You can create a directory whenever you want; you do not have to create directories all at once. You may prefer to use the icons in the Drives folder to create the directories, or you can use the OS/2 command MKDIR (or enter **MD**) at a command line prompt. To remove a directory, first delete the files and any subdirectories in the obsolete directory. (OS/2 warns you if the directory is not empty.) Then use the icons in the Drives folder or enter RMDIR (RD, for short) to remove the directory.

To specify a drive letter, directory structure (called a *path*), file name, and extension, you use the notation shown in the following example:

C:\LOANS\SECURED\EXXON.WK1

In this example, C is the drive letter, \LOANS\SECURED\ is the directory structure (path), EXXON is the file name, and .WK1 is the extension. OS/2 requires you to use the backslash character (\) to separate each of the directory names.

You use the drive letter, path, name, and extension to refer to a file that is not in the *current directory*. For a file in the current directory, you need to specify only the name and extension. At a command line prompt, you enter the CHDIR (or CD, for short) command to change directories. Many applications provide menus to enable you to change to a different directory without typing an OS/2 command.

FROM HERE...

For Related Information

▶▶ "Expanding and Collapsing a Directory List," p. 267.

▶▶ "Learning the Commands for Managing Directories," p. 295.

Formatting Hard Disks and Floppy Disks

As mentioned earlier, a hard disk partition or floppy disk must be formatted before you can store files on it. You probably can format your computer's hard disk only once—after allocating its partitions. Formatting erases existing information on the floppy disk or hard disk partition, so the FORMAT program asks you to confirm your actions. If you do not want to run the FORMAT program from a command line prompt, OS/2 supplies a Format Disk menu item you can choose.

You use the same FORMAT utility to format hard disks and floppy disks. Behind the scenes, however, OS/2 treats hard disks and floppy disks a little differently during the formatting process.

Formatting Hard Disks

You can instruct FORMAT to put either an HPFS or a FAT file system on a disk partition. Files in an HPFS partition can have long names, and applications generally access HPFS files faster than FAT files. You can use HPFS files with OS/2 applications and, if you do not use long names, with DOS applications you run in a DOS session under OS/2. HPFS files are invisible to DOS programs if you give them long names or if you boot your computer with DOS rather than OS/2.

For a hard disk, the FORMAT program creates the initial, empty root directory and checks the surface of the disk to make sure each of the data blocks can be read and written on. FORMAT marks questionable data blocks as unusable so that OS/2 does not later try to store your files in those blocks.

Formatting Floppy Disks

FORMAT creates the initial, empty root directory on floppy disks, as well. In addition, FORMAT actually electronically subdivides the disk surface into data blocks (manufacturers do this subdividing for hard disks at the factory). Finally, FORMAT checks the surface of the disk and marks defective blocks as unusable.

> If you keep a supply of formatted disks, you can avoid the annoyance of having to run the FORMAT utility just to copy a few files to give to someone.
>
> **T I P**

Knowing What Can Go Wrong

With early versions of DOS, reformatting your hard disk was an easy mistake to make. Early FORMAT programs did not have the built-in safeguards contained in the OS/2 FORMAT program. Even though FORMAT asks you twice for confirmation that you really want to format your hard disk, you may someday reformat by mistake. This accident is not likely, though. If you have recently backed up your hard disk, the mistake only costs you the time you must spend in copying the files back to your disk.

Hard and floppy disks have imperfections; FORMAT notices these defective spots and marks them accordingly. If FORMAT finds bad spots on a floppy disk, you may want to consider throwing it away (or sending it back, if the disk is under a warranty). Your data is worth much more than the cost of a disk. Because a hard disk has a greater capacity than a floppy disk, bad spots are not as significant. FORMAT and the CHKDSK utility tell you the number of bytes in bad *sectors* (data blocks). If the number is less than about 3 to 5 percent of the total disk capacity, you probably should not be concerned. A larger number may signify a malfunctioning disk or some other hardware problem.

For Related Information
▶▶ "Formatting and Copying Floppy Disks," p. 277.

FROM HERE...

Copying Disks and Files

You copy disks and files to share information with others, make backup copies of your application software and the work you do, and establish different versions of your work. In this last situation, you make a copy of a file that contains current information; run your application to update the copy with tentative, new information; and then later, may delete the older version if it does become out-of-date.

Copying Floppy Disks

The DISKCOPY command (or the Copy Disk item on the drive icon's menu) makes an exact copy of an entire floppy disk. Both the original and the copy must be the same type of disk. If the original holds 1.44 megabytes of data, the target disk also must be a 1.44 megabyte disk. DISKCOPY actually copies data blocks, not files. Copying a nearly empty disk takes the same amount of time copying a full disk takes.

The following example shows the syntax of the DISKCOPY command:

    DISKCOPY A: B:

This command tells OS/2 to copy the disk in drive A to the disk in drive B.

If you have only one floppy disk drive (A), you still give the same command. When OS/2 prompts you for the *source disk* (the original disk) and the *target disk* (the copy), you insert them into the same disk drive. OS/2 keeps track of which disk is which.

Copying Files

You can copy files by using the COPY command (which you type at a command prompt) or by using the Workplace Shell. With its menus and graphical representation of files, the Workplace Shell provides an easy way to copy files. You can use the mouse to identify which file you want (called *selecting* a file) and then drag its icon to another directory or disk drive.

The following example shows the most commonly used syntax for the COPY command:

    COPY C:\PROSPECT\ACME.DOC C:\LOANS\SECURED\ACME.DOC

This example shows how to copy the ACME.DOC file from the PROSPECT directory to the SECURED subdirectory in the LOANS directory.

The following command is a slightly more complex example that uses wild cards to copy more than one file:

COPY C:\PROSPECT*.DOC C:\LOANS\SECURED*.DOC

This second example of the COPY command shows how to copy all the PROSPECT directory files that have the .DOC extension to the LOANS\SECURED directory.

If the disk that is the target of the COPY command does not have enough room left (that is, enough unoccupied data blocks) to hold the target file, OS/2 displays an error message and stops the copy operation. You also see an error message if you try to copy a file to itself (the source and target are the same drive, same path, and same file name).

If you have only one disk drive, you can still copy files from disk to disk. You can copy the files to an empty directory on your hard disk, switch disks, and then copy the files to the target disk. Or you can use the A and B drive letters as if you did have two disk drives; OS/2 prompts you to insert the appropriate disk at the appropriate time.

For Related Information

▸▸ "Learning the Commands for Managing Files," p. 301.

FROM HERE...

Deleting, Renaming, and Moving Files

After you have used your computer for a while, it will seem like home to you. As a consequence, you may have to do some periodic housecleaning of your files. You can use commands or the Workplace Shell to tidy up your hard and floppy disks.

The ERASE (or DEL) command removes files. You can use wild cards to delete many files at once (be sure you know which files match your wild cards). If you tell OS/2 to delete all the files in a directory, OS/2 asks you if you are sure. The following is an example of the DEL command:

DEL *.TMP

This command deletes all the files with an extension of TMP in the current directory.

Renaming a file changes the file's name but otherwise leaves it intact. You cannot rename a file onto a different disk (use COPY instead). The following is an example of the RENAME (REN) command:

RENAME ACME.DOC ACME.OLD

Similarly, you can use the OS/2 MOVE command to move a file from one directory to another (but not to different disks). The following command moves the ACME.DOC file from the PROSPECT directory to the LOANS\SECURED directory:

MOVE C:\PROSPECT\ACME.DOC C:\LOANS\SECURED\ACME.DOC

FROM HERE...

For Related Information

▶▶ "Command Reference," p. 647.

Chapter Summary

If you have not used DOS before, you should feel a little more at ease after reading this chapter. The basic principles and operations of personal computers were covered. You learned what makes up an operating system, how to start DOS, what attitudes you need to use your computer productively, how to protect your work by making backup copies, how DOS treats hard and floppy disks, files, and directories, how to name files, how to format disks and copy files, and how to delete, rename, and move files.

The next chapter explains the differences between DOS and OS/2.

Learning OS/2 If You Know DOS

IBM describes OS/2 2.1 as "a better DOS than DOS." In this chapter, you explore how and why this statement is true. IBM further describes OS/2 as a "better Windows than Microsoft Windows." You also meet Microsoft Windows in this chapter.

OS/2 2.1 runs DOS applications compatibly, and it runs them in ways that DOS cannot. With OS/2, you can run multiple DOS applications at the same time, each in a window on-screen or in a full-screen session. Each application has more internal memory available to it under OS/2 than it had under DOS. You can start a specific version of DOS in a DOS session and manage that session separately from your other DOS sessions.

OS/2 utilizes the hardware features of the 80386 and 80486 Intel CPU chips to give you these advantages. The DOS inside OS/2 is a special DOS that uses the 32-bit architecture of these CPU chips, the overlapped input/output capabilities of OS/2, and the preemptive multitasking of OS/2. Your DOS applications run faster on OS/2 and have more internal memory available to them, but they assume that they are running on a regular version of DOS.

To run OS/2 2.1, you need a computer with an 80386 or 80486 CPU chip, a hard disk, a VGA- or XGA-compatible screen and video adapter, and at least 4M (megabytes) of internal memory. Although a mouse is optional, it is strongly recommended. (If you're familiar with Microsoft Windows, note that these are the same requirements for running Windows in Enhanced Mode.) You learn more about these hardware requirements in Chapter 5, "Using Non-IBM Computers and OS/2."

If you just finished Chapter 2, "Learning OS/2 If You Don't Know DOS," you looked briefly at DOS. If you have used DOS in the past, you probably skipped Chapter 2. Now you're ready to discover how OS/2 improves on DOS.

Matching OS/2 with DOS

OS/2 is like DOS in many ways. If you choose to use OS/2, its command line prompt looks like the one that DOS gives you. OS/2 uses many of the same commands as DOS, and OS/2 can use the same files as DOS if you follow certain rules—an important advantage. You can use OS/2 to just run DOS applications and still have many benefits beyond what DOS alone offers.

Comparing OS/2 and DOS Files

Disk files in a File Allocation Table (FAT) partition are completely compatible between DOS and OS/2. If you use the OS/2 System Editor to create a text file on a FAT disk drive, for example, you can boot DOS on your computer and use the DOS TYPE command to type the contents of the file on-screen. Both DOS and OS/2 treat FAT files exactly the same way. (Chapter 2 discussed File Allocation Table partitions.) OS/2 offers a High Performance File System (HPFS). The HPFS is somewhat compatible between DOS and OS/2, but only if you use the DOS built into OS/2 and then only if you follow certain rules. The "Looking at DOS and OS/2 Incompatibilities" section of this chapter covers these rules and restrictions fully.

Comparing OS/2 and DOS Commands

Most OS/2 commands are similar in appearance and function to their DOS counterparts. With OS/2, however, you can use Workplace Shell utilities to accomplish many of the administrative and maintenance tasks you need to do. But you will occasionally find that you have to start the OS/2 command processor, either full-screen or in a window (by using the Command Prompts icon in the OS/2 System folder). Chapter 12, "Learning the Commands You Use Most Often," and Part VI of this book, "Using the Command Reference," explain the OS/2 commands in detail.

The OS/2 installation process inserts PROMPT statements into your startup files (CONFIG.SYS for OS/2 and AUTOEXEC.BAT for DOS) to make OS/2 and DOS command line prompts look different, helping you to distinguish between the two prompts. By default, the OS/2 command line prompt looks like the following example:

    [C:\]

For DOS sessions under OS/2, the DOS command line prompt has the following appearance:

    C:\>

Both examples assume that the root directory is the current directory.

Commands that work the same in both environments include CLS, DATE, TIME, BACKUP, RESTORE, COPY, ERASE, PRINT, RENAME, TYPE, XCOPY, CHDIR (CD), MKDIR (MD), RMDIR (RD), and, except for HPFS files, the DIR command. If you have used these commands under DOS but without OS/2, you will be pleased to know that they operate the same way; these are the commands you use most often in a DOS or OS/2 environment.

Using DOS Applications under OS/2

The DOS inside OS/2 is highly compatible with DOS Version 5.0. This compatibility means that business-related and general purpose DOS applications run under OS/2 the same way they ran under DOS 5.0. Even most entertainment software products (games) run under OS/2. Disk utilities and disk diagnostics are one category of DOS-based software that does not run successfully under OS/2, however. The section of this chapter on DOS and OS/2 compatibility issues talks about this category of software.

For Related Information

▶▶ "Beginning the Command Line Interface," p. 293.

▶▶ "Understanding DOS Sessions," p. 386.

FROM HERE...

Understanding How OS/2 Expands upon DOS

OS/2 2.1 offers more than DOS compatibility, of course. By taking advantage of the features of the 80386 and 80486 CPU chips, OS/2 protects applications in different DOS sessions from crashing into one another (*system integrity protection*). Before OS/2, under plain DOS a bug (software error) in an application often meant that your computer would lock up or become unresponsive; you would have to use the power switch to reboot the computer. OS/2 catches these situations, ends the offending DOS session and its application, and enables you to continue your work without rebooting the computer.

OS/2 also implements a scheme of overlapped access to the hard disk (*overlapped I/O*), which enables applications to run faster. This same input/output scheme tries to anticipate what disk data your application will need next by reading ahead and putting the read-ahead data into a memory buffer. The scheme also performs *lazy writes* (if you have turned the option on). A lazy write puts the data onto the surface of the disk a few short milliseconds after an application has told OS/2 to write that data, allowing the application to continue processing in those short moments as if the data had actually been written. Lazy writes make your system more responsive, although they present a minor risk of data loss if power is interrupted before data is written.

OS/2 provides better support than DOS for different languages. Called *National Language Support (NLS)* you set this OS/2 attribute with a configuration option at installation time. The country and language you select determine the display format of such country-dependent items as time of day, calendar date, and currency amounts and symbols.

Chapter 2, "Learning OS/2 If You Don't Know DOS," discussed the Multiple Operating System Tool, Boot Manager, when it explained hard disk partitions. If you choose to install it, Boot Manager is an option that takes up a small disk partition of its own. When your computer boots, Boot Manager gets control first and allows you to select from OS/2, UNIX, or some other operating system. If you are upgrading your computer from UNIX-and-DOS to UNIX-and-OS/2, Boot Manager makes switching between operating systems easier.

Both DOS and OS/2 use a configuration file named CONFIG.SYS at boot time. CONFIG.SYS is a text file, which means that you can change it with a text editor (such as the OS/2 Enhanced Editor). The changes you make take effect the next time you boot your computer.

OS/2 expands upon DOS in several other ways, too. Your applications have more internal memory available to them when you run them in DOS sessions.

If you start one application that takes a long time to finish an operation (recalculating a spreadsheet, for example), you can start other applications in other sessions so that you can continue to be productive. Your DOS and OS/2 applications can share the printer without confusion about which printout is which. Your DOS, Microsoft Windows, and OS/2 applications can work alongside each other; you can often share information among your applications without having to retype it.

As you might expect, the list of OS/2 commands you can use is longer than the DOS list. Chapter 12, "Learning the Commands You Use Most Often," explains some of these commands, and the command reference in Part VI is a complete dictionary of OS/2 commands. Finally, the Workplace Shell and Presentation Manager are easy-to-use features of OS/2 that you do not find in DOS.

Providing More Memory for DOS Applications

PC users often hear and talk about the number *640 kilobytes* (or 640K). In a plain DOS environment, or DOS-and-Microsoft-Windows environment, the *real mode address space* (also called *conventional memory*) is a maximum of 1 megabyte of internal memory. Real mode address space is the space in which DOS applications run. After allowing for video adapter cards, network adapter cards, hard disk controller cards, and the so-called ROM BIOS, only 640 kilobytes are left.

DOS takes up part of the 640 kilobytes. Each statement in the CONFIG.SYS file causes more of the 640K to be taken up. Your DOS applications have to work in the remainder. On a local area network using plain DOS, you may only have 500K in which to run applications. If your computer is also connected to a host (mainframe) computer, the communications software occupies another portion of the 640K.

OS/2 gives you back some conventional memory in two ways. The memory used by CONFIG.SYS statements (your device drivers) comes from a separate memory area, not from the 640K. In addition, because you can have several DOS sessions under OS/2, you can put your host communications software in one session and run applications in a different DOS session. Each session starts out with 640K of available memory, and typically each has about 620K free for DOS applications to use.

Some DOS applications use *expanded memory* (often referred to as EMS memory). Expanded memory was invented by Lotus Development Corporation (developer of Lotus 1-2-3), Intel (inventor of the PC CPU chip), and Microsoft (maintainer of the DOS operating system); the standard for expanded memory is called the LIM 4.0 Specification. *LIM* comes from the initials of these companies.

Expanded memory was originally provided by special memory boards, but OS/2 provides expanded memory to your applications automatically, without the need for special boards. Each DOS session under OS/2 has a maximum of 512M of expanded memory for DOS applications. Before OS/2 2.1 and the use of the special memory boards, DOS applications could use a maximum of 32M of EMS. Microsoft Windows provided an EMS maximum equal to four times the physical memory in your system.

Extended memory is another type of memory that your applications may use. By supporting a specification known as the DOS Protected Mode Interface (DPMI), OS/2 makes 512M of extended memory available to DOS applications.

You probably have noticed that these memory amounts exceed the physical memory in your computer. Under plain DOS, both the 640K limit and the amount of physical EMS memory in your computer were "hard" boundaries, and you would see out-of-memory error messages when your applications reached a boundary. Under OS/2 and in DOS sessions under OS/2, your hard disk becomes an extension of the internal memory in your computer. OS/2 can overcommit memory by swapping internal memory to your hard disk and back again as necessary.

Your system may seem to run more slowly when applications begin to surpass your installed physical internal memory, but you still can finish your work. The file SWAPPER.DAT, which by default resides in the \OS2\SYSTEM directory, contains the overflow; the size of SWAPPER.DAT gives you a clue as to when you need to install more memory in your computer. SWAPPER.DAT starts out as a 512K file. As a rule of thumb, if it increases to 2M or more, you should consider installing more internal memory in your computer.

Not all DOS applications use expanded or extended memory. Check your software products to see if they can use the special types of memory that OS/2 provides.

Running Multiple DOS Applications

Chapter 1, "Taking a Quick Tour of OS/2 and Your Computer," mentioned that you can run several DOS applications at the same time. OS/2 creates a Virtual DOS Machine (VDM) for each application, with each VDM having about 620K of internal memory free to run programs. You might have a DOS word processor in one VDM, a communications program in a second VDM, and just a command line prompt in a third VDM so that you can easily enter DOS commands in that third session.

A DOS session under OS/2 can be full-screen or it can be windowed. In the case of a windowed DOS session, OS/2 displays the DOS command prompt or the textual output of an application in a font you choose. The size of the window depends on the font (smaller fonts cause smaller windows, which you may prefer).

OS/2 provides *clipboard services* you can use to copy information from one DOS session to another. With these services, you mark a region of one screen (OS/2 highlights that region), copy the information in that screen region to the clipboard, and then paste the information into another window.

Unless it is waiting for keyboard input, an application in a DOS session under OS/2 continues to process even while you use another application in a different DOS session. The system integrity protection afforded by OS/2, as mentioned earlier, does not allow one application in a session to lock up the computer and cause you to lose the work you have not yet saved. This feature is important when you have more than one application running at the same time.

The first question most people ask about running multiple applications is, why do it? The answer is productivity. You no longer have to wait for your computer to finish a long-running operation (printing a large report, transferring a large file in a communications session, or recalculating a large spreadsheet, for example). You can go on to other tasks after starting a long-running operation.

Getting More from OS/2 Applications

The DOS sessions and DOS compatibility provided by OS/2 2.1 are important because more than 20,000 DOS applications exist today. People rely on these applications to get their work done, but a DOS application can use no more than the 640K of memory when it is supported by DOS.

Applications written especially for OS/2 do not have this 640K memory limitation, and they can take advantage of other features of OS/2, such as the Presentation Manager interface. When they develop OS/2 applications, software developers have more operating system resources from which to draw. In general, an OS/2 application can be faster and can process more data than a similar DOS application. Some of the resources available to developers are rather complicated and technical, but you should understand two significant ones, *threads* and *32-bit architecture*.

■ *Threads*. Not only can you run several OS/2 applications at the same time on your computer, each application may in turn run portions of itself concurrently. Each portion is a thread. Applications use threads to perform long-running tasks that do not need your attention, and you see an enormously increased performance in such applications. You might instruct your word processor to save the current document, for example, so that you can go on to the next. If the application uses a thread to do the work of saving the current document, it can immediately begin processing your request to load the next document. The saving of the first document file occurs in the background.

■ *32-bit architecture*. OS/2 utilizes the 32-bit architecture of the 80386 and 80486 CPU chips, and applications can also take advantage of this architecture. Basically, these CPU chips have the capacity to process larger amounts of data at one time (the older 80286 CPU chip in the IBM AT could process only 16 bits at a time, while the original IBM PC, first released in September 1981, could process data only 8 bits at a time with its 8088 CPU chip). When software developers write computer programs based on the 32-bit architecture, the result is increased performance.

OS/2 applications can be text-based (as most DOS applications are), or they can be Presentation Manager-based. You can run text-based applications in an OS/2 window or full-screen. The user guide or manual that comes with your application tells you whether it uses Presentation Manager.

Printing from DOS and OS/2

Multiple concurrent applications need to share the printer; you don't want pages from a spreadsheet report mixed with pages from a word processing document. To keep printouts separate, OS/2 spools each one to the hard disk and then prints each as a separate print job. OS/2 comes with a Workplace Shell utility (called the *Printer object*) for managing these print jobs. Chapter 15, "Printing with OS/2," discusses this Presentation Manager utility in detail.

In Chapter 1, "Taking a Quick Tour of OS/2 and Your Computer," you read about printer fonts and how they should match the fonts you see on-screen. Presentation Manager contains services that applications use to put characters on-screen and on the printer, but the fonts themselves—their shape, size, and other attributes of their characters—come from both Presentation Manager and a product called Adobe Type Manager (ATM), licensed by IBM and included on your OS/2 disks. The computer industry recognizes Adobe and its ATM product as having the highest quality fonts for both print and display purposes.

Examining New and Changed Commands

Some commands that you type at an OS/2 command line prompt function slightly differently from the way their DOS counterparts do. In particular, the DIR command, which displays the names of the files in a directory, shows HPFS file names in a different format so that OS/2 can show you the long file names you can use in an HPFS partition. In a FAT partition, the OS/2 DIR command functions the same way it does under DOS.

Some of the commands that accept file name options (including the wild-card characters * and ?) can process multiple options under OS/2. The DIR command in an OS/2 session is the best example. You can type **DIR *.DOC *.TXT** to see a display of those files with either DOC or TXT as the file's extension.

The on-line HELP command, introduced by IBM in DOS 5.0, takes on an entirely new dimension under OS/2. When you type **HELP CHKDSK** at an OS/2 command line prompt, for example, OS/2 gives you information about the CHKDSK command (just as DOS 5.0 does). The information is provided by the OS/2 on-line command reference. This reference is a Presentation Manager utility that allows you to explore OS/2 concepts, commands, and options. Chapter 13, "Using the Built-In Help Facility," describes the on-line command reference in more detail.

You may be accustomed to using the ANSI.SYS device driver supplied with DOS. ANSI.SYS processes screen color change commands, cursor positioning commands, and clear-screen commands issued from within an application. Under OS/2, ANSI.SYS functions the same in DOS sessions as it always has. In OS/2 sessions, you have a new ANSI command you can use to turn the processing of these screen commands on or off. ANSI.SYS does not affect OS/2 sessions.

The CHKDSK command, under both DOS and OS/2, verifies that file storage and file allocation on your disk are correct. Each data block within the partition must be allocated to a file or marked as unoccupied (free), and no data block can be allocated to more than one file. For an HPFS partition under OS/2, CHKDSK also verifies the internal structure of the special list of physical location information for directories and files.

The following commands are unique to OS/2 or DOS sessions within OS/2. Part VI of this book, "Using the Command Reference," describes each command in detail. This list gives you an idea of the extra commands you can use in an OS/2 session.

Command	Description
AUTOFAIL	Specifies how you want "Abort, Retry, Ignore" situations processed.
BOOT	For Dual Boot, starts the other operating system.
CACHE	In CONFIG.SYS, specifies how you want HPFS managed.
DISKCACHE	In CONFIG.SYS, specifies how you want non-HPFS files managed.
CHCP	Change Code Page (NLS).
DPATH	In CONFIG.SYS, tells applications where to look for data files, such as the system message file.
IFS	In CONFIG.SYS, tells OS/2 to use an Installable File System (such as HPFS).
IOPL	In CONFIG.SYS, indicates whether you want applications to have I/O Privilege Level.
KEYS	In CONFIG.SYS, indicates whether you want OS/2 to keep a list of commands you have entered so that you can recall and reuse them later.
LIBPATH	In CONFIG.SYS, specifies where to find Dynamic Link Library (DLL) files.
MAXWAIT	In CONFIG.SYS, indicates the maximum number of seconds each application should have to wait before getting to use the CPU.
MEMMAN	In CONFIG.SYS, specifies how to manage memory swapping.
MOVE	Moves files from one directory to another on the same disk drive.
PAUSEONERROR	In CONFIG.SYS, specifies whether to pause when OS/2 detects errors in the CONFIG.SYS file.
PRIORITY	In CONFIG.SYS, specifies whether OS/2 can dynamically change application priorities to allow better access to the CPU.
PROTECTONLY	In CONFIG.SYS, specifies whether you want DOS sessions.

Command	Description
PROTSHELL	In CONFIG.SYS, specifies which command shell you want to use (Workplace Shell is common).
RMSIZE	In CONFIG.SYS, tells the memory size for each DOS session (maximum 640K).
RUN	In CONFIG.SYS, starts a program in the background at boot time.
SETBOOT	Tells Boot Manager your defaults for how you want to boot your computer.
SPOOL	Starts a Printer object; redirects print from one device to another.
SWAPPATH	Specifies where you want your SWAPPER.DAT file.
THREADS	In CONFIG.SYS, specifies the maximum number of threads OS/2 should allow.
TIMESLICE	In CONFIG.SYS, sets the minimum and maximum amounts of CPU time, in thousandths of a second, that OS/2 allots to each application and its threads.
VIEW	Interactively displays document files that have an INF extension.

The Workplace Shell and Presentation Manager

As you learn in Chapter 9, "Using Your Computer Screen as a Desktop," and Chapter 10, "Managing the Workplace Shell," Presentation Manager (PM) is OS/2's graphical interface, and the Workplace Shell uses PM to make your computer look and work like a desktop. You organize your desk by placing papers in folders; Workplace Shell enables you to group files in the same way. For example, a data file is represented by an icon, a small picture that looks like a piece of paper. You can use the mouse to pick up the icon and drop it into a folder to file the data file away. Or you can get a printed copy of the data file by dropping its icon onto a printer object—just like putting a real piece of paper into the office copier when you need a copy. To delete a file, you drop its icon onto a picture of a paper shredder.

In the Workplace Shell, everything appears as an object, just like the papers, folders, printer, and paper shredder in your office. You use all these objects in basically the same way; after you learn how to work with one object, using the others comes naturally. Even programs are objects, and the basic keystrokes, menus, and mouse actions you use to get your work done are the same for every PM program because the interface is consistent. Best of all, with the Workplace Shell you never need to type instructions at a command prompt because you can use the mouse to manipulate objects.

FROM HERE...

For Related Information

▶▶ "Using the Workplace Shell," p. 218.

▶▶ "Introducing Presentation Manager," p. 221.

▶▶ "Adding DOS Programs," p. 389.

▶▶ "Switching between OS/2 and DOS with Dual Boot," p. 397.

Using Microsoft Windows with OS/2

OS/2 has built-in support for both Windows 3.0 and Windows 3.1 applications. You don't have to buy a separate copy of Microsoft Windows just to run an application written for the Windows environment. Your Windows applications function the same under OS/2 as they would have functioned under Microsoft Windows. If you already have a copy of Microsoft Windows on your computer, you may want to consider removing Windows (but not your Windows applications) to save disk space.

Version 3 of Microsoft Windows operates in one of the following three modes, depending on how much internal memory you have and what type of CPU you have:

■ *Real Mode.* The operating mode that provides maximum compatibility with Version 2 of Microsoft Windows. Real mode is the only mode available if you have less than 1M of internal memory (RAM).

■ *Standard Mode.* This mode provides access to more internal memory; standard mode enables you to run multiple large Windows applications simultaneously.

■ *Enhanced Mode*. Takes advantage of the 80386 and 80486 Intel CPU chip's virtual memory capabilities, just as OS/2 does.

OS/2 runs Windows applications in either Standard Mode or Enhanced Mode.

For Related Information

▶▶ "Adding DOS Programs," p. 389.

FROM HERE...

Looking at DOS and OS/2 Incompatibilities

In general, OS/2 runs business-related DOS applications the same way plain DOS did. As mentioned earlier, however, one category of software presents a potential problem to OS/2's preservation of system integrity. This category consists of utilities that perform hard disk diagnostics, sort directory entries, and rearrange file physical location information to make each file contiguous ("defragment").

If you use DOS applications under OS/2 to access files in an HPFS partition, you need to be careful about your filenames; also, you cannot access HPFS files if you boot DOS (without OS/2).

Non-IBM computer equipment *may* present you with an OS/2 compatibility problem. Chapter 5, "Using Non-IBM Computers and OS/2," goes into detail on this issue. Basically, the degree of compatibility depends on the manufacturer's adherence to IBM's standards. Most manufacturers are very careful to ensure their equipment's level of IBM compatibility.

Finally, some DOS applications use the *Virtual Control Program Interface (VCPI)* to store information in extended memory. VCPI, by its nature, allows a DOS application to directly control and modify all of extended memory, subverting the system integrity protection that OS/2 enforces. VCPI applications cannot run under OS/2. If you have an application that uses VCPI to access extended memory, you should use Dual Boot to boot DOS before running that application, and you should set up a FAT (not HPFS) partition. Later in this chapter, DOS compatibility with HPFS partitions is discussed.

Using Hard Disk Utilities

Probably the most popular DOS-based hard disk utility product is
Norton Utilities from Symantec Corporation. This set of computer programs enables you to set your screen colors, search for text strings in
files, find files, set volume labels, test your system's performance,
change file attributes, print text files, and do a number of other useful
things. These other things can compromise OS/2's integrity. Norton
Utilities also contains computer programs for sorting directories, un-
erasing files, undeleting directories, and modifying the internal physical
file allocation tables. These computer programs, while useful, are dangerous in a multitasking environment. If you sort a directory in one DOS
session while another DOS session is using that same directory, you
"pull the rug out from beneath" the second session.

Other popular hard disk utilities that potentially compromise OS/2's file
integrity include PC Tools Deluxe from Central Point Software, HDTest
from Peter Fletcher, SpinRite from Gibson Research, OPTune from Ga-
zelle Systems, and Mace Utilities from Fifth Generation Systems, Inc. If
you want to use one of these products on your computer, you should
use only FAT (not HPFS) partitions, and you should use Dual Boot to
boot DOS on your computer before you run the utility.

What if you have an HPFS partition and accidentally erase a file? Are
you out of luck? No; providers of utility software are developing OS/2
utility applications to help you out of such predicaments. One of the
first is HPFS Utilities for OS/2 from GammaTech. Among other functions, this product enables you to restore erased files.

Working with HPFS Partitions and HPFS Files

The File Allocation Table scheme was really designed to work with the
small-capacity disks that were popular when DOS was first released.
Performance suffers when applications access FAT files, especially
large files. DOS and OS/2 have to read and process long chains of physical disk location information to satisfy application requests for files.

OS/2 offers a High Performance File System (HPFS) option especially
designed for hard disks. Outside of OS/2, DOS cannot recognize files on
an HPFS partition. If you use the OS/2 System Editor to create a text file
on an HPFS drive, and then reboot your computer with DOS (perhaps
by using Dual Boot or a system-formatted floppy disk), DOS does not
show you the HPFS disk drive. DOS reassigns your computer's drive

letters, and the HPFS drive is invisible. On the other hand, if you use the DOS that is built into OS/2, your DOS applications can use files on an HPFS partition, with the exception of long file names.

HPFS enables you to use long file names (up to 254 characters) and to include spaces and several periods in such a name. If you use long file names, your DOS applications cannot see or use those files. Your OS/2 applications can, of course, see and use these files.

If this sounds like a problem, remember that you use an application (DOS- or OS/2-based) to create most of your files. DOS applications do not allow you to create files with long names, so only rarely should you have to be careful about naming files. You will probably only notice the difference when you start a DOS session under OS/2 and ask DOS to list the files in a directory on an HPFS drive. If files with long names exist in that directory, DOS shows you only the files with short names. You will recall that a short name has from one to eight characters of name and, optionally, an extension containing a period and from one to three characters.

For Related Information

▶▶ "Switching between OS/2 and DOS with Dual-Boot," p. 397.

▶▶ "Learning What You Cannot Do in a DOS Session," p. 398.

FROM HERE...

Chapter Summary

You now understand the differences between DOS and OS/2, and you know that OS/2 is like DOS in many ways. In this chapter, you learned that OS/2 and DOS files are usually indistinguishable and that many OS/2 commands behave just as they did under DOS. Not only can you run your DOS applications under OS/2, but when you do, the applications have more of the 640K of memory available to them. OS/2 also can run multiple DOS applications at the same time. OS/2 applications are not constrained by the 640K limitation. You also learned about Microsoft Windows applications working under OS/2, why some DOS-based hard disk utilities cannot run under OS/2, and that OS/2 is highly configurable.

In the next chapter, you decide how you want to use OS/2.

Installing and Configuring OS/2

PART

II

OUTLINE

Deciding How You Want To Use OS/2

In the last two chapters, you learned how DOS operates; you also learned that OS/2 is a superset of DOS with capabilities that far exceed those of DOS. By now, you may feel that you want to try out OS/2 immediately. If you rush ahead with the installation, however, you might miss some key points about tailoring OS/2 to your own work habits. The OS/2 installation process might even fail to complete properly. Take your time and thoughtfully work your way through this chapter before you start the installation process. You will find that the time is well spent and that your use of OS/2 is much more productive after you learn the many ways in which you can customize OS/2 to work the way you want.

You can set up OS/2 in literally hundreds of different configurations. You begin making your setup choices when you install OS/2. The installation program creates disk files on your hard disk that contain your preferences; OS/2 uses these preferences when it loads itself and later while you use your computer.

The installation process asks you how OS/2 should set up your computer system's hard disk, what brand of mouse you have, and which tools and utilities to use. Also, you indicate the maximum number of threads your applications might use and the way in which OS/2 should manage your swap file. OS/2 supplies default answers to many of these types of questions, but you want to be aware of the meanings of these options so that you can determine for yourself what is appropriate. This chapter gives you that information.

If you change your mind later about how you installed OS/2, you may be able to use OS/2's configuration tools (such as Selective Install) to reconfigure your system. OS/2 is definitely not rigid and unyielding; you will find that the operating system probably functions properly even if you made an inappropriate choice during installation. Your computer system may run more slowly than it might otherwise, however, or OS/2 may not make the best use of your computer's internal memory. The worst situation is a computer that may not work at all—a remote but definite possibility. This chapter helps you prevent that from happening.

To help you organize your thoughts, you will find the discussion of the configuration options categorized into the following areas:

- Coexistence with other operating systems
- Disk and disk file considerations
- Application and general system options
- Device support
- Personal preferences

In each area, you learn advantages and disadvantages of the various options you can choose and receive recommendations suitable for most people. Use these recommendations as a guide, but don't be afraid to experiment with other options that seem to fit your needs better.

Examining Other Operating Systems

OS/2 2.1 wants to be a good neighbor to the other operating systems you might use with your computer system. As Chapter 1, "Taking a Quick Tour of OS/2 and Your Computer," and Chapter 3, "Learning OS/2 If You Know DOS," discussed, you can start specific, older versions of DOS by booting them in a Virtual DOS Machine (VDM) environment under OS/2. You also can boot other operating systems on your computer, alternating between OS/2 2.1, OS/2 1.3, UNIX, and/or "pure" DOS. In this latter case, you reboot your entire computer rather than boot a DOS version in a VDM within OS/2.

Employing Dual-Boot

If booting a specific DOS version (such as 3.3) inside a VDM under OS/2 does not allow you to run a particular application, you may have to close all your current OS/2 applications, choose Shutdown from the OS/2 desktop menu, and reboot your computer with the "real" version of DOS in order to use that finicky application. You also can reboot by inserting a DOS boot disk (system-formatted) into drive A and pressing the Del key while holding down the Ctrl and Alt keys. Or you can use OS/2's Dual Boot feature.

Dual-Boot keeps a set of DOS system files on your hard disk beside the OS/2 system files. Dual-Boot also stores your DOS CONFIG.SYS and AUTOEXEC.BAT files in the C:\OS2\SYSTEM directory. When you type BOOT /DOS, the BOOT utility saves the current OS/2 CONFIG.SYS and AUTOEXEC.BAT files, restores the DOS files, and boots DOS. When you later (under DOS) type **BOOT /OS2**, the BOOT utility reverses its previous actions and boots OS/2.

> *Advantages:* You may want to run a DOS disk diagnostic program like Norton Utilities on your hard disk. OS/2 does not allow the diagnostic program access to the hard disk if OS/2 currently has files open on that disk. Dual-Boot lets you boot DOS, run the disk utilities, and then reboot OS/2. You don't have to keep a DOS system-formatted disk handy for such situations. Dual-Boot uses very little hard disk space.

> *Disadvantages:* None, but you may still want to keep a DOS system disk handy for emergencies, as explained in Chapter 8, "Troubleshooting OS/2."

> *Recommendation:* Allow the OS/2 installation process to set up Dual-Boot on your computer.

Using the Multiple Operating System Tool (Boot Manager)

The Multiple Operating System Tool (Boot Manager) is much more complicated than Dual Boot. Fortunately, you almost certainly will not need it. Boot Manager sets up a small portion of your hard disk with a special program that controls the boot process. At boot time, this program enables you to choose which of several different operating systems you want to use; each operating system is in a hard disk partition of its own. You might use Boot Manager for a non-OS/2 operating system such as UNIX that insists on booting from drive C, or you might use Boot Manager to boot OS/2 2.1 from drive D if you have a drive D.

Advantages: Boot Manager allows you to install a second operating system such as UNIX and then switch between OS/2 and the second system. Boot Manager is useful for operating systems too cumbersome to be booted from a single disk.

Disadvantages: Boot Manager slows the boot process and requires that you partition and format your hard disk differently. Boot Manager isn't difficult to install on a new computer; however, if you already have files on your hard disk, you have to back up your files before you use Boot Manager to partition and format your hard disk. Boot Manager also takes up a little disk space.

Recommendation: Avoid using Boot Manager unless you need to use a non-DOS, non-OS/2 operating system such as UNIX.

FROM HERE...

For Related Information

▶▶ "First Step: Text Mode," p. 123.

▶▶ "Choosing the OS/2 Features You Want," p. 134.

▶▶ "Switching between OS/2 and DOS with Dual-Boot," p. 397.

Considering Disks and Disk Files

Several OS/2 options relate to the disk drive or drives in your computer. You may have a CD/ROM drive that requires special driver software, for example, or you may want to take advantage of OS/2's High Performance File System.

Installing CD/ROM Drives

Deciding whether to use this option is easy. If you have a CD/ROM drive attached to your computer, install the support for it. You can access your CD/ROM from within OS/2. This option takes up very little disk space. The following list identifies the CD-ROM drives supported by OS/2 2.1.

Manufacturer	CD-ROM drive model
Hitachi	CDR-1650S, CDR-1750S, CDR-3650, CDR-3750
IBM	CD-ROM I, CD-ROM II
NEC	CDR-36, CDR-37, CDR-72, CDR-73, CDR-74, CDR-82, CDR-83, CDR-84
Panasonic	CR-501, LK-MC501S
Sony	CDU-541, CDU-561, CDU-6111, CDU-6211, CDU-7211
Texel	DM-3021, DM-5021, DM-5024
Toshiba	XM-3201, XM-3301

The CD-ROM drive uses a cable to attach to an adapter card in your computer. The following table lists of the OS/2-supported adapter cards you can use.

Manufacturer	SCSI adapter or interface
Adaptec	AIC 6260, AHA 1510/1512/1520/1522, AHA 1540/1542/1544, AHA 1640/1642/1644, AHA 1740/1742/1744
DPT	PM2011/2012
Future Domain	TMC-850/860/875/885, TMC-1660/1670/1680, MCS-600/700, TMC-700EX, TMC-850IBM
IBM	PS/2 SCSI Adapter, PS/2 SCSI Adapter with cache

Offering the High Performance File System

DOS uses a software mechanism called a File Allocation Table (FAT) to access disks. OS/2 also can access FAT-based disks. The File Allocation Table scheme was really designed to work with small-capacity disks, however. Applications that access files (especially large files) on FAT-based hard disks run slowly. Each file access causes DOS or OS/2 to search long chains of physical disk location information inside the FAT.

OS/2 offers a High Performance File System (HPFS) option especially designed for hard disks. The HPFS works much faster than a FAT when applications access large files. On a FAT-based disk, your file names can be only 11 characters long—eight characters for the root name, one period, and three characters for an extension. With HPFS, you can give files longer, more meaningful names—up to 255 characters long— and your file names can include embedded spaces and lowercase letters (for example, October 1st Sales Projection).

Advantages: Your computer will seem much faster, your DOS applications can access HPFS files from DOS sessions under OS/2, long file names are convenient, and HPFS uses little disk space.

Disadvantages: HPFS files are invisible unless OS/2 is running (if you use Dual Boot to start DOS, for example, you cannot access your HPFS files). Files with long file names are invisible in DOS sessions. (In fact, the entire HPFS partition is invisible unless you are running OS/2.) The first disk partition must be FAT-based if you use Dual Boot. At this time, few Norton-like utilities for disk diagnostics exist for HPFS. Finally, HPFS requires that you format your hard disk, so you must back up and restore existing files.

Recommendation: Set up part of your hard disk as an HPFS partition for the files you access from within OS/2 (using either DOS-based or OS/2-based applications). Avoid using long file names for files you access from DOS-based applications.

Using Buffers, Disk Caches, and Lazy Writes

Because disks are partly mechanical, they are relatively slow in comparison to your computer's internal memory. You can make your computer faster by using some of the internal memory to hold portions of disk files while they are accessed.

Buffers

A buffer is 512 characters of internal memory. When an application reads or writes blocks of data that are not exactly the same size as a disk sector (512 characters), OS/2 uses a buffer as an intermediate holding area. Buffers also take part in OS/2's overlapped input/output feature. Data in a buffer can be processed and handed to an application even while other disk activity continues.

Advantages: You can increase the speed of your system by increasing the number of buffers OS/2 uses.

Disadvantages: When you increase the number of disk buffers, you decrease your available internal memory. Additional buffers may cause large, memory-intensive programs to run more slowly or not at all because OS/2 must perform memory-swapping to allow these applications to share the same internal memory space.

Recommendation: Experiment with the number of buffers to get the best performance. Start with the OS/2-supplied default value. Increase the number if you run many programs concurrently.

Disk Caches

You can set aside a portion of your computer's internal memory as a disk cache. OS/2 can remember previously accessed disk file data stored in a cache and give that data to an application without waiting for the relatively slow hard disk. When an application program requests hard disk data already in the cache, the disk cache sends the data directly to the application program. This procedure is much faster than if the data were read from the disk each time.

A disk cache has the same advantages and disadvantages as buffers.

Recommendation: Base your setting of the size of the disk cache on the amount of physical internal memory in your computer. The following table lists the recommended cache size per computer memory size.

Computer memory	Cache size
2-3M	64K
4-5M	192K
6M or more	256K

Lazy Writes

Disk caching can be applied to disk data write operations as well as read operations. When lazy writes are enabled, OS/2 uses its multitasking capability to perform physical write operations in the background while you continue to use the computer. If you turn off lazy writes, OS/2 actually places the data on the disk surface before allowing your application to continue processing.

Advantages: Lazy writes make your computer system faster.

Disadvantages: A power failure that occurs at just the wrong moment can cause data to be lost.

Recommendation: Unless you use your computer in life-and-death situations, such as running a heart/lung machine, you probably want to take advantage of lazy writes.

Working with RAM Disks

IBM supplies what is called a RAM Disk utility (or VDISK) with OS/2. A RAM Disk utility uses internal memory to simulate the operation of a disk drive.

Advantages: The RAM Disk is fast and is a convenient place to put temporary files.

Disadvantages: The files on the RAM Disk disappear when the computer's power is off. A RAM Disk large enough to be useful may preempt more internal memory than you are willing or able to allocate.

Recommendation: If your applications use temporary files and if you have more than about 12M of internal memory (a rough guideline), you should have OS/2 set up a RAM Disk and then you should instruct your applications to use it.

FROM HERE...

For Related Information

▶▶ "First Step: Text Mode," p. 123.

▶▶ "Understanding the Drives Object Display," p. 259.

▶▶ "Manipulating Files," p. 273.

▶▶ "Learning the Commands for Managing Directories," p. 295.

▶▶ "Learning the Commands for Managing Files," p. 301.

Understanding Application and General System Options

You can set or change several OS/2 options to control how OS/2 functions internally and how it uses your computer's resources. These resources include the CPU (how it should be shared among the various applications), the hard disk (how OS/2 should use the hard disk when the demand for physical memory exceeds the actual amount installed, as well as how OS/2 should report disk errors), and the internal memory (whether a DOS environment should be created and what size it should be).

Using Autofail

If you have ever seen a DOS `Abort, Retry, or Ignore?` message, you will recognize the importance of the AUTOFAIL option. If a serious disk error occurs and AUTOFAIL is OFF, you see a pop-up window that notifies you of the error. You have the opportunity to retry the disk operation, notify the application that the operation failed, or end the application. If AUTOFAIL is ON, no pop-up window appears, and the application is automatically told the disk operation failed.

> *Advantages:* When a computer runs unattended, you can set AUTOFAIL ON to ensure that you do not have to periodically check on the hands-off application to see if it is still running.

> *Disadvantages:* You don't see serious disk errors when they happen. Not all applications correctly handle the FAIL notification.

> *Recommendation:* Leave AUTOFAIL set to the default OFF.

Looking at PauseOnError

If OS/2 detects an error while it processes the CONFIG.SYS file at startup, it looks at the value of PauseOnError. If this option is ON, OS/2 displays an error message and waits for you to press Enter before OS/2 continues. If this option is OFF (the default), OS/2 continues to process the remainder of the CONFIG.SYS file.

> *Advantages:* The ON setting may be useful for unattended computers that need to begin processing without human intervention when power is restored following a power failure.

> *Disadvantages:* You do not get a chance to read and correct CONFIG.SYS error messages.

> *Recommendation:* Change the setting of PauseOnError to ON.

Working with Input/Output Privilege Level

For OS/2 applications to multitask and share computer resources successfully, those applications must not try to take over the computer.

OS/2's job is to manage the computer hardware. An application should ask OS/2 to perform services that require direct hardware control. When the IOPL option is set to NO, any application that tries to access the computer hardware directly is ended. If you set IOPL to YES, OS/2 allows the application to perform the hardware access and to continue processing.

The IOPL option gets its name from the names of the CPU instructions that perform direct hardware access—INPUT and OUTPUT. OS/2 uses the setting of this option to grant or refuse Input/Output Privilege.

Advantages: Setting IOPL to NO prevents a program that contains errors (bugs) from continuing to process.

Disadvantages: A few applications exist that multitask correctly and yet require I/O privilege. Check the documentation that came with your application to see if it requires IOPL to be set to YES.

Recommendation: Leaving IOPL at its default setting is best in most instances.

Examining Threads

In OS/2's multitasking environment, several applications can run at the same time. In various sessions, for example, you might be entering information into a spreadsheet program, printing a report, formatting a floppy disk, and downloading a file from another computer. In turn, each application may be doing multiple things at the same time. Each one of these running processes is called a *thread.* An OS/2-aware word processing program will likely have separate threads for repaginating, saving a file to disk, and printing. OS/2 supports a maximum of 4,095 simultaneous threads. The default (if no option is supplied) is 256 threads. You use the THREADS option to tell OS/2 to allow more than 256 simultaneous threads. When an application tries to exceed the allocated number of threads (to calculate results in the background, for example), OS/2 forces the process to run serially and thus more slowly.

Advantages: A higher value for THREADS allows more multitasking to occur under OS/2.

Disadvantages: Each allocated thread takes up a small amount of internal memory.

Recommendation: Experiment with a setting of 512 threads to see if your computer performs faster. If it does not, drop back to the initial setting of 256 threads.

Considering MaxWait

The essence of multitasking is the sharing of the computer's resources, especially the CPU. Only one process can use the CPU at one time, however, and this limitation is a design flaw of the CPU. OS/2 gives each application its fair share of CPU time by allowing each one to have the CPU for a few milliseconds and then handing the CPU resource to the next application.

The MaxWait option specifies the longest amount of time, in seconds, that an application has to wait for the CPU. The system default is three seconds. To help an application that has waited MaxWait seconds for the CPU, OS/2 boosts the application's priority so that it is next in line.

Advantages: Setting a lower value for MaxWait causes all applications to seem to move along more smoothly.

Disadvantages: The processing that occurs inside OS/2 when the MaxWait setting is exceeded is small but significant. A too-low value for MaxWait causes OS/2 to spend unproductive time trying to determine which application to run next.

Recommendation: Leave the system default at three seconds; you may want to experiment with values of two or perhaps even one, however.

Using Memory Management

OS/2 can assume that you have in your computer more internal memory than is physically present. OS/2 does this by using a portion of your hard disk as an overflow area. You may have only 4M of physical memory, yet run a set of concurrent applications that together require 6M of memory. OS/2 overcommits memory by using the overflow area on the disk, called the Swap File, to temporarily hold sections of internal memory. OS/2 also can move sections of internal memory around to make more room.

The Memory Management (MemMan) CONFIG.SYS statement controls how OS/2 uses the Swap File and how it treats sections of internal memory. Setting options are SWAP/NOSWAP, PROTECT, and COMMIT. SWAP allows OS/2 to use the Swap File; NOSWAP denies OS/2 the use of the Swap File. PROTECT enables OS/2 to allocate memory for dynamic link library (DLL) software modules. COMMIT (a version 2.1 new parameter) causes OS/2 to deny an application's memory allocation request if that request would expand the Swap File beyond your CONFIG.SYS MINFREE setting. If you do not use COMMIT and if the Swap File grows to endanger your MINFREE setting, OS/2 warns you that you need to close applications and delete unneeded files. The COMMIT setting prevents OS/2 from allocating further memory to applications and thus makes sure you always have free disk space equal to your MINFREE setting.

> *Advantages:* OS/2's memory management is sophisticated and well-designed, allowing you to run applications that otherwise would not fit in your computer.

> *Disadvantages:* Swapping and moving memory take time, and you will notice that your computer runs more slowly when OS/2 needs to use the Swap File.

> *Recommendation:* Leave the system defaults (SWAP, PROTECT) alone. Use COMMIT for PCs that are low on disk space and that usually run in unattended mode.

Working with Priority

As mentioned in the discussion of the MaxWait option, OS/2 can change the priority of threads waiting to use the CPU. You use the Priority option to override OS/2's manipulation of thread priorities. A setting of Absolute tells OS/2 not to change thread priorities; Dynamic tells OS/2 to do what is necessary to activate a thread and have it use the CPU. The default setting is Dynamic.

> *Advantages:* A value of Absolute may help achieve predictable results by allowing applications to control their own priorities.

> *Disadvantages:* Some threads may not run for a long time.

> *Recommendation:* Use the default Dynamic value.

Examining SwapPath and Initial Swap File Size

The discussion of the MemMan option mentioned the Swap File, the special disk file that OS/2 uses to temporarily hold sections of memory. You specify the disk drive and directory in which the Swap File (named SWAPPER.DAT) exists by using the SwapPath option. You also specify the starting (minimum) size of the Swap File. The default location is C:\OS2\SYSTEM. The default initial file size is 512K.

> *Advantages:* Overcommitment of memory through the use of the Swap File enables you to run more applications and larger applications.

Disadvantages: You cannot erase the SWAPPER.DAT file while OS/2 is operating. A Swap File on a relatively slow hard disk severely affects performance. At times, the Swap File may grow quite large.

Recommendation: Never place the Swap File on a floppy disk. If you have more than one hard disk, put the Swap File on the disk you think is fastest.

Using DOS Environment Control

OS/2 offers extensive support for DOS-based applications. Several OS/2 configuration options (Break, ProtectOnly, and Real Mode Size) pertain only to DOS and enable you to better control and manage your DOS sessions.

Break

Holding the Ctrl key and pressing the Break key terminates a DOS application. BREAK instructs OS/2 to determine whether you pressed the Ctrl/Break keys before it performs an Input/Output operation for the DOS application. The default for BREAK is OFF.

Advantages: You can use the Ctrl/Break keys to more quickly stop an errant computer program if BREAK is ON.

Disadvantages: The computer may run slightly slower.

Recommendation: The default setting of OFF should suffice for most people.

ProtectOnly

The ProtectOnly option indicates whether or not you have DOS sessions. PROTECTONLY=YES tells OS/2 that all your applications run in protected mode and that you don't need DOS sessions. PROTECTONLY=NO indicates that you have DOS-based applications to run. (See Chapter 3, "Learning OS/2 If You Know DOS," for an explanation of protected mode.)

Advantages: DOS sessions require an amount of internal memory (see the explanation of the RMSIZE option). You have more memory available to your OS/2 applications if you specify PROTECTONLY=YES.

Disadvantages: 20,000 DOS-based applications exist; you will probably want to run at least one of them at some point.

Recommendation: Unless you are very short of internal memory and you only run OS/2 applications, specify NO.

Real Mode Size

The size of each DOS session under OS/2 can be up to 640K. You can specify a smaller memory region for DOS under OS/2 by using the Real Mode Size (RMSIZE) option.

Advantages: If you don't have much memory, you can allocate a smaller amount to DOS and a correspondingly larger amount for OS/2 applications by using this option.

Disadvantages: When you want to run a DOS-based application that requires a substantial amount of memory, OS/2 displays an error message instead of running the application.

Recommendation: Unless you are very short on internal memory, use the default 640K.

FROM HERE...

For Related Information

▶▶ "Choosing the OS/2 Features You Want," p. 134.

▶▶ "Adding DOS Programs," p. 389.

▶▶ "Command Reference," p. 647.

Using Device Support

OS/2 includes built-in support for many computer devices you might connect to your system. The designers and developers of OS/2 paid particular attention to graphical displays, printers, and downloadable fonts. If you have an application that uses a communications (serial) port, the application will probably configure the COM1, COM2, COM3, or COM4 port itself. OS/2 lets you provide default startup options for devices connected to communications ports, however.

Increasing Display Resolution and Colors

Depending on the video adapter card installed in your computer, OS/2 2.1 can display more information on your monitor. You can use more and larger windows on the Workplace Shell desktop. You can increase the display resolution (the number of horizontal and vertical dots) and the number of possible colors on your display. You can take advantage of higher resolutions to see more of your work at the same time. In a graphics-based word processing application such as WordPerfect for OS/2, Microsoft Word/PM, or Ami Pro for OS/2, for example, you see a greater portion of each page of the document while you work.

The following table lists several IBM-established display standards that OS/2 2.1 supports.

Adapter	Common name	Resolution
Color Graphics Adapter	CGA	640x200
Enhanced Graphics Adapter	EGA	640x350
Video Graphics Array	VGA	640x480
8514 Display Adapter		1024x768
Extended Graphics Array	XGA	1024x768

OS/2's support for CGA is quite limited; IBM strongly recommends that you upgrade from CGA to a more modern video adapter and monitor if you want to use OS/2. If you have an EGA video adapter, you will find the amount of information displayed on-screen is similarly limited. You should consider upgrading your video adapter and monitor if you presently use CGA or EGA.

In addition, OS/2 2.1 supports several brands of Super VGA video adapters. IBM did not create the Super VGA display standard. Several manufacturers of IBM-compatible computers and peripheral devices formed a committee, the Video Electronics Standards Association (VESA), to promote higher resolution displays. VESA has defined a Super VGA standard that offers a resolution of 640x480 with 256 colors and a resolution of 800x600 with 16 colors. Some manufacturers go beyond the VESA specification to provide even higher resolutions, such as 1024x768. IBM built device drivers for Super VGA video adapters as well as some higher-resolution video adapters into OS/2. You select your level of video adapter support during the installation process. You can use an OS/2 configuration option, as Chapter 7, "Modifying Your OS/2 Configuration," explains, to further increase the resolution produced by your video adapter.

IBM now makes a Super VGA video adapter, the IBM VGA 256c. OS/2 2.1 supports the following VGA 256c and the video adapters:

Headland Technology VRAM II

Tseng Laboratories ET4000

Trident Microsystems TVGA

ATI Technologies VGA Wonder

Western Digital Imaging Paradise

Before you install OS/2, refer to the documentation supplied with your computer system to determine the type of video adapter your computer has, as well as the amount of video memory (VRAM) on the adapter. Greater amounts of VRAM allow higher resolutions and more colors. During installation (see Chapter 6, "Installing OS/2") and configuration (see Chapter 7, "Modifying Your OS/2 Configuration"), you choose the video resolution and color possibilities that best suit the work you do.

Working with Printers and Fonts

In OS/2 2.1, IBM offers support for many makes and models of printers besides IBM's own printers. This support is all the more impressive when you realize how different these printers are. In addition to the character data they print, printers accept commands that do not show up on the printed page but that tell the printer how to handle subsequent character data. These commands vary widely among the different printers.

OS/2 supplies printer driver software modules for the following general categories of printers:

- IBM/Epson-compatible dot-matrix printers
- PCL printers (Hewlett-Packard LaserJet and InkJet)
- PostScript printers
- IBM laser printers

In addition, OS/2 supports other printers with a generic printer driver that does not include printer command functions. The type of control you can exercise over each kind of printer driver is extensive; the Hewlett-Packard LaserJet driver allows you to specify such settings as number of copies, type of form, orientation (portrait or landscape), manual or automatic paper feed, 1- or 2-sided (duplexed) printing (for selected models), dots-per-inch resolution, and font cartridge selection, for example.

If you have a laser printer and a WYSIWYG (What You See Is What You Get) word processor application, you know that getting fonts for the printer, especially ones that match the fonts you see on-screen, can be difficult. Your application and Presentation Manager (PM) have to cooperate with each other to make the best use of your fonts. Generally, PM and the printer both choose the closest one available to match your choices.

OS/2 comes with a set of fonts, fortunately, and these fonts provide an excellent match between what you see on-screen and what is actually printed. OS/2 groups the fonts into the following typeface families: Courier, Helvetica, System (mono-spaced), Times Roman, Courier (Adobe), Helvetica (Adobe), and Times New Roman (Adobe).

Advantages: Installing all the fonts gives you the greatest accuracy between what you see on-screen and what is actually printed. If you use a laser (or other font-based) printer with your desktop publishing application or WYSIWYG word processor, the fonts you install save you time because you need to do fewer trial-and-error printouts. Even without a laser printer, you may just want to be able to select your on-screen fonts from the variety supplied with OS/2.

Disadvantages: The screen and printer fonts supplied with OS/2 occupy disk space. The amount of space varies according to which font families you choose to install, ranging from about 100K up to 1.5M.

Recommendation: Unless you have a shortage of disk space, install all the fonts.

Connecting with Communications Ports

You may have no communications port, one port, or a full complement of COM1, COM2, COM3, and COM4 on your computer. These serial device ports enable you to connect a modem or plotter to your system. In addition, some mice connect to computers through serial ports.

With OS/2 you can supply startup options for the communications ports; these options take effect when you boot the computer. Most applications that use these ports, however, automatically reconfigure the ports when the applications are started. If you have an application that does not initialize a communications port before using it, the options you specify to OS/2 remain in effect so that the application can successfully use the port. The options you can specify for a communications port are baud rate, number of data bits, parity, number of stop bits, and whether the computer should use a hardware handshaking protocol. Consult your application's documentation to find out what these options mean and what values to use.

Advanced Power Management and PCMCIA Support

IBM assumes that some day you may want to use OS/2 on a small, battery-operated notebook computer. The Advanced Power Management (APM) and Personal Computer Memory Card International Association (PCMCIA) specifications are two emerging standards for notebook computers. OS/2 2.1 includes support for both these specifications. During installation, you choose to configure OS/2 for either or both of the APM/PCMCIA environments.

OS/2's support for the APM specification means that OS/2 will help you run your notebook computer for a longer time on one battery charge. OS/2 detects that it's running on a computer based on the APM specification and cooperatively uses APM to consume fewer of the computer's battery-draining resources. The relatively new technology standard of PCMCIA allows add-ins such as modems, network adapters, and even disk drives to exist in the form of a device approximately the size of a credit card. If your computer offers an APM feature or a PCMCIA slot, you will want to configure OS/2 2.1 to support these options.

FROM HERE...

For Related Information

▶▶ "Choosing the OS/2 Features You Want," p. 134.

▶▶ "Learning OS/2 Printer Basics," p. 367.

▶▶ "Learning about Fonts," p. 374.

▶▶ "Printing with OS/2," p. 378.

Reflecting Personal Preferences

You're a unique person, and you like to get your work done in a style distinctly your own. The designers of OS/2 realize this and want OS/2 to reflect your preferences and personal tastes. OS/2 therefore supports many categories of options you can select to tailor OS/2 in highly personal ways. These options include screen colors, mouse usage, keyboard usage, national language, on-line documentation, tools, games, utilities, a sophisticated batch processing language, command history/recall, and the Workplace Shell.

Are you the only person who uses the computer system? If not, when you consider each of these options (especially in the area of screen colors), keep in mind that the selections you make also affect other people.

Selecting Screen Colors

You can express a great deal of artistry and personal taste by selecting screen colors for the different parts of each Presentation Manager window. You can easily spend an hour or two—or more—adjusting these colors, if you want. The PM window has 26 different parts you can color, and you can choose from literally thousands of colors for each part. You also can set the width of each window border.

Advantages: Color choices and adjustments are personal matters of taste; you can make your computer system look exactly the way you want.

Disadvantages: If you begin adjusting colors, you may have to remind yourself to stop playing and get back to work. On a serious note, you do need to choose some of the color combinations carefully. You might make on-screen components invisible by selecting, for example, the same foreground and background colors for a part of the screen.

Recommendation: Don't try to make all your color selections in a single session. Make a few adjustments and try out the new color scheme for a while before you make further changes. With this approach, you will not get frustrated when you attempt to make the colors come out exactly right, and you are less likely to make on-screen components invisible.

Specifying Mouse Usage

Of all the devices ever connected to computer systems, the mouse (and its cousin, the trackball) probably undergoes the most varied techniques and styles. People double-click at different rates, people like to give the mouse buttons different meanings—and not everyone is right-handed. OS/2 allows you to configure the mouse to work the way you want.

If you are left-handed, you can tell OS/2 to reverse the meanings of the mouse buttons. You can specify which mouse button is the selection button and which is the manipulation button, and you can indicate to OS/2 which combination of buttons you want to use to pop up the Task List window.

Varying Input Methods

People type on the computer keyboard in almost as many different ways as they use the mouse. Some people have special needs when it comes to using the keyboard. With OS/2, you can enable what IBM calls input methods and then select how you want the keyboard to react to your key strokes. You can type with one finger and still use keys like Shift, Ctrl, and Alt—you tell OS/2 to make these keys "sticky," for example. When you press a key, it remains active (even after you release it) until after you press the next key. With OS/2 you can specify the length of time the stickiness persists and which keys to regard as sticky. You also can change the rate at which a key repeats when you hold it down and the delay before it starts repeating.

Examining National Language Support

IBM is an international company, of course, and its products are sold worldwide. To make OS/2 easy for people in different countries to use, the designers of OS/2 provide support for different display formats for time of day, calendar date, numbers in general, and currency.

Using On-Line Documentation

OS/2 comes with a set of documentation files on disk that you can view on-screen. To learn about OS/2 in general, you choose Start Here on the Workplace Shell desktop. When you need help with an OS/2 command or utility, you type HELP at an OS/2 command line prompt or you use a HELP menu item (or pushbutton) if one is visible on-screen. You also can choose OS/2 Command Reference in the Information folder to browse through the IBM documentation on OS/2 commands and their syntax. Chapter 13, "Using the Built-In Help Facility," describes each of these facilities in more detail.

> *Advantages:* On-line help is quick, handy, and often context-sensitive—it shows you information that relates to the current task at hand.

> *Disadvantages:* The help files use 1.5M of disk space. The tutorial needs only about 200K, and the command reference occupies about 500K. You may not like the way the help windows and command reference windows pop up over your application and obscure your view of the application.

> *Recommendation:* If you have the disk space, install the on-line documentation.

Installing Tools, Games, and Utilities

As Chapter 1, "Taking a Quick Tour of OS/2 and Your Computer," mentioned, OS/2 is a full-featured operating system. It comes with utilities and small applications (called *applets*). With the applets you can become productive immediately after you install OS/2. You may need to obtain and install other applications to use your computer effectively, of course. The tools and utilities will serve you well and help you manage your computer system, however.

You can choose to install or not install each component. Disk space requirements range from about 100K to 2.5M, depending on how many components you choose.

The tools, games, and utilities you can choose to install include the following:

- Calendar and Diary
- Address Book
- Mini-spreadsheet and Database
- Calculator
- FAX software
- Alarm Clock
- Business graphics charting
- Enhanced Editor (text editor)
- Seek and Scan (file search utility)
- Cat and Mouse (cursor finder/chaser)
- Solitaire game
- Other miscellaneous games

Working with the REXX Language

With Batch files you can construct and run scripts of OS/2 commands on your computer. The REXX language goes a step further and enables you to write sophisticated computer programs that automate many of the repetitive tasks you need to do. REXX complies with the standards set forth in IBM's System Applications Architecture (SAA). Appendix G, "Programming with REXX," shows you how to program with REXX, and Chapter 18, "Batch File Programming with OS/2," gives an overview of the similar, simpler Batch language.

Advantages: When your experience with OS/2 increases, you will find that batch file programming saves you time and effort in typing. Because batch file programming is somewhat restrictive, you may find that REXX is exactly what you need to overcome these restrictions.

Disadvantages: REXX and its on-line help files take up about half a megabyte of disk space—only a small disadvantage. Perhaps the biggest considerations are your own intentions and objectives for how you want to use your computer. The idea of computer programming may be not be appealing to you.

Recommendation: Install REXX and spend a little time learning to do batch file programming and REXX programming to see if you enjoy it.

Using Command History/Recall

For the commands you enter at an OS/2 command line prompt, you can save typing time and reduce typing errors by installing and using the command history/recall feature. This feature is automatically enabled at installation time.

Suppose that you type a command or program name at an OS/2 command line prompt and then you type another. Next you want to redo the first command you typed. Command history/recall enables you to scroll through previously entered commands (by using the cursor keys) and to choose one to execute again. You can edit a previously entered command before you execute it.

FROM HERE...

For Related Information

▶▶ "Choosing the OS/2 Features You Want," p. 134.

▶▶ "Installing Features Selectively," p. 172.

▶▶ "Configuring Your Desktop," p. 174.

Chapter Summary

This chapter showed you the different options and features that you can choose during the installation of OS/2. You learned about the following options and features: Dual Boot; the Boot Manager; CD/ROM drive support under OS/2; the High Performance File System; application and general system options; printer and serial port device support; custom screen colors and mouse usage; selecting special keyboard conventions; National Language Support; on-line documentation; tools, games, and utilities; REXX programming; and command history/recall.

The next chapter discusses OS/2 considerations for non-IBM computers and non-IBM computer hardware components. If your computer system is manufactured by IBM, you can move on to Chapter 6, "Installing OS/2." If some component in your computer system is not made by IBM, go to the next chapter to learn about the compatibility issues you face when you install and use OS/2 on your non-IBM computer.

Using Non-IBM Computers and OS/2

I f all of your computer equipment is made by IBM, you can safely move on to Chapter 6, "Installing OS/2," and install OS/2. If you have an IBM computer and an IBM display adapter but your computer monitor is non-IBM or if you have an IBM computer but some of the internal memory chips (RAM chips) are non-IBM, you can safely move on to Chapter 6 to learn about the installation procedure. This chapter is for you if you own a personal computer made by another company or if some part of your computer system (such as a video adapter card, mouse, hard disk, hard disk controller card, or keyboard) is non-IBM.

In this chapter, you learn about the differences between true IBM and IBM-compatible computers and components that affect OS/2. You may find that your computer system supports OS/2 perfectly or, less likely, that you need to make some adjustments to your system so that you can install and use OS/2 2.1.

If you're thinking of buying a computer and you suspect that the one you choose will not be IBM-manufactured, you can follow the number-one rule for buying a computer system—purchase your software, including the operating system and initial applications, first. Then try these applications on the hardware you want to buy. You can easily save yourself some time, effort, and expense. When they can, wise computer buyers purchase software first, and then hardware. You may even want to follow this maxim if you purchase an IBM computer to see whether the model you choose performs as well as you want it to perform.

Some companies make computers and parts that look quite a bit like IBM's equipment, and you may have difficulty identifying non-IBM components in your computer. The following list gives some tips on identifying non-IBM equipment:

- When you boot your computer, you see messages (perhaps only briefly) that mention the name of a manufacturer other than IBM.

- You have user manuals and user guides for add-in boards (adapter cards) or disk drives that you or someone else has added to your computer.

- The computer case is similar to IBM's, but you cannot find an IBM logo/sticker on the front of the case.

- The FCC certification sticker on the back of the computer case identifies a manufacturer other than IBM.

Working with IBM-Compatible Computers

Legally, manufacturers cannot exactly duplicate IBM's personal computers, but they can make computers that behave and work the same (or, with respect to such things as video monitor resolution and hard disk speed, perhaps even better). The engineers at Compaq, Dell, Gateway 2000, CompuAdd, AST, Toshiba, Texas Instruments, and hundreds of other companies work hard to design electronic circuits that use the same chips IBM computers use but that are laid out differently. These engineers also have to write ROM BIOS software that works the same as IBM's software but looks different from it; like this book, software is copyrighted. (You learn more about ROM BIOS software later in this chapter.)

Companies in the United States are careful to design personal computers that run DOS and OS/2 applications as perfectly as possible so that the applications appear to be running on IBM hardware. These companies are equally careful to create computers that do not infringe upon IBM's patents and copyrights, however. Ironically, manufacturers in places like Taiwan and Korea have duplicated the IBM personal computers almost exactly, without as much regard for legalities, but their computers sometimes have more problems running DOS and OS/2 applications.

Most people categorize the manufacture of PCs into three tiers. IBM occupies the first tier. Companies such as Compaq, Dell, Tandy, Gateway 2000, AST Research, Texas Instruments, and Toshiba fall into the second tier. The third tier of manufacturers includes companies in Taiwan and Korea as well as some U.S. companies.

Some companies try to compete with IBM by producing computers that are compatible in all respects but that go beyond IBM's hardware capabilities to provide special options and features. Occasionally, some of these manufacturers get together to form standards committees that proclaim these options and features as new standards. An example is VESA, the Video Electronics Standards Association. VESA came into being to promote high-resolution computer monitors and adapter cards. Soon after the formation of VESA, IBM announced a new, high-resolution video adapter and monitor combination called XGA (Extended Graphics Array). Now the other manufacturers are working overtime to create XGA clones.

In general, OS/2 works (or works best) on computer equipment that functions exactly like IBM hardware. OS/2 2.1 doesn't support every extension and enhancement, such as the ones being promoted by VESA. Version 2.1 of OS/2 does offer support for the most popular non-IBM PC components and peripherals, however.

Before you go much further with the discussion on IBM-compatible computers, take a moment to review the hardware requirements for OS/2 2.1 as outlined in the next section. Then, when you move ahead into specific areas of compatibility (such as hard disks and video adapters/monitors), you have a solid foundation on which to judge your own computer's compatibility with OS/2.

Examining OS/2 2.1 Hardware Requirements

OS/2 is necessarily more stringent than DOS about the hardware on which it runs. Version 2.1 takes advantage of the Intel-designed 80386 or 80486 CPU chip to offer the multiple DOS sessions and the system integrity protection mentioned earlier. OS/2 cannot offer these capabilities on the older 80286 or 8088 CPU chips used in the IBM AT and the original IBM PC. Intel created two distinct types of 80386 CPU chips; OS/2 works with both the sx and dx designations.

OS/2 needs at least four megabytes (M) of internal memory (RAM); the operating system performs better if you give it even more memory. You should consider putting at least 8M of RAM in your computer before you install and begin using OS/2.

OS/2 is also selective about the type of hard disk, hard disk controller, and video display that you have. While it operates, OS/2 controls these devices to an extent beyond that imposed by plain DOS. The extra control allows OS/2 to perform faster and more reliably than DOS.

OS/2 supports several types of hard disks and hard disk controllers, but you may have to obtain software device drivers from the manufacturer of the disk or controller to use a hard disk with OS/2 2.1. Usually, the types of disks known as MFM and ESDI do not require drivers; IDE and SCSI disks may require software drivers. Hard disk controllers that behave exactly like the Western Digital WA1003 and WA1006 controllers should not require software drivers, but other hard disk controllers may.

You need a high-capacity floppy disk drive to install and use OS/2. If you use 5 1/4-inch disks, the disk drive must be a 1.2M drive. If you use 3 1/2-inch disks, the disk drive must be a 1.44M or 2.88M drive. You can use the lower capacity 360K (5 1/4 inch) or 720K (3 1/2 inch) drives to store files you create, but you cannot use these drives to install OS/2.

IBM originally used a chip with the designation 8250 on its asynchronous communications adapters. This adapter contains the COM1, COM2, and/or COM3 port. You can connect a modem to this adapter when you want to dial a bulletin board or information network, for example. OS/2 does not support the now-obsolete 8250. Beginning with the IBM AT computer, IBM has installed chips with the designation 16450 or 16550 in its personal computers. OS/2 works with communications adapters based on these chips.

You can use a variety of video displays (adapters and monitors) with OS/2, but VGA (Video Graphics Array) and XGA (Extended Graphics Array) work best.

The following list summarizes the hardware requirements of OS/2 2.1:

- 80386 (sx or dx), 80486, or Pentium CPU chip

- 4M or more of internal memory (RAM)

- MFM or ESDI hard disk, probably no software driver needed
- SCSI or IDE disk drive, possibly with a software driver
- IBM/Western Digital (or compatible) hard disk controller
- Floppy disk drive; 1.2M drive, 5 1/4-inch disk; 1.44M drive, 3 1/2-inch disk; or 2.88M drive, 3 1/2-inch disk
- A mouse and printer, optional

NOTE   OS/2 is easier to use if you have a mouse.

You can use one of the following types of video systems:

- CGA (Color Graphics Adapter)
- EGA (Enhanced Graphics Adapter), color or monochrome
- VGA (Video Graphics Array), color or monochrome
- Some Super VGA (SVGA) displays
- 8514/A, with or without memory expansion
- XGA (Extended Graphics Array)

Making OS/2 Vendor-Neutral

You might think that IBM designed OS/2 2.1 to be incompatible with other vendors' personal computers. This is not the case. In fact, IBM has enlisted the aid of many PC vendors to ensure that OS/2 2.1 runs on the greatest variety of computers. These PC vendors include: ALR, Apricot, AST, AT&T, Compaq, CompuAdd, Dell, Grid, Everex, Hewlett-Packard, NCR, NEC, Netframe, Olivetti, Reply, Siemens, Tandon, Tandy/Grid, and Trichord.

Someone at IBM coined the phrase "vendor-neutral" to describe IBM's positive attitude about making sure that OS/2 2.1 runs on both IBM and IBM-compatible hardware.

For Related Information

◀◀ "Understanding Hardware and Software," p. 13.

▶▶ "Booting the Installation Disk," p. 122.

FROM HERE...

Understanding CPU Chips

Intel Corporation manufactures a variety of 80386, 80486, and Pentium (80586) CPU chips. These chips provide your computer with its "brainpower." Intel is even now designing, building, and testing the next generation of personal computer CPU chips. Internally, Intel refers to the 80386, 80486, and Pentium chips as the iAPX386, i486, and P5 Microprocessors. Just as computer manufacturers have cloned the IBM personal computer, chip makers have recently cloned the Intel 80386. A computer capable of running OS/2 2.1, whether that computer is made by IBM or another manufacturer, contains an 80386, 80486, or a Pentium (80586) CPU chip.

Examining the Intel 80386 Chip

Intel rates its microprocessor chips at different running speeds. Naturally, higher speeds mean better performance and increased cost. Intel expresses the speed ratings in *megahertz* (often shortened to MHz), a unit of measurement equal to one million that tells the number of times per second the CPU chip is driven to perform its work. An 80386 chip running at 33 MHz is about twice as fast as one running at 16 MHz. Don't depend solely on this rating to measure the speed of your computer, however; other components, such as the hard disk, weigh heavily as factors in how well the computer performs.

Intel makes two kinds of 80386 chips, sx and dx. An 80386sx computer can address up to 16M of internal memory. An 80386dx computer (sometimes the dx designation is omitted when discussing these computers) can address up to 4G (G represents gigabytes, or four billion bytes) of memory. In all other respects, the two kinds of 80386 CPU chips are virtually identical. OS/2 runs equally well on sx and dx chips.

Some computers have math coprocessors installed, or you may install one as an option. Such chips are designated as 80387 chips, and you can purchase one to help your applications run more quickly. The 80387 chip helps the CPU perform certain kinds of arithmetic operations faster. OS/2 does not benefit from the presence of a math coprocessor.

Your 80386 CPU can operate in three modes. In the simplest mode (*real mode*), the CPU is a fast version of the older 8088 chip, and it can address up to 1M of memory. If you install DOS on your computer instead of OS/2, you get this mode by default.

In *protected mode*, the CPU can address up to 4G of internal memory. Practically speaking, however, you're unlikely to have a computer with this amount of RAM installed. One of the benefits of protected mode is the 32-bit architecture you read about in Chapter 4, "Deciding How You Want To Use OS/2." OS/2 and OS/2 applications run in protected mode.

Finally, *virtual 8086 mode* allows the 80386 CPU to act as if it were several real-mode computers. This mode is what OS/2 uses to give you multiple concurrent DOS sessions.

You sometimes see advertisements for 80386 accelerator cards that you can add to an existing computer. In general, these cards cannot run OS/2. An example of such a card is the Intel AboveBoard.

Examining the Intel 80486 Chip

The 80486 CPU chip is an enhanced edition of the 80386. The 80486 contains circuitry enabling it to operate faster than an 80386. The 80486 CPU also incorporates the functions of a math coprocessor. You don't need to purchase an 80487 math coprocessor if you have an 80486 CPU. Intel produces a particular 80486sx CPU, however, that is an 80486 chip without the math-coprocessor functions. This specialized 80486 CPU chip is for unique purposes, and you probably should not consider getting one.

Examining the Intel Pentium (80586) Chip

Intel found, to the company's dismay, that it could not register the number *80386* or the number *80486* as a trademark. Other companies, as explained in the next section, have produced CPU chips that function in exactly the same way as Intel's 80386 and 80486 chips. These other companies use variations of the numbers *80386* and *80486* to identify the clone CPUs. Intel wants to protect its competitive edge and keep other companies from using Intel's names for PC CPU chips. Toward this end, Intel named the latest generation of CPU chips *Pentium* rather than 80586. The situation is confusing because the 80586 designation is a natural progression from earlier CPU designations. Clone CPU makers who use the name 80586 will take advantage of the progression. Intel, on the other hand, plans a multimillion dollar advertising campaign to bring name recognition to the Pentium.

At any rate, you should be aware that the Pentium CPU chip is the next generation CPU beyond the 80486. A Pentium CPU typically operates two to three times faster than an 80486.

Examining 80386 and 80486 CPU Chips from Other Manufacturers

At least two companies have either reverse-engineered the Intel 80386 and 80486 CPU chips or claim to have licensing arrangements with Intel that allow them to produce the chips. These companies are Advanced Micro Devices, and Chips and Technologies.

> **NOTE** *Reverse engineering* is the process of duplicating the function of a chip by carefully and thoroughly understanding that function and then creating a chip that behaves the same way without actually copying someone else's design. As you might imagine, this process is subject to interpretation; Intel, Advanced Micro Devices, and Chips & Technologies have filed lawsuits to encourage the courts to clarify such interpretations.

Interestingly, IBM has a license from Intel to produce CPU chips. Some IBM computers contain CPU chips manufactured by IBM; some contain Intel-made chips.

FROM HERE...

For Related Information

◄◄ "Understanding Hardware and Software," p. 13.

▶▶ "Booting the Installation Disk," p. 122.

▶▶ "First Step: Text Mode," p. 123.

Using ROM BIOS

The *ROM BIOS* is software built into your computer. This software is always in the computer—even when you turn it off. The BIOS software is burned into special memory chips; the contents of those chips do not depend on the presence of electrical power. ROM stands for Read-Only Memory, and BIOS stands for Basic Input Output System.

The ROM BIOS takes control when you turn on your computer and checks out your computer with a series of diagnostic steps. It then transfers control of the computer to the operating system (OS/2, in this case), and the operating system loads into memory. Because the ROM BIOS software is always present and available, OS/2 sometimes uses the ROM BIOS functions as if they were part of OS/2.

An IBM or IBM-compatible computer is likely to contain an 80386 or 80486 CPU chip made by Intel. An IBM computer contains a ROM BIOS written and copyrighted by IBM, however. A compatible computer contains a ROM BIOS written by another company that specializes in such software. IBM designed OS/2 to take advantage of the IBM-written ROM BIOS, if it is present. Otherwise, OS/2 loads and uses its own BIOS program code.

If the ROM BIOS in an IBM computer is computer software copyrighted by IBM, how do other companies avoid infringing upon IBM's intellectual property rights? They hire programmers who sign affidavits saying that the programmers have never seen or worked with IBM's software and give those programmers specifications on how the ROM BIOS should behave. The programmers write their own computer software (without copying IBM's). The result, if the specifications are accurate, is an IBM-compatible ROM BIOS. People often call this process the "clean room" approach.

Sometimes you find that companies who do not manufacture IBM ROM BIOS provide extra setup parameters, including such options as *ROM BIOS shadowing*. You may need to turn off shadowing, or perhaps make other setup changes, to successfully install OS/2.

T I P

Making BIOS Criteria Compatible

Despite OS/2's loading of its own BIOS code, the computer's internal ROM BIOS does play a part in the loading and initial installation of OS/2. Non-IBM manufacturers of ROM BIOS program code are aware of this fact and have, for the past few years, developed ROM BIOS software that is compatible with OS/2.

An adapter card often contains its own ROM BIOS software that augments the BIOS built into the computer. In general, OS/2 operates these adapters through device drivers, without using the built-in ROM BIOS. In a DOS session under OS/2, you may find that your software runs okay, but OS/2 applications might not be able to use the adapter/device unless the manufacturer supplies an OS/2 device driver with the hardware. Check with the manufacturer to find out whether an OS/2 device driver is available for non-IBM adapter cards. If the adapter requires a device driver under DOS, it almost certainly needs one under OS/2.

IBM's own ROM BIOS is actually two distinct sets of ROM BIOS code. The first, called the *ABIOS*, is compatible with and used by DOS. The other, *CBIOS*, is for use by OS/2.

Manufacturing ROM BIOS Software

The biggest manufacturers of IBM-compatible ROM BIOS software are Compaq, Phoenix Technologies, American Megatrends (sometimes referred to as AMI), Award, and Quadtel. New versions appear from these companies all the time, so pinpointing compatibility issues with a particular manufacturer's ROM BIOS is difficult. These difficulties represent another reason why trying out your software, and even the operating system, on a computer before you buy it is important. Bugs (programming errors) in early versions of the AMI BIOS prevented OS/2 from installing successfully on machines equipped with the early AMI BIOS chips, for example. OS/2 2.1 installs on and runs successfully with recent versions of ROM BIOS software from each of the companies just mentioned, however.

AMI designed its BIOS to display a Screen ID Code which you see each time you boot a computer equipped with an AMI BIOS. The Screen ID Code appears in the lower left portion of the screen at boot time and has one of the following formats:

AMI BIOS and AMI BIOS Plus:

aaaa-bbbb-mmddyy-Kc

AMI Hi-Flex BIOS:

ee-ffff-bbbbbb-gggggggg-mmddyy-hhhhhhhh-c

If you have a BIOS written by AMI, make a note of the Screen ID Code. If you want to use an IDE hard disk drive in your computer (with any operating system, not just OS/2), the BIOS date (the "mmddyy" part of the Screen ID Code) should be 040990 or later. AMI modified the BIOS code on that date (April 9, 1990) to accommodate the special timing requirements of IDE drives. A BIOS date of 092588 or later allows OS/2 to install on other types of disk drives, as explained in the next section. The Keyboard Controller Revision Level (*c* in the Screen ID Code format) must be *F* or later to support OS/2 2.1.

For Related Information

◄◄ "Understanding Hardware and Software," p. 13.

►► "Booting the Installation Disk," p. 122.

FROM HERE...

Working with Disks and Disk Controller Cards

Hard disk drive companies manufacture several different kinds of hard disks for personal computers. The following table shows the acronyms by which these disk types are known.

Acronym	Meaning
MFM	Modified Frequency Modulation
RLL	Run-Length-Limited
ESDI	Enhanced Small Device Interface
SCSI	Small Computer System Interface
IDE	Integrated Drive Electronics

Disk drives vary not only by type but also by capacity, number of surfaces, information density, and access rate.

Understanding Disk Drive Types

As mentioned earlier, MFM and ESDI disk drives are likely to work with OS/2 2.1 without a special device driver from the manufacturer. IBM uses primarily MFM and ESDI drives, and a few types of SCSI drives, in its computers. SCSI and IDE drives may need a device driver from the disk drive or disk controller manufacturer, depending on the hard disk controller card's degree of IBM compatibility. The next section discusses hard disk controller cards. RLL drives do not work with OS/2.

A disk cylinder is made up of tracks. A track is one of the concentric circles on the surface of the disk for storing information. A cylinder is the set of tracks that, one on top of the other, are all equidistant from the edge of the disk surface (the platter). Figure 5.1 illustrates disk drive cylinders and their tracks.

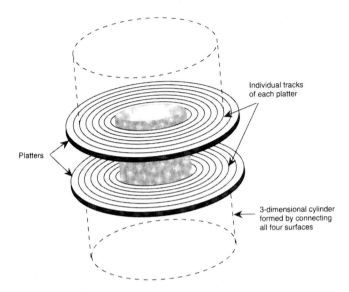

Individual tracks
of each platter

Platters

3-dimensional cylinder
formed by connecting
all four surfaces

Fig. 5.1

A disk drive
cylinder.

Some disk drives have more than 1,024 cylinders, which may be a problem for OS/2. DOS has this problem, too, but DOS users install special
device drivers to allow DOS to use these disk drives. (Two popular
drivers are Disk Manager from OnTrack Computer Systems and
SpeedStor from Storage Dimensions.) Under OS/2, people commonly
use (or switch to) disk controller cards that do sector translation, as
described in the next section. You may find that your hard disk controller vendor has written an OS/2 device driver to provide compatibility.
One such vendor is Adaptec.

Learning about Disk Controller Cards

Each type of disk drive (MFM, SCSI, IDE, ESDI) requires its own particular kind of disk controller. For years, IBM has used controller cards
made by Western Digital in addition to manufacturing its own controllers. This practice has made Western Digital controllers something of a
standard. For compatibility, other manufacturers ensure that their controller cards behave the same as Western Digital cards.

MFM drives commonly place 17 sectors on each track. With their
higher capacity, ESDI and other drives use more sectors per track (34
or 63, for example). Some controller cards have options that enable you
to set the number of sectors per track and to set aside some sectors as

spares in case bad spots develop. Bad spots on the disk surface cause disk read/write errors; some controller cards recover from these errors automatically.

The Western Digital WD1007VSE2 is an example of a controller card that enables you to use an ESDI disk with OS/2 that has up to 1,700 cylinders. This type of card employs sector translation, which enables the ROM BIOS and OS/2 to treat the disk as having fewer than 1,024 cylinders. The actual sector numbering scheme on the disk is translated into a different scheme that's acceptable to the ROM BIOS and to OS/2 (or DOS) without the need for a device driver.

On the other hand, some people have reported problems getting the SCSI Future Domain TMC 850 controller card to work successfully with OS/2. If you have doubts or questions, contact the manufacturer.

For Related Information

◄◄ "Understanding Hardware and Software," p. 13.

►► "First Step: Text Mode," p. 123.

►► "Understanding Installation Errors," p. 191.

FROM HERE...

Using the Keyboards and Mice

Most non-IBM keyboards and mice are compatible with OS/2. The few keyboards that are not are older models whose electronics do not closely match IBM's. Similarly, the few incompatible mice (or other pointing devices) do not behave electronically like the IBM and Microsoft mice.

Looking at the 101-Key Keyboard

As Chapter 1, "Taking a Quick Tour of OS/2 and Your Computer," pointed out, the 101-key keyboard has become an industry standard. The number of keys on the keyboard, however, is not a compatibility issue. Notebook computers have fewer keys (you sometimes use a combination of two keys to equal a single key on the 101-key keyboard) yet are usually quite compatible with OS/2. Toshiba's computers, the CompuAdd Companion/SX, and the Texas Instruments TravelMate 3000 are examples of notebook computers that run OS/2 well.

Personal computers contain what is called a keyboard controller chip. You can think of this chip as part of the ROM BIOS. Some years ago, a few makers of IBM-compatible computers did not design this chip exactly right. The computers ran DOS successfully, but not OS/2. These computers also have difficulty with some DOS Extender software products and with Microsoft Windows. An earlier section of this chapter on Manufacturing ROM BIOS Software explained how to determine the proper revision level for machines equipped with AMI BIOS chips.

Considering Serial, Bus, and PS/2 Mice

IBM makes a two-button mouse that connects directly to the mouse port in an IBM computer. The IBM mouse works exactly the same as the Microsoft mouse, and the two pointing devices are interchangeable. In fact, when you purchase a Microsoft serial mouse, one of the cables in the package connects the Microsoft mouse to the mouse port on a PS/2.

Microsoft offers three kinds of mice. The most popular is the serial mouse, which connects to a serial port or to the mouse port on a PS/2 (using the special cable). Microsoft also makes a bus mouse that requires its own adapter card and a mouse called the InPort.

During the installation process, OS/2 tries to identify the type of mouse you have (if any). In many cases, this automatic detection eliminates compatibility problems. You may find, however, that OS/2 has chosen the wrong type of pointing device. Check the documentation that came with your mouse to see whether it emulates one of the mice in the following list:

- IBM PS/2 mouse
- Microsoft serial, bus, or InPort mouse
- PC Mouse (from PC Mouse Systems)
- Visi-On Mouse (from Visi-On)
- Logitech Serial Mouse

OS/2 directly supports the mice in this list. For pointing devices that are not on the list or that do not emulate these mice, you may need to experiment by telling OS/2 that you have each of the mice on the list until you find a combination that works. You also may see that your mouse, trackball, or other pointing device connects to the computer like one of these other mice, and that may give you a clue as to what to tell OS/2. Logitech manufactures a bus mouse, for example; you would select the Microsoft bus mouse during the OS/2 installation process.

For Related Information

◀◀ "Understanding Hardware and Software," p. 13.

▶▶ "Upgrading Your Hardware," p. 165.

FROM HERE...

Working with Video Adapter Cards and Monitors

The IBM Video Graphics Array (VGA) specification has existed long enough that almost every manufacturer of video adapter cards and monitors is highly compatible—sometimes indistinguishably so—with IBM. The Extended Graphics Array (XGA) specification, on the other hand, is relatively new. Other manufacturers have not yet copied the IBM XGA design in a manner that does not infringe upon the patent. Many of these manufacturers, to compete with IBM's VGA standard, formed the Video Electronics Standards Association (VESA) to promote higher-resolution, fuller-color displays. Video modes supported by VESA are often called Super VGA, and the non-IBM hardware always has two modes: standard VGA and Super VGA.

In addition, IBM has three older standards—the Color Graphics Adapter (CGA), Enhanced Graphics Adapter (EGA), and 8514/A color adapter.

NOTE   The video adapter card and software drivers, not the computer monitor, determine OS/2 compatibility.

Using VGA

IBM's VGA specification describes color and monochrome displays. A monochrome VGA display can show text with a resolution of 132 columns horizontally and 50 rows vertically; most people and applications use 80 columns and 25 rows. In graphics mode, a monochrome VGA display can show a resolution of 640 dots horizontally and 480 dots vertically.

A color VGA display for text has a 132-column by 50-row mode, also. Most people and applications use 80 columns and 25 rows, however. Each character on-screen has a foreground color and a background color using colors chosen from a range of 16 possibilities. In high-resolution graphics mode, a color VGA display also shows 640 dots horizontally and 480 dots vertically in 16 colors. In medium-resolution graphics mode, a color VGA display shows 320 dots horizontally and 200 dots vertically in 256 colors.

Most people use VGA color systems for OS/2, which operates in high-resolution graphics mode for Presentation Manager (PM) applications.

Using XGA

The Extended Graphics Array (XGA) is IBM's most recent specification. XGA is compatible with the earlier VGA and 8514/A video adapters from IBM. (This chapter discusses the 8514/A and other adapters in the next few sections.) With an XGA-equipped computer, you get a high-resolution mode that shows 1,024 dots horizontally and 768 dots vertically in 256 colors. You also get a medium-resolution mode that shows 640 dots horizontally and 480 dots vertically in 65,536 colors. Of course, you can still have 80 columns by 25 rows of text.

Using CGA and EGA for OS/2

The Color Graphics Adapter (CGA) and Enhanced Graphics Adapter (EGA) standards are officially obsolete, but OS/2 supports them. Basically, the CGA video adapter offers a high-resolution graphics mode that shows 640 dots across and 200 dots vertically in black and white. The EGA adapter is similar, but it can show 350 dots vertically. These resolutions are coarse; OS/2 cannot make effective use of your monitor if you have either CGA or EGA. You should consider upgrading to a higher resolution video adapter and monitor.

Using 8514/A

The 8514/A video adapter standard was IBM's highest-resolution personal computer display offering until XGA. It offers a 1,024 by 768 dot resolution, like XGA, but XGA operates much faster. XGA has superseded the 8514/A video standard.

Using Super VGA

When VESA was formed, initial participants included ATI Technologies, Genoa Systems, Orchid, Renaissance GRX, STB, Tecmar, Video-7, and Western Digital/Paradise. At the present time, members of VESA include Panacea, Western Digital, Everex, Hewlett-Packard, Intel, ATI Technologies, Headland, Chips and Technologies, Mitsubishi, Genoa, Tandy, NEC, and Willow. VESA exists to promote the so-called Super VGA standard, which calls for an 800 horizontal by 600 vertical dot resolution.

Video adapters made by these companies all support VGA and should work with OS/2 in VGA mode. In some cases, a non-IBM Super VGA mode requires that you load an OS/2 device driver (you must use a text editor to change the CONFIG.SYS file). If you have a video adapter made by one of these companies, check with your manufacturer to find out whether that company has written an OS/2 device driver so that you can use the special 800 by 600 mode (or other non-IBM mode).

IBM built device drivers for the most popular Super VGA video adapters as well as some higher-resolution video adapters into OS/2 2.1. You select your level of video adapter support during the installation process. You use an OS/2 configuration option to further increase the resolution produced by your video adapter.

IBM now makes a Super VGA video adapter, the IBM VGA 256c. OS/2 2.1 supports the IBM VGA 256c and the video adapters in the following list:

> Headland Technology VRAM II
>
> Tseng Laboratories ET4000
>
> Trident Microsystems TVGA
>
> ATI Technologies VGA Wonder
>
> Western Digital Imaging Paradise

For Related Information

◀◀ "Understanding Hardware and Software," p. 13.

▶▶ "Upgrading Your Hardware," p. 165.

FROM HERE...

Chapter Summary

This chapter helped you understand the potential problems you may encounter if part or all of your computer system is made by a company other than IBM. In particular, you covered what makes a computer IBM-compatible and how OS/2 runs successfully on most non-IBM computers. Other topics emphasized were the 80386, 80486, and Pentium CPU chips, the computer's ROM BIOS, non-IBM disk drives and disk controller cards, non-IBM keyboards and mice, and compatibility issues with video adapter cards.

In the next chapter, you install and begin using OS/2. Now that you know what issues you face if you have non-IBM computer hardware, you are well prepared for any problems you may encounter during the installation. In most cases, you find that OS/2 installs onto your computer without your realizing that it isn't made by IBM.

Installing OS/2

You're now ready to install OS/2. If you're familiar with DOS and have a computer system made by IBM, you reached this chapter quickly. You quickly toured OS/2 in Chapter 1, "Taking a Quick Tour of OS/2 and Your Computer," discovered the differences between OS/2 and DOS in Chapter 3, "Learning OS/2 If You Know DOS," and decided how you want to configure OS/2 in Chapter 4, "Deciding How You Want To Use OS/2."

On the other hand, if you used DOS before, Chapter 2, "Learning OS/2 If You Don't Know DOS," brought you up to speed; if another manufacturer besides IBM made your computer system, Chapter 5, "Using Non-IBM Computers and OS/2," helped you identify potential compatibility problems.

OS/2 installation is a simple process, for the most part. The installation software preselects common choices for you, and you can install many options just by clicking buttons or pressing the Enter key. The installation of HPFS and/or Boot Manager works differently, however, and you use a multistep process to set up these optional features of OS/2. If you want to install HPFS or Boot Manager, use the instructions later in this chapter.

You can install OS/2 on a computer's hard disk that already has DOS on it, or you can install OS/2 on a "fresh" (not previously formatted) hard disk. The installation software prompts you to do the formatting step.

If you want to use HPFS or Boot Manager, you must set up new partitions on your hard disk and go through the formatting process. When you install HPFS and/or Boot Manager on a computer already formatted with DOS, you must make a backup copy of your hard disk files; the partitioning and formatting process does not preserve existing hard disk files. You then restore your files to the hard disk after installation by copying them from your backup copy.

The following list describes the basic steps you use to install OS/2. You can use this list as a roadmap when you explore the details of the installation process in this chapter.

- Insert the OS/2 2.1 Installation Disk and turn on the computer.

- When prompted, insert OS/2 Diskette 1 and press Enter.

- View some introductory screens of information.

- Indicate whether you want to partition and/or format the hard disk.

- Select your type of mouse.

- Insert OS/2 Diskettes 2 through 5 when prompted.

- Reinsert the OS/2 Installation Disk when prompted.

- Remove the disk and reboot the computer into the Presentation Manager portion of the installation.

- Select the features you want to install.

- Change configuration settings, if desired.

- Insert the remaining disks, when prompted.

- Migrate your existing applications.

- Reboot; OS/2 is installed.

The installation process takes from 40 minutes to as long as two hours, depending on the number of features you choose to install and the processing power (speed) of your computer system.

If you encounter any difficulty installing OS/2, recheck the instructions in this chapter first. Then use Chapter 8, "Troubleshooting OS/2," to fix the problem.

NOTE The OS/2 installation software contains foreground and background threads. You learned about OS/2 threaded applications in Chapters 3 and 4. The foreground installation thread displays information on-screen and interacts with you. The background thread copies files and performs other internal tasks. During the installation process, you may notice hard disk activity even while you're inserting the next disk. This is a sign that the background thread is working, even while the foreground thread prompts you for a disk.

Installing from a CD-ROM Disk

If you have a CD-ROM drive supported by OS/2 and you purchased the CD-ROM edition of the operating system, you will have an easier time installing OS/2. You will not have to insert several floppy disks during installation. You simply boot your computer with the two floppy disks supplied with the CD-ROM disk and continue the remainder of the installation from the CD-ROM disk.

To install OS/2 from the CD-ROM drive, first make sure that your CD-ROM drive is on and ready (if the drive has a power switch). Close any open files and exit your applications to save any work you're doing. Turn off the computer.

Insert the OS/2 CD-ROM disk into the CD-ROM drive. Then insert the floppy disk labeled OS/2 2.1 Installation into the first floppy disk drive (the A: drive). Turn on your computer. When the blue IBM logo screen appears, remove the OS/2 2.1 Installation floppy disk and insert the OS/2 Diskette 1 floppy disk into the first floppy disk drive. Press Enter. After a few moments, you see the Welcome to OS/2 screen shown in figure 6.1. After you press Enter, the installation program uses the CD-ROM disk for the remainder of the installation process.

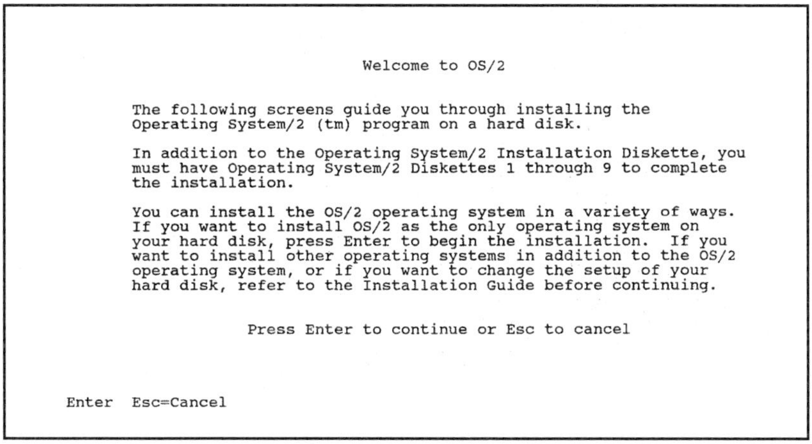

```
                          Welcome to OS/2

           The following screens guide you through installing the
           Operating System/2 (tm) program on a hard disk.

           In addition to the Operating System/2 Installation Diskette, you
           must have Operating System/2 Diskettes 1 through 9 to complete
           the installation.

           You can install the OS/2 operating system in a variety of ways.
           If you want to install OS/2 as the only operating system on
           your hard disk, press Enter to begin the installation.  If you
           want to install other operating systems in addition to the OS/2
           operating system, or if you want to change the setup of your
           hard disk, refer to the Installation Guide before continuing.

                     Press Enter to continue or Esc to cancel



      Enter   Esc=Cancel
```

Fig. 6.1

The Welcome to OS/2 screen.

You still need to read the rest of this chapter; you have choices to make during the installation and you should follow the steps and guidelines presented in this chapter to make correct choices. You don't have to insert floppy disks into your computer during the process, however. OS/2 installs from the CD-ROM disk.

If you see an error message after the OS/2 Diskette 1 floppy disk loads into memory and you press Enter, you may have a CD-ROM drive that OS/2 doesn't support. To determine if this is the case, verify that you have properly inserted the CD-ROM disk into the CD-ROM drive, that the CD-ROM drive is turned on, and that all connections are tight. Restart the installation from the beginning. If the error message appears again, you probably do not have a CD-ROM drive supported by OS/2. You should contact the company that sold you the CD-ROM edition of OS/2 and explain the problem. You may have to obtain the floppy disk edition of OS/2 and install from floppy disks.

Setting Up the Installation Floppy Disks

IBM distributes the basic operating system on 27 disks. (Many features of OS/2 are optional; don't be overly concerned about the number of disks. You can install as much or as little of OS/2 as you want.) Check your OS/2 distribution disks now to make sure that you have one disk labeled OS/2 2.1 Installation and 19 others labeled OS/2 Diskette 1 through OS/2 Diskette 19. You should have five other disks labeled Printer Driver Diskette 1 through Printer Diskette Driver 5 and two disks labeled Display Driver Diskette 1 and Display Driver Diskette 2.

Following your installation of OS/2, or perhaps even before installation if you already have a working computer, make copies of all the distribution disks in case something happens to the originals. The fastest way to copy disks is with the DISKCOPY command, explained fully in Part VI, "Using the Command Reference."

FROM HERE...

For Related Information

◀◀ "Understanding Hardware and Software," p. 13.

Booting the Installation Disk

If you already have DOS or an earlier version of OS/2 on your computer, make sure that you have a backup copy of your files before continuing. If you want to use Boot Manager or HPFS, you *must* have a backup copy of your files at this time. When you install Boot Manager or HPFS, you repartition and reformat your hard drive, which erases any and all existing files.

> **T I P**
>
> If your computer system is on, save your work and turn the computer off. On a few kinds of non-IBM hardware, the OS/2 Installation Disk has trouble initializing the computer if the previously run DOS-based application leaves the hardware in an unusual state. Installing OS/2 onto a just-powered-on computer sometimes helps the OS/2 Installation Diskette boot properly because it allows the installation software to avoid the left-over hardware state.

Insert the OS/2 Installation Diskette into drive A and turn the machine on. The first part of the installation software takes several moments to load from the disk. After a while, you see an IBM logo and a message asking you to remove the OS/2 Installation Diskette and replace it with the disk labeled OS/2 Diskette 1. After you insert OS/2 Diskette 1, the next part of the installation software loads from the disk. You then see the Welcome to OS/2 screen (refer to fig. 6.1).

> **CAUTION:** Make sure that you follow the disk insertion instructions carefully. Removing a disk at the wrong time can cause the installation process to fail part way through.

For Related Information

◄◄ "Understanding Hardware and Software," p. 13.

FROM HERE...

First Step: Text Mode

You install OS/2 in two steps. The first step uses a text mode interface; the second step uses the graphical interface of Presentation Manager. OS/2 reboots your computer between these steps. Step 1 uses the OS/2 Installation Disk, the OS/2 Diskettes 1 through 5, and then the Installation Diskette again. Step 2, the graphical portion of the installation, uses OS/2 Diskette 6 through OS/2 Diskette 19, the Printer Driver Diskettes, and the Display Driver Diskettes.

After you use the Installation Diskette and OS/2 Diskette 1 to reach the screen, press Enter to continue or press the Esc (escape) key to stop the installation process. Pressing Esc presents you with an OS/2 command line prompt. Because OS/2 is not yet installed, you can execute commands only from the distribution disks after you press Esc. If you press Esc by mistake at this point, restart the installation process by reinserting the OS/2 Installation Diskette and rebooting your computer.

The next screen displayed is the Introduction screen. This screen provides tips on selecting choices and obtaining help from OS/2 during the installation. You only need to read the Introduction screen, which does not ask you any questions. When you press Enter to leave the Introduction screen, the File System screen appears. This screen reminds you to repartition and reformat your hard disk to use HPFS. The File System screen also only requires that you read it. Upon pressing Enter, you see the Installation Drive Selection screen, shown in figure 6.2.

```
                        Installation Drive Selection

        If you are interested in having multiple versions of DOS, OS/2
        or other operating systems on the same hard disk, refer to the
        Installation Guide for information on OS/2 Hard Disk
        Management before continuing.

        If you have multiple primary partitions set up on your hard
        disk, select option 2 to verify that the correct partition is
        active.

        OS/2 will be installed on drive C :


        Select an option:

          1. Accept the drive

          2. Specify a different drive or partition

        If you select option 2, the FDISK screen is displayed.

  Enter  Esc=Cancel  F3=Exit  F1=Help
```

Fig. 6.2

The Installation Drive Selection screen.

The Installation Drive Selection screen is another information display. You use this screen to confirm whether you want to install OS/2 on drive C (your first bootable partition). If you have used DOS on your computer before and don't want to install Boot Manager or HPFS, choose option 1. Choose option 2 if any of the following conditions fit your situation:

- Your hard disk has not been previously formatted by DOS or an earlier version of OS/2.

- You want to install HPFS in place of the DOS File Allocation Table formatting.

- You want to install Boot Manager.

Choosing option 2 on the Installation Drive Selection screen presents you with the Installation FDISK screen. You use this screen to indicate partition and formatting changes. Figure 6.3 shows this FDISK screen.

```
               Formatting the Installation Partition

    The partitions on a hard disk must be formatted before information
    can be placed on them.  If the partition in which you are going to
    install the OS/2 operating system has been formatted by DOS or the
    OS/2 operating system, it is not necessary to format it again.

    The installation partition can be formatted to use either the High
    Performance File System (HPFS) or the FAT file system.  If you have
    other partitions on your hard disk, you can format them to use either
    file system after you have completed installation.  Files can be
    copied between partitions that use different file systems.

    Formatting erases all files.  If you need these files, or if you want
    to repartition your hard disk, refer to the Installation Guide before
    continuing installation.

    Select an option.

        1. Do not format the partition

        2. Format the partition

  Enter  F1=Help
```

Fig. 6.3

The Installation FDISK screen for repartitioning your hard disk.

If your hard disk is already partitioned and formatted the way you want for OS/2, you can move on to the next section.

Partitioning and Formatting Your Disk

Because partitioning and formatting your hard disk erases any existing files on your hard disk, including application software files, data files, and operating system files, make sure that you make a backup copy of any files you want to save before you partition or format your hard disk.

> **CAUTION:** When you partition and format your hard disk, you erase *all* data on the disk. If you want to save the data on your disk, make a backup copy before you partition or format.

Installing OS/2 on a Non-Formatted Machine

If you're installing OS/2 on a new machine and you want to use the Dual-Boot feature, you first should install the appropriate version of

DOS on your computer. *Que's MS-DOS 5 User's Guide,* Special Edition, leads you through booting DOS, running the DOS FDISK program, and running the DOS FORMAT program.

If you don't want Dual-Boot, you can proceed to FDISK and format your hard disk as part of the OS/2 installation procedure.

Before you tell the OS/2 or DOS FDISK programs to set up your hard disk partitions, you should decide whether to use Boot Manager or HPFS.

Installing OS/2 on a DOS-Formatted Machine

To change your partition sizes, to use Boot Manager, or to use HPFS, you first should make backup copies of the data on your computer, and then treat your computer as if it had not been formatted before (see the previous section). Remember that the FDISK and FORMAT programs erase existing data on your hard disk.

If you want OS/2 to recognize your existing version of DOS and automatically install Dual-Boot, use the instructions and guidelines later in this chapter.

Choosing Boot Manager

To install the Multiple Operating System Tool (Boot Manager), you must tell FDISK to create a primary disk partition for each of the operating systems you will use, in addition to the disk partition you set aside for Boot Manager. Boot Manager needs only a 1M partition. When you create partitions, make the first partition the one for Boot Manager.

To use Boot Manager and HPFS, designate the last partition on the disk as the HPFS partition. (All installable file systems for all operating systems generally should be placed in partitions at the end of the partition list.) Be aware of the disk partition restrictions, if any, for the non-OS/2 operating systems you will use. If you create a partition for use by DOS 3.3 (that you can select with Boot Manager at boot time), for example, ensure that the DOS 3.3 partition is located within the first 32 megabytes of the hard disk.

After you use FDISK, your list of allocated partitions might look like the following example.

Alias	Status	Access	FS type	Size (MBytes)
BOOT MGR	Startable	Primary	Boot Manager	1
DOS 3.3	Selectable	Primary	FAT 16	20
OS/2 2.1	Selectable	Primary	FAT 16	32
Common	None	Logical	FAT 16	32

In the preceding table, BOOT MGR represents the Boot Manager partition.

To set up the Boot Manager partition, first tell FDISK to delete any existing partitions on the hard disk. Use the up-arrow and down-arrow keys to select (highlight) the partition you want to delete, and then press Enter to see the Options menu. Select Delete and press Enter. Repeat these steps for all the partitions on the hard disk.

NOTE Changes you make in FDISK take effect only after you press F3 to exit from FDISK. You then have a chance to accept or abandon your FDISK modifications.

After you delete any existing partitions, you can create the Boot Manager partition and the partitions for the other operating systems. Select (highlight) the unused partition entry with the up- or down-arrow keys. Press Enter to access the Options menu, and then choose the Install Most... item. You next specify whether you want the Boot Manager partition to occupy the beginning or end of the hard disk. You probably should use the first 1M of the hard disk for Boot Manager.

You have allocated your Boot Manager partition, but the OS/2 installation process has not yet copied Boot Manager to it. The installation of Boot Manager occurs later in the installation process.

You now can create partitions for other operating systems, unless that operating system requires you to use its own FDISK-type utility to allocate disk space. You can create DOS and OS/2 partitions now. Some UNIX operating systems, such as IBM's AIX, must allocate their own space. If you plan to use an operating system such as AIX, leave sufficient unallocated (unused) space in the partition table; AIX allocates the space during its installation procedure.

To create a DOS or an OS/2 partition that you can select from the Boot Manager menu when you start the computer, press Enter to see the FDISK Options menu. Choose Create and press Enter. Type the number of megabytes you want the partition to occupy on the hard disk, and specify whether the partition should be a primary partition or a logical drive within an extended partition. You should set up the first DOS or OS/2 partition as a primary partition. Tell FDISK where on the disk the new partition should exist.

After you create the partition, use the Options menu to change the characteristics of that partition. If you have multiple primary partitions, choose the Access menu item to tell FDISK which primary partition is active (you can have only one active primary partition). Use the Startable menu item to select which partition you want to have control when you start the computer. When you install Boot Manager, you normally make the Boot Manager partition the Startable partition. At boot time, Boot Manager then gives you the opportunity to select one of the other partitions. Use the Selectable menu item to designate which partitions (and therefore which operating systems) you want to see in the Boot Manager menu at boot time. You also can give each partition a meaningful name, or *alias*, at this time.

You now told FDISK about the Boot Manager partition and about any other partitions for other operating systems you will use except for OS/2 2.1. You left unallocated space for an operating system such as AIX (UNIX operating systems supply their own FDISK cquivalents).

To continue installing OS/2, you now create its partition. Choose Create from the Options menu, and specify the size of the OS/2 2.1 partition. Make sure that the new OS/2 2.1 partition is marked Installable by choosing that FDISK menu option.

Finally, before you continue with the installation of OS/2, you can configure Boot Manager by selecting the Startup Values menu option. You can tell Boot Manager whether to start one of the partitions' operating systems by default each time the computer boots, and you can tell Boot Manager how long to display its menu before booting that default operating system.

When you are satisfied with the changes you made to your partition table, press F3. FDISK asks you to confirm your changes; you then proceed with the installation of OS/2 2.1.

Selecting HPFS

You install the High Performance File System by creating a partition on your hard disk that contains HPFS data, formatting that partition with a special form of the FORMAT command, and inserting the appropriate HPFS statements in your CONFIG.SYS file. You run FDISK, and perhaps the FORMAT command, during the installation procedure.

First, use FDISK to delete any existing partitions on the hard disk. Use the up- and down-arrow keys to select (highlight) the partition you want to delete. Then press Enter to see the Options menu. Select Delete from this menu and press Enter. Repeat these steps for all the partitions on the hard disk.

 NOTE Changes you make in FDISK take effect only after you press F3 to exit from FDISK. You then have a chance to accept or abandon your FDISK modifications.

After you delete any existing partitions, you can create the HPFS partition. You might choose to have a combination of FAT and HPFS partitions, or you might choose to install Boot Manager and HPFS on the same computer, with perhaps a combination of FAT and HPFS partitions. You create the partitions when you run FDISK as part of the installation process. The actual formatting of the HPFS partition occurs later.

To create an HPFS or FAT partition, press Enter to see the FDISK Options menu. Choose Create and press Enter. Type the number of megabytes you want the partition to occupy on the hard disk, and select whether the partition should be a primary partition or a logical drive within an extended partition. (Your HPFS partition should be a primary partition.) Indicate to FDISK that the HPFS partition should be allocated at the end of the disk, if you are creating multiple partitions.

After you create the partition(s), use the Options menu to change the characteristics of the partition(s). If you're installing Boot Manager, follow the directions given earlier for setting these characteristics. If you want only a single HPFS partition, be sure to mark that partition primary, startable, and installable. For a combination FAT and HPFS set of partitions, tell FDISK to put the FAT partition at the beginning of the disk and the HPFS partition at the end of the disk. Ensure that the FAT partition is marked startable and installable. You also can give each partition a meaningful name at this time.

When you're satisfied with your changes to the partition table, press F3. FDISK asks you to confirm your changes, and you then continue to install OS/2 2.1.

Continuing with the Installation

Depending on the OS/2 functions, features, and mini-applications you select, OS/2 needs from about 15M of disk space to about 40M. The installation software detects an insufficient disk space condition and warns you that the installation may not succeed. Figure 6.4 shows the warning screen titled Hard Disk Space Requirement.

```
ëëëëëëëëëëëëëëëëëëëëëëëëëëëëëëëëëëëëëëëëëëëëëëëëëëëëëëëëëëëëëëëëëëëëëëëëëëëëëëf
¤                                                                        ¤
¤                    Hard Disk Space Requirement                         ¤
¤                                                                        ¤
¤                                                                        ¤
¤                                                                        ¤
¤     The OS/2 operating system requires 16MB of hard disk space.        ¤
¤     You now have less than that amount available.  If a previous       ¤
¤     version of the OS/2 operating system is installed on your hard     ¤
¤     disk, or if you want to reformat your hard disk later in the       ¤
¤     installation process, you might not need as much space.            ¤
¤                                                                        ¤
¤     Be sure that you have 16MB of hard disk space available.           ¤
¤                                                                        ¤
¤                                                                        ¤
¤                                                                        ¤
¤     Do one of the following:                                           ¤
¤                                                                        ¤
¤     - Press Enter to continue with installation.                       ¤
¤                                                                        ¤
¤     - Press F3 to exit to the OS/2 command prompt.                     ¤
¤                                                                        ¤
¤ Enter  Esc=Cancel  F3=Exit                                             ¤
àëëëëëëëëëëëëëëëëëëëëëëëëëëëëëëëëëëëëëëëëëëëëëëëëëëëëëëëëëëëëëëëëëëëëëëëëëëëëë¥
```

Fig. 6.4

The Hard Disk Space Requirement warning screen.

You can safely ignore the warning if you simply restart the installation process or you install version 2.1 of OS/2 over an earlier version (files are replaced in both situations).

If you're not replacing files during the installation and you truly lack the disk space to continue, you have the following three options:

- You can press F3 to exit from the installation software. An OS/2 command line prompt appears. At the prompt, use the DIR, CD, and ERASE commands to perform housecleaning on your old files and directories. When you regain enough free disk space, restart the installation process by rebooting the OS/2 Installation Diskette. This option appears on the Hard Disk Space Requirement warning screen.

- You can press Enter to continue with the installation. The installation of OS/2 probably will not complete if you choose this alternative. This option also appears on the Hard Disk Space Requirement warning screen.

- You can boot DOS and use your favorite file manager to do the housecleaning. Choose this option if you don't feel comfortable finding and deleting files at a command line prompt. When you recover enough disk space, restart the OS/2 installation.

Installing Dual-Boot

OS/2 2.1 automatically installs its Dual-Boot feature if you have an existing version of DOS on your computer. If OS/2 cannot completely install the Dual-Boot feature, you may see a screen similar to the one in figure 6.5. If you see such a warning during installation, you must note the problem and fix it after OS/2 is installed. You usually can fix the problem by using the OS/2 System Editor to correct your DOS CONFIG.SYS file or by moving files to their usual directories as specified in the *DOS User's Guide and Reference.*

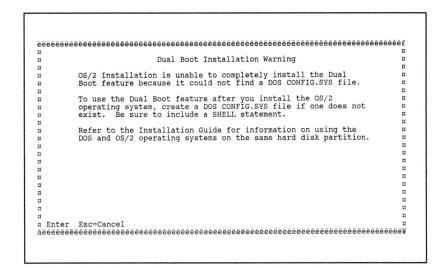

Fig. 6.5

The Dual-Boot
Installation
Warning screen.

If Dual-Boot does not successfully and completely install on your computer, use the following guidelines to correct your DOS AUTOEXEC.BAT and CONFIG.SYS files and to put the files into the proper subdirectories. Dual-Boot successfully installs if the following conditions are true on your computer:

- DOS is already installed.

- The DOS operating system is version 3.3 or later.

- DOS is installed in the first partition on the hard disk and that partition is marked bootable.

- Your DOS partition has sufficient free disk space for the installation of OS/2.

- All DOS commands and utility programs exist in a subdirectory (such as C:\DOS) and not in the root directory of the disk. In particular, the file COMMAND.COM must reside in this subdirectory.

- You do not select the FORMAT option during OS/2 installation.

■ The file C:\AUTOEXEC.BAT contains at least the following statements, exactly as shown:

```
PATH C:\DOS

SET COMSPEC=C:\DOS\COMMAND.COM
```

■ The file C:\CONFIG.SYS contains at least the following statement, exactly as shown:

```
SHELL=C:\DOS\COMMAND.COM C:\DOS\ /P
```

Your SHELL statement in the CONFIG.SYS file may also contain the /E:*XXXX* option where *XXXX* represents the number of bytes of environment space to reserve. Your DOS CONFIG.SYS file and AUTOEXEC.BAT file may also contain other statements. The preceding entries are the minimum requirement for the correct installation of the OS/2 Dual-Boot feature.

Selecting Your Mouse

OS/2 needs to know whether you have a pointing device (a mouse) and what brand it is. You have an opportunity to change this selection later in the installation, just in case you make a mistake. You can use a mouse to choose options during the graphical second part of the installation, and so you need to tell OS/2 now what sort of mouse you have.

You can select your mouse from the following list:

■ IBM Personal System/2 Mouse

■ Microsoft Mouse, Bus Version

■ Microsoft Mouse, InPort Version

■ Microsoft Mouse, Serial Version

■ Microsoft Mouse, PS/2 Version

■ PC Mouse Systems Mouse

■ Visi-On Mouse

■ Other Pointing Device for Mouse Port

■ No pointing device support

If you choose Other Pointing Device, you use the mouse driver file on the disk that contains an OS/2 device driver. You received this disk from the manufacturer of your pointing device. OS/2 prompts you to insert this disk.

If your brand of mouse is not on the list, you often can choose a mouse similar to and compatible with your brand. You can choose Microsoft Mouse, Bus Version, for example, if you have a Logitech Bus Mouse.

If you select Microsoft Mouse, Serial Version, OS/2 asks you to confirm which serial port to use. OS/2 tells you how many COM ports it has found, suggests one, and allows you to change the COM port assignment.

Copying Files from the First Few Disks

After you have determined how you want to set up your disk partitions (or decided to use your already-formatted ones), selected your pointing device, and made a note of any warning screens that you see, you're ready to continue. After you select your mouse and confirm its serial port usage (if necessary), the following message appears on-screen:

```
Remove the diskette from Drive A. Insert Operating System/2
Diskette 2 into Drive A. Then press Enter.
```

When the installation program prompts you, follow the instructions on-screen to insert OS/2 Diskettes 2 through 5 and the Installation Diskette. which contains the installation software and some other OS/2 files. While OS/2 copies the files of each disk onto your hard disk, the program indicates the process is underway by displaying the message Transferring Files from Diskette and by showing you the name of each file being installed.

When you install OS/2 files on your hard disk, you may see a screen that contains the following message:

```
The installation program has failed due to an error. To view
the error, you need to look at the INSTALL.LOG file that was
created for you. Press Enter to display INSTALL.LOG.
```

The OS/2 installation program suggests that you fix the problem by exiting to a command line prompt and issuing commands. Alternatively, if you have a DOS-bootable floppy disk, you can boot DOS and use a file manager or your favorite text editor to correct any errors.

Note that most files on the distribution disks are compressed. You should let the installation software copy the files to your hard disk. If you attempt to copy them with the COPY command, your computer system will not work. If you absolutely must copy a file from one of the distribution disks by hand, use the UNPACK command described in the command reference section of this book.

When OS/2 has copied and installed the contents of the OS/2 Installation Diskette and OS/2 Diskettes 1, 2, 3, 4, and 5 onto your hard disk, a screen with the following message appears:

> The hard disk preparation is complete. The next step will be OS/2 system configuration. Remove the diskette from the disk drive. Press Enter to start OS/2 system configuration. When you take the disk out of the drive and press Enter, the computer reboots (do not be surprised) and the second part of the installation begins.

FROM HERE...

For Related Information

◄◄ "Understanding Hardware and Software," p. 13.

◄◄ "Examining Other Operating Systems," p. 78.

◄◄ "Considering Disks and Disk Files," p. 80.

Choosing the OS/2 Features You Want

After the computer reboots into the graphical portion of the installation process, the first screen displayed is an IBM OS/2 logo. You then use the Presentation Manager interface to confirm the type of mouse you have, the type of keyboard, type of computer monitor, your country, and other configuration settings. Next, you choose the OS/2 features you want—CD/ROM support, on-line documentation, printer/screen fonts, optional system utilities, tools and games, HPFS, the OS/2 DOS environment, the REXX batch programming language, serial device support, and the serviceability and diagnostic aids. Finally (and optionally), you can modify your DOS environment and OS/2 configuration parameters.

Using the Initial PM Installation Screen

The first screen of the graphical portion of the installation asks you if you want to learn how to use a mouse, if you want to install all of OS/2 (including all the mini-applications, games, options, and features), or if you want to select which features OS/2 should install. You would normally choose this last item, Select features and install, because OS/2 is so feature-rich you almost certainly will not use every option or utility.

The Learn how to use a mouse option takes you through the Mouse-familiarization section of the OS/2 Tutorial. If you select this option, you spend a few moments learning how to interact with OS/2 through your mouse movements and button presses. Exiting from the mouse tutorial returns you to the installation screen.

The Install all features option tells the OS/2 installation program that you want every last bit of OS/2 on your computer—no questions asked. Even if you have ample free disk space, you probably do not want to choose this option. OS/2 includes a rich set of options, features, utilities, and games that you probably will not get around to exploring or using.

The Select features and install option takes you to the System Configuration screen. The next several sections of this chapter discuss how to choose which OS/2 features you want on your computer. Before you do that, however, confirm your mouse, keyboard, country, and type of computer display (monitor) to OS/2. This step is important because it lets you and OS/2 know that you see and hear one another, in the correct language, during the remainder of the installation process.

 NOTE   OS/2 has a Selective Install feature you can use after you have OS/2 up and running. If you want to install a feature you did not install initially, you can use Selective Install to add the feature later, as explained in Chapter 7, "Modifying Your OS/2 Configuration."

Confirming Your Configuration

Figure 6.6 shows an example of the screen on which you confirm your system configuration. Note that this figure is only an example; your screen will contain other values for the preselected choices if you have a different computer configuration (such as an XGA display screen or a mouse that does not connect through a serial port).

You typically will find that the preselected choices for mouse, keyboard, country, type of display, and other peripherals are correct for your computer. You can press Enter or click the OK button if this is the case.

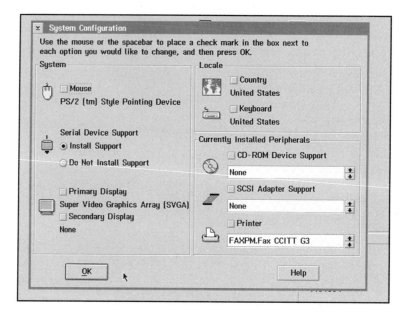

Confirming your
mouse, key-
board, display,
printer, and other
peripherals.

If the Mouse Doesn't Work

If you find that the mouse cursor doesn't move when you roll your
mouse on the surface of your desk or if you want to change the country
settings for your computer, for example, use the up- and down-arrow
keys to select (highlight) the item you want to change. Press the space
bar to put a check mark next to that item and then press Enter. (Pressing Enter is equivalent to clicking the OK button.) You see a screen on
which you can change the value for that item, as described in the next
few sections. Choose the value you want and press Enter. The OS/2
installation program returns you to the system configuration screen.
Press Enter, with no check marks showing, when you finish.

If the OK button is highlighted and you want to go back to one of the
items to put a check mark next to it, use the Tab key to move the selection highlight.

Selecting Serial Device Support

If you have a modem or plotter connected to a serial port on your computer (COM1, COM2, COM3, or COM4), you need to install OS/2's serial
device support. These software driver modules take very little room on
your hard disk. In most cases, you will want to check the box labeled
Install Support under the Serial Device Support heading.

Setting Up Your Display

If you put a check mark in the Primary Display check box and click OK, OS/2 lets you choose your computer's video adapter and display resolution from a list. The list of adapters will look similar to that shown in figure 6.7. Click the type of video adapter your computer uses (OS/2 may already have highlighted your adapter in the list for you if OS/2 was able to automatically detect the adapter type) and click OK. On the next screen, choose the display resolution you feel you will be most comfortable using. Be aware that higher resolutions, such as 1,024 by 768, present more information on-screen at one time but require a larger screen to be readable. If your video adapter is not listed, choosing plain VGA is usually a safe choice.

Fig. 6.7

Choosing your
video adapter.

If you later upgrade or change the video adapter in your PC, or just want to change the display resolution, you can use OS/2's Selective Install feature, as explained in the next chapter, "Modifying Your OS/2 Configuration," to reconfigure OS/2 for the different display mode.

Verifying CD-ROM, SCSI Adapter, and Printer Support

Under the screen heading Currently Installed Peripherals, you see buttons, called *spin buttons*, with headings labeled CD-ROM Device Support, SCSI Adapter Support, and Printer. You use these spin buttons to see the types of these peripherals that OS/2 thinks you have attached to your computer. To operate a spin button, click the mouse button 1 on the up arrow or down arrow located to the right of the current text value for that peripheral. The spin buttons let you see the list of peripherals OS/2 has detected in your computer but do not let you change those values. You click the mouse to put a check mark next to the labels CD-ROM Device Support, SCSI Adapter Support, and Printer if you want to make changes to the lists you see. Then click OK.

Changing CD-ROM and SCSI Adapter Settings

If you click the check box next to CD-ROM Device Support and then click the OK button, OS/2 displays a list of the CD-ROM drives that OS/2 can access. The following list identifies these supported CD-ROM drives:

Manufacturer	CD-ROM drive model
Hitachi	CDR-1650S, CDR-1750S, CDR-3650, CDR-3750
IBM	CD-ROM I, CD-ROM II
NEC	CDR-36, CDR-37, CDR-72, CDR-73, CDR-74,CDR-82, CDR-83, CDR-84
Panasonic	CR-501, LK-MC501S
Sony	CDU-541, CDU-561, CDU-6111, CDU-6211, CDU-7211
Texel	DM-3021, DM-5021, DM-5024
Toshiba	XM-3201, XM-3301

By clicking the SCSI Adapter Support check box and then clicking OK, you tell OS/2 which kind of SCSI adapter you have in your computer. You can choose from the items in the following list:

Manufacturer	SCSI adapter or interface
Adaptec	AIC 6260, AHA 1510/1512/1520/1522, AHA 1540/1542/1544, AHA 1640/1642/1644, AHA 1740/1742/1744
DPT	PM2011/2012
Future Domain	TMC-850/860/875/885, TMC-1660/1670/1680, MCS-600/700, TMC-700EX, TMC-850IBM
IBM	PS/2 SCSI Adapter, PS/2 SCSI Adapter with cache

Selecting a Printer

If you check the Printer check box under Currently Installed Peripherals and click the OK button, a list of printers appears on-screen (see fig. 6.8). Select your printer from the list. OS/2 may ask you a few questions about your printer; you will probably have to refer to the manual that came with your printer to answer these questions.

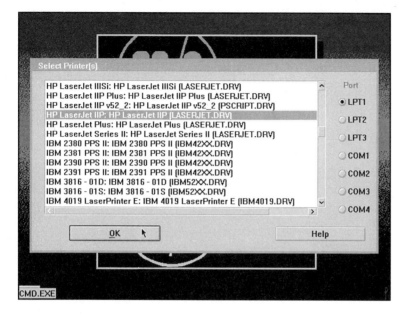

Fig. 6.8

Selecting your
printer.

Selecting Your Features

After you confirm or change your mouse, keyboard, display, printer,
and other system configuration settings, the OS/2 installation program
displays the Setup and Installation screen, as shown in figure 6.9.
Choose the features and options you want by checking the items you
want and by unchecking the items you do not want. These items include on-line documentation, fonts, system utilities, tools and games,
DOS and Windows support, the High Performance File System, Advanced Power Management support (available in some notebook computers), PCMCIA Support (a new way of connecting adapter cards to
computers), REXX, serviceability and diagnostic aids, and the optional
OS/2 bitmaps.

You check and uncheck the items, also called selecting and deselecting,
until you're satisifed with the set of features you want to install. When
you make changes, OS/2 displays in the lower right corner of the screen
a running status of the amount of disk space your selected options
require. Many items on the Setup and Installation screen have subcategories of items. These items appear with a More... button next to
them. If you have selected the item and you click the More... button,
you see a list of the subcategories for that item; you can make further
selections of those subcategory items.

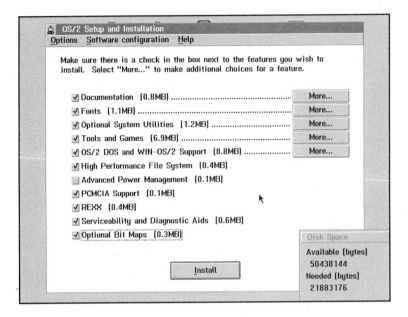

Fig. 6.9

Selecting OS/2
features.

When you complete the selection process, click the Install button to
continue with the installation process. OS/2 then asks if you're ready
to proceed with the installation.

The next few sections of this chapter discuss each of the selectable
items on the Setup and Installation screen.

Using On-Line Documentation

You certainly will want to install at least a portion of the on-line documentation for OS/2 2.1, but you may not want all the files on your hard
disk. To choose the subcategories you want, put a check mark in the
box labeled Documentation on the Setup and Installation screen. Click
the More... button to view the screen illustrated in figure 6.10.

If you're new to computers or feel the least bit timid about them, leave
the OS/2 Tutorial button checked. After you install OS/2, you can run
through the tutorial to strengthen your familiarity with OS/2. You also
may want to install the tutorial for curiosity's sake, even if you are familiar with computers.

The second subcategory, the OS/2 Command Reference, is the heart of
the on-line documentation. You will almost certainly want to install this

part so that you can refer to the on-line help whenever you have a question. Chapter 13, "Using the Built-In Help Facility," shows you how to ask questions and receive answers from the on-line help that OS/2 supplies.

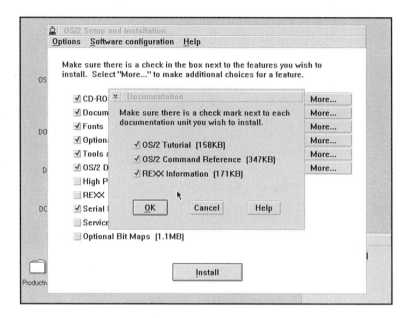

Fig. 6.10

Selecting on-line documentation.

The third option, REXX Information, tells OS/2 you want the on-line help available for the REXX programming language. If you plan to do sophisticated batch file programming under OS/2, leave this box checked. Otherwise, you can safely uncheck the box.

When you have made your selections, click the OK button or press Enter with the OK button highlighted. The OS/2 installation process returns you to the Setup and Installation screen.

Installing Fonts

Chapter 4, "Deciding How You Want To Use OS/2," explained the pros and cons of installing the fonts that come with OS/2. When you check the Fonts option and click the More... button for that option, you receive an opportunity to indicate which fonts you want to use. Figure 6.11 shows the screen that appears.

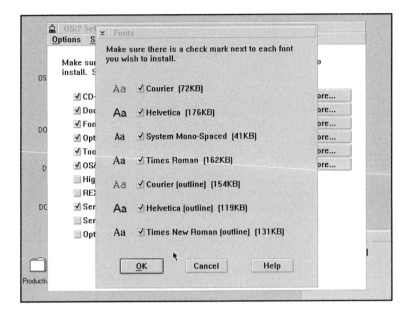

Fig. 6.11

Selecting fonts.

Note that if you just check the Fonts option without clicking the More... button, OS/2 installs all the fonts. If you uncheck the Fonts option, however, OS/2 doesn't install any of the fonts. The Fonts selection screen shown in figure 6.11 appears only if you check the Fonts option and click the More... button to view the subcategories for that option.

The fonts supplied with OS/2 include Courier, Helvetica, System Mono-Spaced, Times Roman, Courier outline, Helvetica outline, and Times New Roman outline. The last three fonts are products of the Adobe company and are quite handsome. These special outline fonts do take a larger amount of disk space, however. The Fonts selection screen shows you exactly what each font looks like.

After you make your selections, click the OK button, or press the Tab key to highlight the button and then press Enter.

Selecting Optional System Utilities

The optional system utilities selection screen allows you to choose from the list of system utilities supplied with OS/2 (see fig. 6.12).

The following table shows the purpose of each of these optional utilities so that you can judge whether you want to install that utility.

Utility	Purpose
Backup Hard Disk	Make backup copies of your data on floppy disks
Change File Attributes	Change a file to/from Read-Only status
Display Directory Tree	View the structure of your hard disk subdirectories
Manage Partitions	Change partition sizes
Label Disks	Record internal volume labels on your disks
Link Object Modules	A programmer development tool
Picture Viewer	View OS/2 metafiles
PMREXX	A Presentation Manager interactive REXX programming environment
Recover Files	A rarely used, CHKDSK-like command for emergency recovery of files from a badly corrupted hard disk
Restore Backed-up Files	Copy backed-up files to your hard disk
Sort Filter	Sort text files; used most within batch file programs
Installation Aid	A portion of the installation process that you might need later when you want to do a selective install

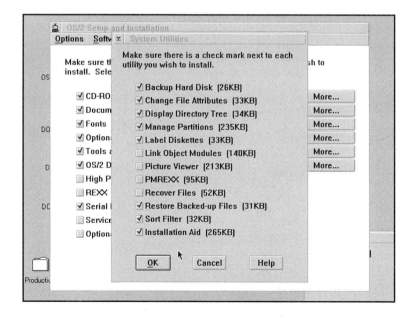

Fig. 6.12

Selecting system utilities.

After you check the items you want to install, click the OK button (or press the Tab key to highlight OK and press Enter). You return to the Setup and Installation screen.

If you're uncertain about which system utilities to install even after you looked over the preceding list, you may want to choose the same items checked in figure 6.12. You can selectively install other portions of OS/2 later, if you want, but for now the sample configuration shown in figure 6.12 will probably suffice for all your day-to-day work and for the occasional disk file administration you will do.

Adding Tools and Games

When you check the Tools and Games box and click its More... button, the screen shown in figure 6.13 appears. On this screen, you select the OS/2 tools and games components you want, just as you did on the previous screens.

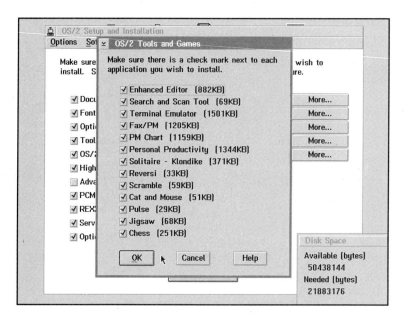

Fig. 6.13

Selecting tools and games.

To help you decide which components you want, the following table lists the purpose of each of the items on the Tools and Games selection screen.

Tool or game	Purpose
Enhanced Editor	Edits text files
Search and Scan	Enables you to search for files by name as well as search the contents of files
Terminal Emulator	Connects to other computers through your modem
Fax/PM	Sends or receives a single fax page through your fax modem
PM Chart	An application for preparing graphs and charts from spreadsheet data
Personal Productivity	A collection of mini-applications (applets); includes a calendar, a calculator, to-do list, simple spreadsheet, notepad, and other helpful software
Solitaire	The one-player card game
Reversi, Scramble	Puzzles for you to solve and play
Cat and Mouse	The animated cat follows your cursor
Pulse	Graphs how hard your computer is working
Jigsaw	Another puzzle
Chess	A 3-D chess game; play against the computer or over a local area network against another player

If you're uncertain about which tools and games to choose, select those that you think will give you a good starting point and suffice for most day-to-day computer work. You can make changes later with OS/2's selective install capability.

Working with the OS/2 DOS Environment

Figure 6.14 is the screen you see when you check the OS/2 DOS and Windows Support box and click the More... button. The first three boxes, labeled DOS Protected Mode Interface, Virtual Expanded Memory Management, and Virtual Extended Memory Support, enable you to install all of OS/2's built-in memory managers. If you install these three items, they provide the same functions and features as the popular DOS products QEMM (from Quarterdeck Office Systems) and 386MAX (from Qualitas). A growing number of applications take advantage of the memory management interfaces created by products such as QEMM and 386MAX, and OS/2 has a built-in capability to also provide these interfaces. The DOS Memory Management section in this chapter covers DOS memory management in detail.

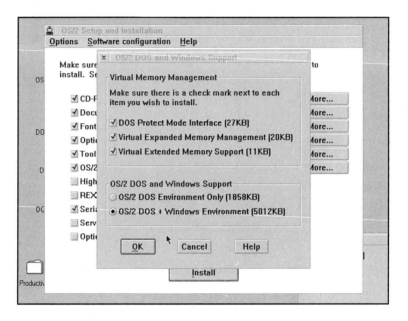

Fig. 6.14

Selecting DOS/ Windows options.

Because you will almost certainly run DOS applications under OS/2 and DOS applications now commonly use these memory management interfaces, you should leave all three boxes checked. The disk space taken by these memory management modules is minimal.

The other two items on the DOS and Windows Support screen represent somewhat larger amounts of disk space. Unlike the first three items, which have boxes next to them for your check marks, the DOS Environment Only and DOS + Windows Environment items have *radio buttons* next to them. You learn more about radio buttons in Chapter 9, "Using Your Computer Screen as a Desktop." For now, all you need to know is that you select one or the other option for DOS and Windows support by clicking its radio button. With the keyboard, you use the Tab key to move the selection highlight to one of the radio buttons. Use the up- and down-arrow keys to change the selection.

As explained in Chapter 16, "Running DOS and Windows under OS/2," OS/2 gives you multiple simultaneous DOS sessions and, if you choose,

Microsoft Windows sessions. On this DOS and Windows Support installation screen, you decide whether you want Microsoft Windows sessions under OS/2.

After you make your selections, click OK (or use the Tab key to move the selection highlight to the OK button and press Enter). You return to the Setup and Installation screen.

Memory management programs work with the following types of memory:

- *Conventional memory*. The memory that is directly addressable by the CPU chip in real mode. The upper boundary is normally the well-known 640K limit, but some memory managers raise that ceiling.

- *Upper memory*. The memory between 640K and 1M. Video adapters, ROM BIOS chips, hard disk controller ROMs, and network adapters are in this region, but some memory managers can map "holes"—Upper Memory Blocks—as regular memory.

- *Extended memory*. Memory above the 1M threshold, addressable only in protected mode.

- *High Memory Area*. The first 64K of extended memory, minus 16 bytes, beginning at the 1M threshold. Because of a quirk in the design of the 80286, 80386, and 80486 CPU chips, you can address these 65,520 bytes in real mode.

- *Expanded memory*. Invented jointly by Lotus, Intel, and Microsoft, expanded memory enables an application to bank-switch RAM, in 16K blocks, from an EMS memory card into conventional or upper memory. The specification is the Lotus/Intel/Microsoft (LIM) Expanded Memory Specification (EMS). The most recent EMS version is Version 4.0. OS/2 can transform extended memory into expanded memory.

- *Extended Memory Specification (XMS)*. Also developed by Lotus/Intel/Microsoft, this standard provides the means for DOS applications to use portions of extended memory.

- *Virtual Control Program Interface memory (VCPI)*. Quarterdeck Office Systems and Phar Lap Software developed the VCPI standard so that DOS applications can cooperatively share extended memory without conflict.

- *DOS Protected Mode Interface (DPMI)*. Developed by Microsoft, DPMI offers functions similar to VCPI but allows OS/2 to enforce control over extended memory access.

Adding High Performance File System Support

In Chapter 4, "Deciding How You Want To Use OS/2," you learned the pros and cons of using the High Performance File System. The next box you can check on the Setup and Installation screen, the HPFS box, enables you to choose to use HPFS. If you put a check mark in the box, the OS/2 installation process takes the following actions:

- Copies the HPFS support modules to your hard disk.
- Inserts a statement in your CONFIG.SYS file to load the HPFS software drivers at boot time.

Checking the HPFS box does not automatically format one of your disk partitions with the new file system. You must do that formatting at a later time; the HPFS check box does not have a More... button.

Installing REXX

You also learned about REXX in Chapter 4. If you want to try your hand at batch file programming, check the box marked REXX on the Setup and Installation screen. The OS/2 installation process copies the REXX modules to your hard disk.

Note that you can do simple batch file programming without REXX. REXX enhances your batch file programs by enabling you to use more sophisticated techniques in your programs. The REXX check box does not have a More... button.

Choosing Serviceability and Diagnostic Aids

If you check the box marked Serviceability and Diagnostic Aids, the OS/2 installation process copies certain optional OS/2 software modules to your hard disk. These modules enable you to "take a snapshot" of the contents of memory if you encounter an error in OS/2 that halts your computer. Such errors are rare. If you have IBM-trained support people in your company who can make sense of the "post-mortem" memory snapshot, however, you probably will want to install these optional modules. If you do not install them, you do not change the performance of OS/2.

Working with Optional Bit Maps

You may someday tire of having a computer screen desktop that appears in a solid color. If you are the flamboyant type, you perhaps will want to select a different background image for your OS/2 desktop. OS/2 comes with a variety of pictures and images you can install by checking the Optional Bit Maps box. Later, after the installation process is completed, you can choose one of these pictures (an OS/2 logo screen, a New England lighthouse, and other images) to be the background of your desktop.

Changing Your Configuration Settings

After you have checked all the boxes on the Setup and Installation screen you want (and perhaps have used the More... buttons to further select or deselect items within each category), you can modify the configuration settings for your OS/2 sessions and your DOS sessions. Making such changes is optional; you may not want to change the defaults at all.

On the Setup and Installation screen, click the Software Configuration menu item (or press Alt-S) to see the configuration pull-down menu. Choose the OS/2 or the DOS menu option. The screen shows various CONFIG.SYS entries. If you have used DOS and a text editor to modify CONFIG.SYS, you will appreciate the ease with which you can change these settings. The OS/2 configuration screen, illustrated in figure 6.15, shows such items as the number of Buffers, the Diskcache size, the MaxWait option, the Swap Minfree option, the number of Threads, the settings for MemMan Protect, MemMan Swap, Priority, and SwapPath. The DOS configuration screen, illustrated in figure 6.16, shows items such as the setting of the Break switch, the amount of memory you want for each DOS session, and the number of FCBs (file control blocks).

The defaults for all these settings are almost certainly correct for you. Leave them alone for now. If you discover you want to change a setting, you can go back and make changes later. The next chapter, "Modifying Your OS/2 Configuration," discusses how to make such changes.

Installing Your Selected Features

When you finish with the Setup and Installation screen, click the Install button (or press Alt-I) to continue with the installation process. A popup message box appears; confirm that you want to proceed. The message You're about to begin the installation of your selected configuration appears on-screen, and OS/2 asks you to insert the remaining disks.

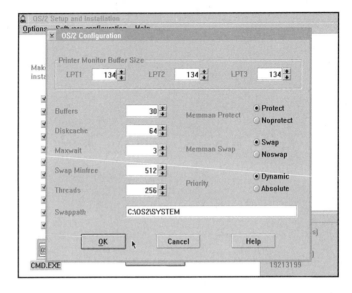

Fig. 6.15

The OS/2 Configuration Window in which you make CONFIG.SYS changes.

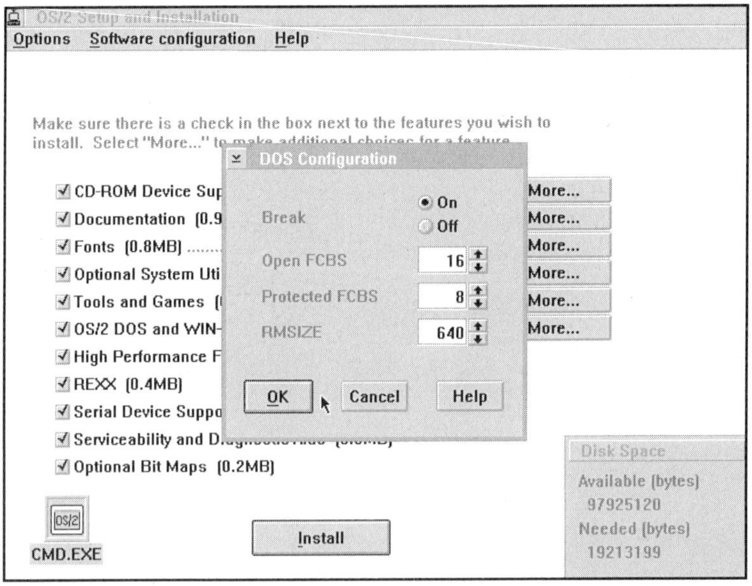

Fig. 6.16

The DOS Configuration Window, for DOS-related CONFIG.SYS changes.

While the OS/2 installation process copies the components of the operating system you selected, you see the progress of the installation on-screen. OS/2 displays a bar chart to show how much of the installation has been completed. It also displays images of the disks so that you can tell which ones you have processed. OS/2 tells you the name of each file while it installs the file on your hard disk.

After OS/2 copies the last file from the disk labeled Diskette 19, the installation process displays a message box telling you OS/2 Setup and Installation is updating the system configuration. This update may take several minutes. When OS/2 finishes updating your system configuration, you're almost finished with the installation of your new multifaceted operating system. The Advanced Options window screen appears (see fig. 6.17).

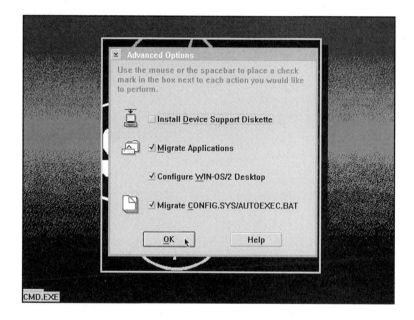

Choosing Advanced Options

You next need to tell OS/2 how you want OS/2 to configure itself for your Windows applications, whether you want OS/2 to automatically make icons for your existing DOS and Windows applications, whether you have optional device support disks to install, and whether the installation process should examine your existing CONFIG.SYS and AUTOEXEC.BAT files to migrate their contents into your new environment.

On the Advanced Options menu, put check marks in the boxes for the actions you want to take and click the OK button. OS/2 leads you through the all the selections, one by one.

Migrating DOS and Windows Applications

If you checked the Advanced Option box labeled Migrate Applications, the screen shown in figure 6.18 appears.

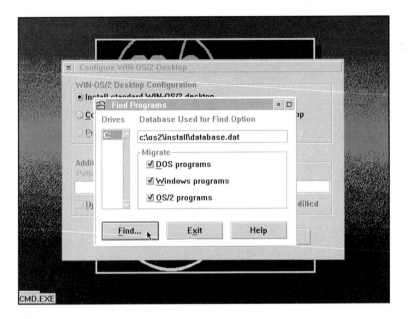

Migrating your
DOS and
Windows
applications.

Icons (objects) represent applications, data files, and utility programs on your OS/2 desktop. You can tell the OS/2 installation process to automatically search for your existing DOS and Windows applications and make icons for them. Later, when you reboot your computer and OS/2 is running, you do not have to manually tell OS/2 about each of your applications. You almost certainly should select this option.

Configuring Your Win-OS/2 Desktop

If you chose to install support for Windows applications on your OS/2 computer, the screen shown in figure 6.19 appears.

You can choose the standard Win-OS/2 desktop, you can copy your existing Windows desktop, or you can preserve an existing Win-OS/2 desktop configuration. The last two options only apply if you already have Windows installed on your computer.

You also can tell OS/2 the path to your existing Windows directory, and you can instruct OS/2 to update your existing Windows desktop settings to reflect your new Win-OS/2 settings.

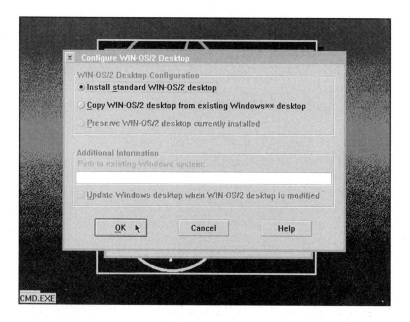

Using Optional Device Support Disks

The standard set of OS/2 distribution disks does not include device
support disks. Third-party (non-IBM) manufacturers supply these disks
along with hardware components. The disks contain optional software
driver modules. If you have such a disk, you should follow the instructions that came with the disk to install the drivers. You probably will
not have any device support disks.

Migrating CONFIG.SYS and
AUTOEXEC.BAT File Contents

OS/2 can determine whether you have statements and commands in
your existing CONFIG.SYS and AUTOEXEC.BAT files that OS/2 should
include in your new environment. You almost certainly should select
this option. OS/2 will migrate the contents of the previous files into the
new CONFIG.SYS and AUTOEXEC.BAT files it creates.

The five disks labeled Printer Driver Diskette 1 through Printer Driver
Diskette 5 contain software drivers for a variety of printer makes and
models. If you chose to install a printer earlier (in the Currently Installed Peripherals section of the System Configuration screen), OS/2
asks you to insert one or more of these disks now. (The System Configuration screen is the one illustrated in figure 6.6.) OS/2 then copies

the appropriate printer to your hard disk. Next OS/2 may ask you to insert one or both of the Display Driver diskettes.

When you finish with the Advanced Options portion of the installation of OS/2, you then see the message `OS/2 Setup and Installation is complete. Remove the disk from Drive A: Press Enter to re-start your system.` When you remove the last installation disk from the disk drive and press Enter, OS/2 reboots your computer. After OS/2 loads into your computer, a screen similar to the one in figure 6.20 appears. You're now running OS/2!

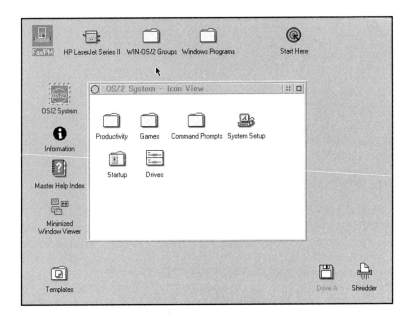

Fig. 6.20

The initial OS/2 screen, showing your new desktop.

> **NOTE** The first time the Workplace Shell initializes itself, it has extra work to do. Don't be concerned if this process takes several moments. The next time you boot your computer, the Workplace Shell will appear much more quickly.

If you asked for tutorial help during the installation process, the first software OS/2 runs will be the OS/2 Tutorial. Spend a few minutes exploring this tutorial material to make yourself more comfortable with your new operating system.

HPFS and Boot Manager—the Finishing Touches

If you chose either Boot Manager or HPFS, you have a little more work to do. For Boot Manager, you need to install the other operating system(s) that Boot Manager allows you to select each time you reboot your computer. Follow the directions that came with the operating system(s).

For HPFS, you may need to format the separate disk partition you designate for HPFS. If you chose to use HPFS for your primary OS/2 partition, the installation process formatted that partition before installing OS/2 on it. If you designated a second, separate partition for use by HPFS, however, you should format that partition now. Double-click the icon labeled OS/2 System. After the folder opens, double-click the icon labeled Command Prompts. Then double-click the icon labeled OS/2 Full Screen. When you see the command line prompt, enter the following command:

> FORMAT <drive letter:> /FS:HPFS

The <drive letter:> is the logical drive that FDISK assigned to the HPFS partition you set up.

For Related Information

FROM HERE...

◄◄ "Understanding Hardware and Software," p. 13.

◄◄ "Examining Other Operating Systems," p. 78.

◄◄ "Considering Disks and Disk Files," p. 80.

◄◄ "Understanding Application and General System Options," p. 84.

◄◄ "Reflecting Personal Preferences," p. 94.

Chapter Summary

This chapter led you step-by-step through the installation of OS/2. You found out how many distribution disks you should have, and you started the installation process. You proceeded through the text mode portion of the installation, partitioning your hard disk as necessary for Boot Manager and HPFS. You learned how to set up your computer so that Dual-Boot would install without incident. You told OS/2 what sort of pointing device you have, and you learned how OS/2 uses that device.

You next confirmed your mouse, keyboard, country, printer, type of computer display, and other peripherals to OS/2. You may have told OS/2 to install all components on your computer, or you more likely told OS/2 that you wanted to indicate which features and options you use.

You learned about the DOS and OS/2 configuration settings, which the next chapter explores in more detail. You then used the Advanced Options menu of the installation process to indicate whether OS/2 should turn your DOS and Windows applications into icons and whether OS/2 should automatically migrate your CONFIG.SYS and AUTOEXEC.BAT file contents into your new environment. You may possibly have installed optional device support disks. You then completed the installation and booted your computer with its new operating system.

In the next chapter, you learn how to modify your OS/2 configuration.

Modifying Your OS/2 Configuration

As part of the installation process, you might want to tailor OS/2 to your own tastes before you use your new operating system. You also might want to know about the several configuration options before you use OS/2. You need to feel comfortable using the OS/2 Workplace Shell before you make changes to your new operating system, however. If OS/2 is your first graphical user interface-based operating environment, you might want to explore Chapter 9, "Using Your Computer Screen as a Desktop," and Chapter 10, "Managing the Workplace Shell," before you make any configuration changes. You can come back to this chapter later if you first want to try out OS/2 before changing anything.

If you don't have a mouse, read Chapters 9 and 10 before proceeding. OS/2 has keystrokes you can use instead of moving the mouse and pressing the mouse buttons. Chapters 9 and 10 cover these special keyboard operations.

The OS/2 installation process created new CONFIG.SYS and AUTOEXEC.BAT files. You learn in this chapter how to modify these startup files. You also learn about the OS/2 STARTUP.CMD file, an optional file of boot-time commands you can create.

> **NOTE**   If your computer had a copy of DOS on it before you installed OS/2, the OS/2 installation process saved your old AUTOEXEC.BAT and CONFIG.SYS files in the C:\OS2\SYSTEM directory. When you use Dual-Boot (the BOOT command), OS/2 moves its AUTOEXEC.BAT and CONFIG.SYS files to C:\OS2\SYSTEM and moves the DOS versions of these files to your root directory before booting DOS. Using Dual-Boot to return to OS/2 causes the opposite actions to occur.

When you add new hardware options to your computer, you need to change your OS/2 configuration. This chapter discusses adding a printer, a new font, a mouse, and a hard disk, as well as changing your display adapter.

During installation, you may have chosen to leave out certain features of OS/2. This chapter shows you how to selectively install OS/2 features without reinstalling all of OS/2.

The desktop is one of OS/2's most configurable elements. This chapter shows you how to express your preferences by selecting screen colors, background images (wallpaper), and different views of your system.

When you use the objects on your new OS/2 desktop, keep the following basic procedures in mind:

- Use mouse button 1 for selection (opening folders and running programs); use mouse button 2 for manipulation.

- Click an icon or an empty space on the desktop with mouse button 2 to bring up pop-up menus.

- Alt-F4 is the universal "close window" signal in OS/2 utilities and applications.

- *Always do a shutdown before powering down or rebooting.* Click an empty part of the desktop with mouse button 2 and then choose the Shutdown option on the pop-up menu.

- When an object's icon is selected, OS/2 displays a gray backdrop around the icon. This is *selection emphasis*.

Using CONFIG.SYS and AUTOEXEC.BAT

Each time you boot your computer, OS/2 uses the contents of the CONFIG.SYS file to load its device drivers and to configure ditself for your use. At boot time, OS/2 also uses the contents of the STARTUP.CMD file to automatically execute commands and programs. Each time you start a DOS session under OS/2, your AUTOEXEC.BAT file tells DOS what programs and commands to run as part of setting up that DOS session.

 NOTE　Here is a summary of when the different startup files take effect. At boot time: CONFIG.SYS statements and STARTUP.CMD statements; each DOS session: AUTOEXEC.BAT statements.

If you have used DOS before, you may be surprised at the number of entries you find in the CONFIG.SYS file. OS/2 is more sophisticated than DOS and requires many more setup options. The CONFIG.SYS file for OS/2 is correspondingly more sophisticated because it expresses these setup options.

NOTE　After first using the Shutdown option, remember to reboot your computer when you make changes to your CONFIG.SYS file. The changes take effect only after you reboot.

After rebooting, you may decide you do not like the changes. Before changing your CONFIG.SYS file, make a copy of the file (COPY C:\CONFIG.SYS C:\CONFIG.HLD, at an OS/2 or DOS command line prompt, does the trick). If you decide to undo your changes, you can copy your saved file over the CONFIG.SYS changes and reboot.

Appendix F, "The Default CONFIG.SYS File," identifies and explains the typical contents of the initial CONFIG.SYS file that OS/2 creates for you.

Changing CONFIG.SYS Statements

To make changes to the portions of the CONFIG.SYS file, you can use OS/2's Enhanced Editor. Chapter 14, "Using the OS/2 Text Editors," explains OS/2's built-in text editors in detail. However, the basic process of editing a text file (such as CONFIG.SYS) with the Enhanced Editor is a simple one.

To use the Enhanced Editor to change CONFIG.SYS, run the text editor by opening the Productivity folder and double-clicking the Enhanced Editor's icon. Choose the File/Open menu option, specify the file C:\CONFIG.SYS, and make your changes. Use File/Save when you finish, followed by Shutdown and a reboot.

The following listing shows some of the CONFIG.SYS entries you might want to change:

```
LIBPATH=C:\OS2\DLL;C:\OS2\MDOS;C:\;C:\OS2\APPS\DLL;C:\NETWARE;

SET PATH=C:\OS2;C:\OS2\SYSTEM;C:\OS2\MDOS\WINOS2;
  C:\OS2\INSTALL;C:\;C:\OS2\MDOS;C:\OS2\APPS;F:\PUBLIC\OS2;
  C:\NETWARE

SET DPATH=C:\OS2;C:\OS2\SYSTEM;C:\OS2\MDOS\WINOS2;
  C:\OS2\INSTALL;C:\;C:\OS2\BITMAP;C:\OS2\MDOS;C:\OS2\APPS;

SET PROMPT=[OS2] $p$g

BUFFERS=30

DISKCACHE=64,LW

BREAK=OFF

SET TEMP=C:\

PROTECTONLY=NO

SHELL=C:\OS2\MDOS\COMMAND.COM C:\OS2\MDOS /E:1024 /P

RMSIZE=640

DEVICE=C:\OS2\MDOS\ANSI.SYS

DEVICE=C:\OS2\VDISK.SYS 2048 512 128
```

The LIBPATH statement tells OS/2 where to find the parts of your OS/2 application programs called Dynamic Link Libraries (DLLS). The PATH statement, as with DOS, tells OS/2 where to find executable programs. The PATH statement in CONFIG.SYS refers only to OS/2 applications. You put a separate PATH statement in your AUTOEXEC.BAT file for DOS sessions and the applications you run in those sessions. The

DPATH statement works for OS/2 applications and indicates where OS/2 or an OS/2 application can find data files that are not in the current directory. The OS/2 DPATH statement is similar in purpose to the DOS APPEND statement.

You can change the appearance of your OS/2 command line prompt with the PROMPT statement. Unlike other CONFIG.SYS statements, the PROMPT statement also works at a command line prompt. The BUFFERS entry tells OS/2 how many disk buffers to use. The DISKCACHE statement lets OS/2 know how much memory you want allocated for OS/2's disk cache feature and whether you want OS/2 to use "lazy writes." The BREAK parameter, which applies to DOS sessions, enables you to press Ctrl-C to interrupt a running program. Some OS/2 applications use the TEMP environment variable, set in the listing's example to C:\, to know where to store temporary files. The SET statement specifies the environment variable and its value.

PROTECTONLY tells OS/2 whether you will use DOS sessions. The SHELL statement expresses the location of the DOS command processor, COMMAND.COM. SHELL also enables you to allocate more memory to DOS environment variables that you might set in your AUTOEXEC.BAT file. The RMSIZE parameter indicates the maximum size of any DOS session you might start. The DEVICE statement loads a device driver; in the statement listing, the two DEVICE statements load the ANSI.SYS driver and the OS/2 RAM disk driver.

You now understand the basic function of each statement in the example listing. If you want to know more about one of these CONFIG.SYS statements, or about other CONFIG.SYS entries, see Appendix G of this book for a complete explanation.

Changing DOS and Windows Settings

The changes you make to CONFIG.SYS affect all future OS/2, Windows, and DOS sessions after you reboot. But you can change several DOS and Windows settings on a session-by-session basis. You can modify all the settings before you start a session; for an already started session, you can change a subset of the DOS and Windows options.

To see the list of settings, follow these steps:

1. Open the Command Prompts folder by double-clicking it. (Unless you have moved this folder, you can find it inside the OS/2 System folder.)

2. Display the pop-up menu for the DOS Full Screen object by placing the mouse cursor over the object and pressing mouse button 2.

3. Place the mouse cursor on the arrow next to the Open menu item. Press mouse button 1 once to see the Settings/Program menu.

4. Place the mouse cursor on the Settings menu item. Press mouse button 1.

5. Select the Session tab on the notebook that appears on-screen.

6. Click the button labeled DOS Settings. Your screen should now look similar to the one shown in figure 7.1.

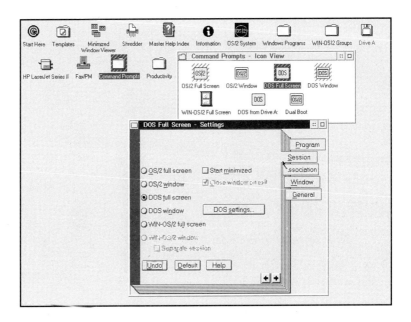

Fig. 7.1

The DOS Full Screen Settings Session notebook page.

Figure 7.2 shows part of the list of settings you can change on a session-by-session basis. One of the settings, PRINT_TIMEOUT, is highlighted; the Description and Value fields that you see apply only to PRINT_TIMEOUT. Other settings' fields have their own descriptions and methods for changing their values. To change the current setting, you can type a new value in the text box or you can use the slider box to increase or decrease the value. When you finish, click the Save button.

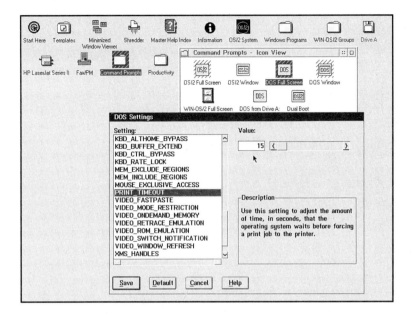

Fig. 7.2

Changing DOS/
Windows settings
on a session-by-
session basis.

Migrating CONFIG.SYS Statements

If you use the Enhanced Editor to view the CONFIG.SYS file, you may notice that some device driver statements have been turned into comment statements because they are preceded by the word REM. The OS/2 CONFIG.SYS Migration utility may have made these changes for you during installation. Some device drivers, designed to work with DOS, may not function correctly with OS/2. The OS/2 Migration utility turns the statements that load these device drivers into comments. You can delete the word REM from these statements with a text editor and then reboot your computer to see whether the device driver operates correctly. If the driver malfunctions, you can copy your saved CONFIG.HLD file (mentioned earlier in this chapter) over the CONFIG.SYS file and reboot again to remove the driver from memory.

If your computer doesn't boot properly after you "unremark" the device driver statement in CONFIG.SYS, you can recover by following these steps:

1. Insert the OS/2 Installation disk in the disk drive and reboot your computer.

2. When prompted, insert OS/2 Disk 1.

3. At the next prompt, press the Esc key to obtain a command line prompt.

4. Use the Copy command to overlay the CONFIG.SYS file with your saved CONFIG.HLD file.

5. Reboot by pressing the Ctrl-Alt-Del.

Updating CONFIG.SYS Statements for Application Programs

The installation software programs for some applications may contain their own configuration editors. For example, the Novell NetWare Requester for OS/2 versions 2.0 and 2.1 comes with such a configuration aid. If an application requires CONFIG.SYS changes, such a configuration aid makes it easy to complete the application's installation. You indicate your preferences to the configuration aid, and the software automatically updates the CONFIG.SYS file for you.

On the other hand, some applications tell you to use a text editor to make CONFIG.SYS changes. In such cases, you need to use the OS/2 Enhanced Editor to make your changes.

Executing AUTOEXEC.BAT Statements

OS/2 executes the statements in your C:\AUTOEXEC.BAT file each time you start a new DOS session. The following is an example of the statements that OS/2 automatically inserts in your new AUTOEXEC.BAT file at installation time. You can use a text editor to insert other statements.

```
@ECHO OFF
ECHO.
PROMPT $p$g
SET DELDIR=C:\DELETE,512;
PATH C:\OS2;C:\OS2\MDOS;C:\OS2\MDOS\WINOS2;
  C:\;C:\WORD;C:\DOS;
LOADHIGH APPEND C:\OS2;C:\OS2\SYSTEM;
LOADHIGH DOSKEY FINDFILE=DIR /A /S /B $*
SET DIRCMD=/A
```

Executing STARTUP.CMD Statements

The STARTUP.CMD file is the OS/2 equivalent of the DOS AUTOEXEC.BAT file. OS/2 executes the STARTUP.CMD file at boot time. The installation process does not create a STARTUP.CMD file because the file is optional, but you can make one if you want to run certain commands and utilities each time you start your computer. Alternatively, you can create a CMD file that executes OS/2 commands and programs, make a shadow of the CMD file, and place the shadow in your Startup folder. (Chapter 10, "Managing the Workplace Shell," explains how to make shadows of objects and perform drag-and-drop operations.)

If your computer is part of a local area network (LAN), you will find that the STARTUP.CMD file is a good place to put the commands that you use to log on to the network.

For Related Information

◀◀ "Understanding Disk Partitions and Disks," p. 44.

▶▶ "Understanding DOS Sessions," p. 386.

▶▶ "Command Reference," p. 647.

FROM HERE...

Upgrading Your Hardware

When you add hardware options to your computer, you need to indicate the changes for OS/2. In particular, you need to give OS/2 information about a new printer, new font, new mouse, new display adapter, or additional hard disk.

NOTE You might receive special device driver installation disks from hardware manufacturers. OS/2 provides a facility for using these disks—the Device Driver Install program. If you need to access this program, you can find it in the System Setup folder. Figure 7.3 shows the Device Driver Installation window.

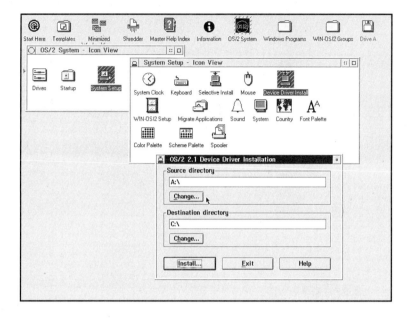

Fig. 7.3

The Device Driver
Installation
window.

Adding a Printer

To install a printer, first connect it to your computer according to the
directions that came with your printer. These directions probably tell
you to connect the device to your LPT1 or COM1 port. Note which port
you use. Next, indicate to OS/2 that you have a new printer and the
special things your new printer can do. You do this with a settings
notebook entry for a printer object. If you do not have a printer object
on your desktop (it appears as an icon labeled Printer or labeled with
the make and model of your printer), create one by following these
steps:

1. Open the Templates folder. By default, it is located inside the OS/2
    System folder.

2. Use mouse button 2 to pick up the icon labeled Printer, drag it
    onto the desktop, and drop it (release the mouse button). The
    Create Another Printer window opens automatically. Click the
    Output Port to which you attached the printer. Click the Create
    Another button.

3. If you want the equivalent Windows printer driver installed, click
    the Yes button that appears in the message window labeled
    Printer.

4. You are prompted to insert the appropriate printer disks. Choose
    a printer driver and follow the on-screen instructions to finish
    creating your new printer object.

5. Open the settings notebook for the printer object. Use the Printer driver tab to specify the printer driver for your printer. Figure 7.4 shows a sample Printer Driver page of the settings notebook.

6. To copy a printer driver file from one of the OS/2 distribution disks, insert Printer Disk 1 in drive A and double-click the drive A icon to select that disk drive. When you see the list of printer driver icons appear on-screen, select the one appropriate for your printer and drag it onto an empty place on the desktop.

7. Double-click the Printer Driver icon to see the Job Properties notebook page, on which you tell OS/2 about the paper-handling and font capabilities of your new printer. Figure 7.5 shows the Job Properties notebook page for a Hewlett-Packard LaserJet printer.

8. Use the tab marked Output to tell OS/2 which port the printer uses (LPT1 or COM1, for example).

9. Use the Queue Options tab to tell OS/2 which queue driver to use for this printer.

10. Close the settings notebook by pressing Alt-F4, or clicking Close in the window's system menu.

You probably will not need to use the other tabs on the settings notebook to specify your new printer. If you want more details on printers and fonts under OS/2, however, please see Chapter 15, "Printing with OS/2."

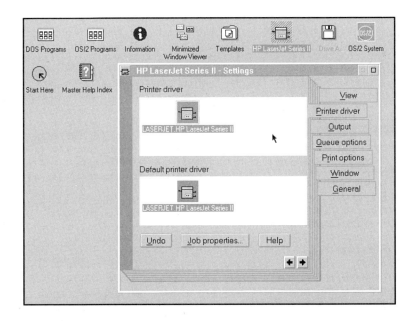

Fig. 7.4

The Printer driver page of the settings notebook for your printer object.

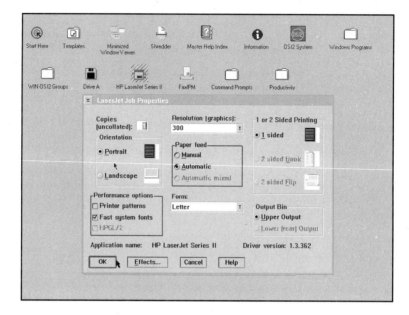

Fig. 7.5

Telling OS/2
about the
capabilities of
your new printer
on the Job
Properties
settings note-
book page.

Adding and Changing Fonts

OS/2 comes with a wide range of printer and screen fonts, some of
which are fonts supplied to IBM by Adobe Systems. You may want to
selectively install some of these IBM and Adobe fonts at a later time if
you did not select them during the OS/2 installation process. Or you
may purchase additional font files you need to install.

To install a font, first open the System Setup folder (located by default
in the OS/2 System folder). Then double-click the object labeled Font
Palette. The Font Palette (the top window shown in figure 7.6) enables
you to edit the characteristics of existing fonts in your computer, as
well as add new fonts. Choose the Edit font option in the Font Palette
window to see the Edit Font window shown in figure 7.6.

Figure 7.6 shows how to select an existing font on your computer for
editing, but you can use the same window to add a new font (the Add
button is hidden by the list of fonts). Click the Add button to install a
new font from a floppy disk. Choose an existing font from the list to
change its characteristics.

If you click the Add button, OS/2 asks you to insert the floppy disk containing the new font file. OS/2 then adds that font to your collection. If
you choose an existing font from the list, you can specify its size and
emphasis (outline, underline, or strikeout).

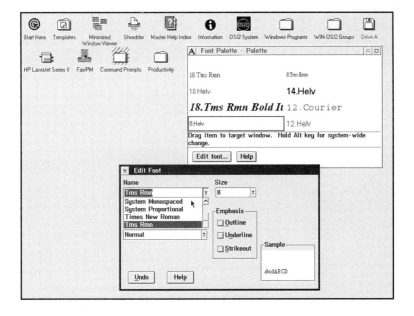

Fig. 7.6

The Font Palette and Edit Font window.

Try this: Select a font on the Font Palette by clicking it with mouse button 1. This highlights the font item. Use mouse button 2 to drag the highlighted font to a window title bar or to the name of an icon on the desktop. Drop the font by releasing the mouse button. You have changed the appearance of the title bar or icon name.

As yet, not too many OS/2 objects display the different font when you drop a font on them. This situation will change as more applications become OS/2-aware.

Adding a Mouse

To add a mouse to your computer, or to change the type of mouse that you have, first connect the mouse according to the directions that came with the pointing device. Then open the Selective Install object in the System Setup folder. You see the System Configuration window, which may look familiar to you. It is the same window you used during the installation process to confirm your mouse, keyboard, country, and display. Check the box labeled <u>M</u>ouse and press Enter. Then select your mouse from the list that OS/2 displays and click OK.

If the manufacturer of your new mouse gave you a floppy disk with an OS/2 device driver on it, use the manufacturer's instructions to install the driver.

Changing the Display Adapter or Resolution

You follow the same steps to upgrade your display adapter that you do to install a new mouse. Install your new adapter according to the manufacturer's instructions. If the manufacturer supplied a disk containing an OS/2 device driver, install that driver by using the manufacturer's instructions.

If your new display adapter does not support the video mode and resolution of the old one, you may find that simply installing the new hardware and booting OS/2 results in an incoherent screen. Before you power off your PC in preparation for the new display adapter, you should first reconfigure OS/2 to use a mode (such as plain VGA) commonly supported by both the old and new display adapters. After inserting the new adapter and booting OS/2, you can then reconfigure for different display resolutions.

To reconfigure OS/2's display system, or to simply increase or decrease the screen resolution produced by your present display adapter, click the Selective Install object that's located by default in the System Setup folder inside the OS/2 System folder. The Selective Install object lets you select a supported display adapter and the screen resolution you want the display adapter to use. OS/2 2.1 supports the IBM VGA 256c and the display adapters in the following list:

> Headland Technology VRAM II
>
> Tseng Laboratories ET4000
>
> Trident Microsystems TVGA
>
> ATI Technologies VGA Wonder
>
> Western Digital Imaging Paradise

When using DSPINSTL, you click the check box labeled Primary Display and then click OK to bring up a window entitled Primary Display Adapter Type, as shown in figure 7.7. You choose your display adapter from the list and click OK. OS/2 will likely ask you to insert one or both of the OS/2 distribution disks labeled Display Driver Diskette 1 and

Display Driver Diskette 2. After OS/2 reconfigures itself for the new display adapter and screen resolution, you should perform a shutdown operation and reboot your computer.

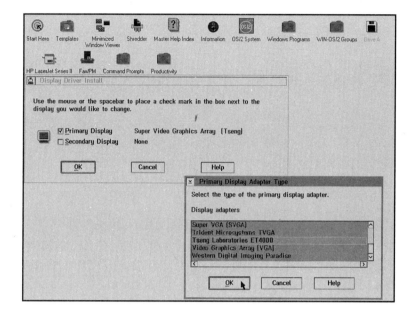

Fig. 7.7

The Primary Display Adapter Type configuration window.

Adding a Hard Disk

You add a hard disk to a computer running OS/2 in much the same way you add a hard disk to a DOS-based computer. You may want to confirm with the manufacturer that the drive is compatible with OS/2 before you purchase the extra disk. See Chapter 5, "Using Non-IBM Computers and OS/2," for a discussion on disk drives and OS/2.

First, install the new drive according to the manufacturer's instructions. Then power up your computer and run the FDISK and FORMAT utilities to prepare the new disk drive for use. You can run these utilities from the OS/2 command line by selecting an OS/2 Full Screen or Windowed session from the Command Prompts folder. Or you can run the Presentation Manager versions of these programs. To do the latter, choose PMFDISK and PMFORMAT from the OS/2 System folder, or execute these programs from an OS/2 command line prompt. You find both programs in the C:\OS2 directory, assuming that you selected them for installation when you installed OS/2.

FROM HERE...

For Related Information

◀◀ "Understanding Hardware and Software," p. 13.

◀◀ "Using Device Support," p. 90.

◀◀ "Reflecting Personal Preferences," p. 94.

◀◀ "Working with IBM-Compatible Computers," p. 102.

◀◀ "Learning about Disk Controller Cards," p. 112.

◀◀ "Using the Keyboards and Mice," p. 113.

◀◀ "Working with Video Adapter Cards and Monitors," p. 115.

Installing Features Selectively

In addition to enabling you to confirm or change your mouse, keyboard, display, and country, the Selective Install object (in the System Setup folder) allows you to add the following features to your system:

- *CD-ROM Device Support.* Provides system support for CD-ROM devices.

- *Documentation.* Adds the OS/2 Tutorial, the OS/2 Command Reference, or REXX Programming Information.

- *Fonts.* Determines the typefaces you can use on your system. The OS/2 operating system gives you both bit-map fonts and fonts in Adobe Type 1 format for displaying and printing data on many output devices. Vector devices, such as plotters, cannot use the bit-map fonts. When you haven't installed the optional fonts, OS/2 uses the system default font and the Helvetica fonts.

- *Optional System Utilities.* These utilities enable you to do the following:

    Back up the hard disk

    Change file attributes

    Display the directory tree

Manage disk drive partitions

Put internal labels on disks

Link object modules (a programmer's tool)

Convert, display, and print pictures

Use PMREXX

Recover files

Restore backed-up files

Sort files

■ *Tools and Games.* Installs productivity aids, such as a simple database manager, a spreadsheet application, a calculator, a calendar, and a notepad, as well as some games.

■ *OS/2 DOS and Windows Support.* Enables DOS and Microsoft Windows programs to run under the OS/2 operating system.

■ *High Performance File System.* Provides fast access to large files and supports file names up to 254 characters in length.

■ *REXX.* Installs the REXX Operating System/2 procedures language. This batch programming language is Systems Application Architecture (SAA) compliant and extends the capabilities of the statements you embed in your CMD files.

■ *Serial Device Support.* Provides system support for serial devices, such as a modem, a serial plotter, or a serial printer assigned to a communication port. You don't need to select this option for a serial mouse.

■ *Serviceability and Diagnostic Aids.* This option provides information to a technical support person, who typically forwards the information to IBM so that IBM can isolate and correct system problems.

■ *Optional Bitmaps.* Provides a set of images (sometimes called wallpaper) that you can use to change the background of the desktop.

To add one or more of the listed features after installation, open the Selective Install object in the System Setup folder. Click the OK pushbutton in the System Configuration window. In the OS/2 Setup and Installation window (the same window you used during the installation of OS/2), check the box for each feature that you want to add to your computer. If you want to select a subset of that feature, click that feature's More... button.

After you select the additional features, click the OK button. When prompted, insert the installation disks to let OS/2 copy the features to your hard disk.

For Related Information

◄◄ "Choosing the OS/2 Features You Want," p. 134.

Configuring Your Desktop

You can configure your OS/2 desktop in a variety of ways. You can change general system parameters and the appearance of the information the desktop presents to you. You can alter the desktop's settings for sound, country, mouse behavior, and keyboard usage. You can choose how you want the system clock to appear, and you can choose background colors and images for the desktop. You can create objects on the desktop that represent your applications. The next sections of this chapter explain these configuration settings.

To access the Desktop settings notebook, move the mouse cursor to an empty part of the desktop and click the right mouse button. The desktop's pop-up menu appears. Click the arrow next to the Open menu option to make your screen look like the one shown in figure 7.8. Then click the Settings option.

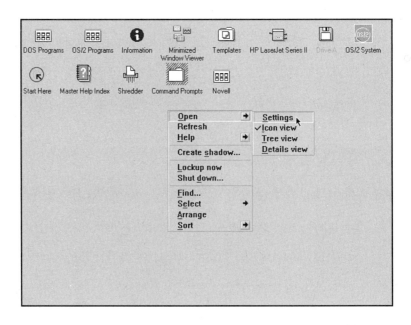

Fig. 7.8

The pop-up menu for the OS/2 desktop.

When the Desktop settings notebook appears, you see tabs labeled View, Include, Sort, Background, Menu, File, Window, General, and Lockup. Click the View tab to see a screen similar to the one shown in figure 7.9.

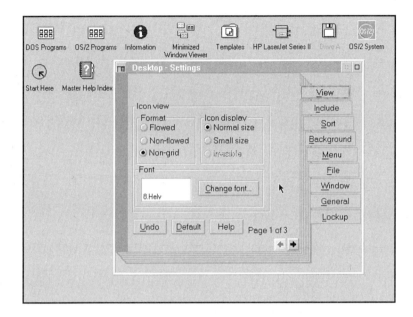

Fig. 7.9

The View page of the Desktop settings note-book.

Selecting Icon, Tree, and Details Views

Each settings notebook, including the one for the desktop itself, en-ables you to change the way objects appear on the desktop. You can select Icon View, Tree View, or Details View from the pop-up menu shown in figure 7.8.

Selecting Icon View

Icon View is the default view. Each object is an icon with the icon's name positioned next to it.

The View page of the settings notebook allows you to customize the Icon View format, icon display, and font.

Icon View has three formats: *Flowed*, *Non-flowed*, and *Non-grid*. The default is Non-grid. In this mode, icons can appear anywhere on the desktop. In Non-flowed mode, each object is a separate line that shows the object's icon followed by its name. Flowed mode is a multiple-column version of the Non-flowed mode. Each column is just wide enough to hold the longest icon's name.

You can configure the icon's size and font independently for each of the three formats, in any font and point size. Icons may be normal size (default) or small size. In Flowed and Non-flowed modes, you can suppress the icon itself so that you see only the name of the icon on the desktop.

Selecting Tree View

To select Tree View, click Tree View in the pop-up menu shown in figure 7.8. Tree View shows the contents of the desktop or a folder as a directory tree. The folder is at the root of the tree. You can collapse or expand the subtrees by clicking the + (plus) and – (minus) buttons. The desktop, or each folder, shows the icon and the name for each folder contained within the view. Figure 7.10 illustrates the Tree View for the OS/2 desktop.

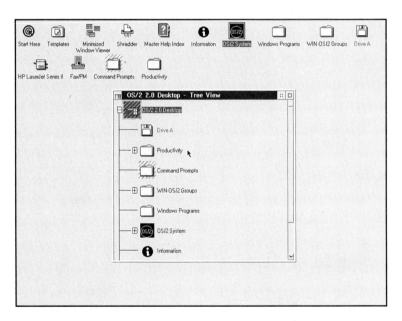

The View page of the settings notebook allows you to customize the Tree View's format, icon display, and font. You can customize the icon display and font, just as for Icon View. The format can be "lines" or "no lines." In lined mode, the tree structure is emphasized with lines that highlight the objects.

Selecting Details View

To select Details View, click Details View in the pop-up menu shown in figure 7.8. Details View uses one line for each object. The view is split vertically into two panes. The left pane shows the object's icon and descriptive name. The right window pane gives details about the object. You can adjust the placement of the boundary between the panes. Figure 7.11 shows the Details View for the OS/2 desktop.

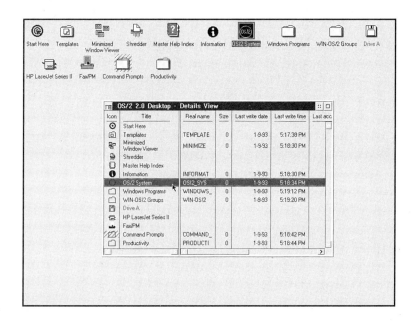

Fig. 7.11

The Desktop
Details View.

The View page of the settings notebook allows you to customize the Details View display. You can select the font, and you can specify which of the object's details you want to see.

Using Other Notebook Settings

In addition to the View page, the settings notebook has eight other pages: Include, Sort, Background, Menu, File, Window, General, and Lockup.

The *Include* page allows you to select which objects to display in the views.

The *Sort* page selects the object ordering that occurs when you perform an Arrange operation. You can choose to sort objects by name or by type.

The *Background* page selects the background for the views. You can select a color or a bit-map image. You learn more about configuring the desktop's screen colors in the next section of this chapter.

The *General* page enables you to customize the folder's icon.

The *Menu* page enables you to customize the folder's pop-up menu.

The three *File* pages provide the following information about the object whose settings notebook you have selected:

- Descriptive and physical names
- Created, modified, and last accessed time and dates
- Data and extended attribute sizes
- Attribute flags
- Subject, comments, key phrases, and history information

Some of the information that you enter on the File pages applies only if you have an HPFS partition.

The *Window* page enables you to customize window behavior in ways that seem most natural and comfortable to you.

The three *Lockup* pages allow you to specify security options. You can indicate whether OS/2 should password-protect your computer when you step away from it, what OS/2 should show on-screen while you're away, and how many minutes of no keyboard activity should cause OS/2 to activate password protection. When you return to your computer, you enter a password to regain use of the PC.

Altering Screen Colors and Background Images

You can change screen colors for both the desktop and each of the folders. To choose a different color for the background of the desktop, click the Background tab of the settings notebook for the desktop. You see a screen similar to the one shown in figure 7.12. Select the Image button if you want to see a bit-map image (picture) on the desktop instead of the default solid color. You can preview and select from the bit-map images supplied with OS/2. If you want to use this option, you should first tell the installation process to install the optional bit-map files.

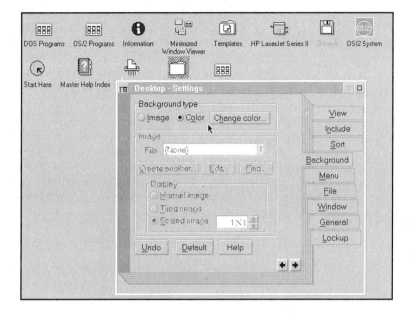

Fig. 7.12

The options on the Background tab in the Desktop settings notebook.

Click the Change Color button if you want to select a solid color for the desktop's background. You see a palette of colors from which you can choose.

The Display options enable you to specify how you want an image to appear: normal, tiled, or scaled. Normal Image tells OS/2 to show the image file, in its original size, as a single picture on the desktop's background. Tiled Image instructs OS/2 to place several copies of the image on the desktop's background. And Scaled Image informs OS/2 that you want the image blown up or reduced as necessary to fit on-screen.

To change the colors that appear inside each of your folders, select the Color Palette object in the System Setup folder. The Color Palette enables you to customize the screen colors of various other objects. When you select the Color Palette, you see a window that contains several circles, each a different solid color. You can edit the color of a circle if you want.

Try this: use the right mouse button (button 2) to drag a non-white color circle from the Color Palette window. When the circle moves out of the Palette window onto the desktop, it changes into a picture of a paintbrush. Drop the resulting paintbrush image on the background of a open folder on the desktop. The color of the folder changes.

Unfortunately, not too many OS/2 objects currently understand having a color dropped on them. This situation will change as more applications become OS/2-aware.

Customizing with System

The System object enables you to customize the behavior of certain aspects of the system. This object has only a settings view, with six pages: Confirmations, Title, Window, Print Screen, Logo, and General. To change one of these settings, select the System object located in the System Setup folder. Click the Window tab of the settings notebook that appears. You see a screen similar to the one shown in figure 7.13.

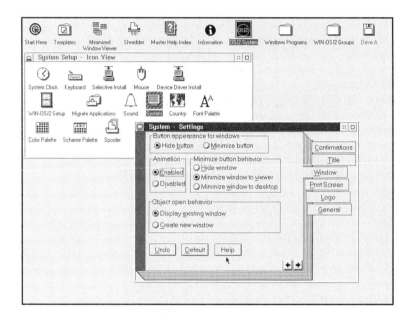

Fig. 7.13

The Window page of the settings notebook for the System object.

The *Window* page of the settings notebook allows you to enable or disable the animation that occurs when a window opens or closes. You can specify how minimized windows are to be handled and specify what happens when you open an object that already exists on the desktop. By default, the Workplace Shell resurfaces the existing object. You can tell the Shell to create a new view of the object instead of reshowing the existing object.

The *Confirmations* page, illustrated in figure 7.14, allows you to enable or disable the confirmation dialogs you get when you attempt to shred folders and objects.

Fig. 7.14

The Confirma-
tions page of the
settings notebook
for the System
object.

The *Logo* page allows you to specify how long applications should display their product information window when they start up.

The *General* page allows you to alter the System object's icon.

The *Print Screen* page enables and disables the capability of the Print Screen key to send output to the printer.

Changes in these settings take effect immediately.

Modifying the Sound

The Sound object, shown in figure 7.15, allows you to enable or disable OS/2's warning beep. Sound has only a settings view. You find the Sound object in the System Setup folder.

Altering the Country

The Country object, also located in the System Setup folder, allows you to customize OS/2 to use national language support. Country has only a settings view, with five pages whose tabs are labeled Country, Time, Date, Numbers, and Icon. The Country tab display appears in figure 7.16.

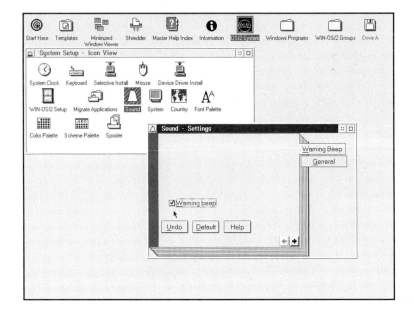

Fig. 7.15

The Sound object in the System Setup folder and its settings notebook.

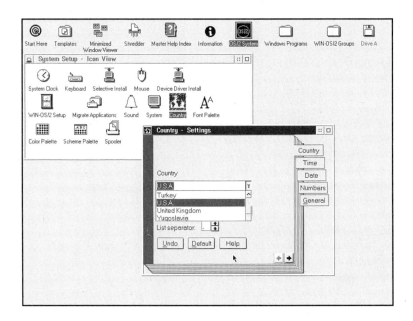

Fig. 7.16

The Country tab settings for the Country object.

Customizing the Mouse

The Mouse object enables you to customize the behavior of the mouse. This object has a five-page settings view, with tabs labeled Timing, Setup, Mappings, Window, and General.

The *Timing* page enables you to set the double-click interval and the tracking speed. Changes take effect immediately. In fact, the tracking speed of the mouse actually changes as you manipulate the slider control to increase or decrease the tracking speed.

The *Setup* page enables you to configure the mouse according to whether you're right- or left-handed. Figure 7.17 shows the Setup page of the Mouse settings notebook.

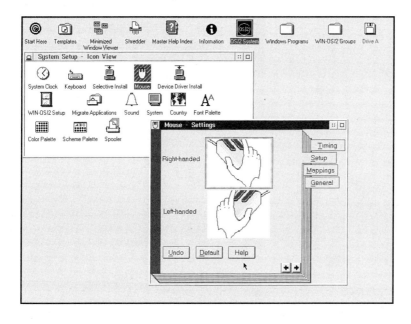

Fig. 7.17

The Setup tab settings for the Mouse object.

The *Mappings* page enables you to define which combination of mouse buttons, single/double-clicking, and Shift/Ctrl/Alt keys perform selection functions and other actions. You can configure which button performs a drag operation (the default is mouse button 2), which button displays pop-up menus (the default is a single click of mouse button 2), and which button enables you to edit icon and window title text (the default is a single click of mouse button 1, in combination with holding down the Alt key). Figure 7.18 shows the Mappings page of the Mouse settings notebook.

The *General* page of the Mouse settings notebook allows you to customize the Mouse object's icon.

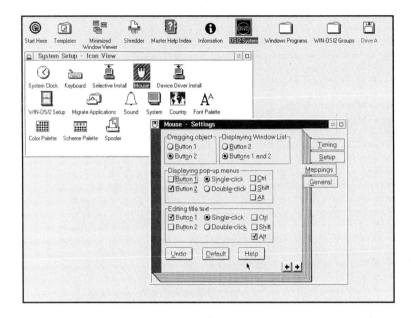

Fig. 7.18

The Mappings
tab settings for
the Mouse
object.

Changing the Keyboard

The Keyboard object in the System Setup folder allows you to customize the keyboard configuration of the system. This object only has a settings view, with five tabbed pages: Timing, Mappings, Special Needs, Window, and General.

The *Timing* page allows you to customize the repeat rate, repeat delay rate, and cursor blink rate by using slider controls. A test box appears so that you can test your changes. Figure 7.19 shows the Timing page.

The *Mappings* page provides keyboard equivalents for certain mouse operations. By default, Shift-F10 displays pop-up menus. Shift-Ins enables you to edit window title text.

The *Special Needs* page allows configuration of the system for people who have special requirements. For example, if you cannot simultaneously press several keys, such as the Shift key along with a letter key, you can use the Special Needs page to tell OS/2 to treat the Shift key as a "sticky" key, which means that when you press Shift, the key remains active for a period of time you specify. This time period allows you to press another key that OS/2 will deem to be shifted.

Four slider controls appear on the Special Needs page: Acceptance Delay, Delay Until Repeat, Repeat Rate, and Settings Time-out. Figure 7.20 shows the Special Needs page of the Keyboard settings notebook.

The *General* page enables you to customize the Keyboard object's icon.

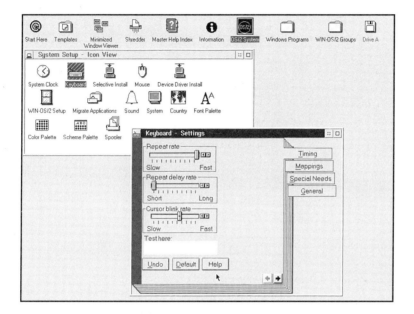

Using the System Clock

The System Clock object displays the current time. You also can use the System Clock to change your computer's date and time. The settings notebook has four tabbed pages: View, Alarm, Date/Time, and General.

The *View* page determines the appearance of the clock. You can select digital or analog, time and/or date, and hide/show title bar. In analog mode, you can select hour marks, minute marks, and a second hand.

The *Alarm* page allows you to set an alarm. You can specify both a time and date for when the alarm sounds; you also can specify whether you want an audible alarm or message box.

The *Date/Time* page allows you to change the system date and time. You change the hours, minutes, seconds, month, day, and year fields with spin buttons.

The *General* page allows you to customize the System Clock object's icon.

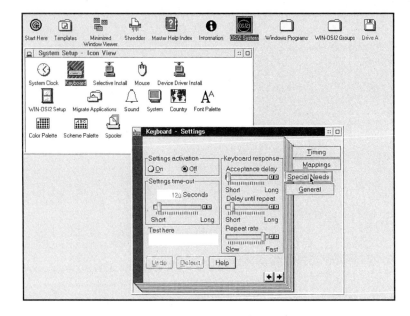

Fig. 7.20

The Special Needs tab settings for the Keyboard object.

Adding Applications to Your Desktop

Earlier in this chapter, when you learned how to install a printer, you used the Templates folder to create a new print destination object. You dragged a printer icon out of the Templates folder and configured the printer through the icon's settings notebook. When you want to create an icon object on the desktop that represents one of your applications, you perform a similar set of steps.

Using the Program Template in the Template Folder

To place a new Program object icon on the desktop, open the Templates folder. Use mouse button 2 to drag the icon labeled Program onto the desktop. (Don't double-click the Program icon in the Templates folder.) The icon automatically opens its settings notebook for you. The tabs on the five pages contain the names General, Association, Program, Window, and Session.

You use the *General* page to specify the window title and icon for your application program. The *Association* page enables you to tell OS/2 the kinds of files and names with which your application works. The *Program* page is where you tell OS/2 the name and directory location of the executable file for that application. On the *Session* page, you specify whether the application is a DOS or OS/2 program and whether the application should run full screen or in a window on the desktop. For a DOS application, you also can specify DOS settings (as discussed earlier in this chapter) if that application requires other than the OS/2 defaults. Use the *Window* page to customize window behavior.

Choosing To Migrate Applications

When you installed OS/2, you had an opportunity to migrate your DOS and Windows applications into the OS/2 environment. If you did not select this option during installation, you can select it later by choosing the Migrate Applications object in the System Setup folder. You see a screen similar to the one shown in figure 7.21. You indicate whether you want OS/2 to search for DOS applications, Microsoft Windows applications, OS/2 applications, or all three. You tell OS/2 which drive letter to search and then click the Find button. The Migrate Applications object then searches your disk for applications. When it finds each application, Migrate Applications identifies that computer program in a list, by name. You can deselect items in the list that you do not want to migrate onto your desktop. You also can add to the list of applications by clicking the Add button and specifying additional computer programs. When the list meets with your satisfaction, click the OK button to cause the Migrate Applications object to create a new folder and put the migrated applications, in icon form, in the new folder.

For Related Information

▶▶ "Using the Workplace Shell," p. 218.

▶▶ "Understanding the Drives Object Display," p. 259.

▶▶ "Understanding DOS Sessions," p. 386.

▶▶ "Adding DOS Programs," p. 389.

FROM HERE...

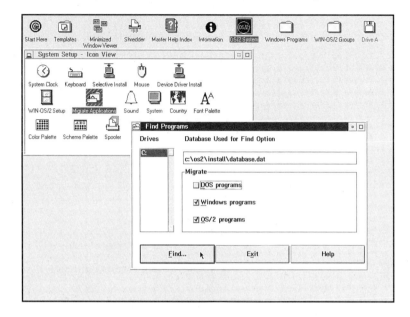

The Migrate
Applications
object.

Chapter Summary

In this chapter, you learned how to configure OS/2 to suit your day-to-day work habits and your computer's particular needs. You found out how to modify the startup files AUTOEXEC.BAT, CONFIG.SYS, and STARTUP.CMD, discovered how to tell OS/2 about new hardware options you might add to your computer, and explored the selective installation of OS/2 options and features. You now know how to configure the OS/2 desktop itself.

In the next chapter, you learn how to troubleshoot OS/2.

Troubleshooting OS/2

You may never have any trouble with OS/2 2.1. If you do have problems, however, this chapter explains the steps you can take to solve the problems; it also explains how to prevent problems.

Computers are not foolproof. People occasionally run into problems with DOS, UNIX, and other operating systems, and OS/2 is no different from other software in that regard. OS/2 does have some built-in safeguards, however, and the OS/2 error messages are generally clear and self-explanatory. In fact, the OS/2 designers went to some lengths to make both the error messages and informational messages as easily understood as possible.

Unlike DOS and some other operating systems, OS/2 provides a great deal of on-line help and information. The OS/2 files of error messages are sizable. You can appreciate the amount of information OS/2 is prepared to give you in case of trouble by looking at the sizes of the message files and help files within the OS/2 system. Take a moment now to locate and identify these files. Open (double-click) an OS/2 Full Screen session in the Command Prompts folder. At the command line prompt, type **CD \OS2\SYSTEM**, and then type **DIR *.MSG**. OS/2 displays the names and sizes of the message files. Type **CD \OS2\HELP** followed by **DIR *.HLP**. The names and sizes of the OS/2 help files appear. Finally, type **CD \OS2\BOOK** and then type just **DIR**. The names and sizes of the OS/2 information files appear. (Type **EXIT** to close the OS/2 Full Screen session.) The message, help, and information files exist to help you whenever you encounter problems with OS/2.

If you have used DOS before, you know that when DOS or a DOS application fails, the entire computer stops and you have to reboot. If you're logged into a local area network, booting and logging in can take a considerable amount of time away from your personal productivity. Under OS/2, when OS/2 itself, an OS/2 application, a DOS application, or a Windows application fails, OS/2 notifies you of the error, enables you to terminate the application that failed, but does not crash. Only in rare circumstances (if a device driver fails to work properly, for example) does OS/2 fail in such a way that you must reboot your computer.

The type of error that causes you to reboot OS/2, no matter how rare, is serious, so this chapter first presents how to prepare your computer system for such errors. Errors that require you to reboot your computer are easy to recognize. This chapter also helps you identify and deal with other types of less obvious errors. You learn the steps you take to gracefully recover from error situations, including diagnosing the problem, issuing commands to correct the problem, using the installation disks to reboot your computer to deal with unusual problems, and even booting a DOS disk so that you can fix the really stubborn problems.

This chapter organizes errors into the following categories:

- The Installation process encounters a problem.
- The computer fails to boot.
- An application, or the entire computer, stops suddenly.
- An application does not behave as expected.
- The screen is garbled.
- Pressing keys produces no reaction from the computer.
- The mouse fails to move the cursor, or the mouse buttons fail to select items on-screen.
- Nothing prints.
- Printouts are garbled.
- Performance is slow.

Understanding Installation Errors

Figure 8.1 shows the screen displayed if the OS/2 installation process encounters a problem and cannot continue without your intervention. OS/2 may find, for example, that one of the sectors of your hard disk is damaged and cannot reliably hold the information written to it. If a screen similar to the one in figure 8.1 appears, you must boot the OS/2 Installation Disk to fix the problem (as detailed later in this chapter).

```
An error occurred when System Installation tried to copy a
file. The installation program has failed due to an error.
To view the error, you need to look at the INSTALL.LOG file
that was created for you. That file gives the condition
that caused the error.

   Press Enter to display INSTALL.LOG.

To take action to correct the error, insert the Operating
System/2 Installation Disk in drive A. Press and hold the
Ctrl and Alt keys, then press the Del key.

When the Logo panel appears, remove the Installation disk,
insert OS/2 Disk 1, and press Enter. When the Welcome
screen appears, press Esc.

After you correct the error, restart OS/2 Installation by
inserting the Operating System/2 Installation Disk in Drive
A. Press and hold the Ctrl and Alt keys, then press Del.
```

Fig. 8.1

Notification that the OS/2 installation process encountered a problem.

For Related Information

◄◄ "Booting the Installation Disk," p. 122.

FROM HERE...

Preparing for Trouble

Before trouble strikes, you can do certain things to prepare yourself and your computer. You can minimize the effect of some problems by configuring your computer in a way that allows you to get at the hard disk from DOS as well as from OS/2. You can further prepare yourself by keeping a DOS boot disk handy for emergencies, by making copies of your configuration files in case the originals get damaged, by knowing which files OS/2 considers sensitive, and by making sure that you can access OS/2's files of messages.

Configuring Your Hard Disk

If you want to use HPFS, you don't have to make the entire disk a single HPFS partition. You may benefit from creating a FAT partition for the OS/2 system files and an HPFS partition on the remainder of the disk. You then can use CHKDSK to repair HPFS damage on the separate partition, or you can boot DOS to fix errors in the primary FAT partition. Depending on how much of OS/2 you decide to install, you can designate the first 40M or so as the FAT partition that will hold the OS/2 system files.

While OS/2 is active, you cannot use CHKDSK with the /F parameter to repair errors in the partition containing the OS/2 system files. OS/2 keeps many of its system files open when it runs your applications and manages the desktop. Because files are open in the partition containing the OS/2 system files, CHKDSK cannot move portions of files or change file attributes. If you make the entire disk a single partition, either FAT or HPFS, you have to boot the OS/2 Installation Disk to get a command line prompt at which you can run the CHKDSK utility; this procedure is outlined later in this chapter.

If you create a FAT partition for the OS/2 system files and an HPFS partition for your data files, however, you can use CHKDSK on the HPFS partition without having to reboot your computer with the Installation Disk.

Even if you don't want to use HPFS, you can use the two-partition approach to divide your disk into separate FAT partitions. You can use the second partition for your data files and manage that partition separately. You can access both partitions with either OS/2 or DOS.

Using the DOS Boot Disk

Perhaps a power failure occurs just when one of your applications updates a file, and you want to use a DOS-based disk diagnostic tool to inspect the damage. Perhaps you want to run a disk reorganizer utility to defragment the files on your hard disk, or perhaps you chose not to install OS/2's Dual-Boot feature but want to use plain DOS (outside of OS/2) to play a game that is copy-protected or that reboots the computer when you finish playing the game. For these and similar situations, you should keep a DOS boot disk handy. A later section of this chapter explains how to use the DOS boot disk.

> **NOTE** When one of your applications writes a file to a FAT partition, both DOS and OS/2 put the contents of the file into sectors on the disk. These sectors don't have to be contiguous. The next time you access the file, DOS and OS/2 retrieve the contents of the file for your application without the application having to know that the file may have come from disk sectors that aren't contiguous.
>
> Your application seems to run slightly slower, however, because DOS or OS/2 must move the read/write mechanism of the disk drive back and forth to the various locations of the file. This phenomenon is most apparent on large files. You can speed things up by periodically running a disk utility that rearranges the files so that their sectors are contiguous. Such a utility is called a disk defragmenter or *defragger*. Such low-level disk utilities cannot run under OS/2; you must boot DOS to use them.
>
> HPFS partitions don't need to be defragmented. HPFS automatically organizes the contents of your files in a way that enables OS/2 to access the files quickly.

Making Copies of Important OS/2 Files

You know the importance of your CONFIG.SYS file. OS/2 uses the contents of the CONFIG.SYS file at boot time to determine how to configure the operating system for your use and what device drivers you want loaded. OS/2 uses other files to hold configuration information, too. You should make copies of these files periodically (perhaps daily or at least weekly) in case you need to recover from an OS/2 configuration error.

In addition to the CONFIG.SYS file (located in the root directory of drive C) the other files whose current state you want to preserve are the OS2.INI and OS2SYS.INI files (located in the OS2 subdirectory). You also need to make a copy of the desktop's directory structure.

For a FAT-based system, the name of the desktop directory is OS!2_2.0_D. For an HPFS-based system, the name is "OS!2 2.0 DESKTOP". (The directory name may be OS!2_2.1_D or "OS!2 2.1 DESKTOP"; use the DIR command to determine the name OS/2 uses on your computer.) You should make a backup copy of your desktop directory structure. To do so, follow these steps:

1. Boot with the OS/2 Installation Diskette; insert OS/2 Diskette 1 when the prompt for the disk appears.

2. After the second part of the installation software loads from OS/2 Diskette 1, use the Esc key to obtain a command line prompt.

3. Type **C:** and press Enter.

4. If the hard disk partition OS/2 starts from is FAT-based, insert a blank, formatted disk in the A drive and enter the following command (substituting the directory name appropriate for your computer):

    BACKUP OS!2_2.0_D A: /S

5. If the hard disk partition from which OS/2 starts is HPFS-based, insert a blank, formatted disk in the A drive and enter the following command (substituting the directory name appropriate for your computer):

    BACKUP "OS!2 2.0 DESKTOP" A: /S

6. Use the XCOPY command to also make a backup copy of the OS2SYS.INI and OS2.INI files. These two files, located in the OS2 directory, contain information about how you have customized your desktop. The following command puts the backup copy of these files on the same floppy disk you used in the preceding steps:

    XCOPY C:\OS2*.INI A:

7. Putting a copy of your CONFIG.SYS file on the floppy disk is also a good idea; to do so, use the following command:

    XCOPY C:\CONFIG.SYS A:

8. You should now store the floppy disk in a safe place. This floppy disk contains a copy of your computer's OS/2 configuration, including the state of your desktop.

If you need to restore your configuration files from the floppy disk, including the appearance of your desktop, follow these steps:

1. Boot with the OS/2 Installation Diskette; insert OS/2 Diskette 1 when the prompt for the disk appears.

2. After the second part of the installation software loads from OS/2 Diskette 1, use the Esc key to obtain a command line prompt.

3. Type **C:** and press Enter.

4. For an HPFS-based system, type the following command:

    RESTORE A: "OS!2 2.0 DESKTOP" /S

5. If your system is FAT-based, type the following command:

    RESTORE A: OS!2_2.0_D /S

6. You can make your backup copy of the OS2SYS.INI and OS2.INI files current by typing the following command:

    XCOPY A:*.INI C:\OS2*.INI

7. Make the copy of your CONFIG.SYS file on the floppy disk current with the following command:

    XCOPY A:\CONFIG.SYS C:\CONFIG.SYS

You can use a second method to back up and, if necessary, restore your OS2SYS.INI, OS2.INI, and CONFIG.SYS files. You may want to consider using this second method in addition to the first method already discussed. The OS/2 installation process copied your original OS2SYS.INI and OS2.INI files into the \OS2\INSTALL directory. Unless you copy newer files over the original ones, the files in \OS2\INSTALL reflect the original (installed) state of your desktop.

If you simultaneously press the Alt and F1 keys during the boot process, OS/2 restores your computer's configuration to a previous state by copying OS2.INI and OS2SYS.INI from \OS2\INSTALL to \OS2, and copying CONFIG.SYS from \OS2\INSTALL to the root directory.

If the OS2.INI, OS2SYS.INI, and CONFIG.SYS files in the \OS2\INSTALL directory are the ones left by the installation process, pressing Alt and F1 during system boot puts your desktop back to its original (first time) state. You can periodically update the files in the \OS2\INSTALL directory to reflect your current desktop settings, however.

As a first step toward establishing an automated backup copy of your OS/2 desktop, use a text editor (such as the Enhanced Editor) to insert the following four lines at the end of your CONFIG.SYS file:

```
CALL=C:\OS2\XCOPY.EXE C:\OS2\INSTALL\*.INA
     C:\OS2\INSTALL\*.INB
```

```
CALL=C:\OS2\XCOPY.EXE C:\OS2\*.INI
   C:\OS2\INSTALL\*.INA

CALL=C:\OS2\XCOPY.E2XE C:\INSTALL\CONFIG.SYA
   C:\OS2\INSTALL\CONFIG.SYB

CALL=C:\OS2\XCOPY.EXE C:\CONFIG.SYS
   C:\OS2\INSTALL\CONFIG.SYA
```

These four additions to the CONFIG.SYS file give you two copies of your OS2.INI, OS2SYS.INI, and CONFIG.SYS files. The files whose last character in the extension is A are the most recent copy. The files with a final extension character of B are the next most recent copy. The copies exist in the \OS2\INSTALL directory, and you automatically make new copies every time you boot your computer.

If you need to restore your desktop to an earlier state, follow these steps:

1. Boot with the OS/2 Installation Diskette; insert OS/2 Diskette 1 when the prompt for the disk appears.

2. After the second part of the installation software loads from OS/2 Diskette 1, use the Esc key to obtain a command line prompt.

3. Type **C:** and press Enter.

4. Type **CD \OS2\INSTALL** and press Enter.

5. Type one of the following commands, depending on whether you want to use the "A" set or the "B" set of files (you may want to start with the older "B" set, unless you know the "A" set isn't corrupted in any way):

   COPY *.INA *.INI

   or

   COPY *.INB *.INI

6. Type one of the following commands:

   COPY CONFIG.SYA CONFIG.SYS

   or

   COPY CONFIG.SYB CONFIG.SYS

7. After you set up the "A" or "B" filesets to become the current desktop and CONFIG.SYS, press Ctrl-Alt-Del to reboot the computer. During the boot procedure, hold down Alt and F1 so that OS/2 uses the backup files in the \OS2\INSTALL directory.

Of course, you should make a separate copy of these files in *addition* to the regular backup procedures you use.

Working with Sensitive OS/2 Files and Directories

OS/2 creates and manages certain files that you should not attempt to modify or delete. You should ensure that you back up these files along with the other files on your hard disk, however. In general, these files contain information about other files. OS/2 gives these special files the Hidden and System attributes so that you normally don't see them. A DIR command does not show these files. You run across the files, however, if you boot DOS and inspect your hard disk with a low-level disk utility. Depending on how you have your desktop's Detail View file criteria set up, you also may see the files in a Detail View window.

The first special file is named EA DATA. SF. Notice that the file has spaces in its name; you cannot access this file with most OS/2 and DOS software. EA DATA. SF contains extended attributes for the files on your computer system. OS/2 uses this file to hold information about other files that does not fit into a directory entry (the 32 bytes of information you see when you use the DIR command). OS/2 2.1 relies heavily on EA DATA. SF. If you use low-level disk diagnostic software, make sure that you do not disturb this file.

The WP ROOT. SF file is another special OS/2 file. The Workplace Shell uses this file to hold information about your desktop settings. As with the EA DATA. SF file, you should be careful that you do not disturb WP ROOT. SF.

> **CAUTION:** Some defragmenters don't work with OS/2 disks, regardless of whether the disk is formatted as FAT or HPFS. The defragmenter might scramble the EA DATA. SF file, and that file is critical to OS/2, as discussed in this chapter. Make sure that your disk defragmenter is OS/2-compatible before using it on your hard disk.

The C:\DELETE directory holds copies of files you have deleted. OS/2 automatically reclaims the space used by these deleted files as necessary, but maintains the copies as long as possible in the C:\DELETE directory should you want to undelete them. OS/2 also marks the copies of the deleted files with the Hidden and System file attributes. If you use a DIR command in the C:\DELETE directory, you see what appears to be an empty directory. You should not try to remove this directory.

OS/2 created a set of directories on your hard disk at installation time. The directory names are OS2, SPOOL, NOWHERE, DELETE, and either OS!2_2.0_D or OS!2_2.1_D. You almost certainly should leave this directory structure alone. In particular, the OS!2_2.0_D directory (perhaps named OS!2_2.1_D) holds information the Workplace Shell needs to function properly. The directories underneath the OS!2_2.0_D directory typically include TEMPLATE, MINIMIZE, OS!2_SYS, COM-MAND_, GAMES, and PRODUCTI. You may find additional directories in C:\OS!2_2.0_D, depending on which applications you install on your system. You should make backup copies of this directory structure, as discussed in the previous section.

The following table explains OS/2's uses of the directories in C:\OS2.

Directory	Contents
SYSTEM	Message, swap, and Dual Boot files
DLL	Dynamic Link Library (OS/2 program) files
HELP	On-line help files
INSTALL	Installation program and data files
BOOK	The OS/2 command reference
BITMAP	Image files for your desktop
APPS	The applets that come with OS/2
MDOS	DOS and Windows environment files
WINOS2	Microsoft Windows files (WINOS2 is a subdirectory of the MDOS directory)

Appendix E, "OS/2 Files by Function," contains a complete list of files that OS/2 installed on your PC. The list groups the files by function so you can understand why OS/2 installed a particular file.

Accessing the Message Files

Finally, before a problem happens, make sure that OS/2 can locate your message files. As the beginning of this chapter mentioned, the OS/2 installation process put the files in the C:\OS2\SYSTEM directory. For many types of errors, OS/2 retrieves the explanation for the error from one or more of the message files and then displays the result to you. If the message files cannot be found, OS/2 cannot fully explain the error.

The DPATH entry in the CONFIG.SYS file tells OS/2 where to find the message files for errors that happen in OS/2 sessions. The APPEND statement in the AUTOEXEC.BAT file does the same thing for DOS ses-sions. If you make changes to either the CONFIG.SYS or AUTOEXEC.BAT files, be careful about the DPATH and APPEND entries. Make sure that you use APPEND in your DOS sessions so you get the benefit of the message files in C:\OS2\SYSTEM. For OS/2 sessions, ensure that C:\OS2\SYSTEM is in the DPATH statement in the CONFIG.SYS file.

Make sure that you have installed the OS/2 on-line command reference. If trouble strikes, you may be able to solve the problem by simply referring to OS/2's on-line help.

For Related Information

◄◄ "Making the Computer Work for You," p. 42.

▶▶ "Command Reference," p. 647.

FROM HERE...

Recognizing Trouble

When OS/2 displays an error message or error screen, the error appears as a textual response to a command you have entered at a command line prompt or as a window of explanatory information. Sometimes you notice a problem, however, and no error explanation appears. This latter situation happens when one of your applications does not behave as expected; when the screen becomes garbled and unreadable; when you press keys on the keyboard or move the mouse or press its buttons, but the computer doesn't respond; when the printer does not print your documents properly; or when performance suddenly degrades. Any one of these occurrences is reason to suspect a problem.

Understanding Error Messages

When OS/2 displays an error message in response to a command you have entered at a command line prompt, you see something similar to the examples shown below:

Example 1

```
ERROR: The name specified is not recognized as an
internal or external command, operable program, or
batch file.
```

This error is equivalent to the DOS Bad command or file name error message.

Example 2

```
ERROR: You tried to write to a disk, but it is
write-protected.

ACTION: Make sure that the proper disk is being
used, or remove the write protection. Retry the
command.
```

Example 3

```
ERROR: A file contains a reference to an
extended attribute that does not exist. Either the
disk partition is damaged or the extended attribute
system file has been improperly modified.

ACTION: Run CHKDSK /F on the disk or disks.
```

Example 4

```
ERROR: The system cannot find the file "<filename>"
specified in the <statement> command on line <line
number> of the CONFIG.SYS file. Line <line number>
is ignored.
```

You can usually take corrective action when you see an error message such as one of those shown in the preceding examples by choosing an appropriate action from those suggested, by typing the command correctly, or by making sure that the appropriate files are located in the proper directories.

Understanding the *The system is stopped* Message

When OS/2 detects an error that halts the entire computer, you typically see a screen similar to the one illustrated in figure 8.2. You then must reboot OS/2.

Catching Application Program Errors

The safeguards built into OS/2 can catch an application program's error that otherwise would cause you to reboot your computer. Figures 8.3, 8.4, and 8.5 show such an error. You can respond to the error by clicking the button labeled End program/command/operation. Figure 8.3 illustrates the initial notification screen.

```
Exception in device driver: TRXNET$
TRAP 000e        ERRCD=0000  ERACC=****  ERLIM=********
EAX=fdce0001  EBX=fff311c0  ECX=000000fc  EDX=ffe302e0
ESI=fd415d96  EDI=feb40008  EBP=00000000  FLG=00010216
CS:EIP=0700:00000c69  CSACC=009b  CSLIM=00000fce
SS:ESP=00e8:000007dc  SSACC=0093  SSLIM=000007ff
DS=2310  DSACC=0093  DSLIM=0000fdff  CR0=fffffffe1
ES=0708  ESACC=1093  ESLIM=00003fff  CR2=00015d96
FS=0000  FSACC=****  FSLIM=********
GS=0000  GSACC=****  GSLIM=********
The system detected an internal processing
error at location ##0160:fff6986f - 000d:986f.
60000, 9084
038600d1


The system is stopped.  Record the location number of the
error and contact your service representative.
```

Fig. 8.2

The *The system is stopped* error screen.

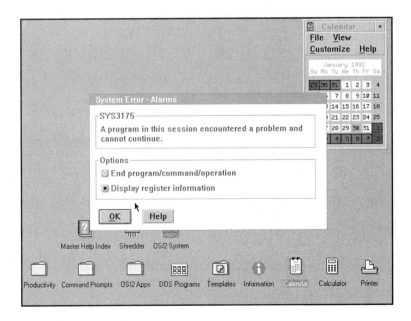

Fig. 8.3

OS/2's notification that it has caught an application error before the application can crash your computer.

If you click the Help button shown in figure 8.3, OS/2 displays an explanation of the error (see fig. 8.4). Usually, the explanation tells the programmer what he or she has done wrong. If you purchased rather than developed the application that caused the error, you may want to record the system error number (SYS3175 in the examples shown in figures 8.3 and 8.4) and send the error number to the customer support personnel at the company that makes the software.

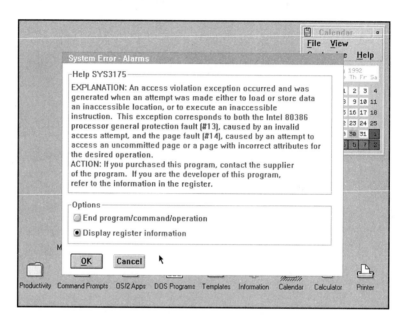

Fig. 8.4

OS/2's explanation of what the application was doing at the time of the error.

Clicking the Display register information button shown in figure 8.3 makes the screen illustrated in figure 8.5 appear. This screen shows the contents of the CPU chip's internal registers at the time the application error occurred. Note that figure 8.5 is only an example; the actual values in the registers vary from application to application. As with the system error number information shown in figure 8.3, the register display is for the programmer who wrote the software. You may want to record the information so that you can send it to the customer support people at the company that makes the software. The system error number and the register values give the programmer enough information to fix the software.

After you have ended the program, you can continue using OS/2 and your other applications. You can restart the application that failed, but be aware that you have discovered a bug in that application. The application may fail again.

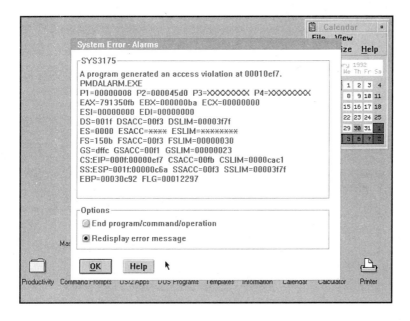

Fig. 8.5

OS/2's display
of registers when
an application
fails.

For Related Information

◄◄ "Understanding Operating Systems," p. 34.

◄◄ "Matching OS/2 with DOS," p. 60.

◄◄ "Looking at DOS and OS/2 Incompatibilities," p. 71.

FROM HERE...

Knowing What Steps To Take

If you encounter an error, the first step is to diagnose the problem. You
can categorize and identify the error by using the later sections of this
chapter. These sections explain how to recover from problems that
happen during the boot process, when an application (or the entire
computer) stops suddenly, when an application does not behave as
expected, when the screen becomes garbled, when pressing keys on
the keyboard produces no reaction from the computer, when the
mouse fails to move the cursor or the mouse buttons fail to work, when
your printouts don't appear or are garbled, and when the performance
of your computer suddenly becomes slow.

If your computer cannot recover from the error by your responding to an error message, changing a setting, or issuing a command, this chapter explains how to use the OS/2 installation disk, or perhaps a DOS boot disk, to fix the problem.

Diagnosing the Problem

This chapter has shown you OS/2 error messages, The system is stopped error message, and application error messages. An error may appear in a different form, however. The next several sections of this chapter discuss unusual kinds of errors.

Knowing Why the Computer Fails To Boot

If your computer does not display the Workplace Shell desktop screen within several minutes after booting, look carefully at the screen for error messages that explain why the computer stopped. If no message appears, you may have a hardware problem. (Hardware problems are beyond the scope of this book.) If no message appears and you don't have a hardware problem, you may need to reinstall OS/2. First, though, try booting the OS/2 Installation Disk, as outlined later in this chapter. If the Installation Disk boots successfully, try the CHKDSK /F command to see if it repairs your hard disk so that you can reboot.

Also note whether you made configuration changes recently to your computer. One of your changes may have disabled the computer's capability to boot properly.

Reacting When the Computer or Application Stops Suddenly

The computer's or application's stopping suddenly is perhaps the rarest of errors. If OS/2 does not show you even a The Computer is Stopped error message, and you cannot get a response from the computer, look for a hardware problem in your computer.

If you suspect your computer has stopped working entirely, the first thing to do is move your mouse. Does the cursor on-screen move with it? If so, your computer is still running, although it is perhaps not running the software you intended.

If the mouse cursor does not move, reboot the computer with the power switch or the computer's reset button. Note that with OS/2's built-in safeguards, running into the situation where you need to use the power switch is highly unlikely.

The problem may be that the full-screen or windowed application session you're using has simply lost the current focus; another application is using the keyboard and/or the screen. Click the title bar of the window of the application you're using. Does this action highlight (activate) the window? If so, you should be able to resume using that application.

Before you reboot your computer, try pressing Ctrl-Esc to bring up the list of active applications on your desktop. If Ctrl-Esc has no effect, reboot. Don't forget to have your computer checked for hardware malfunctions.

Checking an Application that Does Not Behave

If your application's behavior causes you to suspect a strange interaction between OS/2 and your application, first make sure that you have followed the correct steps to obtain results from that application. You may simply have typed an incorrect file name or clicked a button unintentionally. Also, inspect the settings notebook for the session in which the application is running. Perhaps you changed a setting and need to restore it to its original value. Also, you may need to change a setting to make the session's environment better suited to your application.

This category of error is the broadest and the most difficult to pin down. You must verify whether the application is in error, OS/2 is in error, or you have a hardware problem. Perhaps you misunderstand how the application is supposed to behave. One step you can take is to see if the error is repeatable. If you cannot make the error happen a second time, the error may be the result of a typing error.

If you have a DOS application that is supposed to run in the background but that does not run properly, look at the DOS settings for that session. You should make sure that timer interrupts in the background are enabled, and you should try increasing idle sensitivity from the default 75 percent to a higher value. By increasing the idle sensitivity, you allocate more CPU time to the DOS program.

If the application is a communications program that uses one of the serial ports (COM1, COM2, COM3, or COM4), you may want to substitute the COM02.SYS file for the default serial port device driver. Change your CONFIG.SYS file to DEVICE=C:\OS2\COM02.SYS rather than DEVICE=C:\OS2\COM.SYS. Unpack COM02.SYS from Disk 5 of the distribution disks. In an OS/2 full-screen session, insert Disk 5 in your A: drive, make C:\OS2 your current directory, and type **UNPACK A:\SERIAL**. You should see a message telling you COM02.SYS is unpacked. After using the Shutdown option, reboot your computer; the change then takes effect.

If you find that a serial mouse doesn't function properly on an IBM PS/2 model 90 or model 95 computer, you may need to use the Setup/Diagnostics disk that came with the computer to disable the serial port arbitration levels.

If a DOS application requires VCPI memory, that application does not run under OS/2. You must use Dual Boot to run the VCPI application by itself and under DOS, without the benefit of OS/2's multitasking.

Perhaps the software you're trying to run is a low-level disk utility that reads and writes to disk sectors (rather than files). Or perhaps the software is copy-protected or is a game, and you need to use Dual-Boot to run the software under plain DOS.

Unscrambling a Garbled Screen

If your screen appears garbled (not just confused—actually unreadable), you first want to ask yourself if you recently made configuration changes to your computer, especially the CONFIG.SYS file. If so, you should reset your changes and reboot. You also can explore the possibility that your computer has a hardware problem.

To see if OS/2 can regain control of the video adapter, try pressing Ctrl-Esc to bring up the list of active sessions on the desktop. If this action fails to work and because you cannot read the screen, try rebooting the computer.

Freeing a Keyboard that Fails To Work

If pressing keys on the keyboard produces no response from the computer, you first should work through the material given earlier in this chapter in the section titled, "Reacting When the Computer or Application Stops Suddenly." The problem may be that a different application is using the keyboard.

Try pressing the Caps Lock key. Does the green light on the keyboard toggle on and off each time you press Caps Lock? If so, the computer is still active, but the other keystrokes are not getting through to the intended application. Try pressing Ctrl-Esc to bring up the list of active desktop sessions. If this action is effective, select your application from the list and try to resume your work. If you still have a problem, the application is simply not looking for keyboard input (despite what may appear on-screen). The application software may have a bug in it. Consult the application documentation to pursue this further.

Solving Mouse Problems

Most of the suggestions and discussion you covered earlier in the sections titled "Reacting When the Computer or Application Stops Suddenly" and "Keyboard Fails to Work" apply also to the mouse. The mouse cursor should always move in response to moving the mouse, whether or not an application is looking for mouse input. If the mouse cursor fails to move, you probably have a hardware problem. (If the mouse cursor fails to move and you have just installed OS/2, you may have made an incorrect selection regarding the type of mouse you have. Double-check your selection before you proceed.) Also, make sure that the mouse is connected properly to the computer. A loose connection can cause the mouse to appear unresponsive.

Checking the System When Nothing Prints

Obviously, the first thing to check when the printer does not print is that it is plugged in, turned on, and selected (on-line). Also check with the documentation that came with the printer to see why it might fail to print.

If you are trying to print for the first time after you have installed OS/2, you should go back to Chapter 6, "Installing OS/2," and Chapter 7, "Modifying Your OS/2 Configuration," to make sure you have configured OS/2 for your make and model of printer. Ensure that you have a properly set up print destination object on your desktop (refer to Chapters 6 and 7).

If your printer is connected to your serial port and you have an IBM PS/2 model 90 or model 95 computer, you should make sure that you set the Serial Transmit and Serial Receive Arbitration Levels to Dedicated and assign different numbers to each. Use the Setup/Diagnostics disk to make this configuration change, as outlined in the documentation that came with your computer.

Clearing Garbled Printouts

If your printer worked fine yesterday but prints unreadable characters today and you haven't made configuration changes to your OS/2 print destination object, the problem may simply be that the printer is in the wrong mode. Turning the printer off and on again or using its reset button usually clears things up. If these actions don't cure the problem, you probably have a hardware problem in the printer or the printer cable is bad.

If your printer does not print correctly right after you install OS/2, you should review Chapters 6 and 7 to make sure that you have given OS/2 the correct data for your printer. In particular, look at the printer driver settings to see if they match the type of printer you use.

Analyzing Performance Problems

If your computer produces the correct results but slowly, you may have a performance problem. "May have" is the operative phrase because performance is a perceived thing; you may think the computer is slow, but another person may think it is fast.

Here are some tips you can use to make your computer run as fast as possible. First, look at the number and complexity of the applications you're trying to run simultaneously under OS/2. Your computer has only a certain amount of horsepower. OS/2 divides up that horsepower among the active applications on your desktop. To get better performance, try reducing the number of applications you have open at the same time.

Next, realize that OS/2 uses the hard disk as a memory-overflow device. When OS/2 begins to run out of physical memory in which to run applications, the SWAPPER.DAT file in the C:\OS2\SYSTEM directory becomes very active. Choose a command line session and look at the size of the SWAPPER.DAT file. If the size exceeds about 2 or 3M, you should probably consider installing more physical RAM in your computer. (Under DOS, when applications reach the 640K threshold, they simply stop working altogether. Because OS/2 uses the SWAPPER.DAT file for overflow, the computer just slows down.)

You can enhance the performance of a FAT partition by using the Lazy Write (LW) parameter on the DISKCACHE statement in the CONFIG.SYS file. If you change this parameter, remember to reboot your computer so your change takes effect. You also can make sure that the third parameter on the DISKCACHE statement is 128, as shown in the following example:

```
DISKCACHE=64,LW,128
```

If you have a performance problem with an application that uses graphics and you're running that application in a windowed session, you can get a much better performance from the application by running it in a full-screen session. If you run Windows applications on your desktop, you should realize that OS/2 must serialize access to the screen. Windows can write to the screen or OS/2 can write to the screen, but both cannot write to the screen at the same time.

For Related Information

◀◀ "Understanding Disk Partitions and Disks," p. 44.

◀◀ "Considering Disks and Disk Files," p. 80.

◀◀ "Using the Keyboards and Mice," p. 113.

◀◀ "Working with Video Adapter Cards and Monitors," p. 115.

▶▶ "Using the Workplace Shell," p. 218.

▶▶ "Introducing Presentation Manager," p. 221.

FROM HERE...

Using the Installation Disks in an Emergency

If your computer does not boot or if you need to run the CHKDSK command with the /F parameter on a partition that OS/2 is using, you usually can fix the problem by following these steps:

1. Insert the disk labeled OS/2 Installation Diskette in the disk drive and reboot your computer.

2. At the prompt for the next floppy disk, insert the disk labeled OS/2 Diskette 1.

3. At the next prompt, press the Esc key to obtain an OS/2 command line prompt.

If the problem is caused by errors in the CONFIG.SYS file, you can use the procedures given earlier in this chapter to restore the CONFIG.SYS file to a previous state. You also can use those procedures to restore the appearance and configuration of your desktop.

If you need to run the CHKDSK program, you can type the following command at the command line prompt to repair the damage:

CHKDSK C: /F

After you restore files and repair the disk format, reboot your computer.

FROM HERE...

For Related Information

▶▶ "Beginning the Command Line Interface," p. 293.

▶▶ "Learning the Commands for Managing Directories," p. 295.

▶▶ "Learning the Commands for Managing Files," p. 301.

▶▶ "Learning the Commands To Back Up Your Hard Disk," p. 313.

▶▶ "Command Reference," p. 647.

Booting a DOS Disk

You can stop OS/2 by selecting the Shutdown option from the desktop's pop-up menu, inserting a DOS boot disk in drive A:, and rebooting your computer. At the DOS prompt, you can run disk diagnostic tools, disk defragmenters, copy-protected software, and games. If you have an HPFS partition, it is invisible under plain DOS. You can access your FAT partitions normally, however, after booting DOS.

You also can use the Dual-Boot feature to run DOS. Dual-Boot *does* need to write files on your hard disk just before it restarts your computer. You should use a DOS disk if you suspect you need to repair a Sector Not Found error or other error requiring the use of low-level disk diagnostic tools. In this case, you probably don't want to even use the Shutdown option. Your first action after seeing signs of a hard disk malfunction might be to insert the DOS disk and press Ctrl-Alt-Del.

Note that the DOS version of the CHKDSK utility cannot repair damage to OS/2's extended attributes. Running CHKDSK under DOS is not as satisfactory as running the OS/2 version.

Also note that utilities such as PC Tools and Norton's Utilities cannot repair damage to an HPFS partition.

For Related Information

▶▶ "Understanding DOS Sessions," p. 386.

▶▶ "Switching between OS/2 and DOS with Dual-Boot," p. 397.

FROM HERE...

Chapter Summary

In this chapter, you have covered a number of unlikely situations. Being prepared for these kinds of situations is important. You're now ready in case problems arise.

You learned what OS/2 error messages look like, including the ones that appear when you issue commands at the command line and the ones that appear when OS/2 detects that an application is misbehaving. You can recognize `The system is stopped` error screen that you now know means you must reboot your computer.

You learned how to deal with installation errors, you know what to do if the computer fails to boot, and you understand the different problems causing an application (or the entire computer) to stop suddenly. When an application does not behave as expected or displays a garbled screen, you can diagnose the problem. If the keyboard or mouse produce no reaction from the computer, you know what to look for. If you have problems with your printouts, you can correct the problem. You also know ways you can deal with performance problems so that you get the most productivity from your computer system.

Using the Graphical Interface

P A R T

III

O U T L I N E

Using Your Computer Screen as a Desktop

Y ou now have OS/2 2.1 up and running on your computer. If you
didn't have a problem installing OS/2, you probably skipped Chapter 8, "Troubleshooting OS/2," and came directly to this chapter's explanation of the OS/2 graphical user interface. This approach is a good one; you can return to Chapter 8 when you need to (or if you just get curious).

Presentation Manager—the OS/2 graphical user interface (GUI)—is easy to learn, easy to use, and consistent. PM gives you on-screen objects that you can manipulate in several ways. In this chapter, you learn how to identify these objects readily. You also discover that PM and the Workplace Shell make these objects behave similarly to the objects on a desk, with which you are already familiar. This behavior is OS/2's *desktop metaphor*.

The PM standard for consistency and ease of use comes from a team of IBM people who spent a number of years investigating user interfaces. The team's findings parallel the findings of Xerox Corporation at the Palo Alto Research Center (PARC) and the findings of the Apple Computer, Inc., makers of the Macintosh computer. IBM published these findings in the form of suggested standards and called them *Common User Access*, or CUA. CUA is part of a larger set of standards, termed *Systems Application Architecture* (SAA) by IBM. SAA covers communications, programming, database design, and user interfaces.

When applications have a consistent appearance, operational interface, and terminology, you naturally develop a conceptual model for how to use computer software. If you encounter a new application that presents a consistent appearance, you transfer previously learned skills and experience to the new application. You accurately can predict how the new application may behave and can expect your skills to carry over to the new application. This carryover translates into productivity.

Non-PM-based applications have little or nothing in common in terms of their appearance and interface with other applications you use. Inconsistency costs more in training time and increases the likelihood of errors, resulting in decreased productivity and increased frustration.

Common User Access treats the computer screen as a desktop that holds as many or as few objects on your *desk* as you prefer. (Some people like a clean desk, others don't.) PM is a bit object-oriented; the Workplace Shell is even more so.

Understanding CUA Principles

IBM based the Common User Access standard on seven principles that describe how people and computers should work together. The following table describes these principles.

Principle	Description
Actions should be reversible.	In a dialog between you and the computer, the application should provide a Cancel option to return the application to a previous state. You should be able to easily undo a wrong menu choice and be able to back up more than one step. When appropriate, an application should offer a Refresh option for restoring input values to a default state.
Preserve the display context to sustain orientation.	Primary windows, window titles, secondary windows, pop-up windows, and scrolling information should appear and behave in a way that suggests the context in which the action takes place. (These terms are defined later in this chapter.)

Principle	Description
Don't rely on a person's memorization of steps.	You shouldn't have to remember how to type commands and what every command does. Pull-down menus and other means of selection should offer available options from which you can choose.
Give immediate feedback for every action.	The application should acknowledge each step or action you take. An application should use screen colors, emphasis, and other selection indications to denote what item is chosen, what may not be chosen, and whether an error condition exists.
Confirm potentially destructive actions.	An application should verify your intent and provide options to perform or cancel an action that erases or deletes information.
Common definitions enhance consistency.	Applications should use common definitions for concepts, appearance of displayed information, and interaction techniques.
The keyboard and mouse are interchangeable.	You should be able to use the keyboard to perform actions that you can perform with a mouse (or with another pointing device). You should be able to switch to and from the mouse and the keyboard in the middle of an operation.

The best way to begin identifying and working with the objects on the Workplace Shell desktop or in Presentation Manager is to start with the outermost parts first. After you understand the overall screen display, you can work inward, focusing more closely on the detail of the smaller components. In the following sections, you look first at the Workplace Shell. You explore a basic PM screen, application windows, and then so-called *dialog boxes*.

For Related Information

◄◄ "Examining Presentation Manager," p. 12.

◄◄ "Understanding How OS/2 Expands upon DOS," p. 62.

FROM HERE...

Using the Workplace Shell

IBM designed the Workplace Shell to be an easy-to-use, object-oriented environment. You do some computer work directly on the Workplace Shell's desktop, but most often you probably use the Workplace Shell to run your applications. In the next few sections, you learn about the objects on your OS/2 desktop and how to manipulate them.

Understanding Workplace Objects

The icons you see when you start OS/2 are objects. You can use these objects when you use the objects on your desk—as tools and as places to file information. When you first boot OS/2, your screen should look like figure 9.1.

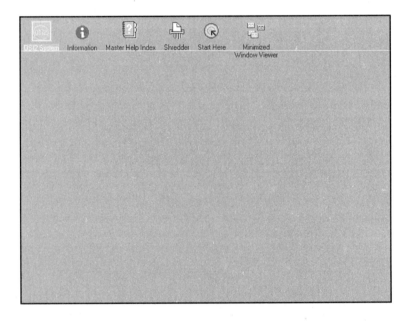

Fig. 9.1

The initial OS/2 screen, showing your new desktop.

The icons you see on-screen and in figure 9.1 are *objects*. Those labeled OS/2 System, Information, Main, and Templates are *folders*. Place the mouse cursor over the OS/2 System folder and quickly click mouse button 1 twice. This mouse operation, known as *double-clicking*, opens the folder. Hold down the Alt key and press the F4 key to close the folder.

Dragging and Dropping Objects

Now you should take something out of a folder so that you can see how objects behave on your desktop. Double-click the OS/2 System folder to open it. Then follow these steps:

1. Move the mouse cursor over the icon labeled Command Prompts.

2. Press and hold down mouse button 2 and move the mouse cursor to an empty place on the desktop screen. The Command Prompts folder moves with the mouse cursor.

3. Release the mouse button. You have dragged the folder to your desktop and dropped it.

4. Double-click the Command Prompts folder. It opens to reveal objects representing the DOS, OS/2, and Windows sessions you can start under OS/2.

5. Press Alt-F4 to close the Command Prompts folder, and then press Alt-F4 again to close the OS/2 System folder. The Command Prompts folder remains on your desktop.

Navigating the Workplace Shell

The techniques you learn in this section serve you well when you use other CUA-compliant computer software. Figure 9.2 shows a typical Presentation Manager utility, the OS/2 System Editor. The System Editor is a good example of CUA compliance.

You can use the keyboard to make your screen look like figure 9.2 by following these steps:

1. Press Alt-Tab until you highlight an icon. The highlight appears as a gray rectangle around the icon.

2. Press the arrow keys to move the highlight from icon to icon. Watch how the highlight moves.

3. Highlight the icon labeled OS/2 System. Press Enter to open this object (a folder).

4. You see another group of objects in the OS/2 System folder. Highlight the Productivity object and press Enter.

5. Highlight the OS/2 System Editor object and then press Enter. The System Editor screen appears.

6. Press Alt-Tab to move the Productivity folder to the foreground.

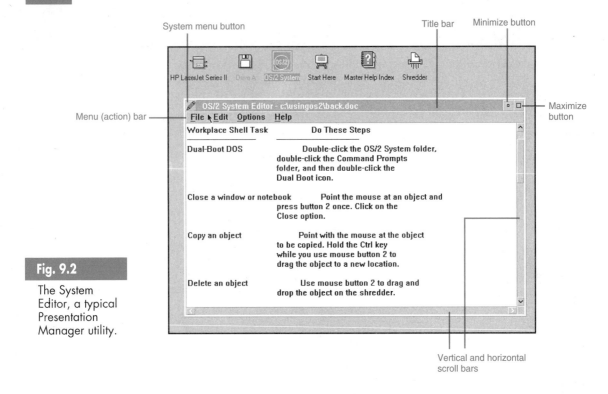

System menu button

Title bar

Minimize button

Menu (action) bar

Maximize button

Fig. 9.2

The System Editor, a typical Presentation Manager utility.

Vertical and horizontal scroll bars

7. Press Alt-F4 to close the Productivity folder.

8. Press Alt-F9 to *minimize* the OS/2 System folder. (The folder is still open but doesn't take up space on your OS/2 desktop.)

9. To bring the System Editor to the foreground, press Alt-Tab again.

NOTE   The preceding steps assume that you don't have a mouse attached to the computer. You can use a mouse in several of these steps, but now you are somewhat familiar with the keystroke equivalents for some basic Workplace Shell operations.

FROM HERE...

For Related Information

◄◄ "Understanding How OS/2 Expands upon DOS," p. 62.

◄◄ "Configuring Your Desktop," p. 174.

Introducing Presentation Manager

By looking at figure 9.1, you can tell that the previously outlined CUA principles are fully effective. These principles probably seemed to be obvious, common-sense ideas when you first read about them. Now you have seen these principles put to use. The screen preserved the related display context, you received immediate feedback for each action you took, and you used the keyboard to perform actions that you may have believed would require a mouse. Not all application environments are as consistent, easy to learn, and easy to use as Presentation Manager and Workplace Shell.

Using the Keyboard in PM

In figure 9.1, the System Editor is the *active* window, and the desktop is an *inactive* window. To switch to another window and make the next window active, you can press Alt-Tab, or move the mouse cursor over the inactive window and click mouse button 1 once after the mouse cursor is in the inactive window. The keyboard and the mouse perform equivalent operations.

With the System Editor as the active window, press Alt to highlight the menu item labeled File in the upper left corner of the System Editor window. (If File isn't highlighted, you may have pressed the Alt key twice. Press Alt again.)

Now press the right-arrow key until you highlight the word Help and then press Enter. A menu appears (drops down) on-screen. Press the down-arrow key until you highlight the word Copyright; press Enter. These steps make the About dialog box (listing product information for OS/2) appear. Your screen should resemble figure 9.3. Press Enter to remove the About box from the screen.

You can move, maximize (to take up the entire screen), or minimize (to become icons) PM application windows. You learn more about these procedures in later sections of this chapter and in the following chapter. For now, just minimize the System Editor by pressing Alt-F9. The only objects left on the desktop are the icons.

To activate windows that you previously minimized to icons, press Ctrl-Esc. The Window List appears. Use the arrow keys to highlight the OS/2 System Editor entry in the Window List. Press Enter to bring the System Editor window to the foreground.

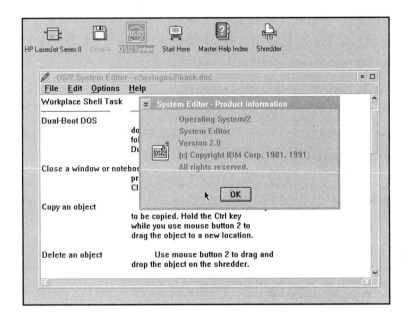

The System
Editor's About
box.

Now to make your screen look like figure 9.4, press Alt-space bar. You
have activated the System Editor's pop-up system menu. (You can
press Alt-space bar or Shift-Esc to invoke the pop-up system menu for
the currently active window.)

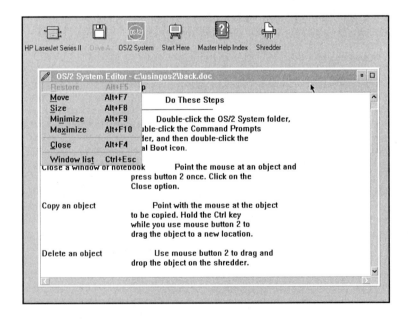

The pop-up
system menu.

To maximize the Editor window, press Alt-F10. To restore Editor to the former position and size, press Alt-F5. You can see that focusing on the current application (maximizing it), or making the window the same size as the other windows on-screen is a simple matter.

Using the Mouse in PM

Up to this point, you have not used the mouse. You can use the keyboard or the mouse to perform the same operations, according to your preferences.

Study figure 9.1 again for a moment. The pencil icon in the upper left corner is the system menu icon. If you click the system menu icon, you activate the system menu. To deactivate the system menu, click mouse button 1 again.

In the upper right corner are the Minimize and Maximize icons. Clicking these icons causes the window to minimize or to take up the entire screen. In the latter case, the Maximize icon becomes a double arrow that you can use to restore the window to its former size.

 NOTE At various times and in various areas of the screen, the mouse cursor may change from an arrow into an I-beam, an hourglass, a cross, a hand, and other shapes. Each shape indicates a different mode for the application.

So far, you have concentrated on managing the desktop as a whole. In the following sections, you delve deeper by focusing on the interior of a Presentation Manager application window.

Understanding the Elements of a PM Window

Presentation Manager windows have elements in common: title bars, action (menu) bars, window borders, dialog boxes, and the Client Area. The following sections explain each element.

Title Bars

All Presentation Manager windows have a *title bar*, which contains the name of the application and sometimes the name of a file on which you are working. Some applications insert extra material in the title bar, such as the name of the file on which you are working.

When the screen contains several windows at the same time, title bars identify each window. As a result, title bars serve as your first line of defense against confusion on a cluttered screen.

Action Bars

Below the title bar all primary windows and many secondary windows offer *action bars* (known as *menu bars* in other applications).

Notice that for the System Editor, the action bar contains the words File, Edit, Options, and Help. In each word, one character (for System Editor, the first character) of the word is underlined. When you use the keyboard to activate an item in the action bar, you press the Alt key and the underlined character; for example, press Alt and then E for the Edit item. The selection becomes a pull-down menu, an extension of the action bar item. The menu items you see for the Edit menu are Undo, Cut, Copy, Paste, Clear, Find, and Select all (see fig. 9.5). Some menu items appear in a shade of gray, which means these menu items are now unavailable. When you are ready to close the menu, press Alt or Esc.

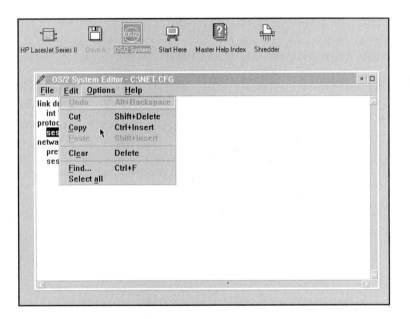

Fig. 9.5

The System Editor, with the Edit menu pulled down.

You also can use the mouse to access the Edit menu by clicking the menu's name on the action bar. Then click to choose an option from the pulled-down menu.

Presentation Manager often gives you several ways to take the same action. With the System Editor, for example, you can choose the Copy option from the Edit pull-down menu with any of the following actions:

- Press Alt-E, C (the underlined letters in the menu and the option) to activate the command.

- Use the command's shortcut keystroke, Ctrl-Insert. (The shortcut is listed to the right of the command on the pulled-down menu.) With shortcut keystrokes, you don't have to access the menus.

- After you pull down the Edit menu, use the arrow keys to highlight Copy and then press Enter. Alternatively, click the command.

The important thing to note about action bar menu items is that these items are consistent across all Presentation Manager applications. You used the System Editor in this example, but you just as easily can use a different utility or application.

Sizable Window Borders

So far, each window you have used has remained its original size, expanded to maximum size, or shrunk to an icon. You also can size each window the way you want, as discussed in this section. You can give a window virtually any dimensions you want.

By using the keyboard, you can size the currently active window by first pressing Alt-F8 and then using the arrow keys to move window borders inward or outward. By using the mouse, you move the mouse cursor directly over a window border until the cursor changes to a double-arrow shape. Then press mouse button 1 and drag the border until the window is the size you want it.

The Client Area

The body of a window inside the border and below the action bar is the *client area*. The client area is the workspace for viewing, entering, and selecting information.

Scroll Bars

Often, the information that an application presents to you exceeds the viewing area of the current window—vertically, horizontally, or in both directions. If you are faced with this situation, you can scroll the information on-screen. The presence of a horizontal or vertical *scroll bar* is a visual cue that more information is available and that you can bring the unseen information into view.

Earlier in this chapter you saw and used scroll bars. If you look again at figure 9.5, you see scroll bars along the bottom and right side of the System Editor's client area. These scroll bars are *grayed* to indicate that no off-screen information is present. (If you are looking at a text file that is several lines long, the vertical scroll bar is darkened.)

In figure 9.4, however, the display of text in the System Editor window extends beyond the bottom of the window. The vertical scroll bar is active (not grayed) and you can use the up- and down-arrows and the Page Up and Page Down keys to see more of the directory list.

So far, you have become acquainted with the PM screen as a whole and have learned to manipulate objects and windows on this screen. Now, prepare to focus even more closely as you look at a type of secondary window known as the dialog box.

Working with Dialog Boxes

Most applications use pop-up windows, or *dialog boxes*, to gather information from the user. These secondary windows appear inside a primary window and contain a variety of information display, entry, and selection tools. Dialog boxes usually are movable and fixed in size. A menu option name followed by an ellipsis (for example, Open...) calls up a dialog box or a secondary (cascaded) menu. Figure 9.6 shows the dialog box the System Editor uses to ask you which file you want to edit.

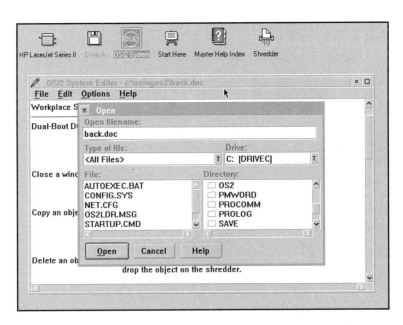

Fig. 9.6

The System Editor dialog box for opening a file to edit.

To bring up a dialog box, follow these steps:

1. From the System Editor window, press Alt-F to drop down the File menu.

2. Choose the Open... menu command.

3. After you finish viewing the information in the dialog box, press Esc to close the dialog box.

Title Bar and System Menu

Like most other windows, dialog boxes have title bars for easy identification. Some dialog boxes also have minimize/maximize icons and a system menu. Usually, the system menu for the dialog box contains only two menu items: Move and Close.

Buttons and Boxes

When an application directs you to specify a value (or select an option) from a list, the application displays a set of buttons. Beside or inside each button, you see a word or phrase that tells you what the button does.

You can use the mouse or the keyboard to choose a button. You can click the button with the mouse. If you're using the keyboard, press Tab and the arrow keys to move to the button you want to choose and then press the space bar. A button with a *selection highlight* (a visual emphasis) around it means that you now can choose this button.

In a dialog box, you can choose options marked with a pushbutton, radio button, spin button, slider box, or check box. Figure 9.7 shows the Autosave dialog box displayed by the System Editor. It contains pushbuttons, a spin button, and a check box.

The various button types are described as follows:

■ *Pushbutton*. The most common button, a pushbutton looks like a rectangle with rounded corners and text inside. When you choose a pushbutton, the application performs the indicated action. Figure 9.5 shows three pushbuttons: Open, Cancel, and Help. If you choose the Open button, the System Editor uses the other information in the dialog box, including the file name, to open a disk file for you to edit. The text you see in a pushbutton is application- and context-specific. You often see action-oriented words, such as OK, Accept, Save, Yes, and No.

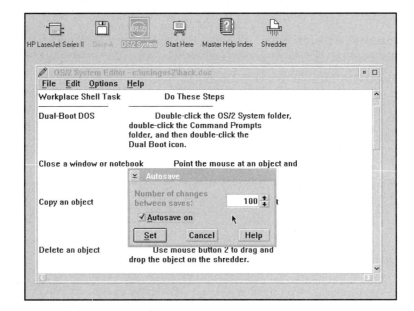

Fig. 9.7

The System Editor Autosave dialog box.

■ *Radio button.* Unlike pushbuttons, radio buttons don't cause the application to take immediate action. You use radio buttons to choose one of a mutually exclusive, fixed set of options. A radio button is a small circle with text beside it. When selected, the option has a partially filled-in circle.

■ *Spin buttons.* Sometime you may need to make a choice from a consecutive list with values that don't all fit in the dialog box window. The application may use a spin button with which you can make your selection—for example, the months of the year or the hours in a day. The spin button shows the current value next to two icons and up and down arrows. Clicking the up arrow selects a previous item in the list; clicking the down arrow selects the following item. (You also can activate the up and down buttons by pressing the up- and down-arrow keys.) This button is called a spin button because the current value "spins" if you continue to click the up or down buttons. The Number of changes between saves option in figure 9.6 is a spin button.

■ *Check boxes.* Pushbuttons cause immediate action, radio buttons select mutually exclusive options, and spin buttons change the current value from a range. To make one or many choices that are not mutually exclusive, you use check boxes. OS/2 displays a check mark in the *check box* when its corresponding option is selected. The Autosave on option in figure 9.6 is an example of a check box.

■ *Slider box.* You already saw one kind of slider box when you explored scroll bars earlier in this chapter. On a scroll bar, the slider
box shows you the relative position and size of the visible information in a window. Slider boxes also appear in dialog boxes so
that you can select a value by positioning the slider within a
range. The Mouse object (in the System Setup folder), for example, uses a slider box on the Timing page of its settings notebook to ask you how fast the mouse cursor should move.

List Boxes

Look at figure 9.6 again. The Open dialog box from the System Editor
contains four list boxes (sometimes known as *selection lists*). Two of
these boxes, Type of file and Drive, serve as drop-down list boxes and
text boxes. The other two boxes, File and Directory, are ordinary list
boxes. A list box contains a set of scrollable choices from which you
can choose. You select one entry from the list with the mouse or the
keyboard. The ordinary list box always shows the scrollable list, with
the currently selected item highlighted in the list.

The drop-down list box shows the currently selected value in a separate text box. To pull down the list so that you can select a different
value, you click the text box, or use Alt-down arrow to display the list.
You also can type the information in the text box.

Another kind of list box, the combination box, is a cross between the
other two kinds of list boxes. The scrollable list always appears (it
doesn't drop down). You make a selection from the list or you enter
text in the text box.

Data Entry Fields

All the selection and data entry mechanisms you just covered assume
that the application knows ahead of time what you may want to choose
to enter. Of course, the computer cannot possibly know what you may
type in the next memo or what name and phone number you may want
to track next. For these kinds of situations, you use a special area on-
screen known as an *entry field.* In figure 9.5, the Open filename text box
is a data entry area.

One thing that the application does know about what you type in an
entry field is the maximum number of characters you can type for the
field. The application can gather your information from a single-line,
nonscrollable entry field (much like the text box mentioned in the discussion on drop-down list boxes). The application also can offer a

single-line text box that scrolls; if you reach the right side of the text box while you type, the characters to the far left disappear while you continue to type at the right edge of the text box. If the application is prepared to accept several lines of typed text, you may see a multiple-line entry field.

Of all the selection and data entry mechanisms you learned to identify, the entry field is one you sometimes see in a primary window client area, outside a dialog box.

FROM HERE...

For Related Information

◀◀ "Examining Presentation Manager," p. 12.

▶▶ "Using the OS/2 Editors," p. 336.

▶▶ "Mastering Basic Editing Techniques," p. 338.

▶▶ "Understanding the System Editor Menus," p. 346.

▶▶ "Learning Commands Shared by Most General Purpose Applets," p. 517.

Chapter Summary

This chapter showed you how to operate the basic elements of the Workplace Shell screen (the desktop) and a Presentation Manager application. You now should be able to understand the CUA principles on which PM is based, and identify and manipulate title bars, action bars, window borders, dialog boxes, and the client area in your PM windows. You also have learned how to drag and drop the objects on your OS/2 desktop.

In the next chapter, you learn more about "Managing the Workplace Shell."

Managing the Workplace Shell

The Workplace Shell is OS/2's graphical interface. As you learned in Chapter 9, the Shell resembles a desktop covered with objects. On a real desk, a memo and a manila folder are objects. The Workplace Shell has many objects that look and work like the things with which you are familiar, such as notebooks and a paper shredder. Because the Workplace Shell uses the 1991 Common User Access standard, you can work these objects (and also the desktop) with the keyboard or the mouse, or both. Because this interface is consistent, the way you work with one object carries over to the other objects.

In this chapter, you gain hands-on experience working with three main kinds of objects: programs, data files, and folders. Folders contain other objects and help you organize the way you work with information.

Each kind of object appears initially as an icon—a small picture that tells you something about the object. You learn how to do many things by working directly with icons. To erase a file, for example, you can click the related icon with the mouse, and drag and drop the icon on the Shredder.

When you use an object, a window on the desktop usually opens. Several windows can be open at the same time. You can change each window's size and location, and you can move between windows. After working through this chapter's examples step by step, you will know how to arrange the desktop to best fit the way you work.

You also learn how to personalize the Workplace Shell. You can control how fast the mouse moves and how fast a key repeats when held down. You find out how to choose the fonts you like best and change the color of all parts of the windows on-screen. If solid colors seem too plain, you even can put a picture in each window.

If you previously installed DOS and Windows applications, you can still use these applications. This chapter shows how to put these applications on the desktop by default.

IBM designed the Workplace Shell to be easy to learn and easy to use. If you previously used a graphical interface like Windows, you may notice that many things are easier to do in the Workplace Shell. When you want to change a program's settings, for example, you don't have to open the Windows PIF Editor and type the program's name. Instead, click mouse button 2 on the program's icon. Invest the time to work through this chapter at the computer, and all these procedures soon will become second nature.

Working with Program Objects

Everything on the Workplace Shell desktop, even programs, is an object. The best way to become familiar with objects is to use them. In this section you start with a useful program object: the System Clock.

Starting a Program Object

When you start OS/2 for the first time, the Workplace Shell desktop is clear except for a few icons. One icon, called OS/2 System, contains many other objects. Open this icon and look inside. If you're using a mouse, move the mouse cursor to OS/2 System and double-click with mouse button 1. If you prefer to use the keyboard, use the arrow keys to move the cursor to OS/2 System and press Enter.

Inside OS/2 System, an icon labeled System Setup looks like a keyboard, mouse, and screen combined. Open System Setup like you did OS/2 System. Now, find and open the System Clock object. A window appears on-screen with a clock inside.

Displaying an Object's System Menu

Every program object has a system menu from which you control the program. To use the clock's system menu, move the mouse cursor to the clock and click mouse button 2, or press and release the Alt key.

The screen should look like figure 10.1. Actually, two menus are available. These menus are *cascaded*; one menu flows from the other. On the main menu, Window is already selected for you because this choice is probably where you want to start most of the time. The arrow to the right of Window means that a cascade menu listing several things you can do with the clock window is available. For now, you focus on the Window menu.

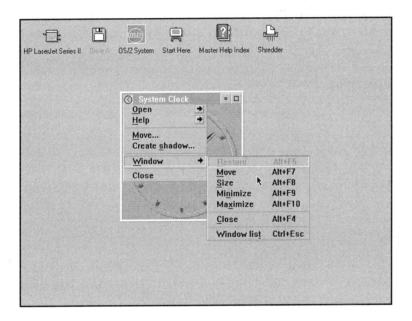

Fig. 10.1

The System Clock and its system menu.

Maximizing a Window

To expand the clock to fill the whole screen, you can maximize it (or any other icon) in the following ways:

- With the mouse button 1, click Ma<u>x</u>imize from the system menu.

- Press X. (X is the underlined letter in the word Ma<u>x</u>imize.) M would be easier to remember, but M already stands for <u>M</u>ove. Fortunately, Workplace Shell applications are consistent, and X always means Maximize on every application Window menu.

■ Hold down Alt and press F10. You need not memorize this key-stroke combination, because you always see the combination listed on the Window menu beside the Maximize option.

■ Double-click mouse button 1 on the clock's title bar, the shaded area at the top of the window that says System Clock. This method is faster than other ways because you can click at any time without first popping up the Window menu.

■ Click once with mouse button 1 on the Maximize button. This button has a large square and is located in the upper right corner of the window.

Minimizing a Window

You can go to the opposite extreme and shrink the window to an icon. As with maximizing, you can minimize a window in the following ways:

■ Pop up the Window menu, and click with mouse button 1 on the word Minimize.

■ While the Window menu is displayed, press the N key. N is the underlined letter in Minimize.

■ Hold down Alt and press F9.

■ Click once with mouse button 1 on the Minimize button. This button contains a small square and is located to the left of the Maximize button.

By default, a minimized window disappears into the Minimized Window Viewer. You can restore the window on your desktop by double-clicking the icon in the Minimized Window Viewer, or you can click the object's name in the Window List. In the section of this chapter titled "Working with Minimized Views," you learn how to minimize objects into icons that remain on your desktop.

Restoring a Window to Original Size

To reset the window to original size and position, choose Restore from the Window menu. You can move the highlight to Restore and press Enter, but pressing R is easier. Alt-F5 produces the same result.

To restore a maximized window with the mouse, two quick ways are available. When you maximize the clock window by clicking the Maximize button, the button changes to a Restore button, which looks like a picture of a medium-size square between two vertical lines. Click this button to restore the window to the original state. Or if you prefer,

double-click the title bar in the maximized window to restore it to
original size.

Moving a Window

Another choice on the Window menu is Move. Choose Move and you
can reposition the window anywhere by moving the arrow keys or the
mouse. The shortcut key for Move is Alt-F7.

If you're using a mouse, you have an easier way to choose Move. Follow
these steps:

1. Click either mouse button on the window's title bar.

2. Position the window to the desired location on-screen by moving
   the mouse while you hold the button down. This *drags* the window
   to its new location.

3. Release the mouse button when the window is at the desired
   location.

Resizing a Window

To change the clock window's size by using the keyboard, follow these
steps:

1. Choose Size from the Window menu, or press Alt-F8.

2. Move either the arrow keys or the mouse. The mouse cursor
   changes to a double arrow.

3. Press Enter or click a mouse button when the window is the size
   you want.

You may find resizing windows an easier task by using the mouse directly, without going through the Window menu. First, move the mouse
cursor to any edge or corner of the window, and notice that the cursor
changes to a double arrow. Hold down either mouse button to grab the
window frame at this spot, move the mouse to get the exact window
size you want, and then release the button.

Closing a Window

To close a window, click Close or press **C** while the Window menu is
displayed. Alt-F4 is the shortcut keystroke. The mouse shortcut is to
double-click the Menu button, which is in the upper left corner of the
window.

When you close the System Clock, the program ends, and the clock vanishes. If you experiment with closing a window now, remember that you must open the clock again before you go on to the following section, which tells how to change the clock display to suit your personal preferences.

FROM HERE...

For Related Information

◄◄ "Examining Presentation Manager," p. 12.

◄◄ "Understanding How OS/2 Expands upon DOS," p. 62.

Viewing an Object in Different Ways

You usually place a clock so that you can view the time. If you want to change the time, however, you turn the clock around to see the knobs on the back. Workplace Shell objects like the System Clock work in the same way. To change an object's display, you open a view of the object's settings.

Viewing the Settings Notebook

To open a view of the object's settings, follow these steps:

1. Move the clock to the far right side of the screen so that it is still visible in the background when you open the settings notebook.

2. Click the mouse button 2 on the clock. The System Clock main menu appears, with the Open option at the top of the menu.

   To the right of Open, you see an arrow button, which means that more than one way to open the clock program exists—more than one view is available.

3. Move the highlight to Open and press the right-arrow key, or just click the arrow button.

   A cascaded menu appears, giving you a choice between Settings and Program. These selections are available for all Workplace Shell program objects. The check mark next to Program means that starting the program is the default.

4. Choose Settings. The settings notebook appears.

5. Resize this window so that you can also see the open program view of the clock, as shown in figure 10.2. The notebook contains several pages grouped in sections, and each section has a tab— just like a real notebook.

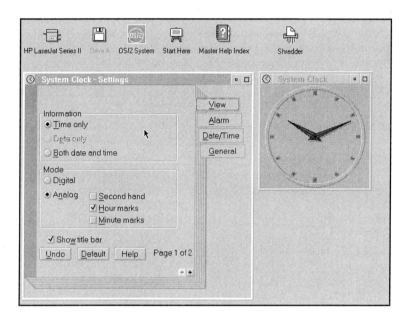

6. Choose the Underline{V}iew tab, either by clicking mouse button 1 on the tab, or by flipping the pages with Alt-PgDn or Alt-PgUp.

Experimenting with Different Settings

The first page in the View section, as shown in figure 10.2, enables you to change the clock from an analog (a round clock face with hands) to a digital (numeric) face. Click Digital, or use the arrow keys to select the button and press Enter. Two things happen immediately. The clock changes to a digital display; and in the settings notebook, options that don't apply to digital clocks, such as showing the second hand, are *grayed*. You still can see the grayed options faintly, but clicking them does nothing. This condition is typical of the Workplace Shell; changing an option produces a visible effect instantly. You don't have to close Settings to see the effect.

The View screen says Page 1 of 2. To go to the next page under the View tab, press Ctrl-PgDn or click the right-arrow button at the bottom of the page. Experiment with different fonts and colors. You can display the available choices by clicking the *spin buttons*—the buttons with an arrow that points downward. To activate a spin button from the keyboard, highlight the button and press Alt-down arrow.

The System Clock also is an alarm clock. You can set alarms by choosing the _A_larm tab in the settings notebook. The _D_ate/Time tab enables you to change the date and time. Experiment with these tabs now if you want. Remember, however, that the computer remembers new times or dates that you set, even after you turn off the power.

Undoing Changes

What happens if you change several settings on a page in the notebook and then decide that you prefer your previous settings? To cancel all the changes you just made, choose the _U_ndo button. To restore all options to the way you originally set them when you installed OS/2, use the _D_efault button.

FROM HERE...

For Related Information

◀◀ "Configuring Your Desktop," p. 174.

◀◀ "Using the Workplace Shell," p. 218.

▶▶ "Understanding the Enhanced Editor Menus," p. 354.

▶▶ "Learning OS/2 Printer Basics," p. 367.

▶▶ "Adding DOS Programs," p. 389.

Moving between Windows

By now, the desktop may be getting cluttered. The clock's settings notebook takes up much of the screen, hiding the objects beneath. To use the other open windows, you need a way to bring the windows to the top of the screen. Alt-Esc performs this job.

By pressing Alt-Esc repeatedly, you can move through all the different object views currently open on the desktop. When you move to each view, the related window appears on the top of the stack. As long as you also can see part of a window in the background, you can click the window to bring it to the top.

What happens if you close the OS/2 System folder? Should this step terminate the clock because it's contained in the folder? Many people may expect the clock to stay open, so this result is what normally happens. Later in this chapter, you learn how to change this default behavior.

For now, tidy up the screen by closing any open folders, and then minimize both open views of the clock. Alt-Esc still moves between the minimized views and by default does not restore them to the original size. Instead, this key combination shows the related system menus, and you can choose to restore the views or pick any other action you want.

Having two minimized icons may seem odd—especially if you have used another graphical interface previously. After all, only one clock exists. The explanation is that the clock is an object, and you can never actually see an object directly; you can see only a *view* of the object. The icons symbolize two different views of the clock object. This state is different from the way many other systems work. If you haven't used another interface, however, this state probably seems completely natural.

For Related Information

◀◀ "Understanding CUA Principles," p. 216.

◀◀ "Introducing Presentation Manager," p. 221.

FROM HERE...

Using the Window List

At any time, you can pop up a special menu known as the Window List by pressing Ctrl-Esc. Pop up this menu, and you see a list of every open view of an object. First comes the object's name—for example, System Clock. Indented beneath this list item are the two open views—Program and Settings.

Choosing an Object View

The object view that was active when you popped up the Window List is highlighted. You can move the highlight to any other view with the up- and down-arrow keys. If you press Enter, the highlighted view surfaces on the desktop, and the Window list disappears. You also can choose a view from the Window List by double-clicking mouse button 1 on it. If you press Esc or click anywhere outside the Window List, the Window List vanishes.

A special menu for each view is available from the Window List. To display the menu, move the highlight to a view with the up- and down-arrow keys and press Shift-F10. To display a menu by using the mouse, click mouse button 2 on any view.

The menu that you pop up within the Window List is different from the view's system menu. The first choice the menu lists is Show. This does the same thing as Restore on the system menu; the name is different so that you do not confuse the two menus. The second choice, Hide, does the same thing as Minimize on the system menu.

Displaying More Than One Open View of an Object

The Tile and Cascade options are useful when you have multiple views of an object open, such as the clock's Program and Settings. The Tile and Cascade options arrange the different views either side by side with no overlap, like tiles, or in an overlapped, cascaded stack. The best way to see this is to try it. First, show both views of the clock, because Tile and Cascade do nothing if minimized. Next, pop up the Window List and select System Clock, either by clicking it with mouse button 1 or by moving there with the arrow keys. This highlights not only the clock object, but also both its open views. Pop up the menu by using Shift-F10 or mouse button 2, and choose Cascade. Try the same thing with Tile.

You also can close a view of an object from the menu in the Window List. A Help selection is available as well, in case you get lost. Some of these items will not be present on the menu for certain objects. The desktop shows up on the Window List, for example, but you cannot close it. Think of it this way: you can close a folder and put it away, but you cannot close the top of the desk. The menu offers only the choices that make sense for the current object.

The Window List is especially handy for keyboard users. You also can pop up the List with the mouse by clicking both buttons at the same time on any blank part of the desktop.

For Related Information

◀◀ "Examining Presentation Manager," p. 12.

FROM HERE...

Summarizing What You Have Learned So Far

Now that you are halfway through this chapter, take a break and review what you have learned. You saw how to open a folder, or start a program, by double-clicking its icon. This opens a window, giving you a view of the object. You know how to rearrange windows, change their size, and move between them. You also learned how to view and use an object's settings notebook. In the next section, you see that you can work with objects without even opening them.

Manipulating Icons

Remember how the Workplace Shell desktop looked when you first started the system? It was blank except for a few icons at the top. Icons are graphical representations of objects, and you can do lots of things with them without opening them first. You already learned how to open a view of an object by double-clicking its icon. This section shows several other things you can do with the icons on the desktop and inside folders.

The documentation calls these actions *direct manipulations* because you are dealing directly with the icon instead of going through menus. Each form of direct manipulation gives you a distinctive kind of visual feedback.

Before you start exploring, clear off the desktop by closing all views of the clock. Then open the OS/2 System folder as you did earlier, so that you have a selection of icons to experiment with—some on the desktop, and others in the folder.

Selecting an Icon

Click any icon once to select it. Selecting does not actually do anything to the object. Instead, it means that the next action you take will apply to that object. Pressing Enter, for example, opens any object you select. The Workplace Shell gives you immediate visual feedback by highlighting the icon you select in gray. The documentation calls this *selection emphasis*.

With the keyboard, you can select an icon by moving to it with the arrow keys. Because OS/2 System is the currently open folder, however, the keys move only among the icons the folder contains. To select an icon on the desktop, use Window List to show the desktop.

Opening a View

You have already learned how to open a view. Press Enter to open a view of the currently selected object. Double-clicking mouse button 1 on an icon selects and opens the icon. The icon gets *in-use emphasis*—a horizontally shaded pattern that tells you at a glance which objects are open.

Popping Up the System Menu

As mentioned previously, clicking mouse button 2 on an icon brings up the icon's related system menu. Selecting the icon first isn't necessary.

Moving an Object

The following procedure is the first of several direct manipulations that you haven't yet used. To move an icon, press and hold down mouse button 2 on an icon while you move the mouse. This is called *dragging*. The icon moves on-screen with the movement of the mouse cursor.

Drag the Information icon to an empty place on the desktop and release the mouse button. The icon is placed there. You can arrange the icons in any way you like.

You also can move objects between folders. Drag the Information icon to an empty spot inside the OS/2 System folder. Drop the icon. The original icon on the desktop vanishes and reappears inside the folder.

You can perform the same process by dragging Information onto the OS/2 System icon. First, drag the Information icon back to the desktop and drop it. Then drag the Information icon to the OS/2 System icon and drop it on top. This icon again vanishes from the desktop and appears inside the folder.

Creating a Copy of an Object

Making a copy of an object is like putting a memo through a copy machine. You get a new object that appears to be an exact duplicate of the original, but the two are distinct. To copy an object, follow these steps:

1. Hold down the Alt key.

2. Drag the icon to any blank spot on the desktop or in a folder.

3. Drop the icon; then release the Alt key.

When you move the icon, the on-screen representation looks dimmer than usual, which gives you visual feedback that a copy is in progress.

Creating a Shadow of an Object

A shadow is a great deal like a copy, except that the shadow is just an alias for the original object. Like a reflection in a mirror, the shadow has no independent existence of its own. The advantage of using shadows rather than copies is that these objects don't take disk space, and copies do use disk space. You can delete a shadow without affecting the original object.

If you want a program object to run (execute) when you boot your computer, you can make a shadow of the object and move the shadow to the Startup folder. You also might put shadows of the objects you open and close frequently during the day right on your desktop. This makes the objects immediately accessible, yet leaves the original in an appropriate folder. You don't have to move such an object onto the desktop, then later move the object back to its proper folder.

You may have noticed that you cannot open two identical views of the same object. You cannot have, for example, two program views of a single System Clock. If you want two clocks, make a shadow of the original and open the shadow.

You create a shadow the same way you make a copy, but you hold down the Ctrl and Shift keys instead of the Alt key. To emphasize the difference, the Workplace Shell draws a line that connects the original icon to the shadow icon while you move the mouse.

The result of a drag operation—move, copy, or shadow—actually depends on whether you are holding down Alt or Shift and Ctrl when you release the icon. Holding down these keys isn't necessary when you start the operation, but the visual feedback, like the line connecting the original object to a shadow that you create, depends on the current state of these keys.

Dropping One Icon on Another

Dropping an icon on top of another icon is one of the Workplace Shell's most exciting features. As you saw previously, you can move an object to a folder by dropping the object on the folder's icon. This procedure works even if the folder isn't open. To print an object, drop the object on the printer icon. To delete an object, drop the object on the Shredder. OS/2 applications may enable you to drag a number from a phone book, drop the number on a telephone icon, and have the application place a call.

Suppose that you copied the System Setup object from the OS/2 System folder to the desktop. As mentioned earlier, the copy operation wastes considerable disk space. To clean up the disk, drag and drop the copy from the desktop to the Shredder. Be careful that you shred only the copy, not the original. If you made a Shadow, the shadow disappears when you shred the original object.

As another experiment, drop the OS/2 System icon on the icon for the Master Help Index. You see a circle with a bar through it, similar to a *do not enter* road sign. Master Help Index is a program, not a folder, and dropping the system on a program makes no sense. The *do not enter* symbol tells you that dropping the icon here has no effect.

Canceling a Move, Copy, or Shadow Operation

When dragging an icon, you may change your mind and decide not to complete the operation. Just press the Esc key before you drop the icon.

Changing an Object's Name

You can change the name of any object by typing the new name in the Title box, which comes under the General tab of the related settings notebook. A shortcut is available for mouse users. Hold down Alt and click mouse button 1, either on the icon or on the Title bar of an open view. Backspace over the old name, type the new name, and then click the icon or title bar.

Working with Minimized Views

When you minimize an open view, it becomes a special kind of icon, which is surrounded by a gray box to emphasize that the view is open. Because you are working with a view and not an object, most direct manipulations don't work. You can only move the view or pop up the related system menu. You cannot create a copy or shadow, and dropping a view on another icon, such as the Shredder, has no effect.

Performing a Select, Move, Copy, or Shadow Operation with the Keyboard

Keyboard users cannot perform direct manipulation, but several operations can be done indirectly with the keyboard. These options are available as choices on an object's system menu.

Take a moment to review direct manipulation. Following chapters explain the results of dropping icons on the Printer or the Editor. The following section of this chapter discusses the system menu for Folder objects, which includes the desktop.

For Related Information

◄◄ "Examining Presentation Manager," p. 12.

◄◄ "Understanding CUA Principles," p. 216.

◄◄ "Introducing Presentation Manager," p. 221.

FROM HERE...

Using a Folder's System Menu

Earlier in this chapter, you studied the system menu for the System Clock program object—especially the cascaded menus for Open and Window. The OS/2 System folder open on the desktop now has a system menu specific to the folder, which contains these options and also some new ones. You just covered several of the options, which are keyboard equivalents for direct manipulation with the mouse. An option to arrange icons also is available, and Open has new selections on the related cascaded menu.

First, you need to know how to pop up a folder's system menu. Keyboard users can press and release the Alt key to perform this step. Mouse users can click with mouse button 2 on any blank spot inside the folder or with either button on the menu box in the upper left corner of the window.

Arranging Icons by Default

In a random order, move around a few of the icons in the OS/2 System folder's pop-up menu inside the folder. Now, pop up the folder's system menu and select Arrange. The icons are placed in a tidy straight line.

Next, choose Resize to change the folder from a short, wide window to a tall, narrow window, so that you no longer see one or two of the icons. A scroll bar appears at the bottom of the window. You can use the scroll bar to scroll to the other icons, but a better way is available. Select Arrange again; the icons are placed regularly within the window so that you see all the icons at one time (providing that the window is large enough), and the scroll bar vanishes.

Changing Folder Settings

After you open the settings notebook for the OS/2 System folder, you see options that weren't available for program objects. Some of these options are advanced settings normally used by programmers, but you may find some of the other icons helpful.

Under Format on the View page, you see the following three settings:

- *Flowed* arranges icons in straight rows and columns.

- *Non-Flowed* puts all icons in a single column.

- *Non-Grid* enables you to place icons anywhere in the window. Non-Grid is the default.

The three radio buttons under Icon Display enable you to make icons large, small, or invisible. If you choose Invisible, the names of objects are displayed on-screen, but no icons appear next to them. Invisible icons are unavailable with the Non-Grid arrangement.

The final option on the View page enables you to change the font for the names of objects. You can choose different typefaces, styles, and sizes. Just for fun, try the Symbol Set font.

Changing the Window Background

If the normal gray background seems unexciting, flip to the Background tab and choose a different color. By choosing Change Color, you call up the Color Editor and design your own background. Drab solid colors generally work best, but choose whatever background fits your mood.

If you prefer to see a picture, select Image. If you copied pictures included with the system during installation, or if you created pictures with the built-in paint program, you can choose from these pictures. Try drawing a simple picture and then select Scaled Image 10x10. The window becomes tiled with little copies of the drawing.

For Related Information

◄◄ "Using the Workplace Shell," p. 218.

FROM HERE...

Using the Workplace Shell's System Menu

Because the Workplace Shell desktop also is a folder, it has a system menu. Although you don't usually see an icon for the desktop, you can get to this menu by clicking mouse button 2 on any blank spot on the desktop.

Using the keyboard is only a little more difficult. To open the Workplace Shell's system menu using the keyboard, follow these steps:

1. Pop up the Window List by pressing Ctrl-Esc.

2. Select Desktop, and press Enter.

3. Press the space bar to unselect the current icon.

4. Hold down Shift, press F10, and release both keys.

You see a menu slightly different from the system menu for other folders. The Copy, Move, and Window choices are unavailable because using these choices with the desktop makes no make sense. Two extra choices that appear nowhere else are found here—Lockup and Shutdown. You need to understand how to use Shutdown, but Lockup is optional.

Locking Up the System

The computer may contain confidential files that you don't want others to examine if you step away from the computer. The LOCKUP command on the Workplace Shell's system menu provides simple protection. When you choose this option, you are asked to type a password, which can be anything you want. You type the password twice, just to ensure that you don't misspell the word accidentally.

The screen is replaced by the OS/2 logo, and a picture of a padlock appears. When you return, type the password to restore the desktop.

If you forget the password, you can restart the system by turning the power off and back on again. Of course, anyone can access the computer by flipping the power switch. If the files are really sensitive, save them on a floppy disk that you can lock in a drawer or carry with you.

Shutting Down the System

Shutting down a DOS system is easy. Just turn off the computer. Avoid taking this step with OS/2, however; instead, always use Shutdown from the Workplace Shell's system menu.

By default, OS/2 doesn't always write data to the hard disk immediately, even when you save a file. OS/2 waits until you or the programs aren't working the computer very much and then writes the data during slack times. By performing an orderly shutdown, you ensure that all open files are closed properly and saved. Shutdown also saves the state of the Workplace Shell, so that when you turn on the computer again, the screen you saw at Shutdown is the same screen you see when you re-enter OS/2.

When you use Shutdown, you may notice some disk activity. A message asks you to wait a few seconds for the activity to finish. You then see a `Shutdown has completed` message telling you that you can safely turn off the power.

Although a reliable system, OS/2 also is large and complex. No system this big is completely free of bugs. If you encounter a severe bug, the system may lock up so that you cannot even perform a shutdown. If this error occurs, wait for a minute to see if the system comes back by itself. If not, hold down the Alt and Ctrl keys at the same time, press Del, and then release all three keys. OS/2 tries to close all open files and then reboot. You also can try pressing Alt-Esc repeatedly; this sometimes will bring control back. If neither of these methods works, the only remaining option is to turn off the power.

If you have to turn off the system without running Shutdown, the CHKDSK program runs immediately after you turn back on the computer. Chances are good that CHKDSK can recover from any damage. For more information, see the instructions for CHKDSK in this book's command reference section.

Saving the Arrangement of Open Objects on the Desktop

When you use Shutdown, all open objects on the desktop are saved in the Startup folder, which is inside OS/2 System. The next time you turn on the system, these objects reappear in the same locations. You may never need to do anything with this folder directly because it works automatically. You can drag and drop extra objects into the Startup folder, however. To try this, use a Shadow (hold down Ctrl and Shift when you drop the object). This step leaves the object in the original location so that you can still use it without opening the Startup folder. Use Shadow rather than Copy because Copy creates a duplicate of the object, which takes up disk space.

Congratulations! You now have learned everything you need to know about running the Workplace Shell. The following section shows several settings you may want to change to fit your personal preferences.

For Related Information

◀◀ "Configuring Your Desktop," p. 174.

FROM HERE...

Customizing the Workplace Shell

After studying the previous parts of this chapter, you should feel comfortable working with the Workplace Shell. Now that you have learned how to use the system the way it was installed, you are ready to explore ways to personalize the system to suit your tastes. The System Setup folder inside OS/2 System has objects that enable you to customize many details. Most of these objects have only one view—Settings. Experiment with these objects when each is discussed in the following sections.

The Mouse

The tabs in the Mouse object's settings notebook cover several aspects of using the mouse:

- *Timing* controls how fast the cursor moves when you move the mouse, and how quickly you need to double-click.

- *Setup* gives you a choice between right- and left-handed mouse operation.

- *Mappings* enables you to pick a custom combination of mouse clicks and Alt, Shift, and Ctrl keys for the different kinds of direct manipulation.

> **CAUTION:** You should not touch these default settings if you share a computer with another person.

The Keyboard

The following Keyboard object options enable you to change the speed of the keyboard and to customize the actions that the keys perform:

- *Timing* enables you to adjust the rate at which a key repeats when held down. A short delay occurs before the key starts to repeat; you can customize this delay. You also can make the cursor blink slower or faster.

- *Mappings* is similar to the Mouse Settings tab of the same name.

- *Special needs* gives you several options that may help if you find certain keyboard actions uncomfortable. If you cannot easily hold down the Shift key and press Tab to move backward, for example, you can make Shift *sticky*, which means that you get the desired effect when you press and then release Shift, and then press and release Tab.

The System Object

The System object enables you to customize the appearance of all windows on-screen and to control the safety feature that asks you for confirmation when you drop an object on the Shredder.

- *Confirmations* determines whether you get a last chance to change your mind when deleting an object or folder. You probably want to leave this option turned on.

- *Window* enables you to turn off the *exploding window* graphical effect you see when you open a window. Window also controls whether minimized object views are visible as icons on the desktop, and whether opening a minimized icon restores the original view or opens a fresh copy.

- *Logos* gives you control over the menu button at the upper left corner of a window. If you don't want a miniature copy of the icon to appear here, you can turn off the menu button. You can even tell logos displayed by applications to show for a number of specified seconds and then to disappear, or not appear at all.

The Sound and Country Objects

The Sound object has only one useful tab—Warning Beep. If you don't like the beep, turn it off here.

The Country object enables you to tell the system in what country you live. Numbers, times, and dates are displayed in the format of that country.

The Palettes

A *palette* is the thin board that painters use for mixing colors. Using the Color Palette, you can mix colors to use with Workplace Shell objects.

You can pick a color or design your own. If you drag the color somewhere, the mouse cursor turns into a picture of a paint roller. If you
drop the color on the title bar of an open window, for example, the bar
turns that color.

The Scheme Palette, similar to the Color Palette, works with an entire
color scheme at one time. Dragging and dropping the Scheme Palette
on a window sets different colors for the border, title bar, text, background, and other areas. You can choose from preset color schemes
named for the seasons of the year, or you can design custom color
schemes.

What the Color and Scheme palettes do for color, the Font Palette does
for fonts. You can pick from, and change the size of, any of the previously installed fonts.

FROM HERE...

For Related Information

◄◄ "Installing Features Selectively," p. 172.

◄◄ "Configuring Your Desktop," p. 174.

Setting Up Other Applications

The Workplace Shell includes objects for all related built-in applications, but you also probably use some other applications. You can add
other applications in two ways: automatic and manual. Automatic setup
was an option when you installed OS/2, but if you didn't choose the
automatic setup when you installed OS/2, you can run this setup now.

Migrating DOS and Windows Applications

To set up icons for your DOS and Windows applications in the Workplace Shell, open the Migrate Applications object in the OS/2 System
folder. This program creates two new folders, one folder each for DOS
and Windows programs, searches the hard disk for applications, and
enables you to choose the programs you want to put in the folders.
When you open the folders, you find the chosen programs ready to use.

Applications written before OS/2 Version 2.0 cannot take full advantage of all the Workplace Shell's features. Many software companies, however, are writing new OS/2 versions of the old programs that will work better with the new interface.

Creating Folders

You probably want to arrange your favorite applications to fit the way you work. Suppose that you want to make a new folder for word processing. All you have to do is open the Templates object and drag the Folder template onto the desktop. As you may have guessed, Templates contains a model for each kind of Workplace Shell object. Whether you move or copy a template—or create a shadow—doesn't matter. Dragging a template always creates a new, empty object.

Using the techniques you learned previously, customize the new folder any way you like. You at least want to give the folder a name. Putting a shadow of your word processor into the new folder makes sense. You also can store memos in the folder; this procedure is shown in a following section. First, however, you should know about another useful option on the folder's Settings view.

Go to the File tab in the new folder's Settings and click Work Area. Now, whenever you close this folder, every open object it contains—for example, the word processing program—also closes. When you open the folder again, every object inside is restored to the last view. You may want to drag in and customize a printer object for the document settings you use.

The following section shows how to find programs and documents on the hard disk. You can put shadows of these files in the new folder you just created.

Using the Drives Object

Migrate Applications recognizes most popular programs, but may miss one of your favorites. You can fix this oversight by finding the program yourself.

Open Drives in the OS/2 System folder and double-click the drive you want to examine. A good place to start is drive C (usually, the main hard disk), but you can choose any drive. A folder with an icon of a hard disk appears; click the plus sign beside the icon to see more detail.

Figure 10.3 shows the Tree View of the directories on the hard disk. Directories are the same thing as folders, and indeed the directory icons are pictures of folders. This is the way your hard disk looks to the Workplace Shell—folders and icons.

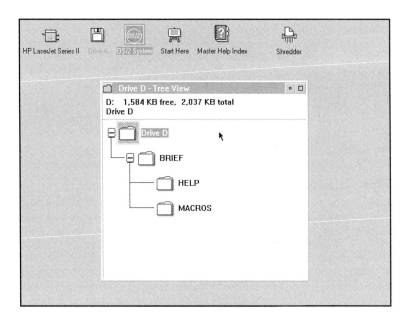

Fig. 10.3

The Tree view of a Drive object.

To examine the contents of any folder, you double-click the folder. Figure 10.4 shows the Details View of the files contained in the folder. This list shows the name and size of each file, and tells when you saved the file. You can perform direct manipulations (drag-and-drop, for example) with the icons that you see on the left side of the list.

Suppose that you want to put a word processor program and documents into the folder you just created. Just drag shadows of these objects from Drives and drop them on the folder. Remember that shadows are better than copies because these items don't consume extra disk space.

The system menus for Drives objects have a Check Disk option. This diagnoses disk problems and draws a chart that shows how the disk is used and how much space is available. From time to time, run Check Disk, especially if you turn off the computer without first performing a complete Shutdown. For information on fixing disk problems, see the CHKDSK command in the command reference. Chapter 8, "Troubleshooting OS/2," also discusses using the CHKDSK command to repair disk problems.

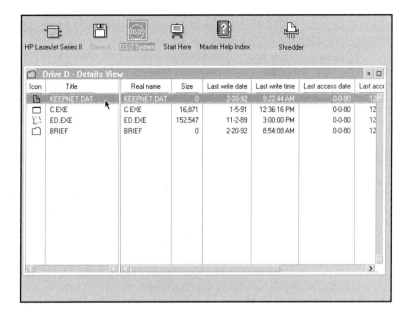

Fig. 10.4

The Details view
of a Drive object.

For Related Information

FROM HERE...

◄◄ "Choosing the OS/2 Features You Want," p. 134.

◄◄ "Installing Features Selectively," p. 172.

►► "Associating a File with an Application," p. 281.

►► "Adding DOS Programs," p. 389.

Chapter Summary

In this chapter, you mastered the Workplace Shell. You learned how
to arrange and customize the desktop to suit your preferences. This
graphical interface is object-oriented. You choose an object, decide
what to do with it, and receive immediate feedback. You briefly explored the Drives object in this chapter. The next chapter, "Using the
Drives Object," explains many more ways you can use the Drives object
to manage your work.

Learning the Basic Features of OS/2

P A R T

IV

OUTLINE

Using the Drives Object

⬛⬛⬛⬛⬛⬛⬛⬛⬛⬛⬛⬛⬛⬛⬛⬛⬛⬛⬛⬛⬛⬛

I n Chapter 10, you learned how to manage the Workplace Shell. Armed with this knowledge, you are now ready to learn how to use the basic features of OS/2. This chapter introduces the Drives object, the file management program for your disk drives. From the Drives object, you can view your files and their arrangement on the disk as well as select, copy, open, and move files. The file association features help you organize your files further by providing an association between a file's name and an application program.

This chapter first describes the parts of Drives object displays. The chapter also teaches you how to configure your file viewing options in different ways, manipulate directory lists and manage each disk drive, format and copy floppy disks, and assign attributes to files.

Understanding the Drives Object Display

When you create memos, spreadsheets, and databases, you fill your disks with files. Eventually you will need to move, copy, or delete the files to keep them organized, regardless of how many application programs you run under OS/2.

In some cases, you may need to get involved with files immediately after installing OS/2 so that your favorite application program can run. You perform file management tasks from the Drives object.

The Drives object is located in the OS/2 System window. To open the OS/2 System folder, double-click the OS/2 System icon. The OS/2 System window appears. Then double-click the Drives icon to view the drives available to you. The Drives window opens (see fig. 11.1).

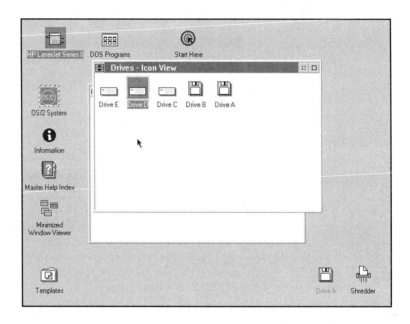

The Drives window, in Icon View.

When you open the Drives object, a list of all the disk drives on your computer appears. This list includes the floppy disk drives and any networked drives. Logically, the icon for a floppy disk drive is shaped like a floppy disk, and the icon for a hard disk drive is shaped like a hard disk.

Your computer designates drives by letters. Drives A and B are floppy disk drives and hard disks are drive C and higher. The computer used to generate the figures has two floppy disk drives, as well as three hard disks or partitions, named C, D, and E. Your computer may have a different number of drives. If your computer does not have a floppy disk drive, you will not see an icon for drive A or B. If your computer only has one floppy disk drive, you will not see an icon for drive B. The first hard disk on your computer is always named drive C. In most cases, your computer boots from drive C. This chapter focuses on drive D as an example.

OS/2 can show the available drives in any of three different ways—Icon View, Tree View, and Details View. Note that in figure 11.1, the drives are shown in Icon View. In figure 11.2, the drives are shown in Tree View, and in figure 11.3, they are shown in Details View.

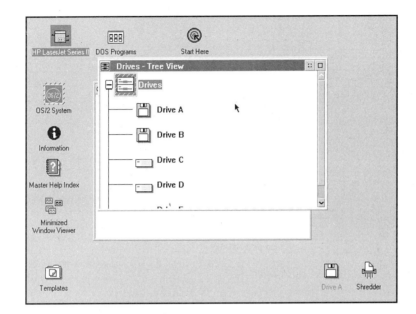

Fig. 11.2

The drives displayed in Tree View.

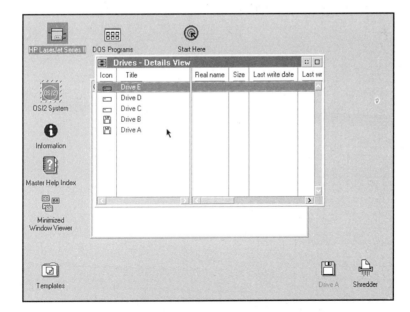

Fig. 11.3

The drives displayed in Details View.

To select the view type, choose Open from the system menu and then choose your view type from the cascaded menu by clicking the appropriate option with mouse button 1. From the keyboard, access the system menu by pressing Alt-space bar (or Shift-Esc). Then use the arrow keys to reach Open. Press the right-arrow key to list the view types. Highlight your selection and press Enter.

You view your files depending on the level of detail required. For example, Icon View is generally used for viewing the drive icons. Tree View is for seeing the general arrangement of your directories (or folders) on a particular disk, and Details View displays all the information on particular files within a directory or file folder.

Icon View

After double-clicking the Drives object in the OS/2 System folder, you will probably see an icon view of your drives. (If not, open Icon View as described in the preceding section.) OS/2 displays each drive that you can access from your computer.

As is typical with OS/2 icons, a drive icon's image changes depending on your selections. In figure 11.4, for example, the diagonal lines behind the Drive D icon indicate that drive D is open; the Drive E icon is highlighted, showing that drive E is your current selection.

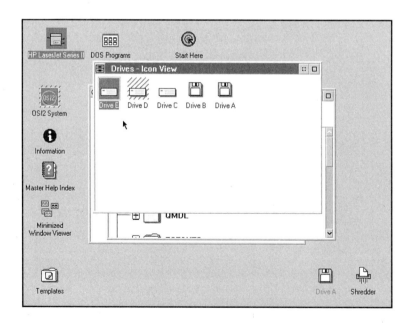

Fig. 11.4

The Drives - Icon View showing one open drive and the currently selected drive.

To view the contents of a drive, double-click its icon; or use the arrow keys to highlight the icon and then press Enter. You see a new window displaying the files and directories on this drive.

Tree View

After double-clicking the drive icon, you see a tree view of your chosen disk. (If you see an icon or detail view, open Tree View from the system menu as described earlier.) Figure 11.5 shows the Drive D - Tree View window maximized to fill the screen.

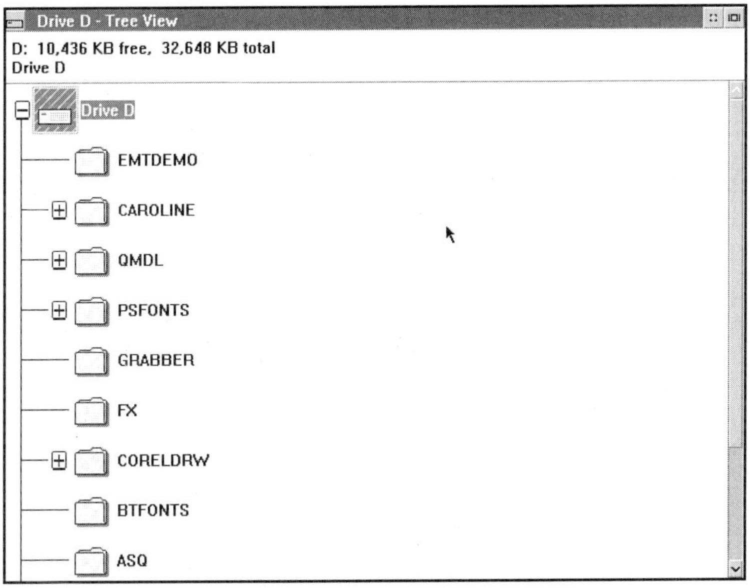

Fig. 11.5

Drive D shown in Tree View.

The Tree View window shows the directories (or folders) on your disk arranged in a tree-like form. (This form is more like a family-tree structure than the growing tree kind.) The drive icon (Drive D in figure 11.5) is at the top. All the directories found in drive D are listed below the Drive D icon. They are linked by a series of lines intended to represent branches of a tree. The directories are represented by file folder icons, and the name of each directory is beside the file folder icon. The example disk includes directories called EMTDEMO, CAROLINE, and GRABBER.

264

As in Icon View, any currently open object in Tree View has a background with diagonal hatching on it. The currently selected object, in this case the Drive D icon, has a shaded background.

The minus sign to the left of the Drive D icon indicates that you can see all the directory levels within drive D. A plus sign, such as the one in front of the folder named CAROLINE, indicates that there are additional levels of subdirectories that are not currently visible. Later in this chapter, you learn how to expand and collapse the directory tree.

Details View

Details View shows a list of all the files and directories for the selected object. Double-click a file folder to open a details view. (If you are looking at a tree or icon view of a file folder's contents, open Details View from the system menu as described earlier.) Figure 11.6 shows the directory CAROLINE in Details View.

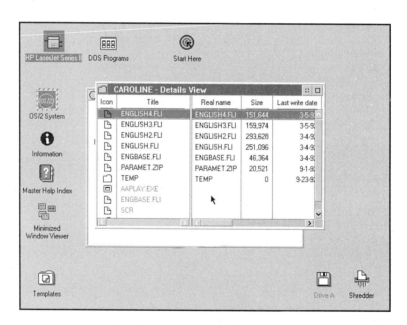

Fig. 11.6

The CAROLINE directory shown in Details View.

The files and subdirectories are listed in tabular form. The left column shows the file type. Notice that nonexecutable files, such as ENGLISH.FLI, have icons that resemble pieces of paper with a folded corner. The icon shape for an executable file looks like a miniature window. The shadowed items, such as AAPLAY.EXE, are shown in grayed-out text. The names of the shadowed items appear on the list, but the detailed information, such as the size and date, does not appear. See the "Shadowing Files" section of this chapter for more on shadowing.

The Title column lists the file names as they appear next to the icon; the real name column shows the file name as it is stored on the disk. If you create a folder named My Scrapbook, for example, its title is My Scrapbook, but its real name is MY_SCRAP to conform with correct file-naming procedures. (If you are using the high performance file system (HPFS), the real name is the same as the title. See Chapter 4, "Deciding How You Want To Use OS/2," for more information on HPFS.) As another example, your OS/2 drawing program may name its icon Best Drawing Program, but the executable file has a different name, such as BESTDRAW.EXE, on the disk. You can change the names associated with any icons without altering the file name stored on the disk.

The title and real name are separated in the Details View window by a double line. You can move this line to the left or right by pointing at it with the mouse. The cursor changes to a double-headed arrow, and you can drag the line to a new position. Moving this line to the left, for example, leaves less room for the icon and title columns but shows more of the other detail information.

You view the rest of the detail information by enlarging the window or by using the window's scroll bars.

In addition to the title and the real name, OS/2 displays the following attribute information in this window:

- ■ Size
- ■ Last write date
- ■ Last write time
- ■ Last access date
- ■ Last access time
- ■ Creation date
- ■ Creation time
- ■ Flags

The file size is given in bytes. Notice that directories do not have file sizes. A directory's name is stored on the disk, in the directory area, but the directory itself does not occupy any data area. Creating a lot of directories on your disk to make finding files easier does not result in wasted disk space.

The last write date and time indicate the time and date when the file was last changed. The last access time and date show when the file was last read, and the creation date and time show when the file was originally created. If OS/2 does not know the date and time information, typically because the file was created prior to OS/2's installation, OS/2 displays a time of 12:00:00 AM and a date of 0-0-80.

The Flags column at the far right of this window has four letters or dashes in it. The letters may be R, A, S, or H, referring to read-only, archived, system, or hidden flags (or indicators). A file may have any combination of these flags.

A read-only file cannot be changed or deleted while it is marked as read-only. When you back up a file or use a copy command with a suitable switch you can set (or reset) the archive switch on a file to indicate that it has been backed up.

The system flag appears on files that are part of the OS/2 operating system. System files are most typically used when you boot your computer. The hidden flag appears on files that are normally hidden from view. You make them visible from the Settings menu. A typical end user never alters or moves system files or hidden files.

Display Configuration

If you want to customize your drive views, you adjust the settings from the Open option on the system menu. Many of these settings are similar to the options detailed in Chapter 10, "Managing the Workplace Shell." Click the system menu icon for the drive you want; click Open and then Settings to reach the settings options shown in figure 11.7.

You adjust each view's appearance with the View option. As covered in Chapter 10, you can alter the format, icon size, and font for Icon View and Tree View. The first page alters Icon View. The second page alters Tree View, and the third page alters Details View. You can select the details that you want displayed in Details View, as well as alter the font size. Move from page to page by clicking the arrow buttons at the lower right corner of the page.

When set to the default, the Include option prevents hidden files from appearing in the views. You can alter this setting to limit the files that are displayed. As a beginner, however, you should avoid altering this setting because you may reveal and later erroneously delete or move important system files that have been hidden to reduce the chance of their accidental deletion or moving. You can restore the default setting at any time by clicking the Default button on the Include Settings screen. The Default button works the same way with other setting options.

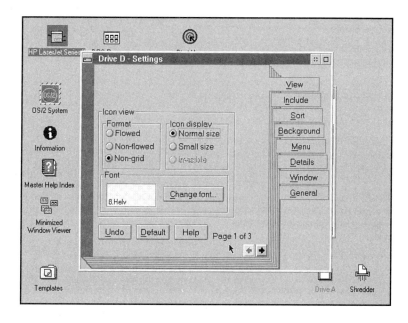

Fig. 11.7

The Drive
Settings window.

Although you may prefer a smaller or larger font size for your views, you are unlikely to need the other settings in this menu. You should realize that OS/2 is fully customizable and that you can alter every aspect of your views by creating, for example, special icons, limiting the file display, and altering screen colors.

For Related Information

◄◄ "Offering the High Performance File System," p. 81.

◄◄ "Using a Folder's System Menu," p. 246.

FROM HERE...

Expanding and Collapsing a Directory List

In order to manipulate directory lists, you first must open a Tree View for the drive of interest. Figure 11.8 shows a Tree View display of drive D.

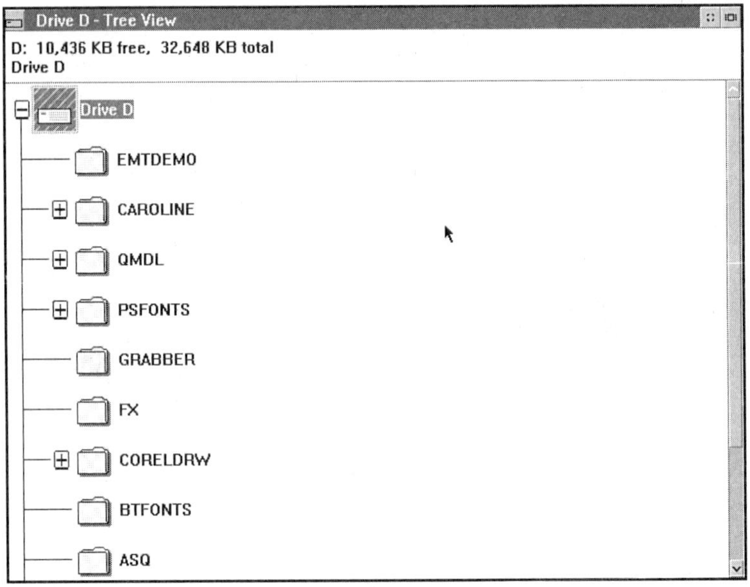

Fig. 11.8

The Tree View
display.

To see the divisions within a folder, click the plus sign to the left of the folder and expand the Tree View listing. Figure 11.9 shows the subdivisions of the folder named CAROLINE, for example.

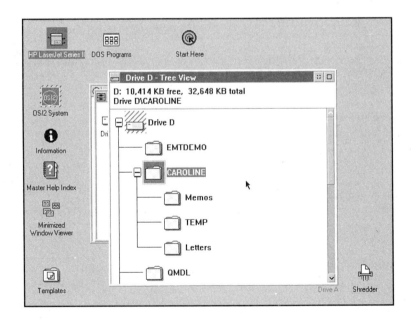

Fig. 11.9

The expanded
Tree View of the
folder named
CAROLINE.

To collapse the Tree View and make the subdivisions of a folder disappear, click the minus sign to the left of the folder. Figure 11.10 shows a completely collapsed Tree View.

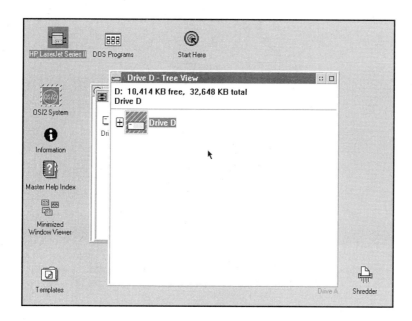

Fig. 11.10

A completely collapsed Tree View of drive D.

Expand your Tree View until you can see the folder you want to examine in more detail. For example, you may want to examine the folder named Memos. When you can see the folder, double-click it to open a view of its contents. Figure 11.11 shows the contents of the Memos folder in Icon View.

Finding Files

So far in this chapter, you have looked at lists of files and selected the items of choice. Sometimes, you may know a file name but not the location of the file. You can make OS/2 search for your file in a folder.

From the Tree View of a drive, click a folder with the right mouse button to display its pop-up window. Your screen resembles figure 11.12.

Click Find to open the Find window. Your screen resembles figure 11.13.

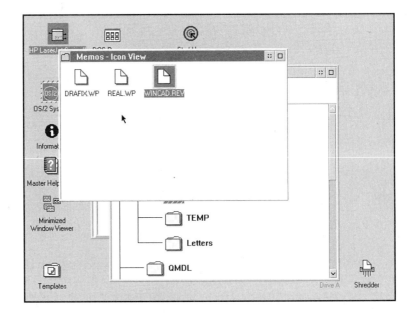

Fig. 11.11

The Icon View of the contents of the Memos folder.

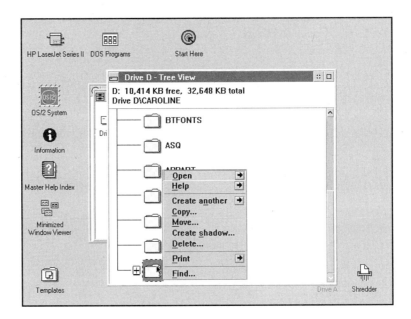

Fig. 11.12

An Object's pop-up menu.

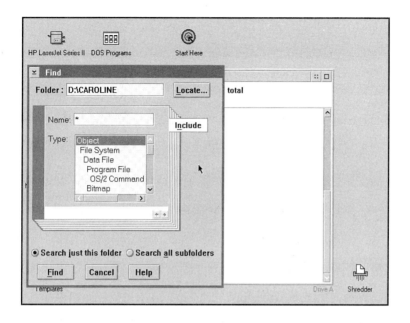

Fig. 11.13

The Find
window.

The Folder text box lists the folder's name. If you want to pick a different folder, click the Locate button and choose a new folder from the
list.

You pick the items to find from the area of this window that contains
the Name text box and the Type list box. The Name text box shows the
file names for inclusion. An asterisk (*) is the wild-card character and
means all files of the specified type will be found. Wild cards are explained in Chapter 2. If you know your file's name, you type it in this
box.

The Type list box lists all the possible OS/2 object types. For example,
you can look for a data file, a folder, or a bit-map file. Notice that this
list has a hierarchy. The subsets are indented from the left.

When you open the Find window, the Object type is highlighted. This
selection causes OS/2 to look for all objects in the folder. The File System type is indented one character to the right, showing that all the File
System objects comprise a subset of OS/2 objects. If you use the scroll
bars to view the rest of the list, you see that OS/2 considers Abstract
objects, such as indexes, and Transient objects, which are typically
temporary files, as equivalent objects to File System objects. The File
System subset contains Data Files and Folder objects that have subdivisions of their own.

You can limit your search by picking one of the divisions rather than all
the objects. For example, you can choose the Program File type and
find only executable files, or choose Network and find only network

folders. When you have highlighted the object type of interest, choose the appropriate radio button to search only within the current folder or to widen the search into all the subfolders of the current folder. Click Find to start the search. Your screen resembles figure 11.14.

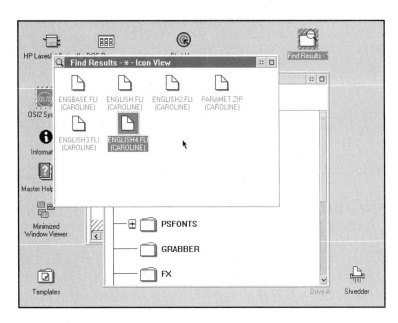

Fig. 11.14

The Find Results window.

You can change the view of this display to Tree View or Details View, as described earlier in this chapter.

Each file that is found and its folder's name is shown in this window. If you do another search using different criteria, any additional objects found are placed in another Find Results window.

You can manipulate the found objects in the same way as objects in other windows. For example, you can move, copy, or create shadows of objects. The Find Results folders are placed on the desktop when you close them.

Delete the Find Results folders to remove them from the desktop. Deleting the Find Results folder does not delete the objects, only the found copies. To delete a folder, open its system menu and click Delete. Confirm the deletion by clicking Yes when prompted.

OS/2 also supplies a more sophisticated file finding and examining program called Seek and Scan. If you selected this program during installation, it was placed in the OS/2 System folder in the Productivity folder. Chapter 21, "Using the OS/2 General Purpose Applets," details how to use this powerful utility program. See Chapter 7, "Modifying Your OS/2 Configuration," for information on installing selective portions of OS/2.

For Related Information

◄◄ "Installing Features Selectively," p. 172.

▶▶ "Using Seek and Scan Files," p. 533.

FROM HERE...

Manipulating Files

You can manipulate files in the same way as other OS/2 objects. For example, you can move one or multiple files, copy one or more files, or create shadows of one or multiple files.

This section covers the basics of working with OS/2 files: opening files, selecting files, moving files, copying files, and shadowing files. You can display the program files in any view type when you manipulate the files; however, you probably will prefer to use Icon View.

Opening Files

To open a file, double-click its icon, or use the arrow keys to highlight its icon and press Enter. When you open a file, OS/2 takes different actions depending on the file type.

If the file is an executable program and you open its icon, for example, the program starts. If the file is a text file (the file type OS/2 assumes if it cannot identify the file's type) OS/2 starts the System Editor and tries to load the file into the editor for viewing.

Selecting Multiple Files

As with any OS/2 object, you select a file by clicking it with mouse button 1. The selected item becomes highlighted. When the file is selected, you can do things to it, such as move or copy it. In many cases, however, you want to do the same action to more than one file. For example, you may want to move three files to another folder or copy a whole folder to another disk. In such cases, you need to select more than one object at a time.

If you want to select all the files in a folder, click the window's system menu. Choose Select and then choose Select All from the pop-up menu. All the objects are highlighted. From the keyboard, press Ctrl-/ to select all the objects in a folder.

To select more than one file, but less than all the files in a folder, you can use one of following methods:

■ Position the mouse cursor on the first file for selection. Press and hold mouse button 1. Using the mouse, point to each of the other files you want to select. Each file becomes highlighted when you select it.

■ Draw a box around the desired files. Use this method when the desired files are arranged in a rectangle. Move to a point in the window that is below and to the left of the lower left file and then press and hold mouse button 1. Move the mouse to the upper right corner of a rectangle that encloses the desired objects.

■ If the desired files are in separate places within the window, press Ctrl and then click the first file with mouse button 1. Hold Ctrl and click each of the other files for selection. Many users prefer to use this method of selecting files.

Canceling Selections

To cancel all your selections, click a blank area of the window with mouse button 1 or press Ctrl-\. OS/2 removes all the icon highlighting.

To cancel some of your selections, rather than all of them, you essentially reselect the icons. If you have selected only one file, select it again to remove the highlighting.

If you have selected several icons either by drawing a box or by using the Ctrl key method, but decide you do not want one of the files selected, use the Ctrl key method. Hold down Ctrl and click the undesired file. Many users prefer this method of file selection.

Selecting and canceling selections can be frustrating unless you remember the Ctrl key method. Unless you are careful, it is easy to accidentally deselect all your icons by clicking a blank area of the window and have to reselect them all again.

Moving Files

To move files from one folder to another, or to or from a folder and the desktop, follow these steps:

1. Arrange your windows so that you can see the files you want to move and the position to which you want to move them.

2. Select the file or files that you want to move.

3. Position the mouse cursor on one of the selected files. Press and hold mouse button 2 and drag the files to their new position.

   When you start to move the mouse, the cursor changes to show that you are moving the file. Figure 11.15 shows the icon that appears when you move three text files.

   If you move a variety of file types, the cursor icon reflects these types. If you move an executable file, a folder, and a text file, the cursor you see while you are dragging the files shows a stack of icons—one a text file icon, one a folder icon, and one an executable file icon.

4. Release the mouse button. Your files are moved to their new position. You can cancel the move by pressing Esc before you release the mouse button.

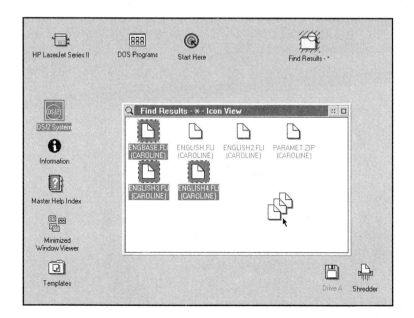

Fig. 11.15

The cursor displayed when you move figures.

Copying Files

The method for copying files is similar to the method for moving them. Follow these steps:

1. Arrange your windows so that you can see the files you want to copy and the position to which you want to copy them.

2. Select the file or files that you want to copy.

3. Press Ctrl and click one of the selected files with mouse button 2. While continuing to hold down the Ctrl key and the mouse button, drag the files to their new position.

    When you start to move the mouse, the cursor changes to show you are copying the files. The cursor is similar to the one that appears when you move files, except the outlines of the icons are dashed lines rather than solid.

4. Release the Ctrl key and the mouse button. Your files are copied to their new position.

Shadowing Files

As explained in Chapter 10, you can create shadows of objects, including files. Shadowing creates a duplicate icon for a file but does not duplicate the file itself, thereby saving disk space. Shadowing files is similar to moving them. Follow these steps:

1. Arrange your windows so that you can see both the files you want to shadow and their potential shadow's position.

2. Select the file or files that you want to shadow.

3. Position the mouse cursor on one of the selected files. Press and hold Ctrl, Shift, and mouse button 2. Drag the files to their new position.

    When you start to move the mouse, the cursor changes to show you are shadowing the objects. The cursor is similar to when you move files, but a line extends from the original file position to the new file position, as shown in figure 11.16.

4. Release the Ctrl and Shift keys and the mouse button. Your files are shadowed to their new position.

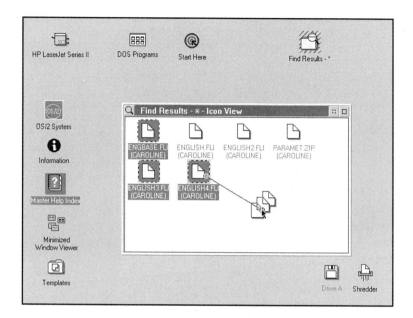

Fig. 11.16

The cursor icon showing that you are shadowing files.

Formatting and Copying Floppy Disks

Formatting and copying disks are typical routine chores you have to do to create copes of your data. You may want to give others the disks or use them as backups for some of your data files.

Formatting Floppy Disks

You must format new floppy disks to prepare them for use. The formatting process establishes the positions for the data that you store on a disk. You can think of the formatting process as laying out and numbering the spaces in a parking lot so that when cars are parked you can easily find any car by its position.

You can reformat floppy disks. The formatting process prevents your accessing any data previously stored on your floppy disk, however. Consider formatting an irreversible procedure.

To format a blank floppy disk (or one that you are sure does not contain valuable data), insert the disk into the floppy disk drive, click the
floppy disk drive icon with mouse button 2 to open the system menu,
and choose Format disk. If the floppy disk drive icon is not visible,
open the Drives window from within the OS/2 System folder. Your
screen resembles figure 11.17.

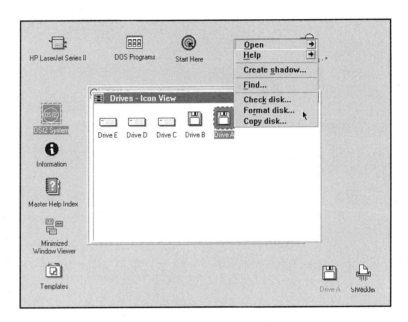

Fig. 11.17

The system menu
for the Drive A
icon.

When you choose Format disk, a pop-up window resembling
figure 11.18 appears.

The volume label is the disk's electronic name. When you display a
directory of this disk, this name is shown. You should label your floppy
disks electronically as well as with paper labels so that you can still
identify them even when a paper label falls off. Type in your label for
the floppy disk in the Volume Label text box.

Next, select a disk capacity. Chapter 1 introduces floppy disks and their
capacities. Be sure to choose the capacity that matches the physical
floppy disk you insert in the drive; you choose the capacity by using
the arrows at the far right of the Capacity box. Note that if you format a
floppy disk at the wrong capacity, you may see a large number of data
errors, depending on your error. Check your floppy disk's capacity and
the formatting capacity you select carefully.

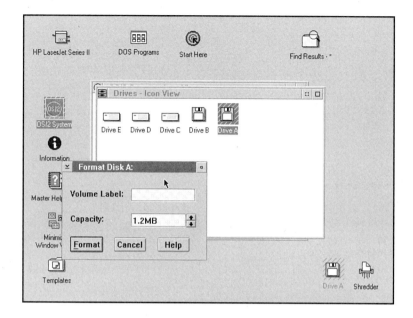

Fig. 11.18

The Format Disk A pop-up window.

Click Format to start the formatting process. A progress window appears showing the percentage of the disk that has been formatted. When complete, this window shows the total space on the disk and the space available. Click OK to complete the operation.

If the space available differs from the total space available on the disk, OS/2 has determined that certain areas of your floppy disk are defective and has marked them as unavailable to store data. Do not use a floppy disk with many defects because you may have a marginal disk and lose data later. Most floppy disks are warrantied to be defect-free by the manufacturer, so you may be able to exchange it for another floppy disk.

Copying an Entire Floppy Disk

You also can make copies of your floppy disks with the Copy disk command from the drive icon's pop-up menu. Note that this command copies the whole floppy disk rather than a selection of files on a floppy disk.

OS/2 refers to the floppy disk you are copying from as the *source* floppy disk and the floppy disk you are copying to as the *target* floppy disk.

During the copying process, the target floppy disk is formatted, so you lose any existing data on that disk. All the files on the source disk are copied to the target floppy disk.

To copy a floppy disk, insert your source floppy disk into a floppy disk drive. Click the floppy disk drive's icon in the Drives - Icon View window with the mouse button 2. The system menu opens. Choose the Copy disk command from this window. OS/2 opens a command line menu and starts the Copy command. Your screen resembles figure 11.19.

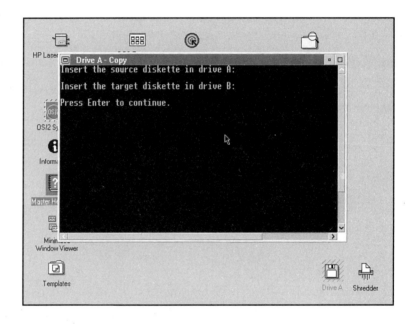

Fig. 11.19

The Copy command window.

If you have two floppy disk drives, place your target floppy disk into drive B. If you only have one floppy disk drive, OS/2 prompts you to swap source and target floppy disks when necessary. Press Enter to start the copying process. OS/2 displays a status line showing the status of the copying process. Exchange floppy disks when prompted, if necessary, until the process is complete. *Note:* Diskcopying between different size disks does not work.

For Related Information

◄◄ "Understanding Disks, Disk Files, and Disk Directories," p. 18.

Associating a File with an Application

OS/2 enables you to link (or associate) your data files with particular application programs. If you open a text file, for example, OS/2 automatically starts the OS/2 System Editor and loads your selected text file into it. You can create your own associations with other application programs. Three approaches are supported.

You can specify that a data file is a particular type and have OS/2 start the associated application program automatically, or you can add the application program to a data file's pop-up menu so that you can start the associated application program. Alternatively, you can create associations so that all data files with similar file names are considered associated with a particular application program. When you open a data file that fits the pattern, the associated application program starts.

Note that these processes will not be successful unless you choose appropriate file associations. If you are a beginner, you are unlikely to set up these associations. After you are familiar with the concepts of program files, data files, and their locations, you will probably take advantage of the power and convenience of file associations, however.

Associating by File Type

When you associate by file type, all files of a particular type, such as bit-map, metafile, Pascal code, or Plain Text files, are considered associated with a particular application program. You create the association by adjusting the program's settings by using its icon settings menu selection.

Click the program icon with the right mouse button to see the system menu. Click the arrow alongside Open to see the Settings menu. Click Settings to open the Settings window. Figure 11.20 shows a typical program icon Settings window.

Click Association to adjust the data file associations. To associate by file type, pick the desired file type from the Available types list at the top of the window. You can add and remove file types as desired. When complete, close the Settings window.

When you open a data file of the appropriate type, OS/2 starts the associated application program and loads your data file into it.

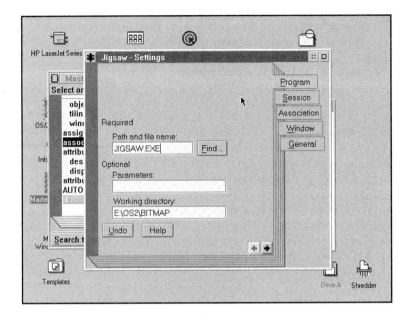

Fig. 11.20

The Settings window for the program Jigsaw.

Associating by File Name

When you associate by file name, all files with a similar name are considered associated with a particular application program. As with associating by file type, you create the association by adjusting the program's icon settings.

Click the program icon with mouse button 2 to see the pop-up menu. Click the arrow beside Open to see the Settings menu. Click Settings to open the Settings window. Figure 11.21 shows a typical program icon Settings window.

Click Association to adjust the data file associations. To associate by file name, type the file name in the box labeled New Name and then click Add to add it to the Current Names list. You can use OS/2 wild cards for this association.

If you want all files with the file name extension DOC to be considered word processing documents, for example, open the Settings window for your word processor and type ***.DOC** in the New Name text box. If you want all files that have file names beginning with CAD to be considered drawing files for your CAD program, open your CAD program's settings menu and type **CAD*.*** in the New Name text box.

You can add or remove files from the Current Name list. When you are finished, close the Settings window. When you open a data file with an appropriate name, OS/2 starts the associated application program and loads your data file automatically.

Notice that although this feature is powerful, you need to use consistent file naming methods for it to be successful. For many users, particularly those users who run several different application programs, this process is intuitive, but for many beginners, the desirability of this practice is not obvious.

Associating from the Pop-up Menu

To associate a data file with an application program, you can add the application program's name to the pop-up menu. Unlike the other association methods that link a set of data files with an application program, this method links one data file with an application program. You can add several application programs to one data file and choose between them from the pop-up menu.

You alter your pop-up menus by adjusting the menu settings. Be aware in the following explanation that you are adjusting the configuration of your pop-up menu. You need to realize when you are to choose an item from the pop-up menu and when you are adjusting the items that make up the pop-up menu. You pick Open from the pop-up menu to start the adjustment and then alter the Open menu to add the association, for example.

To associate a data file with a program, follow these steps:

1. Click the data file icon by pressing the right mouse button. The pop-up menu appears.

2. Click the arrow to the right of the Open option.

3. Choose Settings from the menu. The Settings window appears.

4. Choose Menu from within the Settings window. Your screen resembles figure 11.21.

5. Click ~Open in the Available menus list. Your screen resembles figure 11.22. The Actions on menu scroll bar in the lower half of the Settings window shows the items that appear when you select the Open menu.

   Before continuing, look at this window in detail to understand the lists. The Available menus scroll box shows a list of available menus—a primary pop-up menu and the Open menu—for the data file object. The tilde (~) in front of the word *Open* indicates that the Open menu contains a selection of items.

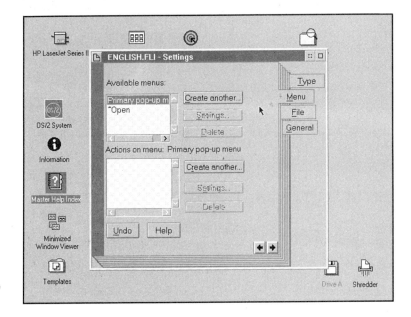

Fig. 11.21

The Settings
window with
Menu displayed.

The list of options in the Actions on menu scroll box in the bottom half of the window are the menu options you see when you click the arrow to the right of Open on the pop-up menu. In this example, you see ~Settings and OS/2 System Editor. The OS/2 System Editor appears because OS/2 assumes that all data files can be loaded into the System Editor. You want to add your application program name for the data file to this list.

6. Click Create another... in the bottom half of the window to add an application program to the pop-up menu. Your screen resembles figure 11.23.

7. In the Menu item name text box, type in the name of your application program. This name will appear in the pop-up menu.

8. Type the executable file name for your application program in the Name text box. You can use the Find program option to search for your program if you are unsure where the executable file is located.

9. Click OK to accept the change. Your application program appears in the Actions on menu list below OS/2 System Editor.

10. Close the Settings window by double-clicking the system icon. Now when you open the pop-up menu for the data file and click the arrow to the right of Open, you see your application program name.

You can start the application program by double-clicking its name from the pop-up menu's Open list. Alternatively, if you select Open, or double-click the data file object, OS/2 opens your application program and loads your data file into it.

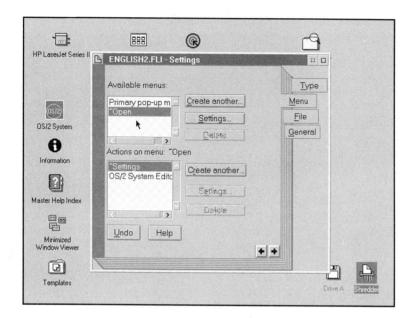

Fig. 11.22

Settings window with Menu Open selected.

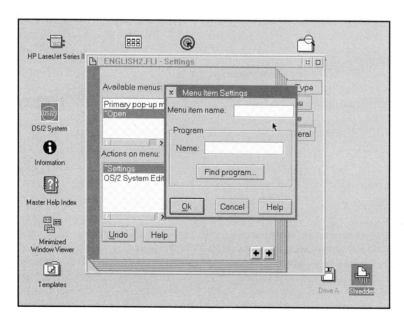

Fig. 11.23

The Menu Item Settings window.

You can make the application program the default setting so that the program automatically runs when you select Open. To do this from the ~Open option in the Available menus list, click Settings. Then click the radio button labeled Conditional Cascade. Choose your application program's name from the text box list to make the program the default setting. Click OK to accept the changes. (Click Undo if you want to reject any changes.)

Assigning Attributes to Files

Each file within a directory has certain attributes. For example, a file has a name and size. It was created or last modified on a particular date and at a particular time. OS/2 can store a variety of attribute information about each file on your disk. If you have two files with similar names but know that the one you want is the one you were working on yesterday, for example, you can use the attribute information (the date the file was last modified) to find the file of interest.

You can attach two main types of attributes to your files: attributes and extended attribute flags. As covered in the "Details View" section, a file can have up to four flags associated with it. These flags are read-only, archive, system, and hidden. You also can attach descriptive information about the file by using the extended attribute features.

Flags

In practice, you are unlikely to need to change the flags for a file although you may execute a command on a set of files based on their flag settings. For example, you probably will not need to make a file read-only or a read-only file editable. You may use an application program that does that for you, however. You may make a spreadsheet data file read-only, for example, but you will probably use the application program's features rather than set it yourself.

When you use backup or copying commands, you may choose options that only back up files that do not have an archive flag set. You are unlikely, however, to use OS/2 features to reset the archive flag for any files individually.

If you do want to alter the flags for a file, open the pop-up window for the file by clicking it with mouse button 2. Choose the arrow to the right of Open, and click Settings to open the Settings window. Click the File tab to open the File Settings window.

The File Settings window consists of three pages. Page one contains the file's name and its icon's name. Click the right arrow to move to page two. Your screen resembles figure 11.24.

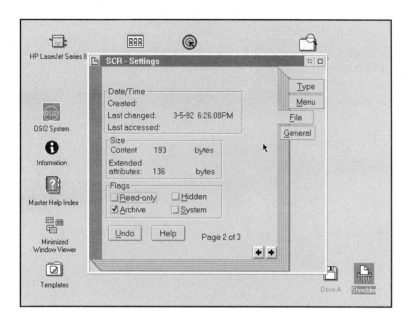

Fig. 11.24

Page 2 of the File Settings window.

The window shows information about when the file was created and last accessed as well as the file size. Its flag settings are shown at the bottom of the window. In the example, the selected file has its Archive flag set. You toggle each of the flags by clicking the check box to the left of the flag's name.

Extended Attributes

With OS/2 you can store extra information with a file. You can add, for example, a file description in the extended attribute area.

You are much more likely to want to add descriptive information about your files than to alter a file's flags. This information is known as extended attribute information. You add extended attribute information on page three of the File Settings window. From the second page of the File Settings window (refer to fig. 11.24), click the right arrow at the bottom of the window to move to page three. Your screen resembles figure 11.25.

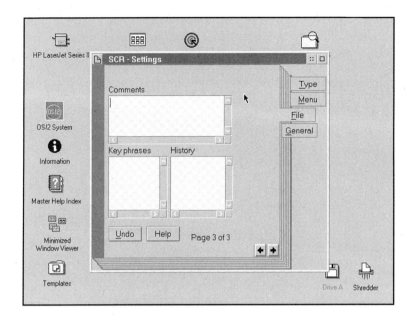

Page 3 of the File
Settings window.

You add the extended attribute information about your file in this window. You can search this information by using the Find procedure explained in an earlier section. You typically add this information to keep an audit trail or description of your files. The information is particularly valuable if more than one person will be accessing the file or if a traditional file name isn't descriptive enough.

Type any general notes you want to keep about the file in the Comments section. If the file were a preliminary budget spreadsheet, for example, you might include a couple of the assumptions you made during its creation.

In the Key phrases section, you type important words or phrases that you might want to use later in an index. Using the spreadsheet example, the key phrases might be *budget, five-year plan,* and *ten-percent growth.*

After adding your extended attributes, close the Settings window by double-clicking the system menu icon in the upper left corner of the window. (To undo any changes, click Undo before closing the window.)

Chapter Summary

In this chapter, you learned about the Drives icon and file management features of OS/2. You now know how to use Icon, Tree, and Details Views to see your file arrangements. You also can find files by file type or by searching for key phrases previously stored in a file's extended attribute area. This chapter covered the basics of working with files, including selecting one or more files at a time, copying files, and shadowing files. Copying and formatting floppy disks from the Drives icon was described. Finally, you learned how to alter or add to a file's attributes from its Settings menu and link data files with application programs by one of three methods.

The next chapter covers the commands you use most often in OS/2.

Learning the Commands You Use Most Often

In the preceding chapters you learned about Presentation Manager—OS/2's graphical interface that makes available to you all of the program's features. When you use Presentation Manager, you simply choose an option from a menu or click an on-screen icon.

OS/2 also offers a command line interface. Initially, you may find the command line interface more difficult to use than Presentation Manager. Because the command line interface has no menus, you must know the name of the command you want to use and how to use the command. When you master the command line interface, however, you may find it quicker and easier to use than the graphical interface. Further, the command line interface enables you to perform functions you cannot perform with Presentation Manager. Give both interfaces a try, to see which you prefer.

To explore the command line interface, you first must start an OS/2 or DOS session under OS/2. Several session objects are in the Command Prompts folder. The names of the session objects suggest their purpose—full-screen or windowed, OS/2 or DOS. The Command Prompts folder also contains a Windows full-screen object. Chapter 17, "Configuring Your DOS and Windows Sessions," discusses the different kinds of DOS and Windows sessions.

Open an OS/2 windowed session by double-clicking the OS/2 Window object. You now have opened a window on the past—this feature was the only interface in early computers. Your computer screen is no longer a desktop; it is now a line-oriented teletypewriter. In this mode, you type a line of command text and OS/2 (or DOS, in a DOS session) responds with one or more lines of information that explain the command's action. Although the plain white text on a black background may make this interface appear less exciting than Presentation Manager's colorful graphical environment, the interface is no less powerful. You can use the command line interface to run applications and issue commands. This chapter concentrates on issuing OS/2 and DOS commands.

You can look up commands in OS/2's on-line command reference (as explained in Chapter 13, "Using the Built-In Help Facility") or in the command reference section of this book. You want the most frequently used commands to become second nature to you, however, and this chapter focuses on those commands. You actually learn the commands for two operating systems because the commands presented in this chapter work for both OS/2 and DOS sessions. You learn that some of the more powerful commands have built-in safety features that protect against accidental misuse. This chapter also explains some important concepts about using OS/2 and provides you with a variety of expert tips.

You learn best by doing, and this chapter presents many examples to reinforce the information contained in the text. Type these examples as you go, and feel free to make up your own. The following list presents a roadmap of the topics discussed in this chapter:

- Opening, clearing, and closing a command-line window
- Setting the system time and date
- Understanding, creating, removing, and navigating directories
- Listing, copying, erasing, and renaming files
- Backing up your hard disk and restoring files from the backup
- Displaying files on the screen and printer

Beginning the Command Line Interface

To use the command line interface, choose either OS/2 Window or OS/2 Full Screen from Presentation Manager's Main Group. When you choose OS/2 Window, you find a new menu selection available only in windowed sessions, font size, in the pull-down menu bar. Set the characters to the size you prefer and maximize the window so you can see it all at once. Alternatively, you can choose DOS Window or DOS Full Screen; the commands are basically the same in OS/2 and DOS modes.

You begin this session by learning to use the commands for changing the system's date and time. These commands are useful in themselves, and you can practice working with them before tackling more complicated commands. The discussion concludes with commands for clearing the screen and ending the session.

Viewing or Changing the System Date (DATE)

In the OS/2 window you just opened, type **DATE** and press Enter. The information that appears on-screen should resemble the following:

```
DATE

The current date is: Sat 11-15-92

Enter the new date: (MM-DD-YY)
```

If the date is correct, just press Enter. To change the date, type a new date, such as the following, and press Enter:

```
4-15-93
```

If you prefer, you can separate the numbers with slashes instead of hyphens or type the year as a four-digit number. You even can type the date command and the new date all on one line:

```
DATE 4/15/1993
```

Try an invalid date, such as 2-31-93, and see what happens.

T I P   You can use the DATE command as a calendar. Suppose that you want to know on what day of the week 1995 will begin. You can type the following command to find out:

DATE 1-1-95 (this changes the date)

DATE (this reports the date)

The system returns the following message:

```
Current date is: Sun  1-01-95
```

This technique tricks the system into believing that the current date is January 1, 1995. The system obligingly reports that the day of the week is Sunday. Be sure to reset the system to the true date, or your computer will remember the wrong date even after you turn the power off.

Viewing or Changing the System Time (TIME)

The OS/2 TIME command works much like the DATE command. To use the TIME command, type **TIME**. OS/2 then displays the following messages on-screen:

```
The current time is: 14:31:25.78

Enter the new time:
```

TIME uses a 24-hour clock, so that a minute before midnight is 23:59:00.00 and a minute after is 0:01:00.00. To set the clock to 3:31 p.m., for example, you add 12 to the number of hours and type the following at the Enter the new time prompt:

15:31

If the system shows the correct time, just press Enter.

As you saw with DATE, you can type the command and the new time all on one line, for example:

TIME 15:31

Notice that you can choose not to specify seconds and hundredths of seconds. You even can leave out the minute and type the following, for example, if you want to set the clock exactly to midnight:

TIME 0

You also can follow the custom of many countries and use periods to separate hours, minutes, and seconds, as shown in the following example:

TIME 15.31.59

Try setting an impossible time, such as 65 minutes past 25 o'clock. OS/2 recognizes that no such time exists, and asks you to try again.

Clearing the Screen (CLS)

When you practiced with the TIME and DATE commands, the screen filled, and some lines scrolled off the top. You can unclutter the screen before going on to the next section by using the CLS command.

CLS, which stands for Clear Screen, is the simplest of all commands. To use it, just type **CLS**. Everything vanishes from the screen, and you start at the top again. Be certain you want to remove all the information on-screen before you use this command. When CLS removes information from the screen, the information is gone forever.

Closing the Command Line Session (EXIT)

When you finish using an OS/2 window and want to close it, you use the EXIT command. You type **EXIT**, the window disappears, and the system returns you to the Main Group. You also can close the window from Task Manager. If you try EXIT now, remember to open another OS/2 window before continuing with the next section.

For Related Information

◀◀ "Understanding Disk Partitions and Disks," p. 44.

◀◀ "Storing Files and File Names," p. 46.

FROM HERE...

Learning the Commands for Managing Directories

As you learned in Chapter 2, "Learning OS/2 If You Don't Know DOS," OS/2 organizes its files into directories. Figure 12.1 shows an example of a directory structure for a word processor.

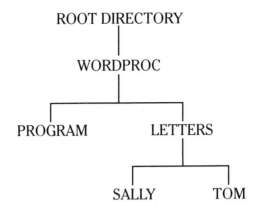

ROOT DIRECTORY

WORDPROC

PROGRAM   LETTERS

SALLY   TOM

Fig. 12.1

A sample
directory
structure for a
word processor.

This structure groups the word processor's program files in a
PROGRAM directory and contains a separate branch for letters. Two
people, Sally and Tom, use the word processing program, and each has
a private directory for the letters they type. This section shows you
how to set up, manage, and navigate this directory layout. Your first
step in learning these techniques is to familiarize yourself with the
following terms and concepts:

- *Current Working Directory.* Think of the directory structure as a
  tree, with each directory representing a branch. You can climb up
  and down from one branch to another, but you are always in some
  directory on the tree. The prompt that OS/2 displays, such as
  [C:\OS2], when it waits for your next command, tells where you
  are. This is the current directory.

- *Paths.* You can tell someone how to get anywhere in a tree by
  specifying which branches they must climb. Similarly, you can
  specify any directory's location by spelling out the path to that
  directory. A complete path starts at the root directory, but you
  also can use a shorter form that starts from the current working
  directory.

- *Shorthand Directory Names.* You use three special abbreviations in
  paths:

Abbreviation	Represents
\	The root directory
.	The current working directory
..	The *parent* of the current working directory—the directory one level closer to the root. (In figure 12.1, WORDPROC is the parent of LETTERS, and LETTERS is a *child* of WORDPROC.)

Making a Directory (MD or MKDIR)

OS/2 creates several directories in which it stores its files; DOS and Windows applications do the same. You can create your own set of directories to organize your files. You create directories by using the MD (Make Directory) command. MKDIR is another name for the command, but MD is easier to type.

The first step in creating the layout for the word processing example is to open an OS/2 window and create the \WORDPROC directory. To create the directory, type the following:

    MD \WORDPROC

The backslash before the name indicates that this directory is a child of the root directory. You can create a subdirectory by typing its full path, for example:

    MD \WORDPROC\PROGRAM

Both preceding examples give the full path from the root to the new directory because they start with the backslash character (\). An easier way to create children of the current directory is to use the CD command to make \WORDPROC the current directory. The next section explains the CD command in detail. For now, type the following command lines, pressing Enter at the end of each line:

    CD \WORDPROC

    MD LETTERS

These commands create the subdirectory \WORDPROC\LETTERS. To complete the directory structure, type the following commands:

    CD LETTERS

    MD SALLY

    MD TOM

You now have created the directory structure pictured in figure 12.1.

The last command you typed is equivalent to MD \WORDPROC\LETTERS\TOM, but MD TOM is shorter and reduces the risk of typing errors. This command works, however, only if \WORDPROC\LETTERS is the current directory. Each command form has advantages, and you work most efficiently when you learn to use both forms.

Changing the Current Directory (CD or CHDIR)

Both CD and CHDIR are names for the Change Directory command. Most users prefer the shorter command name, CD. You use this command to move to any directory on a hard disk or floppy disk. The directory you move to becomes that disk's current working directory.

Suppose that you want to work with the \WORDPROC\PROGRAM directory you created earlier. You can use any of several techniques to make this the current directory. To use a direct method, you type the following command:

CD \WORDPROC\PROGRAM

This form of the CD command gives the complete path from the root to the desired current directory. This command always works, no matter what directory you are in when you type it.

If you are already near the directory you want to make current, however, you can use a shorter command form to reach the directory. If you are in the \WORDPROC directory, for example, you can change to \WORDPROC\PROGRAM by typing the following command:

CD PROGRAM

Alternatively, you can move to \WORDPROC\LETTERS\TOM with this command:

CD LETTERS\TOM

If you're in \WORDPROC\LETTERS, and you want to move to the \WORDPROC\LETTERS\SALLY directory, type the following command:

CD SALLY

This method of changing directories is quick and helps you avoid typing errors.

When you want to know what directory you're in, type **CD** without any path following it. This command instructs OS/2 to tell you the name of the current directory.

T I P

Here is another shortcut to help you work faster. If you're working in the \WORDPROC\PROGRAM directory and want to move back to the \WORDPROC directory, type the following:

> CD ..

Remember that the double period is shorthand for the parent directory, one level closer to the root. You can use this shorthand symbol with the name of another subdirectory that is a child of the same parent. For example, suppose that you want to move from \WORDPROC\LETTERS\TOM to \WORDPROC\LETTERS\SALLY. These subdirectories share the same parent, \WORDPROC\LETTERS, which you abbreviate with a double period:

> CD ..\SALLY

You can use the double period more than once. To move to the parent directory's parent, type the following:

> CD ..\..

To return to the root directory, you use this special form:

> CD \

Removing a Directory (RD or RMDIR)

As your needs change over time, you can remove directories that you no longer use. You need not keep, for example, the directories you created in the two preceding sections of this chapter. You can use the RD (Remove Directory) command to delete directories. RD has a built-in safety feature that prevents you from removing a directory that contains any files or subdirectories.

Because \WORDPROC\PROGRAM is empty, you can remove it. You can either specify the full path by typing **RD \WORDPROC\PROGRAM,** or you can move to \WORDPROC and use the short form, as shown in this command sequence:

> CD \WORDPROC
>
> RD PROGRAM

Do not attempt to use the following command:

RD \WORDPROC\LETTERS

If you try this command, you receive an error message. You cannot delete this directory because it contains two child directories. Although this safety feature may seem an inconvenient obstacle when you want to remove an entire directory, it has its benefits. The feature averts the potential disaster of mistakenly wiping out a whole branch of your directory tree. OS/2 provides this feature as a built-in safety net.

To remove the \WORDPROC\LETTERS branch, you must first remove its subdirectories by typing the following command sequence:

CD\WORDPROC\LETTERS

RD SALLY

RD TOM

Again, however, don't try typing this command:

RD \WORDPROC\LETTERS

If you type this command now, you run into another safeguard. OS/2 does not let you remove the current directory. You easily can get around this safeguard; simply switch to another directory, such as the root, and remove the remaining directories in the opposite order in which you created them, as shown in the following command sequence:

CD \

RD \WORDPROC\LETTERS

RD \WORDPROC

You have learned how to create, move, and remove directories. Directories are just containers, however, useful only because of the files you put in them. The next section discusses several commands for managing files.

FROM HERE...

For Related Information

◄◄ "Organizing Directories," p. 51.

►► "Command Reference," p. 647.

Learning the Commands for Managing Files

As you learned in Chapter 2, "Learning OS/2 If You Don't Know DOS," files are sets of data you store on a disk. This section covers several important commands you use to do the following:

- Obtain a list of the files in a directory

- Copy a file

- Back up a group of files to a floppy disk

- Delete a file you no longer need

- Change a file's name

In this section you learn that these commands can manipulate more than one file at a time.

Every file has a *name* and an *extension*—these are like your first and last names. Your last name tells what family you belong to, and file extensions work the same way.

Program files usually have the extension EXE, which means they are files of the executable program family. A file's name tells which member of the family it is. The file MURAL.EXE, for example, is part of the program family whose members can paint a background on the Presentation Manager screen. A period usually separates the name and extension.

If you use OS/2's High Performance File System (HPFS), you can give files very long names; other systems limit filenames to eight characters and extensions to three characters. With this bit of background, you are ready to start working with files.

CAUTION: HPFS files with long file names are invisible in DOS sessions under OS/2. OS/2 applications and OS/2 command prompt sessions can access the files, but DOS applications and DOS command prompt sessions cannot.

Listing Files (DIR)

The first question you may ask about a directory is, what files does it contain? The DIR command answers that question. To see a list of the files in the current directory, type **DIR**. To list the files in a non-current directory, type **DIR** followed by the name of the directory, for example:

    DIR \OS2\BOOK

If you type this example, the system returns the following messages:

```
The volume label in drive C is HARDDISK.

The Volume Serial Number is 3F58:12C9

Directory of C:\OS2\BOOK

    .             <DIR>       7-31-92    9:04p

    ..            <DIR>       7-31-92    9:04p

REXX     INF    174936       7-03-92    4:19a

CMDREF   INF    364447       7-03-92    3:21a

SAMPLE         <DIR>         8-10-92    2:40p

    5 File(s)   13117440 bytes free
```

What do these messages mean? First, the directory contains two files. REXX.INF is 174,936 bytes long and was created or last modified on July 3, 1992, at 4:19 a.m. The other file, CMDREF.INF, is about twice as big as REXX.INF and was created about an hour earlier. About 13 million bytes are available on this disk.

If only two files are located on this disk, why does the last line displayed by DIR say 5 File(s)? The three extra "files" are marked <DIR>, which labels them as directories. Technically, directories are files of a special type. They have a date and time stamp but no size. The first directory name is shown as a period, meaning the \OS2\BOOK directory, and the second directory name is shown as two periods, meaning the parent directory, \OS2. If you run DIR on a drive that you formatted with the High Performance File System, DIR displays the same information, but in a different order.

Most directories have many more files than this example illustrates. The \OS2 directory, for example, contains about 100 files. If you type **DIR \OS2**, the filenames zoom by on your screen faster than you can read them. To help you manage lengthy directories, OS/2 provides two options called *switches*. A switch is an option that you type after a command; the switch always follows a slash (/). If you type the switch **/P**, for example, you tell OS/2 that you want your scrolling screen to pause after every page. To look at the files in the \OS2 directory one screen at a time, type:

DIR \OS2 /P

OS/2 displays as much information as it can fit on the screen, followed by the message Press any key when ready. When you press a key, OS/2 shows the next screen and pauses again.

If you want to see only the filenames and not the size and date information, use the /W (Wide Listing) switch. This switch makes DIR list the filenames five columns across. Type the following:

DIR \OS2\BOOK /W

The system returns the following message:

```
The volume label in drive C is HARDDISK.

The Volume Serial Number is 3F58:12C9

Directory of C:\OS2\BOOK

.              ..              REXX     INF     CMDREF
INF            SAMPLE          DIR
        5 File(s)    13117440 bytes free
```

These switches can help you wade through a large directory list, but sometimes you want to display only the names of certain files. You can narrow the scope of DIR by telling it, for example, to show only files with names containing a particular sequence of characters. The next two sections explain the techniques for producing these listings and provide some practice examples.

Using Wild Cards

In some card games, certain cards are *wild*; wild cards match any other card. In OS/2, when you want to refer to a set of computer files that have similar names, you can use wild-card characters. If the following explanations seem complicated at first, you can skim through them for now and then skip ahead to the examples in the next section. Practice is the best way to become familiar with wild cards and to appreciate their usefulness.

OS/2 uses two wild cards—the asterisk (*) and the question mark (?). The asterisk matches any *group* of characters, as you can see in the following examples:

*.EXE indicates the set of all files with the extension EXE, regardless of the filename.

C*.EXE indicates all EXE files with names beginning with the letter C. These files include CALENDAR.EXE but not ABC.EXE or CC.TXT (ABC.EXE does not start with C, and CC.TXT's extension is not EXE).

C.* indicates all files whose names contain the letter C, regardless of their extension. The group includes files CONSYS, ACE.TXT, and ABC.DEF. It does not include AAA.CCC, however, because the letter C occurs only in the file's extension, not in its name.

The question mark is OS/2's other wild-card character. While the asterisk matches any group of characters, the question mark matches any *single* character, as shown in the following examples:

?.EXE indicates all files with one-character names whose extension is EXE. This category includes the file A.EXE; it does not include file AB.EXE.

???.* indicates all files whose names are up to three characters long, regardless of their extensions. It matches ABC.DEF, but not ABCEF.GHI.

You also can combine wild cards. The example ?O*. means any file with O as the second letter of its name and no extension. This example matches COMMENTS and COOKIES but not MEMO or OOO.OOO.

In DOS sessions, the asterisk wild card works a little differently. DOS ignores characters following the asterisk. In DOS mode, therefore, A*C matches ABC, AAA, or any other name beginning with A.

You also can insert filenames containing wild cards in your command lines. In these situations, the filename containing the wild card becomes a *file specification*. OS/2 looks for every file that matches the file specification and applies the command to each of those files in turn. The remaining sections of this chapter provide many examples that illustrate the use of wild cards with a variety of commands.

Using DIR with Wild Cards

Now that you're acquainted with wild cards, the time has come to reinforce the concepts with practical examples. Suppose that your word processing program applies the extension TXT to the documents you type. To view a list of these documents, you can type DIR and search the entire directory for TXT files. The following command, however, provides a more efficient tool:

DIR \WORDPROC*.TXT

This command produces a list of only the TXT files; you easily can compare their names, dates, and sizes. If the listing of TXT files does not fit on one screen, add a switch to the command, for example:

DIR \WORDPROC*.TXT /P

As another example, if you use Lotus 1-2-3 for Presentation Manager, you may save spreadsheets with extensions WK1, WK2, or WK3. To list them all, type the following:

DIR \123G*.WK?

If you have a series of spreadsheets with names like BUDGET1 and BUDGET2, you can display all names in the series by typing the following:

DIR \123G\BUDGET*.WK?

In OS/2 mode only, you can specify more than one set of files in a single command:

DIR \123G\BUDGET*.WK? \123G\SALES.WK?

You can create your own examples and use them to experiment with the wild cards. Practice until you feel comfortable with wild cards—they are an important tool for extending the power of many commands.

Deleting a File (DEL or ERASE)

DEL (Delete) and ERASE are two names for the command you use to delete files. If you use the delete command by mistake, it can erase a file you don't want to erase. To practice safely with the command, type the following command sequence to set up a directory of files you can afford to delete:

MD \ERASE.ME

CD \ERASE.ME

XCOPY \OS2

The last line above copies the OS/2 files into your new directory. To protect its most critical files, OS/2 does not copy them to the new directory. You can confirm with the DIR command, however, that you have enough files in the new directory to experiment with DEL. You can begin experimenting by deleting XCOPY.EXE, the program you used to copy the files. To delete it, type:

DEL \ERASE.ME\XCOPY.EXE

Alternatively, make sure that you are in the \ERASE.ME directory first, then type:

    DEL XCOPY.EXE

DEL also works with wild cards. Many of the files in \ERASE.ME begin with the letters PM. To erase them all in one operation, type the following:

    DEL PM*.*

In OS/2 mode (but not in DOS mode), you can delete more than one set of files with a single command. To delete all files whose names or extensions contain the letter E, type:

    DEL *E*.* *.*E*

Finally, type the following to try to delete all the files remaining in \ERASE.ME:

    DEL .

Remember, the single period is shorthand for the entire current directory. Wiping out this directory is a drastic action, so OS/2 asks you to confirm that you really want to do so. For now, answer no to leave some practice files for the next command.

CAUTION: Be extremely careful when you use wild cards with the DEL command. You inadvertently may delete more files than you intended to.

Changing a File Name (RENAME or REN)

The RENAME or REN command changes the name of a file. If you worked through the examples in the previous section and are still in the ERASE.ME directory, your practice directory still has a file called CHKDSK.COM. To give it a more pronounceable name, type this command:

    REN CHKDSK.COM CHEKDISK.COM

REN works with wild cards. If you find the command names DISKCOPY and DISKCOMP too long for your taste, try typing the following command:

    REN DISK*.COM D*.COM

Now you have two new commands, DCOPY and DCOMP, which work exactly like the originals.

Copying Files (COPY)

The COPY command has many uses. In its most basic form, it duplicates a file and gives the duplicate a different name than the original, or
it places the duplicate in a different directory. Before changing your
CONSYS file, for example, which records the particular way you have
customized OS/2, you first make a backup copy as a safeguard. To
create the backup copy and name it CONOLD, type the following
command:

COPY \CONSYS \CONOLD

If you're already in the root directory, you can omit the backslashes
and just type the following:

COPY CONSYS CONOLD

In either situation, first type the name of the file you want to copy, followed by the name of the file you want to create. Use care when assign-
ing names to files you create with COPY. If you create a file using a
name that is already assigned to another file, COPY overwrites the
original file and replaces its contents with those of the new file. The
original file's contents are lost forever.

What if you want to copy the file to a different directory? You may create a directory named \BACKUP, for example, specifically for saving
old files. In this case, you need not change the file name to CONOLD
because two files can have the same name if they are in different
directories. You can type the full path of each file with this command:

COPY \CONSYS \BACKUP\CONSYS

You must do some extra typing to specify the path and file name completely, but this command always works no matter in which directory
you are currently working. If no \BACKUP directory exists, your screen
displays an error message.

If the \BACKUP directory exists, you can use this shorter command
form and achieve the same results:

COPY \CONSYS \BACKUP

Because this method specifies the path but not the name of the copy,
OS/2 uses the name of the original file. If the \BACKUP directory
doesn't exist, OS/2 interprets \BACKUP as the name of a file that you
want to create in the root directory.

If \BACKUP is the current directory, you need only type the following
to get the same result:

COPY \CONSYS

OS/2 sees that you have not specified a name for the new file, so it assumes that you want a duplicate, with the same name as the original file but in the current directory. If you're in the root directory, however, this command gives you an error message because you cannot copy a file onto itself.

OS/2 offers shortcuts that can help you work more quickly, but you must be aware of the dangers of using shortcuts. You always are safest when you spell out what you want in full detail. Practice that way at first until you feel proficient. The next section introduces another powerful technique—one that enables you to copy whole groups of files with a single command.

Copying with Wild Cards

Suppose that you have four Lotus spreadsheets in your \123G directory and you want to copy them all to a disk so that you can work on them at home. You can type a separate COPY command for each spreadsheet, but you have an easier option because the spreadsheets share the same file extension. You type the following to take advantage of the easy method:

    COPY \123G*.WK1 A:

This single command copies all four spreadsheets because the asterisk wild card matches any file name.

If you have January sales and payroll figures in spreadsheets named JANSALES.WK1 and JANPAYRL.WK1, and you want duplicates for entering February results, type the following:

    COPY \123G\JAN*.WK1 \123G\FEB*.WK1

If you're in the \123G directory, you can simplify the command to the following:

    COPY JAN*.WK1 FEB*.WK1

Remember that OS/2 applies the command to every file that matches the wild-card specification. If your coworker Janet had a spreadsheet JANET.WK1 in this directory, you just made a copy called FEBET.WK1.

COPY with wild cards is a very powerful command that can save you a lot of typing. You must be careful, however—a typing mistake can mean you don't get what you want. If your finger slips, for example, and you accidentally omit the colon in this section's first example, then OS/2 interprets **A** as the name of a file:

    COPY \123G*.WK1 A

OS/2 creates a file called A and copies each of your spreadsheets to it. Further, if you already had a file named A, it is gone forever. Of course this outcome is not what you intended; but the command is valid, so the system produces no error message. The more powerful the command, the more carefully you must work with it.

Copying and Combining Files

COPY also enables you to combine files. Suppose that you have used a spreadsheet to create several exhibits, which you want to print out and attach to a memo. Putting them all in one file makes this task a little easier and ensures that the files remain together. To use COPY to accomplish this task, you join the names of the files you want to combine with plus signs and then give a name for the file that is to contain them, as shown in the following example:

COPY EXHIBIT1.PRN+EXHIBIT2.PRN+EXHIBIT3.PRN EXHIBITS

If you don't supply a new name for the combined file, COPY uses the first name you listed. For example,

COPY EXHIBIT1.PRN+EXHIBIT2.PRN+EXHIBIT3.PRN

adds EXHIBIT2.PRN and EXHIBIT3.PRN to the end of EXHIBIT1.PRN.

T I P

Every file has a date and time stamp that shows when you last changed the file. COPY usually duplicates this information along with the file's data; but when you use COPY to combine files, the new file gets the current date and time. Here is a neat trick to change the date and time of an old file to the current date and time:

COPY MYFILE+

The plus sign means add another file at the end of MYFILE, but you have not indicated what file is to be added. The contents of MYFILE, therefore, are unchanged. You can give a file any date you want by first using the DATE command to set the computer's internal date.

Consider the following command:

COPY .+

This command puts the current time and date on every file in the current directory. This unusual trick works only with OS/2 and not DOS.

Using COPY and Devices

This section contains somewhat advanced information. You may want to skip this section entirely unless you have enjoyed the expert tips in earlier sections.

COPY treats devices—such as the keyboard and the printer—as though they are files. As a result, you can use the following command to copy from the keyboard to the printer:

    COPY CON PRN

This command makes your computer behave like a typewriter. PRN is the name of the printer device, and CON (short for console) represents the keyboard and screen. You also can copy a file to the PRN device. However, the PRINT command, discussed later in this chapter, is a more versatile tool for producing printouts.

When you COPY from CON, you need a way to tell COPY that you are finished typing your file, so that the command can stop copying and return you to the OS/2 prompt. You stop the copying action by pressing the special end-of-file character, Ctrl-Z, and then pressing Enter. This feature is easy to remember, because Z comes at the end of the alphabet, so Ctrl-Z marks the end of the file.

You can copy from the console to a file by using the following command:

    COPY CON MYFILE.TXT

You can use this command to create a new file quickly; just type the text and press Enter after each line. This feature is handy when you want to quickly copy a short file. You cannot change a line after you type it, however, so this technique does not replace your editor or word processing program. Remember to press Ctrl-Z and then Enter when you are finished typing.

What happens if you COPY a file to CON? You can try this experiment by typing the following command:

    COPY \CONFIG.SYS CON

This command copies the file to your screen. Remember, the console represents the keyboard and the screen. When you COPY *from* the console, you copy from the keyboard. When you COPY *to* the console, you copy to the screen.

You also can copy a file to the printer by typing this command:

    COPY \CONFIG.SYS PRN

You cannot copy *from* the printer, however, because it is not an input device like the keyboard.

Copying files to the screen and printer are such important operations that they have their own commands, TYPE and PRINT, which are discussed later in this chapter.

Copying Directories (XCOPY)

XCOPY (Extended COPY) is a specialized version of the COPY command. The XCOPY command copies groups of files more flexibly than COPY. XCOPY can even copy whole branches of a directory tree. This command is not a complete replacement for COPY, however, because it does not combine files or work with devices such as the printer.

In early OS/2 versions, XCOPY ran faster than COPY under DOS, but that advantage has all but disappeared in later OS/2 versions. Compare the speed of both commands on your system. XCOPY may be the quicker of the two commands. Even if XCOPY is not faster, the command is worth learning because of the power of its optional switches. Some of these switches tell the command to copy whole directories, including their subdirectories and all the files they contain. Other switches enable you to copy only certain files—based, for example, on the date you last changed them or whether you have backed them up. The following paragraphs describe these XCOPY switches.

/S   With this switch, you can copy an entire directory tree. If you have several subdirectories on a floppy disk and want to copy them with all their contents to your hard disk, for example, type the following:

     XCOPY A: C: /S

This command creates all the subdirectories automatically and then copies every file to its proper location. If you have two hard drives and want to move an entire spreadsheet package with all its subdirectories and files from the first drive to the second, type the following:

     XCOPY C:\123G D: /S

/E   Perhaps your spreadsheet setup includes a separate subdirectory for files you plan to create for a future project, but you have not yet put any files in the subdirectory. XCOPY with the /S switch does not copy this empty subdirectory unless you also include /E, as in the following example:

     XCOPY C:\123G D: /S /E

You should make a habit of including /E whenever you use /S, because in most circumstances you want to copy all subdirectories, even those that are empty.

/P   Sometimes you want to copy only certain files from one directory to another. Suppose that you have a dozen memos in your \MEMOS directory, for example, and you want to copy five of them to a disk. If you use the command

    XCOPY \MEMOS A: /P

OS/2 displays the name of each file in turn, and asks whether you want to copy it.

/D   This switch enables you to copy just the files that you created or changed after a certain date. For example,

    XCOPY \MEMOS A: /D:1-1-92

selects every file in your \MEMOS directory that bears a date later than 1991, and copies it to a floppy disk.

/A   This switch copies files that have not been backed up. Back up your files regularly by using the BACKUP command, which is discussed later in this chapter. Suppose that you do this every Friday, but this is Tuesday and you just finished an important project. You may want to copy your latest files to a disk for extra safety. Instead of running BACKUP, you type the following:

    XCOPY \PROJECT A: /A

The /A switch stands for archive because backing up files is like packing papers into a box and shipping them off to an archive. Every file has an archive flag that indicates whether or not you have backed up the file; the flag is turned on when you create or change the file, and off when you run BACKUP. When you run XCOPY with /A you do not change this flag.

/M   This switch works exactly like /A except that it turns off the archive flag of each file you copy. This feature is useful when you want to use XCOPY as a substitute for BACKUP. BACKUP writes files in a special format, and you must use RESTORE to convert them back to their original format before you can use them. XCOPY does not have this drawback, but because BACKUP makes more efficient use of space, it uses fewer disks than does XCOPY. BACKUP also can copy a file that is too large to fit on a single disk. You may prefer to use BACKUP rather than XCOPY, therefore, in some situations.

For Related Information

◄◄ "Copying Disks and Files," p. 56.

►► "Command Reference," p. 647.

FROM HERE...

Learning the Commands To Back Up Your Hard Disk

If your hard disk stops working correctly, you can replace it. The data you have stored on the disk, however, is probably worth more to you than the computer. You may have to put forth enormous effort to re-place the data—unless you have a backup copy. Hardware failures are rare, fortunately, and you are more likely to lose data because of a de-fective program or a mistaken command. In either case, however, the BACKUP command is your insurance policy against losing valuable data.

BACKUP copies data on your hard disk to floppy disks. It uses a special format for your data, so you cannot use commands such as COPY to read the data. Instead, you must use RESTORE to copy files from your backup disks back to the hard disk.

BACKUP and RESTORE intentionally refuse to work with some of OS/2's most critical files. These files are the OS2.INI, OS2SYS.INI, EA DATA. SF, and WP ROOT. SF files. When it multitasks, OS/2 keeps these files open and continually updates the files. BACKUP and RESTORE cannot access these files while OS/2 is using them. Chapter 8, "Troubleshooting OS/2," provides steps you can take to make backup copies of these critical files.

If you have a large hard disk, consider buying a tape backup unit. Tape cartridges can hold as much data as your hard disk, so you can back up your hard disk without having to continually swap floppy disks. As a rule, tape drives come with their own software; make sure that the one you get can run under OS/2 as well as DOS.

Making a Backup (BACKUP)

BACKUP copies the files on your hard disk to floppy disks. After you have a complete backup of every file, you can update the backup by directing BACKUP to affect only the files that you have changed or added. User opinions vary, but one rule of thumb is to do a complete backup every couple of months and update it weekly.

Making a Complete Backup

Most users need several floppy disks for a complete backup, because each floppy disk holds far less data than a hard disk. If you have a 60 megabyte hard disk that is half full, for example, you need about 20 floppy disks if you are using a high-density, 3 1/2-inch drive. To find out how many disks you need, follow these steps:

1. Run the CHKDSK program to find out how much space your files consume. The command's response should resemble this:

   ```
   29935872 bytes in 827 user files.
   ```

2. Look up the capacity of your disk drive in the following table:

Disk drive type	Capacity in kilobytes
5 1/4-inch double density	360
5 1/4-inch high density	1200
3 1/2-inch double density	720
3 1/2-inch high density	1440
3 1/2-inch ultra density	2880

3. Divide the number of bytes used on the hard disk by the number of bytes on each disk; divide the result by 1,000 and round the result up. If you're using 3 1/2-inch, high-density disks, 29,935,872 / 1,440 is approximately 21,000, so you need about 21 disks. Add a few extra disks to be sure you have enough. Twenty-five disks should be plenty for this backup.

To do a complete backup from your hard drive C to a high-density, 3 1/2-inch disk drive A, first prepare the necessary number of disks. You don't need to format them, but stick a label on each and number them in order. Then type:

BACKUP C:*.* A: /F:1440 /S

This command uses the two following optional switches:

/F This switch tells BACKUP to format each disk, so you can use new disks right out of the box. You have to include the disk capacity (in kilobytes), shown in the preceding table. If you already formatted the disks, BACKUP doesn't format them again, which makes the backup process go a little faster. Further, if you format the disks first, you can discard any that have bad sectors.

/S This switch tells BACKUP to copy not only the files in the root directory of C but also each subdirectory and all its files.

After you type the preceding command, your screen displays the following messages:

```
BACKUP C:\*.* A: /F:1440

Insert backup disk 01 in drive A:

Warning!  The files in the root directory

of target drive A: will be erased.

Press Enter to continue or Ctrl+Break to cancel.
```

The warning simply states that any data you may have on the disk will be replaced with the backup. If this condition is acceptable, press Enter. If the disk is unformatted, BACKUP takes care of that first:

```
Insert a new disk in drive A:

and press Enter when ready.

Formatting has been completed.

The Volume Serial Number is 6217-1815

Enter up to 11 characters for the volume label,

or press Enter for no volume label. BACKUP01
```

A *volume label* is similar to the paper label you stick on the disk except that the volume label is a file on the disk. This label is optional.

```
        1457664 bytes total disk space

        1457664 bytes available on disk

        512 bytes in each allocation unit.

        2847 available allocation units on disk.

Format another disk (Y/N)? N
```

After formatting the disk, BACKUP moves your files onto it.

```
The files are being backed up to drive A.

Disk number 01
```

The name of every file appears on the screen after it is backed up. When a disk is full, BACKUP asks you to remove the disk and insert the next one.

Updating the Backup

Later on, when you want to refresh your complete backup by adding newly created or modified files, type:

BACKUP C:*.* A: /F:1440 /S /M

Notice the new switch, /M. This switch tells BACKUP to add only the new files. OS/2 marks the files it backs up, so it can pick out those that are new or have changed. After you type the above command, the following message appears on-screen:

```
Insert backup disk 01 in drive A:

Warning!  The files in the root directory

of target drive A: will be erased.

Press Enter to continue or Ctrl+Break to cancel.

The files are being backed up to drive A.

Disk number 01
```

BACKUP lists the files on-screen, enabling you to watch its progress.

Making a Partial Backup

In some situations you may want to back up only a certain directory or a certain set of files. If you want a separate backup copy of the memos you keep in your \MEMOS directory, for example, and they all have the extension MEM, type:

BACKUP C:\MEMOS*.MEM A:

The following two switches can help you make selective backups:

/D   Backs up files created or changed since a given date

/T   Backs up files created or changed since a given time

You can use these switches together. To make a backup of the memos in \MEMOS, excluding files that were present before noon on March 1, 1992, and have not changed since then, type the following command line:

BACKUP C:\MEMOS*.MEM A: /D:3-1-92 /T:12:00

Restoring from Backup (RESTORE)

In the preceding section, you learned how to use the BACKUP command to store the contents of your hard disk on a set of disks. You cannot use the stored data immediately, however; to put it back on the hard disk, you use BACKUP's companion, the RESTORE command.

Suppose that you backed up the hard disk you use at work and want to re-create all the files and directories on your computer at home. You first must install OS/2 at home—remember, BACKUP and RESTORE do not work with OS/2's system files. After you complete the installation, type the following:

RESTORE A: C: /S

Insert the disks in order, and OS/2 places all the files and directories on the hard disks, and your screen displays these messages:

```
Insert backup disk 01 in drive A:

Press Enter when ready.

The files were backed up on 09-28-1992.

Files will be restored from drive A:

Disk 01
```

RESTORE then displays the name of each file and prompts you to change disks as needed.

You also can restore a single file, for example,

RESTORE A: C:\CONFIG.SYS

or all the files in a single directory,

RESTORE A: C:\DATABASE*.*

or a certain set of files that you specify by using wild cards, as in

RESTORE A: C:\DATABASE\CUSTOMER.*

If you backed up files from the \DATABASE directory, however, you cannot restore them to a different directory, such as \DATA.

Several optional switches extend the flexibility of RESTORE. They enable you to restore files in all subdirectories or restore only files that you have modified or deleted since the last backup. You can limit the command to files that you modified either after or before a given time and date, and you can tell RESTORE to ask your permission before writing over a file that you have modified. The following paragraphs list and describe these switches.

/S   By default, RESTORE only restores files in the hard disk's current directory. Use this switch when you want to restore files in all subdirectories.

/N   With this switch, RESTORE processes only files that don't exist on the hard drive, such as files you deleted after making the backup.

/M   This switch tells RESTORE to restore only those files that you have deleted or changed since the backup and to ignore all other files. Use /M if you have made accidental changes to your files and want to put them back the way they were.

/P   If you want RESTORE to ask your permission before replacing any file that you have changed since its last backup, use /P. This safety feature protects you against accidentally wiping out the changes you have made after the backup.

/A and /L   Suppose that you finished a project last Friday at 6 p.m. and then immediately did a backup. If a misguided co-worker dropped in over the weekend and deleted or changed some of the files, these switches let you undo the damage. To put your files back the way they were at a given date and time, type the following:

RESTORE A: C: /S /A:3-1-92 /L:18:00

/B and /E   These switches correspond to /A and /L, but they tell RESTORE to replace files that you changed *before* the data and time you specify.

For Related Information

◀◀ "Formatting Hard Disks and Floppy Disks," p. 54.

▶▶ "Command Reference," p. 647.

FROM HERE...

Learning the Commands for Viewing and Printing Files

The preceding sections of this chapter have presented commands that treat files as sealed boxes. You have learned how to change the labels on file folders and move them from one file cabinet to another. You haven't learned, however, how to open the folders up and look at what they contain (except within the "expert" sections on using COPY to display files on-screen and the printer). The following sections examine two commands that display a file's contents.

Displaying a File On-Screen (MORE)

The MORE command displays a file on-screen. MORE uses a syntax unlike the other commands in this chapter. To use MORE to display your system configuration file, for example, one screen at a time, type the following command line:

MORE< \CONFIG.SYS

You must type the less-than sign, because MORE is a special type of program known as a *filter*. The advanced topic of filters is beyond the scope of this book. For now, consider the less-than sign as part of the command's name.

Printing a File (PRINT)

Most OS/2 and DOS applications have built-in options for printing the files they create. You also can print files with the PRINT command. For example, to send the file \CONFIG.SYS to the printer, type the following:

PRINT \CONFIG.SYS

You can print more than one file at once, by typing the following:

PRINT \LETTERS\LETTER1.TXT \LETTERS\LETTER2.TXT

You also can use wild cards, for example, type the following:

PRINT \LETTERS\LETTER*.TXT

The PRINT command works correctly only for plain text files. If you try to print a Lotus 1-2-3 spreadsheet with a WK1 extension, you do not get a spreadsheet printout because WK1 files have a special internal file format that only the spreadsheet program understands. (You would get a garbled printout of the internal file format.) If you use 1-2-3's Print to File option, however, 1-2-3 will create a plain, unformatted file with a PRN extension that can be printed with the PRINT command. 1-2-3 in this instance converts the WK1 file contents to a plain text file format the printer can print.

The following paragraphs list and describe the optional switches you can use with PRINT.

/D   If you have more than one printer, you can use this option to choose among them. Follow the /D switch with a colon and then the name of the printer. The names for the first three printers are LPT1, LPT2, and LPT3; network printers can have higher numbers. To print a file on the second printer, for example, type:

     PRINT MYFILE.TXT /D:LPT2

If you don't use the /D switch, your files go to the first printer.

/C   This option tells PRINT to stop printing the file it is currently working with. PRINT goes on to print any other files you have sent to the printer.

/T   This option cancels all files you have sent to the printer.

You cannot use the /C and /T switches together. You cannot cancel printing of a particular file by name.

FROM HERE...

For Related Information

◀◀ "Storing Files and File Names," p. 46.

▶▶ "Command Reference," p. 647.

Chapter Summary

In this chapter, you saw how to use the command line interface and mastered its most important commands. Working through examples, you saw that this interface is very powerful, although it is harder to learn than Presentation Manager. OS/2 has more than 100 commands, and the command reference in Part VI, "Using the Command Reference," discusses them in detail.

Fortunately, you don't have to remember all the options and switches for each command. Chapter 13, "Using the Built-In Help Facility," explains how to obtain extensive on-line help for both command line and Presentation Manager sessions.

Using the Built-In Help Facility

In the last chapter, you learned several OS/2 commands, but you undoubtedly did not memorize every option and switch. If you did memorize them, congratulations! The rest of us, however, can use OS/2's built-in help facility to look up the command for every option and switch.

Even if you remember the exact command, the built-in help feature can be a valuable tool by deciphering OS/2 error messages for you. Suppose that you make a mistake typing a command, and OS/2 replies with an error message that you don't understand. You can use the HELP command to obtain a full explanation of the error message, including possible causes for the error and steps you can take to correct it.

The Presentation Manager application also includes a built-in help feature. The feature offers many pages of information to assist you in learning and using the program. The help feature presents its information in a book format, with a table of contents and an index. You also can search the help information for key words, or print the information if you want a paper copy.

Presentation Manager's on-line Command Reference program offers extensive help on every OS/2 command. The Command Reference includes many examples and cross-referenced related commands.

No matter how you use OS/2, you have immediate access to help in many ways and in many forms. This chapter groups the discussion of the HELP command into the following three categories:

- Understanding a command line window
- Learning Presentation Manager
- Using the Command Reference utility

Understanding a Command Line Window

What if you are working in an OS/2 window, and you cannot recall exactly how to use a needed command? Or what if you receive a puzzling error message and don't understand it? You easily can get assistance in both situations if you simply type **HELP**. After you type the HELP command, the following messages appear on-screen:

```
[C:\]HELP
Alt+Esc to switch to the next session.
Ctrl+Esc to switch to the Task List.
Type HELP ON for help text.
Type HELP OFF for no help text.
Type HELP message-number for message help.
Type HELP [ BOOK ] SUBJECT to receive online information.
Type EXIT to end this OS/2 session.
```

The following paragraphs discuss each of these HELP messages and how to use them. Even if you already know how to switch from one session to another, you can benefit from learning the forms of the HELP command.

Turning the HELP Reminder On and Off

You can use the HELP ON and HELP OFF commands to instruct OS/2 to display or not to display help reminders. When you opened the window, for example, you may have noticed this brief reminder at the top:

```
Ctrl+Esc = Task List   Type HELP = help
```

The reminder remains on-screen even when other text scrolls off. If you type **CLS** to clear the screen, the reminder remains. If you want to instruct OS/2 not to display the reminder, type **HELP OFF**. You can redisplay the message at any time by typing **HELP ON**.

Using HELP To Remember a Command

Suppose that you want to list your files one screen at a time. You remember that DIR is the command you need but cannot recall the necessary switch. Is it /W for *Wait* or does that stand for *Wide*? You can look up the switch in the reference section if you have this book handy, or you can type the following:

HELP DIR

When you type **HELP** followed by the name of a command, you bring up OS/2's on-line command reference and go right to the command you named. In a later section of this chapter, you learn how to use the powerful Command Reference utility.

Using HELP To Explain an Error Message

If you ask OS/2 to do something impossible, such as to show the directory of a drive that doesn't exist, you receive an error message similar to the following:

```
[C:\]DIR Z:  SYS0015: The system cannot find the drive specified.
```

Perhaps you wanted drive A but typed **Z** by accident. You have no idea that you typed the wrong letter, and therefore you don't understand why the system cannot find drive A.

In the previous example, you may go back and check your DIR command line and discover your error. Many of OS/2's error messages, however, are more complex than the one just displayed. You can obtain a further explanation of any error message by typing **HELP** followed by the number that appears at the beginning of the message (you need not type the letters and zeros at the beginning of the number.) HELP then repeats the error message, explains the message's meaning, and suggests other ways to issue the command.

To obtain help on SYS0015, for example, you type **HELP 15** and receive the following explanation:

```
SYS0015: The system cannot find the drive specified.
EXPLANATION: One of the following has occurred:
  1. The drive specified does not exist.
```

```
2. The drive letter is incorrect.
3. You are trying to RESTORE to a redirected drive.
   ACTION: For situations 1 and 2 above; retry the command by using
the correct drive letter. For situation 3, you are
not allowed to RESTORE to a redirected drive.
```

In this example, the second explanation is the hint you need.

FROM HERE...

For Related Information

◀◀ "Beginning the Command Line Interface," p. 293.

Learning Presentation Manager

All Presentation Manager programs share a common user interface. As a result of this shared interface, you can get help regardless of which PM program you are using. Further, you obtain help by using the same methods in every application. You use the following methods to obtain help:

- ■ Press F1 to bring up a Help menu or screen.

- ■ Use the application Help selection. Every PM application has a Help selection on its action bar. Clicking that selection, or pressing Alt-H, pulls down a Help menu.

- ■ Use the Help buttons (located in most dialog boxes) that give you specific help for that dialog box.

Getting Help on Help

OS/2's Help system is extensive. You can explore the Help system to find out what it offers, although you may spend a great deal of time doing so. Fortunately, the Help system contains information on how to use Help.

To see the Help feature in action, open the Desktop settings notebook by clicking an empty place on the desktop with mouse button 2 (the right mouse button). Click the arrow next to the word Help. Choose the menu item labeled Using Help. The window now displays Help for Using the Help Facility. If you want more information on this category, press F1 and Help for the Help Window appears.

As this exercise has demonstrated, Help has several levels. You can back up one level by pressing Esc.

Getting Help for Menu Options

Sometimes you encounter menu items whose operations are not immediately apparent to you. In most circumstances, you want to know what a menu item does before you try to use it.

Click an empty place on the desktop with mouse button 2 to bring up the desktop's pop-up menu. Click the Select menu item once to highlight it. Press the F1 key to get help for that menu option.

You can get instant help on a highlighted option only by pressing F1. If you click Help on the action bar, the Help menu replaces the pop-up menu. Not all ways of getting help work in all situations, so you benefit from mastering every technique for obtaining help.

You can use another technique to learn more about an action before you select that action. Bring up the desktop's pop-up menu again and choose the Find option. A dialog box pops up that contains a Help button you can click. You also can use F1 in this box.

In most situations, you can choose between several methods of obtaining help. If you practice them all, you find it easier to learn new applications. Most of the methods you learn also apply to other programs, because of Presentation Manager's common interface.

Using an Application's Help Menu

The Help menu mentioned in the preceding two sections deserves a detailed discussion. The menu is a gateway to extensive help on each Presentation Manager application. In many cases, the help information is so complete that you can use it to learn a new application without studying the manual. The information is tailored to each application, but the ways you use the Help feature are always the same. Any time you spend now exploring all the available Help features, therefore, is time well spent. You already have opened the desktop's pop-up menu, so it can be your first example.

A Presentation Manager application's help system is like a book. The system has an introduction that gives you an overview, and a table of contents and an index that help you easily find the information you need. Because you can search the entire help system for a key word that interests you, the system is easier to use than most books.

Introduction

The introduction is the first section many people turn to when they pick up a book. To read the introduction to the desktop's on-line manual, select the Help option on the action bar, pull down the menu, and choose General Help. This selection displays a brief summary of the OS/2 desktop.

Table of Contents

Like most books, the Help facility has a table of contents. Pull down the Options menu on the General Help screen you just opened, and select Contents. You can scroll through the topics to get an idea of the desktop's capabilities. You may want more information, for example, on the Help for Folders topic. You can move the highlight to that topic and press Enter to get a brief explanation of folders.

Index

You also can learn about folders by looking up the topic in the index, which you call up with the Index option on any Help menu. The Help index contains an alphabetic listing of topics. As a result of this arrangement, when you know what you want to look up, the index can be a quicker source of help than is the table of contents. Help's index works just like a book's index, except you don't have to flip through pages to find a reference. You find the reference instantly when you press Enter.

For practice, open the index and look under F to find the word *folder*. Highlight the word and press Enter, or double-click the word. OS/2's on-line description of folders appears.

Search

Imagine reading through an entire book and marking every occurrence of a given topic. That task may be a chore for you, but it is the type of job a computer does well.

To start a search any time you are in the Help facility, press Ctrl-S or select Search from the Services menu. A Search window pops up. Type **folder**, press the All Sections button, and then press Enter. A menu appears listing every topic that contains the word *folder*, including some topics you may not have considered. When you press Enter again to explore any topic further, Help highlights in the text the word you searched for.

Instead of searching all sections, you can look through the current section only, or just the index. You even can search across the entire OS/2 Help system if you pick All Libraries on the Search menu. In most situations, however, you can limit your search to All Sections.

Print

On-line help is easier to explore than a printed book, but you must be at your computer to use Help. You may want information on a piece of paper, so you can make notes on the paper, then fold it up and put it in your pocket. This capability is built into on-line help through the Print option.

The Print option on the Services menu gives you several choices for printing Help text. You can print the current section, or the index, or the table of contents. You can print an entire Help manual by selecting All Sections.

Copy and Append to File

OS/2 stores Help files in a special format that saves space on your hard disk. You cannot examine the files directly by using tools such as the System Editor. If you want to put help information into a file you can access with a text editor, choose Copy or Append from the Services menu. These options put the currently displayed topic into a file. The file, named TEMP.TXT, is in the root directory of your hard disk. The Copy option replaces anything that was already in this file. The Append option adds the current topic to the file and leaves the file's previous contents intact.

Previous Topics and Previously Viewed Pages

As you wander through on-line help, you may want to retrace your steps. To backtrack one screen, press Esc or select Previous on the Options menu. You also can choose Viewed Pages on the same menu to obtain a list of all topics you have viewed. You then can jump immediately back to any page you want to see again.

Shortcut Keys

The pull-down menus provide an easy way to learn how to use help because they display every option. When you become proficient at using Help, however, you may want to maneuver the system more quickly. You can use single keystrokes, or shortcut keys, for the operations you need most often. The menu lists these shortcut keys. The Options menu, for example, shows the shortcut key Ctrl-C next to Table of Contents. You can press this key to move right to the table of contents, even if the menu is not displayed. The Keys option on the Help menu gives a list of these shortcuts.

New Window

You can view more than one Help topic at a time. The New Window option enables you to do this by placing each topic in a separate window.

As an example of this option's uses, you can search all sections for help on folders. Help for Folder sounds useful, so you highlight it and press Ctrl-N to display this help panel in a new window. You can make the window smaller and drag it to the bottom of the screen so you can see the search list again. Now, you highlight the Help for Open entry and press Ctrl-N. If you resize this new window and move it to the top right corner, your screen resembles figure 13.1.

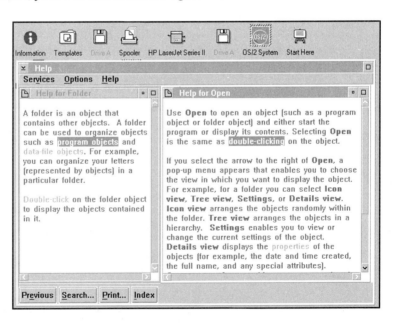

Fig. 13.1

Viewing more than one help window at a time.

The New Window option enables you to display several help panels at one time. You can maximize the Help window first, to provide more room for on-screen information. If the screen becomes crowded, you can minimize or close some of the windows.

Branches

A table of contents is an outline and, like all outlines, it can have more than one level. Levels are like branches of a tree, in that each branch can have subbranches. The Command Reference utility has several levels. The following section explains this program and shows how to view the table of contents in whatever level of detail you want.

For Related Information

◄◄ "Introducing Presentation Manager," p. 221.

FROM HERE...

Using the Command Reference Utility

The OS/2 Command Reference utility explains every OS/2 and DOS command. Because the Command Reference utility is a Presentation Manager program, it uses all the features you learned in the previous section of this chapter. As you learned in the first section, you can start the Command Reference utility from an OS/2 command-line session by typing **HELP** followed by the name of any command. You also can start it from the Information folder.

Selecting Levels of Detail in the Table of Contents

In addition to containing help for each command, the Command Reference contains general help for concepts that apply to your command-line sessions.

You can explore this utility by starting the Command Reference from the Information folder now. The table of contents appears, displaying a plus sign (+) next to the first entry, Information about OS/2 Commands. When you press the plus (+) key on the keyboard or click the plus sign in the window, you see another level of detail with three sub-topics indented under the main heading. You click the first one, File and Directory Concepts, to see the screen illustrated in figure 13.2.

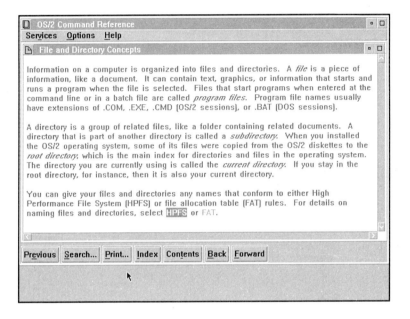

Fig. 13.2

Selecting a topic from on-line Help's table of contents.

When you no longer want to view this branch of the outline, click the minus sign (–). The plus and minus keys are shortcut keys for the Expand One Level and Collapse Branch choices on the Options menu.

You can have more than one extra level of detail. To explore this capability, you first can expand the OS/2 Commands by Name heading. Next, scroll down a page, and you see the CHKDSK command with a plus sign before it. Click the plus sign, and yet another level of the outline appears.

To collapse the entire outline and see only the highest level, you press Ctrl-minus (–). To show the outline in full detail, you press Ctrl-asterisk (*).

Getting Help on a Command

To find out more about a particular command, you expand the OS/2 Commands by Name branch, move to the command, and press Enter. You can try this operation with the TIME command, located near the bottom of the alphabetical list. This command shows a Help screen with the following features (the screen is shown in figure 13.3):

■ A brief description of the command's action. The TIME command, for example, sets the time on your computer's built-in clock.

■ A railroad diagram that includes the command's name, (in this example, TIME), followed by several lines pointing to the options you can use with the command (here, to set the hour, minute, and second). Railroad diagrams are explained later in this section.

■ An Examples button that you click to get an illustration of how to use the command. One of the examples for TIME shows how to set the clock to 6:45.

■ A list of related commands. In addition to DATE, the TIME example includes COUNTRY, because the country you live in determines how OS/2 displays the time.

■ Notes that elaborate on what the command does and how you use it. The comments on TIME, for example, say that it uses the 24-hour clock.

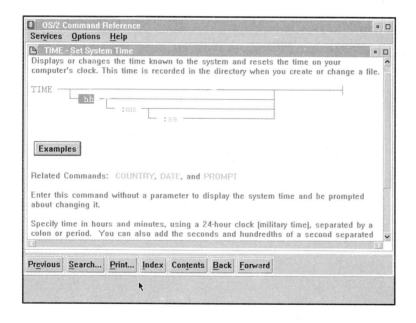

Fig. 13.3

Obtaining on-line help for the TIME command.

In figure 13.3, hh is highlighted. Highlighting indicates that more help is available for that word or phrase. Press Tab to move to a highlighted word, then press Enter to obtain more information about the word or phrase.

A few commands work only in DOS sessions or only in OS/2 sessions. The Help screen for these commands has a DOS or OS/2 icon in the upper left corner. To see an example of these icons, you can ask for help on the APPEND command, which works only under DOS. TIME has no such icon because the command is available in either operating system.

The Command Reference expresses the syntax of each command by drawing lines between each of the command's parts. These lines are *railroad diagrams* that help you understand how to use the command. The following section discusses these diagrams.

Railroad Diagrams

Railroad diagrams are a compact, graphic illustration of every valid technique for using a command. Although the diagrams initially may appear confusing, with a little practice you can learn to read them. On the left and right sides of the railroad diagram are *stations*, where a train must begin and end its trip. The train must start on the left side and end on the right side, but in between, the train can take any path. The train represents the command you type, including any parameters you can or must supply.

Paths on the Diagram

You can perform a simple exercise to learn how to use railroad diagrams. For this exercise, you use the OS/2 Command Reference screen for the TIME command (refer to fig. 13.3). You begin by typing **TIME**, because the command is at the left side of the diagram. You need not type anything else because a line (the railroad track) goes directly to the right side of the screen. That direct line indicates that the word TIME is a valid command on its own. You use the TIME command in the following manner to ask what time it is.

Suppose that the train takes the southern path whenever it comes to a junction. That situation means you type **TIME hh:mm:ss** to reset the clock to a certain hour, minute, and second. Whenever the train passes through capital letters or punctuation marks, like the colons here, you have to type them exactly as shown. When you come to something in lowercase letters, you have to plug in a value. TIME 13:20:59, for example, is a legal command.

Can you use TIME 13:20 as a valid setting? Yes, because the train can pass through the hh (hour setting) and mm (minute setting) stations and bypass the ss (seconds setting) station to return to the main TIME track line. The diagram illustrates, however, that you cannot reach the minute setting without first specifying the hour.

Lines and Arrows

In a railroad diagram, the train has no reverse gear; normally, it cannot move to the left. In some circumstances, however, you can backtrack through a command. The diagram marks with an arrow each command phase, or optional switch. The CHKDSK command, for example, has several optional switches, such as /F to fix any problems CHKDSK finds and /V to show the name of each file it checks (see fig. 13.4). You can use either switch, neither switch, or both switches. To see how you can use both, tell the train to pass through /F, turn left, backtrack along the upper path with an arrow, and then pass through /V.

The arrows also keep the train from running off the page. Because this route map is too wide to fit on the screen, the system breaks the map into two pieces. When the train gets to the right end of the top line, it continues at the left end of the next line, as the arrows pointing to the left show.

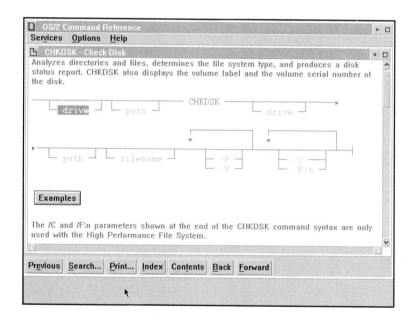

Fig. 13.4

Viewing the railroad diagram for the CHKDSK command.

For Related Information

◄◄ "Using the Workplace Shell," p. 218.

◄◄ "Introducing Presentation Manager," p. 221.

▶▶ "Command Reference," p. 647.

FROM HERE...

Chapter Summary

In this chapter, you learned that on-line help is always available in OS/2, and you mastered the help menus for Presentation Manager applications. Although you may not need to use the command-line interface often, you learned how to get help on error messages and how to look up information on DOS and OS/2 commands.

In the next chapter, "Using the OS/2 Text Editors," you learn how to view, create, and change text files.

Using the OS/2 Text Editors

OS/2 includes two text editors, the System Editor and the Enhanced Editor, that you can use to view, create, and change simple text files. The System Editor is simple to learn and easy to use. You can think of the Enhanced Editor for Presentation Manager (EPM) as the System Editor's bigger brother. EPM was developed by an IBM employee, and people who work at IBM have used EPM for years. Because EPM works like the System Editor but adds many extra features, IBM decided to distribute EPM free with OS/2 versions 2.0 and higher.

In this chapter, you learn how to use the System Editor and EPM. This chapter discusses all techniques—including the basic ones—you need to know in order to use a text editor. If you have some experience using a text editor, you may want to skim the first few sections quickly as a refresher.

The first sections of this chapter present a short file that contains several typographical errors, then demonstrate various ways you can use the text editor to correct the errors. You gain valuable practice as you work through these steps. The illustrations show what your screen should look like along the way.

After you master the basics, you learn advanced techniques that make your work easier and more efficient. These powerful commands enable you to do the following:

- Copy and rearrange lines and paragraphs

- Scan files for a particular phrase

- Automatically replace one word or phrase with another throughout a file

- Move and copy text

- Undo the last change you made

- Use different fonts and colors

- Wrap words at the end of a line, as you do with a word processing program

EPM provides additional commands that enable you to do the following:

- Edit several files at once

- Move and copy text between files

- Undo any or all changes you have made

- Customize the appearance of the editor

As the above lists indicate, the OS/2 editors have many useful features. You may find the text editors handy for many tasks, even if you have a word processing program.

Using the OS/2 Editors

The System Editor and the Enhanced Editor work with pure text files, also called *flat files* or *ASCII files*. The files contain only the text you put in them. Word processing programs use special format codes to keep track of paragraphs, page breaks, and more. Because the OS/2 editors do not understand these special codes, the text editors may not work well with documents produced with word processing software. Most word processing programs enable you to save documents as flat files, however, so you can edit them with tools like the System Editor or EPM.

The System Editor is handy for creating simple files like memos or to-do lists. You can use the System Editor to make changes in your system setup files, such as the CONFIG.SYS file. In addition, you can use the

System Editor to display a file without making any changes. While you learn how to use the System Editor in the next few sections, remember that you can use the same techniques with EPM.

You start the System Editor by opening the Productivity folder (located inside the OS/2 System folder) and clicking the System Editor icon. Figure 14.1 shows the System Editor's initial screen.

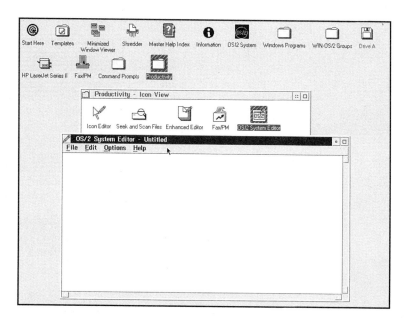

Fig. 14.1

The System Editor startup screen.

The editor window provides you with much information. The title bar displays the name of the file you are editing. In the figure, the name *Untitled* indicates that you have not yet named the file. Below the title bar is a menu bar from which you can pull down several menus. Later sections of this chapter discuss these menus in detail.

For Related Information

◄◄ "Examining Presentation Manager," p. 12.

◄◄ "Using the Workplace Shell," p. 218.

FROM HERE...

Mastering Basic Editing Techniques

After you type a memo, you may see an error that needs correction, or a sentence that you want to change. In this section, you learn how to use the text and mouse cursors to move directly to the text you want to alter and then make the alterations.

Practice makes perfect. To begin this section, therefore, you must type some erroneous text upon which you can practice the basic editing techniques by correcting the errors. You enter text simply by typing on the keyboard. Type the text shown in figure 14.2 now, pressing Enter at the end of each line. Include all the typing errors; you correct them in the following sections.

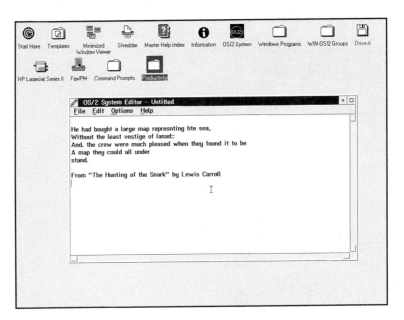

Fig. 14.2

A poem excerpt with typographical errors.

Understanding the Text Cursor

While you type, you see that a flashing vertical black line moves one space ahead of your typed characters. This line, the *text cursor*, indicates your current position in the file.

Text cursor movement is one of the most frequently performed operations you use when revising a file. The shortcut keystrokes in table 14.1 enable you to move the cursor quickly. These shortcuts are worth learning; they can make your work easier and more efficient.

As you might expect, the PgUp and PgDn keys move the cursor up or down a page. When you press and hold down the Ctrl key, Ctrl changes the meaning of any cursor-movement key you press. For example, Home moves the text cursor to the beginning of the current line, but Ctrl-Home moves the cursor to the beginning of the file.

Table 14.1 Keystrokes To Move the Cursor

Keystroke	Action
Left arrow	Left one letter
Ctrl-Left	Left one word
Right arrow	Right one letter
Ctrl-Right	Right one word
Up arrow	Up one line
Down arrow	Down one line
PgUp	Up one page
PgDn	Down one page
Home	Beginning of line
Ctrl-Home	Beginning of file
End	End of line
Ctrl-End	End of file

Understanding the Mouse Cursor

In Chapter 9, "Using Your Computer Screen as a Desktop," you used the mouse in conjunction with the scroll bars to scroll the screen forward or backward. You also can move around in the System Editor with the *mouse cursor*. In figure 14.2, the mouse cursor appears in the center of the screen. The mouse cursor looks like a fancy capital I. Move anywhere in the file and click once with mouse button 1, and the text cursor moves to that place. If you click beyond the end of a line, the text cursor moves only to the end of that line.

Many people find the mouse cursor easier to learn and use than the text cursor. With the keystrokes listed in table 14.1, however, you can move the text cursor without taking your hands away from the keyboard. You can experiment with both methods to see which you prefer.

Inserting or Replacing Text

Now that you have learned how to move the cursor, you are ready to learn how to manipulate the text. Move to the first line of the file and place the cursor after the letter *s* in *represnting*. Type an **e** to correct the spelling of the word.

The text editor inserts into the text the letter you typed. Letters to the right of the insertion shifted to make room. The editor is in Insert mode, the editor's default mode.

Now, press Ctrl-right arrow to move to the beginning of the next word. Press the Ins key once, then type **th** to correct the misspelling of *the*.

When you pressed Ins, you may have noticed that the text cursor grew larger. The text cursor enlarged because you put the editor in Replace mode. In this mode, each letter you type replaces the letter to the right. You can toggle back to Insert mode by pressing Ins again.

Deleting Text

Sometimes you need to remove a letter or phrase from a document. At the end of the second line of the sample text, for example, you need to remove the second *a* from the word *lanad*. Move the cursor to the left of the extra *a*, and press the Del key to delete the letter *a*. Now go to the end of the line and press Backspace to remove the extra colon.

Both the Del and Backspace keys delete one letter at a time. You must move the cursor to the letter you want to delete. The Del key deletes the letter to the right of the cursor. The Backspace key erases the letter to the left of the cursor. If you hold down either Backspace or Del, you continue to delete letters (the key action repeats until you release the key).

Joining, Splitting, and Inserting Lines

You may want to divide a line, or join two lines together. In the sample text, line four breaks in the middle of the word *understand*. To reconnect the two parts of the word, move the cursor to the end of *under* and press Del. You also can remove the break by moving the cursor to the beginning of the word *stand* and pressing Backspace.

To break a line in two, move the cursor to the place where you want to make the break, and press Enter. If you want to insert a blank line beneath the current line, move the cursor to the end of the current line and press Enter. You can insert a blank line above the current line by pressing Enter while the cursor is at the beginning of the current line.

For Related Information

◄◄ "Understanding CUA Principles," p. 216.

FROM HERE...

Learning Advanced Editing Techniques

In the last section, you learned the basic techniques of entering and revising text one letter at a time. In this section, you learn how to work with whole blocks of characters, such as paragraphs. You practice moving blocks of text within a file, and you learn how to search for words or phrases and replace them with others.

Understanding Blocks

When editing, you frequently need to move or alter whole sentences or paragraphs that span many lines. The System Editor has convenient commands to copy and paste blocks of text. The title of the poem in the sample text appears at the end of the poem selection. To move the poem's title to the beginning, follow these steps:

1. Move the cursor to the beginning of the line of text containing the poem's title.

2. Hold down Shift and press End to highlight the entire line.

3. Hold down Shift and press Del. The highlighted text disappears.

4. Move the cursor to the beginning of the first line of the sample text. Press Enter twice to insert two blank lines; then move the cursor back to the beginning of the first line.

5. Hold down Shift and press Ins. The title appears at the top of the window.

In this operation you marked and moved a block of text. The following sections discuss in detail each step of the operation you performed.

Marking a Block

Before you can delete, move, or copy a block of text, you must tell the System Editor what block you want to work with. You accomplish this task by *marking* the block. To mark a block of text, move the cursor to the beginning of the text you want to include in the block, hold down Shift, and move the cursor to the end of the text you want to include in the block. You can use any of the shortcut keys in table 14.1 to move the cursor. When you release the Shift key, the system highlights the block of marked text, as shown in figure 14.3. Note that you need not begin blocks at the beginning of a line.

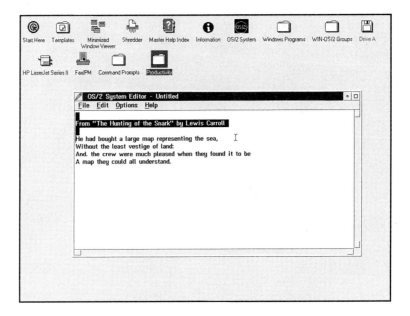

Fig. 14.3

Marking a block of text.

You can use the mouse to mark a block of text easily. Move the mouse cursor to the beginning of the text you want to mark. Hold down mouse button 1 and move the mouse cursor across the text you want to mark. The text highlights as you move the mouse across it. Release the button when you reach the end of the text you want to include in the marked block.

Clearing, Cutting, Pasting, and Copying Blocks

When you want to edit whole sections of text, marking a block is only the first step. With the keystrokes in the following list, you can remove or insert blocks in the editor, in a manner similar to cutting and pasting paper documents.

- *Cutting.* You press Shift-Del to remove a marked text block from the screen and into a temporary holding area called the *Clipboard*. You can insert the block elsewhere in the document by using the Paste command.

- *Copying.* You press Ctrl-Ins to copy a block of text to the Clipboard. Unlike Cutting, Copying does not delete the original block.

- *Pasting.* To paste a block of text from the Clipboard into a document, move the cursor where you want to insert the block, and press Shift-Ins. The block appears at the new location and the surrounding text moves down to make room. Pasting does not clear the Clipboard. You can press Ctrl-Ins repeatedly to insert multiple copies of the same text.

- *Clearing.* To erase a marked block of text, press the Del key. Note that a cleared block is gone forever. You cannot retrieve a cleared block.

Finding and Replacing

In some documents, you may use a single phrase repeatedly throughout the text, and later discover you want to change the phrase. Searching for and correcting each occurrence of a phrase can be a time consuming task, particularly in a long document. To make this task easier, you can use the OS/2 text editor's find-and-replace capabilities to locate and change every occurrence of the text you designate. The following sections discuss this operation in detail.

Finding Text

The FIND command has some fancy options, and this section explores them all. The following exercise, however, demonstrates the basic use of this command.

To use the FIND command to locate *vest* in our sample text, follow these steps:

1. Move to the top of the file, to search from the beginning to the end of the document.

2. Press Ctrl-F to pop up the Find menu.

3. Type **vest**. These letters then appear in the Find field.

4. Press Enter.

The System Editor finds and highlights the word. Your screen now resembles figure 14.4.

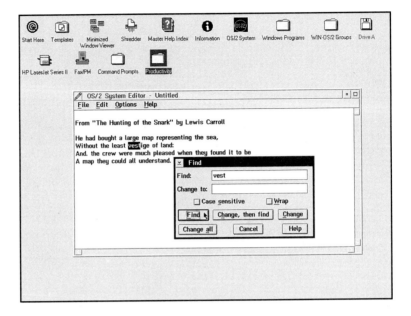

Fig. 14.4

Finding a string
of letters.

Note that the search was successful, even though it located the word *vestige*. The FIND command looks for strings of letters, not whole words.

Replacing One Text String with Another

One typing error remains in our sample text—the period after *And* at the beginning of the second line. You can practice using the Replace command by following these steps to correct the error:

1. Move to the top of the file to search the document from beginning to end.

2. Press Ctrl-F to pop up the Find menu.

3. Type **And.** in the Find field (be certain to include the period).

4. Press Tab to move to the Change To field, and type **And** without the period.

5. Click the Find button to search for the text, click the button labeled Change, and then click Find again.

Your screen now resembles figure 14.5. Note that the replacement is complete.

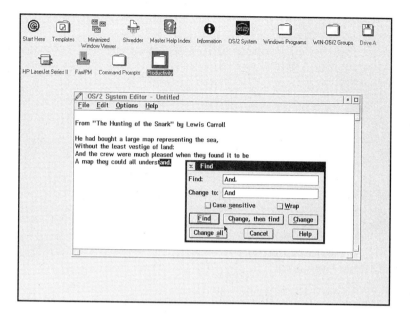

Fig. 14.5

Replacing a string
of letters.

If you look again at figure 14.5, you see that something interesting has happened. The editor has found another occurrence of *and.* at the end of the fourth line. You could change this occurrence, too, by pressing the Change button, and then the Find button again. In this occurrence, however, the period is correct and you need not change the word. Instead, you press Esc to clear away the Search screen.

With these operations under your belt, you are ready to study the items on the rest of the Find menu. You can customize these operations to make them work exactly the way you want.

Using Find Options

The Options section of the Find menu contains two buttons. The following paragraphs describe the function of each button.

■ *Case sensitive* tells the FIND command to distinguish between uppercase and lowercase characters in its search. If you turn case sensitivity off, FIND treats all letters the same. Case sensitive is the only option the editor activates by default.

■ *Wrap* tells the System Editor to search the whole file. In Wrap mode, the editor searches from the cursor to the end of the file, then wraps around and searches from the start of the file to the cursor.

Each of the six buttons at the bottom of the Find menu performs a different function. You can click them with the mouse. If you prefer to use the keyboard, move the cursor to your selection with the Tab and arrow keys, and then press Enter; or press Alt plus the letter underlined in your selection.

- *Find* locates the next occurrence of the string of letters you have typed in the Search field and draws a circle around the found text.

- *Change* locates the next occurrence of the text you typed in the Search field and replaces that text with the text you typed in the Replace field.

- *Change, then find* performs a Change operation, then finds and highlights the next occurrence of the text in the Find field. You can repeat this action to continue changing and finding the text. If you reach an occurrence of the text that you do not want to change, select the Find button to leave that occurrence unchanged and search for the next.

- *Change all* automates a Change operation. Use this option to tell the System Editor that you want to replace every occurrence of the text string you have supplied without confirming each one separately.

- *Cancel* makes the Search menu disappear. You can press the Esc key to accomplish the same action.

- *Help* brings up the help system. This action is similar to selecting Help on the Menu bar.

For Related Information

◄◄ "Introducing Presentation Manager," p. 221.

Understanding the System Editor Menus

You now know the techniques for entering and editing text and are ready to tackle the menus. In this section, you learn commands that enable you to load and save files and to customize many editor options. You also learn how to undo and redo the most recent change you have made—a useful tool if you have made a mistake.

The items on the Menu bar are called pull-down menus, because they hang from the bar when you access them. To go to the Menu bar, press and release the Alt key. Now press the first letter of the menu you want to use; for example, press F to pull down the File menu.

The status line tells you the function of the current menu option. If you want more information on a menu item, use the arrow keys to move to that item, then press F1. F1 is the Help key, and it activates a complete on-line help system. Chapter 12, "Learning the Commands You Use Most Often," and Chapter 13, "Using the Built-In Help Facility," explain how to use on-line help.

As you study the menus, you see shortcut keystrokes listed next to many items. You already used one of these shortcut keystrokes when you pressed Ctrl-F to activate the Find menu. Try learning the shortcuts for the commands you use most often. The shortcuts help you work more efficiently.

Working with the File Menu

The File menu enables you to load and save files. Pull down the menu (with Alt-F or the mouse) to see the choices offered by the File menu. You can move among the items with the up-arrow and down-arrow keys. The following sections discuss each item on the menu, after enabling you to experiment with a couple of the most useful operations.

Now that you have corrected all the typing errors in the sample file, you need to save your corrections. Using the down-arrow key, move to Save As... on the File menu. Press Enter, and the Save As... window pops up, as shown in figure 14.6.

The first field, Save as filename:, asks what you want to call the file. *Snark* seems an appropriate name, so type the name in the first field. You can skip the next field, Save file as type:, a field useful mostly to programmers. The Drive and Directory options enable you to put the file anywhere on any disk. For now, use the default, which is the root directory of the C: drive. The box labeled File shows the names of all files in the chosen directory. You could pick one of these, but avoid this option for now. This option replaces the highlighted file's contents with the poem in the editor. Now press Enter to save the file. The new name appears on the title bar.

Next, pull down the File menu again and move to Open.... This command loads a different file into the System Editor, where it replaces the file with which you previously were working. The three periods after Open indicate that this item offers you additional options. With Open... selected, you press Enter, then type the name of a new file, or pick one of the files listed.

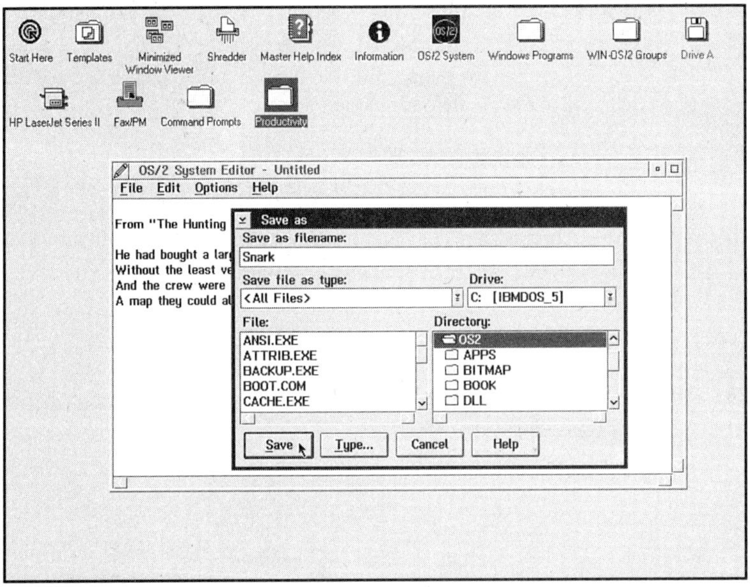

Fig. 14.6

The Save As...
menu.

Through the preceding exercises, you have learned to use some of the basic File functions. To better acquaint you with this versatile tool, the following list discusses each option on the File menu.

- *New* wipes out all the text in the current editor window, and gives you a blank screen to begin a new file. Before using this option, be certain that you really want to wipe out the text in the current window. You cannot get the original text back unless you have saved the file.

- *Open* loads a different file in the editor, where it replaces the file you were previously editing.

- *Save* writes the current file to disk. Save your files often—this operation is your best insurance against losing valuable data.

- *Save As* is a combination of Rename and Save, as you saw in the example in figure 14.6.

- *Autosave* automatically saves your file at set intervals. You protect your work by saving your files often. When you are working on a large document, however, you may not want to repeatedly interrupt your progress in order to perform frequent save operations. To avoid this problem, you can use the Autosave option to instruct the System Editor to handle the chore automatically. To take advantage of this valuable insurance, click the Autosave On button. The System Editor then saves the file after every 100 changes. You can change the save interval by clicking the arrows in the Number of Changes between Saves box.

Using the Edit Menu

The Edit menu has several options that you can use to activate the Mark, Cut, Copy, and Paste block commands you learned earlier. You may prefer using the keyboard shortcuts, however, rather than the Edit menu. The Edit menu also lists the Find command that you learned earlier.

The System Editor keeps track of the last change you made to a file so that you can undo a mistaken change if you catch the error quickly. This feature is very helpful if you accidentally delete something and want to get the original text back.

To undo your most recent change, select Undo from the Edit menu, or press Alt-Backspace. Try changing something now in the file you have loaded, then undoing your change. When you pull down the Edit menu again, a Redo option appears. Redo enables you to reverse the Undo operation.

The System Editor remembers only the last change you made (but forgets that change when you save the file). Later in this chapter, you learn that the Enhanced Editor has a more versatile Undo option. EPM enables you to undo or redo many changes, one at a time.

Using the Options Menu

In this section, you explore the three items on the Options menu. You learn how to select different fonts and colors, and how to use word wrap to make the System Editor work more like a word processing program.

Choosing Colors

Pick the Colors option from the Options menu, and a new window appears, as shown in figure 14.7. Move the text or mouse cursor up and down in the Foreground area to pick a text color. The text in the Color Sample box changes immediately, to show you how the new color scheme looks.

Now try picking a contrasting color from the Background box. You can move to this box with the Tab key, or just place the mouse cursor there and click a new color. Again, the Color Sample area displays your changes.

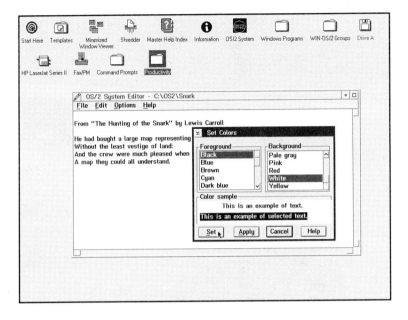

Fig. 14.7

The Set Colors
pop-up window.

When you are satisfied with your new color scheme, click the Set button. The System Editor saves these colors, and uses them the next time you start your computer. If you want to see how the new colors look in the editor before making your final decision, click the Apply button. Apply has an action similar to Set, but Apply leaves the Set Colors window open and doesn't change the colors permanently.

When you select colors, try to choose colors that are different enough for easy readability but don't contrast too sharply. Many people prefer light text on a dark background, but experiment to find the combination you like best.

Selecting a Font

When you choose the Font option from the Options menu, a new window appears (see fig. 14.8). The options in this window enable you to customize the typeface of the text you see in the System Editor window. The following paragraphs list and discuss these options in detail.

■ *Font* enables you to choose from a variety of type fonts. Some fonts are proportionally spaced, so that the letter *i* takes up less room than the letter *m*. The default System Proportional font is an example. Some fonts use equal spacing between letters. Some fonts have serifs, and others do not.

■ *Style* enables you to customize the font you have chosen. You can use this option to apply italics, for example, or boldface. Not all options are available with all fonts.

■ *Size* enables you to control the type size. The number in this box is the size in *points*, a measurement that printers use. Seventy-two points equal one inch. Some fonts are available in only one point size.

■ *Display* makes the System Editor use the font you pick to display text in the text edit window.

■ *Emphasis* presents options similar to Style. You can choose Outline, Underline, or Strikeout emphases. Some of these options are not available with every font.

The Sample box immediately reflects each of your choices. Click Apply to see how the editor screen looks with the font and options you have chosen. When you're satisfied with the results, click OK.

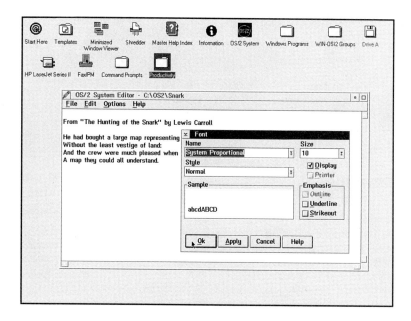

Fig. 14.8

The Font pop-up window.

Using Word Wrap To Reformat Paragraphs

The System Editor isn't a full-featured word processing program. If you leave Word Wrap enabled on the Options menu, however, you can type past the end of a line, and the editor continues the text on the next line, breaking between words. If you resize the editor window, the editor rearranges the text to fit the new window size.

If you use this feature, you might be surprised when you print a file. With the System Editor, word wrap applies only to the screen display, not to printed output. The following sections of this chapter discuss the Enhanced Editor, which handles word wrap more consistently on the screen and the printed page. Better word wrap is only one of EPM's many features.

FROM HERE...

For Related Information

◄◄ "Introducing Presentation Manager," p. 221.

Comparing the System Editor to the Enhanced Editor

The System Editor is handy for changing small files, and perhaps that's all you need. If you long for a more powerful tool, however, read on. EPM, the Enhanced Editor, is similar to the System Editor, but offers many more options. Although some of the menus are slightly different, EPM operates much like the System Editor, so you can be productive in EPM right away with the techniques you already have mastered.

The Enhanced Editor is similar to the System Editor, but EPM does a lot more. Like the System Editor, EPM works with pure text files, but EPM also gives you the following extra capabilities:

- You can edit several files at once, and copy text between them.

- EPM's Undo and Redo commands are much more powerful than those of the System Editor, as you learn in a later section. You can replay all the changes you make backward and forward—a very useful capability if you mistakenly delete an important block of text.

- A status line at the bottom of the EPM screen tells you at a glance the line and column where the text cursor is located, and indicates whether you are in insert or replace mode.

- EPM's message line gives a simple explanation of every menu option when you are exploring the menus.

■ You can customize the appearance of the EPM screen to fit your own preferences.

■ You can use various fonts and colors for different parts of your file.

Command names in the editors differ in two minor respects. The System Editor's Find command has a parallel in EPM's Search command, and the EPM Search shortcut key is Ctrl-S instead of Ctrl-F. When EPM finds text you have designated for a search, the editor highlights the found text by drawing a circle on the screen around the characters. Aside from the highlight, the commands work the same in the two editors. And EPM's Edit menu has a Delete option to remove a marked block of text. This EPM option works in the same manner as the System Editor's Clear option.

Starting the Enhanced Editor

You start the Enhanced Editor by opening the Productivity folder (inside the OS/2 System folder) and clicking the Enhanced Editor icon. Alternatively, you can type EPM at the command line in an OS/2 window to start the editor. Figure 14.9 shows the Enhanced Editor's initial screen.

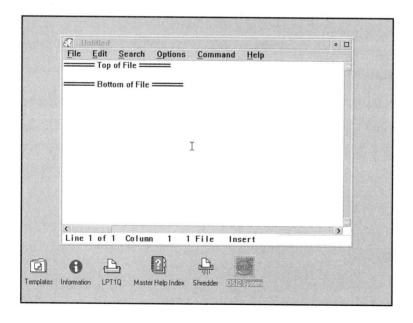

Fig. 14.9

The Enhanced Editor startup screen.

FROM HERE...

For Related Information

◄◄ "Using the Workplace Shell," p. 218.

Understanding the Enhanced Editor Menus

EPM's pull-down menus look very much like those of the System Editor you studied earlier in this chapter. In this section, you learn how EPM differs from the System Editor, and discover new commands to load and save files and to customize many editor options. You also explore EPM's great flexibility in undoing and redoing changes you make in your text.

The EPM status line tells you the function of the current menu option. As with the System Editor, you can get more information on a menu item by pressing F1.

Working with the File Menu

Pull down the EPM File menu, and you see some familiar options. Previously in this chapter, you mastered the New, Open, Save, and Save as... options. The menu also contains some new options, which you learn to use in this section of the chapter.

When you move the cursor to Open..., the status line message reads Open a file in a new window. That message tells you that you can edit more than one file at a time with EPM. The three periods at the end of this menu option name indicate that you can use additional options with the command.

After you select Open..., press Enter. You can type a new file name, or you can choose from the list of files you have recently edited, as shown in figure 14.10. Editing multiple files is handy, for example, when you want to Cut (or Copy) text from one window and Paste the text into another.

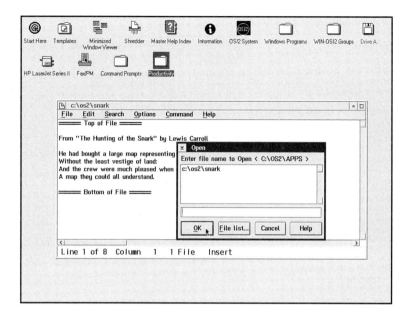

Fig. 14.10

The Enhanced Editor's Open window.

The following list describes the EPM File menu options. You used some of these options when you worked with the System Editor, but others are unique to the EPM editor.

- *New* wipes out all the text in the current editor window and gives you a blank screen to begin a new file. Use this option with care. You cannot retrieve information wiped out by this option unless you saved the file.

- *Open Untitled* opens a new, empty editor window. The new window overlaps the original one.

- *Open* creates a new editor window and loads a file.

- *Import Text File* inserts any file you name at the current cursor position of the file you are editing. You can use this option to combine files.

- *Rename* enables you to change the name of the current file.

- *Save* writes the current file to disk. Save your files often—this is your best insurance against losing valuable data.

- *Save As* acts as a combination of Rename and Save. You can use this option to save a file under a new name.

- *Save and Close* combines the functions of Save and Quit.

- *Quit* closes the current window. If this is the only open EPM window, Quit also closes the editor. If you have made changes since you last saved a file, Quit prompts you to save the file before the window closes.

- *Print File* enables you to print a copy of your file.

Using the Edit Menu

You are familiar with most of the functions on the Edit menu, such as Marking, Cutting, Copying, and Pasting blocks. In this section you learn to use the EPM Styles option. You also work with EPM's Undo feature, which is much more flexible than Undo in the System Editor.

Using Styles

Although EPM's style options are not as fancy as some word processing and desktop publishing programs, EPM does allow you to pick different fonts and type sizes. Figure 14.11 shows an example of EPM's versatility. In the figure, each line is set in a different style. This EPM option is similar to the System Editor's Font options, except that you can use many different Styles within an EPM file.

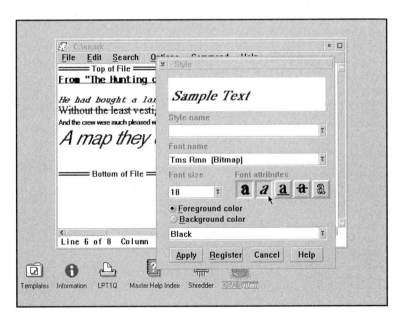

Fig. 14.11

Viewing different style selections.

To experiment with styles, mark a block of text—it need not be a whole line—and bring up the Styles screen. You then select a font, change the font's size, and choose one or more attributes, such as boldface or italic. The sample text at the top of the window immediately reflects every change you make. You can choose different colors for the text, the background, or both. When you are satisfied with the style, choose the Apply button to apply the change to the marked block.

Undoing Changes

Even if you are just skimming this chapter and something has yet to grab your interest, please read this section.

The Enhanced Editor keeps track of every change you make to a file, and enables you to undo each change in reverse order. After you undo changes, EPM enables you to redo them. This undo feature is very helpful if you accidentally delete something and want to get the text back.

When you choose Undo from the Edit menu, a slider bar appears on-screen. To undo your changes one by one, press the left-arrow key repeatedly. Use the right-arrow key to reapply each change in order. You also can drag the slider with the mouse. To accomplish this action, you move the mouse cursor to the slider, hold down mouse button 1, and move the slider back and forth.

Every change you make to a line is saved when you move the text cursor to a new line. If you type a word, for example, and then press Enter to move the text cursor to a new line, you can use Undo to remove the word you typed. Undo will not remove the letters in the word one by one, however.

You can use Undo only with changes you make in the current session. EPM does not save the change history with the file. If you modify and then save the file, you cannot undo the changes when you later reopen the file.

Using the Search Menu

When you need to search for or replace a string of text, use EPM's Search feature. Search works in a manner similar to the Find option on the System Editor's Edit menu. EPM includes enough additional features that Search deserves a separate menu.

T I P   The shortcut key for Search is Ctrl-S—not the Ctrl-F shortcut you learned for the System Editor.

The Options section of the Search menu contains five buttons. The following list describes the functions of these buttons:

- *Ignore case* directs the Search function to pay no attention to the distinction between upper- and lowercase letters. This option is the editor's default option, and perhaps its most useful setting. This option is similar in function to the System Editor's Case Sensitive option.

- *Marked area* confines the search to a marked block of text.

- *Reverse search* searches backward through the file. The default is a forward search.

- *Grep* is an advanced option that enables you to work with patterns of characters. Grep is powerful, but Grep can be subtle and tricky even for experts. The text box below gives more information about Grep. You can find complete details for using Grep in the Help system for EPM.

- *Change all occurrences* automates a Replace operation. Use this option to tell EPM that you want to replace each occurrence of the specified text string without confirming each one separately. This option is similar to the System Editor's Wrap option.

Using GREP

When you check the Grep option, EPM searches for patterns of characters. If you want to find every numeric digit in a file, for example, check the Grep option and type **[0123456789]** in the Search field. EPM finds any character you included in the set between square brackets. You get the same result if you type **[0-9]** in the Search field, because EPM understands that you mean all the digits from 0-9.

With the Grep option checked, you also can tell EPM to find all characters except the ones you specify, by typing ^ as the first character in the set. For example, **[^0-9 A-Za-z]** finds all characters that are neither digits, spaces, nor upper- or lowercase letters. This Search string finds all the punctuation marks and other less common characters in a file.

In a Grep expression, a period represents any single character. If you type **t.e** in the Search field, for example, EPM finds *the*, *tie*, and *little*. The search is unaffected by what single character comes between *t* and *e*. The search does not identify *true* as a match, because the word has two characters between the *t* and the *e*.

A potential problem exists in the preceding example, because *The*, with its capital *T*, does not match the search string. To fix that, you can type your search expression as **[Tt].e**. As you can see, Grep search expressions can be quite complicated. The great power Grep makes available to you, however, repays you for the time you spend mastering its uses.

Using the Options Menu

In this section, you explore the most useful items on the Options menu. You learn how to do the following:

- Customize margins, tab stops, colors, and fonts
- Use word wrap to structure paragraphs in the manner of a word processing program
- Edit several files in a single window
- Save files automatically
- Change the appearance of the editor

Using the Settings Notebook

As you learned in Chapter 9, "Using Your Computer Screen as a Desktop," you can flip through the pages of the settings notebook to select various options. To access these options, you choose Preferences from the Options menu, then select Settings. Figure 14.12 shows the settings notebook opened to the Margins page.

Each page of the settings notebook presents you with various choices. After you change options on one or more pages, press one of the following buttons at the bottom of the notebook page:

- *Set* saves the options you have selected as your personal default for all files.

■ *Apply* uses the selected options only on the current file. You clear the option settings when you quit the editor.

■ *Defaults* restores the original settings, clearing any you saved with Set.

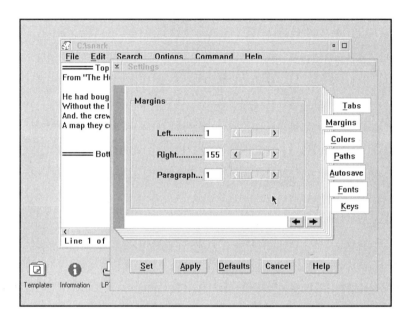

Fig. 14.12

The Margins page of the Enhanced Editor's settings notebook.

The following sections describe the settings notebook pages under the Enhanced Editor's Options menu.

Setting Tab Stops

Choose Tabs and type a single number in the input field on-screen to tell EPM how many spaces to insert when you press the Tab key. The default Tab setting is eight spaces. You can use Tab stops to create table columns. This technique works best with a monospaced font, where all characters are the same width. If you want to line things up in columns 10, 15, and 28, type those three numbers on-screen after choosing Tabs.

Setting Margins

On this page of the notebook you set the left and right margins for your file. The paragraph margin controls the number of spaces the editor indents the first line of each paragraph.

Unlike a word processing program, the Enhanced Editor formats in lines rather than paragraphs. If you use EPM to type memos, you need a way to reformat each paragraph to fit within the margins. The Alt-P keystroke performs the reformatting, based on the margins you set.

Choosing Colors and Fonts

The Colors tab and the Fonts tab resemble the Style option on the Edit menu (refer to fig. 14.12). The choices you make here apply to the entire document, not just a marked block of text. You can make the changes permanent with the Set button.

Saving Files Automatically

You protect your work best by saving your files often. The settings on the Autosave page enable you to instruct EPM to handle this chore automatically. By default, EPM saves a file after every 100 changes. This setting is generally satisfactory, but you can change the value according to your preferences. To turn off this feature, set the number to zero.

By default, EPM stores autosave files in the current directory. The settings on the Paths page enable you to place autosave files somewhere else. Don't store files on a temporary disk, however, or you could lose your work if the power goes off.

Redefining Keystrokes

With the options on this notebook tab, you can redefine several keystrokes to perform different actions. The Enter key on the numeric keypad, for example, normally adds a new line after the cursor. You can redefine the Enter keystroke to move the cursor to the beginning of the next line.

Editing Several Files in a Single Window

As you learned when exploring the File menu, the Enhanced Editor can edit several files at once and display the files in separate windows. You may discover that viewing files side by side is convenient, but the desktop gets cluttered if you have four or five files open at the same time. EPM answers this problem by allowing you to edit several files in one window.

To see how this works, pick Ring Enabled from the Options Preferences menu. Two *rotate buttons* appear near the right end of the title bar. The rotate buttons look like two circles, one with an arrow pointing clockwise and the other with a counterclockwise pointing arrow. You can arrange several files in a ring pattern and move around the ring with these buttons.

Now pull down the File menu, and you notice a new option, *Add File*. This option enables you to add a new file to the ring. Use the Quit option to remove a file from the ring. If you want to see what files are in the ring, pick *List Ring*, a new choice that appears on the Options menu when you edit a ring of files. Figure 14.13 shows the List Ring dialog box. List Ring shows the names of the files you are editing and enables you to move to any one without using the mouse. Use the up- and down-arrow keys to move to the file you want, and then press Enter.

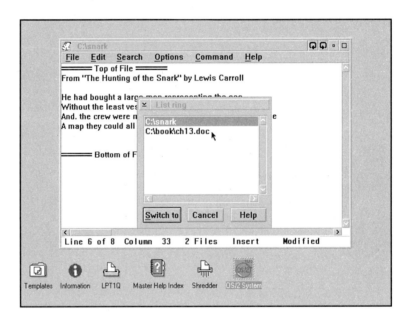

Fig. 14.13

The List Ring
dialog box.

Changing the Window Display with Frame Controls

The frame surrounding EPM's main window provides useful information, such as telling you in which line and column the text cursor is located. The frame provides scroll bars so that you can move through the file with the mouse. You can customize the frame's appearance to suit your preferences. Select Frame Controls from the Options menu. This choice brings up a menu with six items that you can turn on or off. The following list describes the six optional Frame Control features.

- The *status line* at the bottom of the screen displays the current row and column numbers. The status line also indicates whether you are in Insert or Replace mode and whether you have modified the current file since you last saved your changes. In most situations, leave the status line turned on.

- The *message line* is the area at the bottom of the screen where EPM gives you information, such as describing the action of a menu. If you turn the message line off, the messages appear on the status line.

- You can turn the *scroll bars* off, and may want to do so if you are using the keyboard instead of the mouse.

- *Rotate buttons* enable you to move around a ring of files.

- *Info at top* puts the status and message lines at the top of the window. Most people prefer that the messages appear at the bottom of the window, but you can choose the location you like.

- *Prompting* refers to the messages you see when you move around the menus. This item is helpful to you, particularly while you learn to use the editor.

Reviewing Messages from the Editor

EPM gives you useful information on the message line, but old messages disappear to make room for new ones. You can see a list of all the messages you have received from EPM. To produce this list, pick the Messages item on the Options menu.

Saving Options

After you set the options you like best, you can preserve them so that they take effect whenever you load EPM. To save the options, select Save Options from the Options menu.

Using Other Menu Options

The Enhanced Editor has some additional capabilities that may interest programmers only. If you want to learn about these exotic options, explore the Help facility, as discussed in Chapter 12, "Learning the Commands You Use Most Often."

Editing Files without Typing Their Names

This section gives you one last tip to make your work easier. When you double-click a data file's icon, the file is automatically loaded into the System Editor. If you prefer to use the Enhanced Editor, you can drop the file icon onto EPM instead. You can accomplish this switch using the drag-and-drop techniques you learned in Chapter 10, "Managing the Workplace Shell."

For Related Information

◀◀ "Introducing Presentation Manager," p. 221.

Chapter Summary

In this chapter, you learned how to use the System Editor and its more powerful cousin, the Enhanced Editor. With these versatile tools, you can examine the files on your computer and create new ones. You learned how to use the text editors' powerful features to make your work easier.

After you create a file, you may want to print it. In the next chapter, you learn the techniques for printing with OS/2 2.1.

Printing with OS/2

B efore the advent of OS/2, your applications dealt with the printer without asking for much help from DOS. DOS provided a device name for the printer (LPT1, LPT2, or LPT3) and offered a PRINT command. DOS did not deal with such printing issues and application options as font selection, page orientation, and two-sided printing.

Microsoft Windows was a great step forward toward device-independent printing. Print Manager inside Windows acts as a waiting room (a queue) for your printouts, until your printer is ready to print them. Control Panel enables you to configure your printer for page orientation, fonts, and other characteristics. With Windows, your applications no longer have to provide their own interface for setting up and configuring your printer.

OS/2 includes a spooler (described later in this chapter) and a print manager for printouts you request in DOS and OS/2 sessions. Because Windows is a part of OS/2, OS/2 includes Windows' Print Manager for printouts you request in Windows sessions. Instead of remembering how to tell your application to change printer features, you now use OS/2's printer-awareness to control the appearance of your documents, reports, memos, and other printouts.

OS/2, like Windows, gives you more control over your printer and better enables your applications to make use of your printer's features. OS/2 can print multiple applications at the same time. OS/2 prints as easily to a network printer as it does to a local printer. Further, OS/2 understands fonts, page orientation, two-sided printing, and other printer features.

You may find that you rarely need to refer to the printer or spooler icons on your desktop to make settings changes. You may rarely open the printer icon's Icon View or Details View to see your printouts in the output queue. The information in this chapter prepares you for what you see when you do open these icons and teaches you how to gain maximum benefit from the OS/2 printing facility.

You start this chapter by learning the basics of printing with OS/2. You learn how OS/2 keeps your printouts separate when you use OS/2's multitasking feature to tell multiple applications to send printouts to the printer. You come to understand the role of the spooler. You explore the different printer features that OS/2 helps you manage and set. You may come to view your printer as just another object on your OS/2 desktop, as you learn about print jobs, print queues, and print job properties.

Your exploration of OS/2 printing leads you next to printer fonts. You cover font basics—what it means to download a font, what a font cartridge contains, and how to work with font metrics. You learn about the OS/2 system fonts and the Adobe Type Manager fonts, and you discover how to install soft fonts for your printer.

You can print from your applications or directly from the Workplace Shell. You learn in this chapter how to send files to your printer by using your mouse, either on your desktop or within your OS/2 applications.

This chapter explains what you see in the printer icon's list of print jobs, both in the Icon View and the Details View. You learn how to change the status of a print job. You find out how to set up multiple printer objects to represent different forms and multiple printers. Further, you learn how to send your printouts to a file instead of directly to the printer.

> **NOTE** If during OS/2 installation you did not enter information about your printer, you do not have what is called a *printer object* on your desktop. You must have a printer object before going further in this chapter. You can find step-by-step instructions for creating an initial printer object in Chapter 7, "Modifying Your OS/2 Configuration."

Learning OS/2 Printer Basics

In the next few sections, you become acquainted with printer basics in an OS/2 environment. When you have started one printout from an application, you need not wait for the printer to finish before you continue your work. This capability is the biggest advantage to printing with OS/2 rather than printing with DOS. OS/2 also enables you to use the special features of your printer—landscape or portrait printing, fonts, and duplex printing.

Each time you request a printout, you create a print job. OS/2 enables you to manage these print jobs individually. You use the printer icon on your desktop to see the list of print jobs. The printer icon is the object on your desktop that represents your printer. The *Spooler* is the OS/2 desktop object that holds your printouts until the printer is ready to receive them.

Using Multiple Applications with One Printer

When you tell one of your applications to print something, OS/2 accepts the print material on behalf of the printer. OS/2 begins printing the data in the background. As a result, your application "frees up" even before the printout finishes, and you can continue working in the application. If you need to print two reports or documents from two applications in a hurry, you can switch to the second application and tell it to print, even while the first application is still giving print material to OS/2. Both applications can send printouts through OS/2 to the printer, and OS/2 keeps them separate.

Understanding Printer Differences

Some years ago, dot-matrix printers could print characters in two or three sizes and produce rather coarse-looking graphics output. Dot-matrix printers are faster now, and they can print a greater variety of character sizes. Some dot-matrix printers can display italics and other special effects on the printed page.

Laser printers, which are generally faster and more expensive than dot-matrix printers, offer better-looking characters, more character shapes and sizes, the capability to accept different paper stock from separate trays, duplex (two-sided) print, and higher-resolution (300 dots per inch) graphics. You can add extra character shapes and sizes (fonts) to most laser printers in the form of *downloadable character sets* or *font cartridges*. You learn more about these special printer features later in this chapter.

In Chapter 4, "Deciding How You Want To Use OS/2," you learned that printers accept commands that don't show up on the printed page. These commands—which vary widely among different printers—tell the printer how to handle subsequent character data.

OS/2 supplies printer driver software modules for the following general categories of printers:

- IBM/Epson-compatible dot-matrix printers
- PCL printers (Hewlett-Packard LaserJet and DeskJet)
- PostScript printers
- IBM laser printers

In addition, OS/2 supplies a generic printer driver that doesn't include printer command functions. This driver supports other printers.

In each case, the printer driver software presents a common, generic interface to your OS/2 and Windows application software. You need not configure each of your OS/2 and Windows applications to use your printer's special features. You tell the OS/2 Print Manager and the Windows Print Manager what kind of printer you have. When your Windows and Presentation Manager applications print, OS/2 handles the details of fonts, page orientation, duplexing, and other printer capabilities. If your printer doesn't support a particular capability, such as duplex print, your applications cannot take advantage of that capability.

You may have one or more DOS applications that don't use the OS/2 print driver interface. Such applications ask you what sort of printer you have and provide their own non-PM support for your printer's features. When you use these applications, follow the application software's instructions for printing. Configure the application's print environment as though you are using plain DOS rather than OS/2.

Seeing the Printer as an OS/2 Object

When you choose a printer during OS/2 installation, or if you add a printer to your computer system, your printer selection becomes an icon on your desktop. OS/2 labels the icon with the make and model of your printer or with the generic label "Printer." This printer icon is an OS/2 object that, like the other objects on your desktop, has a settings notebook and other object-like characteristics.

The printer object (icon) is OS/2's desktop representation of your printer. When you want to manage your printer's features and configuration, you manipulate the printer object. You can create and set up more than one printer object on your desktop. A second printer object may represent a second printer, or it can represent a different configuration of the same printer. A later section of this chapter explains creating multiple printer objects.

One of the settings for the printer object is the *printer driver*. The printer driver understands the features and capabilities of your printer. You can use the printer driver's *job properties* settings to tailor the default appearance of your printouts. If you want OS/2 to prompt you for specific job property settings for each printout, you can check the box marked Prompt for Job Properties on the Queue Options settings page. Each printer object has its own *queue driver* as well as a setting that indicates which printer port (usually LPT1, LPT2, or LPT3) the printer object uses. Figure 15.1 shows the Queue Options page of the printer object's settings notebook.

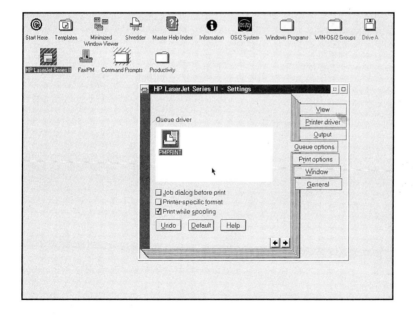

Fig. 15.1

The Queue Options page in the settings notebook for the printer object.

The settings notebook for the printer object includes pages labeled View, Printer Driver, Output, Queue Options, Print Options, and General. The following list describes how to use these pages:

- You can change the name of the printer object on the View page.

- The Printer Driver page enables you to specify the printer driver name and properties. Figure 15.2 shows a typical Printer Driver settings notebook page.

- You indicate the printer port on the Output page, as shown in figure 15.3.

- On the Print Options page, as shown in figure 15.4, you can tell OS/2 to defer the printing operation until a time of day you specify. The Print Options page also enables you to enter the name of a file that OS/2 is to print before each print job. OS/2 prints this file on *job separator pages* between each of your printouts.

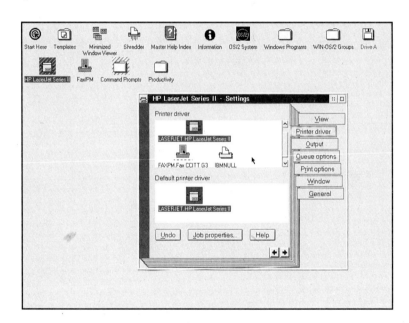

Fig. 15.2

The Printer Driver page in the settings notebook for the printer object.

Working with the Spooler and Queue Driver

When you send data to the printer, OS/2 sometimes has to convert the data file to a form the printer can accept. OS/2 also must hold the print data in a queue until the printer is ready to receive it. Print jobs can come from multiple applications, PRINT commands, and other printer operations you initiate.

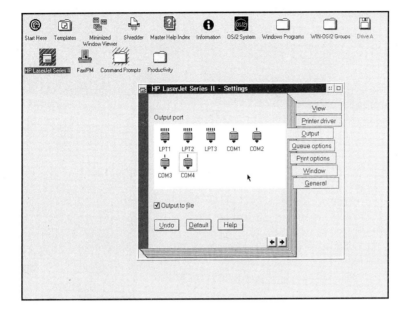

Fig. 15.3

The Output page in the settings notebook for the printer object.

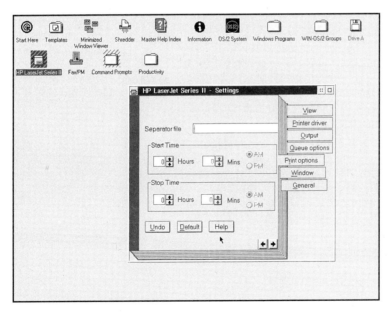

Fig. 15.4

The Print Options page in the settings notebook for the printer object.

The Queue driver individually tracks each print job and sends the jobs, one by one, to the Spooler object. The Spooler object holds the print data until the printer is ready to accept it. The Spooler object receives print jobs from each of your Queue drivers. By default, the OS/2 Spooler object is in the System Setup folder.

The OS/2 Spooler object holds the material waiting to be printed in the *spool directory*. The installation process created this directory, named C:\SPOOL. You can change your spool path on the settings notebook page for the Spooler object. You also can disable the Spooler with a menu option on the Spooler's pop-up menu. If you disable the Spooler, you must be careful not to send two print jobs to the printer at the same time. You may find that the printed pages contain a confusing mixture of interspersed data from both print jobs.

Creating Print Jobs

Each printout you request, whether from an application, a PRINT command, or other print operation, is a print job. You can see a list of print jobs by double-clicking the printer object. The list shows each print job's associated properties. You may want to change some print job properties before printing starts. You can see in the list the size of the print job and when the job was submitted.

Viewing Your Print Jobs

The list of print jobs for a printer object represents the printer's output queue. To see this list, open the printer object (by default, the installation process leaves the printer object on your desktop). You can specify on the printer object's settings notebook whether you want to see an Icon View or a Details View of the print job list. Figure 15.5 is an example of the Icon View of a job list. Figure 15.6 shows the Details View of the same list.

The job list changes dynamically as the printer finishes each print job. You can change the frequency with which OS/2 updates the on-screen list of print jobs. To make this change, use the Refresh Interval field of the View page of the printer object. You also can use the Refresh menu option to cause OS/2 to update the list immediately.

Changing Print Job Status

The pop-up menu for the printer object contains options for changing the status of the printer driver. You can set the status to *Hold* (to hold print jobs without printing them) or *Release* (to release previously held print jobs). When you use the printer object's pop-up menu to hold or release print jobs, your action affects all print jobs in that print queue. You can use this technique to release print jobs you previously held, or hold print jobs that haven't yet printed. You also can use the printer object's pop-up menu to switch to a different default printer if you have more than one printer object defined.

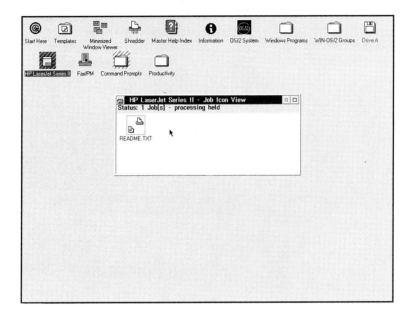

Fig. 15.5

The Icon View for print jobs that are waiting print.

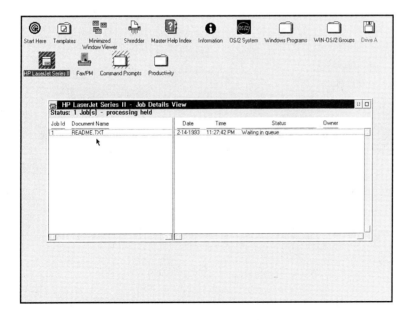

Fig. 15.6

The Details View for the print jobs in the queue.

The individual print job icons have pop-up menus, too. Before a print job begins printing, you can use the job's pop-up menu to change its print job properties. You can specify a new *job position*, to make the printout appear before or after other print jobs. You can tell OS/2 to print a different number of copies of the job. You can give the print job a different priority, and you can change the *form name* on which OS/2 is to print the job. If you specify a different form name from the default for that printer object's properties, OS/2 prompts you to change the paper in the printer when it is ready to print that job.

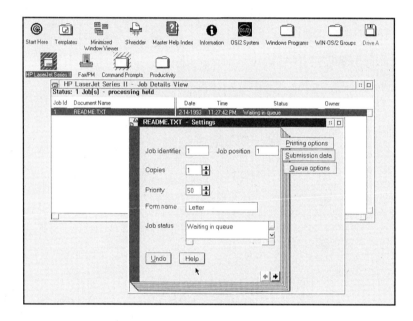

Fig. 15.7

The Print Options settings notebook page for a particular print job.

For Related Information

◀◀ "Understanding How OS/2 Expands upon DOS," p. 62.

FROM HERE...

Learning about Fonts

During the OS/2 installation process, you indicated which of the optional fonts you wanted to install. The fonts you chose control the appearance of the screen and the appearance of the printouts you produce. In the next few sections, you learn more about the fonts on your computer system. You start with the basics and then move up to important details about OS/2 system fonts and Adobe Type 1 fonts. You discover how to install new soft fonts and how to tell OS/2 that you have a font cartridge in your printer.

Understanding Font Basics

A font is a set of characters that have a particular size and shape. Each font has a name, usually supplied by the font's designer. To represent a font on-screen and on your printouts, the computer must know how each character is shaped, and it must know the font's spacing, pitch, height, style, stroke weight, symbol set, and typeface. These characteristics of a font are, collectively, its *font metrics*.

You're looking at an example of a font right now. This book uses Garamond, a pleasant, easy-to-read font that doesn't intrude on your efforts to understand the information contained in the text.

The *spacing* characteristic determines the size of the distance between the font's letters and numbers. *Pitch* expresses the number of characters that occur per horizontal inch for a font that has equidistant (fixed) spacing. Pitch does not apply to proportionally spaced fonts, because the spacing varies in these fonts on a character-by-character basis. A font's *height* is specified in *points*, and each point is 1/72 of an inch.

Style denotes the angularity of the font's characters; popular styles are upright and *italic*. *Stroke weight* describes the thickness of the lines that make up the characters. You sometimes see a **bold** stroke weight, but most characters appear with a medium stroke weight.

A font's *symbol set* reveals the font's intended purpose. The symbols may be ordinary letters and numbers, or the symbols may be specific to a particular kind of work. Lawyers, engineers, and mathematicians use special symbol sets.

A font's *typeface* identifies its design and corresponds to the name of the font. A group of fonts that have similar characteristics make up a *font family*. Font designs are either *serif*, with characters having curved, adorned shapes, or *sans serif*, with straight characters having little or no adornment.

The fonts that come with OS/2 are *soft fonts*. Soft fonts come on a floppy disk and must be downloaded into the printer. OS/2 Presentation Manager takes care of this task automatically when you print from a PM application. The Windows Print Manager performs the same job if you use a Windows application. DOS applications, however, must use their own printer management methods to download fonts as necessary.

Using OS/2 System Fonts

You received four IBM Core Fonts with your OS/2 operating system. These fonts are Courier, Helvetica, System Monospace, and Times Roman. The installation process copied the appropriate files to your hard disk automatically. The IBM Core Fonts are *bit-map* fonts, which means that each character is a simple matrix of dots.

NOTE   IBM Core Fonts can be used by PostScript printers.

OS/2 cannot arbitrarily scale (resize) or reshape bit-map fonts. A bit-map font can only be enlarged by multiplying it by a whole number scaling factor. At larger sizes, bit-map fonts look coarse, because the software is only doubling or tripling the matrix of dots. Type 1 fonts, on the other hand, can be easily scaled and reshaped. The next section discusses Type 1 fonts.

Working with Adobe Type Manager Fonts

In addition to the four IBM Core Fonts, OS/2 gives you 13 Adobe Type 1 fonts. Adobe Systems is a company well known for its font technology. Adobe created what it calls *Type 1* fonts to be easily scaled and managed by computer software. A Type 1 font file contains directions and shape information that computer programs can use to render that font, either on-screen or on your laser printer.

Adobe Type Manager (ATM) is built into OS/2. ATM is a font manager software module that does the job of managing, scaling, and rendering Type 1 fonts. Because each character exists in the Type 1 font file as a series of directions that tell how to draw that character, ATM can scale the character in an arbitrary fashion. Each character in the font retains its good resolution and quality when enlarged.

The following list shows the names of the 13 Adobe Type 1 fonts you received with OS/2. These fonts work with Hewlett-Packard laser printers (which use PCL, *Printer Command Language*) and with PostScript printers. PostScript is a page description language developed by Adobe.

- Times New Roman
- Times New Roman Bold
- Times New Roman Bold Italic

- Times New Roman Italic
- Helvetica
- Helvetica Bold
- Helvetica Bold Italic
- Helvetica Italic
- Courier
- Courier Bold
- Courier Bold Italic
- Courier Italic
- Symbol

Installing Soft Fonts and Font Cartridges

Adobe Systems and other companies that specialize in computer font technology offer thousands of fonts. You can add new fonts to your computer system by purchasing and installing extra Type 1 fonts (contact IBM or Adobe for more information on what fonts you can add to your system). You also may be able to install a font cartridge in your printer, if your printer supports this option.

To install soft fonts, and to tell OS/2 about a font cartridge you have installed in your printer, open the settings notebook for the appropriate printer object. Select the Printer Driver notebook page. Next, open the settings notebook for the default printer driver object.

To tell OS/2 about a font cartridge you have purchased, select the appropriate font names (up to two) in the list box of available choices.

To install soft fonts for a Hewlett-Packard or a PostScript laser printer, select the Fonts option. For an IBM laser printer, select the Download Fonts option. OS/2 displays the Font Installer window. Insert your disk of new fonts and click the Open button to display a list of fonts. From the list box, select (highlight) the fonts you want to install and click the Add>> button.

NOTE Type 1 fonts come in pairs of disk files. One file has an AFM extension and the other has a PFB extension. The Font Installer window must have both files available to it at the same time, to install a given font. If you received more than one disk containing your new fonts, create a temporary directory, copy all the disk files to the temporary directory, and install the new fonts from the temporary directory.

To delete fonts from your system, follow the preceding directions but click the Delete button after you have selected the fonts you want to remove.

You can change your default fonts with the Font Palette (located in the Setup folder inside the OS/2 System folder). The Font Palette contains font samples and an Edit Font option. You can add or delete fonts in the Font Palette window by selecting (highlighting) a font, checking the Edit Font option, and using the Add or Delete buttons to indicate the operation you want to perform. Chapter 7, "Modifying Your OS/2 Configuration," contains more information on using the Font Palette.

For Related Information

◀◀ "Understanding Hardware and Software," p. 13.

FROM HERE...

Printing with OS/2

The preceding sections of this chapter introduced you to the way OS/2 and your printer work together to make your printouts look their best. At this point, however, you have yet to print anything. This chapter now turns to the different ways you can send your printouts to the printer.

You can print with OS/2 by the following methods:

- You can drag and drop a data file object onto a printer object.
- You can use the PRINT or COPY commands at an OS/2 command line prompt.
- You can instruct your application program to print.
- You can use the Print Screen key on the keyboard.

The following sections cover these OS/2 printing techniques.

Using Drag and Drop

The printer object understands that it is to print a file that you drop on it. Remember, however, to drop only text files or other printable files on the printer object. The printer object uses its default print job properties to send your printout through the queue to the printer.

Sending the Print and Copy Commands

If you want to send a text file to the printer and you are currently looking at an OS/2 command line prompt, you can use the PRINT command. Part VI of this book provides details of the PRINT command. Generally, however, you type the PRINT command as shown in the following example:

PRINT MEMO.DOC

If you prefer a command line interface over OS/2's drag-and-drop mechanism, you can use a simple COPY command, as shown in the following example, to print a text file:

COPY MYFILE.TXT LPT1

Printing from an Application

OS/2 is a multifaceted environment. You can send printouts to the printer from your Presentation Manager, Windows, or DOS applications. You can print from two or more applications at the same time. OS/2 turns each printout into a separate print job and queues each print job for printing.

Printing with PM Applications

Most PM applications have at least two printer-related menu options on the File item's drop-down menu. The Print menu item brings up a dialog box in which you can specify details about what you want to print. The application's Print dialog box enables you select which parts of the document you want to print, and enables you to change other application-related print options. In most applications, the dialog box tells you the name of the printer object it is to use for printing.

The other drop-down menu item, Printer Setup, enables you to choose a printer object. You click the Setup button to see the Printer Properties window. In this window, you can specify such things as which paper tray to use and which font cartridge is active. You also can manage your fonts, forms, and printer device defaults in the Printer Properties window, just as you can in the settings notebook pages for the printer object.

Printing with Windows Applications

You notice little or no change in the way your Windows applications print under OS/2's WIN-OS2 environment, as compared to printing with Microsoft Windows under DOS. The Print Manager controls your printouts (and you control the Print Manager). When you print from a Windows application, OS/2 routes your printouts through a printer object. Windows' Print Manager is closely tied to the OS/2 desktop's printer objects.

Windows' Print Manager enables you to pause or resume a printout. Its window shows you a list of Windows print jobs currently waiting to print. You can use the Options menu item to set the priority of your print jobs. Another setting on this menu enables you to determine how Print Manager signals you when the printer has a problem or is offline. The View menu item enables you to specify what information about each print job you want to see (Time/Date Sent and Print File Size). You also can use Windows' Print Manager to print jobs from the queue.

If you previously installed Windows on your computer, the OS/2 installation process migrated your Windows printer setup to your new Windows-under-OS/2 environment. If you installed OS/2's Windows support on a machine that did not already have Windows (when there was nothing to migrate), you must tell Windows about your printer. You find Control Panel in the Main window. Double-click Control Panel and then the Printers icon to see the Printer Setup window. In this window, you can choose a default printer, you can configure Windows to use that printer to your specifications (click the Configure button), and you can toggle Print Manager on or off.

 NOTE   Toggling Print Manager off may result in intermixed printouts if you print from more than one Windows application at the same time.

You see the Printer Configuration window when you click the Configure button on the Printer Setup window. To configure Windows for your particular printer, choose a printer port (the one labeled LPT1.OS2 is an alias, or synonym, for the OS/2 printer object connected to the LPT1 printer port) and click the Setup button. For now, you can leave the Device Not Selected and Transmission Retry fields set to their default values.

The Windows Printer Setup window behaves like the OS/2 desktop's Printer Properties window. You use both windows in the same way to specify your printer's features.

Printing with DOS Applications

As this chapter mentioned earlier, non-PM, non-Windows applications have their own methods of enabling you to specify printer options and of downloading fonts and printer commands to the printer. DOS applications do not use Presentation Manager to format and prepare their printouts. When you tell a DOS-based computer program to print something, that application manages the final appearance of the printed output completely without PM's help. The printout does appear, however, as a print job that you can view with the printer object's Icon View or Details View window.

Handling Printer Errors

Any mechanical process is subject to occasional errors, and this rule holds true for computer printing operations. When OS/2 sends spooled output to the printer, for example, the printer may run out of paper or develop a paper jam. OS/2 notifies you of printer errors with a screen similar to the screen in figure 15.8. After you fix the problem with the printer (consult the printer's reference manual as necessary), you can click Retry to tell OS/2 to resume the print job. Alternatively, you can click Abort to end that print job, or Ignore. The Ignore option probably will result in part of the printout not appearing.

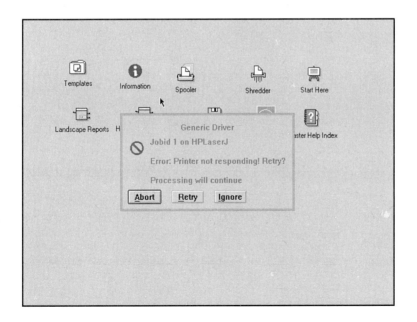

Fig. 15.8

An OS/2 pop-up window notifies you of printer errors.

Using Multiple Printer Objects

You can use multiple printer objects in a variety of ways. Each printer object can represent a different printer, or different default configuration settings for the same printer. You can use a second printer object for landscape printing, for example, if your printer supports this feature. When you drop a text file object on the printer object configured for landscape printing, your printout appears across the page instead of down the page.

To create a second printer object, open your Templates folder. Drag the Printer template onto an empty place on your desktop. When the Create Another Printer window appears, give the new printer object a unique name and choose a printer port. You also can select a different printer driver in this window. OS/2 may prompt you to insert a Printer Driver Disk after you click the Create Another button.

If you want to change the printer driver for a printer object, insert Printer Driver Disk 1 in drive A and select Drive A: on the desktop. A printer driver folder appears, from which you select the make and model of the printer driver you want to install. Drag and drop that printer driver icon onto your printer object.

If you are unsure which printer driver to select for your particular make and model of printer, you can double-click the data file object labeled PRDESC.LST. You then see a list of printer models and their associated printer drivers. You can use the Help menu item on the pop-up menu for the printer object and its printer driver to get information about the specific features that the driver supports.

To make changes to the settings notebook (including job properties) for your printer object, click mouse button 2 on the printer object, open the object's settings, and modify the items on the notebook pages. The job properties settings appear on the notebook page labeled Printer driver.

Printing to a File

You can set up a printer object to produce a disk file containing your printouts instead of sending the printouts to a printer. You can use this operation if your computer is not connected to a printer, and you have to perform print operations on another computer that is connected to a printer. (This approach assumes that your computer is not part of a local area network with a shared LAN printer.) You begin this task on your computer by creating a printer object with a printer driver matching the characteristics of the printer that is attached to the other computer. In the printer object settings notebook, check the Output to File box.

Each time you print to a file, OS/2 asks for the name of a file to use in place of an actual printer. You can specify a drive letter and path to send the printout to a directory of your choosing. When you are ready to produce a printout of the file, copy the file to a disk and take the disk to the other computer. On the other computer, you can drag and drop the disk file onto a printer object, or you can copy the file to the appropriate printer port (LPT1, for example).

For Related Information

◄◄ "Understanding How OS/2 Expands upon DOS," p. 62.

◄◄ "Using the Workplace Shell," p. 218.

◄◄ "Introducing Presentation Manager," p. 221.

◄◄ "Learning the Commands for Viewing and Printing Files," p. 318.

FROM HERE...

Chapter Summary

In this chapter, you learned how OS/2 helps you make your printouts look their best. After surveying the basics of printing with OS/2, you learned how to configure OS/2's print-related options. The chapter presented information on printer objects, print jobs, and print job properties. After coming up to speed on fonts, you learned about the OS/2 system fonts, Adobe Type 1 fonts, and font cartridges.

You have explored various methods of printing with OS/2—from the command line, with a drag-and-drop action, or from within your applications. In this chapter, you saw how OS/2 notifies you of printer problems. You also learned how to look at the entries in the awaiting-print queue and how to manage those entries. You know how to set up multiple printer objects and how to use multiple printer objects to send printouts to a file rather than to a printer.

In Chapter 16, you learn more about working with DOS and Windows under OS/2.

Running DOS and Windows under OS/2

M any high-quality OS/2 applications are available, and more are being written each day. Still, tens of thousands of DOS applications exist, and you don't want to turn your back on them. Fortunately, you can run almost any DOS or Windows program under OS/2. In fact, if you have enough memory (or disk space), you can run up to 240 different DOS programs at one time. OS/2 runs DOS and Windows programs better than real DOS or Windows. Consider the following, for example:

- OS/2 can run several programs simultaneously. You can type a letter or memo in Word for Windows, recalculate a DOS spreadsheet in another window, and download a bulletin board file in the background with an OS/2 terminal program.

- If a DOS or Windows program crashes, you just close its session. No harm comes to the other programs you're running at the same time. You don't need to reboot the computer when one program goes astray, as is so often necessary with real DOS or Windows.

- DOS programs may actually run faster under OS/2 because OS/2 does a better job of managing disk files.

- OS/2 can make more total memory available to your DOS programs than you have actually installed in your computer. When OS/2 runs out of memory, it uses free disk space instead.

- Today's most powerful DOS applications use clever tricks to bypass the memory limitations of DOS. Configuring these applications properly can be a tough challenge. OS/2 configures these applications for you.

- Windows 3.1 is included. You do not have to buy it separately. In addition, Windows applications run on the Workplace Shell desktop, enabling you to get the advantages of the new user interface.

- Even if you find a DOS program that doesn't run well under OS/2, you can easily load your old copy of DOS.

This chapter is arranged so that you master one concept at a time and build on what you have learned. After a quick overview of DOS sessions, you see how to get to DOS's usual interface, the command line prompt. You then learn how to incorporate the advantages of the Workplace Shell interface by setting up your DOS and Windows applications on the desktop. Next, you explore options that increase your DOS session's memory and speed. The chapter concludes with a troubleshooting guide and a discussion of a few types of DOS programs that you cannot run under OS/2.

Understanding DOS Sessions

Imagine having several separate computers linked together so that they share one monitor and one keyboard, with each computer running a different DOS program. If one computer crashes, you reboot it while the other computers continue to run independently, unaffected by the mishap. This scenario is what DOS sessions under OS/2 are like. Each program runs in its own DOS session, and you can run several programs at a time. Although the programs share the resources of a single machine, each program functions as though it were running alone on a separate computer.

A DOS session under OS/2 is difficult to distinguish from DOS running by itself, which we call *real DOS* in this chapter for clarity. IBM engineers took great pains to make DOS sessions work the same as real DOS, testing OS/2's DOS support with dozens of popular applications. You can run almost any DOS or Windows program under OS/2, including applications that require expanded or extended memory, such as large spreadsheets. You can even play graphical DOS games, which run so smoothly that you might forget you're running OS/2.

Because DOS sessions run under OS/2, they can access files on a High Performance File System (HPFS) partition. All the features of this advanced file system are available except for long file names, which DOS programs cannot understand anyway. Even the File Allocation Table (FAT) file system runs faster under OS/2 than under real DOS.

You must install DOS support before you can run DOS programs. Windows programs require additional support. If you did not load these options when you installed OS/2, add them now. See the description of Selective Install in Chapter 7, "Modifying Your OS/2 Configuration."

For Related Information

◄◄ "Matching OS/2 with DOS," p. 60.

◄◄ "Understanding How OS/2 Expands upon DOS," p. 62.

FROM HERE...

Opening a DOS Command Line Session

Inside the OS/2 System object is the Command Prompts folder. This folder contains objects that open command line sessions for DOS and OS/2, either windowed or full screen. A full-screen DOS session looks exactly like real DOS. A windowed session is similar, except that you usually see only part of the DOS screen in a window on the Workplace Shell desktop. Open a full screen session and a windowed session now to experiment with their properties.

Run the DIR command in each session. You may immediately notice one major difference: the full-screen session seems several times faster than the windowed session. Although the programs run at about the same speed, screen output in a windowed session is much slower because it runs in graphics mode. Full-screen sessions can use text mode, which takes advantage of fast video hardware to write a whole character at a time.

Making Sessions Full-Screen or Windowed

Go to your windowed DOS session, hold down the Alt key, and press Home. The DOS session turns into a full-screen session. Pressing Alt-Home again returns you to the windowed session.

Having both options is convenient. Full-screen sessions have snappier video response and show you the whole screen at one time. Windowing, however, enables you to see more than one session at a time. Although you normally see only part of the application's screen in a window, you can view the entire screen if you maximize the window.

Moving among Sessions

As you learned in Chapter 10, "Managing the Workplace Shell," you can go from one session to the next by pressing Alt-Esc. Another combination keystroke, Alt-Tab, also enables you to go from one session to the next, but with one important difference. Alt-Tab cycles only between your windowed desktop applications and sessions. Alt-Tab does not switch to or from full-screen sessions.

When a windowed DOS or OS/2 session is active, pressing the Alt key alone reveals that session's system menu, shown in figure 16.1. From the system menu, you can use the Window list option to switch to another session or application. You can see from the list of menu options in figure 16.1 that several other choices are also available.

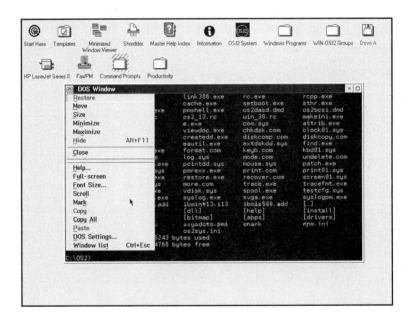

Fig. 16.1

A DOS session's system menu.

Starting a Windows Session

If you open the Windows Full Screen object in the Command Prompts folder, you see the Windows Program Manager, just as though you started Windows under real DOS.

The first release of OS/2 2.0 incorporated Windows 3.0, but OS/2 2.1 now includes Windows 3.1 support, as well. Many applications have been written for the Windows environment, and you can run these applications in addition to your DOS and OS/2 programs.

You have now learned everything you absolutely need to know in order to run most DOS programs under OS/2. You can start them by typing their names at the command line, the same as if you were running real DOS. You also know how to run Windows programs the way you are used to. In the rest of this chapter, you will become even more productive with your DOS and Windows applications. You learn how to do the following:

- Run applications from the Workplace Shell desktop, without using the command line interface

- Start an application by double-clicking one of its data files, such as a word processing document

- Protect Windows sessions from each other so that if one terminates with an Unrecoverable Application Error, you do not lose work in other Windows applications

- Cut and paste between sessions

- Fine-tune sessions for maximum performance

- Fix common problems

- Leave OS/2 and boot real DOS

For Related Information

◄◄ "Beginning the Command Line Interface," p. 293.

FROM HERE...

Adding DOS Programs

As you learned in Chapter 10, you can add DOS and Windows applications to the Workplace Shell desktop or to any folder. Automatic installation, using the Migrate Applications program in the OS/2 System folder, is the easiest way to add applications. If you want to add applications manually, however, complete the procedures provided in the following sections, which illustrate how to install Borland's Quattro Pro spreadsheet for DOS.

Creating a New Program Object

To create a new Program object, you drag a Program icon from the Templates folder to the desktop. Then you assign a program to that icon. To create an example Quattro Pro Program object, follow these steps:

1. Open the Templates folder by double-clicking it.

2. Select a Program icon by clicking it once with mouse button 1.

3. Hold down mouse button 2 and drag the Program icon onto the desktop; then release the mouse button, dropping the icon on the desktop.

   These steps create a new program object, whose settings notebook opens automatically. To move to a specific notebook page, you can click the tabs on the right side of the notebook.

4. Click the General tab to open the General page.

5. Type in a title for the program, in this case **Quattro Pro**.

   Your new title appears underneath the Program object's icon.

Telling OS/2 How To Run the Program

You now need to establish Program settings, which tell OS/2 how to run the program. Follow these steps:

1. Click the Program tab on the settings notebook.

2. Type the program's complete file name in the Path and file name field; for this example, type **C:\QPRO\Q.EXE**.

   You can specify any program here as long as its name ends in EXE, COM, or BAT.

3. Move to the Parameters field and type any options you need, such as switches that you would type after the program's name if you were running it from the DOS command line. Quattro Pro does not need any optional parameters.

4. Fill in the Working Directory field, which tells OS/2 where to find the program's data files. For this example, type **C:\QPRO**.

Figure 16.2 shows the completed Quattro Pro Program page.

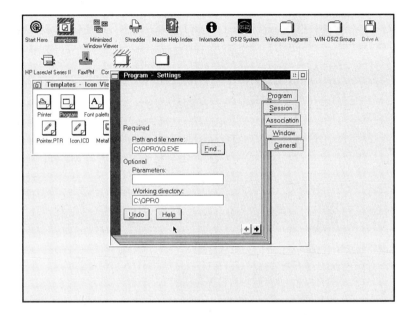

Fig. 16.2

Adding a DOS program to the Workplace Shell desktop.

Telling OS/2 How To Recognize Files

You can use the Association page to specify what sort of files the application uses. The built-in types are mostly for programmers, so you usually need to create your own.

Quattro Pro worksheets, for example, use the file extensions WQ1 and WQ!. Type ***.WQ1** in the New Name field, and choose A<u>d</u>d>> to move it to the Current Names field. Then do the same for the WQ! extension by typing ***.WQ!** in the New Name field, as shown in figure 16.3. The asterisk is a *wild card* that tells OS/2 to associate, with the program, *any* file that has the specified extension(s).

Whenever you double-click a spreadsheet's data file icon—for example, while viewing the working directory with the drive C object—this association tells the system to load the file into Quattro Pro. You don't need to start the spreadsheet program explicitly. You have already told OS/2 to associate Q.EXE (Quattro Pro) with any file that has an extension of WQ1 or WQ!.

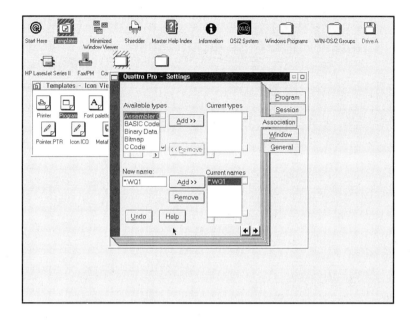

Fig. 16.3

Identifying a program's data files.

Telling OS/2 What Kind of Session To Open

Figure 16.4 shows the settings notebook's Session page. As soon as you filled in the Program page, OS/2 analyzed the program file and determined that Q.EXE is a DOS program. Therefore, OS/2 only offers you a choice between windowed and full-screen DOS sessions. Click whichever button you prefer. For this program, full screen gives you the best performance. A windowed DOS session, on the other hand, enables you to see your program run in a window on your desktop, alongside other desktop windows.

Sometimes, when you set up what you think is a DOS program, the Session page insists that you load it in an OS/2 session. This feature means that you have a *bound* program, which can run under either operating system, DOS or OS/2. Many Microsoft applications are bound programs. Running them in an OS/2 session yields better performance and fewer memory constraints.

The Close window on exit check box is selected automatically because you normally want to end the session when you leave the program. If you turn this option off, the session remains open when you exit from the program so that you can view any last minute error messages the application might display upon exiting.

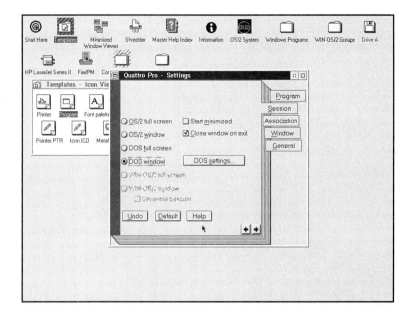

Fig. 16.4

Types of DOS
sessions you can
choose.

The DOS settings button offers you many options to tune the performance of the application. The next chapter, "Configuring Your DOS and
Windows Sessions," discusses DOS Settings in detail. For now, close the
settings notebook by pressing Alt-F4, or by choosing Close from the
notebook's system menu.

Your new Program object is now an icon on your desktop. Before you
store the Program object in a folder, explore some of the things you
can do with the new object. Double-clicking the object runs the program. Clicking mouse button 2 displays the object's pop-up menu.

Double-click the object to start the program now. If you chose to run
the program in full-screen mode, use Alt-Home to window the DOS session on your desktop.

Using a DOS Session's System Menu

The system menu you saw in figure 16.1 has the usual items you would
expect after reading Chapter 10, but some new choices also are
present. Full-screen does the same thing as Alt-Home. DOS Settings
enables you to customize many options that fine-tune DOS's performance, as detailed in Chapter 17, "Configuring Your DOS and Windows
Sessions."

Go to your windowed DOS session and pull down its system menu by pressing Alt. You see even more choices. Full-screen does the same thing as Alt-Home, and DOS Settings is again available. The other new choices control font size and enable you to cut and paste, as explained in the next few sections.

Controlling the Font Size

Windowed DOS sessions offer you a choice of character sizes. The largest characters are easiest to read, although the smaller fonts enable you to see an entire DOS screen in a small window. Figure 16.5 shows the options available when you load a DOS application, in this case Quattro Pro. Choose Font Size from the system menu.

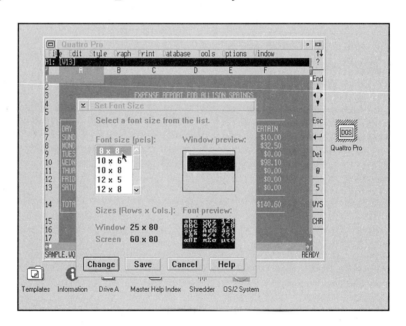

Fig. 16.5

Choosing a font size for a windowed session.

The Set Font Size window describes font sizes in terms of *pels* (sometimes called *pixels*), which are the tiny dots that make up each character. With the 12 x 5 font, for example, each character is 12 dots high and 5 wide. For comparison, the standard font you see in a full-screen DOS session is 14 x 8 on a VGA monitor. An additional column of blank dots always occurs between characters, to separate them.

The numbers beneath the Font size menu labeled Window tell you the size of your DOS window. The size is usually 25 rows of 80 characters, but many applications allow you to use 50 rows instead. Another pair of numbers, labeled Screen, tells the maximum number of character rows and columns that can be shown on-screen. This number depends on the font size, and it changes when you move through the various options with the up and down arrows. The Window preview area, which graphically shows how large an area the window would fill, also changes for each font size. The Font preview gives you a snapshot of sample characters in each size.

After you have made your selection, press the Change button to activate it for the current DOS session. If you press Save instead, the selected font size becomes the default for all DOS sessions. Many people prefer the 12 x 5 font, which enables you to see a whole screen in a small window, or the 18 x 8 font, which is the easiest to read.

Cutting and Pasting in DOS Sessions

In Chapter 14, you learned how to cut, copy, and paste text in the Enhanced Editor. You can use this feature in windowed DOS or OS/2 sessions, too. For example, you might want to cut or copy a table of numbers from a spreadsheet and paste it into a word processor document. You cannot cut and paste between applications by using the handy shortcut keys you learned, like Ctrl-Ins, however. Remember, programs running in DOS sessions think that they are running on a separate computer of their own, so they don't know how to communicate with other sessions. For windowed DOS or OS/2 sessions, you need to use the session's system menu.

To mark a block of text that you want to copy, choose Mark from the system menu. If you want to use the keyboard, notice that the text cursor changed to a box shown in reverse color. Move this cursor to a corner of the block, hold down the Shift key, and use the arrow keys to highlight the whole block. Then release the Shift key.

You also can mark text with the mouse; its cursor changed to a picture of a box to let you know it is ready. Move the mouse cursor to a corner of the block you want to copy, hold down mouse button 1, and move the mouse to highlight the whole block. Release the button when you are done.

After marking a block, press Alt to pull down the system menu again, and this time pick Copy. The text you selected is now in OS/2's Clipboard.

Finally, go to the session into which you want to copy the block, position the cursor where you want to insert it, and pick Paste from that session's system menu.

Closing a Session

Each session's local menu includes a Close option. Avoid using it except as a last resort; instead, exit from the application as though you were running real DOS or Windows. Otherwise, the program doesn't have a chance to shut itself down properly, saving any files it has opened. If the program crashes and you cannot get its attention even to terminate it, Close allows you to end the session. This action is like rebooting the computer when you are running real DOS and a program locks up.

Running Individual Windows Applications

Under real DOS, you cannot run a Windows application directly; you must load Windows first. You open the Windows Full Screen object (in the Command Prompts folder) and run your application from Windows' Program Manager. If you're an experienced Windows user, you will feel at home with the familiar interface. This method takes up less memory if you run several Windows applications at a time because only one copy of the Windows program code is loaded. If you get an Unrecoverable Application Error in one Windows application, however, it can crash the whole Windows session, and other applications might lose data.

OS/2 gives you another option. You can create an OS/2 desktop object for your Windows application and run that application directly. The procedure is the same you used earlier to place Quattro Pro on the desktop. To create a Word for Windows object, for example, type **C:\WINWORD\WINWORD.EXE** on the top line of the Program screen in the settings notebook. OS/2 automatically recognizes Windows applications and installs the special support they need.

When you open the Word for Windows object, it loads its own copy of the Windows code. Each Windows application runs in a separate Windows session. If you get an Unrecoverable Application Error in another session running a Windows spreadsheet (such as Excel), it does not harm the Word for Windows session. Running Windows applications in separate sessions consumes more memory, but that is a small price to pay for the error protection OS/2 provides.

For Related Information

◄◄ "Using Microsoft Windows with OS/2," p. 70.

◄◄ "Setting Up Other Applications," p. 252.

FROM HERE...

Switching between OS/2 and DOS with Dual-Boot

When you start a program, the operating system does the nitty-gritty work of loading it. But when you start an operating system, it must load itself—like pulling itself up by its own bootstraps. The colorful term *booting* describes this process.

You can switch back and forth between OS/2 and real DOS with the BOOT command. To start DOS, double-click the Dual-Boot icon in the Command Prompts folder, which is inside the OS/2 System folder; or in any OS/2 or DOS session, type the following command:

    C:\OS2\BOOT /DOS

To go back to OS/2, type the following at the DOS prompt:

    C:\OS2\BOOT /OS2

When you use Dual-Boot to switch from OS/2 to DOS, OS/2 goes through its normal shutdown procedure first.

For Related Information

◄◄ "Looking at DOS and OS/2 Incompatibilities," p. 71.

FROM HERE...

Booting DOS without Leaving OS/2

Some finicky programs run only under a specific version of real DOS. If you want to run such a program at the same time as OS/2, you can boot that version of DOS from a floppy disk. Change the DOS_STARTUP_DRIVE setting in the OS/2 DOS Settings window to reflect the drive you are using, insert your DOS boot disk there, and start the DOS session. What you get is not the normal OS/2 emulation of DOS: it is actually real DOS. You cannot boot versions of DOS before 3.0, however. The next chapter covers the DOS_STARTUP_DRIVE and other DOS settings in more detail.

For Related Information

▶▶ "Changing DOS Settings for Each Session," p. 410.

Learning What You Cannot Do in a DOS Session

OS/2 was designed to isolate sessions from each other so that a bug in one program cannot crash the system. To protect programs from each other, OS/2 must take exclusive control of the hardware. This step means you cannot run DOS programs that try to take such low-level control themselves. But in most cases, OS/2 gives you another way to do the tasks for which these DOS programs were designed.

Preventing Viruses

Many DOS viruses cannot do their dirty work because of OS/2's protection. Because OS/2 is a nearly crash-proof operating system, it protects crucial parts of your disk and system memory, which these nasty programs often try to modify. You should continue to take your usual precautions, of course, such as obtaining programs only from legitimate retailers and quality bulletin boards, and running virus-check software regularly.

Using Disk Utilities

PC Tools and Norton Utilities include examples of low-level disk utilities that do not work under OS/2. Used improperly, such programs can crash your system, and OS/2 does not permit that. It does not even allow you to run the potentially dangerous commands in DOS. For example, while OS/2 is running, you cannot format the hard disk from which you booted OS/2.

You still can use most of the programs in these packages, such as PC Tools Shell and Norton Commander. Only programs like DiskFix and Norton Disk Doctor, which try to take complete control of the disk, are not allowed to execute. For the same reason, you cannot run Stacker in a DOS session under OS/2.

Many of the jobs these programs do are built into OS/2. For example, OS/2 includes an UNDELETE command that you can use to get back files that you accidentally erase and a cache program to speed up your hard disk.

> **CAUTION:** Using a DOS disk cache under OS/2 is not safe. Many programs, such as Norton Cache, recognize that OS/2 is active and refuse to run anyway.

> **CAUTION:** Do not use disk defragmenters (sometimes called disk organizers) like Speedisk, Compress, and Disk Optimizer. You can run them if you boot real DOS first, but they may damage the extended attributes of files you used under OS/2. Make sure that you use a defragmenter compatible with OS/2.

Running Diagnostic Utilities

You can run DOS diagnostic programs like Norton Sysinfo or Quarterdeck Manifest, but they may crash or give incorrect information. Such programs usually rely on undocumented quirks of DOS and try to access the hardware directly. You may need to use Dual-Boot to run plain DOS if you want to run such a diagnostic utility.

Working with Memory Managers

Most people who run DOS on 386 PCs use memory management software such as QEMM, 386MAX, or EMM386, which allows DOS applications to access all the computer's memory. To accomplish this, they must take full control of the 386 chip, and OS/2 does not permit that. You don't need these programs in DOS sessions because their function is built into OS/2. Best of all, OS/2 takes care of memory management automatically, whereas configuring real DOS memory managers can be a time-consuming task even for experts.

Using Applications that Use Obsolete DOS Extenders

A few DOS applications still use an outdated technique to access memory beyond 640K. Their documentation should mention the words VCPI, or Virtual Control Program Interface. This early DOS extender tries to get around the wall that OS/2 puts between DOS sessions. A bug in such a program can crash the computer, so OS/2 doesn't let the program run. OS/2 supports the modern DPMI DOS extender, and most software companies are upgrading their products accordingly.

Employing Windows Enhanced Mode

Almost all Windows applications run in *Standard* mode. Windows also offers an *Enhanced* mode, which can run several Standard mode programs simultaneously. As the name indicates, Windows accomplishes this step by taking exclusive control of the 386 chip. OS/2 does not let that happen, but it does enable you to multitask Windows applications by loading them in separate sessions. This step is an improvement over Windows because OS/2 protects these sessions from each other, whereas an error in one application can crash Windows Enhanced mode.

FROM HERE...

For Related Information

◀◀ "Looking at DOS and OS/2 Incompatibilities," p. 71.

Chapter Summary

OS/2 applications are the wave of the future, but you don't have to leave behind your favorite DOS and Windows programs. In fact, they will run better than ever under OS/2. You learned how to run these programs from the Workplace Shell desktop. You also learned how to tailor your DOS sessions for maximum performance, and how to troubleshoot common problems.

The next chapter expands your knowledge of DOS and Windows sessions under OS/2.

Configuring Your DOS and Windows Sessions

M ost DOS applications work well without any special configuration changes. Some applications may benefit from extra memory, however, and any program is more fun to use if it runs faster. In the next few sections, you learn how to change global DOS settings by using CONFIG.SYS commands to get more memory and more speed and how to fix common problems. You also learn how to modify the global settings to affect each DOS session.

Changing Default Settings in CONFIG.SYS

There are many settings that you will want to apply in all your DOS sessions. The best approach is to place those settings in your system configuration file, CONFIG.SYS. You can edit this file with the Enhanced Editor discussed in Chapter 14, "Using the OS/2 Text Editors." Try editing your configuration file now, and follow the recommendations in the next few sections. Generally, the installation defaults are appropriate, but a few improvements are recommended.

Telling DOS To Make the Best Use of Memory

DOS normally can use only 640K of memory. Part of that space is occupied by DOS, which leaves less memory for your applications. You can free this space by loading DOS in *high memory*, memory beyond 640K.

Another special kind of memory, *upper memory*, enables DOS to load programs that run in the background. The AUTOEXEC.BAT file in your root directory, for example, contains the following line:

```
LOADHIGH APPEND C:\OS2;C:\OS2\SYSTEM
```

When you type LOADHIGH before the name of the APPEND program, DOS loads it into upper memory.

You don't need to know the technical details of high and upper memory. Just remember that this memory is outside the 640K where DOS loads your applications. You have more room to work in DOS if you tell DOS to use these special kinds of memory. To do so, make sure that your CONFIG.SYS contains this line:

```
DOS=HIGH,UMB
```

Delete any other line beginning with DOS=.

Setting the Number of Files DOS Can Use

DOS applications use disk files to store programs and data. The maximum number of files a DOS session can use is set in CONFIG.SYS. This maximum was set to 20 when you installed OS/2. That number is enough for most applications, but some programs, such as Windows, may occasionally need more. Search through CONFIG.SYS for the line that says the following:

```
FILES=20
```

Change the number to 50.

Expanding the DOS Environment

The environment is part of DOS's 640K memory area, where programs can store information. DOS sessions normally set aside only 256 bytes for the environment, which is not enough for some applications. Find the following line in CONFIG.SYS:

```
SHELL=C:\OS2\MDOS\COMMAND.COM C:\OS2\MDOS /P
```

Change it to the following:

```
SHELL=C:\OS2\MDOS\COMMAND.COM C:\OS2\MDOS /E:1024 /P
```

The /E:1024 you added sets aside a full kilobyte—1024 bytes—for the DOS environment. This size is enough for almost any application that adds environment variables to your system.

For Related Information

◄◄ "Changing Your Configuration Settings," p. 149.

◄◄ "Using CONFIG.SYS and AUTOEXEC.BAT," p. 159.

FROM HERE...

Changing Settings in the System Menu

The changes you made to CONFIG.SYS apply to all DOS and Windows sessions, but several other settings enable you to customize each program's session to better fit its particular needs. You have the following two ways to access these settings:

■ Click mouse button 2 on the program or command prompt object to open its settings notebook, and choose DOS or Windows Settings from the Session page.

■ Press Alt when a windowed session is open, and pick DOS Settings from the local menu.

Some settings do not appear when you use the second method because they cannot be changed while the program is running.

Figure 17.1 shows the DOS Settings screen. When you move through the settings in the list box on the left side, the Description field is updated to give a brief explanation of the setting. More information is available by pressing the Help Button. When you have changed one or more settings, press Save to apply those changes to the object. The Default button restores all settings to the values they originally had when you loaded OS/2.

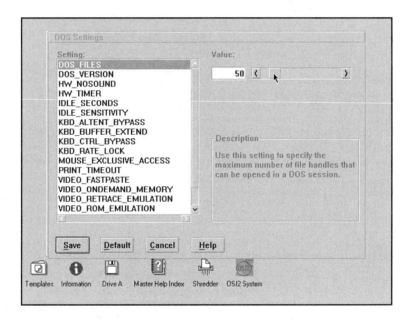

Fig. 17.1

The DOS Settings screen.

Using Special Kinds of Memory

Some DOS applications manage to break the 640K barrier and use all your computer's memory. These applications use several methods, known as EMS, XMS, and DPMI, to break this barrier; each method requires you to configure special support when running under real DOS. But with OS/2's DOS sessions, you don't need to wade through this alphabet soup of memory enhancements, because a couple of megabytes of each type of memory are automatically available to every program.

You might want to change the defaults to provide even more memory to a particular DOS program, or to strip out these extra features and streamline your DOS sessions. This section explains the techniques for determining which sort of memory your application requires and optimizing the settings.

By looking for certain key words in your program's documentation, you can figure out which setting controls its use of extra memory:

■ Use the XMS_MEMORY_LIMIT setting if the documentation mentions Extended Memory or XMS.

■ Use the EMS_MEMORY_LIMIT setting if you find the words Expanded Memory, LIM, EMS, or EEMS.

■ Use the DPMI_MEMORY_LIMIT setting if you see DOS Protected Mode Interface or DPMI.

No matter what type of memory your program requires, OS/2 provides all the memory the program asks for, up to 2M. You can change this limit. Increase the limit when you need more—for example, when you run out of memory when loading a large spreadsheet. On the other hand, some programs rudely grab all the extra memory they find, whether they need it or not. Tame these programs by experimenting with lower limits.

Most DOS programs don't use EMS, XMS, or DPMI. Turning all three options off is a good idea when you don't need them; change all their limits to 0. This step reduces the memory the DOS session takes up. DOS loads faster and leaves more room for other sessions.

To see how much EMS and XMS memory is available, run the MEM command from a DOS command prompt. As you can see in figure 17.2, this step also tells you how much regular memory DOS can use, and whether DOS was loaded in high memory by specifying DOS=HIGH in CONFIG.SYS.

Getting More than 640K of Memory for DOS

You have probably heard that DOS can access only 640K of memory—so why does figure 17.2 show more memory than that available? An OS/2 DOS session can get well over 700K, as long as you use only the normal 25-line text mode and very low resolution graphics. Just change the VIDEO_MODE_RESTRICTION setting to CGA.

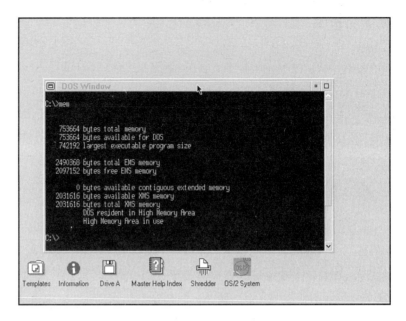

Fig. 17.2

Different types of
memory a DOS
Session can use.

The graphics capabilities are primitive, and you cannot use enhanced
text modes that display 50 lines on-screen. These limitations may not
matter to you, however. With the extra memory, you can run a combination of programs that would not fit in a normal 640K session.

Tuning the Priority of DOS Sessions

When a DOS program waits for input from you, it continually checks
the keyboard, perhaps a thousand times a second. If you are running
real DOS, this feature doesn't matter; DOS runs only one program at a
time because it has no better use for your computer's resources.

Under OS/2, on the other hand, this approach is wasteful because OS/2
tries to speed up the programs doing useful work by giving relatively
less attention to others. OS/2 continually checks whether a DOS program is sitting idle, waiting for input from you. It keeps track of how
long a program has waited for input, and how much time a program
spends checking whether you have pressed a key or moved the mouse.
OS/2 uses this information to adjust the priority of each session.

Usually, this method gives you the best overall performance, but sometimes you don't care how fast programs run in the background, as long
as the foreground program is responsive. Two settings enable you to
adjust the idle checking, or even turn it off:

- *IDLE_SECONDS*. Normally, OS/2 gives a program a lower priority if it sits idle for three seconds. You can change this number to any number of seconds you want. Setting the number to 0 completely disables this checking.

- *IDLE_SENSITIVITY*. OS/2 reduces the priority of any program spending 75 percent or more of its time checking the keyboard. You can set this time period as you like. If you set this period to 100 percent, the system stops checking, and the program always runs at a high priority.

Choosing Performance Enhancements

The following settings affect the performance of your system. You can tune OS/2 to give you faster DOS sessions by experimenting with these settings.

- *HW_ROM_TO_RAM*. Deep inside your computer, built-in programs that control devices such as the keyboard and disk drive are stored on relatively slow, permanent memory chips. When you turn this option on, these programs are copied to the system's main memory, which is much faster. This step consumes about 100K of memory, but it does not come from DOS's 640K, and the speedup is usually worthwhile.

- *HW_TIMER*. This option gives DOS sessions direct access to the computer's timer chip. Turn this option on for applications that need precise timing control, such as music programs or action games. If you use this option in more than one session, the sessions may interfere with each other.

- *KBD_BUFFER_EXTEND*. You can type ahead when your DOS program is busy. Your keystrokes are saved in a buffer and played back when the program is ready for input. In real DOS, the buffer is only 17 characters long. OS/2 DOS sessions extend this buffer to 128 characters. Some programs, however, do an end-run around DOS and buffer keystrokes themselves, in a way incompatible with OS/2's keyboard buffer enhancement. If a particular program doesn't work correctly when you type ahead, try turning off this setting.

- *VIDEO_FASTPASTE*. When you paste text to a DOS session, the text is entered at about the rate that a fast typist can manage. If you turn this option on, text is pasted much faster. The option is off by default, however, because the high speed is faster than some programs can handle. Experiment to find out whether your application can benefit from the faster pasting speed.

- *VIDEO_ROM_EMULATION*. This setting tells the system to use fast OS/2 routines to move the cursor and scroll the screen. Turning this setting on usually speeds up your screen. Some fancy video cards have their own built-in routines, however, which are even faster. Try both ways to see which works better on your computer.

- *VIDEO_WINDOW_REFRESH*. DOS windows are usually redrawn every tenth of a second, almost as fast as the eye can see. Heavy-duty graphics applications spend much of their time redrawing the screen, however, which makes them smooth but slow. If this is a problem, increase the redraw delay to get a snappier response. If you increase the delay too much, though, the graphics may get jerky.

Accommodating Special Needs

As you have seen, several keystroke combinations have special meaning with OS/2. Your DOS programs, therefore, cannot ordinarily use Alt-Home, Alt-Esc, or Ctrl-Esc. If you have a DOS program that must use these keystrokes, change the KBD_ALTHOME_BYPASS or KBD_CTRL_BYPASS settings. You cannot reassign both Alt-Esc and Ctrl-Esc to a DOS session because you need one key combination to switch to a different session if your DOS program crashes.

Some DOS programs work only if you load a specific device driver first. If you list the driver in CONFIG.SYS, the driver loads in every DOS session. To load the driver only for a particular program, open that program's settings and type the name of the driver in its DOS_DEVICE field. Be sure to include the driver's complete path and file name.

Troubleshooting DOS Settings

Although almost any DOS program runs in an OS/2 DOS session with the default configuration, you may encounter problems. The most common problems are listed here, along with the settings you should change to fix them.

The modem doesn't work with a DOS communications program.

Type the following line in the DOS session, before you start the communications program:

> MODE COM1: 9600,,,,OCTS=OFF,RTS=OFF,DTR=OFF,ODSR=OFF,IDSR=OFF

Enter the actual communications port and data rate you are using. If you have a 2400-bit-per-second modem on the second port, for example, use the following:

> MODE COM2: 2400,,,,OCTS=OFF,RTS=OFF,DTR=OFF,ODSR=OFF,IDSR=OFF

If your program then works, you may want to add the MODE command to the AUTOEXEC.BAT file in your root directory C:\.

The modem disconnects the line when you temporarily exit from a DOS communications program.

Turn on the COM_HOLD setting. This step prevents OS/2 from reclaiming the modem port when you exit from the DOS program temporarily. Until you close the current DOS session, no other session can use the modem.

A DOS program uses the speaker, and you want the program to run quietly.

Turn on the HW_NOSOUND setting.

After a certain DOS program runs, the keyboard speeds up or slows down in other sessions.

Turn on the offending program's KBD_RATE_LOCK setting. Some programs change the keyboard speed, which is usually what you want. Leave this setting off unless the program interferes with other programs.

A program in a windowed DOS session has two mouse cursors.

Turn on the MOUSE_EXCLUSIVE_ACCESS setting, and then click the mouse in the DOS window. The Workplace Shell desktop's cursor disappears. To get the cursor back, press the Alt key.

You print a report from a DOS application, such as a spreadsheet graph, and the report prints in several pieces.

Increase the PRINT_TIMEOUT setting. The system normally assumes that your report is finished if nothing is sent to the printer for 17 seconds. But your program may take longer to format different parts of your printout.

When you switch between windowed and full screen with Alt-Home, the screen is garbled, or it goes blank.

Turn VIDEO_RETRACE_EMULATION off, and turn VIDEO_SWITCH_NOTIFICATION on. If the problem persists, turn VIDEO_ON_DEMAND_MEMORY off. This last setting should be necessary only with graphics programs. It usually fixes the problem, but uses more memory and makes your program load slower.

When you run a particular program, you get an error message as shown in figure 17.3.

End the program, and contact the developer of the application. The application contains a bug. Such problems often go unnoticed for a while under real DOS, until the problems eventually result in puzzling sporadic errors. OS/2 catches such problems before they can affect other applications. Usually, the error indicates the computer program tried to change a location in memory when it had no right to do so. Many DOS programmers develop applications in OS/2 DOS sessions so that they can catch bugs before the bugs cause problems. Chapter 8, "Troubleshooting OS/2," contains more information about such bugs.

Changing DOS Settings for Each Session

The last section discussed global settings that you can make by using CONFIG.SYS commands. This section, however, details the configuration settings available for you to improve individual DOS sessions' performance and functioning ability. Refer to the earlier sections of this chapter for tutorial information on adjusting these settings and troubleshooting your DOS and Windows sessions.

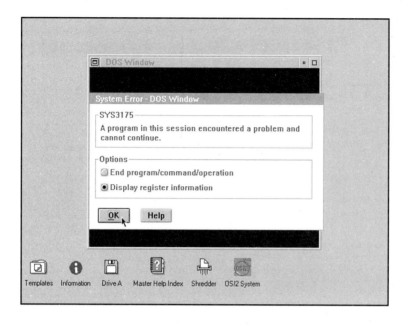

Fig. 17.3

OS/2 discovers
a bug in a DOS
application.

The available configuration settings are divided into the following
topics:

- Improving DOS session performance
- Configuring the keyboard, mouse, and touch screen
- Modifying display settings
- Maximizing available memory
- Using miscellaneous DOS settings for improving printing and Windows session performance, and controlling DOS environment parameters

Most DOS session settings are either ON or OFF. Adjust the settings by
selecting a radio button in the settings window for the DOS session's
icon. In some cases you select a number, typically a time in seconds,
for a setting.

Making DOS Sessions Perform Better

As a multitasking operating system, OS/2 divides the CPU time between
each of the open sessions. To alter the proportion of time allocated to
DOS sessions, OS/2's responsiveness to DOS sessions, and the way in
which OS/2 redistributes time allocations to open sessions, you need to
use the settings described in the following sections.

DOS_BACKGROUND_EXECUTION

When DOS_BACKGROUND_EXECUTION is ON, the default setting, a DOS session continues to operate in the background. When OFF, the DOS session in the background is suspended. The setting can be changed before or during the DOS session.

OS/2 can run multiple sessions (windows) at once; however, you can only interact with one of those sessions at a time. The currently active window is known as the *foreground session* and all the others are *background sessions*. Use this DOS setting to alter the DOS session's behavior when it is a background session.

Suspending the DOS session in the background improves the performance of your other open OS/2 sessions because OS/2 does not have to allocate time to support it. In some situations, the suspension is appropriate because nothing happens unless you interact with the program.

If you type in a word processor and then switch it to the background, for example, nothing happens until you make it a foreground session again.

In other situations, however, you will want to switch the DOS session to the background as you perform other functions, and you will return to the session only when the action is complete. If you generate an index for a large document, in, say, the word processing example, you may want to use another program during the regeneration. In this case, you will not want the DOS program's operation suspended in the background.

Consider your actual use of a DOS application program before you switch this setting off. An electronic Rolodex or game program is a likely candidate for an off setting; a communications, network, Windows, or printing program is not a likely candidate.

HW_ROM_TO_RAM

ROM (read only memory) is an electronic memory chip that can store information even when your computer is off. The contents of the ROM are used, in part, when you boot your computer. RAM (random access memory) stores more temporary information; when power is removed, the data stored in RAM is lost. These two chip types are made in different ways, and, as a result, have different access times. (Typically, data can be retrieved from RAM ten times faster than from ROM.)

When you turn the HW_ROM_TO_RAM setting to ON, the ROM's data copies into the faster RAM; when your DOS program accesses this data, the data is retrieved from RAM instead of ROM. Your DOS session's performance may improve because your computer can access information stored in RAM faster than information stored in ROM. The default setting is OFF; you can only change this setting before you start a DOS session.

If your DOS program makes extensive use of the ROM contents, you will see a performance improvement in your DOS application. However, the percentage of time that your DOS application spends accessing ROM instead of performing other functions may be small, so the improvement may be minimal. In addition, you may experience compatibility problems, or your computer hardware may do this swapping automatically.

IDLE_SECONDS

OS/2 divides its time between all the open sessions and automatically adjusts the time allocation for each session. If OS/2 determines that a session is idle, perhaps waiting for you to type something, it gives the program less time until the program becomes active again.

Consider the action of pouring a cup of coffee as an analogy. If the person pouring says "Say when," that person continues to pour until you speak, like a program that awaits input, but continues to operate as it waits. OS/2 determines that it is waiting for your input, and reduces the time allocation for the program's session because it considers the program inactive. As a result, the rate of "pouring coffee," or time allocated to the program, goes down. If this is undesirable, increase the IDLE_SECONDS value. OS/2 then delays checking whether the program is idle for the number of seconds specified.

The IDLE_SECONDS setting defines the number of seconds that OS/2 waits before it determines whether a DOS session is idle. You can choose a value between 0, the default value, and 60. This setting can change before starting or during a DOS session.

OS/2's idle detection can make your DOS program seem sluggish because your program appears idle when it is not and OS/2 lowers the time allocation for the DOS session.

IDLE_SENSITIVITY

OS/2 allocates time to each open session automatically. To make each session operate more efficiently, OS/2 checks to see whether a session is idle and waiting for input. If a session is found idle, that session's proportion of time is reduced so that the remaining sessions operate more efficiently.

The IDLE_SECONDS value discussed in the previous section delays the start of OS/2 to determine whether a session is idle; IDLE_SENSITIVITY determines "how idle" a session must be before it is judged as idle. The IDLE_SENSITIVITY setting is a percentage between 0 and 100, with a default value of 75 percent. OS/2 uses this value to determine when a DOS session is idle or only waiting for input.

A DOS session has a predetermined maximum polling rate (the number of times per second that the program checks for an input). When a program requires input, from say, a keyboard or a communications port, the program polls the input to see whether the input is ready, like checking a mail box to see whether mail has arrived. The polling rate is the number of times per second the input is checked. Because this polling is done by OS/2, OS/2 can determine how often a program polls the input. If the DOS session polls for input more often than the percentage of time given as a value for the IDLE_SENSITIVITY setting, OS/2 considers the program idle and reduces the time allocation for the DOS session.

If this setting is inappropriate, you may experience sluggishness with certain DOS sessions, most likely when a program waits for input but continues to operate. For example, if a program increments a number on-screen automatically, and stops only when you press a key, you may find that the number increments more slowly than you would expect; OS/2 thinks the program is only waiting for you to press a key.

If you experience sluggish performance, try setting IDLE_SENSITIVITY to a higher percentage. If you do not see an improvement, however, return IDLE_SENSITIVITY to its previous value. You can change this value either before starting or during a DOS session.

Configuring the Keyboard, Mouse, and Touch Screen

Because DOS is not a multitasking operating system, DOS application programs almost always are written with the assumption that you have exclusive use of the keyboard and mouse. When you run these programs as DOS sessions under OS/2, the program shares the computer resources with other OS/2 applications.

In most cases, OS/2 can divide the resources so that the DOS session operates and "shares" without any problem. Some DOS application programs, however, may not work properly because those programs expect settings to remain constant or to have exclusive rights to a resource such as the keyboard. For example, OS/2 uses the Alt-Home key combination to switch between sessions. If your DOS application program uses the Alt-Home key combination, you need to alter a setting because the DOS program is not expecting OS/2 to use the Alt-Home key.

The other settings in this category alter the DOS session so that the DOS application program has access to the features it needs.

DOS_BREAK

Many DOS programs use Ctrl-C or Ctrl-Break as an interrupt or canceling command. To stop a BASIC program that is running, for example, you press Ctrl-C (or Ctrl-Break). To allow this interrupt, DOS must be prepared to receive the key combination even as it processes other information.

When the DOS_BREAK setting is OFF, the typical default setting, OS/2 does not continually check for the Ctrl-C or Ctrl-Break key combination used by many DOS programs to abort the current command or program. When DOS_BREAK is ON, OS/2 performs this check. Note that the line BREAK=OFF is placed in your CONFIG.SYS file during installation, unless you specify otherwise. If you change this setting, OFF will not necessarily be the default setting for BREAK. This setting must be made before you start a DOS session.

When running a DOS session under OS/2, it takes more overhead for OS/2 to be continually looking for this key combination. As a consequence, your programs can be very sluggish if you set DOS_BREAK ON.

If you set DOS_BREAK to OFF, you still can use the Ctrl-C and Ctrl-Break key combinations for keystroke input to your DOS program. These key combinations, however, do not act as interrupting keystroke mechanisms when your program is actually doing something else.

In general, unless you have a specific program in which you really need to use Ctrl-C or Ctrl-Break to interrupt the program, leave DOS_BREAK turned OFF.

KBD_ALTHOME_BYPASS

In OS/2, the key combination Alt-Home switches a session from a window to a full-screen session. Setting KBD_ALTHOME_BYPASS to ON means that within your DOS session you can use Alt-Home for other reasons. The default setting is OFF. You can change the setting either before starting or during a DOS session.

If you have a DOS application program that uses the Alt-Home key combination, you must set KBD_ALTHOME_BYPASS to ON. Otherwise, every time you try to press Alt-Home, OS/2 changes your window between a window and a full-screen session.

KBD_BUFFER_EXTEND

A *type-ahead buffer* is an area of memory that stores your keystrokes until your program is ready to process them. If you fill this buffer, your computer beeps each time you press a key until your computer can accept more keystrokes.

Most users, even those who type by hunting and pecking, take advantage of the keyboard type-ahead buffer. If you press a key to save a file in a word processor, you can anticipate that the program will next ask whether you want to overwrite the existing file, and press Y to speed the process. Most touch typists frequently overflow a 16-byte buffer. Consequently, increasing this buffer to 128 bytes, which enables you to type as quickly as you like, is a good idea in almost all cases.

The price you pay for the larger buffer, however, is that it uses memory—if you run a DOS program, these few extra bytes allocated to the type-ahead buffer instead of your DOS program may make the difference between being able to run your DOS program or not.

To allow your DOS program to increase the type-ahead buffer from 16 to 128 bytes, set KBD_BUFFER_EXTEND to ON, the default value. Set to OFF to prevent this increase. You can change this setting before starting or during a DOS session.

KBD_CTRL_BYPASS

In OS/2, by default the key combination Ctrl-Esc activates the window list, and Alt-Esc switches between sessions. Changing KBD_CTRL_BYPASS from the default NONE means you can use either Alt-Esc or Ctrl-Esc within your DOS session for other reasons. You can change the setting either before starting or during a DOS session. If you select ALT_ESC, you can use Alt-Esc within your DOS session. If you select CTRL_ESC, you can use Ctrl-Esc within your DOS session.

If you have a DOS application program that uses the Alt-Esc key combination, set KBD_CTRL_BYPASS to ALT_ESC. Otherwise, every time you press Alt-Esc, OS/2 swaps to the next session.

If you have a DOS application program that uses the Ctrl-Esc key combination, set KBD_CTRL_BYPASS to CTRL_ESC. Otherwise, every time you try to press Ctrl-Esc, OS/2 displays the window list.

KBD_RATE_LOCK

When you press a key on your keyboard, the action is transmitted to the computer and recorded as a single keystroke. If you hold down the key instead of releasing it, after a delay, known as the *typematic delay period*, the computer automatically repeats the keystrokes until you release the key. The rate at which the keystrokes repeat is called the *keyboard repeat rate*, which can be altered by your programs.

Most DOS programs, however, do not alter this rate; even if they do alter it, they reset it again. In the rare event that you experience keyboard problems when you switch to another session after using a DOS session, consider altering the KBD_RATE_LOCK setting. The symptoms of a repeat rate problem show up when you press and hold down a key (the key's function repeats unusually slowly or rapidly).

To allow your DOS program to adjust the keyboard repeat rate, set KBD_RATE_LOCK to OFF, the default value. Set it to ON if you want to prevent this change. You can change this setting before starting or during a DOS session.

MOUSE_EXCLUSIVE_ACCESS

As a graphical user interface, OS/2 controls the mouse and mouse cursor, and shares this resource among all the open windows. DOS programs, which were not typically written to share the computer's resources with other programs, either do not use a mouse, or expect exclusive use of the mouse.

In many cases, a DOS program that uses the mouse controls the mouse's behavior as well as its position. For example, some programs use different mouse sensitivities so that you may have to move the mouse longer or shorter distances to make the mouse cursor move.

If your DOS program creates and manages its own mouse cursor, change the MOUSE_EXCLUSIVE_ACCESS default setting from OFF to ON. You can change the setting before starting or during a DOS session. When this setting is ON, click within the DOS session window to remove the Presentation Manager mouse cursor. Press Alt, Ctrl-Esc, or Alt-Esc to restore it.

Change MOUSE_EXCLUSIVE_ACCESS to ON for any DOS session that manages its own mouse. If you get two unsynchronized mouse pointers, one in OS/2 and one in your DOS session, for example, change the setting.

TOUCH_EXCLUSIVE_ACCESS

This setting is important only if you use a touch screen connected to a Personal System/2 mouse port. The setting prevents OS/2 from sharing the mouse port with other OS/2 sessions and allows your DOS program exclusive use of the touch screen.

If you experience problems with your touch screen in a DOS session, change the TOUCH_EXCLUSIVE_ACCESS default setting from OFF to ON. You can change the setting before starting or during a DOS session. When this setting is ON, the position you touch on-screen represents the position in the DOS session's window. Alter the DOS session's window size to full screen if you want the position you touch to match the DOS session's.

To avoid changing this setting, run your DOS sessions as full-screen sessions if you use a touch screen. Full-screen sessions are also probably preferable because of the connection between the position you touch on-screen and the displayed image. If you run a paint program in a window one-quarter the size of the screen, for example, your drawings would display at one-quarter their actual size, which might be a bit disconcerting.

Modifying Display Settings

DOS application programs were not designed to share resources like the display, keyboard, or mouse. When you try to run these resources under OS/2, you may experience problems.

In the case of the display, problems usually arise because an OS/2 window overwrites the DOS session's window display or changes the video mode so that when the DOS application program runs, the video screen is corrupted. The DOS application program does not anticipate the change in the video screen because the application expects exclusive use of the computer's resources. Consequently, you may need to adjust the following settings to compensate.

VIDEO_8514A_XGA_IOTRAP

This setting is used only if you have an 8514/A or XGA board. In order to operate faster, many DOS programs that support these high-resolution video boards directly manipulate the hardware instead of using the operating system video services. When a program runs under DOS, this direct manipulation is good because the program is the only one running at the time. Under OS/2, however, many application programs can run at the same time, and the video is a shared resource; therefore, OS/2 must keep firm control so that all the programs work together. Consequently, your DOS program may operate more slowly than usual.

To regain speed, you can turn VIDEO_8514A_XGA_IOTRAP to OFF. When you switch back to the DOS program after working in another OS/2 session, however, this setting can be a problem. The DOS program probably will be unaware of any video mode changes and will not update your screen automatically. But if you set VIDEO_SWITCH_NOTIFICATION to ON, OS/2 notifies your DOS session that the screen needs updating when you switch back to the DOS session.

To allow your DOS program direct access to the 8514/A or XGA video adapter, change the VIDEO_8514A_XGA_IOTRAP setting from ON to OFF. Change this setting only before starting a DOS session. When you turn off this setting, change the VIDEO_SWITCH_NOTIFICATION setting to ON so that your screen is redrawn when you switch back to the DOS session. When VIDEO_8514A_XGA_IOTRAP is OFF, OS/2 also releases the 1M of memory normally reserved for video data in a DOS session.

VIDEO_FASTPASTE

When you copy or paste text information, the characters transfer between the session and OS/2's Clipboard. OS/2 uses the Copy command to transfer characters between a DOS session and the Clipboard, and the Paste command to transfer text characters between the Clipboard and a DOS session. OS/2 transfers that information faster than you can type it; and when you set VIDEO_FASTPASTE to ON, OS/2 sends the information even faster.

In most cases this speed increase is not a problem for your DOS program, which thinks you are typing fast. If the characters arrive too quickly in DOS programs that buffer keystrokes internally, however, you may fill the temporary buffer (storage area) where the keystrokes are being stored before processing. Your program may not be able to handle the overflow. Also, you will see no change from setting

VIDEO_FASTPASTE to ON with DOS programs that directly monitor the keyboard interrupts. You also can try expanding the keyboard buffer by changing KBD_BUFER_EXTEND, but note that you use precious DOS memory to do this. (See the preceding section.)

The default value for this setting is OFF, and you can change the setting either before or during a DOS session.

VIDEO_MODE_RESTRICTION

A few DOS programs use only CGA or monochrome video modes. With these programs, the area of memory normally used to store video information for other video modes can be used for your application program, instead of keeping that memory reserved for video information.

You can use the VIDEO_MODE_RESTRICTION setting for programs that run only in CGA or monochrome text modes. If your DOS program uses these modes only, you can take advantage of the extra memory for your program. This method of gaining extra memory is useful on computers with limited memory and monochrome text or CGA video adapters. Your computer does not have limited memory by DOS standards, however; you would not be able to run OS/2 if it did. Your computer is also unlikely to only have a monochrome or CGA video board.

On the other hand, higher resolution video boards, such as EGA or VGA, emulate the CGA and monochrome text video modes, so in theory you could use this setting on most computers. The advantages, however, are negligible except with unusual (or very old) application programs that do not use any VGA or EGA video modes. Do not use this setting if your program uses any modes other than CGA or monochrome text modes.

The default setting is NONE, and you change this setting before starting a DOS session. If you choose CGA mode, 96K of memory space is added to low DOS memory. If you choose MONO mode, 64K of memory space is added to low DOS memory.

 DOS_RMSIZE must be set to 640 to use the VIDEO_MODE_Restriction setting.

VIDEO_ONDEMAND_MEMORY

One way OS/2 can handle multiple programs at the same time is by storing each program's current video image in memory as you view another session. When you switch from a full-screen session, OS/2 stores the image in memory and restores it when you return to the session.

If you run a DOS program that uses a lot of memory, or if you run many different programs at once, switching from the DOS session to another session, OS/2 may not have enough memory to enable you to switch back to another session without losing the current image. Your DOS session asks OS/2 for the memory, and the memory is not available. Consequently, the DOS session fails.

If your DOS program fails because of lack of memory when you switch from a full-screen view of the program, set VIDEO_ONDEMAND_MEMORY to OFF. The default value is ON, which allocates memory to the DOS program at the time you switch from the full-screen view instead of when you start the program. Adjust this setting either before starting or during the DOS session.

If you set VIDEO_ONDEMAND_MEMORY to OFF, the memory needed for the DOS session is allocated when you switch to the session. Your program is less likely to fail because of lack of memory, but there are disadvantages, too. The memory allocated to your DOS session is unavailable for other programs. Additionally, the time taken to switch to the DOS session increases because OS/2 has to reserve the memory before you start the program.

VIDEO_RETRACE_EMULATION

Setting VIDEO_RETRACE_EMULATION to OFF can improve the performance of your DOS session by causing OS/2 to retrace your DOS session's window at the speed of the DOS program's video mode instead of more frequently. Most DOS programs' speeds are unaffected by this OFF setting; for the exceptions, however, you do gain performance. Unfortunately, you may find that with the setting turned OFF, screen switching is not reliable. You can get incorrect palettes or even a blank screen.

The default setting is ON, and you can change that setting either before starting or during a DOS session.

VIDEO_ROM_EMULATION

When VIDEO_ROM_EMULATION is ON (the default setting), OS/2 provides emulation of the following text-mode video functions: full-screen scroll, WriteChar, and WriteTTY. When this setting is OFF, your programs use the equivalent routines supplied by your video board. You change this setting either before starting or during a DOS session.

In most cases, leaving this setting ON gives the best video performance because OS/2's emulation is faster than that of most video boards. Some manufacturers produce video boards whose routines are faster, however. If you have such a video board, selecting OFF enables you to scroll your screen and display text on-screen faster.

VIDEO_SWITCH_NOTIFICATION

When VIDEO_SWITCH_NOTIFICATION is ON, OS/2 notifies your DOS programs when you switch the session between foreground and background. If this setting is ON and your DOS program checks for screen switching, it saves or redraws the screen when you switch. You can change this setting either before or during a DOS session.

If you have one of the common video adapters, such as VGA, EGA, and CGA, you probably do not need this setting. Most video modes you can access with these adapters do not support screen-switch notification. To avoid getting a blank screen when you switch to the DOS session, however, you need to change the setting when you use VIDEO_ONDEMAND_MEMORY.

VIDEO_WINDOW_REFRESH

When you run a DOS session, OS/2 updates the screen at regular intervals, known as the *refresh rate*. If you set this value too low, your screen is always current, but your program runs slowly because so much time is spent redrawing the screen instead of running your program. If you set this value too high, your screen is updated infrequently.

To choose the time interval in which OS/2 redraws a window, select a value between 0.1 seconds and 60 seconds for VIDEO_WINDOW_REFRESH. The default value is 0.1 second, but you can adjust the setting either before starting or during a DOS session.

Test the effect of altering this value by opening a DOS window and issuing a DOS command such as DIR or TYPE. Change the value and reissue the command. The appropriate value depends on the DOS program you run.

Maximizing Available Memory

Although OS/2 takes away the infamous 640K memory barrier, you may run into memory resource problems when you run DOS application programs under OS/2. Like the display, keyboard, and mouse settings, these problems typically arise because the DOS application program you run expects exclusive use of the computer's resources—in this case, memory. You can adjust the settings to give the DOS application program the memory resources it expects.

Many of these settings deal with memory specifications created to deal with the limitations of DOS, including expanded memory and extended memory. A large number of terms, such as upper memory blocks (UMB), high memory area (HMA), page frames, and handles relate to these specifications. OS/2 has generally eliminated the need to understand these terms unless you run a DOS program in a DOS session and need to use them. The following explanations briefly introduce the terms, but do not attempt a comprehensive explanation.

DOS_HIGH

The DOS_HIGH setting is equivalent to the DOS=HIGH directive available in DOS 5.0 and later versions. By allowing OS/2 to place DOS into high DOS memory, you have more memory available below 640K. Most programs allow this, but some do not work unless DOS is in low DOS memory (the more traditional location).

Change DOS_HIGH from its default value of ON to OFF so that OS/2 places DOS in low DOS memory rather than high DOS memory. You must change this setting before starting a DOS session.

DOS_RMSIZE

The DOS_RMSIZE value indicates the amount of memory available to DOS programs. The default setting is 640, but you can select between 128 and 640. The units are kilobytes. You must change this value before starting a DOS session.

You are unlikely to need to change this setting, because almost all DOS programs work best with 640K of memory. In exceptional situations, however, such as times when your video board uses some of the base memory, you need to change this value.

DOS_UMB

Upper memory blocks (UMBs), which are areas of memory between 640K and 1M, can be used to load DOS device drivers and DOS TSRs. One way to load these programs is to use DOS's features and add

DEVICEHIGH and LOADHIGH statements to your DOS CONFIG.SYS file. In this case, DOS controls the UMBs and handles their creation and the loading and unloading of the data they contain.

An alternative method is to use a memory management program instead of DOS. Typically, the memory management programs have more features or are more flexible than DOS. In this case, the memory management program needs to control the UMBs. When running a DOS session under OS/2, change the DOS_UMB setting to OFF to allow the memory manager to control the UMBs. Change this setting before starting a DOS session.

DPMI_DOS_API

To overcome the 640K memory limitation, some DOS programs incorporate a DOS extender program for memory management. Many large DOS application programs, especially databases and CAD programs, include a DOS extender. These programs include their own memory management features. As you require more memory, the program organizes the available memory to accommodate. Some DOS programs (such as Windows), however, expect the operating system to supply these services. OS/2 can supply them, but you need to enable the DPMI_DOS_API setting.

If you run programs that include a DOS extender that conforms with the DOS Protected Mode Interface (DPMI), use the default DPMI_DOS_API setting of AUTO. Change the setting to ENABLED if you want the operating system to handle your program's requests for DOS services. Change the setting to DISABLED if your programs do not use DPMI. You must change this setting before starting a DOS session.

If you do not know whether your programs can take advantage of DPMI, leave the default value; the services are then available, but not used if your programs do not support DPMI.

DPMI_MEMORY_LIMIT

This value limits the amount of memory available to your DOS session for programs that use DPMI services. Note that Windows uses DPMI services; you may want to increase this value if you run several Windows programs at once.

To make more or less memory available for DPMI memory allocation, change the DPMI_MEMORY_LIMIT from its default value of 2. Choose a number between 0 and 512, with the units in megabytes. You must set the value before you start a DOS session.

See the other DPMI settings for further adjustments. If your DOS program does not use DPMI services, select 0 for this setting.

DPMI_NETWORK_BUFF_SIZE

The DPMI_NETWORK_BUFF_SIZE controls the size of the buffer used when you transfer data across a network from programs using DPMI. This setting is important only if you are running on a network and using programs that take advantage of DPMI and transfer data across the network.

If you experience problems transferring data over the network from a DOS session, try increasing this buffer size. Change the default value of 8 (K); the available range is from 1 to 64. You must change the setting before starting a DOS session.

EMS_FRAME_LOCATION

Most DOS programs use the Lotus/Intel/Microsoft Expanded Memory Specification (EMS), which gives your DOS program access to more memory than 1M. The vast majority of these programs behave predictably, so you can ignore this setting. The operating system handles the allocation and deallocation of the areas of memory, known as page frames.

In a few rare cases, which may be due to your specific hardware configuration and/or your particular DOS program, you need to actually specify the page frame location. If you experience problems running programs with expanded memory, adjust EMS_HIGH_OS_MAP_REGION, and then change the EMS_FRAME_LOCATION if the problem is not resolved.

To designate the expanded memory specification page frame location instead of letting the session handle the memory allocation, adjust the default setting of AUTO for the EMS_FRAME_LOCATION to a different address. Choose a value from the list in the settings menu. You must change this setting before starting a DOS session.

EMS_HIGH_OS_MAP_REGION

There are several versions of the expanded memory specifications. Most newer programs are written to the latest version of these specifications, which allows page frames to be larger than 64K. If you run into expanded memory problems with your DOS program, however, try limiting the page frame size to 64K by setting EMS_HIGH_OS_MAP_REGION to 0, which may clear up your program's confusion over memory allocation. If this fails, try explicitly specifying the expanded memory page frame location with EMS_FRAME_LOCATION setting.

To allow your DOS programs to create EMS page frames larger than 64K, place a value for the EMS_HIGH_OS_MAP_REGION setting. The value can be between 0 and 96; the default value is 32. This number indicates the number of kilobytes larger than 64K that your page frames can be. You must change this setting before starting a DOS session.

EMS_LOW_OS_MAP_REGION

To allow your DOS programs to create EMS page frames in low DOS memory (memory below 640K), place a value for the EMS_LOW_OS_MAP_REGION setting. The value, which indicates the number of kilobytes of low DOS memory that can be allocated, can be between 0 and 576; the default value is 384. You must change this setting before starting a DOS session.

The page frame position is handled automatically by the operating system and should not be a problem for programs. If you find you need more expanded memory, however, try raising this value. Note that any memory allocated for expanded memory will not be available as low DOS memory.

EMS_MEMORY_LIMIT

The operating system automatically creates expanded memory page frames and handles their contents. The EMS_MEMORY_LIMIT indicates the maximum amount of expanded memory that can be allocated at once.

To specify the maximum amount of EMS memory your DOS programs can allocate, place a value for the EMS_MEMORY_LIMIT setting. This number indicates the number of kilobytes of EMS memory that can be allocated. The value can be in increments of 16 between 0 and 32768; the default value is 2048. The default value of 2048K (2M) may not be sufficient for some larger programs, such as large spreadsheets, but is adequate for most situations. You must change this setting before starting a DOS session.

Even though you can set a lower value, you typically do not need to do so; the memory is assigned only when needed. If your program does not use expanded memory or uses less than the assigned value, you will not reach this limit.

MEM_EXCLUDE_REGIONS

Your operating system automatically handles memory allocation and deallocation. In some cases, the operating system assumes that an area of memory is not in use when it actually is. This occurs most often with video boards with advanced features, which may require a larger area of memory than the operating system assumes.

If you experience problems with your hardware when you run a program using expanded memory or extended memory, or even when you copy the ROM contents to memory, you may have excluded the memory areas that the particular piece of hardware occupies. This information is usually specified in the hardware documentation.

To exclude specific areas of upper memory from being used for other purposes, such as expanded or extended memory, use MEM_EXCLUDE_REGIONS setting. This setting has no default value. You must specify the addresses before starting a DOS session. Type the hexadecimal address for the range. Either specify the starting address for a 4K region, or type an address range separated by a hyphen. Specify multiple ranges by separating each range by a comma, but do not use spaces. To specify a range from B8000H to C0000H and a 4K region starting at C8000H, for example, type **B8000-C0000,C8000**.

MEM_INCLUDE_REGIONS

Your operating system automatically handles the allocation and deallocation of memory. Just as the operating system assumes that an area of memory is not in use when it actually is, the operating system may assume that an area of memory is in use when it is not.

You can improve program performance by finding additional areas of memory that it can use for expanded or extended memory. You need to be careful, however, that you do not specify an area that is used occasionally.

To allow specific areas of upper memory to be used for other purposes, such as expanded or extended memory, use MEM_INCLUDE_REGIONS setting. This setting has no default value. You must specify the addresses prior to starting a DOS session. Type the hexadecimal address for the range. Either specify the starting address for a 4K region, or type an address range separated by a hyphen. Specify multiple ranges by separating each range by a comma, but do not use spaces. To specify a range from B8000H to C0000H and a 4K region starting at C8000H, for example, type **B8000-C0000,C8000**.

XMS_HANDLES

Each area of extended memory that the operating system generates has a unique name known as its *handle*. The XMS_HANDLES setting limits the number of different areas of extended memory to which your program can have access. In general, you do not need to change this setting; however, too large a number can slow your system.

The XMS_HANDLES value dictates the number of extended memory specification handles that can be assigned. Acceptable values range from 0 to 128, and the default setting is 32. You must change this setting before starting a DOS session.

XMS_MEMORY_LIMIT

The XMS_MEMORY_LIMIT value dictates the maximum amount of extended memory that can be assigned. Acceptable values range from 0 to 17384; the default setting is 2048 and the values are in kilobytes. The maximum limit is equal to 17M. If you set too large a value for the extended memory limit, your system may slow. You must change this setting before starting a DOS session.

XMS_MINIMUM_HMA

The High Memory Area (HMA) is an area of memory, the first 64K immediately above 1M, that can be accessed as low DOS memory. You use this setting when you run multiple programs within a DOS session. In most cases, however, you can ignore this setting and allow the first program that wants HMA to have it. Consider opening another DOS session if you want a second program to use HMA memory.

Your DOS program must support HMA to be able to use it. Only one DOS program per session can use HMA, though, and you may want to restrict which program can access this memory. After this memory is assigned, all other programs are unable to use it. If the first program that requests HMA asks for only a couple of kilobytes, you are wasting the remaining 62K, so you may want to insist that a program ask for at least 20K. That way access to HMA is no longer given on a first-come, first-served basis; the first program that requests a value over your setting (over 20, in the example) would receive access.

To specify the minimum size of HMA that must be requested before it is allocated, change XMS_MINIMUM_HMA. Acceptable values are from 0 to 63; the default setting is 0 and the units are in kilobytes. You must alter this setting before starting a DOS session.

Tuning Other DOS Session Settings

OS/2 uses configuration settings comparable to those used by DOS. When you run a DOS session under OS/2, however, you may need to adjust the DOS session's settings so that you provide the DOS application program with the required settings.

For example, your DOS application program may need the LASTDRIVE setting changed or the DOS version changed. Alternatively, you may need to change Windows' operating mode if you run a Windows application program in OS/2.

COM_DIRECT_ACCESS

If your DOS program needs to have direct access to your serial ports (such as COM1 and COM2), you can change the COM_DIRECT_ACCESS default setting from OFF to ON. You must change the setting before starting a DOS session.

As a multitasking operating system, OS/2 typically controls any access to system resource, such as the serial ports and shares this resource between all the open windows. Some DOS programs which were not written to share the computer's resources with other programs expect exclusive use of the serial ports.

Not only are some programs unwilling to share resources, but they also circumvent the operating system, DOS, and manipulate the hardware directly. The programs typically do this circumvention to improve performance or because the DOS features supplied are not adequate for their needs. When you then run these programs in a DOS window under OS/2, they do not operate correctly because OS/2 is limiting their access to the hardware. Change the COM_DIRECT_ACCESS setting to overcome the problem.

COM_HOLD

DOS programs were not typically written to share resources with other programs. Consequently, if a program decides to send or receive information with a COM port, that program does not expect to share this COM port with other programs. If you communicate with an on-line service or bulletin board and your computer has a modem attached to its serial port, for example, a DOS program expects to have exclusive use of the modem.

An OS/2 communications program, on the other hand, is written so that other programs can use the serial port. If a program needs exclusive use of the serial port for some or all of its operations, the program includes the necessary instructions to prevent other programs from accessing the port.

If you use a DOS communications program to exchange files with other computers, you need to alter the COM_HOLD setting. Otherwise you may experience problems when you switch your DOS session to the background, because OS/2 releases the COM port as soon as your DOS program finishes with it, even if the DOS program needs to use it again.

To give your DOS session exclusive use of a serial (COM) port, change the COM_HOLD setting from the default value of OFF to ON. You must change this setting before starting a DOS session.

COM_SELECT

To allocate a particular serial port (such as COM1 or COM2) to a DOS session, change the COM_SELECT default setting from ALL. You must change the setting before starting a DOS session. Compare this setting with COM_HOLD, which keeps the serial port assigned to the DOS session until the DOS session is ended.

When OS/2 is controlling your computer resources rather than DOS, it allocates the serial port use. When your DOS program stops using the serial port, OS/2 is able to assign it to another program wanting the port. Because most DOS programs are written to expect exclusive use of resources, however, you may run into problems with this reallocation; a subsequent DOS program may assume that it has control of the serial port when in reality it has been reassigned.

You may run a DOS communications program that has two parts, for example (one to establish the connection and another to do file transfer). The first program signals that the second can use the serial port at an appropriate time. Unless you have used the COM_SELECT setting, OS/2 may decide to reallocate the serial port to another session. The second DOS program, which does not expect to share a serial port, assumes that it has the serial port to itself and will conflict with the other program.

The available options are ALL, COM1, COM2, COM3, or COM4. Choose the port name from the list box in the settings window.

DOS_AUTOEXEC

When OS/2 starts a DOS session, it runs the AUTOEXEC.BAT file found in the root directory of the boot drive unless you specify the DOS_AUTOEXEC setting. Add a path and file name to the settings text box, indicating the location and name of the substitute AUTOEXEC.BAT. The default value is blank and, obviously, you must set this value before starting a DOS session.

This setting is valuable for specifying different environments for different DOS sessions. If you want different environment variables in different sessions, for example, you can place them in different batch files and then have OS/2 use a particular batch file for a particular DOS session.

DOS_DEVICE

When you boot your computer, OS/2 records any DOS device drivers in CONFIG.SYS. When you start a DOS session, these device drivers are loaded automatically. You can use the DOS_DEVICE driver setting to tailor the CONFIG.SYS device driver settings for a particular DOS session, however. When you start this DOS session, it then has the modified device driver values instead of those loaded by CONFIG.SYS when you booted the computer.

To change the device drivers for every DOS session, modify your CONFIG.SYS file. To modify the device drivers for only one session, use DOS_DEVICE. For example, if you need to load a device driver for your scanner, but you only want to do it when you run your desktop publishing program, use DOS_DEVICE to add the device driver. If you always want to have access to the scanner, add the device driver to CONFIG.SYS.

You can add, remove, or change any DOS device driver loaded with CONFIG.SYS by using the DOS_DEVICE setting. You must change this setting before starting a DOS session. To remove or change existing device drivers, select the driver from the list in the settings dialog box and modify. To add new drivers, type in the new value.

DOS_FCBS

When you run a program, DOS opens and closes small areas of memory called *file control blocks (FCBs)*. If your program requests a file control block, DOS sets aside an area of memory for that program. The area cannot be used for anything else until DOS closes it. A larger number of open FCBs can improve your program's performance, but when running under OS/2, the overall performance of all the open sessions can deteriorate. OS/2 may be kept so busy handling all the open FCBs for a DOS session that your other background sessions, in particular sessions transmitting data across the network, do not have sufficient resources to be efficient.

To limit or expand the number of file control blocks that your DOS session can open at once, change DOS_FCBS. The acceptable range is from 0 to 255, and the default value is 17. You must change this setting before starting a DOS session.

If a program requests an FCB when the maximum number of blocks is open, your DOS session closes the least recently used FCB to free memory for the new one. (For information on preventing DOS from automatically closing FCB, see the section "DOS_FCBS_KEEP.")

DOS_FCBS_KEEP

The DOS_FCBS_KEEP setting tells DOS to keep a certain number of file control blocks (FCBs) open and not automatically close them. The valid range is from 0 to 255, and the default value is 17. You must change this setting before starting a DOS session. (See the preceding section, "DOS_FCBS," for more detailed information about file control blocks.)

You may want to prevent DOS from automatically closing an FCB when a program requests one more than the maximum FCB setting. After a program has requested the number of FCBs stored in DOS_FCBS_KEEP, DOS does not automatically close an FCB to supply the program with an additional one. The program can continue to request FCBs up to the maximum specified in DOS_FCBS. If more FCBs are required, however, DOS can only supply them by closing existing ones provided the value in DOS_FCBS_KEEP is equal or higher than the number of open FCBs.

DOS_FILES

All DOS and Windows programs open multiple files at once, and in many cases you are unaware of it. A word processor, for example, may enable you to work on two documents at once. When you have two documents loaded, you have at least three files open—the two documents and the word processing program (excluding the files STDIN, STDOUT, and STDERR which all DOS programs open). Many programs, however, do not just operate with a single program file, but use many other files as temporary storage and reference files and as places to hold less frequently used features. A word processor may keep backup files, allow user-generated dictionaries, and keep its graphics viewing features in separate files, all of which may be open at once.

Most large DOS application programs specify a minimum value for your FILES setting in DOS's CONFIG.SYS. To run that application program under OS/2, you need to set at least that value for the DOS_FILES setting.

This setting does not apply to your OS/2 sessions. As a multitasking operating system, OS/2 can keep many files open at once. To allow your DOS or Windows program to have access to as many files as it requires, however, you need to adjust the setting within the DOS session or Win-OS/2 session.

Change DOS_FILES to alter the number of files your DOS or Win-OS/2 session can have open simultaneously. Acceptable values are between 20 and 255. The default settings, which are also the minimum settings, are 20 for DOS sessions and 48 for Win-OS/2 sessions. You can change this setting before or during a DOS or Win-OS/2 session. In most cases, you will not need to change these values unless a particular application program instructs you to increase your DOS files setting.

DOS_LASTDRIVE

This setting is similar to using the LASTDRIVE setting in your CONFIG.SYS on a DOS-based computer, but its purpose on the OS/2-based computer is slightly different. OS/2 automatically enables you to access all drive letters up to Z. (You can use OS/2 settings to limit this choice.) Consequently, with OS/2 you do not need a LASTDRIVE setting for your DOS session.

On the other hand, you can restrict a DOS session's access to drives with this setting. If you do not want your DOS session to access network drives, for example, add a DOS_LASTDRIVE setting. Suppose that you have two hard disks on your computer (with drive letters C and D). To prevent them from accessing the network drives (with drive letters E and above), set DOS_LASTDRIVE to D.

Change DOS_LASTDRIVE to limit the last drive letter accessible to your DOS sessions. The default value is Z, and any setting between A and Z is acceptable; but you must include all drive letters physically in your computer. You must change this setting before starting a DOS session.

DOS_SHELL

One of DOS's flexible features is its capability to run an alternative command processor. As the name suggests, the command processor is the program that translates into instructions the commands you type at the command line, such as COPY, DEL, and DIR. You can purchase alternative command processors, such as 4DOS, which typically includes all the DOS commands and adds functioning ability or speed. For example, 4DOS includes a directory deleting command that deletes the files in a subdirectory and removes the subdirectory. (With DOS you must use two commands for this action.)

On a DOS-based computer, you specify the alternative command processor in your CONFIG.SYS file; but on an OS/2-based computer, use the DOS_SHELL setting. You must change this setting before starting a DOS session. Type the full path and file name, along with any command line switches, for the alternative command processor. The default value is as follows:

```
C:\OS2\MDOS\COMMAND.COM /P
```

Although the alternative command processor's drive is not required if your processor is on the boot drive, you should still include the drive in this setting.

DOS_STARTUP_DRIVE

For most applications, OS/2's DOS emulation is suitable for your DOS programs. In certain cases, however, the emulation is inadequate. You may not be able to load a particular device driver into a normal OS/2 DOS session, for example, or a DOS program may not run properly.

Add the drive and path for an alternative version of DOS in DOS_STARTUP_DRIVE. Instead of allowing OS/2 to emulate DOS, use this setting to load a version of DOS between 3.0 and 5.0.

The DOS_STARTUP_DRIVE setting is used for a different purpose than the DOS_VERSION setting. The DOS_VERSION setting lets a particular program assume that it is running a different version of DOS, although the DOS_STARTUP_DRIVE is part of the method used to actually run a different version of DOS.

Note that several other operations are necessary for this alternative DOS version to operate correctly.

DOS_VERSION

Similar to DOS 5.0's SETVER command, the DOS_VERSION setting enables you to run older programs that expect a particular version of the operating system to run. Suppose that a program uses a feature added only to DOS 3.0. That program may consult the operating system and determine that the DOS version number is 3.0 before it runs. If the DOS version is later, however, the program may run successfully because the feature is available, but it may not get past the version checking procedure. (Some programs include this check to avoid any potential incompatibility problems with later versions of the operating systems.) If you run DOS 5 before you install OS/2 and have program names in the SETVER region, you can add them to your OS/2 installation via this DOS_VERSION setting.

To change the DOS version number that a program encounters when operating in a DOS session, and to change the number of times OS/2 reports this version to your program, add that program to the DOS_VERSION setting. Type the program's executable file name, followed by the version number, a comma, the subversion number (two digits are required), a comma, and the number of times this version number can be reported to the program. A value of 255 for the latter parameter makes OS/2 report this simulated version number every time the program requests the information. If, for example, a program named WORDPROC.EXE requires DOS version 3.2, and you want the program to determine that the DOS version is 3.2 every time it asks, type **WORDPROC.EXE,3,20,255**.

HW_NOSOUND

Because DOS programs do not expect to share resources such as the speaker, they do not turn off the speaker when you switch to another session. You may want to hear the sound from another program, or you may have switched from the DOS session as the speaker was sounding and ended up with a continuous noise.

You can change HW_NOSOUND default setting of ON to OFF. The OFF setting turns off the sound created by a DOS program. Remember to turn this setting back on to hear the sounds again. You can change this setting before or during a DOS session.

HW_TIMER

This setting is important for timing critical applications. The emulation supplied by OS/2 may not be suitable in all situations, and you may have to allow the DOS session to access the hardware timer directly.

Timing-critical applications require very precise time measurements. For example, a data acquisition program that samples data every millisecond must be able to time accurately, or your measurements are meaningless. The most common timing-critical programs are more frivolous than data acquisition, however, and include many game programs. A game program may use the time to determine how fast aliens are approaching, for example.

When you run a DOS session under OS/2, the operating system emulates the system's timer instead of allowing the program direct access to the hardware. This emulation allows multiple programs simultaneous access to timing features and is a feature of multitasking operating systems.

DOS programs, however, expect exclusive use of the timer. Because the OS/2 timer emulation does not and cannot include the time between the period when the program requested the time and when OS/2 actually determined the request, the time supplied to a program may not be completely accurate.

Change HW_TIMER from the default setting of OFF to ON, to allow your DOS session to access the hardware timer ports. When set to OFF, OS/2 intercepts any hardware timer port requests and provides a timing emulation. You can change this setting before or during a DOS session.

INT_DURING_IO

If you want to permit the DOS programs to receive interrupts during a file read or write, change the INT_DURING_IO setting from its default of OFF to ON. You must change this setting before starting your DOS session.

In many situations, you do not want OS/2 to interrupt a DOS program while it is reading or writing a file from or to disk; you are avoiding the potential of corrupted data. Some programs, in particular multi-media programs, need to receive interrupts during the reading process, however. Some CD ROM programs read data from the disk but are playing music or speech at the same time, for example. This is what the DOS program is doing when it processes interrupts while data is being read from the disk. You can think of it as if the program is reading the next thing to be said while the words are actually being spoken.

PRINT_TIMEOUT

If you are running your DOS application program under DOS when you print from that program, the information is typically sent directly to the printer port. Under OS/2, print information is sent first to disk in a spool file; then the OS/2 print spooler prints the file, allowing multiple sessions to print at once. The print spooler handles the printing sequence.

When you run a DOS session and print from the DOS program, OS/2 handles the print spooling. OS/2 waits a period of time defined by the setting in PRINT_TIMEOUT and then transfers the print data to a spooler file ready for printing.

You need to alter this setting if your program takes longer than the specified time to create the print file. The symptom of too short a time is that your print job is divided. You may find that features, such as fonts or highlighting, are lost part way through a document because OS/2 treated the job as two print files rather than one.

To alter the time delay between the time when a DOS program starts to create a print file, and the time when the file is sent to OS/2's spool file, change the PRINT_TIMEOUT setting. The default value is 15, but values between 0 and 3600 seconds are acceptable. You can change this setting either before or during a DOS session.

WIN_RUNMODE

You are most likely to change the WIN_RUNMODE setting so that you can run an old Windows program in real mode. OS/2 normally starts the Win-OS/2 session in standard mode. Forcing OS/2 to start a WIN-OS/2 session emulating real mode enables you to run a Windows program that does not support the more advanced features of standard mode.

For Win-OS/2 sessions, change WIN_RUNMODE to specify whether the session operates in real or standard mode. Acceptable values are REAL, STANDARD, or AUTO. The default setting of AUTO causes OS/2 to start a session in standard mode if the required OS/2 virtual device drivers are loaded. Otherwise, AUTO causes OS/2 to start a real mode session. You must change the setting before starting the Win-OS/2 session.

Chapter Summary

This chapter introduced each of the DOS and Windows session settings. Although some DOS application programs run with the default settings, you may need to make adjustments in particular instances because typically, your DOS applications were not written so that they could share your computer's resources, such as the screen, printer, or memory.

You can vary settings so that you can allocate more time to your DOS session; share computer resources, including keyboard, mouse, touch screen, display, and memory; alter the memory allocated to the DOS session; and adjust DOS settings commonly altered in CONFIG.SYS when you run DOS as the primary operating system.

Batch File Programming with OS/2

B atch files are to command line sessions what macros are to spreadsheets. Batch files store a series of commands that, in combination, perform a useful task. You store the commands in a file and type the file name when you want to run that sequence of commands. This procedure is easier and more foolproof than typing each command individually. You may have noticed that some software products use batch files to automate the products' installation processes; an INSTALL.BAT (or INSTALL.CMD) file enables you to use the software sooner than if you installed the product's components by hand.

You can create a batch file easily with the Enhanced Editor, the System Editor, or some other text editor. Type the commands you want to execute, one to a line, exactly as you would type them at the command line prompt. Save the file, in one of your PATH directories, with any name you choose. Use the extension BAT for a DOS batch file; use the CMD extension for a batch file you want to run in an OS/2 session. Batch file programming is that easy.

As you explore batch files, you may find that you want the batch programs you write to do more than run commands, utility programs, and application programs. When this realization occurs, you are ready for more serious computer programming. OS/2 offers a higher-level batch file programming environment called REXX. Appendix G, "Programming with REXX," discusses this more advanced form of batch file programming.

OS/2 and DOS batch files can contain commands and directions in addition to commands and directions you type at a command line prompt. You can combine regular DOS commands and these extra commands to create small, flexible programs that automate many of the tasks you perform on your computer. In this chapter, you learn how to save keystrokes and prevent typing errors by storing the DOS commands you frequently use in batch files.

Learning Batch File Program Basics

In DOS sessions, the operating system program COMMAND.COM executes the commands and statements in your batch files. In OS/2 sessions, CMD.EXE executes the commands and statements. COMMAND.COM and CMD.EXE are the same operating system components that process the commands you enter at a command line prompt. COMMAND.COM and CMD.EXE process your batch file commands by simulating keyboard entry of those commands. Because the commands are stored in a text file, however, you don't have to worry about typing errors. This benefit is especially important if you use a long sequence of commands frequently or if one or more of the commands requires command line parameters that are difficult to use.

The command processors in OS/2, for both OS/2 and DOS sessions, execute your batch file programs one line at a time. The command processor begins with the first line of your batch file. Unless you direct otherwise, the statements in your batch file execute one after the other, from the top of the file to the bottom. You can use the GOTO statement to change the order in which the commands and statements execute.

In the next few sections, you learn to distinguish OS/2 and DOS batch files, you discover ways to run batch file programs, you explore using commands and statements in batch files, and you create a simple, easy-to-understand batch file program.

Distinguishing OS/2 and DOS Batch Files

OS/2 batch file programs have an extension of CMD. DOS batch files use BAT. Most commands work the same whether you run the commands in a CMD file in an OS/2 session or run the commands in a BAT file in a DOS session. Some commands behave differently, however, or are not supported in one kind of session or the other. Part VI, "Using the Command Reference," clearly spells out which commands work only in an OS/2 session or only in a DOS session. START, for example, is an OS/2-only command; MEM is an example of a DOS-only command. MKDIR, on the other hand, works the same in DOS and OS/2 sessions, assuming that you use the same directory names in each session. You can create directories on an HPFS partition, with the OS/2 version of the MKDIR command in a CMD file, that take advantage of HPFS long file names.

Running a Batch File Program

You normally run batch file programs that have a BAT extension in a DOS session, and you run CMD files in an OS/2 session. If you run a BAT file in an OS/2 session, OS/2 automatically starts a temporary DOS session for you and runs the BAT file in that session. The reverse is not true, however. You cannot run CMD files in a DOS session.

OS/2 and DOS search the directories in your PATH statement to find executable programs, including batch file programs. You can explicitly name the directory from which OS/2 should run a program file. You can type the following command at a DOS or OS/2 prompt so that OS/2 searches your PATH prompt directories:

    MYPROG

To avoid the searching of the PATH directories, you can type the following:

    C:\BATDIR\MYPROG.BAT

You run BAT and CMD files at a command line prompt the same way you run application and utility programs that have an extension of COM or EXE. You simply type the file name portion without the extension and press Enter. If you have files with the same name that vary only in the extension (MYPGM.BAT or MYPGM.CMD, MYPGM.COM, and MYPGM.EXE, for example), both DOS and OS/2 run the program file with the COM extension. When the operating system looks for program files, the operating system finds COM files first, EXE files next, and BAT or CMD files last.

This makes naming a batch file program the same name as a utility or application program difficult. OS/2 runs the COM or EXE file rather than the BAT (or CMD) file if the files are in the same directory. You can circumvent OS/2's (or DOS's) preference for COM and EXE files by putting your batch file programs in a directory named earlier in your PATH statement than your other directories that contain programs.

OS/2 can represent a batch file program as an icon (in a folder or on your desktop). You create such a program object in the same way that you create other program objects. Copy the PROGRAM object from the TEMPLATES folder by dragging the object onto the desktop while you press mouse button 2. In the Path and Filename field on the Program page of the settings notebook, you specify the drive, directory, file name, and extension of your batch file program. You then can double-click the resulting icon to run your batch file.

Using DOS and OS/2 Commands in Batch Files

The batch files you create can contain DOS commands, OS/2 commands, or a mixture of commands and invocations of computer programs. The DOS and OS/2 commands you are likely to use most often in batch files are COPY, ERASE, MOVE, RENAME, XCOPY, CHDIR, MKDIR, RMDIR, CLS, and SET. The OS/2-only commands you are likely to use are START and DETACH. Note that many of these commands are file-oriented. You are not likely to find a use for the DATE or TIME commands in your batch files.

Many office environments use a single tape drive to make backup copies of files on a local area network. To include your files in the office's backup procedure, you must copy files from your PC to the file server. Assuming that your file server is drive F and that you customarily put files in the F:\BACKUP directory so that the LAN tape drive can back up the files, you can automate your daily backup chores with the following batch file program:

```
COPY C:\WP\*.DOC F:\BACKUP
COPY C:\123\*.WK1 F:\BACKUP
COPY C:\DATA\*.DAT F:\BACKUP
```

Although you can type each of these commands individually at a command line prompt, you have to wait for one command to finish executing before you type the next command. A batch file accomplishes all of the work of the several commands in one typing operation. You can insert these three lines with a text editor in a DOS batch file (named SAVEWORK.BAT, perhaps) or an OS/2 batch file (named SAVEWORK.CMD).

If you run this three-line batch file program from a DOS-only (non-OS/2-based) workstation and if the files take a long time to copy, you must find something else to do while that computer runs the COPY commands. With OS/2, however, you can start the batch file in one session and continue to work in other sessions.

Later sections of this chapter explain batch file statements in detail. First, however, you create a simple batch file program.

For Related Information

◀◀ "Storing Files and File Names," p. 46.

◀◀ "Beginning the Command Line Interface," p. 293.

FROM HERE...

Creating a Simple Batch File Program

You can use a simple batch file program to work around one of the limitations of DOS. The DOS PATH statement can contain up to 128 characters of information. The count of the characters that make up the drive letters, backslashes, directory names, semicolons, and file names in your DOS PATH must be less than 128. If you have many applications, you probably will find the 128-character limit constraining. (The OS/2 PATH statement does not have the 128-character limit; the limit applies only to DOS.) Several approaches enable you to work around this limit. Consider the following batch file program, for example:

```
C:
CD \LETTERS
PATH C:\DOS;C:\WORDPROC
WORDPROC
PATH C:\DOS
CD \
```

This batch file program, which is one of the most popular, makes drive C current, changes to the LETTERS directory, modifies the PATH to indicate the DOS and WORDPROC directories, runs a program called

WORDPROC, and restores the original PATH and root directory when you finish your word processing tasks. Although the file (WORDPROC) and directory names (LETTERS and WORDPROC) used in the preceding are fictitious, you can substitute directories and files used by your PC's setup.

You can begin the creation of a similar batch file program by taking advantage of a characteristic of the PATH statement. If you issue a PATH statement with no parameters at a command line prompt, DOS displays your current PATH, as shown in the following:

```
PATH=C:\DOS
```

Typing PATH with no parameters produces an executable PATH statement. You can redirect the display output of the PATH statement into a file. If you want to name your new batch file program LETTERS.BAT and if you have a directory named DOS in your PATH, you can start your batch file program by typing the following DOS command:

```
PATH >C:\DOS\LETTERS.BAT
```

Your DOS directory now contains a file LETTERS.BAT. When you type LETTERS at a DOS prompt, the new batch file program issues a PATH command and the result is the same PATH in effect when you typed the name of the batch file.

Use a text editor such as the System Editor to modify the LETTERS.BAT file. You can insert a PATH command to extend the number of directories in your PATH, insert a line that runs a program, and then insert a second PATH statement calling out the directories that were in effect before the first PATH command. After you save the file, you have a batch file program that modifies your PATH, invokes an application, and restores your PATH when you exit the application. You can create other batch file programs for your other applications that similarly set new PATHs for the duration of the application, and you will not have to worry about the 128-character limit imposed by the DOS PATH command.

Using Batch File Program Statements

Batch file programs are not generally interactive; for example, you will not find an easy way to make a batch file program ask questions while the batch file executes. You can use display statements, however, to inform you of the progress of the batch file.

You can insert reminders to yourself (*comments*) in batch files. As your batch file programs grow beyond the three-line example in the previous section, you may find these comments helpful to you or anyone who wants to use and modify your batch files.

Batch file programs can make decisions and execute alternative sequences of commands based on the outcome of the decision. You, as the creator of the batch file program, take three steps to insert decisions in your batch files. You first analyze the requirements of the batch file; then you determine what decisions the batch file program should make; finally, you translate the decision-making process into a series of batch file statements. You may think that this procedure sounds like computer programming, and for a very good reason: it is, indeed, a simple form of computer programming.

Batch files can contain programming language statements as well as DOS or OS/2 commands. The next few sections explain the programming statements you can use to make your batch file programs clearer and more powerful.

Inserting Comments with the REM Statement

Comment lines you place in a batch file program do not execute; the comments serve as documentation to explain what the batch file program does and how the batch file works. You use the REM statement to insert comments in your batch files.

REM stands for remark. Your batch files are easier to understand if you include remarks that explain what your programs do. To insert a remark, begin a line of the batch file with the letters REM. Whatever you type on a line that begins with REM is not interpreted as a command. DOS and OS/2 just skip over REM lines. You might use the following statements, for example, to help document a batch file program that starts the Lotus 1-2-3 application in a DOS session:

```
REM
REM     Always make C:\123 the current directory
REM     while 1-2-3 is running. The WK1 files are
REM     in the C:\123 directory.
REM
C:
CD \123
123
```

The REM statements document your preference for putting worksheet files in the 123 directory on drive C. The last three lines of this batch file program make C the current drive, change to the 123 directory, and run 123.

Writing to the Screen with the ECHO Statement

When DOS or OS/2 runs a batch file program, the command processor by default displays each line of the file on-screen. You can change this behavior—and tidy up your screen in the process—by typing ECHO OFF at the beginning of the batch file program. When the command processor encounters an ECHO OFF statement, DOS or OS/2 stops echoing the lines of the batch file. ECHO OFF does not affect the display of information generated by the commands and application programs you invoke in your batch files; this command only affects the echo of the lines of the batch file. Unfortunately, this command also hides your REM statements when you run the batch program. If you want your batch file messages to appear on-screen while a batch program runs, use the ECHO command to explicitly display the messages, as shown in the following example:

```
ECHO OFF
CD \LETTERS
ECHO    You are now in the LETTERS directory.
```

You don't have to issue an ECHO ON at the end of a batch file. DOS and OS/2 automatically revert to ECHO ON before running the next batch program.

Passing Parameters to a Batch Program

You can expand the usefulness of a batch file program by supplying one or more parameters when you run the batch file. Statements within the batch file can access the parameters. Inside the batch file program, each parameter is a *variable marker*. You can invoke a batch file program named DELMANY.BAT, for example, in the following manner:

```
DELMANY *.TMP *.BAK *.JNK
```

If you write the DELMANY.BAT program to contain the following statements, DOS or OS/2 substitutes the parameters you supply to DELMANY (*.TMP, *.BAK, and *.JNK, in this example) in place of the %1, %2, and other variable markers:

```
ECHO OFF
ERASE %1
ERASE %2
ERASE %3
ERASE %4
ERASE %5
ERASE %6
ERASE %7
ERASE %8
ERASE %9
```

If you don't supply a parameter for every variable marker (which is the case in the following example; only three parameters appear), DOS and OS/2 substitute nothing for the extra markers. As the batch file program in this example runs, the net result is the same as if you typed the following commands at a command line prompt:

```
ERASE *.TMP
ERASE *.BAK
ERASE *.JNK
ERASE
ERASE
ERASE
ERASE
ERASE
ERASE
```

Although ERASE commands that are not followed by file names do no harm, each empty ERASE command produces the following error message in that DOS session:

```
Invalid number of parameters.
```

You learn how to test for the presence of batch file parameters in a later section of this chapter, "Comparing Strings with the IF Statement."

DOS and OS/2 reserve the variable marker %0 for a special purpose. %0 contains the name of the currently running batch file, without the extension. If you inserted ERASE %0 in a batch file named DELZERO.BAT, DOS tries to ERASE the file named DELZERO.

Changing Program Flow with the GOTO Statement

You can use the GOTO statement to change the flow of execution of the lines of your batch file program. You insert a *label* statement in your program to indicate which line a GOTO statement should jump to.

A label begins with a colon (:) and can contain up to eight characters. When DOS or OS/2 encounters the GOTO statement, the command processor uses the line of the batch file following the label as the next executable statement or command. The following batch file program executes continuously until you press Ctrl-C:

```
ECHO OFF
:LINE2
GOTO LINE2
```

Such a batch file, with its unconditional GOTO, isn't very useful. In the next few sections, you learn ways to test for situations in your batch file programs and use the GOTO statement to execute different parts of the batch file depending on the situation.

Testing File Existence with the IF EXIST Statement

You can make a batch file program behave differently depending on the presence or absence of a file. The IF EXIST statement informs your batch file program whether or not a certain file exists. You combine the IF EXIST statement with another command or statement. The command or statement after IF EXIST executes only if the file exists. The following example, which erases the file TEMP.DOC if the file exists, shows the use of a single command with IF EXIST:

```
IF EXIST TEMP.DOC ERASE TEMP.DOC
```

The next example shows an IF EXIST statement used in combination with a GOTO statement:

```
IF EXIST C:\OS2\BOOT.COM GOTO dualboot
ECHO    The Dual Boot facility isn't installed on this PC.
GOTO done
:dualboot
BOOT /DOS
:done
```

As the command processor executes this batch file, one of two things happen. If the file BOOT.COM is in the OS2 directory, execution jumps to the dualboot label, and the command processor then executes the BOOT program. If the file doesn't exist, however, the command processor executes the ECHO statement and the GOTO done statement. In the latter case, the command processor does not attempt to run the BOOT program because the batch file has "jumped over" the lines that invoke BOOT.

Notice the use of the label in the last line of the batch file. Using a label in this way is a common technique for naming the exit point of the batch file program. You also can use the modifier word NOT in your IF EXIST statements. A batch file line that contains the following line sometimes makes more sense and is more readable than an awkward form of IF EXIST:

```
IF NOT EXIST <filename> GOTO NotThere
```

Comparing Strings with the IF Statement

You can examine the variable markers in your batch file programs by comparing strings. You use an IF statement to make the test. The command processor evaluates the IF statement to determine whether to execute the statement that you place on the same line as the IF. If the IF statement, as processed by the command processor, evaluates TRUE, DOS or OS/2 executes the indicated statement or command. Otherwise the command processor proceeds to the next line of the batch file. A double equal sign ("==") denotes the test you want to make. The following example shows how IF works; in the example, the batch file displays the message Please use a filename as the first parameter to this batch file if you run the batch file program with no command line parameters. If you supply a parameter, the example batch file erases the file named in the parameter.

```
IF "%1" == "" GOTO NoParms
ERASE %1
GOTO Done
:NoParms
Please use a filename as the first parameter to this batch file.
:Done
```

If you don't supply a parameter, the "%1" parameter evaluates to a string containing no characters. The "%1" portion becomes back-to-back quotation marks, and the command processor interprets the first line of this batch file as the following:

```
IF "" == "" GOTO NoParms
```

If you do supply a parameter (TEMP.DOC, for example) when you run the batch file, the command processor interprets the first line as the following:

```
IF "TEMP.DOC" == "" GOTO NoParms
```

The preceding example is not a true statement. The command processor ignores the GOTO NoParms part of the first line.

Processing ERRORLEVEL in a Batch File Program

Some utility programs and application software exit with a *return code* or *exit level*. A return code is a number that an application can give to the command processor when the application finishes and exits. (The documentation that comes with the utility or application mentions these return codes.) For these computer programs, you can make your batch files behave differently depending on the computer program's return code. A return code of zero (0) usually means that the program encountered no problems and executed normally.

A return code value greater than 0 usually means that something went wrong. The problem may be that no files were found, for example, or that the program discovered an error in an input file. For programs that use return codes, you can use IF ERRORLEVEL to detect such problems. Your batch file may use a GOTO statement to jump to a different section of batch statements depending on the result of the IF ERRORLEVEL test. The return code is available to you in ERRORLEVEL.

If the return code (ERRORLEVEL) from the utility or application is greater than or equal to the value you specify in the batch file, the IF condition is true. Suppose that you run a program named COMPILE that returns 0 if the program runs without error. If COMPILE encounters errors, the COMPILE program returns the number 4 to the command processor. Your batch file may resemble the following:

```
COMPILE datafile
IF ERRORLEVEL 4 THEN GOTO errors
GOTO done
:errors
ECHO    Compile ended in error!
:done
```

When you use a series of IF ERRORLEVEL statements (for programs that can return alternative exit levels), be sure to test for the highest ERRORLEVEL value first. The command processor considers an IF ERRORLEVEL statement true if the program's return code is greater than the value you specify.

Inserting FOR Loops in Your Batch Programs

A FOR loop in a batch file adds considerable power to your program in only a few lines. You use a FOR loop to make a particular command or statement execute as many times as the FOR loop specifies. A FOR loop enables you to invoke a utility program, DOS command, or OS/2 command for a group of files or drives. You may insert the following lines in a batch file, for example, to make OS/2 perform a CHKDSK operation on drives A, C, and D:

```
FOR %%1 IN (A: C: D:) DO chkdsk %1
```

In a FOR loop, the %%1 variable takes on the value of each item in parentheses. In this example, the items are drive letters. You can use wild-card file names, drives, or paths as items in parentheses. The double percent sign keeps DOS (or OS/2) from treating the variable as a command line parameter.

Calling Batch Files from Other Batch Programs

You don't have to put all the commands and statements you want to execute into a single batch file. You can modularize your programs by creating different batch files for individual tasks. A main, or *primary*, batch file can invoke batch file modules with the CALL statement. The individual module performs its work and, when finished, returns to the main batch file program. The main program continues execution at the statement following the CALL statement. The following batch file shows an example of calling batch files (notice the passing of parameters from one batch file to the other):

MAIN.BAT

```
ECHO OFF
IF EXIST %1 GOTO ParmOkay
ECHO    Please supply a filename.
GOTO Done
:ParmOkay
CALL WORK %1
:Done
```

WORK.BAT

```
ERASE %1
REM    Control now returns to the MAIN.BAT program.
```

These batch file programs, MAIN and WORK, operate in the following way. If you supply MAIN with a command line parameter and that parameter is the name of an existing file, MAIN jumps (branches the flow of the program) to the ParmOkay label. If you do not supply a parameter or if the parameter isn't the name of a file, MAIN echoes the Please supply a filename. message on-screen and jumps to the Done label.

At the ParmOkay label, the MAIN batch file calls the WORK batch file program, supplying the same parameter to WORK that you supplied to MAIN as a command line parameter. WORK simply erases the file whose name is the parameter.

For Related Information

◀◀ "Learning the Commands for Managing Directories," p. 295.

◀◀ "Learning the Commands for Managing Files," p. 301.

▶▶ "Command Reference," p. 647.

Halting a Batch File Program

A batch file program finishes when execution reaches the last line in the batch file. The batch program may execute statements and commands in sequential order, top to bottom. The batch program also may use a GOTO statement to alter the order in which the lines of the batch file execute.

Occasionally, as you create a new batch file program, you may find that you put a GOTO statement in the wrong place. If your batch file program appears to have gone into an *infinite loop*, never reaching the end of the batch file, you can press Ctrl-C to stop the errant batch program. DOS or OS/2 returns you to the command line prompt. You then can use your text editor to examine the logical flow of your batch program to analyze the problem.

Interacting with Batch File Programs

You must use creativity when writing batch file programs that interact with people during file execution. You may want to invoke a computer program, for example, that asks questions and sets ERRORLEVEL depending on the answer given. Your batch file may use a GOTO statement to jump to a section of the batch file appropriate to the given answer. The public domain utilities INPUT.COM and ASK.COM are especially useful in such a situation. Following is an example containing a series of batch file programs that shows how you can create simple menus on your PC:

MENU.BAT

```
ECHO OFF
C:
CD \MENU
ECHO    DIRECTORY MENU
ECHO            1...Change to the LETTERS directory
ECHO            2...Change to the MEMOS directory
ECHO            3...Change to the DATA directory
PROMPT  Type the number (1-3) and press Enter:
```

1.BAT

```
ECHO OFF
REM   reset the prompt
PROMPT $P$G
CD \LETTERS
```

2.BAT

```
ECHO OFF
REM   reset the prompt
PROMPT $P$G
CD \MEMOS
```

3.BAT

```
ECHO OFF
REM   reset the prompt
PROMPT $P$G
CD \DATA
```

Note that MENU.BAT changes the DOS (or OS/2) PROMPT into an actual prompt, which asks the operator to enter a number and press Enter. When the operator types the number and presses Enter, he or she invokes a batch file whose name corresponds to the number typed. The 1.BAT, 2.BAT, and 3.BAT files each reset the DOS PROMPT back to its usual value after changing the current directory to the value specified in each batch file.

Using Startup Batch Programs that Run Automatically

You can create batch file programs that run every time you start a DOS session or when you boot your computer. At boot time, you can have your batch file program run before or after the Workplace Shell appears.

The AUTOEXEC.BAT file in the root directory of your boot drive (usually C:\AUTOEXEC.BAT) runs at the beginning of each DOS command line session you start. You can change this by specifying a different batch file in the DOS_AUTOEXEC setting for that session. DOS_AUTOEXEC is one of the DOS settings you can modify on the Session page of the settings notebook for that command line session.

STARTUP.CMD runs each time you boot OS/2, not in each OS/2 session you start. OS/2 looks for STARTUP.CMD in the root directory of your boot drive.

Use these files for commands that you always want to run. If you want DOSKEY loaded at the beginning of every DOS session, for example, insert the appropriate lines in AUTOEXEC.BAT. If you want your computer to automatically log on to your local area network when you boot OS/2, put your log-in commands in STARTUP.CMD.

A STARTUP.CMD batch file program in the root directory of your boot drive runs before the Workplace Shell displays your desktop. If you use mouse button 2 to drag a CMD batch file program into the STARTUP folder (which the OS/2 installation program puts in your OS/2 SYSTEM folder), however, your batch file runs after the Workplace Shell displays your desktop.

Do not name the batch file STARTUP.CMD because the batch file program will run twice—once because of its special name and once because you moved the CMD file to the STARTUP folder. Give the batch file some other name when you tell your text editor to save the file. Also, to prevent extra copies of the batch file from taking up hard disk space, use the Create Shadow procedure described in Chapter 10, "Managing the Workplace Shell," to drag the CMD file into the STARTUP folder. You also can find a brief description of the Create Shadow procedure on the inside front cover of this book.

FROM HERE...

For Related Information

◀◀ "Customizing the Workplace Shell," p. 250.

◀◀ "Setting Up Other Applications," p. 252.

Chapter Summary

Batch file programs can save you many repetitious keystrokes. You can use batch files to store long sequences of DOS or OS/2 commands or to store commands and parameters that are long or difficult to remember.

Batch file programming is simple and easy. You don't have to be a professional programmer to create and use batch files to make your day-to-day use of your computer more productive.

In the next chapter, you learn about OS/2's advanced features. You begin with an exploration of some of the little-known but useful utility programs that IBM supplies with OS/2.

PART

V

OUTLINE

Exploring OS/2's Advanced Features

Using OS/2 Utilities

O S/2 includes several utility programs that help you customize, manage, and maneuver the OS/2 Workplace Shell, files, directories, programs, and other features while you work in the operating system. Some of these utilities aid in gathering information, others help correct system problems, and each is invaluable if used correctly.

IBM recommends that you use some of these utilities only with the help of a technical coordinator or a service representative. Before you type the utility command on the command line, be sure of your purpose for using the utilities and of the outcome you require.

This chapter discusses in detail the utilities listed in table 19.1. The sections that follow provide information about the purpose of each utility and instructions and examples for its use. In addition, specific warnings for several of the utilities are included. To make finding specific utilities easier, the utilities are organized alphabetically.

Table 19.1 OS/2 Utilities

OS/2 utility	Description
BOOT	Enables you to switch between the DOS and OS/2 operating systems that are on the same hard disk
EAUTIL	Enables you to split (save) and join extended attributes from a data file to a hold file

continues

OS/2 utility	Description
Table 19.1 Continued	
FDISKPM	Enables you to create or delete a primary partition or a logical drive in an extended partition
MAKEINI	Re-creates the OS2.INI startup file and the OS2SYS.INI system file in your OS/2 operating system
PATCH	Enables you to apply software repairs and IBM-supplied patches
PMCHKDSK	Reads and analyzes files and directories, determines file system type, and produces a disk status report
PSTAT	Displays information about current processes and threads, system semaphores, shared memory for each process, and dynamic-link libraries
SETBOOT	Enables you to set time out value, mode, and system startup index of Boot Manager
SORT	Sorts data from standard input by number or letter
SYSLEVEL	Displays the operating system name, version, ID, and current corrective service level
UNDELETE	Restores a file you recently erased
UNPACK	Restores compressed files on the OS/2 floppy to a form you can use
VIEW	Looks up a topic in an on-line help document

RETURN CODES are messages that some utilities display to signal the successful completion of a task, an error, message, or the reason for the termination of a task. A complete list of Return Codes for the utilities that follow appears later in this chapter.

Using BOOT

The BOOT utility enables you to switch between DOS and OS/2 when they are on the same hard drive. To use this utility, you must have installed OS/2 with the Dual-Boot option. When you install Dual-Boot, you add OS/2 to the same partition in which DOS resides. Installing OS/2 in this manner prevents you from operating DOS and OS/2 at the same time; however, you can switch between the two operating systems by using the BOOT command.

The following list explains the requirements and limitations of Dual-Boot:

- You must have DOS 3.2 or higher installed on your hard disk (drive C). For greater compatibility with OS/2, however, using DOS 3.3 or greater is recommended.

- Your primary partition must be large enough to accommodate both the DOS and OS/2 operating systems.

- DOS uses the File Allocation Table (FAT) system only. Because OS/2 and DOS exist on the same partition, you cannot use the High Performance File System (HPFS) with the Dual-Boot feature.

- If you formatted drive C during the OS/2 installation, you cannot use the BOOT command.

Instructions

You can run the BOOT utility in one of three ways: from an OS/2 command prompt, a DOS command prompt window under OS/2, or from DOS. To run the BOOT command, you first must activate the appropriate command prompt.

When you are using the OS/2 operating system, you access the OS/2 command prompt by following these steps:

1. Open the OS/2 System folder in Presentation Manager.

2. From the System folder, open the Command Prompts folder.

3. Open the OS/2 Window or the OS/2 Full Screen to access the command prompt [C:\].

If you are using the OS/2 operating system and want to access the DOS command prompt, follow these steps:

1. Open the OS/2 System folder in Presentation Manager.

2. Open the Command Prompts folder.

3. Choose either the DOS window or DOS Full Screen to access the command prompt C:\.

At the OS/2 command prompt, type the following, and then press Enter:

    BOOT /DOS

OS/2 responds with the following message:

```
SYS1714: Warning! Make sure all your programs have completed or
data will be lost when the system is
restarted.

You requested to start DOS from drive C:

Your system will be reset. Do you want to continue (Y/N)?
```

If you want your system to reboot to DOS, respond with Y. If you respond N, OS/2 remains the operating system.

When you are in the DOS operating system and want to switch to the OS/2 operating system, follow these steps:

1. To change from the DOS command prompt C:\> to the OS/2 directory, type the following and then press Enter:

    CD\OS2

2. To boot the OS/2 operating system, type the following and then press Enter:

    BOOT /OS2

    (Alternatively, you can combine the preceding two steps and type **OS2\BOOT /OS2**.)

    The system displays a warning similar to the warning displayed when you switch from the OS/2 operating system to DOS.

3. If you want your system to reboot to OS/2, press Y. If you want to cancel the operation, press N. DOS remains the operating system.

T   I   P   You can create a batch file, which you can use in DOS, to change the operating system to OS/2. Type the following in a file named OS2.BAT:

C:\OS2\BOOT /OS2

In addition, you can create a DOS or CMD batch file to use in OS/2 by typing the following in a file named DOS.BAT or DOS.CMD:

C:\OS2\BOOT /DOS

Warnings

Before using the BOOT utility, be sure that you have completed all system operations and that you have stopped all programs; if you don't, you will lose data.

Return Codes

BOOT displays a return code of 0 for normal completion and an error message if a problem with the command occurs.

For Related Information

◀◀ "Installing Dual-Boot," p. 130.

◀◀ "Introducing Presentation Manager," p. 221.

◀◀ "Beginning the Command Line Interface," p. 293.

◀◀ "Learning Batch File Program Basics," p. 440.

FROM HERE...

Using EAUTIL

The EAUTIL command enables you to *split*, or cut, extended attributes from a data file and save these attributes to a hold file, a file that contains the split attributes until you need them. You also can rejoin the split attributes to the original file or to another file.

An *extended attribute* is specific information attached by an application to a file or directory. Extended attributes describe that file or directory to another application, to the operating system, or to the file system program that manages the application. Some applications or file systems may not recognize or process extended attributes from another application. When this situation occurs, you can use the EAUTIL command to split the attributes from the file and save them in a hold file to prevent the attributes from being erased. The EAUTIL command also enables you to join those same attributes from the hold file to the file or directory.

Instructions

The syntax of the EAUTIL command is shown in the following:

EAUTIL datafile holdfile */S /R /J /O /M /P*

datafile specifies the name of the file that contains the extended attributes to be split.

holdfile specifies the name of the file that will hold the extended attributes.

/S splits the extended attributes from the data file and places the attributes in the hold file.

/R replaces the extended attributes in a hold file with new attributes you assign.

/J joins the extended attributes from the hold file to the data file.

/O overwrites extended attributes in the data file with the attributes in the hold file.

/M merges the extended attributes in the hold file into the attributes in the data file.

/P preserves extended attributes in the data file after a split or in a hold file after a join.

Examples

To place extended attributes from a data file named MYFILES.TXT into a hold file named ATTRIBUT.EAU, use the following:

EAUTIL MYFILES.TXT ATTRIBUT.EAU /S

To join the extended attributes in the hold file ATTRIBUT.EAU with the data file MYFILES.TXT, use the following:

EAUTIL MYFILES.TXT ATTRIBUT.EAU /J

To replace the extended attributes in the hold file ATTRIBUT.EAU with attributes from a data file named MYNEWFIL.TXT, use the following:

EAUTIL MYNEWFIL.TXT ATTRIBUT.EAU /R /S

To merge the extended attributes in the hold file ATTRIBUT.EAU with attributes in a data file named MYFILES.TXT, use the following:

EAUTIL MYFILES.TXT ATTRIBUT.EAU /M /J

Warnings

Joining, merging, replacing, or overwriting extended attributes may create problems in your files. Applications attach their own unique extended attributes to files; if the files return to the application with the wrong attributes or with no attributes, the application may no longer be able to read or process the file.

Return Codes

EAUTIL issues the following return codes:

0   Normal completion

1   File not found

2   Ended due to error

Using FDISKPM

FDISKPM enables you to create or delete a primary partition or a logical drive in an extended partition. FDISKPM is similar to FDISK except that you perform FDISKPM from the Presentation Manager; you use FDISKPM in OS/2 only. In addition, the Presentation Manager presents FDISKPM with menus and displays, which help you set up your hard disks. Help is also available from within FDISKPM.

The Fixed Disk Utility window displays Partition Information about your present setup (see fig. 19.1). The information includes the number of partitions and an icon for each partition or logical drive within an extended partition. In addition, the window includes the following:

Element	Description
Name	The assigned name displayed on the Boot Manager menu
Status	Installable (a file system that uses a cache for quick access to large amounts of information), bootable (the partition is displayed on the Boot Manager partition), startable (the system restarts to this partition), or none of the above
Access	Accessible (the partition is available for use) and whether partition is primary or a logical drive within the extended partition
File System Type	FAT, HPFS, Unformatted, or Free Space
MBytes	Size in megabytes of the partition or free space

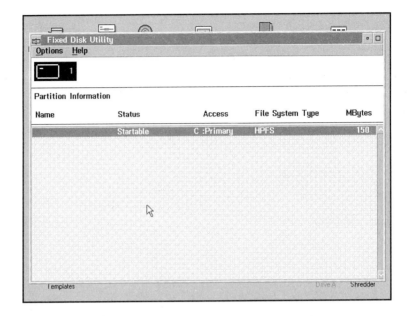

Fig. 19.1

The Fixed Disk Utility window showing partition information.

Two menu items are available: Options and Help. Figure 19.2 illustrates the Options menu. Only three of the commands from the menu are available to you at this point: Delete Partition, Set Installable, and Exit.

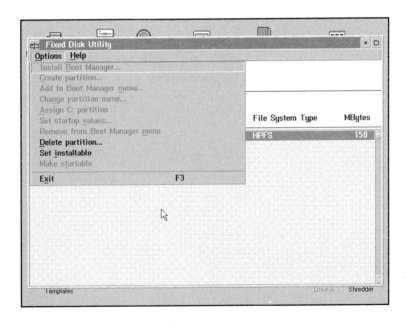

Fig. 19.2

The Options menu in the Fixed Disk Utility window.

The following table describes the Options and Help menu commands.

Command	Function
Options Menu	
Install Boot Manager...	Installs the Boot Manager partition
Create partition...	Creates a primary partition or a logical drive
Add to Boot Manager menu...	Adds a partition to Boot Manager
Change partition name...	Adds or changes an optional name to the partition
Assign partition	Assigns the accessibility of primary partitions
Set startup values...	Sets startup values like a default partition, selection time, or mode for the Boot Manager
Remove from Boot Manager menu	Removes a partition from Boot Manager
Delete partition...	Deletes a primary partition or logical drive
Set installable	Sets a primary partition as installable
Make startable	Specifies a primary partition as startable
Exit	Exits FDISKPM
Help Menu	
Help index	Accesses information about FDISKPM window and descriptions within the window
General help	Provides access to OS/2 General help, search, and more
Using help	Explains how to use Help feature
Keys help	Provides information about using the keyboard instead of the mouse
Product information	Provides information about FDISKPM utility

Instructions

The Boot Manager enables you to create up to four primary partitions on the hard disk. A *primary partition* cannot be shared, and only one primary partition can be active at one time. You can create an extended partition as one of the four primary partitions. You then can divide this partition into *logical drives*, which can be shared and can hold an operating system or data files.

When creating a partition, the Fixed Disk Utility prompts you to choose the type of partition (primary or extended with logical drives) and specify an optional name. You also are prompted to indicate whether the partition will be bootable, the type of files used with the partition (FAT or HPFS), the partition's accessibility, and so on.

You can use the FDISKPM utility in OS/2 only, and you must use it at a command prompt. To access the OS/2 command prompt and run the FDISKPM utility from the command prompt, type the following and press Enter:

    FDISKPM

The Fixed Disk Utility appears and you may now set up partitions.

Warnings

If you have only one partition and delete that partition, you no longer have an operating system.

If you modify any partition, you delete its contents. Be sure to make backup files before using the FDISKPM utility.

Read Hard Disk Information (found in your OS/2 Installation book or in the Command Reference folder) before you operate FDISKPM. In addition, be sure that you know what results you want from this utility and that you know exactly how to get them.

FROM HERE...

For Related Information

◄◄ "Understanding Disk Partitions and Disks," p. 44.

◄◄ "Choosing Boot Manager," p. 126.

◄◄ "Adding a Hard Disk," p. 171.

Using MAKEINI (OS/2 Only)

The MAKEINI utility program re-creates the OS2.INI startup file and the OS2SYS.INI system file in your OS/2 operating system. The OS2.INI startup file contains system settings such as application defaults, display options, and file options. The OS2SYS.INI system file contains font and printer driver information. If either the system or startup file is corrupted, OS/2 cannot start. If you receive a message stating the OS2.INI file is corrupted, re-create both the OS2.INI and the OS2SYS.INI. Use the MAKEINI program from the command prompt to re-create the OS2.INI and the OS2SYS.INI files.

Instructions

Do not use the MAKEINI utility unless you receive a message from OS/2 that the system or user INI file is corrupted.

To re-create a new INI file, use the following syntax:

MAKEINI user system

user is the OS2.INI user file.

system is the OS2SYS.INI system file.

Example

You must first erase the old system and user files before re-creating the new ones. To create new user and system INI files, follow these steps:

1. Insert the Installation disk and reboot your system.

2. When the logo screen appears, remove the Installation disk and insert disk 1 into drive A. Press Enter.

3. When the Welcome screen appears, press Esc.

4. Change to drive C by typing the following:

    C:

5. Change to the OS2 subdirectory by entering the following:

    CD \OS2

6. To erase the current, corrupted OS2.INI user file, type the following:

     ERASE OS2.INI

7. To erase the current OS2SYS.INI system file, enter the following:

     ERASE OS2SYS.INI

8. To re-create the new user INI file, enter the following:

     MAKEINI OS2.INI INI.RC

9. To re-create the new system INI file, enter the following:

     MAKEINI OS2SYS.INI INISYS.RC

10. Remove the floppy disk from drive A and reboot the computer.

This procedure re-creates a new user INI file and a new system INI file on your hard drive, replacing the corrupted INI file.

Warnings

Use this command only if you receive an error message that says your OS2.INI or OS2SYS.INI file is corrupt, or if OS/2 fails to boot. The system INI and user INI files hold vital information that OS/2 needs to run on your computer.

Using PATCH

The PATCH utility enables you to apply software repairs and IBM-supplied patches. A *patch* is a correction or adjustment to the operating system files. Use this utility only if you completely understand the patch process and purpose. Two methods of applying patches to the OS/2 operating system exist: automatically and manually.

PATCH guides you through the process of changing the operating system's software with prompts. Selecting the /A option automatically applies a patch shipped by IBM. PATCH obtains the needed information from the patch information file supplied by IBM. An IBM-supplied patch verifies the problem and makes corrections to the codes. A non-IBM-supplied patch may not offer verification.

If you manually apply a patch, you must enter the command and supply an offset to direct the patch location. After you establish the location, you must enter the patch contents. You must enter the contents and the offset in hexadecimal notations.

After you supply a hexadecimal offset, the operating system displays the 16 bytes at that offset. You can make changes to each byte by typing one or two hexadecimal digits. If you press the space bar, the byte remains unchanged. If you move your cursor past the 16th byte, the operating system displays the next 16 bytes. After you make your changes, press Enter.

Pressing Enter saves the patch information into memory, and the following message appears:

```
Do you want to continue patching filename (Y/N)?
```

If you answer Y, PATCH asks for an offset. When you have completed all patches, OS/2 displays the patches on-screen and asks for verification. If you respond with Y, the patches are written to disk in the same order in which you entered them.

Instructions

PATCH uses the following syntax:

> **PATCH path filename.ext** /A

path is the location of the file to be patched.

filename.ext is the file to be patched; without /A, interactive mode is assumed.

/A is the option to apply the patch automatically.

Examples

To use the automatic mode from a PATCH information file named MYPATCH.TST that resembles

> 123456

enter the following into a patch file called MYFIX.FIL:

> FILE MYPATCH.TST
>
> VER 0 313233
>
> CHA 0 343536

To apply the patch from the OS/2 command prompt, enter the following:

> PATCH MYFIX.FIL /A

Warning

Use PATCH only if you understand the need for a patch, know how to make a patch, and understand the effect the patch has on the operating system. If you apply the wrong patch or apply the patch to the wrong offset, you can corrupt the operating system.

Return Code

PATCH issues a return code of 0 for normal completion.

Using PMCHKDSK

PMCHKDSK is similar to the CHKDSK utility, but PMCHKDSK works from the Presentation Manager. You can use the PMCHKDSK utility only in OS/2; the utility does not work from DOS. PMCHKDSK analyzes files and directories, determines file system type, and produces a disk status report. You can apply PMCHKDSK to the hard disk or a floppy disk.

Run PMCHKDSK to check for errors. If you choose to write corrections to disk when prompted by a dialog box, PMCHKDSK fixes errors when it finds them. PMCHKDSK also detects lost clusters on your disk. A *lost cluster* is a part of a file that the system did not save completely because of a power interruption. Lost clusters take up disk space. By choosing to write corrections to disk, PMCHKDSK automatically converts and deletes lost clusters.

 PMCHKDSK cannot write corrections to the hard disk if the hard disk currently has open files or separate partitions.

Instructions

To run PMCHKDSK from the OS/2 command prompt, follow these steps:

1. From the OS/2 command prompt, type the following and press Enter:

   PMCHKDSK

2. The Check Disk dialog box appears, displaying the following message:

   ```
   Write corrections to disk
   ```

3. You can choose to check the disk without writing corrections to disk, check the disk and write corrections to disk, or cancel the process. To select Check Disk without writing corrections, press Alt-C or select the Check command button. To select Check Disk and write corrections to disk, press Alt-W and Alt-C. To cancel the process, press Esc.

   If you choose to check the disk but not write corrections to the disk, PMCHKDSK displays the warning message shown in figure 19.3 and does not correct the errors.

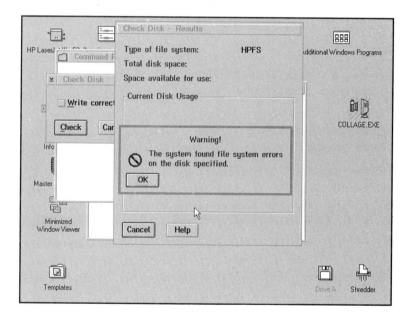

Fig. 19.3

The Check Disk - Results window with a warning message displayed.

If you proceed with the process, the Check Disk - Results window appears (see fig. 19.4). The results include the following:

- *Type of file system*. This information indicates whether the FAT or HPFS file system is being used.

- *Total disk space*. This information informs you of the total number of bytes on the floppy or hard disk.

- *Space available for use*. This information indicates the number of bytes available for storage.

■ *Current disk usage.* A color-coded pie chart displays how the disk is used by directories, files, unusable areas, extended attributes, and reserved space

■ *Cancel.* Choose this option when you want to exit the window.

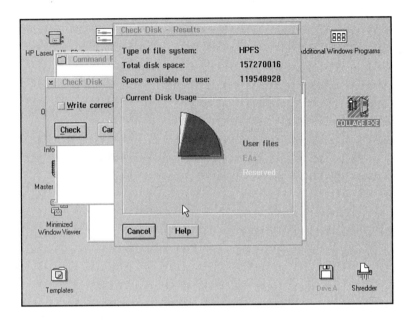

Fig. 19.4

The PMCHKDSK results.

When you finish viewing the disk information, choose Cancel. OS/2 returns to the Check Disk window. Choose Cancel from this window to return to the OS/2 command prompt.

Warning

To receive accurate information about your disk, use PMCHKDSK only when the hard disk is not in use. If the disk is in use, a warning appears when you run PMCHKDSK (see fig. 19.5). Choose OK to cancel the process.

FROM HERE...

For Related Information

◄◄ "Preparing for Trouble," p. 192.

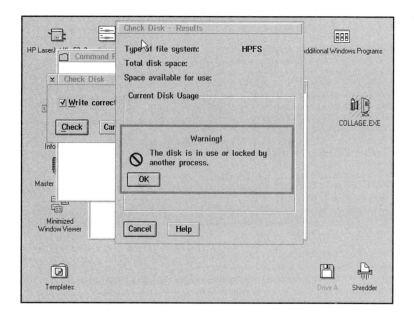

Fig. 19.5

PMCHKDSK
warning that the
command cannot
be completed.

Using PSTAT (OS/2 Only)

PSTAT displays information about current processes and threads, system semaphores (the method of transferring information betwen system components and programs API—Application Program Interface), shared memory for each process, and dynamic-link libraries. Use PSTAT to help you determine which threads are running in the system, their current status, and their current priorities. PSTAT analyzes why a thread may be blocked or running slowly. In addition, PSTAT displays a process ID that you can use with the TRACE utility. PSTAT can be used only in OS/2.

Instructions

The PSTAT utility uses the following syntax:

> **path PSTAT** */C /S /L /M /P:pid*

path specifies the location of the command.

/C shows the current process and thread-related information. Use this parameter to display the process ID, parent process ID, session ID, and the process name for each process. */C* also displays the thread ID, thread state, thread priority, and block ID for each thread.

/S shows the system-semaphore information on each thread. Use this parameter to display the process module name, process ID, session ID, index number, number of references, number of requests, flag (pace holder to indicate a procedure), and the name of the system semaphore for each thread.

/L shows the dynamic-link libraries for each process. Use this parameter to display the process module name, process ID, session ID, and library list for each process.

/M shows shared information for each process. Use this parameter to display the handle (a number that identifies each standard device), selector (identifies the system level address), number of references, and the name of the shared memory for each process.

/P:pid shows information related to the ID of the specified process. Use this parameter to display the process ID, parent process ID, session ID, process module name, dynamic-link libraries, and shared memory data for the ID of the specified process. */P:pid* also shows the thread ID, thread priority, thread status, block ID, and semaphore information for each thread associated with the process.

Examples

To display the current process and thread-related information, type the following and press Enter:

    PSTAT /C

To display dynamic-link libraries for the directory DATAFILE, type the following and press Enter after each line:

    CD\DATAFILE

    PSTAT /L

To display information related to the process ID 0004, type the following and press Enter:

    PSTAT /P:4

Return Codes

Return codes are messages displayed at the completion of some OS/2 commands. A return code signals the normal completion of a task, error messages, or the reason for the end of a task. The most common return code for a command is 0, signifying normal completion. Table 19.2 provides a list of the commands that issue return codes and the meaning of those codes. Many commands that do not issue a return code may issue an error message describing a problem or error in completing the command.

Table 19.2 Return Codes

Command	Return code	Description
ATTRIB	0	Normal completion
BACKUP	0	Normal completion
	1	No files found to back up
	2	Some files or directories not processed because of file errors
	3	Ended by user
	4	Ended because of error
	5	Not defined
	6	BACKUP was unable to process the FORMAT command
BOOT	0	Normal completion (displays error messages if command is not successfully completed)
CHKDSK	0	Normal completion
	1, 2, 5	Not defined
	3	Ended by user
	4	Ended due to error
	6	CHKDSK was unable to execute file system's CHKDSK program
COMP	0	Normal completion
	1	No files were found to compare
	2	Some files or directories were not processed because of file errors
	3	Ended by user
	4	Ended because of error
	5	Files did not compare OK

continues

Table 19.2 Continued

Command	Return code	Description
DISKCOMP	0	Normal completion (displays error messages if command is not successfully completed)
DISKCOPY	0	Normal completion (displays error messages if command is not successfully completed)
EAUTIL	0	Normal completion
	1	File not found
	4	Ended due to error
FDISK	0	Normal completion (displays error messages if command is not successfully completed)
FIND	0	Normal completion
FORMAT	0	Normal completion
	3	Ended by user
	4	Ended due to error
	5	Ended due to NO response when user was prompted to format a hard disk
	6	FORMAT was unable to process another file system's format program
	7	Volume not supported by another file system's format program
GRAFTABL	0	No previously loaded character table exists and a code page is now resident
	1	A previously loaded character table exists; if new table was requested, it replaces previous table at its original location
	2	No previously loaded character table exists; no new table is loaded

Command	Return code	Description
	3	Incorrect parameter
	4	Incorrect DOS version
LABEL	0	Normal completion
MORE	0	Normal completion
PATCH	0	Normal completion
RECOVER	0	Normal completion
	1, 2	Undefined
	3	Ended by user
	4	Ended due to error
	5	Unable to read or write to one of the file allocation tables
	6	Unable to execute another file system's recover program
REPLACE	0	Normal completion
	1	No files were found to replace
	2	Some files not replaced due to file errors
	4	Ended due to error
RESTORE	0	Normal completion
	1	No files were found to restore
	2	Some files were not processed due to file errors
	3	Ended by user
	4	Ended due to error
SORT	0	Normal completion
TREE	0	Normal completion
UNPACK	0	Normal completion
	1	No files were found to unpack or copy
	2	Some files or directories were not unpacked or copied due to file errors

continues

Table 19.2 Continued		
Command	**Return code**	**Description**
	3	Ended by user
	4	Ended due to error
XCOPY	0	Normal completion
	1	No files were found to xcopy
	2	Some files or directories were not copied due to file or directory errors
	3	Ended by user
	4	Ended due to error

Using SETBOOT

SETBOOT helps you set up the Boot Manager. The parameters in the following section enable you to take full advantage of Boot Manager, which governs the startup of multiple operating systems. You can install the Boot Manager feature by using the FDISK utility program during installation. You can use the SETBOOT command only in OS/2.

SETBOOT is a utility that enables you to set the time-out value, the mode, and the system startup index of Boot Manager.

Instructions

SETBOOT uses the following syntax:

SETBOOT */T:x /T:NO /M:m /Q /B /X:s /N:name*

/T:x sets the time-out value of the menu timer in Boot Manager; *x* represents the time in seconds.

/T:NO disables the menu timer so that the Boot Manager menu remains on-screen until you make a selection.

/M:m sets the mode for the Boot Manager menu. *m*=n is normal mode, which displays only the partitions that are selectable; *m*=a sets advanced mode, which displays additional information.

/Q queries the current startup environment.

/B performs a shutdown of the system and then restarts it.

/X:x sets the system startup index. *x*=0 sets the startup index to attended mode; *x*=3 sets the startup index to unattended mode.

/N:name sets the partition or logical drive by the name and its corresponding index value; *N*=0 assigns the specified name as the default operating system; *N*=1 to 3 specifies the name to be started when the corresponding index is started.

Examples

To set the Boot Manager selection timer to 15 seconds, use the following:

        SETBOOT /T:15

To set the normal mode for the Boot Manager menu, use the following:

        SETBOOT /M:n

To set the startup index to put the Boot Manager in attended mode, use the following:

        SETBOOT /X:0

> **CAUTION:** If you are unsure about using the SETBOOT command, consult your technical coordinator or a service representative before you use the command. You could cause damage to the operating system if you use SETBOOT incorrectly.

For Related Information

◀◀ "Choosing Boot Manager," p. 126.

FROM HERE...

Using SORT

SORT reads and sorts data from standard input. You can sort data by letter or by number, and SORT rearranges the lines of text according to your instructions. You can sort the names in a mailing list in alphabetical order, for example, or you can sort the zip codes in a numerical sequence.

NOTE   The input and output files must have different names. The sorted version will not replace the original file.

Files are sorted according to the alphabet of the country you specify with the COUNTRY command. Upper- and lowercase letters are equivalent, and numerals precede letters.

Instructions

SORT uses the following syntax:

SORT <input-file >output-file /R /+n

<*input-file* is the name of the file to be sorted.

>*output-file* is the name of the file receiving the sorted data.

/R reverses the alphabetical sort (from Z to A).

/+n represents the column number where the sort starts. If you do not specify the parameter, the sort begins with column 1.

Examples

To sort alphabetically a file named MAILING and write the output to the file AMAIL, use the following:

SORT <MAILING >AMAIL

To sort a data file beginning in column 3 and send the output to the screen, use the following:

SORT /+3 <MAILING

To sort a mailing list in ADDRESS.DAT, which lists your customers' names in the first 20 columns, street addresses in the next 30 columns, and cities in the next 10 columns, and put the sorted output in SORTED.DAT, use any of the following:

To sort by customer name:

SORT <ADDRESS.DAT >SORTED.DAT

To sort ADDRESS.DAT by street address, which begins in column 21:

SORT <ADDRESS.DAT >SORTED.DAT /+21

To sort ADDRESS.DAT in reverse order by city, which begins in column 51:

SORT <ADDRESS.DAT >SORTED.DAT /+51 /R

Return Code

SORT issues a return code of 0 for normal completion.

Warnings

Large data files may take a few minutes to process.

The maximum file size you can sort is 63KB.

Using SYSLEVEL

SYSLEVEL displays the operating system name, version number, component ID, current corrective service level, and the prior corrective service level. You should run the SYSLEVEL utility before you install the PATCH utility; the SYSLEVEL information may prove helpful. SYSLEVEL is an OS/2-only command.

Instructions

SYSLEVEL uses the following syntax:

        SYSLEVEL

To access the OS/2 command prompt and run the SYSLEVEL utility from the OS/2 command prompt, type the following:

        SYSLEVEL

The message Please wait... appears. Then SYSLEVEL displays the current corrective service level.

Example

After SYSLEVEL determines the corrective service level, a message similar to the following appears on-screen:

```
C:\OS2\INSTALL\SYSLEVEL.OS2
IBM OS/2 Base Operating System
Version 2.10          Component ID 562107701
Current CSD level:    XR02010
Prior CSD level:      XR02010
```

The explanation for each line is as follows:

The first line is the subdirectory and file containing the information.

The second line is the system name.

The third line is the version number and the Component ID of the system.

The fourth line is the current corrective service level.

The fifth line is the prior corrective service level.

Using UNDELETE

UNDELETE restores a file you recently erased. When you delete a file, OS/2 moves the file to a hidden area on your hard disk. If you act quickly, you can retrieve the file by using UNDELETE. If the file is recoverable, UNDELETE restores it to its original path.

Before you use the UNDELETE command, you must use the DELDIR environment available in CONFIG.SYS to define the path and maximum size of directories used to store deleted files, as shown in the following:

> SET DELDIR= drive:\path, maxsize; drive 2:\path, maxsize

Path and maximum size values are separated by a comma; logical drive names are separated by a semicolon. When DEL or ERASE deletes a file, that file moves to the directory specified in the DELDIR statement for that logical drive. If you undelete a file that has the same name as another file, UNDELETE warns you and enables you to change the name.

The area for deleted files is limited in size. When this area fills up, the program discards the oldest files to make room for new files. Files that are available for UNDELETE are reported as used space on the disk.

Instructions

UNDELETE uses the following syntax:

> **UNDELETE dir\files** */A /F /S /L*

dir is the directory that you want to back up, and **files** specifies the files you want to back up. If you don't specify dir or files, UNDELETE looks for all deleted files in the current directory.

/A restores every deleted file in the directory.

/F tells UNDELETE to erase files completely so that no one can recover them.

/L lists the files that can be restored but does not actually restore these files.

/S restores every deleted file in a directory and its subdirectories.

Examples

To display the names of the current directory's deleted files that can be restored, use the following:

> UNDELETE /L

To recover all deleted files without being prompted for confirmation on each file, use the following:

> UNDELETE /A

To erase your performance appraisal in C:\PERSONAL\REVIEW.DOC so that no one can recover it, use the following:

> UNDELETE C:\PERSONAL\REVIEW.DOC /F

Using UNPACK

Many of the files on the OS/2 distribution floppy disk are compressed so that they take up less room and require fewer floppy disks. The installation program automatically unpacks compressed files. If you accidentally lose one of OS/2's files and know which disk contains the file, however, you can use UNPACK to unpack the file. UNPACK restores compressed files on the OS/2 distribution floppy disk to a form you can use. Using UNPACK is easier than reinstalling OS/2.

On the OS/2 floppy disk, if the last character in a file's extension is @, the file is packed. Some packed files contain only one file. Other compressed files contain several files packed together and, when you use UNPACKED, the files may go to different directories. You can view the files' destinations on-screen during decompression.

Instructions

Use the following syntax to unpack and direct the files to a specific target:

UNPACK packed-file target /N:filename *V* */F*

Use the following syntax to show the target path saved in the packed file:

UNPACK packed-file /SHOW

packed-file is the name of the compressed file.

target is the drive and directory to which you want to copy the un-packed file.

/N:filename specifies the name of a single file that you want to extract from a bundle that contains more than one file.

/V verifies that the data was written correctly when it was unpacked.

/F specifies that files containing extended attributes should not be un-packed to a file system that doesn't support extended attributes.

/SHOW displays the names of the files that are combined in a packed bundle.

Do not specify an output file name; UNPACK uses the original file name as the destination file name.

Examples

To extract XCOPY.EXE from the file XCOPY.EX@ on a floppy disk in drive A and to write that file to the OS2 directory on drive C, use the following:

UNPACK A:XCOPY.EX@ C:\OS2

To display the names of the files that are packed into the bundle GROUP.DA@ on drive A, use the following:

UNPACK A:GROUP.DA@ /SHOW

To extract FORMAT.COM from the floppy disk file BUNDLE.DA@ and to put the extracted file in C:\OS2, use the following:

UNPACK A:BUNDLE.DA@ C:\OS2 /N:FORMAT.COM

To verify the compressed files are correctly written to disk, use the following:

> UNPACK A:*.* C:\OS2 /V

To display the path and file name for every compressed file in the packed file, use the following:

> UNPACK BUNDLE.DA@ /SHOW

Return Codes

UNPACK issues the following return codes:

0	Normal completion
1	No files were found to unpack or copy
2	Some files or directories were not unpacked or copied due to file errors
3	Ended by user
4	Ended due to error

Using VIEW (OS/2 Only)

VIEW looks up a topic in an on-line document and displays files that have been compiled by the Information Presentation Facility (IPF) compiler as documents having a INF extension.

OS/2 comes with two on-line document files in its BOOK directory. Applications may add their own on-line document files. On-line document files usually contain specific help and perhaps instructions that are not included in the written documentation.

Instructions

VIEW uses the following syntax:

> **VIEW path book topic**

path is the drive and directory of the INF file to be displayed.

book is the help file with the extension INF.

topic is the subject you want to look up.

Examples

To look up the VIEW command in the on-line command reference, use the following:

VIEW C:\OS2\BOOK\CMDREF VIEW

To find out how the REXX language uses loops, use the following:

VIEW C:\OS2\BOOK\REXX LOOPS

The HELP command does the same thing and is easier to use. The two following commands yield the same results as the VIEW command; that is, the HELP command enables you to view specified on-line documents. In HELP VIEW, you see the on-line documentation for VIEW that explains the VIEW command and its uses. The HELP REXX LOOPS displays on-line references to LOOPS and how to use them.

HELP VIEW

HELP REXX LOOPS

If you do not specify book, then HELP assumes that you mean CMDREF. With VIEW, you must always spell it out.

Chapter Summary

OS/2 provides several utility programs that help you while you work with the operating system. Most of the utilities reviewed in this chapter are safe to use and assist you with disk and file management, error detection and correction, and information gathering. A few utilities covered in this chapter, however, are dangerous to use unless you understand how they affect the OS/2 operating system. If you are unsure about using these utilities—SETBOOT, FDISKPM, MAKEINI, and PATCH, for example—consult your technical coordinator or a service representative.

Finally, a few utilities that you may be interested in are not only complicated commands, but could cause irreparable damage to your data files, programs, or operating system. IBM suggests these utilities— CREATEDD, LOG, TRACE, TRACEBUF, and TRACEFMT—be used only by a technical or service representative. For more information about these utilities, see your technical or service representative. Also, information on each utility is located in the Command Reference in OS/2 Presentation Manager.

Using the OS/2 Time Management Applets

O S/2 includes a set of programs that work together to help you manage your time: Time Management applets. These programs perform all the functions of the appointment book that you might carry around with you, but are more powerful than a paper appointment book. Any entry you make using one program is immediately accessible to all the others. You can easily get summaries that show at a glance how you're spending your time.

The following list of Time Management applets will help you see how you can use these programs to make your time more productive:

■ *Daily Planner* is like each day's page on your desk calendar. This is where you enter the day's schedule, including the time you set aside for each activity. When you finish each activity, you can check the activity off as completed.

- *Monthly Planner* summarizes the information you enter in Daily Planner so that you can see a couple of weeks at a glance.

- *Calendar* shows you an entire month at a time, without any detail. If you need to see the detailed schedule for a particular day, just double-click that day. Calendar also can give you a table of statistics on all your activities for a whole year.

- *Activities List* combines all the activities you have scheduled, no matter on what day they occur, into one list. Here you can easily see which activities are already completed and which remain to be done.

- *Planner Archive* is like a drawer where you keep the old pages you have torn off your desk calendar. Actually, Planner Archive is far better than that, because you can search through all your old activities for key words and phrases.

- *Alarms* works like an alarm clock, with ten independent alarms that are tied into your appointment calendar. You can use this applet, for example, to sound a warning a few minutes before you have to leave for an important meeting.

- *To-Do List* gives you a place to keep track of your most important tasks. You can pop it up any time to make sure that you're focusing on the right things.

If you already use an appointment calendar to manage your time, take a look at what these programs can do for you. You might find them easier to use than your current time management tool. On the other hand, if you cannot be bothered to keep an appointment book because that takes more time than it's worth, these applets might be just what you need. Managing your time is easier when you harness the power of your computer, and this automated approach sure beats pencil and paper methods.

Starting Time Management Applets

To use the Time Management applets, you must first install the applets. If you left them out when you installed OS/2 on your computer, you can add the applets now by running the Selective Install program, which is inside the OS/2 System Setup folder. Chapter 7, "Modifying Your OS/2 Configuration," explains how to run that program.

After making sure that you have installed the Time Management applets, double-click the OS/2 System icon that is on the OS/2 desktop. Next, open the Productivity folder. Inside, you see icons for all the Time Management applets. To start any applet, just double-click the applet's icon. Try starting the Daily Planner applet now. Your screen looks like figure 20.1.

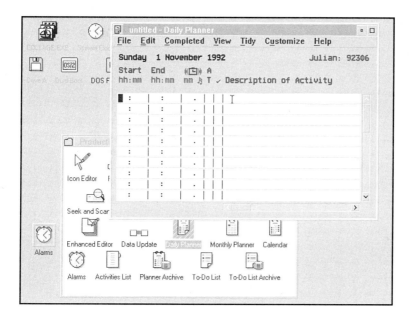

Fig. 20.1

The Daily Planner applet.

For Related Information

◄◄ "Using the Workplace Shell," p. 218.

◄◄ "Introducing Presentation Manager," p. 221.

FROM HERE...

Using Daily Planner

Daily Planner's icon looks like a page from a desk calendar. Daily Planner has one page for each day, and each page gives you space to write things to do, places to go, and people to see. Here you can write down everything you have to do each day and when you plan to do it.

Suppose that your day starts with a meeting from 10:30 to 11:00. Follow these steps to set up the Daily Planner applet:

1. Open Daily Planner by double-clicking its icon in the Productivity folder.

2. In the Start field, type **10** and then **30**.

3. Press the Tab key to go to the End field, and type **11**.

   Daily Planner assumes that the first activity you schedule is in the morning, but you can type the letter **P** after any time to indicate p.m.

4. Press the Tab key again to move to the Alarm field, which is indicated by a picture of an alarm clock. If you want OS/2 to sound an alarm five minutes before your meeting, type **5** here. If you type **15** instead, an alarm will go off at 10:15 to remind you of your meeting. Or just leave the field blank if you don't want a reminder. Later in this chapter, you learn how to customize alarms.

5. Every activity you schedule needs a description. If you press Enter now, Daily Planner pops up a window telling you that you haven't said what you plan to do at 10:30. Tab to the Description of Activity field and fill in a description.

   Each description can be up to 180 characters long. Only the first few characters appear on-screen at once, but you can drag the scroll bar at the bottom of the window to scroll through the entire description. If you enter more activities than fit on one page, you can use the scroll bar on the right to move through the entire day's plan.

Figure 20.2 shows what Daily Planner looks like with this one activity entered. The next step is to save this input, using commands you access from the menu bar.

Using the File Menu

Pull down the File menu by clicking File; or activate the menu by pressing Alt-F. Choose Save to store the information you have entered. Daily Planner asks you to type the name of a file where you want to keep your calendar. Type any name you want; for example, you might want to use your first name.

The File menu has several other commands. Use New to create a completely new Daily Planner file, or Open to access a file that already exists.

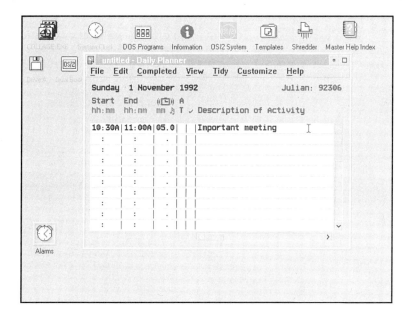

Fig. 20.2

Entering an
activity in Daily
Planner.

The Print command enables you to print a copy of your schedule. You
can print your schedule directly on the printer, or save a copy of the
schedule in any file you name. If you have installed more than one
printer, you can pick which one you want to use. By default, the Print
command prints seven days of your calendar, but you can change this
number on the Print menu and print any number of days you want.

Using the Edit Menu

On the Edit menu, you see a variety of commands that help you manage
your Daily Planner entries. The following list explains these commands:

- *Undo* gives you a chance to reverse the effect of the last change
  you made. This command is very handy when you accidentally
  delete an entry you want to keep.

- *Cut*, *Copy*, and *Paste* enable you to transfer text between Daily
  Planner and other applications, such as your word processor.
  These commands use the OS/2 Clipboard, which you master in
  Chapter 21, "Using the OS/2 General Purpose Applets."

- *Clear Line* deletes everything you have entered on a line so that
  you can start over. *Clear All Lines* erases all the lines on the current day's list.

- *Activity Type* enables you to mark the day as a personal or national holiday. With this command, you also can mark activities that require you to be out of the office. The *Unmark* command allows you to reverse any incorrect Activity Type you have set by mistake.

- *Graphics* pops up a window with 32 different clip-art drawings. Double-click any drawing to copy it into the current activity's Description field. If an activity requires you to make a phone call, for example, you might want to label it with the telephone graphic.

- *Set Alarm Tune* gives you a choice of 26 tunes to play when an alarm is triggered.

- *Propagate/Delete Lines* allows you to schedule a recurring activity. If you have a staff meeting on the third Tuesday of every month, you can enter it once and then copy the entry to each month with a single command.

Using the Completed Menu

If you keep track of activities on your desk calendar, you probably cross them out when you complete them. Daily Planner enables you to do the same thing, but with more flexibility than a paper calendar.

Using the commands on the Completed menu, you can mark an activity as completed and leave the activity on the list. Or you can delete it from the list so that your calendar shows only the things you still haven't finished. You can mark or delete activities individually, or do a whole day's worth at once with a single command.

You probably would prefer to keep a separate record of completed activities, but that takes time with a paper calendar. Daily Planner does this chore for you automatically, however, by storing completed activities in an archive. The command you need is Archive All Completed Lines. This command puts a copy of every completed activity in a separate file. You can examine this separate file with the Planner Archive applet, which you learn about later in this chapter.

Using the View Menu

The View menu has commands that allow you to flip the pages in your Daily Planner calendar forward and backward. On the menu, you see that the shortcut keystrokes for these actions are Ctrl-+ (plus) and

Ctrl-– (minus). If you have moved a few days ahead and want to move back to today, use the Today command, or just press Ctrl-T. The View menu provides no commands to move a month ahead or to go right to a particular date.

Another command on the View menu, View Complete Entry, shows you the entire description for an activity. This command is useful when you type a very long description and want to see it all at once. Figure 20.3 shows a description example.

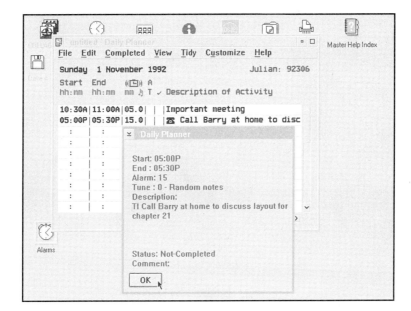

Fig. 20.3

Viewing a complete entry in Daily Planner.

Using the Tidy Menu

If you do not frequently use the Completed menu, your calendar can become cluttered. You can use the commands on the Tidy menu to clean it up all at once. The Tidy commands go through every previous page of your calendar, prior to the current date, and delete many activities with a single command. Before deleting old activities, you can save them in an archive. You can tidy up only the activities you have already marked as completed, or tidy every activity.

You may prefer to leave activities on your calendar for easy reference. In that case, avoid using the Tidy commands because they clear old calendar entries. After you clear old entries, you cannot get them back.

Using the Customize Menu

The Customize menu has two choices, Colors and Fonts. Choosing Colors pops up a window that enables you to pick your own colors for various areas of the Daily Planner window. You also can use special colors for completed activities so that a quick glance can show what you have accomplished and what remains to be done. You even have an option to pick a distinctive color for national holidays.

With the Font command, you can control the size of the characters used to display the Daily Planner window on-screen. Daily Planner starts with a default choice that matches the type of monitor and video card you have installed. You can pick any font size, no matter what equipment you have. If you pick a font designed for a high-resolution XGA display when you have only a VGA monitor, however, the window may be too large to fit on-screen.

So far, you have learned how to enter activities into the Daily Planner, how to set alarms to prompt you a few minutes before important meetings, and how to tidy up old activities that you may no longer want on your calendar. In the next section, you learn how to manage the same list of activities in a different way, with the Monthly Planner applet. If you want, you can close Daily Planner now, by pressing Alt-F4 or double-clicking the menu button at the upper left corner of the Daily Planner window. If you have made any entries since you last saved the file, Daily Planner prompts you to save again before it closes.

Using Monthly Planner

As you have learned, the Daily Planner screen is like a page from your desk calendar. Monthly Planner is like the calendar for a whole month. It uses the same file as Daily Planner, but gives you a perspective of several weeks at a time. You can use the Daily Planner to enter appointments, meetings, and other events that you view with the Monthly Planner.

Open Monthly Planner now, by double-clicking its icon in the Productivity folder. Pull down the File menu and open the same file you used for Daily Planner. Your screen looks like figure 20.4. Each line represents one day, and you can see a couple of weeks at once. The current day is highlighted, as are weekends. All the activities you scheduled in Daily Planner are highlighted so that you can quickly see how much of your time is blocked out from day to day. The first letter or two of each Daily Planner description appears on-screen at the time scheduled.

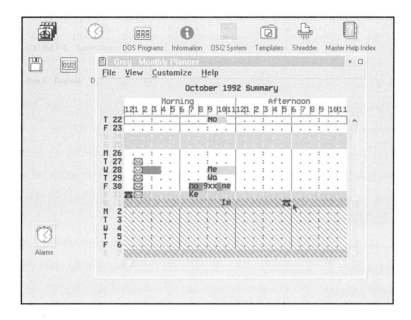

Fig. 20.4

The Monthly
Planner applet.

Monthly Planner draws a box around the schedule for the current date. You can move this box forward or backward with the arrow keys or the scroll bar at right. Select any date and press Enter, and the Daily Planner for that date pops up. You are never more than a keystroke away from the greater detail that Daily Planner provides.

Monthly Planner's File menu has only one choice: Open. No option to save is necessary because you can make schedule changes only in Daily Planner. Now that you have mastered the File menu, the following sections discuss useful commands available on Monthly Planner's View and Customize menus.

Using the View Menu

The View menu has commands that enable you to flip the pages in your calendar a month or a year at a time. The first choice, Month, pops up a list of all the months of the year. This command allows you to look at the calendar for any month instantly. Other options enable you to move forward or backward a month. The hot keys are Ctrl-+ (plus) and Ctrl-- (minus). These are the same hot keys you use for Daily Planner, but with Monthly Planner they move a whole month at a time, rather than just one day.

The Next Year and Previous Year options show you the calendar for the current month, one year in the future, or one year in the past. As with Daily Planner, the Return to Today option brings you right back to the present; its shortcut key is Ctrl-T.

Using the Customize Menu

The Customize menu has Color and Font options that work much the same as Daily Planner's. Monthly Planner's Color option also enables you to pick a different color for entries that trigger an alarm so that you can see which appointments you will be prompted to attend.

Shading is an additional Customize option in Monthly Planner, which allows you to pick shading for all dates outside the current month. You can use Shading in addition to Color to make the current month stand out clearly. Figure 20.5 shows the window that pops up when you choose Shading.

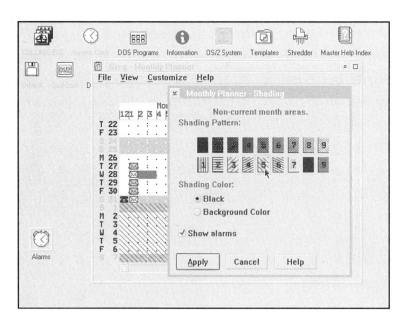

Fig. 20.5

The Shading Options window in Monthly Planner.

You can choose from among 20 different shading patterns by clicking a pattern with the mouse. A pair of radio buttons allows you to decide whether Shading should be in black or in the color that you have chosen for the window background. If you select the Show Alarms check box, any alarms you have set show up in a different color. When you're satisfied with the options you have chosen, click Apply to put them in effect.

Making Changes

While you are using Monthly Planner, you might notice a change you need to make—an appointment you forgot to enter, or perhaps a meeting that was cancelled. Follow these steps to make a change:

1. Using the arrow keys, move to the date where you need to make a change, and then press Enter. Or if you're using a mouse, double-click the date. Either way, the Daily Planner for that date pops up.

2. Change the activity in Daily Planner.

   If you arrange your screen so that you can see both Daily and Monthly Planners, you will notice that the change isn't immediately reflected in Monthly Planner.

3. Now flip a page forward in Daily Planner—by using the Ctrl-+ shortcut key combination, for example. As shown in figure 20.6, a window pops up, prompting you to confirm the change you made. After you select Yes, the applet updates the Monthly Planner screen to reflect the change.

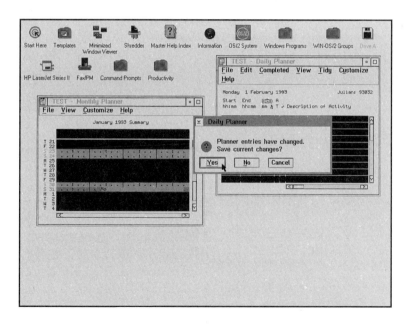

Fig. 20.6

New entries affect other applets only when you save them.

Using Calendar

Like Monthly Planner, Calendar uses the information you enter in Daily Planner, but gives you a broader view. Double-click the Calendar icon in the Productivity folder, and use the Open command on its File menu to load the same file you used for your Daily Planner. Your screen resembles figure 20.7.

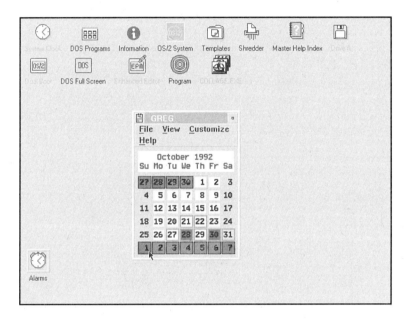

Fig. 20.7

The Calendar applet.

Calendar looks like a monthly wall calendar. Notice that weekdays are shown in a different color than weekends, and today's date is always a special color. If you have entered any Daily Planner activity for a particular date, Calendar draws a box around that date.

To pop up Daily Planner at any time, just double-click a date on the Calendar. You can enter or change activities only in Daily Planner, not in Calendar itself.

Similar to the other applets, Calendar has a menu bar, with many options that are familiar to you by now. In fact, the View and Customize menus are exactly the same as for Monthly Planner, so you have already mastered them. You also have already used the first option on the File menu, Open, to load your Daily Planner file. When you make a change in Daily Planner, use the second option, Refresh Current File, to update the Calendar.

The third option on the File menu is something new. This new option is Shows Statistics for the Current Year. The Statistics display gives you a convenient one-screen snapshot of the whole year. If your Daily Planner entries include graphics or activity types, they are summarized here. If you use the airplane graphic for each flight you schedule, for example, the Statistics screen shows you how many times you have flown this year and how many more flights you have planned. And if you use Activity Types to mark vacation days, you can see at a glance how much vacation you have already taken this year and how many days you have left. Figure 20.8 shows a sample Statistics screen.

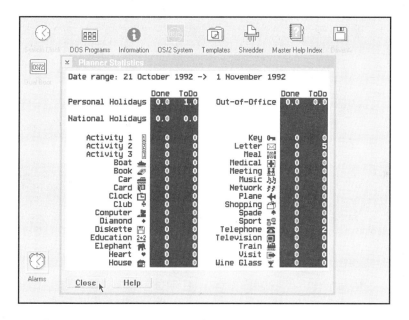

Fig. 20.8

The Calendar's Statistics screen.

Using Activities List

Activities List presents yet another view of the items you have entered into Daily Planner. As the sample screen in figure 20.9 shows, Activities List displays all the activities noted on your calendar. When you start Activities List by double-clicking its icon in the Productivity folder, it lists activities in date order, starting with today's date. Remember to load your Daily Planner file into Activities List, using the Open command on the Activities List File menu.

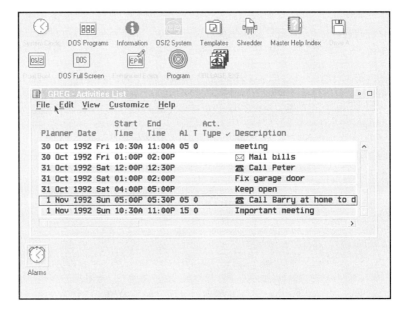

Fig. 20.9

The Activities List applet.

You can examine past and future entries by scrolling the display with the PgUp and PgDn keys or the vertical scroll bar. Use the horizontal scroll bar to view any entries that are too long to fit on one screen. If you have set an alarm to remind you a few minutes before a scheduled activity, the alarm time appears. You also see a check mark next to each activity you have marked as completed. Various Activity Types, such as holidays and vacation days, are highlighted in color.

The menu bar contains commands that enable you to work with your schedule in ways that the other Time Management applets do not. The following sections cover these commands in detail.

Using the File Menu

Along with the Open command that enables you to load your Daily Planner file, you see a Print command on the File menu. This command can print your entire list of activities. You can send the output to a file or to any printer that's attached to your system.

Using the Edit Menu

The Edit menu has two commands. Use the first command, Copy, when you want to copy the currently highlighted activity line to the OS/2 Clipboard. You can then paste it into any other application, such as a word processor.

Figure 20.10 shows the Find command in use. This command searches through the description of every activity on the list and finds whatever string of characters you specify. In the figure, Activities List has found the word *Lunch*. The Find window remains on-screen so that you can look for other Lunch appointments by repeatedly pressing the Enter key. The Find command locates each occurrence in turn. When it gets to the end of the list, Find loops back to the beginning and restarts the search there.

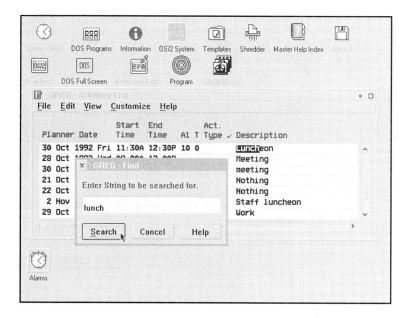

Fig. 20.10

Finding text in the Activities List.

Using the View Menu

The View menu has only one command, Sort. This command enables you to show activities in order by date or by description. Choosing Sort pops up a window that lets you sort in either of these two ways. In the First Field area, pick the button for the sort option that you want and choose the other, if you want, for the Second Field; then press Go. For example, do the first sort by description and the second by date. All appointments with the description *Lunch* are grouped together. Within this group, your lunch dates are sorted chronologically.

If you always want Activities List to be sorted in this particular way, press the Save button. Your preference is stored for future use, even after you turn the computer off. If you have an early release of OS/2, the Help button may not work.

Using the Customize Menu

The Customize menu has two options, Color and Font, that work the same as the corresponding options in the other Time Management applets. The Color option enables you to pick distinctive colors for holidays, days you are out of the office, or weekends, for example. These colors are not used unless you turn on the Color Lines option in this menu.

Using Planner Archive

You have already learned how to archive entries in Daily Planner (by using Daily Planner's Tidy menu, for example). Planner Archive is the Time Management applet that allows you to examine all the activities that you have ever archived. Try archiving an entry or two in Daily Planner, and then open Planner Archive by clicking its icon in the Productivity folder. Your archived entries display on-screen.

Planner Archive looks and works exactly like Activities list. As you can see in figure 20.11, the only difference is the spacing between the lines. The menus are identical, and the commands all work the same. Using the menu bar commands, for example, you can sort archived entries, print them out, or display a summary in a Statistics window.

Using Alarms

You have already seen how to use Daily Planner to set alarms that warn you of impending meetings. The Alarms applet gives you precise control over the alarms you set. In this applet, you can turn alarms on or off, customize the message that displays at the time you set, and even make an alarm start a program of your choice.

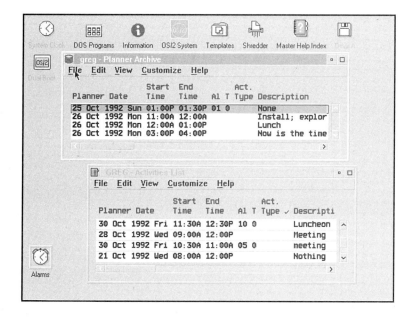

Fig. 20.11

The Planner
Archive re-
sembles the
Activities List.

The Alarms applet automatically starts running in the background
whenever you open one of the other Time Management applets.
(Alarms is like an alarm clock, which cannot go off unless you leave it
plugged in all the time.) Daily Planner can set alarms, but Alarms must
be running for the alarms to sound. If you have already run Daily Planner, find Alarms on the OS/2 Task List and maximize it. Your screen
looks like figure 20.12.

Using the Alarms Menu

Set Alarm is the option you most often use on this menu. Choosing this
option pops up a window as shown in figure 20.13. The various fields
here give you precise control over the alarms you set.

The following list explains the options available in the Alarms SetAlarm
window:

■ *Number* indicates the alarm with which you are working. Ten
alarms are available, and you can set each independently of the
others. You cannot type a number in this field, but you can
change the number by clicking the arrows.

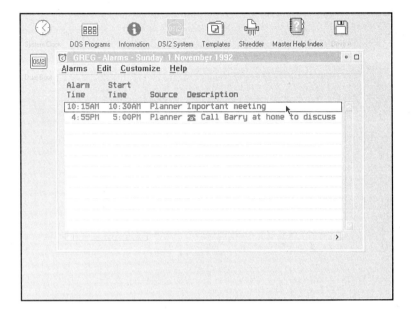

Fig. 20.12

The Alarms
applet.

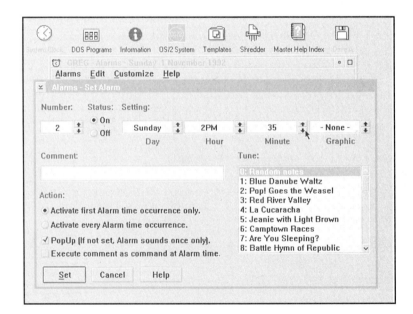

Fig. 20.13

The Set Alarm
window.

■ *Status* can be On or Off. Usually it doesn't make sense to set an
alarm without turning it on. After you have customized the settings for an alarm, however, you can turn it off without wiping out

those settings, just in case you want to reactivate the alarm later. If an alarm's Status is Off, you cannot change any of the other settings until you turn the Status back on.

- *Setting* offers you four input fields. The first three enable you to pick the day, hour, and minute when the alarm should sound. The last field, Graphic, lets you choose a picture that pops up on-screen when the alarm goes off. If you set an alarm to remind you when it's dinner time, for example, you might choose the Meal graphic.

- *Comment* enables you to specify a line of text that displays on-screen in a window that pops up when the alarm sounds. This window pops up only if you check the PopUp box.

- *Tune* allows you to pick from a variety of tunes. The melody you choose plays when the alarm goes off.

- *Action* enables you to decide whether the alarm should sound only once, or every week. You can set an alarm to go off next Tuesday at 11:00, for example, or every Tuesday at 11:00.

- *PopUp* controls whether a window pops up over whatever work you're doing at alarm time. This pop-up window contains whatever you type on the Comment line.

- *Execute comment as command* allows you to start a program automatically at alarm time. Type the name of the program in the Comment field. It can be any program that you could run at an OS/2 session's command line. Be sure to specify the full path and name for the command.

Your alarm clock probably has a snooze button, which turns off the alarm temporarily, but tells it to sound again in a few minutes. The alarms you set in the Time Management applets also have a snooze feature, as you can see in figure 20.14. If you have selected the Snooze button and later decide you want to turn off the alarm before it sounds again, use the Cancel Snooze command on the File menu.

The last item on the File menu is the Print command. This command sends a copy of the Alarms window to whatever printer you choose. Alternatively, you can use this command to put the Alarms window into a file. This capability is useful if you want to use the list of alarms in another software package such as your spreadsheet.

Using the Edit Menu

Copy is the only choice on the Edit menu. This command puts a copy of the Alarms listing into the OS/2 Clipboard so that you can paste it into another application.

Fig. 20.14

An Alarm Popup
Panel.

Using the Customize Menu

The Font and Colors options on this menu work the same way as they
do in the other Time Management applets. The choices you make apply
not only to the Alarms screen, but also to the window that pops up at
alarm time. You might want to pick bold colors for this pop-up window.

Another option on this menu, Sound Limit, controls the number of
times an alarm tune plays before it stops. By clicking the arrows, you
can vary the number from 0 to 30. If you choose 0, the tune does not
play.

If you hit the Snooze button when an alarm sounds, the alarm stops
temporarily, but it sounds again after a certain interval of time. The
Snooze Period option on the Customize menu enables you to set the
length of this time interval. Click the arrows to pick any period between
1 and 60 minutes.

The final option on the Customize menu is Set Master Planner File. You
can use this option to tell Alarms to use a particular Planner file every
time it starts. Pick this option, and take a moment now to tell it the
name you chose earlier for your Daily Planner file. Then press the Set
button, and Alarms will always examine that same file whenever it runs.

Setting a Default Planner File for All Time Management Applets

Perhaps you didn't mind using the Open command on the File menu each time you started one of the Time Management applets, and typing in the name of your Planner file each time. Or maybe you have already grown tired of this repetitive chore. At any rate, you don't want to go through all that trouble each time you want to run these programs. After all, their purpose is to save you time.

Here is a technique you can use to tell each of the Time Management applets to use the same Planner file every time you start the applets. Go through the following series steps once for each applet: Daily Planner, Monthly Planner, Planner Archive, Calendar, and Activities List. Follow along with the example in figure 20.15, which shows how to set up Daily Planner.

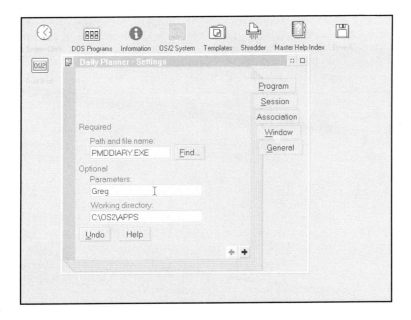

Fig. 20.15

Setting the default file for Daily Planner.

To set a default Planner file, follow these steps:

1. Make sure that the Productivity folder inside OS/2 System is open.

2. Click mouse button 2 on Daily Planner's icon to pop up its local menu.

3. Click the arrow to the right of the <u>O</u>pen command, and pick <u>Se</u>ttings from the pop-up window.

4. Click the Program tab of the settings notebook that now appears.

5. In the Optional Parameters field, type the name of your Planner file.

6. Double-click the menu button in the upper left corner of the settings notebook to close it.

Repeat the preceding steps for each of the Time Management applets, and you will never have to open a Planner file again. For more information on managing the settings notebook, see Chapter 10, "Managing the Workplace Shell."

Using To-Do List

To-Do List looks a lot like Activities List, with one line for each activity. Open the list by double-clicking the To-Do List icon in the Productivity folder. Your screen looks like figure 20.16. You see that each task has a priority and a date. This applet keeps a count of the number of things you have to do and the number you have completed.

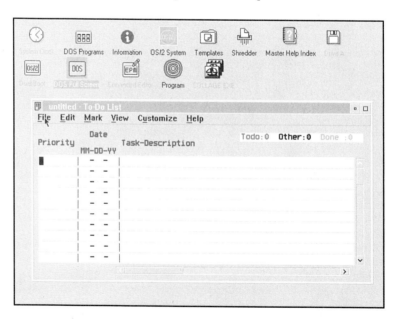

Fig. 20.16

The To-Do List applet.

Unfortunately, To-Do List is not integrated with the other Time Management applets. Tasks you enter in To-Do List are not automatically copied to Daily Planner, or vice versa. If you want to copy entries back and forth, you can use the OS/2 Clipboard, which is explained in Chapter 21.

However, many people who keep detailed appointment calendars also keep a separate list of critical things to do. If you decide not to use the other Time Management applets, you may still find To-Do List helpful on its own. The next section shows how you enter tasks on your To-Do List.

Entering Tasks on To-Do List

To-Do List's screen has three fields for each item. The first field, Priority, indicates the relative importance of each item on the list. You can type one or two characters or numbers here, but you probably will want to use just a single number for simplicity. Use the number 1 for the most pressing task, 2 for the second most urgent, and so on.

The second field is Date. Enter the month, day, and year here. To enter today's date automatically, press Ctrl-C. You can use the date field to show the date on which you added an item to the list; or you might prefer to enter the date when you need to complete the task.

Type a description of the activity in the third field, Task Description. If your description is longer than the part of this field that you can see on-screen, just keep typing when you get to the end of the line. The field scrolls automatically to give you more room.

After you fill in all three fields, press Enter. Because you have not yet completed this task, it shows up in red. The To-do counter in the upper right corner of the window now shows the number 1, to let you know you have one unfinished task on your list.

Now that you know how to enter tasks on the To-Do List, the following sections tell you how to compile and manage your own list of things to do each day.

Using the File Menu

Pull down the File menu by pressing Alt-F, or if you are using a mouse, just click File. Choose Save to store the information you have entered. To-Do List asks you for the name of a file where you want it to store your list. Your own first name will do nicely. You can use the same name for To-Do List that you used for Daily Planner; OS/2 stores the two files separately, with different file extensions.

You see several other commands on the File menu. Use New if you want to create a completely new To-Do List file, Save As if you want to store it under a different name, or Open if you want to load a file that already exists. If you always want to load the same file, type the file name into To-Do List's settings notebook, following the same procedure illustrated in figure 20.15 and the accompanying series of steps.

The Print command prints a copy of your To-Do List. You can print your To-Do List directly to any printer you have installed, or save a copy of the list in any file you name.

Using the Mark Menu

The most pleasant thing about a To-Do List is crossing off a task you have completed. The Mark menu has several commands that enable you to indicate which tasks are finished. Click a task you have entered, pull down the Mark menu, and choose Mark Current Item as Completed. The task's color changes from red to black. The number of things left to do, shown in the upper right section of the window, goes down by one, and the displayed number of tasks completed increases by one.

Other options on the Mark menu allow you to delete lines when their tasks are completed (Add Line to Archive Then Delete), or move the lines to To-Do List's Archive (Mark Item & Add Line to Archive). Another command, Mark Item and Date Stamp, enables you to stamp a completed task with today's date. If you mistakenly mark an outstanding item as completed, you can correct the error by using the Unmark Line command. The last two menu items enable you to choose to Archive All Completed Lines, or to Archive All Completed Lines Then Delete.

Using the View Menu

The View menu has commands that enable you to see entries in their entirety, or to sort them in priority order. The first option, View Complete Entry, pops up a window that shows an entire entry all at once. This option is handy if some of your entries are so long that you cannot read them in the main window.

The other option on the View menu is Sort. You can sort tasks by priority, by date, or alphabetically by description. Choose up to three fields for sorting, specifying the most important one first.

The example in figure 20.17 shows one sort order that will probably suit your needs. The first sort is by Priority, and the second sort field is Date. These settings mean that all items with Priority 1 are listed first, and the items with this top priority display in chronological order. Priority 2 items (sorted by date) are listed next, and so on.

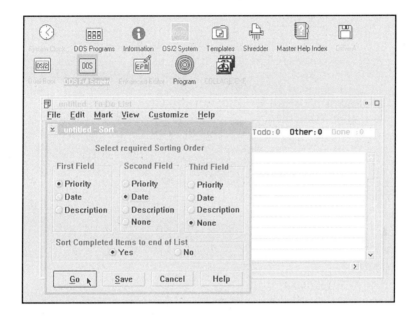

Fig. 20.17

Sorting your
To-Do List.

You probably want to choose Sort Completed Items to End of List so that the things you still need to do appear at the top. When the settings in this window suit your needs, press Go to apply them to To-Do List. Click Save if you want to use the Sort options you have chosen every time you run To-Do List.

Using the Customize Menu

The Customize menu has two choices, Colors and Fonts. When you pick Colors, a pop-up window allows you to select your own colors for various areas of the To-Do List window. You can change the colors of the window background and border, and you can pick special colors to distinguish completed tasks from the items you still have to do.

The Font command works the same way as the Font command in the other applets you learned in this chapter. Using this command, you can make the characters in the To-Do List window larger or smaller. The default, based on the particular type of graphics card and monitor you are using, is usually best.

Using To-Do List Archive

When you use the commands on To-Do List's Mark menu, you can move tasks off the list and into an archive. This archive stores every task you have ever completed. In this way, To-Do List Archive performs a function similar to that of the Planner Archive applet you learned in an earlier section.

In fact, To-Do List Archive's menu commands are exactly the same as the commands you have already mastered for Planner Archive. If you want to experiment with To-Do List Archive, you must first have saved a To-Do List file and archived at least one entry. Archiving the first entry creates the file that To-Do List Archive displays for you so that you can load it using the Open option on the File menu. If you plan to use To-Do List Archive often, set this file as your default, using the settings notebook technique illustrated in a preceding section.

FROM HERE...

For Related Information

◄◄ "Introducing Presentation Manager," p. 221.

Chapter Summary

In this chapter, you learned how to use OS/2's Time Management applets. You saw that Daily Planner, Monthly Planner, Calendar, Activities List, Planner Archive, and Alarms work together, using the same files. You learned how to enter activities in Daily Planner, and work with those activities in various ways with the other applets. You now know how to set alarms that remind you of important meetings. And you have learned how to use To-Do List and To-Do List Archive to keep track of the important tasks you must accomplish each day.

In the next chapter, you master OS/2's General Purpose applets. These programs enable you to write notes and stick them anywhere on your desktop, find files on your hard disk, perform simple arithmetic, monitor usage of your computer's resources, create your own icons, and more.

Using the OS/2 General Purpose Applets

In Chapter 20, you learned how to manage your time with an integrated group of applets that work closely together. In this chapter, you master other applets that serve very different functions, and are completely independent of each other. Each applet has its own section in this chapter, which gives a detailed description of the applet, instructions for using the applet's commands, and some useful hints. The following list tells what each of the General Purpose applets does. You can use it to decide which may be useful to you before reading on.

- *Calculator* looks and works exactly like the electronic calculator you probably have on your desk. With Calculator, you can perform arithmetic and print out your computations step-by-step.

- *Pulse* shows how much work your CPU is performing from one moment to the next by displaying a graph on-screen. If you don't want to clutter your screen with a large graph, you can tell Pulse to display this graph as an icon on the OS/2 desktop.

■ *Clipboard Viewer* enables you to examine the text or graphic contents of the OS/2 Clipboard that you use to transfer information between programs. With this applet, you can move data between OS/2 and Windows programs, as well.

■ *Icon Editor* is a drawing program that enables you to design your own icons. You can substitute an icon that you create for any application's default icon and give the OS/2 desktop a distinctive personal look.

■ *Tune Editor* allows you to compose, play, and print your own melodies. The Alarms applet, discussed in Chapter 20, can use the tunes you write.

■ *Seek and Scan Files* searches your hard disk for any file you specify. This applet is handy when you know the name of a file, but cannot remember the folder or directory where you stored it.

■ *Sticky Pad* supplies you with little yellow notes that you can stick to windows on the OS/2 desktop. You can use these notes as reminders, the same way you use paper sticky notes on the documents and folders on your desk.

■ *Notepad* gives you a stack of index cards that you can use to jot down ideas, using a different card for each topic.

If you choose to study only those applets that interest you, you should still read the first couple of sections of this chapter. Those sections show you how to start the applets, and they cover a few commands that are the same for most applets.

Starting the General Purpose Applets

You need to make sure that you have installed the General Purpose applets before you can use them. To find out whether you have already installed these applets, open the OS/2 System folder and double-click Productivity. Inside the Productivity folder, you see an icon for each applet you have installed. If any applet that you want to learn about is missing, take a moment to install it now by using the Selective Install program that you see in the OS/2 System window. Complete instructions for running Selective Install are in Chapter 7.

You start any General Purpose applet the same way you start any OS/2 application—by double-clicking its icon. Try starting the Calculator applet now. Your screen should look like figure 21.1. The next section uses the Calculator applet as an example to explain several commands that are common to many of the applets in this chapter.

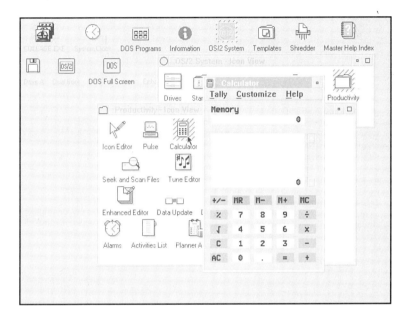

Fig. 21.1

The Calculator Applet.

For Related Information

◄◄ "Using the Workplace Shell," p. 218.

◄◄ "Introducing Presentation Manager," p. 221.

FROM HERE...

Learning Commands Shared by Most General Purpose Applets

Even though the General Purpose applets serve a wide variety of different functions, some of the commands on the applets' menu bars are the same; for example, each applet has a Help menu. You mastered the Help system in Chapter 13. The remainder of this section discusses the Colors, Font Size, and Print options that work the same way on most of the General Purpose applets.

Picking Colors

Figure 21.2 shows the Colors window for the Calculator applet. This window pops up when you choose Colors from the Customize menu. You can select a different hue for each part of the Calculator display. Pick one item from the list of Calculator window areas, select a color, and click Apply to see what the new color scheme looks like. In the figure, the color of the memory buttons is about to be changed to yellow.

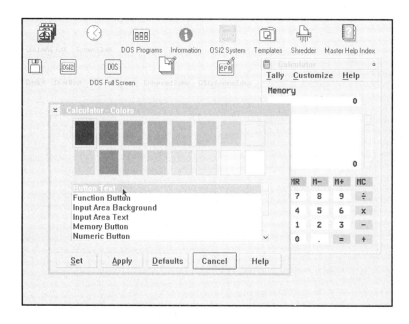

Fig. 21.2

The Calculator's Colors window.

The Apply button shows you the new color scheme, but leaves the Colors window open. If you decide you don't like the new color you chose, you can pick another instead. When you are satisfied with your choices, click the Set button. Set applies your new colors and closes the Colors window. Set also saves your chosen colors so that they are used whenever you start the Calculator.

If you have changed many colors but aren't satisfied with the result, just click Defaults to get back the original color scheme. On the other hand, if you have experimented with a few color changes but decide to discard the changes you have made, choose Cancel.

Choosing a Font Size

OS/2 supplies a separate font for each of the most common video displays. By default, the General Purpose applets all use the font designed for your video card and monitor, but you can pick any of the other fonts. Moving to a larger font size, for example, makes each character in the Calculator window bigger. When you turn on your computer the next day and start Calculator again, it remembers the last font you set.

Figure 21.3 shows how the Calculator looks with an XGA font, displayed on a VGA monitor. The Font Size option on the Customize menu offers a menu of the fonts from which you can choose. The number next to each font's name tells how many little dots are used to draw each of that font's characters on-screen. XGA draws each character in a box 22 dots high by 12 wide, which is about 50 percent bigger than VGA's usual 14 by 8 dots. So using the XGA font makes the Calculator appear about 50 percent larger than it usually does on the VGA screen.

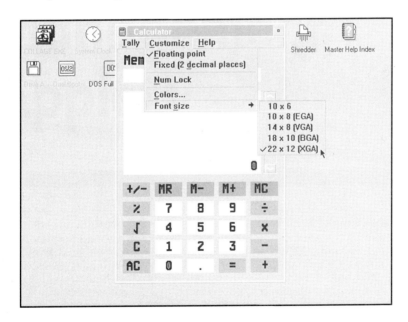

Fig. 21.3

A large font makes the Calculator window bigger.

Printing from a General Purpose Applet

Several of the General Purpose applets have a menu choice that enables you to print a copy of the work you have done in the applet. The Print option on the Calculator's Tally menu, for example, pops up a window that allows you to print the results of your computations. On other applets that offer it, the Print option is usually available on the File menu.

Figure 21.4 shows the Print option in action. The pop-up window enables you to choose between two different destinations for the printout. If you press the Printer button, the output goes directly to any printer you select from the choices offered. Of course, as the figure shows, this procedure does not work if you have not yet installed a printer. If you need to install a printer, refer to Chapter 7, "Modifying Your OS/2 Configuration."

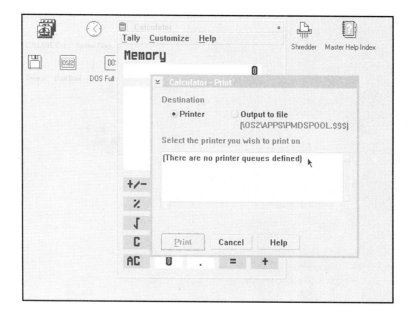

Fig. 21.4

The Calculator's Print window.

Even if you don't have a printer, you can use the Print option to copy your calculations to a file. To send the output to a printable file instead of a printer, click the Output to File button. This option can be handy if your printer is on a network, but the network is temporarily down.

Whichever destination or printer you pick, press the Print button at the bottom of the window to start the printout. Choose Cancel if you decide not to print the calculation after all.

Now that you have mastered the commands that Calculator shares with other applets, you are ready to learn Calculator's arithmetic capabilities.

For Related Information

◄◄ "Introducing Presentation Manager," p. 221.

FROM HERE...

Using Calculator

As you saw in figure 21.3, the Calculator applet looks exactly like the electronic calculator you probably keep on your desk. You can click the Calculator's keys with the mouse, or perform calculations using the keyboard. Calculator has a percent key, a square root key, and a memory. Notice that the results of your calculation display step-by-step in the output area, which works like the paper tape in a desktop printing calculator. You can scroll this tape up or down with the scroll bar, or print it with the Print command on the Tally menu.

The next section tells you what the keys on the Calculator do. If you are already an expert at using your desk calculator, skip to the following section.

Doing Arithmetic with Calculator

If you have ever used a desk calculator, you already know how to perform arithmetic with the Calculator applet. You can click the Calculator buttons with the mouse, or use the keyboard.

Suppose that you want to multiply 1728 by 50 percent. Using the mouse, follow these steps:

1. Enter **1728** by clicking the **1**, **7**, **2**, and **8** buttons in that order.

2. Click the button that shows a times sign (×), and then enter **50** by clicking **5**, then **0**.

   You see 1728 on one line, and 50 on the next.

3. Click the % button.

   The number .5 appears on-screen (.5 equals 50%).

4. Click the = button.

   Figure 21.5 shows that the answer is 864.

If you prefer to use the keyboard, follow these steps:

1. Press the Num Lock key until the Num Lock light on your keyboard comes on.

   This setting enables you to enter numbers from the keyboard's numeric keypad.

2. Type **1728**, and press the * (asterisk) key. The asterisk stands for multiplication.

3. Type **50**, and then press the % key.

4. Press Enter to see the answer.

Whether you use the keyboard or the mouse, the Calculator display looks the same as figure 21.5.

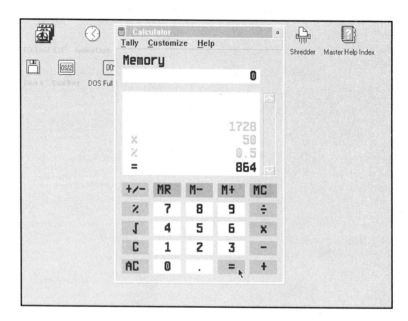

Fig. 21.5

Doing arithmetic in the Calculator.

Every Calculator key you click with the mouse has a keyboard equivalent. Table 21.1 shows the keystroke you use for each operation. Most people prefer to use the keyboard because this method is more like using a desk calculator and faster than using the mouse.

Table 21.1 Calculator Keystroke Summary

Operation	Keystroke
Add	+
Subtract	-
Multiply	*
Divide	/
Equals	Enter
Square Root	S
Change Sign	T
Clear Entry	C
All Clear	A
Add to Memory	F7
Subtract from Memory	F6
Recall Memory	F5
Clear Memory	F8

Using the Tally and Customize Menus

On Calculator's Tally menu, you find the Print option, which is usually on the File menu of other applets. The other Tally option is Clear Tally Roll, which completely erases the calculator tape that shows the steps in each calculation.

The familiar Colors and Font Size options appear on the Customize menu, along with several other options. Two of these options, Floating Point and Fixed 2, work together. You can choose only one at a time. If you choose Floating Point, Calculator displays numbers using however many digits are required. The result of 1 divided by 3, for example, appears as .3333333333. On the other hand, if you choose Fixed 2, Calculator always shows exactly two decimal places so that one-third displays as .33. Any extra digits are rounded to the nearest hundredth.

The Customize menu also has a Num Lock command, which turns your keyboard's Num Lock light on or off. This option is equivalent to toggling the Num Lock key on your keyboard. When Num Lock is off, the keys in the separate numeric keypad move the cursor around. Turn Num Lock on when you want these keys to type numbers in the Calculator.

For Related Information

FROM HERE...   ◀◀ "Introducing Presentation Manager," p. 221.

Using Pulse

The Pulse applet graphically displays how much of your computer's power is being used from moment to moment. You can see at a glance what proportion of your system's resources is demanded by the programs you are running. The closer the graph line is to the top of the window, the more resources the programs are using. This measurement gives you an idea of how much available CPU power remains for other programs that you might want to run at the same time. With this applet, you can keep a finger on your computer's pulse.

If you run Pulse while you have a DOS session open, the Pulse graph generally shows that all of your system's computing power is used. This reading is not an error—Pulse is telling you the truth. OS/2 is a multitasking operating system, designed to run several programs at once. But DOS is single-tasking, and a DOS application thinks it always owns the entire computer.

When an OS/2 program has prompted you for input and is waiting for you to type something, the program takes a brief nap and tells OS/2 to wake it up when you press a key or move the mouse. Meanwhile, other OS/2 applications that are running in the background can use the majority of the computer's resources. Pulse reflects the availability of this spare power.

But when a DOS program is waiting for input from you, it tells the system to check the keyboard continually. OS/2 wrestles control away from the DOS program in order to make sure that other programs have a chance to run. But DOS consumes every spare microsecond, so Pulse correctly reports a 100-percent load on system resources.

Setting Pulse Options

Aside from Help, Pulse has only one pull-down menu: Options. Figure 21.6 shows Pulse running, with its Options menu pulled down and its Background Color menu displayed.

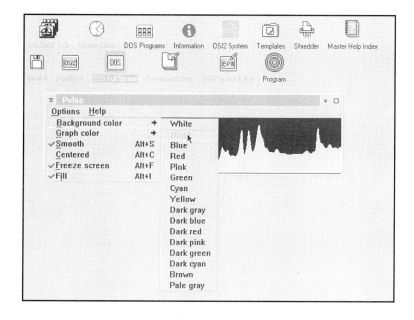

Fig. 21.6

The Pulse applet
and its Options
menu.

The following is a list of the Options commands and explanations of
what each one does:

- *Background Color* gives you a choice of sixteen colors for the main
  Pulse window.

- *Graph Color* enables you to choose any of sixteen different colors
  for the graph. Don't choose the same color for Background and
  Graph, or else you will not be able to see the graph.

- *Smooth* makes the graph less jagged. Instead of displaying exact
  system usage at each instant, it shows a running average that
  doesn't jump around as much.

- *Centered* keeps the graph displayed inside the window's borders.
  You probably will want to turn Centered on so that the graph
  shifts back to the middle of the screen whenever it hits the right
  edge of the window. If you leave Centered off, the graph marches
  past the right side of a window, into an area where you can no
  longer see it.

- *Freeze Screen* tells Pulse to stop updating the graph, but leave it
  displayed on-screen.

- *Fill* colors the area under the graph with whatever graph color
  you choose. If you leave Fill off, the areas above and below the
  graph are the same color, and only the graph line itself is a different color.

Running Pulse as a Graphically Changing Icon

Normally, if you minimize Pulse, you see only its default icon on-screen. This default icon is just a picture that always looks the same. You can set up Pulse, however, to keep updating its graph in a way that you can see even when Pulse is minimized. Figure 21.7 shows Pulse running minimized, with a constantly updated graph of system usage displayed inside the icon.

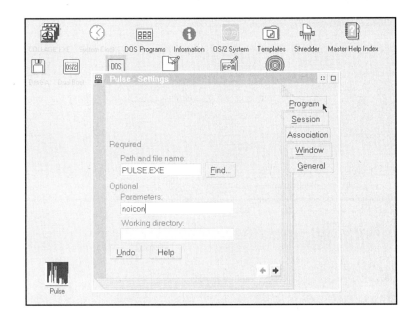

Fig. 21.7

Pulse can graph the load on your system inside an icon.

To configure Pulse this way, follow these steps:

1. Close Pulse if it is already running. Open the Productivity folder (OS/2 installs the Productivity folder in the System folder), and click the Pulse icon with mouse button 2.

2. Click the arrow to the right of Open, and choose Settings to open the settings notebook.

3. On the Program page of the settings notebook, type **noicon** in the Optional Parameters field.

4. Close the settings notebook by double-clicking the menu bar at the top left corner.

5. Run Pulse, and minimize it.

Using Clipboard Viewer

As you learned in Chapter 20 and this chapter, OS/2's Clipboard enables you to transfer text or graphics within or between programs. When you use the Cut or Copy options on an application's Edit menu, for example, the information you highlighted is transferred to the Clipboard. After the text or graphic is on the Clipboard, you can paste it into another location or application.

Clipboard Viewer is minimized automatically when you start it. This makes sense, because you usually want the Viewer out of the way so that it doesn't clutter your screen. When you want to see what's on the Clipboard, double-click the minimized icon to restore the window.

Using Clipboard Viewer, you can display the contents of the Clipboard at any time. As soon as you copy data to the Clipboard, it appears in Clipboard Viewer, as illustrated in figure 21.8. The highlighted line of text in the Enhanced Editor was selected with the mouse, and Ctrl-Ins was pressed to copy the selected line to Clipboard Viewer, where it appears instantly.

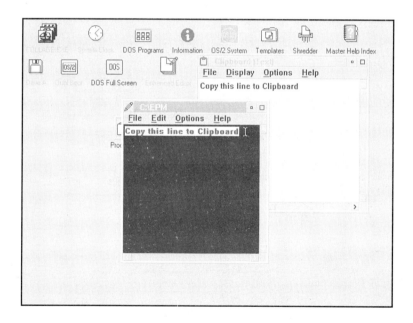

Fig. 21.8

Text cut from an application appears instantly in Clipboard Viewer.

Choosing a Display Format

Skip over the File menu for the moment and pull down the Display menu. This menu has only one choice: Render. When the Clipboard is empty, Render is dimmed and clicking it does nothing. After you copy something to the Clipboard, however, Render pops up a window that offers you a choice of ways to view the Clipboard's contents.

When the Clipboard contains graphics, you have several Render choices. Usually, Clipboard Viewer correctly guesses which one is appropriate. But if the display doesn't look right, try one of the other choices. When the Clipboard contains text, however, it doesn't make sense to Render it as graphics.

Sharing Information between Windows and OS/2

When you run Windows under OS/2, Windows has its own Clipboard which is usually separate from OS/2's Clipboard. You can share information between Windows and OS/2 programs in two ways. The following sections show you how to use each method and how to pick the one that's best for you.

Sharing Information through a Public Clipboard

The easiest way to share information between Windows and OS/2 sessions is through a Public Clipboard. Here, Public means shared: Windows and OS/2 use a common Clipboard. You can copy text or graphics from a Windows session and paste it directly to an OS/2 session, or vice versa. This approach is especially convenient when you are running Windows applications seamlessly so that they appear on the same screen as OS/2 applications. Refer to Chapters 16 and 17 for complete information on Seamless Windows.

The default Clipboard is Private instead of Public. To make it Public, pull down the Options menu on Clipboard Viewer and click Public. After you choose this option, a check mark appears next to the word Public on the Options menu. You can choose a Public Clipboard only when a Windows session is running under OS/2.

Sharing Information through a Private Clipboard

By default, the Public selection on the Options menu is not checked, which means that the Clipboard is Private. With this option, OS/2 and Windows have separate Clipboards. The system behaves exactly as though Windows were running on its own under DOS, completely insulated from OS/2. You might prefer this setup, for example, when you are running Windows in full-screen mode and using the Windows Clipboard to cut and paste graphics, while using OS/2's own Clipboard to move text between OS/2 programs.

The Windows Clipboard and the OS/2 Private Clipboard can communicate with each other, but this takes a little work on your part. To move information from Windows to OS/2, follow these steps:

1. Go to your Windows session. Select some text or graphics.

2. Press Ctrl-Ins to copy your selection to the Windows Clipboard.

3. Open OS/2's Clipboard Viewer. Pull down the File menu and choose Import.

   This command copies the contents of the Windows Clipboard to the OS/2 Private Clipboard. You now can paste your selection into any OS/2 application.

To transfer information in the opposite direction, from OS/2 to Windows, follow these steps:

1. Go to your OS/2 session. Select some text or graphics.

2. Press Ctrl-Ins to copy your selection to the OS/2 Private Clipboard.

3. Open OS/2's Clipboard Viewer. Pull down the File menu and choose Export.

   This command copies the contents of the OS/2 Clipboard to the Windows Clipboard.

You now can go to any Windows application and paste your selection there. Because of the extra effort required when the OS/2 Clipboard is Private, you probably will want to make it Public.

For Related Information

◄◄ "Introducing Presentation Manager," p. 221.

◄◄ "Using the OS/2 Editors," p. 336.

FROM HERE...

Using Tune Editor

Tune Editor enables you to create, save, change, print, and play simple melodies. Each tune can be up to 20 notes long. You can use melodies that you compose with Tune Editor in the Alarms applet that you mastered in Chapter 20. Tune Editor is easier to use if you already know how to read music, but you don't need any musical training to have fun with Tune Editor.

As an example, figure 21.9 shows the first four notes of Beethoven's Fifth Symphony in Tune Editor.

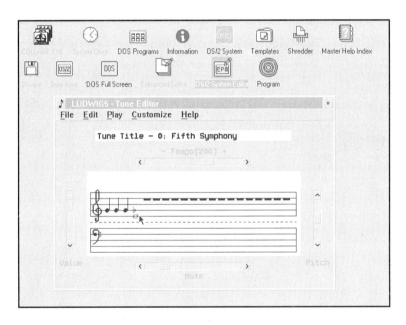

Fig. 21.9

Editing
Beethoven's Fifth
Symphony.

Entering a Tune

To enter a tune, you need to specify the pitch and duration of each note. Follow these steps:

1. Select a note that you want to enter or change by clicking it with the mouse. Alternatively, you can move back and forth between successive notes with the keyboard arrow keys. The note currently selected displays in blue.

2. Choose the length of the note by moving the Value slider at the left up or down. The top position of the slider gives you what musicians call a whole note. A whole note has the longest duration. Move the slider down one step at a time to get a half note, a quarter note, and so on. The current note instantly changes its appearance to the musical symbol for the type of note you have selected. If you continue moving the slider down, the notes change to rests, which take up time but make no sound.

3. Pick the pitch you want by moving the Pitch slider on the right up and down. The current note moves up or down on the music score to indicate the new pitch. An easier way to choose the pitch of a note is to click the mouse right on the score, at exactly the pitch you want. Because rests make no sound, you cannot set their pitch.

Repeat these steps for each note in your tune. If you don't need all 20 available notes, make the ones you don't need into rests. Type the letter **P** at any time to play the tune you're working on. You can change the tune from slow to fast, or anywhere in between, by moving the Tempo slider that is above the musical score.

Notice that you cannot yet enter the exact melody shown in figure 21.9 because the fourth note is E flat. To enter that note, you need the flat symbol, which you learn when you study the menu commands in the sections that follow.

Using the File Menu

The commands on the File menu enable you to save the tunes that you have written in a file so that you can load them again whenever you want to play the melodies. These commands also enable you to change each tune's name and to print your tunes. Each file can contain up to 36 melodies. The following list explains the various File menu commands:

■ *New* clears any tunes you have loaded in Tune Editor and gives you a book of blank pages to compose your own melodies. OS/2's Alarm tune is written on the first page of this book, just to get you started.

■ *Open* allows you to load a file of tunes that you have previously saved.

■ *Open Tune* enables you to select any of the 36 tunes in the file. This procedure is like flipping through the pages of your own songbook. The melody you select is drawn on the music score on-screen.

■ *Rename* allows you to type the name of a tune. The name displays on-screen whenever you open that tune.

■ *Save* is the command that stores a file of tunes. It saves your melodies in the tune file you currently have open.

■ *Save As* stores the current tunes in a file you name.

■ *Print* makes a copy of the current tune appear on the printer. You might be surprised, however, when you look at the printout. You do not get a graphical printout of the on-screen music score. Instead, you see a list of every note's pitch and duration, expressed as numbers.

Using the Edit Menu

The Edit menu displays commands that help you enter or modify a tune. You don't have to pull down the Edit menu to use any of these commands because every command has a hot key that's easier to use. The hot keys are all listed on the Edit menu.

The +, –, and = keys correspond to what musicians call sharps, flats, and naturals, respectively. A sharp looks like a pound sign next to a note, and it raises the pitch of that note slightly. Similarly, a flat, which looks a little like the letter *b*, lowers a note's pitch somewhat. The = sign cancels the effect of a sharp or flat.

When you need to set the duration of a note or rest, you may find that the slider is very sensitive to slight mouse movements. A quick way to pick a quarter note duration is to type the letter **C**, which stands for *crotchet*, a technical term for a quarter note. This command lets you rapidly change a rest into a note so that you can set the note's pitch. If you need to change a note to a rest, press **R**. Other durations, such as whole notes or sixteenth notes, do not have shortcuts.

To delete the current note, press the Del key. By analogy, you might suspect that the Ins key would insert a note, but actually the hot key to insert a note is the I key. And pressing Ctrl-L deletes the entire current tune, replacing it with a blank score.

Playing Your Melodies

You can listen to your tunes with the commands on the Play menu. Here you see an option to play the current tune. You can always play the current tune just by pressing the shortcut key **P**. The other option, Play All Tunes, plays all the tunes in the current file.

The Alarms applet that you learned in Chapter 20 also can play your tunes. You can write your own melody and have Alarms play it automatically at any time of the day. But Alarms doesn't give you a choice of tune files. Alarms works only with the default tune file, which is named PMDIARY.$$A. To change the names and melodies of the tunes available to Alarms, you have to open PMDIARY.$$A in Tune Editor first and then make your changes and save them.

Using Seek and Scan Files

As you learned in Chapter 10, folders and directories are useful tools for keeping your files organized. But sometimes you cannot remember the exact place where you stored an important file. If you can remember the file's name, or at least part of the name, then the Seek and Scan Files applet can sniff it out for you—no matter where the file happens to be on your hard disk.

You also can search files for a string of text. This option is handy if you do not recall the name or location of a file, but know a distinctive word or phrase that the file contains. The next section provides an example for searching for files.

Searching for a File

Suppose that you have the chapters of this book stored in separate files somewhere on your hard disk. You don't know which directory holds them or remember the names of the files, but you know that the names of the chapter files all end with *DOC*. You need to find the chapter that discusses the Time Management applets, and you recall that somewhere this chapter contains the words "alarm tune." Seek and Scan Files comes to the rescue. Figure 21.10 shows the search example.

To access Seek and Scan Files, double-click the Seek and Scan Files icon in the Productivity window. Use the following steps to provide Seek and Scan Files the information needed to search for "alarm tune" in all the DOC files located on your hard disk:

1. In the File name to search for field, type ***.DOC**, which stands for all files with the DOC extension.

   This approach is faster than searching every file.

2. In the Text To Search For field, type **alarm tune**.

   Seek and Scan files will scan each DOC file for this text.

3. Use the Drives to search check boxes to specify which disks the applet should scan. You can select each disk individually and even include floppy disk drives. In this case, you want to search fixed disk C, so check its box.

4. Choose the Options menu and ensure the option Ignore case has a check mark next to it. If there is not a check mark next to Ignore case, choose the option.

   Unless you know exact capitalization, you should generally search for text ignoring the case. Seek and Scan files will find "Alarm tune" or "Alarm Tune" or any other combination of capitalization.

5. After entering this information, press the Search button.

   You hear the disk drive whirring while Seek and Scan Files looks for the misplaced chapter.

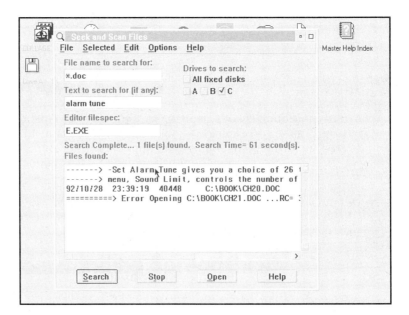

Fig. 21.10

Scanning files for a phrase.

Each time the applet finds something of interest, it prints a message in the Files found box. Take a closer look at this output, which is explained in the following list:

- The first line clearly shows a successful search. You see the words Alarm Tune on-screen. Note that this phrase was found even though you didn't specify in the Text To Search For field that the words should be capitalized. In a later section, you learn a command that tells the applet to require an exact match, including case.

- The second line reports another match, but the reason is not immediately obvious. The search text doesn't seem to be part of the line displayed. The answer to this riddle is that *alarm tune* really does occur later in this line, but only the first few characters of the line are displayed. When this happens, use the horizontal scroll bar to scroll to the right so that you can see the rest of the line.

- The third line gives the name of the file that contains the text shown in the first two lines. This line tells you that the file you seek is called CH20.DOC and is located in the C:\BOOK directory. The numbers tell you the date and time the file was saved and the number of characters it contains.

- You often see something like the fourth line. This line looks confusing at first. Why is Seek and Scan Files giving you an error message? The answer is that the file for Chapter 21 is being edited in a background window at the same time that the Seek and Scan Files applet is running. This file is locked while in use by the word processor, so the applet cannot examine it. This is a normal consequence of the steps OS/2 takes to protect the files an application owns from other applications. You see a similar error message when you try to examine any of OS/2's system files.

This fairly complicated example shows you the power of the Seek and Scan Files applet. Now that you understand what the applet can do, you learn how to use the menu commands in the following sections.

Using the File Menu

File searches can take a considerable amount of time, so you may want to save the results on disk. Saving the results is quicker than performing the search again. The Save command on the File menu puts the results of the search into a file you name. When you save the results of one search and then search for something else, you can use the Save As command to store the second set of results under a different file name that you specify.

Using the Selected Menu

When you have found a file that matches your search criteria, you may want to work directly with that file. You can do that without leaving Seek and Scan Files. Click the file of your choice in the Files found box; then pull down the Selected menu. The following options appear:

- *Open* loads the file into the editor of your choice. The default is OS/2's System Editor. You can specify any other editor by typing its name in the Editor filespec field. You may need to include the full path, for example C:\MM\MM.EXE if you want to use Multimate. The Open button at the bottom of the screen performs the same function as the Open command on the Selected menu.

- *Process* runs the file. This option works only if the file is an executable program, with file extension BAT, COM, or EXE.

- *Command* enables you to perform any OS/2 command on the file. If you want to delete the file you have found, for example, choose Command and then type **Erase** in the window that pops up.

Using the Edit Menu

The Edit menu offers two commands. The first, Copy, puts a copy of the line you have selected on the OS/2 Clipboard. You can then paste the line into any other location or application. The other command you see here, Clear List, erases the contents of the Files found box so that you can start a new search.

Using the Options Menu

The options available on this menu enable you to fine-tune the way Seek and Scan Files works. A check mark appears next to each selected option.

- *Search Subdirectories* tells the applet to look in every file on the disks you have selected. If you do not check this option, the applet confines the search to files in the root directory or in any other directory you specify in the File name to search for field.

- *Display Found Text* instructs Seek and Scan Files to show each match in the Files found box when you have made an entry in the Text to search for field. This option is normally useful. If you expect a lot of matches, however, you may want to turn the option off so that only the names of files containing the text display.

- *Ignore Case* indicates that the text you are searching for must be an exact match, including capitalization.

- *Clear on Search* means that the applet will clear the Files found box whenever you start a new search. Results of any previous search are erased.

- *Set Defaults* saves the current settings on the Options menu. Those settings become the defaults that the Seek and Scan Files applet uses whenever you run it. This command also saves the default editor that you have specified in the Editor filespec field.

Stopping a Search

Some searches take a long time. Even with a fast hard disk, it could take several minutes to seek a key word in every single file. When you see the file that you really need in the Files found box, choose the Stop button to keep Seek and Scan Files from continuing the search.

For Related Information

◄◄ "Storing Files and File Names," p. 46.

◄◄ "Organizing Directories," p. 51.

◄◄ "Introducing Presentation Manager," p. 221.

FROM HERE...

Using Sticky Pad

The Sticky Pad applet enables you to write little yellow notes and attach them to windows on the OS/2 desktop. Minimize a sticky note, and it turns into an icon in the corner of the window. Minimize the window, and the sticky note stays attached. You then can double-click the sticky note to display its contents, without having to restore the minimized window to which you attached the note.

Use this applet the same way you use paper sticky notes. For example, imagine that you are working with your word processor when the phone rings. Your boss is calling to ask you to send a copy of last month's sales spreadsheet across the network—pronto. Write yourself a sticky note that tells what you were typing in the word processor, and then minimize the note and the word processor so that you can open up your spreadsheet and satisfy the boss's urgent request. When you have got that task out of the way, you see the sticky note attached to your word processor, and it reminds you of what you were doing before the interruption.

CAUTION: Don't close the applet, or the sticky notes vanish.

Attaching a Sticky Note

You can attach a sticky note to any open window. Just open the Sticky Pad applet, click the top sticky note's title bar, and drag it to the open window while holding either mouse button down. Release the mouse button when the sticky note is on top of the window, and the note sticks. If you drag the window around the screen, the sticky note moves along with it. If you pop up OS/2's Window List with Ctrl-Esc, you can see the name of the window to which each sticky note is attached.

In figure 21.11, two notes are stuck to the Productivity folder. One of these notes is minimized, so it shows up as a little yellow square in the corner of the window.

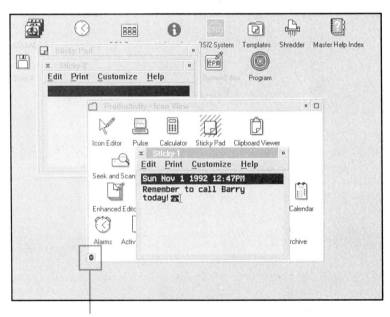

Fig. 21.11

Sticky notes attached to a folder.

Minimized sticky note

If you close the Productivity window in this example, the sticky notes come unglued from the window, and show up on the OS/2 desktop. Closing the Sticky Pad applet clears all sticky notes. Menus available on each sticky note offer you useful commands that are discussed in the following sections.

Using the Edit Menu

Typing a sticky note is like typing in a word processor or an editor. The Edit menu provides commands that make it easier to enter notes. The first command on the menu, Undo, reverses the effect of the last change you typed, which is handy if you make a mistake like inadvertently erasing an entire note. You also see Cut and Paste commands that allow you to exchange information between a sticky note and any other Clipboard-aware application.

The Edit menu also provides commands that clear either a single line or the whole note. The menu also has a Delete Line command. The command to delete a line is only slightly different from clearing the line. Clearing gets rid of the contents of a line and fills in blanks instead, but deleting removes the line and closes up the space it occupied. In addition, the menu has two commands for adding new lines before or after the current line.

The remaining commands give you capabilities not normally available in other text editors. Reset Timestamp inserts the current time and date on the first line of the sticky note. Use this command whenever you modify a note and want to update the time. The Graphics command pops up a window that presents a choice of pictures that you can copy into a sticky note. You might use the telephone graphic in a note, for example, that reminds you to return a phone call.

Using the Customize Menu

In addition to the usual Colors and Font size options, Sticky Pad's Customize menu gives you a command to save the pad's position on-screen. Whenever you start Sticky Pad, it will appear in this same position. Icon is the other special option on the Customize menu. When you choose Icon, you see a menu that allows you to specify to which corner of a window your sticky notes will adhere. The Icon menu also offers you a command that stores this choice so that your sticky notes will always go in the same corner of any window to which you attach them.

Using Notepad

The Notepad applet is like a stack of index cards. There are five cards, and you can write something different on each one. You can use Notepad, for example, to jot down several separate lists of things you have to do during the day. You can have as many Notepad files as you like, with five cards in each. You might want to have a separate Notepad for each of your customers and use the cards to store information such as the customer's address, phone number, and names of key people.

Creating Notes

To begin using the Notepad, you double-click the Notepad icon in the Productivity folder. You can type text on the card that's on top of the other cards, and then click one of the other cards to enter further information. You also can use the View menu, as explained in an upcoming section, to switch to a different card.

The five pages in each Notepad appear in a stack (see fig. 21.12). You can always see the top line on each card, so you might want to use the top line to write down the subject of the notes that you write on each card. Clicking any card brings that card to the top of the stack so that you can view its entire contents.

Through Notepad's menu bar, you access commands to load and save files, edit the text on a card, and view individual cards. You learn these commands in the next few sections. The commands on the Options and Help menus for Notepad are the same as for the other General Purpose applets.

Using the File Menu

You can save Notepad's contents in a file so that they are available whenever you need them. You can have several different Notepad files. The New command at the top of the File menu clears all the contents and gives you a fresh set of five blank cards so that you can start a new file.

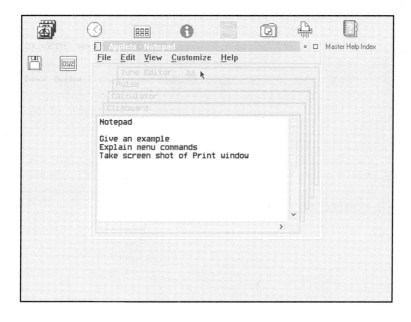

Fig. 21.12

The Notepad
applet.

To load an existing set of cards, use the Open command. The applet prompts you for the name of a card file. Notepad's files are saved in a special format, and you cannot load any other type of file into Notepad. If you try to open the AUTOEXEC.BAT file that always exists in your root directory, for example, Notepad beeps at you. You see the message The requested path does not exist. The message could perhaps be clearer, but it really just means that you tried to load a file that wasn't created by Notepad.

The Save and Save As commands enable you to store the current Notepad in a file on your disk. The difference between these two commands is that Save As prompts you to type the name of the file, whereas Save stores the Notepad into the file currently open. The Save option is not available unless you have made a change to the Notepad contents since you last opened or saved a file.

You also can print the contents of the Notepad. Figure 21.13 shows the window that pops up when you chose the Print command from the File menu. Here you can select a printer and choose whether to send the output to a file or directly to the printer. You can decide whether to print every card or the top one only. The Include blank lines button allows you to print or suppress blanks. You can control the number of lines that print on each page by typing a number in the Lines to print field. Similarly, the Printer line length field enables you to control the number of characters that print on each line.

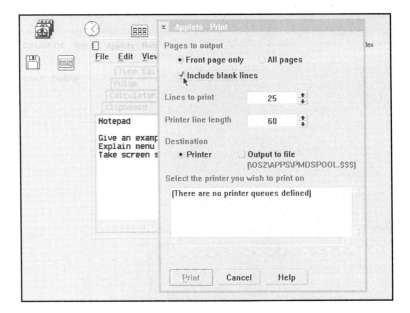

Fig. 21.13

Printing
Notepad's
contents.

Using the Edit Menu

The Edit menu gives you access to commands that modify the
Notepad's contents. Here you see an Undo command, which cancels
the last change you made. The Cut, Copy, and Paste commands permit
you to transfer information between the Notepad and other OS/2 applications. The shortcut key for each of these commands is shown on the
Edit menu; these shortcut keys—Shift-Del, Ctrl-Ins, and Shift-Ins—are
the same ones you use for similar operations in other applications.

On the Edit menu, you also see commands to delete or clear a line, a
card, or the whole Notepad. The Delete Line command is similar to the
Clear Line command. Clearing a line turns it into a blank line, but Delete
Line removes it completely. Other commands insert a blank line before
or after the current line.

The last command, Graphics, pops up a window containing a variety of
little icons. Double-click any of these icons to copy it to the current
cursor position on the top card.

Using the View Menu

A line in the Notepad can be up to 160 characters long, but the screen isn't wide enough to show such a long entry all at once. To see the whole entry, choose the View Complete Line command. Double-clicking any line is a shortcut for doing the same thing.

The other commands on the View menu enable you to bring any card in the background to the top of the stack. An easy alternative method is to click mouse button 1 once on the card you want to see on top.

Using Icon Editor

Icon Editor is a paint program that you can use to design your own icons. You can substitute the icons you create for any of OS/2's default icons, or even modify OS/2's default icons. Figure 21.14 shows Icon Editor during the process of creating a new icon.

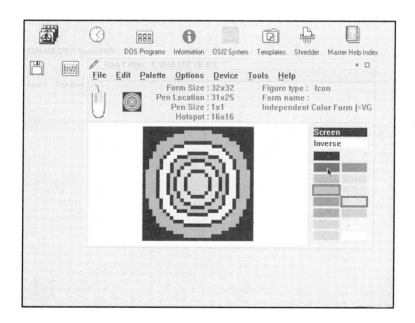

Fig. 21.14

Creating a new icon in Icon Editor.

Creating a New Icon

To draw a picture on-screen, you simply point the mouse to the spot you want to color and click. To draw with a different color, click any color shown in the palette at the right of the window. You can pick a different color for mouse button 1 and mouse button 2, for example; the current color for each is shown on the picture of a mouse near the upper-left corner of the window.

Icon Editor is quite a versatile paint program, with many options and commands available through its menus. The following sections show what you can do with each menu.

Using the File Menu

The New command on the File menu erases the current drawing and presents you with a blank screen for creating a new icon. If you want to change an icon you have already drawn, load your old icon with the Open command. Unfortunately, you cannot directly open the default icon for an OS/2 application. Later in this chapter, you learn a technique to change even the System default icons.

Saving your work often pays; if you make a change that you don't like, you can just reopen the last version you saved. The Save command stores your icon in the file that is currently open. If you want to save your icon under a new name, use the Save As command.

Using the Edit Menu

The Edit menu gives you powerful commands for changing the icon on-screen. The first command, Undo, takes back the last change you made. The Cut, Copy, and Paste commands are used for transferring graphics between Icon Editor and other OS/2 applications. You can copy part of a picture from another program, for example, and paste it into Icon Editor, where it might form the basis of a new icon. And the Clear command erases the current drawing, in case you want to start with a blank screen.

Some commands work with a broad area of the drawing and require you to specify this area first with the Select command. To designate this area, choose Select, hold down mouse button 1 on one corner of the area, drag the mouse to the opposite corner, and release the mouse button. This action surrounds the selected area with a black rectangle. If you want to select the entire icon, use the Select All command.

An example of a command that requires you to select an area is Stretch Paste. This command pastes the OS/2 Clipboard's contents into an area that you outline, stretching or shrinking the contents to fit. With a picture on the Clipboard, you select an area and then use Stretch Paste to insert the picture.

Another command that works on a selected area is Fill. Select an area, choose a color from the palette, and then pick the Fill command from the Edit menu. The entire selected area fills with that color, replacing whatever was in the area before. You also can reverse a selected portion from left to right, or up and down, with the Flip Horizontal and Flip Vertical commands. The Circle command draws a circle that just fits inside the area you have selected.

Using the Palette Menu

The Palette is the group of colors on the right side of the screen. You can create different Palettes with colors that you blend yourself. If you have changed some colors and want to get the defaults back, pick the Load Default command on this menu. To access a Palette that you previously saved, use the Open command. After making changes to a Palette, use the Save command to store your updates, or the Save As command to store your modified Palette in a new file.

The Edit Color command pops up a window that enables you to mix your own custom colors, as you can see in figure 21.15. The three sliders control the amount of red, green, and blue that you blend into your new color. In the figure, the small, equal amounts of these three primary colors result in a dark gray.

Two more commands complete the Palette menu. The Swap command exchanges the colors used by the mouse buttons. When you choose Set Default, your current modified Palette becomes the system default that loads whenever you start Icon Editor.

Using the Options Menu

This menu contains miscellaneous commands that enable you to control how the Icon Editor screen looks and how the drawing tools work. The following list describes these commands:

- *Test* substitutes the current icon for the mouse cursor.

- *Grid* draws a network of black lines that separate every picture element in the icon.

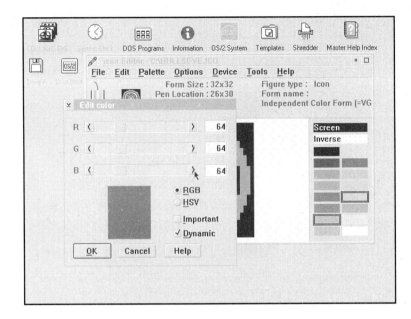

Fig. 21.15

Blending a custom color in Icon Editor.

- *X Background* writes a little X on every picture element that you have not colored. When you use your icon to represent a program on-screen, these uncolored areas let the screen background show through.

- *Draw Straight* forces the mouse to move only in a straight line when you are holding the mouse button down. If your mouse is very sensitive, it can be difficult to draw a straight line without the help of this command.

- *Pen Size* brings up a menu that enables you to pick a width for the "pen" with which your mouse draws. By default, this pen is one picture element wide, but you can make it wider.

- *Preferences* allows you to modify and save the current settings of all your Icon Editor options.

- *Hot Spot* enables you to specify the icon's activation area.

Using the Device Menu

This menu offers two choices that enable you to design icons for displays other than the one you have installed. This feature should not be important unless you are developing OS/2 programs that have to work on all types of video displays. The List option enables you to pick from among the different display types. The Edit Predefined selection gives you an opportunity to change the way these displays work by default. Use caution if you choose to experiment with these options.

Using the Tools Menu

The options on this menu change the way the mouse cursor works. When you pick Color Fill, clicking the mouse on any spot causes the whole area surrounding the icon to fill with the color you choose. The cursor changes to a picture of a paint bucket because this action is like spilling paint into a whole area. The other option, Find Color, turns the cursor into a question mark. When you click any spot on-screen, Icon Editor figures out what color is used at that spot and highlights that color in the Palette by drawing a box around it.

Associating Your Own Icon with a Program

After you have drawn and saved an icon, you will want to associate it with a program. Suppose that you have saved the icon drawn in figure 21.14 under the name Bullseye, and you want to use this icon for the DOS Window program in the OS/2 System Command Prompts folder. Follow these steps:

1. Open the Command Prompts folder in the system menu, and click mouse button 2 on DOS Window.

   A pop-up menu appears.

2. Click the arrow to the right of Open, and then choose Settings.

   This step opens DOS Window's settings notebook.

3. Flip to the General page in the notebook, and click the Find button.

   A Find window pops up, as shown in Figure 21.16.

4. Click the Find button here, and in a few moments you should see the Bullseye icon.

5. Click the Bullseye icon and press OK.

Your icon replaces DOS Window's default icon, as you can see by examining it in the Command Prompts folder on-screen.

Fig. 21.16

Changing an
application's
icon.

Modifying an Application's Default Icon

As mentioned earlier in this chapter, there is no easy, direct way to open an application's default icon. But you can modify this icon if you start Icon Editor from the application's settings notebook.

The default icon for Enhanced Editor, for example, contains the letters OS/2. You might like to change those letters to EPM because, as you learned in Chapter 14, EPM is another name for the Enhanced Editor. Just follow these steps:

1. Open the Enhanced Editor's settings notebook to the General page, as explained in the preceding section.

2. Click the Edit button.

   Icon Editor appears on-screen. The default Enhanced Editor icon loads, and Icon Editor's title bar shows a temporary file name that OS/2 assigns to the editing session.

3. Using the painting techniques described earlier, cover up the letters OS/2 and draw the letters *EPM* instead.

4. Save the icon with the Save command on Icon Editor's File menu. Close Icon Editor, and then close EPM's settings notebook.

   You see the new icon appear on-screen inside the Productivity folder.

Figure 21.17 illustrates this process. If you have created any copies or shadows of EPM, they also display your revised icon.

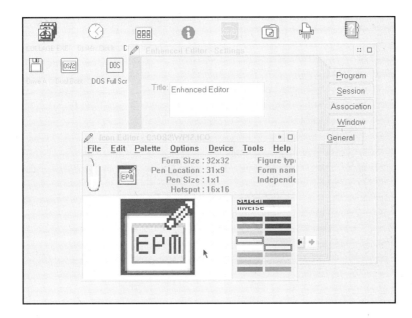

Fig. 21.17

Changing a default icon with the Icon Editor.

For Related Information

◄◄ "Introducing Presentation Manager," p. 221.

FROM HERE...

Chapter Summary

In this chapter, you mastered OS/2's General Purpose applets. You now know how to use these applets to do arithmetic, monitor system resources, manage the OS/2 Clipboard, and edit icons. You also learned how to write tunes, find lost files, and jot down ideas on sticky notes and note cards.

In Chapter 22, you study a group of applets that help you manage your data, using a spreadsheet, a chart program, a database, and a terminal program.

Using the OS/2 Data Management Applets

C hapter 21 introduced the general purpose applets supplied with OS/2. This chapter covers the data management applets: Database, PM Chart, PM Terminal, and Spreadsheet. While they are not full-blown application programs, these applets function adequately for small projects.

Database, as the name suggests, is a small database program where you can store lists of information. Database is comparable to an index card system where you store information about a particular topic on an index card and then have a series of cards in the collection.

Spreadsheet, also as its name suggests, is a small spreadsheet program for storing tables of information. Spreadsheet includes mathematical features, so you can use it for accounting or other arithmetic tables.

PM Chart is a small presentation graphics program that can make simple charts such as bar, line, or area graphs. You also can use PM Chart as a drawing program.

PM Terminal is a communications program for transmitting data to and receiving data from another computer by means of a modem. Although the applet is rather confusing to configure, it is very easy to use.

You probably will use these applets occasionally and will purchase OS/2 application programs with more features and capacities for a business. You can use Database to conveniently store a few names and addresses, for example, but you should buy a more powerful application to manage large mailing lists.

For each applet introduced in this chapter, you learn the following important features:

- Its purpose and typical application
- How to use the applet
- Its limitations
- Examples of typical data entry and manipulation
- What data can be exchanged with other applets and how to make the exchange

Using Database

The Database applet is a small database program. In a database, you can store a series of lists of information. Each list is known as a *record*, and each item in a list is known as a *field*.

Database does not include the sophisticated sorting or reporting features that you can find in full-blown database applications. For small applications, such as keeping a few names and addresses, or for simple project tracking, however, Database is convenient and easy to use. The following table lists the menu options and their functions.

Menu	Menu option	Description
File		
	New	Creates a new database
	Open	Opens an existing database
	Save	Saves your database
	Dialing function...	Dials a phone number in the current record

Menu	Menu option	Description
	Print...	Prints your database
	Print list format...	Arranges your printout's appearance
Edit		
	Restore record	Restores your record
	Copy	Copies highlighted data
	Paste	Pastes copied data
	Clear line	Clears the line in your database
	Clear all lines	Clears the record in your database
	Delete current record	Removes the current record
	Cancel edit	Undoes all the edits made to current record
	Graphics...	Selects a graphics image for your database line
	Edit line headings	Changes or creates headings for your database lines
	Add a new record	Adds an additional record to your database
View		
	Line 1 through Line 8	A check alongside the heading name displays the relevant database line. "Line 1" is replaced by the line's name if you name your lines with Edit line headings in the Edit menu.
	Display statistics report	Lists statistics on your current database
	Print statistics report...	Prints statistic on your current database
Customize		
	Dial setup...	Adjusts the dialing parameters
	Colors...	Changes the colors for your database
	Font size	Changes the font size
Help		

Purpose

The benefit of an electronic database over a series of index cards is found when you search through or organize your data. You can quickly find a database record containing particular information, and you can arrange the records in different sequences. These operations are much more time consuming when you are working with index cards.

Consider a database containing a list of names and addresses. A record is one name, along with its address and other associated data. You may store the first name, last name, street address, phone number, and date of birth on one record, for example. You then can sort your records in alphabetical order by first or last name, by zip code, or in date-of-birth order.

You can use the OS/2 Database as an electronic Rolodex; it can store up to 5000 records, each with eight fields of up to 30 characters. In addition to being able to store data, you can rearrange your database. You even can have your computer automatically dial a phone number stored in a record.

Understanding Database

OS/2 stores its applets in the Productivity folder. To access Database, open the OS/2 System folder and then open the Productivity folder. To open Database, double-click the Database icon. Figure 22.1 shows the Database opening window.

When you first open the database, no database is loaded and the title bar displays the word "untitled." When you save or reload a database, its name appears in the title bar.

The window area is divided into three sections. To understand these sections, you need to understand some database terminology. The terminology is easy to understand if you compare the database with a card index file, like a Rolodex, that contains names and addresses.

When you start Database, you are looking at one record in a database, the equivalent of looking at a particular index card. The left section of the window, which is blank when you have not loaded a database, shows the headings for each field in your database record. You can make these headings be First Name, Last Name, Phone Number, or Zip Code.

The center section has eight blank white bars where you enter your data. Each white bar is called a field. On your index card, this section is where you enter the data, which usually is different for each person in your card index file. The headings on every index card may be First Name and Last Name, for example, but the contents of each line, or field, will vary. Card number 1 may be for Jane Smith and card number 2 for John Jones. On card number 1, a field name is First Name and the field's contents are Jane. On card number 2, a field name is First Name, but the field's contents are John.

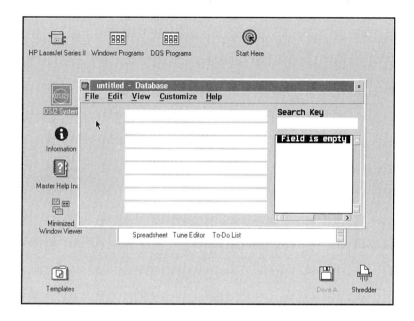

Fig. 22.1

Database
opening window.

The right section of Database's window shows your current organization. The program arranges your database in an order based on a particular field, known as the *key field*. The database may be arranged by first names, for example. In this case, the First Name field is the key field. The list at the right of the window shows all the first names in alphabetical order. (If the fields' contents are numeric, the list places the fields in numerical order.)

To find a particular record based on the key field, you can scroll through the list until you find the record of interest, or you can type the field contents in the Search Key text box. You learn the procedures for retrieving records in later sections.

Because your database can contain up to 5000 records, this list is particularly important when you want to find a record. You can change the key field at any time, and the list is automatically updated. You can arrange the records in Zip Code order or in Last Name order, for example.

Working with Database

To understand how to use the database, you can create a sample data-base of three records. First, you can set up the field name headings and the name of the database by following these steps:

1. Decide on names for your database fields. Each name can be up to eight characters in length.

2. To add headings to your fields, click Edit from the main menu bar and then click Edit line headings. Alternatively, you can press Alt-E to access the Edit menu and press H for the Edit line headings option. Figure 22.2 shows the window that appears.

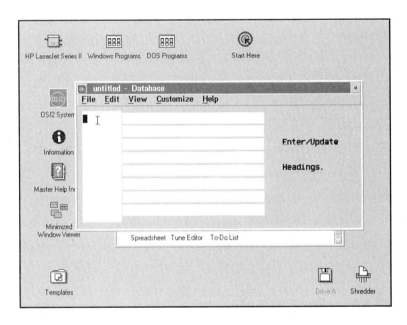

Fig. 22.2

Editing Database headings.

3. Type **First** for the First Name field in your database and press Enter. The flashing cursor moves to the next field heading. Continue entering the headings Last, Street, City, State, ZIP, Phone, and Comments.

   If you need to edit errors, click the field. You can use the typical editing keys such as Delete, Backspace, Insert, and the arrow keys to correct your headings.

4. When you have entered the field names, click File and Save to keep your headings or press Ctrl-S.

5. Type a database name, such as SAMPLE, in the Save as filename: text box and then click <u>S</u>ave to save the new database file. An empty sample database window appears (see fig. 22.3).

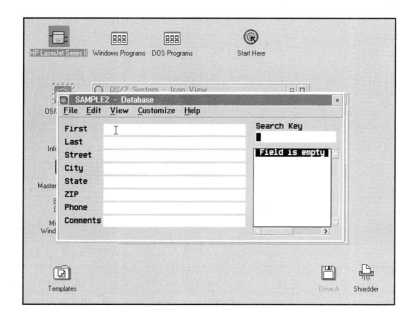

Fig. 22.3

Empty database record.

Your screen shows the first record in your database. To enter data for this record, follow these steps:

1. Click the field area next to the heading First.

2. Type the name *Jane* and press Enter. You can use the arrow keys, Delete, or Backspace key to correct any errors you make as you type.

3. Fill in the remaining blanks with the data in the table that follows.

Heading	Record 1
FIRST	Jane
LAST	Smith
STREET	123 Main St
CITY	Newtown
STATE	IL
ZIP	60089
PHONE	708-123-4567
COMMENTS	new friend

4. When you have finished adding the data for the first record, click File and Save to save the record or press Ctrl-S.

To add other records, choose Edit and then Add a new record, or press Ctrl-A. Database displays a blank record ready for completion. When you have filled in the data, press Ctrl-S or click File and Save to save your file. If you decide not to add another record, press Ctrl-Q or click Edit and then Cancel Edit to cancel the record addition.

You can use the data in the following table to add two more records to the sample database.

Heading	Record 2	Record 3
FIRST	John	Sam
LAST	Jones	Ordinary
STREET	987 Side Rd	555 Primary Ave
CITY	Oldtown	Anytown
STATE	MD	MD
ZIP	21117	21246
PHONE	410-987-4321	301-999-1111
COMMENTS	old friend	business acquaintance

When you have completed entering the data, your screen should look like the one in figure 22.4.

The center section of the window shows the current record, Sam. The right section shows a list of the records in your database. The key field is First and the list shows each first name. When you add more records, this list gets longer.

To find records containing the First Name you want, scroll through the list. To select the name from the list, double-click the desired name and your selection becomes the current record.

To find a record by using the Search Key field, click the text box immediately below the Search Key title and type the first letters of the name you are seeking. Database scrolls through the list automatically to find the record that matches your request.

In the sample database, if you press J, the highlight moves from Sam to Jane. If you then press O, your window displays the John Jones record (see fig. 22.5).

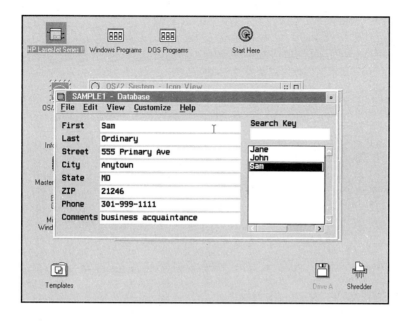

Fig. 22.4

Database with three records.

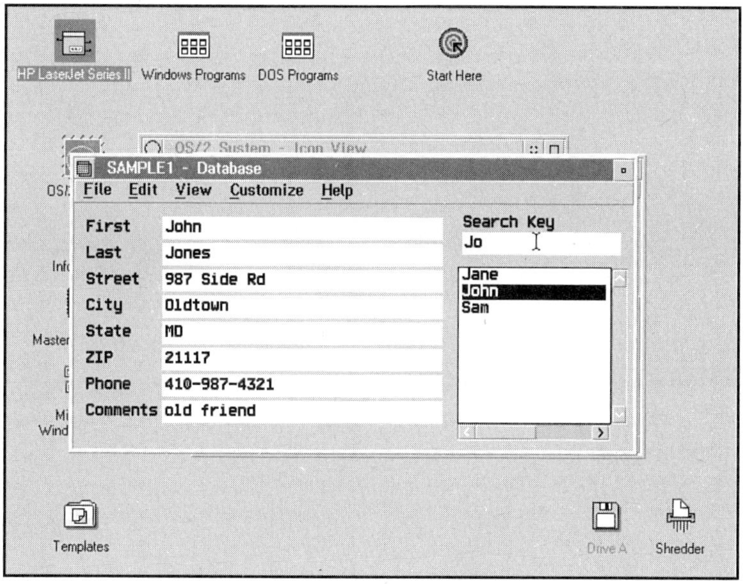

Fig. 22.5

The Search Key text box.

If you want to change the key field (the field used to determine the sorting order), click <u>V</u>iew and then select the field name. If you want the records to be sorted by State, for example, click <u>V</u>iew and then click the field name State.

NOTE If you have not added headings for your field names, the list in the view menu uses the titles Line 1, Line 2, and so on.

Figure 22.6 shows the sample database sorted by State. The list on the right shows the state names rather than the first names.

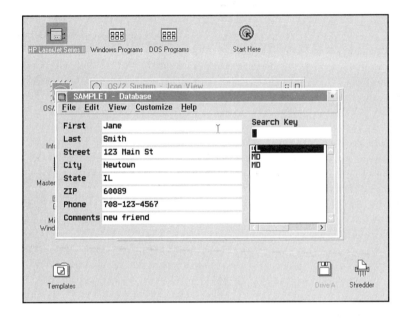

Fig. 22.6

Changing the sorting order.

The Database printing features enable you to print the current record or the whole database. (Unfortunately, you cannot select a few records and print them.) To print a record, make it the current record by finding it in the list or by using the Search Key field. To print all records, you only need to load the database.

When Database displays the data you want to print, click File and then click Print, or press Alt-F and then press P. Figure 22.7 shows the window that appears.

Click the radio button for outputting only the current record. If you want to print all records, click the other radio button for outputting all records. You then can choose between printing to your printer or to a file. After making your choices, click Print.

Database includes a useful tool that uses your modem to dial a phone number from your database. (If you do not have a modem, you cannot use this feature.) Before you can use the automatic dialing, however, you must customize your configuration. Click Customize and then click Dial Setup, or press Alt-C and then D. The Dial Setup dialog box appears (see fig. 22.8).

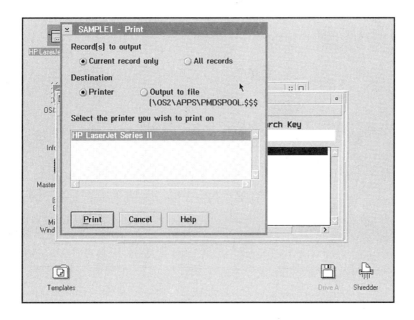

Fig. 22.7

Printing your database.

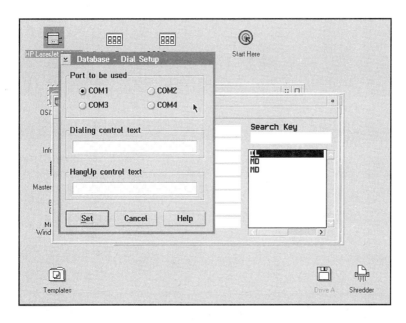

Fig. 22.8

Dial Setup window.

Click the radio button for the serial port where your modem is attached. In the dialing control text box, you can type the control codes
that your modem uses to start dialing. If you are using a Hayes-
compatible modem, for example, you need to add the control codes
that make the modem do the equivalent of taking the phone off the
hook, perhaps pausing for a dial tone, and dialing any numbers to get
an outside line. For the Hayes-compatible modem, you can add the
codes ATDT; this code "wakes up" the modem and prepares it to dial a
number by using tones rather than pulses. The codes you use vary with
the modem. You may have a modem that is attached to a leased line
and is permanently connected to another computer that requires different initial codes, for example.

In the HangUp control text box, you can enter the codes your modem
needs to break the connection. Again, the actual codes you use vary
with the modem type. If you have a Hayes-compatible modem, you
may include the hang up command ATH. Other modems have different
requirements.

After you set the configuration, you can dial a number from your database record. Click File and then Dialing Function, or press Ctrl-D. The
dialog box listing the dialing options from the current record appears
(see fig. 22.9).

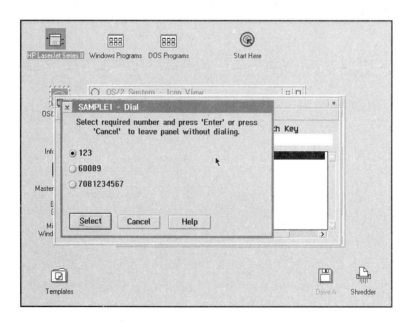

Fig. 22.9

The dialog listing
the dialing
options from the
current record.

Database displays each field that starts with numbers from the current record. Choose the phone number you want the modem to dial. In this example, Database found three fields that begin with numbers and offers you the choice of each as a phone number to dial. Click the radio button alongside the phone number. Although the selection in this example seems ludicrous because you would not want to dial a house number or a zip code, this feature allows you to have more than one field as a phone number. You can keep home and work phone numbers in your database, for example, and you can choose either number. When you have chosen the phone number, click Select. The modem then dials the number.

Understanding Database Limitations

Database has the following capacity:

- You can store up to 5000 records in a database. Each record can contain up to eight fields, each with up to 30 characters. The field names can contain up to eight characters.

- You can sort your data records based on one field name.

- The printing features are fairly limited. You can print the current record or all records, but you do have some flexibility in the output format.

- You can have Database automatically dial a phone number stored in a record.

A full OS/2 database application includes the same features as Database but has far more flexibility. With a full OS/2 database application, you can have more fields, more records, and more options in field names. You can design a format for the presentation of your record. You can design a format, for example, that looks exactly like your current office forms.

The sorting features of a full database application also are more flexible. You can sort records using more than one key field, for example, sorting first by Last Name and then by First Name. You can display, print, or manipulate a subset of a full database—the records belonging to people living in a particular state, for example.

The output features of a full OS/2 database application allow you to design your output format, print a selection of records, and do numerical statistics. For example, a database of items that you sell may include prices. You could print out an order form listing several items and get a total price. You then can print out an order form listing several items and calculate the total price.

Full database applications also usually allow linking between databases. You can link a database containing parts lists, for example, with a customer database to create order entry screens, automatic invoicing, and packing list information.

Database is adequate as a simple Rolodex or other application that requires a short list of items. If you can imagine placing the database on a series of index cards, Database is a good starting application.

Sharing Database Information

As with all OS/2 applications, copying data from Database to another application requires a sequence of steps. To copy data from Database to another application, you highlight the area to be copied and then copy the data. You use the paste command in the other application to place the data into the new application.

To copy data from another application to Database, you highlight the data in the other application and use its copy command. You then use the paste command in Database to retrieve the data.

The final result of what is copied from one application to another depends on the applications being used. Database is a series of fields of data. You can highlight a single field or a series of fields for copying. When you place the data into a receiving application, however, the data is received as a single item, even if you copied multiple fields from your database. If you place the data in Sticky Pad, for example, the multiple fields are copied as a single item. If you place the data in spreadsheet, however, only one field is placed in a spreadsheet cell. You may have to copy each field individually for certain applications to get the expected results.

To copy all or part of a record to the Clipboard, follow these steps:

1. Move the cursor to the first character you want to copy.

2. Press and hold down mouse button 1.

3. Without releasing the mouse button, move to the last character you want to copy. A rectangle appears around the area.

When you release the button, the area is highlighted. If you want to select a different area, click the highlighted area to remove the highlighting.

Click Edit and Copy, or press Ctrl-Insert to copy the data to the Clipboard. In the receiving application, click the position where you want to place the data. Then choose Edit and Paste, or press Shift-Insert to place the data.

Using Spreadsheet

Spreadsheet is a table of information, typically mathematical. It is used most commonly for accounting applications. The table is divided into a series of rows and columns, and each location in the table is called a cell. A cell contains data—either text (such as a title), a number, or a formula. The formula relates the cell to other cells in the spreadsheet.

You can record business travel, for example, in a simple spreadsheet. The left column can contain dates; the next column, the activity; and the right column, the expense. A cell at the bottom can contain a formula totaling the expenses.

Spreadsheets are particularly powerful when they include formulas. If you alter an expense in the business travel report mentioned in the preceding paragraph, the cell containing the total expenses automatically updates to the new value. The following table describes the menu options available in Spreadsheet.

Menu	Menu option	Description
File		
	New	Creates a new spreadsheet
	Open	Opens an existing spreadsheet
	Save	Saves your spreadsheet
	Save as...	Saves your spreadsheet with a new name
	Print...	Prints your spreadsheet
	Print formula/cell data...	Prints the spreadsheet formulas and cell data
Edit		
	Copy	Copies highlighted data
	Paste	Pastes copied data
	Clear input line	Clears the input line
	Home [go to cell A1]	Makes the current cell A1

continues

Menu	Menu option	Description
Recalculate		
	Recalc current cell only	Recalculates the current cell
	Recalc top->bottom, left->right	Recalculates starting at top and moving to the bottom and from the left moving to the right (cell A1 first, A2 second).
	Recalc left->right, top->bottom	Recalculates starting at left and moving to the right and from the top moving to the bottom (cell A1 first, B1 second).
	Auto recalculate	Recalculates after every edit
Customize		
	Colors...	Changes the colors for your spreadsheet
	Font size	Changes the font size
Help		

Purpose

Spreadsheet is a simple spreadsheet, allowing addition, subtraction, multiplication, and division operators in its formulas. Spreadsheet does not include more advanced mathematical operators such as statistical, trigonometrical, or engineering functions.

Typical applications for Spreadsheet include expenses, simple accounts, and record keeping. You can have up to 26 columns and 80 rows of data.

Understanding Spreadsheet

OS/2 stores all its applets in the Productivity folder. To access Spreadsheet, open the OS/2 System folder and then the Productivity folder. To open Spreadsheet, double-click the Spreadsheet icon. An untitled spreadsheet appears (see fig. 22.10).

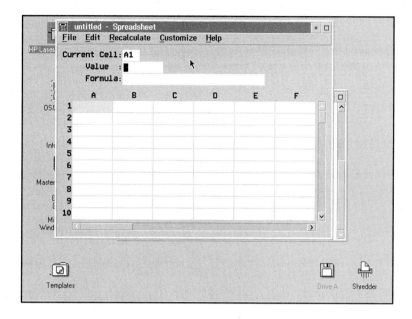

Spreadsheet numbers the rows and labels the columns with letters. To refer to a particular cell, you use its column letter and row number. Cell B3 is on the third row in the second column, for example. The cell where the cursor is currently located is known as the *current cell*.

When you start Spreadsheet, an empty spreadsheet appears. The title bar is labeled *untitled* until you save or reload a spreadsheet. The current cell is A1. Spreadsheet displays the contents of the current cell, along with its name, at the top of the window.

A cell contains either a value or a value and a formula. A value can be a number or text. If the cell contains a formula, the value field is blank, but the result of the formula is shown in the spreadsheet cell.

You can move to any cell in the spreadsheet by clicking the cell or by using the scroll bars and clicking the required cell. To return to cell A1, known as the *Home cell*, press Ctrl-Home, or click Edit and then Home.

Working with Spreadsheet

If you want to practice entering data, labels, and formulas, you can create a spreadsheet showing your utility expenses for the year. You can place the months of the year in the left column, column A, and the total utility expense for the month in the next column, column B.

To insert the column titles into your spreadsheet, follow these steps:

1. Use the arrow keys to move to cell A2 or click cell A2.

2. Type **Month** and press Enter. The label Month appears in the spreadsheet in cell A2 (see fig. 22.11). Note that the word *Month* still appears in the current cell fields at the top of the window because cell A2 is the current cell.

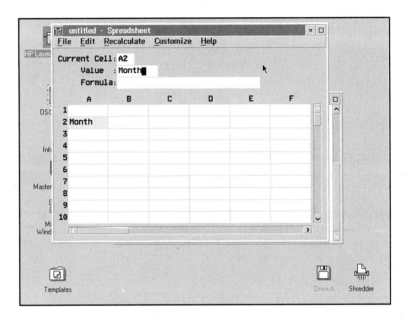

Fig. 22.11

Spreadsheet contents.

3. Use the down arrow key to reach cell A3 or click A3 with the mouse.

4. Type **Jan** and press Enter. Continue entering all the other months of the year until December is in cell A14. You must abbreviate the names of the months because you can only have up to eight characters in a cell.

5. Press Ctrl-Home to return to cell A1.

6. Move the cursor to cell B1 and type the title **Cost in$**. Press Enter (see fig. 22.12).

7. Enter the following dollar amounts of the utility costs per month in cells B3 through B14: 65, 80, 105, 73, 46, 62, 92, 159, 94, 45, 43, and 58.

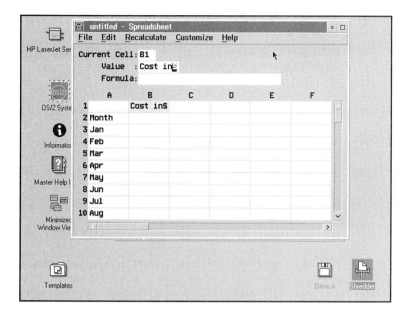

Fig. 22.12

Spreadsheet with labels.

> **NOTE** A Spreadsheet cell can contain three types of information—a formula, text, or a number. If you enter a value that begins with a number, Spreadsheet considers it a number. If you start the value with a symbol such as the dollar sign, however, Spreadsheet considers the value as text.

With Spreadsheet, you can calculate the total annual and the average utility bill. Spreadsheet supports these arithmetic functions—addition, subtraction, multiplication, and division, using the symbols +, -, *, and / respectively. You also can use the @ symbol to add all the cells in a rectangular region. To multiply the contents of cell D4 by the contents of cell E5 and then to place the result in E6, for example, you enter the formula D4*E5 in cell E6.

To determine the total utility costs, Spreadsheet adds all the values found in cells B3 through B14 by using the formula B3@B14. More advanced spreadsheet programs include arithmetic functions such as average or square root. To calculate an average in Spreadsheet, you must use the full formula, B3@B14/12.

You can practice entering the formulas for totaling and averaging utility costs into the sample spreadsheet by following these steps:

1. In cell A16, enter the heading Total.

2. In cell A17, enter the heading Average.

3. Use the arrow keys to move to B16 or click the cell to make it the current cell.

4. Click the formula text box, or press Tab to move the cursor to the Formula text box.

5. Type **B3@B14** and press Enter. Do not leave any spaces between the characters. Your spreadsheet probably looks like the spreadsheet in figure 22.13.

 NOTE You could have used the following formula:

B3+B4+B5+B6+B7+B8+B9+B10+B11+B12+B13+B14

The summation symbol @ is more manageable, however.

6. In cell B17, type the formula B3@B14/12 and press Enter. Spreadsheet calculates the average bill. Your spreadsheet probably looks like the spreadsheet in figure 22.14.

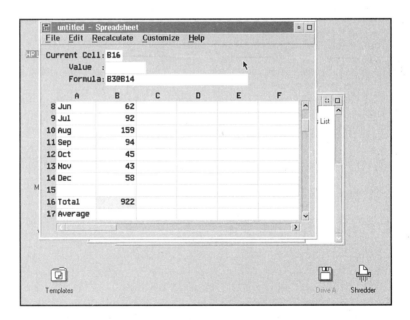

Fig. 22.13

Spreadsheet with a formula.

T I P You also can use the @ symbol when you want to add more than one column at a time. You must define a rectangular area of the spreadsheet by first typing the cell name for the upper left corner of the area followed by @. Then type the cell name for the lower right corner of the area.

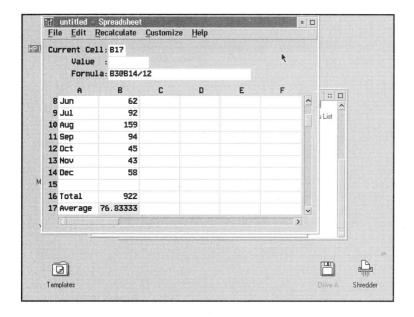

Fig. 22.14

The result of
Spreadsheet's
calculation,
including all
decimal places.

You also can use the formula B16/12, or the following formula:

(B3+B4+B5+B6+B7+B8+B9+B10+B11+B12+B13+B14)/12

Note that in the last OS/2 version you need to use parentheses to make Spreadsheet add all the numbers together before dividing by 12. Without the parentheses, the formula adds cells B3 through B13 and adds 1/12 of B14.

The value shown in B17 includes several decimal places. In other spreadsheet programs, you can alter the display format for the cell and only have the integer part displayed if you prefer. Spreadsheet does not include this formatting feature.

By default, Spreadsheet is set to automatically recalculate your spreadsheet values every time you edit a cell. On small or simple spreadsheets, the time taken to recalculate is minimal. When your spreadsheet becomes larger and includes more interrelated formulas, however, the recalculation time can become significant.

The Recalculate Menu offers alternatives. If you turn off Autorecalculate, Spreadsheet calculates new values only when you press Ctrl-C or Ctrl-R. Ctrl-C recalculates from top to bottom and from left to right; Ctrl-R recalculates from left to right and from top to bottom. Spreadsheet also can just recalculate the current cell.

You should leave Autorecalculate on until the time Spreadsheet uses in recalculation annoys you. By leaving Autorecalculate on, you reduce the chances of getting an incorrect value because you forgot to update the spreadsheet.

Understanding Spreadsheet Limitations

Spreadsheet has a maximum capacity of 26 columns and 80 rows. Each cell can contain a number or text with up to 8 characters. A cell formula cannot exceed 30 characters.

You can do simple arithmetic using addition, subtraction, multiplication, division, and parentheses. No advanced functions such as trigonometric or statistical functions, are supported. You can sum a rectangular area of cells, however, by using the @ symbol.

Sharing Spreadsheet Information

Copying data from Spreadsheet to another application requires the same sequence of steps as all OS/2 applications. To copy data from Spreadsheet, highlight the area to be copied and then choose Copy. Then paste the copied area into the new application. Remember that you can copy and paste within the same application. You can only copy one cell at a time in Spreadsheet, however.

To copy data from another application to Spreadsheet, you highlight the data in the other application and use the application's copy command. You then use the paste command in Spreadsheet to paste the data. The data you paste into Spreadsheet is placed in a single cell. Because a cell can only contain up to eight characters, however, you only get the first eight characters that you have copied.

To use the Clipboard to copy a cell to another application, follow these steps:

1. Click the cell you want to copy with mouse button 1.

2. Click Edit and Copy, or press Ctrl-Insert, to copy the data to the Clipboard.

3. In the receiving application, click the position where you want to place the data.

4. Choose Edit and Paste, or press Shift-Insert, to place the data.

To copy information from the Clipboard, click the cell where you want the data placed and press Shift-Insert or click Edit and Paste to place the data.

Using PM Chart

PM Chart is a presentation graphics program. You can use it to produce charts, such as bar charts or pie charts. You also can use it as a simple drawing program. PM Chart is the most fully featured data management applet in OS/2.

PM Chart enables you to create slides and charts for presentations. You can use the drawing tools to draw circles, ellipses, rectangles, lines, and even freehand objects. You can resize, move, copy, and edit your drawings. You can change the color of your lines and fill areas; you can produce quite complicated drawings.

The real power of PM Chart is its charting capabilities, however. You can chart the contents of a worksheet—a ledger sheet in PM Chart where you enter data to chart. You can type data into a worksheet in PM Chart or you can import data from another spreadsheet program, for example, Excel or Lotus 1-2-3. You cannot import spreadsheets created in the OS/2 Spreadsheet applet, however.

After you have data in the worksheet, you select the information to graph. You also can add annotation to your graphs with the drawing tools and create presentation graphs rapidly and easily. The following table describes the menu options available with PM Chart.

Menu	Menu option	Description
File	New	Creates a new chart
	Open	Opens an existing chart
	ClipArt...	Views clipart
	Save	Saves your chart
	Save as...	Saves your chart with a new name
	Print...	Prints your chart
	Printer setup...	Changes your printer
Edit	Undo	Undoes last command
	Cut	Cuts highlighted data
	Copy	Copies highlighted data
	Paste	Pastes data
	Clear	Clears
	Remove	Removes an object

continues

Menu	Menu option	Description
Change	Align...	Aligns objects
	Combine	Combines objects
	Duplicate	Replicates objects
	Flip	"Turns over" objects
	Move to	Moves objects
	Rotate	Rotates objects
	Smooth	Smooths a jagged object
	Unsmooth	Returns a smoothed object to original form
	Colors/Style	Changes colors and style of objects
Preferences	Crosshairs	Changes mouse cursor to crosshairs
	Pages...	Configures page size, borders, and orientation
	Rulers/Grid...	Defines rulers and drawing grids
	Screen color	Changes screen colors
Help		

Understanding PM Chart

PM Chart is located in the Productivity folder within the OS/2 System folder. Open the OS/2 System folder and then open the Productivity folder. To open PM Chart, double-click the PM Chart icon. Your screen will look like figure 22.15.

To understand how to use PM Chart, you first should become familiar with the elements of PM chart that you see on-screen. The main area of the screen is your drawing area. As you might expect, this area is where you design charts.

On the left side of the screen is the toolbar. The toolbar contains seven tools that you use while creating your presentation. The seven tools and their descriptions are listed in the following table.

Tool	Description
Select arrow	Returns PM Chart to the default pointer tool.
Worksheet	Displays the PM Chart worksheet to load the data for charting.
View	Changes your view of the presentation. For example, changes from full-screen to full-page view.
Draw	Enables you to draw lines, circles, arcs, or freehand objects.
Chart	Accesses the chart options, such as pie chart, bar chart, or line chart.
Text	Enables you to create and adjust text, including changing fonts, styles, and alignments.
Color/Style	Opens the Symbol-Color/Style dialog box to adjust colors and styles of objects.

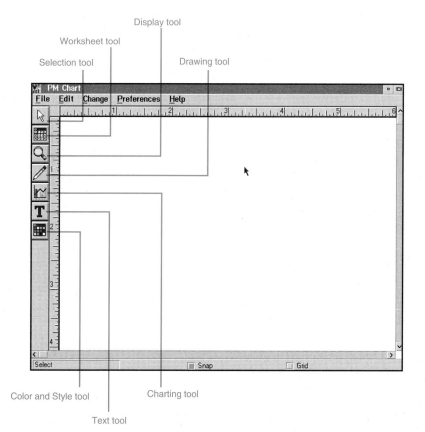

Fig. 22.15

The PM Chart window.

PM Chart includes several options to help you place objects exactly where you want them. One of these options is the ruler (along the top and left sides of the drawing area). You can turn off the ruler or alter the division spacing by using the Preferences menu. Snap and Grid are two toggle settings that also help you place objects accurately. These settings are located at the base of the window.

When you have Snap turned on, the cursor "snaps" to the ruler divisions. You can only place items at each division on the ruler. If you turn Snap off, you can draw an item anywhere on-screen, which is good for freehand drawing; however, it makes aligning and positioning items (such as a series of circles) or drawing boxes very difficult.

The Grid feature draws a grid of dots on-screen, making drawing on-screen equivalent to drawing on graph paper. The grid does not appear on your finished presentation. As with the ruler, you can alter the position and spacing of the Grid with the Preference menu.

You also can change the cursor to make drawing easier. You can choose between the arrow cursor or the crosshair cursor. The arrow is the same arrow that you use throughout OS/2, enabling you to select objects. The crosshair is a vertical and horizontal line that extends the full width of the window. In some cases, the arrow is preferable (when you draw freehand, for example). In other cases, the crosshair helps guide accurate placement.

When you choose to use the crosshair, you do not lose the use of the arrow, however. The arrow appears on-screen when you move the crosshair outside the drawing area.

Working with PM Chart

The best way to learn to use an application is to work through an example using the applications. In this section, you will use sample information that accompanies PM Chart to learn how to create a chart.

First, you must open a worksheet data file that you can chart. When the worksheet is open, you can make changes to the data and see how the changes affect the chart.

To load one of the sample worksheets, click File and then Open.... Alternatively, you can press Alt-F and then O. The File - Open dialog box appears on the screen as shown in figure 22.16.

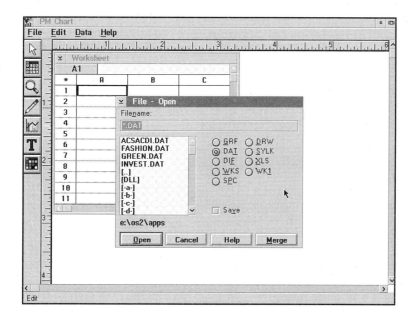

Fig. 22.16

Loading a
worksheet.

By default, you are shown a list of existing files with PM Chart's format, GRF. If you want to use another file format, such as Lotus 1-2-3's WKS or WK1 format, click the radio button to alter the selection list.

NOTE PM Chart can import data from several different file formats such as Lotus 1-2-3 or Microsoft Excel. OS/2's Spreadsheet productivity application is not one of the file formats supported by PM Chart, however.

For this example, you want to read INVEST.DAT, a Micrografx Charisma data file. From the File - Open dialog box, click the DAT radio button. The list of files displays those files with the DAT extension.

Select a file from the list by clicking it. For example, click INVEST.DAT. Click Open to load the data into the worksheet. When the data loads into PM Chart, click the Worksheet tool. Your screen will look like figure 22.17.

Another way to display the worksheet, besides clicking the worksheet tool, is to click mouse button 2, usually the right mouse button.

T I P

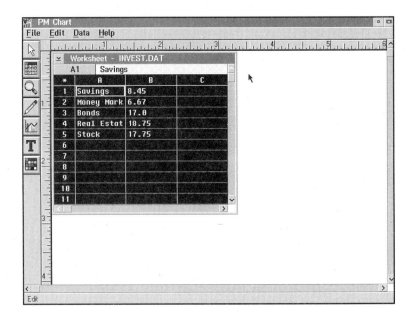

Fig. 22.17

Worksheet loaded with data.

When you load the data into the worksheet, the data is highlighted and ready for charting. To remove the highlighting, click within the worksheet. To highlight a column or row, click in the name of the column or row. To highlight the whole worksheet, click the asterisk in the upper left corner of the worksheet.

With the data highlighted, you are ready to create a chart. Click the Charting tool. As shown in figure 22.18, a button bar displays to the right of the Chart tool.

In the button bar are buttons for choosing mixed bar and line, column (often known as bar or histogram), bar (often known as horizontal bar), area, line, pie, and text charts. For this example, click the Column Chart icon (the button to the right of the chart tool). The Column Chart dialog box appears (see fig. 22.19).

You adjust the options for your chart in the dialog box that opens after you choose the chart type. Each chart type has comparable options. Click the radio buttons to select the items of preference.

For example, in the column chart you can add a 3D effect to your bars, and choose to add a legend and a table of the data. The Auto paste option, which is active by default, automatically creates a chart from the highlighted data and places it directly into your work area. If you turn Auto paste off, the chart is placed into the Clipboard and you must use the Paste command to retrieve it into your drawing.

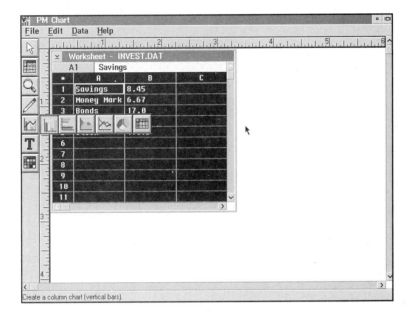

Fig. 22.18

Charting icon
options.

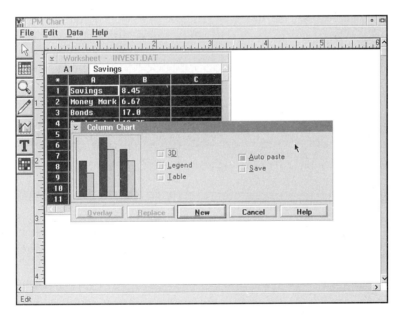

Fig. 22.19

The Column
Chart dialog
box.

After adjusting the options, choose New to create a new chart. If you
already have a chart on-screen, you can choose Overlay to add a second chart or to replace the current chart with a new chart. When you
choose New for the sample chart and close your worksheet, your
screen appears similar to figure 22.20.

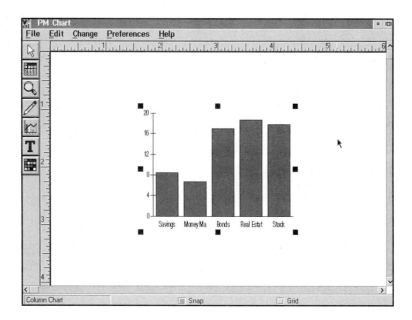

Fig. 22.20

An automatically created column chart.

PM Chart places the text labels as labels for the bars along the bottom of the chart and makes the bars the numerical values. You can make adjustments to the size and position of the chart. If your chart is not selected, click within the chart area (but not on a bar) with the select tool. Small squares, known as *object handles*, appear.

If you click in the selected chart with mouse button 1 and drag the mouse around, you move the whole chart. If you click a corner handle, you stretch the chart horizontally and vertically. Clicking a side or top handle stretches the chart horizontally or vertically, respectively.

Experiment with changing the position and size of the chart. Notice that if you increase the chart size, the bars increase in size but the text does not. When you increase the size, more room is created at the bottom of the bars for their labels.

Besides changing the entire chart, you can change elements within the chart. As with all the objects in PM Chart, you select the object and then pick the editing function. For example, click a bar within the chart. Your screen appears similar to figure 22.21.

Click the Color/Style tool at the bottom of the tool list. A dialog box appears showing the current color settings for the bars. You can pick a different fill color, change the line, text, or background color by using the radio buttons and selecting a color. First click Set so that PM Chart keeps the dialog box open until you have completed all your adjustments. For example, click the Fill radio button and double-click blue. Then click line and double-click red, and background (Bkg) and double-click light blue.

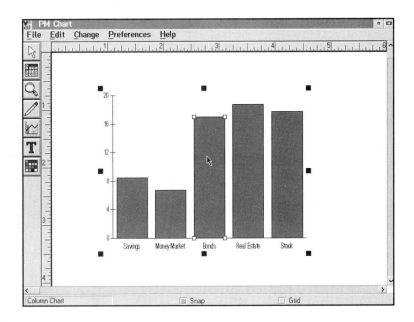

Altering a bar.

You also can alter patterns and fills by choosing patterns from the Style menu. Click Fill and then Style and Bitmap to alter the fill style. Choose a pattern from the dialog box and click OK to select it.

You can continue to alter your bar chart until it has the colors and form you like. You can alter the color palettes, that is the selection of colors, from the palette menu, add a gradient, where one color blends into another, or the style of the fill pattern, crosshatch or color with the style menu. You also can alter the text style, such as bold or underline, with the Style menu when you have the Text radio button selected.

When you have finished tailoring your chart, click Set and then OK to close the Style dialog box. Your screen appears similar to figure 22.22.

Use the other drawing tools to complete your chart. Use the Text tool, for example, to add a title. Put a frame around your chart by using the Rectangle or Rounded Rectangle drawing tool.

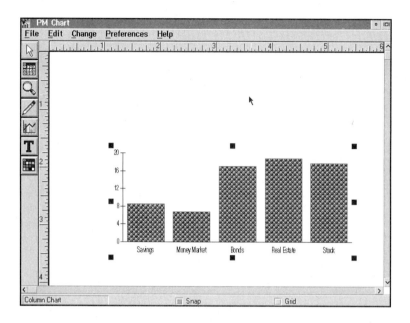

Fig. 22.22

An altered
column chart.

PM Chart includes many drawing features that make it particularly useful. If you have clip art, for example, you can add it to your chart from
the Clip Art option in the File menu. You can create multiple pages,
make them portrait or landscape, and alter their borders by using the
Preferences Page Options dialog box.

In addition to manipulating objects with their handles, you can create a
mirror image, combine multiple objects so that you can handle them as
a single object, or copy objects with the change menu. You also can
align objects from this menu.

Your work area is 34 inches by 22 inches and you can make as many
pages at once as can fit into that size. If you make an A-size drawing
(8.5 inches by 11), for example, you can create 12 pages at once. If you
select a C-size drawing (17 inches by 22), you can only create two
pages at once. The maximum size of the worksheet is 100 rows by
100 columns.

You can print the current displayed view, the current page, or all pages
of your presentation from the File menu. After you make appropriate
changes to your chart, you can save the chart using Save from the File
menu.

Understanding PM Chart Limitations

PM Chart is the most advanced of the OS/2 applets. It can create multiple charts on multiple pages and has many control features to adjust the color and style of your charts and slides.

PM Chart is limited in that you only can produce a few chart types and each file can only contain a few pages. It also does not support Spreadsheet files. Unless you are doing extensive presentation features, however, PM Chart is very suitable.

It does lack clip art and has limited drawing tools, but do not assume that PM Chart is as restrictive as the other OS/2 applets. Its worksheet can accept up to 100 rows and columns, which is more than adequate for most tables and charts.

Sharing PM Chart Information

You can cut and copy from the worksheet and the drawing area. If you cut or copy from the worksheet the data is transferred to the Clipboard as text. If you cut or copy from the drawing area it is transferred to the Clipboard as a bitmap image.

The effect of pasting depends on the receiving application. If you paste into a text editor, for example, text is transferred as text. If you transfer into a field, such as in Database or Spreadsheet, however, only the first few characters are transferred. You must paste a bitmap image into an application that can accept bitmaps. For example, you can paste to another area of PM Chart or into a painting or drawing program.

Using PM Terminal

PM Terminal is a communications program that enables you to link your computer with other computers or terminals. You define a set of parameters, known as a *profile*, that contains the information needed to establish, maintain, and terminate a communications session. When you have established a session, you communicate with the remote computer by means of a session window that is displayed like an OS/2 application program's session window.

Each profile contains different information because you may need to connect with a variety of computers. You can link with a mainframe computer, for example, and may need your PC to emulate a terminal that the mainframe can understand. In another session, you may be connected to another computer by means of an asynchronous modem and regular telephone lines. Typical examples of networking include calling bulletin board systems (BBS), CompuServe, and the Dow Jones News Retrieval Service.

PM Terminal is easy to use if you know how to communicate with the remote computer. The applet is not particularly easy to configure because it requires some knowledge of your communications parameters.

Menu	Menu option	Description
Session	Start	Starts a session
	Stop...	Stops a session
	Add...	Adds a session
	Change...	Changes a session
	Delete...	Deletes a session
	Setup profiles	Configures a session's profile
Options	Save window	Stores the current session window information
	Minimize on use	Makes the window an icon when used
Help		

Purpose

PM Terminal is intended to be configured by a knowledgeable communications person and then activated by an end user who does not need to know that the connection between a PC and a mainframe computer may be completely different than the connection linking two PCs by means of asynchronous modems. Other OS/2 communications programs probably offer more features and more flexibility, but PM Terminal offers the basic features many users need.

Understanding PM Terminal

To start PM Terminal, double-click the PM Terminal icon in the Productivity folder. Figure 22.23 shows the opening PM Terminal window.

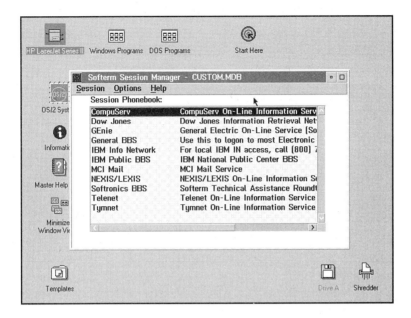

Fig. 22.23

PM Terminal.

The Session Manager window contains a list of named predefined sessions called profiles. After you define your sessions, you double-click on your selection on the list and PM Terminal starts establishing connections with another computer.

Note that most of the predefined profiles access on-line services to which you must subscribe. The profiles define only the information that is not unique to your particular account. This chapter gives an example of connecting to the Dow Jones News Retrieval Service but obviously does not include the unique information, such as an account number or regional phone number.

The second example in this chapter shows how to define your own profile. Because the telephone number and specific connection information is unique to a user and connection system, this information is omitted again.

Working with PM Terminal

The first example shows the principle involved in connecting after a profile has been configured. If you select the Dow Jones Retrieval Service and double-click the entry, for example, PM Terminal opens a session window and prompts you for connection details (see fig. 22.24).

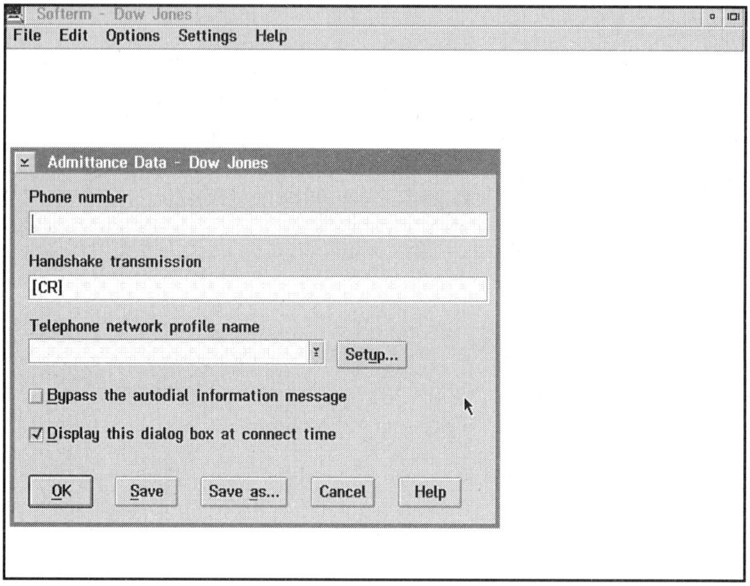

Fig. 22.24

A sample PM
Terminal session.

This profile is configured so that it prompts you for admittance data before making the connection. Note that the button near the bottom of the window is checked, requiring that the dialog box appear. Another profile may already include this information and bypass this dialog box.

In this window, you add the telephone number for the Dow Jones News Retrieval Service. The second line shows the information that PM Terminal must send when you connect with the remote computer. The third box, Telephone network profile name, is a list of all the different ways you can connect with an outside line. If you were to dial the number yourself, for example, you may dial a particular sequence of numbers to get an outside line from your company, another sequence of numbers to link to another division of your company, and perhaps other sequences to use different long distance companies.

This list does not include the part of the phone number or connection sequence that is unique to the Dow Jones Retrieval Service, but contains the sequences that you may use for different connections. The idea is that you have access to the general connection lists within every profile, but only have access to the information unique to the particular profile within that profile.

When you have entered the required phone number and chosen a telephone network profile name, click OK to start the connection. When you start a connection, PM Terminal displays a session window comparable to the window in figure 22.25.

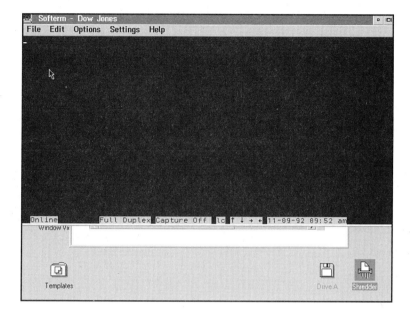

Fig. 22.25

A PM Terminal
Session Window.

In the main area, you see messages from the remote computer. At the bottom on the session window is PM Terminal's status information. In figure 22.25, PM Terminal is using full duplex, is not capturing a record of information to a file, and shows the date and time of the connection.

You can adjust the settings for this session from the menu selections. You can turn on a capture file and have OS/2 capture data to a disk file or to the printer from a data capture selection in the File menu.

To give another example, you can send a file to or receive a file from the remote computer by clicking File and then sending or receiving a file. A dialog box prompts for the file transfer protocol and the file name. (A file transfer protocol, such as XMODEM, ASCII, or Kermit, defines the format of the file being transferred. File transfer protocol defines whether the file is sent in small or large groups, for example, and how each computer acknowledges or rejects the data being transferred.)

Remember that when you use PM Terminal and link with another computer, you have added a level of complexity to your user interface. You have to make both computers communicate with each other. When you want to transfer a file, for example, you have to prepare the receiving computer for file reception and the transmitting computer for transmittal. The methods used for this preparation as well as the actual transmission depend on the type of connection made, the computer software being run on both computers, and the configuration of that software.

If you can connect with a mainframe computer or a bulletin board system, for example, you use different syntaxes and commands for the two systems even though you are using the same computer running OS/2. The remote computers you are connecting with have completely different software and user interfaces.

When you have completed your communications session, click File and Disconnect to break the communications link. PM Terminal then disconnects you from the remote computer and frees the modem for another application program.

With PM Terminal you can have multiple communications sessions active at the same time. You cannot share a modem, however. When a session tries to use a modem that is already in use, PM Terminal displays a dialog box that asks if you want to try a different communications port. When all your modems are in use, you cannot run additional communications sessions simultaneously.

The easiest way to create your own profile is to base it on another profile that has been previously established. If you want to add a new profile for an on-line service, for example, you might use the GEnie, CompuServ, or Dow Jones News Retrieval Service as a template. If you are connecting with a bulletin board system, use the General BBS profile as a template.

To base your profile on an existing profile, you access the Setup profile dialog box after selecting a session. This chapter uses the General BBS profile as an example. Click General BBS and then click Session and Change, or press Ctrl-C. Figure 22.26 shows the Change Session dialog box that appears.

If you want to create your own profile from scratch, click Session and Setup profiles or press Ctrl-P. You need extensive communications knowledge to use this approach.

This dialog box shows the currently selected subprofiles for the General BBS session. The top text box contains the comment that appears on the session list alongside the profile's name. The other four boxes shown the subprofiles. You need to select—or define and select—a terminal emulation, connection path, system environment, and file transfer profile.

The terminal emulation profile defines how your OS/2 PM Terminal session looks to the connecting computer. A BBS usually can communicate with an ASCII terminal. PM Terminal emulates many other terminals. You may use an IBM 3101-10 terminal emulation, for example, when you are communicating with an IBM mainframe. Other emulations include DEC VT100 and TTY. To choose another emulation, click the list button beside the Terminal emulation profile text box and choose an emulation from the list.

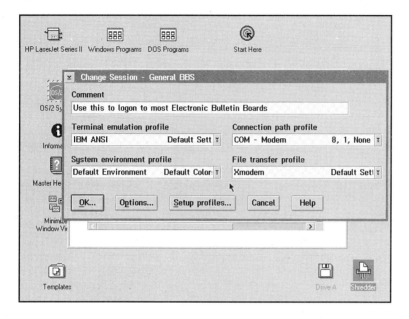

Fig. 22.26

The Change
Session dialog
box.

To customize the emulation or to establish a new emulation, click
Setup profiles and use the dialog boxes for setting up a terminal
emulation. You need extensive communications knowledge for this
procedure.

For a typical BBS, the ASCII terminal emulation is acceptable. When you
register with the BBS, it probably will ask if you want ASCII terminal
emulation as part of your registration procedure. Choose this emulation to make the BBS and PM Terminal communicate optimally.

Choose the other profiles from the lists, or define your own using setup
profiles. The System Environment Profile defines such items as the disk
file path, video code pages, your printers, nationality code page, and
the window colors for your session. PM Terminal supplies only one
profile, but you can create your own.

The Connection Path profile sets the communications parameters that
OS/2 uses to communicate with the remote computer. You set the baud
rate (the rate of communication) in this profile. You also define the
serial port for your modem, the format of the text data, and other modem settings. This profile is most likely to be different for different
types of sessions.

Examine the differences between the Dow Jones News Retrieval profile
and the General BBS profile to see the two most commonly used connection path profiles. You can use other profiles if you have a faster
modem and can connect with computers that also have faster modems.
Similarly, if you have a slow modem, you may need to customize these
profiles.

Note that the on-line services, such as Dow Jones News Retrieval Service, use seven data bits, one stop bit, and even parity. A BBS uses eight data bits, one stop bit, and no parity.

The File Transfer profile sets the default protocol for when you transfer files between computers. A typical communications session may have two different elements. For part of the session, you are typing and reading text from the remote computer. This data is sent one character at a time. The format for this character exchange is set by the number of data bits, stop bits, and parity that you choose from the connection path profile.

In the other part of the session, you may want to send a file to or receive a file from the other computer. Rather than sending one character at a time, you want to send a whole file. The file transfer profile defines how that file is sent. A file normally is sent in sections, each of a particular size. Both computers must be set up to expect the data in a predefined format. They also must use the same format for acknowledging a section of data or for telling the sending computer that a section was corrupted during transmission. The computer industry uses various protocols for file transmission, and you choose one protocol from the file transfer profile text box.

With the profiles chosen, click OK to establish the admittance data. Figure 22.27 shows the Admittance Data form. If you complete this form when you define your profile, you can set it so that the form does not appear when the session starts.

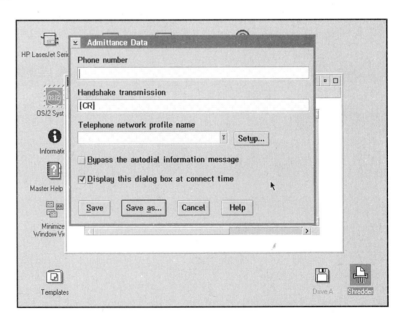

Fig. 22.27

The Admittance Data Form.

This dialog box makes up the second half of your profile for a communications session. You enter a phone number in the top text box and a telephone network profile name in the lower text box. As explained earlier, you can use different telephone network profiles if you use multiple long distance telephone companies or if you have special phone lines installed, such as lines linking different divisions within a corporation.

Click the Bypass the autodial information message if you do not want the end user to see the autodialing information when they select this profile. This message is useful because it gives an intermediate status information while the connection with a remote computer is being made. If the end user does not realize that they are connecting with a remote computer, however, this message may be confusing. If the message is not present, the session gives the impression that the data is being loaded while the connection is being established.

The Display this dialog box at connect time message is used if you want the user to enter information prior to the connection. For example, the Dow Jones News Retrieval example shown earlier did not include the necessary phone number, so the dialog box prompts users for the number when they select the session. If the information is the same every time, you can remove the check from this box to stop this dialog box's appearance when you choose the profile.

After making your selections, click Save as and choose a new session name for your profile. (Remember that you were creating a new session based on an existing profile. You do not want to overwrite your template.) The new profile then appears on the session list.

Understanding PM Terminal Limitations

PM Terminal limits the number of concurrent sessions to 32. You are much more likely, however, to be limited by your hardware. Each communications session needs a communications port and modem. You are limited by the number of ports and modems available on your computer.

A typical PC is limited to four serial ports. You can purchase specialized adapter boards that increase the number of ports available, and you may be able to use these with PM Terminal.

PM Terminal does not emulate every terminal available. If you need a different terminal, you need to acquire a different program.

Sharing PM Terminal Information

PM Terminal does not support the Clipboard. To exchange information with other applets, you use file retrieval and saving methods.

You can save your communications session to a capture file. Additionally, by using the file transfer commands, you can transfer files to and from the remote computer. With the file transfer commands on your computer, you can use the file commands in other applets and application programs to access the file transfer commands.

Chapter Summary

This chapter introduced the data management applets supplied with OS/2. Database is a simple database program that can be used to store lists of information such as lists of names and addresses.

Spreadsheet is a simple spreadsheet program that supports basic arithmetic functions for creating tables of arithmetic information.

PM Chart includes many charting and drawing options for creating presentations of data. It is the most flexible of the data management applets.

PM Terminal is a communications program that enables you to link with remote computers. While relatively complex to configure, it fits many basic communications needs.

Understanding Extended Services

The optional OS/2 product *Extended Services* (ES) is a valuable tool for specialized applications, but not everyone needs it. Extended Services consists of two primary components—Communications Manager and Database Manager—along with a collection of supporting utilities and drivers. Both Communications Manager and Database Manager are high-powered tools for dealing with complex connectivity issues and large amounts of data.

Communications Manager provides your OS/2-based computer with the capability to connect to mainframes or other host computers through terminal emulators and SNA links. Database Manager enables you to create, update, and report relational database tables through SQL, that contain information pertinent to your company or organization. You need these tools if your PC is connected to a mainframe computer or if you maintain a large collection of data in your computer. You don't need ES if you occasionally connect to a bulletin board system or only keep track of a few names and addresses with your computer.

What are SNA and SQL? You learn about these terms and more in this chapter. You begin your exploration of Extended Services by looking at the facilities and functions that ES offers.

Defining the Facilities within Extended Services

IBM has two Extended Services products, *Extended Services with Database Server for OS/2* and the simpler *Extended Services for OS/2*. Both products contain Communications Manager and Database Manager. ES with Database Server also contains database server software and a collection of database client application enabler programs for use with DOS, Windows, and OS/2.

The database server software enables a PC on a local area network (LAN) to share a *database*—a repository of relational tables. These tables, designed by you or someone in your organization, are files of information about customers, sales, products, employees, or other entities. The application enabler programs act as intermediaries, giving applications an interface to the relational tables in a database.

Learning Extended Server Basics

When you install ES, several new folders appear on your OS/2 desktop, as pictured in figure 23.1. The Extended Services, Communications Manager, Database Manager, and User Profile Management folders contain program objects useful for performing ES tasks, as outlined in the following list:

- The program objects in the Extended Services folder help you install, maintain, and understand ES.

- The objects in the User Profile Management folder protect access to your databases by enforcing user-identification security.

- The Communications Manager folder objects are terminal emulation programs and connectivity diagnostics programs.

- The Database Manager folder contains program objects to help you create, repair, update, report, and inquire into your databases.

During installation, you choose the Communications Manager and Database Manager components you plan to use in your application. If you install Communications Manager, for example, you choose terminal emulations—DEC VT100 or IBM 3101 (for ASCII-based hosts), IBM 3270 (for mainframe or AS/400 hosts), or IBM 5250 (for AS/400 or System 36/38 hosts).

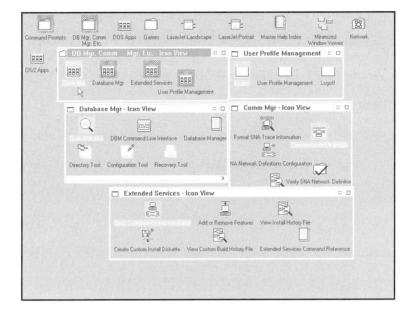

Fig. 23.1

The Extended
Services folders
and program
objects.

The Communications Manager component is especially complicated to install. To help prevent installation problems, read the IBM *Start Here* and the IBM *Workstation Installation Guide* carefully before configuring your computer to use any of the services and utilities within Communications Manager. Fortunately, IBM organized these manuals in the form of road maps that lead you through the installation and configuration processes. The Communications Manager configuration screens, however, are not CUA compliant. (Chapter 9, "Using Your Computer Screen as a Desktop," discusses CUA compliance.)

You definitely need to refer to the IBM manuals the first time you run the Communications Manager configuration and verification tools. The configuration screens are difficult to navigate, and you may have trouble understanding the parameters you must set. If someone in your office has some experience with Communications Manager, by all means, ask that person for help during the configuration process.

Exploring Extended Services with Database Server

You can use Extended Services with Database Server to access a common database from multiple workstations on a network. The database operations (read, update, and search) reside in the database server computer. Perhaps you have a local area network and want one of the PCs on the LAN to store a central database for the other workstations to share. You may have a file server, but you are concerned because response times are slow. The workstations request all or nearly all of the database from the file server each time a user performs a search. The transfer of records to the workstation performing the search consumes too much time. You believe response times can improve considerably if the search operation executes in the same computer that stores the database.

If you're willing to convert from a file server environment to a database server environment, your search operations can execute in the database server computer. With this arrangement, workstations send search requests (or update requests) to the database server and receive the responses.

You have two hurdles to overcome as you convert from one environment to the other. First, the installation and configuration of a database server requires significant effort on your part. Additionally, the software you use to access the database must be compatible with your new database server. You can ask the supplier of your database-oriented application software about compatibility with ES with Database Services. Most companies that sell off-the-shelf database software (Borland International, Computer Associates, and Microsoft, for example) offer ES with Database Services compatibility. If your organization has an in-house programming staff, you can ask one of the staff what plans exist to take advantage of database-server technology.

FROM HERE...

For Related Information

◀◀ "Using Device Support," p. 90.

◀◀ "Upgrading Your Hardware," p. 165.

Securing Access to Your Data

Before you learn about Communications Manager and Database Manager, you need to understand how Extended Services helps you control access to your computer records. User Profile Management (UPM) is the Extended Services tool you use to protect the data in your computer from intruders. UPM consists of logon, logout, and user account management facilities. Figure 23.2 shows the Logon screen that UPM displays when you begin using Database Manager. In this screen, you must identify yourself to the computer in order to access Database Manager files. UPM does not control access to Communications Manager files.

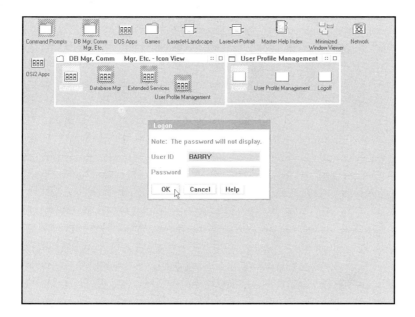

Fig. 23.2

The User Profile Management Logon screen.

You or another authorized person can set up account IDs for the users who need access to the files in Database Manager on your computer. You establish and maintain these account IDs through UPM. Figure 23.3 illustrates the screen you use to update user information. In this screen, you can establish the following identification components for each user:

- You can change user's level of access (from lowest to highest levels of privilege, these are User, Local Administrator, or Administrator).

- You can permit or cancel a user's access to the database information (Logon Allowed or Denied).

- You can change a user's password, or make the entry of a password unnecessary for a particular user.

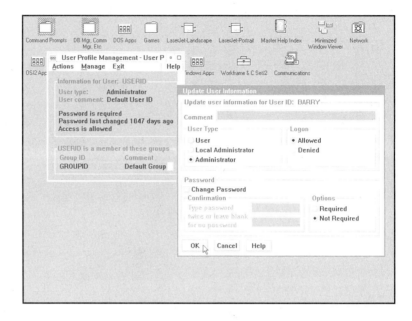

Fig. 23.3

The Update User
Information
screen.

FROM HERE...

For Related Information

◀◀ "Using CONFIG.SYS and AUTOEXEC.BAT," p. 159.

◀◀ "Using the Workplace Shell's System Menu," p. 247.

Using Communications Manager

The software modules that make up Communications Manager enable
your PC to access another computer (typically an IBM mainframe, a
DEC minicomputer, an IBM minicomputer, or another PC). You can
exchange information with or use the resources of the other computer
through Communications Manager. To use Communications Manager,
your PC must be equipped with a serial I/O adapter, a Synchronous
Data Link Control (SDLC) I/O adapter, or a network adapter.

You can use one of Communications Manager's connectivity options
to open terminal emulation sessions with host computers. If you buy
additional software, or if your organization has a staff of in-house programmers, you can establish other kinds of communication links
between a PC running Communications Manager and a host computer.

The programmers may design this link, for example, to transfer information automatically between the PC and the host at preset intervals.

Understanding Connectivity Options

Communications Manager supports four ways to connect your OS/2-based computer to other machines, as shown in the following list:

- SNA Gateway
- X.25 network
- Direct or modem-assisted
- Local area network

The next few sections explain these connectivity options.

Systems Network Architecture (SNA) Gateway

In most system setups, an SNA Gateway PC links an IBM mainframe host (System/370 or System/390) to workstations on a local area network. The workstations on the LAN establish host sessions through the Gateway computer. To the host, the SNA Gateway computer is a single physical unit. To a workstation on the LAN, however, the host is directly attached to the workstation. The SNA Gateway maintains this illusion by distributing host messages to individual workstations and, in reverse, forwarding workstation messages to the host.

The Gateway PC carries on several host sessions on behalf of the workstations. The people at the workstations, through Communications Manager, use these 3270 terminal sessions to log on to the host and run mainframe software without any awareness that the SNA Gateway PC exists.

X.25 Network

X.25 is one of many standards established by the CCITT. CCITT is the Committee Consultatif International Telegraphique and Telephonique, or International Telegraph and Telephone Consultative Committee. An international organization, headquartered in Geneva, CCITT creates and maintains telecommunications standards for the whole world.

The X.25 network protocol defines how mainframes access packet switching networks (*protocols*, also known as *conventions*, are discussed in a later section of this chapter). Packet switching is a data transmission method that sends computer information in messages (packets). The network routes the X.25 packets along the best possible path, in no particular order. Each X.25 packet contains information about itself that enables the receiver to reassemble and reorganize the packets to place the computer information in its original form. An X.25 network is an efficient means of routing computer information. If your company or organization uses an X.25 network, you can connect computers running Communications Manager to the network.

Direct or Modem-Assisted

Your computer may be directly connected to a host computer, or you may use modems and a telephone line. Direct connections may use a coaxial link to a mainframe, a twinaxial link to an AS/400, a Synchronous Data Link Control (SDLC) connection to a mainframe, or perhaps an asynchronous link to either a mainframe or minicomputer. Communications Manager supports serial I/O (COM1, COM2, COM3, or COM4) connectivity options through ACDI, the Asynchronous Communications Device Interface.

ACDI is a communications service within Communications Manager. The terminal emulators that operate through your COM ports (IBM 3101 or DEC VT100) use ACDI to set the baud rate and to send and receive information. Programmers can develop communications software using ACDI, producing customized computer-to-computer links between applications on different computers.

Local Area Network Connectivity

You can connect your OS/2-based computer, running Communications Manager, to other computers through a local area network. The LAN may use token ring network adapter cards, PC Network adapter cards, or EtherNet network adapter cards. IBM uses the name *ETHERAND* to refer to the EtherNet adapters it makes.

Communications Manager can interact with an SNA Gateway over a local area network. Communications Manager also contains drivers you can use to access other computers through specialized interfaces. These specialized interfaces are APPC (Advanced Program-to-Program Communications), APPN (Advanced Peer-to-Peer Networking), the Server-Requester Programming Interface, NetBIOS, and the IEEE 802.2 Protocol. Your programming staff can set up these interfaces and instruct you in their use.

IBM's Advanced Peer-to-Peer Communications (APPC) and Advanced Peer-to-Peer Networking (APPN) are, in essence, conventions computers use to exchange information. Computers need the guidance of conventions to send and receive information efficiently. The computers use the rules and specifications of the convention to determine, for example, which characters in a message denote the destination address and which characters represent incoming information. APPC and APPN are advanced conventions (protocols), because both enable the computers to send and receive information as peers.

Long ago, before PCs, APPN, or APPC, host computers treated all devices as "dumb," because the peripheral devices did not execute applications. The host mainframe controlled the devices, and only the host mainframe could execute application software. The host accepted keystrokes from a terminal and sent screen data back to the terminal. The host mainframe recognized only those messages that were in the form of keystrokes from a terminal.

PCs and the interconnection of mainframes changed this device relationship. A PC can run application software and can act as a peer to the host mainframe. IBM invented APPC (also called *LU 6.2*) to enable computers to exchange information. The PC does not pretend to be a terminal (sending keystrokes and receiving screen data) with APPC. The PC and the host or hosts can establish a communications session and exchange information in the form of predefined fields, records, and files. A programmer defines the layout of these fields, records, and files.

Advanced Peer-to-Peer Networking (APPN) is a further enhancement to APPC. APPN provides for automatic best-path routing of messages in a network. An OS/2-based computer running Communications Manager can use APPC to communicate with other computers and can participate in APPN routing.

Using Terminal Emulations

For many users, the heart of Communications Manager is a terminal emulator session with a host computer. Figure 23.4 shows the main Communications Manager screen, from which you start or stop a terminal emulator session.

The Communications Manager Main Menu is an OS/2 full-screen session that you can leave running in the background. You bring the Main Menu session to the foreground (by using the Window List, for example) only in the following situations:

- When you want to start or stop a terminal emulator session

- When you want to reconfigure Communications Manager

- When you want to terminate Communications Manager

When you install Communications Manager, you select the type of terminal emulation sessions you plan to use—IBM 3270, IBM 3101, DEC VT100, or IBM 5250.

```
Message  Status  Advanced   Exit                      |F1=Help
───────────────────────────────────────────────────────────────
                Communications Manager Main Menu
Active configuration file . . . . . . . . : DEFAULT
Configuration file status . . . . . . . . :
  Verified
Press F10 to go to the action bar or
select an item below and press Enter.
1. Start emulators (3270, 5250, and ASCII)...
2. Stop emulators (3270, 5250, and ASCII)...
3. Transfer file
4. Specify new configuration file name default...
```

Fig. 23.4

The Communications Manager Main Menu screen.

IBM 3270 Terminal Emulator

An IBM 3270 terminal is a device consisting of a screen and a keyboard. In most cases, the terminal is attached to a mainframe computer. A 3270 is a *block-mode* device—the terminal receives and sends entire screens of messages at once, rather than sending one character at a time. Each time you press the Enter key in a 3270 session, Communications Manager sends your typed data to the host computer. When Communications Manager receives the incoming host's response, the host's message appears on-screen.

You can configure the 3270 terminal emulator, using a screen such as the one shown in figure 23.5, to act as a *Distributed Function Terminal* (DFT). DFT is a 3270 mode of operation that enables multiple concurrent logical terminal sessions. You have one physical connection to the host computer(s), through which you can have more than one logical connection. You also can use the screen in figure 23.5 to configure the 3270 terminal emulator to use one of the connectivity options listed earlier in this chapter. As illustrated in figure 23.6, you can select and configure CICS, VM, or TSO file transfer.

Communications Manager supports up to 10 active 3270 sessions at one time. DFT enables five of these sessions; the other connectivity options can create up to five other sessions. Each active 3270 logical session runs in its own windowed OS/2 session. You can perform file transfers with the host computer, cut, copy, and paste information to or from the Clipboard, print locally or direct your print jobs to the host, and run customized computer programs that use Communications Manager services.

```
                    3270 Feature Configuration
DFT terminal/printer emulation
  1. DFT...
Non-DFT terminal/printer emulation (only one may be configured).
  2. SDLC...
  3. Token-Ring or other LAN type...
  4. X.25...
  5. IBM PC Network using Gateway...
  6. ETHERAND Network using Gateway...
DFT and non-DFT options
  7. 3270 color and alarm...
  8. 3270 file transfer...
_____

Esc=Cancel    F1=Help    F3=Exit
```

Fig. 23.5

The 3270 Feature Configuration screen.

```
                    Create/Change CICS Profile
Use the spacebar to select.
Profile name . . . . . . . . . . . . . . . . . . : M14
Comment. . . . . . . . . . . . . . . . . . . . .
   [MODEL PROFILE 3270 FILE TRANSFER  IBM HOST (CICS) TEXT FILES]
ASCII to/from EBCDIC translation . . . . . . . . . : Yes  No
Use CR/LF as record separator. . . . . . . . . . . : Yes  No
PC file code page. . . . . . . . . . . . . . . . . : [437 ]
Host file code page. . . . . . . . . . . . . . . . : [037 ]
IBM host file transfer command
   name . . . . . . . . . . . . . . . . . . . . . : [IND$FILE]
One-to-one character mapping . . . . . . . . . . . : Yes  No
_____

Enter   Esc=Cancel   F1=Help   F4=List
```

Fig. 23.6

The Create/Change CICS Profile screen.

IBM 3101 Terminal Emulator

An IBM 3101 terminal is an ASCII device that connects to a host through an asynchronous (modem or direct-connect) link. The 3101 is one of the simplest terminals. The character sequences that control the 3101 screen (from the keyboard or from the host) are abbreviated versions of ANSI/DEC VT100 sequences. The 3101 is not compatible with ANSI or DEC VT100 protocols, however, because the 3101 character sequences for terminal commands are shorter and fewer in number. The 3101 offers both a block mode and a character mode of operation; most people operate the 3101 in character mode. Communications Manager supports the 3101 terminal in both modes.

You can use the 3101 emulator to access a bulletin board system or an information service such as CompuServe or MCI Mail. The 3101 isn't as popular as the DEC VT100, however, and you may find that you need to use the VT100 emulator to access these services. The 3101 terminal emulator runs in an OS/2 windowed session, and you can use Clipboard-oriented cut, copy, and paste operations to manipulate host session information. You can transfer files with XModem, TSO, VM, or CICS file transfer protocols.

DEC VT100 Terminal Emulator

Digital Equipment Corporation set an industry standard with the VT100 terminal. The VT100 device is a character-mode screen and keyboard that uses ANSI *escape sequences* to manage the appearance of the information on-screen and to indicate cursor-key and other special user operations at the keyboard. Figure 23.7 shows the VT100 terminal emulator as a windowed session on the desktop. You may use the VT100 emulator to access a bulletin board system, a DEC host computer, or an information service such as CompuServe or MCI Mail.

As with 3101 emulation, you can cut, copy, and paste information to and from the host session window. You can use the XModem, TSO, VM, or CICS file transfer protocols to exchange files with the host computer.

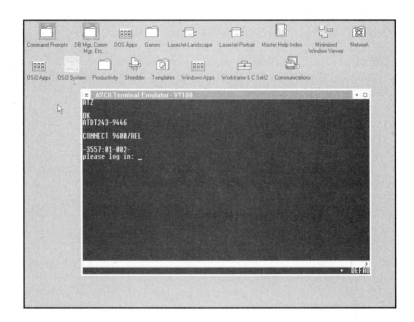

Fig. 23.7

The Communications Manager's VT100 terminal emulator.

IBM 5250 Terminal Emulator

If your host computer is an AS/400, System/36, or System/38 machine, you can access that host by emulating an IBM 5250 terminal from within Communications Manager. The 5250 Work Station Feature of Communications Manager can operate through SDLC, Token Ring, EtherNet, X.25, or twinaxial connections.

The 5250 Work Station Feature manages up to five active terminal or printer sessions at one time. You can transfer files between your PC and an AS/400 host if you purchase PC Support/400, a separate IBM software product.

For Related Information

◀◀ "Choosing the OS/2 Features You Want," p. 134.

◀◀ "Using CONFIG.SYS and AUTOEXEC.BAT," p. 159.

FROM HERE...

Learning Database Manager

The preceding sections of this chapter have concentrated on the Communications Manager portion of Extended Services for OS/2 and the security features of User Profile Management. The discussion now turns to the other primary component of Extended Services, Database Manager.

Database Manager is easier to use than Communications Manager. Many functions within Database Manager make use of CUA-compliant screens under Presentation Manager to help you access your information. In the next several sections of this chapter, you explore the fundamentals of databases and you learn about database services and database tools. These sections introduce you to Query Manager and teach you special techniques for accessing database files in a shared fashion from DOS, DOS-and-Windows, and OS/2 workstations.

Database Manager runs in a single-user (stand-alone) or multiuser (LAN) environment. The Database Manager portion of the Extended Services product consists of Database Services, Database Tools, Query Manager, Remote Data Services, and DOS and Windows Database Client support. You can use Database Manager in any of the following configurations:

- *Stand-alone.* The databases you create exist only on your PC and other people cannot share your access to the files.

- *Database Client/Server.* You and others can share the databases that reside in your PC. You also can access databases on other database server PCs.

- *Database Client.* You share databases that reside on other PCs (database servers); you have no local databases on your PC.

- *Database Client with Local Databases.* You share access to a database server in addition to having one or more local databases on your PC that only you access.

Understanding Database Manager Basics

Database Manager has many components and can do many tasks, but all the functions within Database Manager relate either to designing or manipulating databases. You specify the information you want to store when you design the database. You then add, change, and retrieve information when you use the database.

A database is a repository of relational tables which store information about entities. Each table is, in essence, a list of entities. At design time, you indicate what data fields the columns of the table are to hold. You also indicate the relationships among the tables.

Relational Databases

Database Manager uses the relational model of data. The software stores your information in table-oriented rows and columns. Each row is a different entity. Each column identifies a *data field*—a piece of information associated with each entity. You can designate one or more of the columns (fields) as indexes in the table. An *index* is a key that identifies each row of a table. A database can consist of one or more tables.

A simple example may help you understand relational database technology. Suppose that you work at a bank, and you want to use Database Manager to keep track of mortgage loan accounts. You may at first design a single table, such as the following, for all customer data:

MORTGAGE CUSTOMERS

Name and Address Account Number Loan Amount Monthly Payment

What if the same customer has several mortgages with your bank? You don't want the name and address information replicated several times in the database. To avoid this problem, you can design two tables in your database:

Table 1

MORTGAGE CUSTOMERS

Name and Address	Account Number	List of Mortgage Numbers (1 or more)

Table 2

MORTGAGES

Mortgage Number	Loan Amount	Monthly Payment

In this example, you can use Mortgage Number to relate the contents of one table to the other.

Structured Query Language (SQL)

You use Structured Query Language (SQL) statements to store data in and retrieve data from relational tables. You can learn the details of SQL and issue your SQL statements explicitly. Alternatively, you can use Query Manager, or the facilities of another software product such as Borland International's Paradox, to formulate your SQL statements. Query Manager is a component of Database Manager that you learn more about later in this chapter.

SQL, pronounced *sequel*, is an English-like language. SQL statements occur in layers of increasing complexity and capability. You quickly can learn SQL's basic features, yet SQL provides programmers with considerable control over the database. With SQL, you can do the following:

- Create tables
- Store information in tables
- Select exactly the information you need
- Change the stored data
- Change the structure of the tables
- Combine data from multiple tables

In contrast to other data manipulation languages, SQL is *non-procedural*—you specify operations in terms of *what* SQL is to do, rather than *how* SQL is to do the operations. With a single command, you can update multiple rows of a table without needing to know the location or other physical attributes of the rows.

Popular SQL statements are CREATE, SELECT, UPDATE, and INSERT. The following example SQL statement creates a new staff member table in the database:

```
CREATE TABLE STAFF    (NAME              CHAR(25),
                       JOB_DESCRIPTION   CHAR(50),
                       HIRE_DATE         DATE,
                       SALARY            NUMBER(7,2));
```

This table is to contain the name (25-characters wide), job description (50 characters), hire date (stored in date format), and salary (in #####.## format) for each staff member. The table is empty after the CREATE operation, ready to hold information about the people in your organization. You use INSERT statements to populate the table with data, as shown in the following example:

```
INSERT INTO STAFF
VALUES ('JEFFREY', 'ADMINISTRATOR', 10/1/1982, 55000.00);
```

To update Jeffrey's salary, you issue the following UPDATE command:

```
UPDATE STAFF
SET SALARY = 57500.00 WHERE NAME = 'JEFFREY';
```

Finally, to obtain a list of all administrators and their salaries from the STAFF table, you use the following SELECT statement:

```
SELECT NAME, SALARY
FROM STAFF
WHERE JOB_DESCRIPTION = 'ADMINISTRATOR';
```

These examples illustrate that SQL isn't difficult to use in its basic form. You can formulate much more complicated updates and queries with SQL. To help you in working with SQL, IBM supplies a complete *Structured Query Language (SQL) Reference* with the Extended Services product.

Using Database Services

Database Services is the part of Database Manager that actually manages the data stored in a database. Database Services provides record locking and transaction management. Database Services also ensures the integrity of the data in the database.

Database Services controls all access to the database, performing database operations on your behalf (or those of a computer program you run) by processing SQL statements. You can interact with Database

Services through the Command Line Interface, through Query Manager, through the Extended Services Database Tools, or through a computer program (written by your company's programmers) that issues SQL statements.

Preparing SQL Statements

Database Services accepts SQL statements from Query Manager, from the Command Line Interface, or from an application program. Database Services translates SQL statements into a sequence of internal operations. The translation process is called *preparing* or *binding*. Database Services must prepare all executable SQL statements before performing the operations called out by those statements.

If you use Database Services interactively, through Query Manager or the Command Line Interface, Database Services prepares the statements at run time and then executes the statements. This method of operation is termed *dynamic SQL*. Some custom-written computer programs issue dynamic SQL, but most do not.

A computer programmer can use Database Services to prepare his or her SQL statements before the program actually runs. The programmer runs an SQL precompiler; this mode of operation is termed *static SQL*. Static SQL statements, embedded in the application program, enable Database Services to bypass preparing the SQL statements at run time. The application program executes faster because Database Services has less work to do.

Record Locking and Transaction Management

When you design your tables, you may express data relationships among the tables. You don't want these relationships destroyed by a sudden power failure in your building. Database Services uses the concept of a *unit of work* to ensure that the database is always in a consistent state. A unit of work is a transaction—a collection of updates to related tables. You want all the updates in the collection to be successfully applied. If only some of the updates happen and then a power failure occurs, you want the partial update to be "rolled back" so that the database returns to a consistent state.

To understand consistent and inconsistent database states, consider the tables you created earlier for the bank mortgage records. When you use the MORTGAGE CUSTOMERS and MORTGAGES, you may issue SQL statements against the database to transfer a mortgage from one customer to another. After you remove the Mortgage Number from one customer's records, but before you add that Mortgage Number to the second customer's records, the database is in an *inconsistent* state. Only after you add the Mortgage Number to the second customer's records is the database *consistent* again.

Every time a computer program begins using a database, Database Services automatically starts a unit of work. The program can signal the end of the unit of work by issuing a COMMIT statement (that indicates successful completion of the update) or a ROLLBACK statement (that instructs Database Services to restore the database to the state it was in before the unit of work began). If the computer program disconnects from the database before successfully finishing the update, Database Services issues a ROLLBACK statement. While the unit of work is in progress, Database Services prevents other workstations in a multiuser environment from accessing the data you are updating.

Database Objects

Database Services objects include databases, tables, views, indexes, and packages. The following paragraphs describe these objects in detail, and explain how Database Services groups the objects in the database.

In previous sections, you learned about databases and their tables. Database Manager considers a database to encompass not only the tables but also a set of system catalogs that describe the logical and physical structure of the data, a configuration file, and a recovery log file that contains information about ongoing transactions (updates in progress).

A *view* is an alternate representation of the data in one or more tables of the database. A typical view may include only some of the columns of the tables in a database and thus provide restricted access to the tables. You can create a view, for example, of only 20 or 30 fields that people can query and update, even though the entire table might contain hundreds of fields. You thus impose a measure of security and simplify people's access to the table.

An *index* is a key, a set of table columns you designate as fields that identify the entity stored in a row. You can specify whether the index value is unique or the table can hold duplicate indexes (keys).

A *package* is the result a programmer obtains when he or she prepares a set of SQL statements, in a computer language, for use with the database. The package contains all the information needed by Database Manager to process the programmer's specific SQL statements.

Database Manager groups objects in the database by *qualifier*. The qualifier is an identification code that can contain up to eight characters (numbers and letters). The qualifier identifies each person who accesses a database and helps Database Manager keep separate track of each person's database objects.

Exploring Database Tools

Extended Services offers three tools for configuring Database Manager and administering databases. These tools are the Configuration Tool, Recovery Tool, and the Directory Tool. The following sections describe these tools and their use.

Configuration Tool

You use the Configuration Tool to change Database Manager resources and database characteristics. You can allocate resources for the database buffer pool, database log files, the number of applications that can use a database, and the size of the database sort buffer. You also can instruct Database Manager to use more memory for storage management.

The Configuration Tool also enables you to mark a database as a candidate for *roll-forward recovery* by the Recovery Tool. Roll-forward recovery is the update of the database by the application of changes recorded in the database log. The database log stores all pertinent information about each update operation during a unit of work (a transaction). Figure 23.8 illustrates the Configuration Tool screen.

Recovery Tool

You use the Recovery Tool to make backup copies of your databases and, when necessary, to restore your database files. You can specify that you want a backup of the entire database, or you can specify that the system copy only the changes and updates that are more recent than the last backup. The Recovery Tool can recover or restore a database as new, as a replacement for an existing database of the same name, or as a continuation of a recovery operation you previously started. Figure 23.9 shows the Recovery Tool screen.

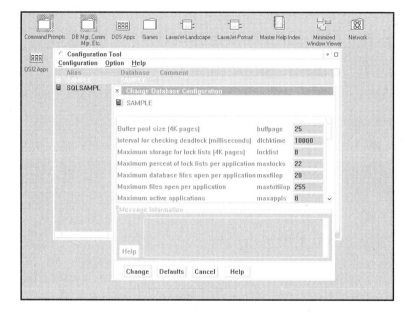

Fig. 23.8

The Configuration Tool screen.

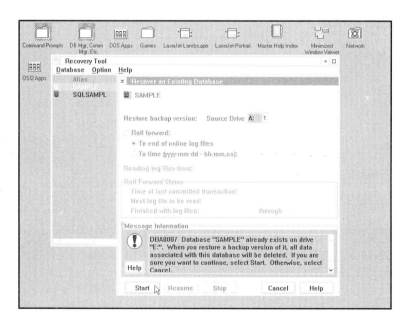

Fig. 23.9

The Recovery Tool screen.

Directory Tool

You use the Directory Tool to create database files and to specify who can access the databases. The Directory Tool can create a new database, catalog a local or remote database, and uncatalog a database. A *catalog* is a published description of the logical and physical structure of the data; other people can "see" a database on your PC if you have cataloged that database. The Directory Tool also can list all the local and remote databases cataloged in the system database directory, or list the volume database directories (the disk drives on which your databases reside). You can use the Directory Tool to catalog or uncatalog workstations (to enable or disable access to your databases), and to list the workstations cataloged on your computer. Figure 23.10 shows the Directory Tool screen.

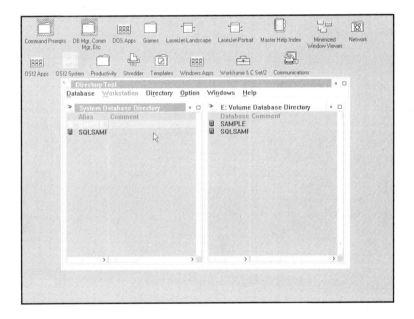

Fig. 23.10

The Directory Tool screen.

Using Query Manager

Query Manager is a Presentation Manager application that provides interactive access to your databases. You don't have to be an expert in SQL to use Query Manager. Query Manager's menus guide you through the steps of creating and executing SQL statements.

You can use Query Manager to create and define a database, request information from a database, review the operational status of a database, and change the authorizations that control who has access to specific database functions, tables, and views. You also can direct Query Manager to create a customized user interface through which users can gain access to your databases.

Creating and Defining a Database

After you double-click the Query Manager icon and identify yourself to the User Profile Management services Logon screen, the Query Manager screen appears. You can choose a database from that screen's list or you can create a new database. Figure 23.11 shows the Query Manager screen.

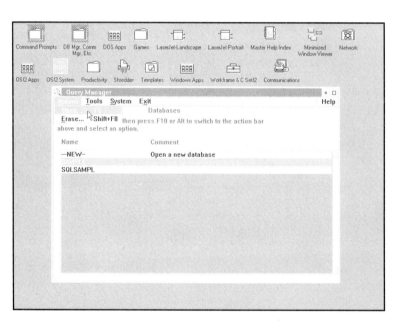

Fig. 23.11

The Query Manager initial screen.

After selecting a database, you use the Query Manager Main Selection screen, shown in figure 23.12, to begin working with that database. The following list describes the Query Manager options available on this screen:

- *Tables and Views.* Use this option to design tables or views, or update table data.

- *Queries.* Use this option to retrieve data from tables and display reports.

- *Forms.* Use this option to design reports.

- *Procedures.* Use this option to develop custom command sequences.

- *Panels.* Use this option to design custom data-entry screens.

- *Menus.* Use this option to design menus for data-entry screens.

- *Profiles.* Use this option to change default database names and other system defaults.

To add a column of information to a new or existing table, you use the Tables and Views option. This option brings up a Table screen, similar to the one shown in figure 23.13. On the Query Manager Table screen, you use menu options to add or delete columns from the table. The screen shows the current layout of the table.

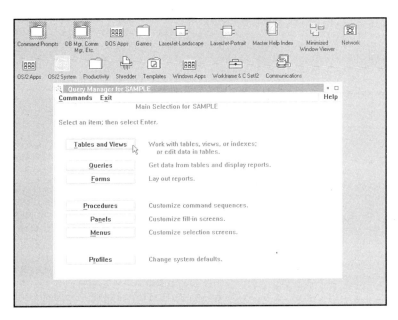

Requesting Information from a Database

You can use Query Manager's menus to formulate a query. If you plan to use the same query several times, you can store the query for future reference. You start the process of building a query by selecting the Queries button on the Query Manager's Main Selection screen.

You use Query Manager menus to build queries. In the menus, you select the columns the query is to display, the criteria for which rows the query displays, and the sort order of the final report. The first pull-down menu contains options for managing the query during the query-building process. You can run the query, save the query, get (load) a query, convert the query to SQL and show the result, and print the query.

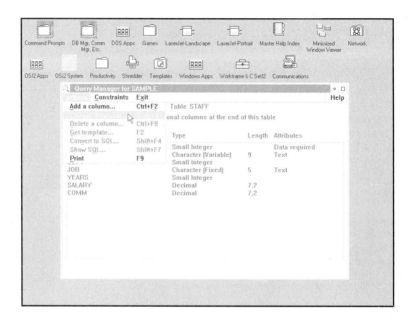

Fig. 23.13

The Query Manager Table screen.

Figure 23.14 shows a query under construction. In this example, the query is to display the columns (data fields) DEPT, SALARY, COMM, and the expression SALARY+COMM. The *Row Conditions* entry of the query states, IF DEPT Is Equal To 15, 20 OR 38. This query will sort information for departments 15, 20, and 38 in ascending order by DEPT.

When you run the query, Query Manager produces and displays a report containing the information you specified in the query construction. The on-screen report shown in figure 23.15 displays the query shown under construction in the previous figure. Notice in the column headings that Query Manager named the combined SALARY+COMM column EXPRESSION 5. You can rename such expression-result headings.

You use the Forms screen, shown in figure 23.16, to create reports containing data from your database. You can customize the appearance of Query Manager reports. You can change several options for the form, and you can specify Column Heading, Usage, Indent, Width, Edit rules, and Sequence for each column in your report.

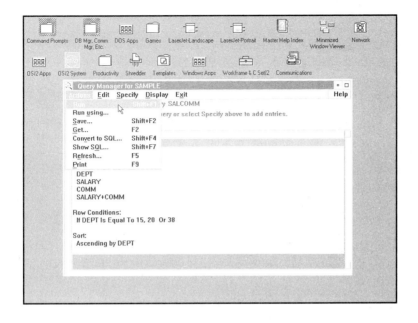

Fig. 23.14

A query under construction.

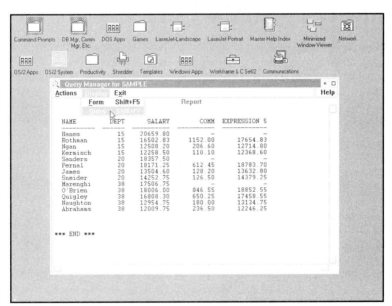

Fig. 23.15

Query Manager displays query results in report format.

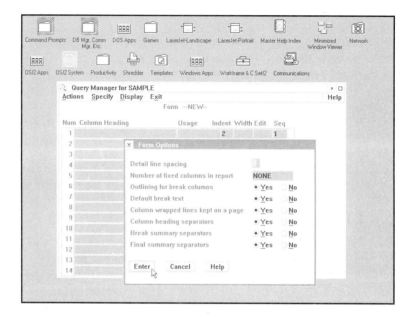

Fig. 23.16

The Query
Manager Forms
screen.

Reviewing the Query Manager Profile

Query Manager maintains a user profile for each account ID assigned
to your database's users. The profile enables Query Manager to know
the computer environment of each user when he or she accesses the
database.

The profile contains *Sign-On Options* and *Printing Options*. The Sign-On
Options indicate the default database name, the qualifier that Query
Manager will use for this account ID, and the row buffer size that Query
Manager is to use for that account ID. The *qualifier* is a prefix that denotes a certain table in the database and which allows a person to refer
to that table without explicitly naming the table. The row buffer size is
a parameter that specifies how much memory should be set aside for
reading and writing rows of a table.

The Printing Options express the printer nickname (an alias by which
you refer to the printer), lines per inch or centimeter, regular or con-
densed print, and number of copies. The Printing Options also include
report title configuration, which you use to indicate whether you want
page numbers and the current date/time to appear on each report.
Figure 23.17 shows the Query Manager Profile screen.

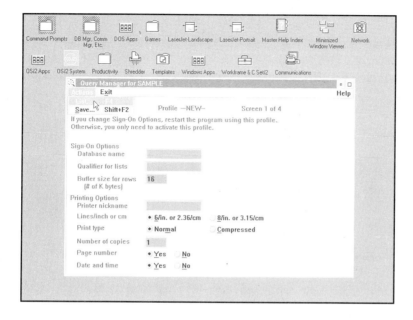

Fig. 23.17

The Query
Manager Profile
screen.

Using Customized Interfaces

You can use Query Manager menus to access your databases, or you
can program Query Manager to present a customized interface to
enable the same access. The interface you design can include menus,
data-entry screens, and simple procedures (in a simple computer programming language). You also can use the customized interface to
print reports of your own design.

You design the custom interface menus with the Menu Actions screen
(see fig. 23.18). You specify Action Text, a Mnemonic (which becomes a
shortcut key), and a Command for each menu option. The commands
you list on this screen appear as Command options on your custom
interface menu. When a user selects one of these options, Query Manager executes the designated Query Manager Procedure.

Figure 23.19 shows the Query Manager screen you use to design the
panels of your customized interface. *Panels* is Query Manager's term
for screens. You type procedural instructions that indicate the Query
Manager processing that is to take place for a panel. You also designate
panel search queries and names of procedures that are to execute under the conditions you specify.

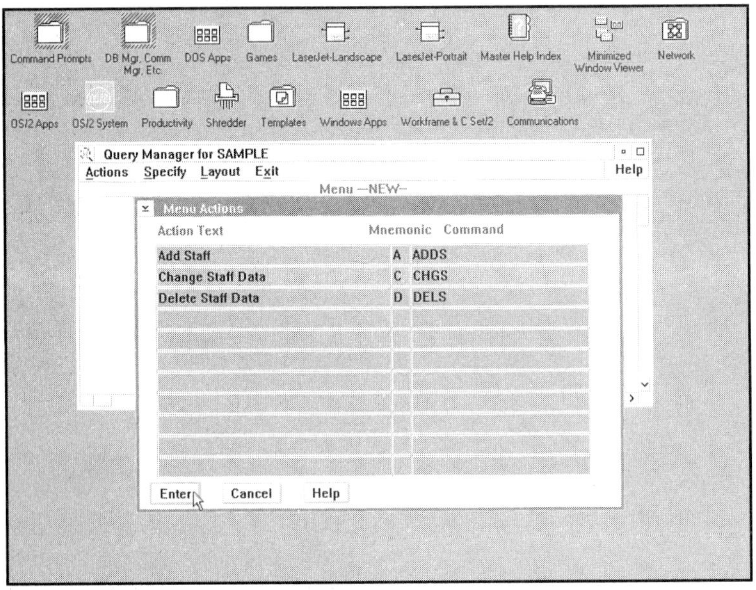

Fig. 23.18

The Query Manager Menu Actions screen.

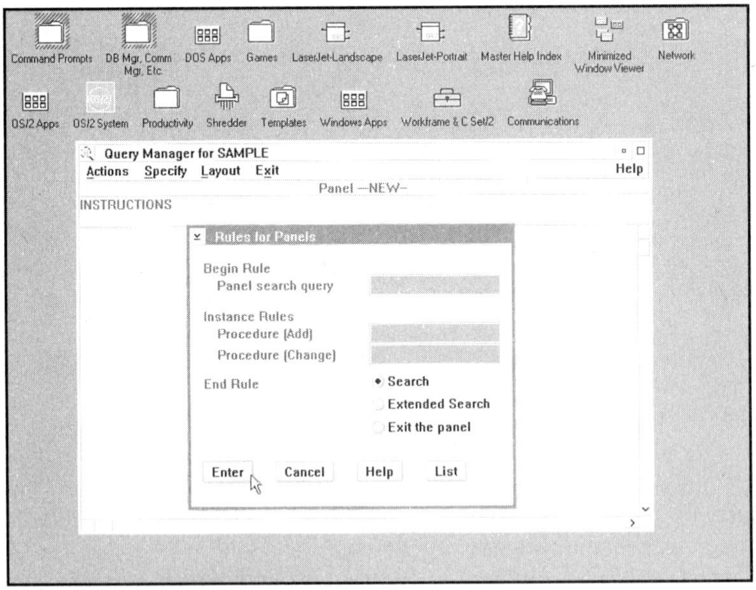

Fig. 23.19

The Query Manager Panel screen for designing customized interfaces.

Figure 23.20 shows the list of Panel Actions you can attach to each panel you design for the custom interface. Each action has a Mnemonic and an Action Key that users of your customized interface can invoke.

You specify the Panel Operation/Command that executes when users invoke the Action. The Mode expresses whether the action is an Add, Change, or Delete operation.

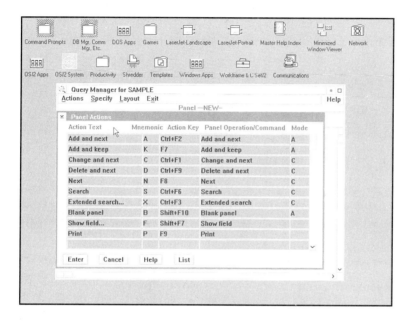

Fig. 23.20

The Query Manager Panel Actions screen.

Applying Remote Data Services

If you install and configure Database Manager as a networked, multiuser application, Extended Services also installs Remote Data Services on your computer. Remote Data Services enables multiple workstations to access a shared, common database. Certain components of Communications Manager also install themselves on your computer to support Remote Data Services. You can use Remote Data Services through any one of the following connectivity options:

- A Token Ring-based LAN
- An IBM PC Network-based LAN
- An EtherNet-based LAN
- An SDLC adapter card
- An X.25 connection

Remote Data Services supplies the database server and database client functions; Communications Manager components supply the means of communicating database requests and replies to and from a remote database. After you establish catalogs of databases and remote workstations, you use Database Manager (through Query Manager, the Command Line Interface, or an application program) to access databases on the LAN in the same way you access databases on your local PC.

Understanding Client/Server Applications

You can use a network operating system such as IBM's LAN Server, Microsoft's LAN Manager, or Novell NetWare to turn a computer on the LAN into a file server. You then can put your databases on that file server.

The network operating system enables workstations to share the database file just as they share any other file. In a file-server environment, however, your database search operations take longer to execute and cause substantially greater LAN traffic. Your workstation must read the entire database from the file server to perform the search. If you have a database with a table of 5,000 entries, and you run a query that displays five rows of the table, for example, your workstation must read all 5,000 rows to find the five desired entries.

In a client/server environment, your workstation uses Remote Data Services to transfer your SELECT statement to the PC on which the database resides. Under the database conditions outlined in this example, the Database Manager running on that remote PC performs your search and returns the five table rows to your workstation. Remote Data Services processes the response through your own Database Manager. The faster running time is the only indication that the database is on a remote PC.

A *database client* workstation requests access to resources made available by a *database server* workstation. Applications that your programmers develop, as well as software that you buy, can take advantage of Remote Data Services. Such applications are client/server applications.

Making a Remote Database Seem Local

A database client workstation uses either NetBIOS or Advanced Peer-to-Peer Networking (APPN) to communicate with a database server. NetBIOS is the default protocol for Database Manager and Remote Data Services, but you can use the Communications Manager configuration screens to work with either protocol.

Remote Data Services reads the Extended Services configuration and catalog files to know where each database resides. You or an administrator sets up these configuration files and catalog files at Database Manager installation time or when your office designs and creates a new shared database.

Supporting DOS and Windows Database Clients

The Extended Services with Database Server product contains computer program "helper" modules that enable client workstations to access shared databases. Your organization's programmers can develop custom applications using these modules. The client workstations need not run OS/2 and Extended Services. Some of the workstations on the LAN can be DOS or DOS-and-Windows based, provided at least one of the workstations runs Extended Services and OS/2. The DOS or DOS-and-Windows database client workstations contain only NetBIOS and a database-access enabler. A user at a DOS workstation, for example, cannot use Query Manager to access a database.

NOTE Check with IBM about the licensing requirements for the database client workstation enabler software.

For Related Information

◀◀ "Introducing Presentation Manager," p. 221.

▶▶ "OS/2 LAN Server and LAN Manager LANs," p. 635.

FROM HERE...

Chapter Summary

Through the information in this chapter, you gained an understanding of IBM's Extended Services product. You explored the features and functions of Communications Manager and Database Manager. You learned how User Profile Management helps protect the privacy of your databases. You also became aware of the advantages of the Extended Services with Database Server product.

In the next chapter, you turn your attention to networking OS/2 on a LAN.

Networking with OS/2

O S/2 is a natural computer network environment. It contains a number of LAN-aware features and facilities. Network operating system vendors such as Novell and IBM can take advantage of these features and facilities to make networks easy to install, administer, and use. You can access the network not only from a command-line session but also from the Workplace Shell's graphical interface.

You can use an OS/2-based PC as a workstation on a LAN or as a file server. Novell offers a NetWare Requester for OS/2 that turns your OS/2 computer into a workstation on a NetWare LAN. Novell also offers a relatively new product, NetWare for OS/2, which can turn an OS/2-based computer into a NetWare file server.

IBM offers LAN Server to customers who want to run a network operating system on an OS/2-based computer. Although in some respects LAN Server and NetWare are competing products, IBM sells both network software products. IBM entered into an agreement with Novell to resell NetWare under the IBM name.

This chapter gives you an understanding of how your OS/2-equipped PC functions on a local area network. In this chapter, you first explore Novell's popular network environment, NetWare. You learn how to install and use the NetWare Requester for OS/2. You also learn about IBM's LAN Server product as well as Microsoft's version of LAN Server, called LAN Manager.

OS/2 Workstations on a NetWare LAN

The NetWare Requester for OS/2 enables a computer running OS/2 2.1 to become a workstation on a NetWare LAN. In the next few sections, you become familiar with the NetWare Requester for OS/2 products.

Understanding NetWare Requester for OS/2

The NetWare Requester for OS/2 is an installable file system that is similar to HPFS. (Chapter 4, "Deciding How You Want To Use OS/2," discusses HPFS.) The file system you access through the Requester is in the file server rather than in your local PC. Through the Requester, you can share disk drives and printers, you can share files with other users, and you can send messages to people at other workstations.

NetWare Requester has several components. The components that enable you to access the file server are device drivers you load through your CONFIG.SYS file. The components that you use to administer and manage the network are available as command-line utilities and also as Presentation Manager (PM) utilities. You can choose the command-line interface or the PM interface. The Requester product contains on-line help files that work in the same manner as OS/2's built-in help files.

The NetWare Requester enables you to access the file server and shared printer from any of your OS/2, DOS, or Windows sessions. Your DOS applications operate the same way in a DOS session, for example, as they operate on a plain DOS workstation. The DOS utility SHARE is always in effect under OS/2. You don't have to remember to load SHARE when you access the network.

Figure 24.1 shows three new folders on your desktop—a Network folder containing PM program objects, a NetWare folder containing a drives object labeled POWERPRO (a file server name), and a third folder representing a tree view of the same drives object. The NetWare Requester installation program put the NetWork and NetWare folders on your desktop. You use the drives object in the NetWare folder in the same way you use the OS/2 drives object for your local floppy and hard disks.

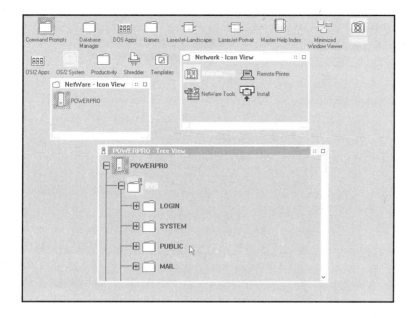

Fig. 24.1

The NetWare
Requester for
OS/2 folders.

Installing the NetWare Requester

The NetWare Requester is easy to install. The installation program is a
PM application. Through a menu-driven interface, you copy the Requester files onto your workstation and configure your workstation's
networking parameters. Figure 24.2 illustrates the initial NetWare Requester Workstation installation screen. You follow the initial screen's
step-by-step instructions to install the software that enables you,
through your network adapter, to access the LAN.

Your organization's network administrator (an individual with SUPER-
VISOR privileges on your LAN) installs the OS/2 versions of the
NetWare utility programs, such as SYSCON, PCONSOLE, and USERLIST.
The installation process places these OS/2 utilities in the PUBLIC\OS2
directory on the file server. The OS/2 utilities have to be installed only
once, and your network administrator already may have made the installation. If you are the network administrator, you use the Attach to a
NetWare File Server screen similar to the screen shown in figure 24.3 to
gain supervisor-level access to the file server.

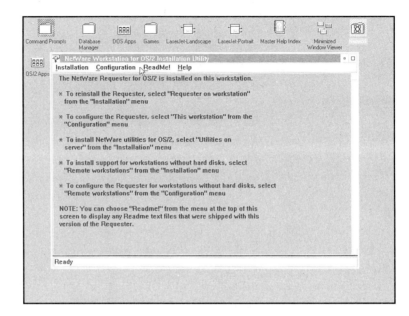

Fig. 24.2

The NetWare Requester for OS/2 installation screen.

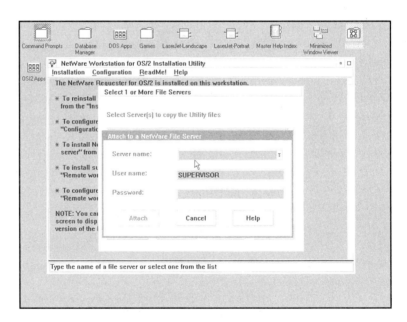

Fig. 24.3

The Attach to a NetWare File Server screen.

Setting Up the NET.CFG File

During installation, the Requester installation program prompts you to set up your NET.CFG file. This file contains the parameters your workstation uses to control access to the LAN. The installation process, in true PM form, presents a list of the parameters you can set and offers values for those parameters. You (or your network administrator) choose the parameters that are appropriate for your workstation. Assuming that your PC already has a network adapter in one of the computer's slots, you merely reboot your computer after installing and configuring the Requester and you are ready to log in to the LAN.

Figure 24.4 illustrates the Requester installation program's screen for creating or updating a NET.CFG file on your workstation. When you highlight and click the items in the NET.CFG Options window, explanations of those items appear in the bottom window. You can select text from the explanations window (by using the mouse or the keyboard) and paste the result into the window labeled Current NET.CFG File Contents. When you finish making your selections, choose the Save pushbutton to write your selected entries to the NET.CFG file. The Requester installation program provides good on-line help, as shown in figure 24.5.

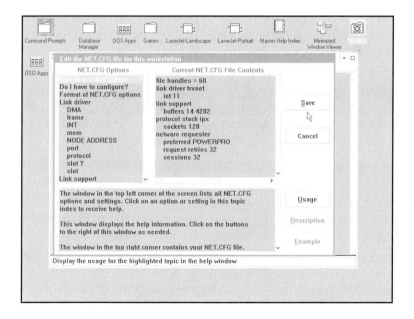

Fig. 24.4

The Requester installation program used to construct an appropriate NET.CFG file for the workstation.

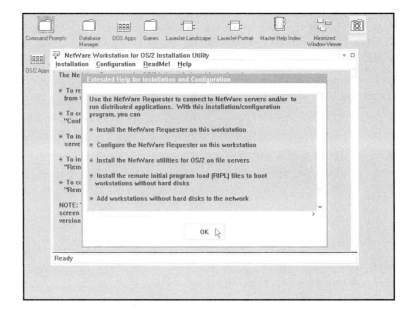

Fig. 24.5

One of the
Requester
installation help
screens.

Logging In and Mapping Drives

You can perform the log-in sequence in a variety of ways with the
NetWare Requester for OS/2. You can point and click your way onto
the LAN through the NetWare Tools, you can log in manually at a command-line prompt, you can create a STARTUP.CMD file in the root directory of your hard drive to automate the log-in process, or you can
create a program object (consisting of a CMD file that executes the
LOGIN program) and place that program object in your StartUp folder.
The best way to accomplish the latter alternative is to use a text editor
to create the CMD file, build your program object from the model in the
Templates folder, and then do a Create Shadow operation to move the
program object into the StartUp folder.

The CMD file you place in the StartUp folder or that you name
STARTUP.CMD contains entries similar to those in the following
example:

```
L:
CD OS2
LOGIN BARRY
MAP G:=POWERPRO\SYS:
MAP L:=POWERPRO\SYS:PUBLIC\OS2
CAPTURE Q=LASERJET
```

Note that this log-in sequence is quite similar to the one you used under DOS, before you installed OS/2 (if you had a DOS workstation in the past). After you perform the log-in sequence (which you may have automated to happen at boot time by using the STARTUP.CMD batch file that runs when you start OS/2), you can access the shared network disk drives and printers from any application or command-line session you start.

Figure 24.6 shows the NetWare Tools screen. NetWare Tools is a PM application that lists the network disk drives you currently have mapped. NetWare Tools also provides menu options for attaching to file servers, logging in to file servers, mapping drives, and sharing a LAN printer.

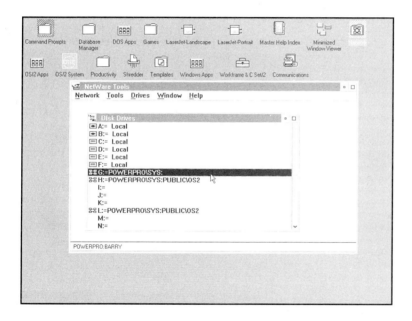

Fig. 24.6

The NetWare Tools screen.

If you prefer using a PM interface (rather than a command-line interface) to map drives, you can use the screen shown in figure 24.7. You double-click one of the disk drives in the list presented by NetWare Tools, then indicate the server, volume, and directory you want to map as that disk drive. You gain access to a shared LAN printer in a similar manner. Figure 24.8 illustrates the Add Remote Printer screen of NetWare Tools. You select the printer server and printer name from the lists and then click the Add pushbutton to share access to that printer.

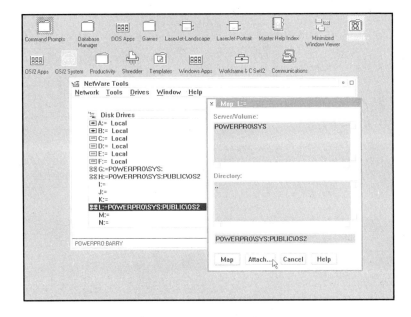

Fig. 24.7

Mapping drives
with NetWare
Tools.

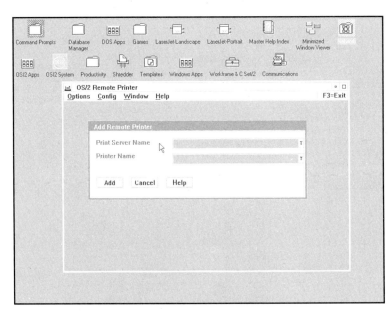

Fig. 24.8

Sharing a printer
with NetWare
Tools.

Exploring IPX/NETX Support for DOS Sessions

The NetWare Requester for OS/2 distinguishes between two types of networking sessions, global and private. By default, every DOS and OS/2 program runs in a global session. Private sessions are optional. A global session uses the log-in name and drive mappings you establish when you first log in to the network. A private session, on the other hand, can use a separate log-in name and set of drive mappings. The next few paragraphs explain the distinction more fully.

After you log in to the LAN, map your drives, and set up your access to shared printers, you can use network resources. Every DOS or OS/2 session you start becomes a global session that can access the shared drives and printers. You have the maximum amount of memory available in your DOS sessions because you don't have to load network TSR (terminate-and-stay-resident) programs (such as IPX.COM or NETX.COM).

You cannot perform certain network tasks in a global DOS session. If you try to run NetWare utilities (USERLIST, PCONSOLE, WHOAMI, and MAP, for example) in a global DOS session, you receive error messages. You also cannot run network-aware programs that use IPX to do PC-to-PC communications. You must convert to a private session in order to run these programs.

Novell supplies a version of the NETX.COM program that you can run in a DOS session and that converts the session from global to private. After you run NETX, you must log in to the network from that session, remap your drives, and reestablish your access to shared printers. You then can run NetWare utilities such as USERLIST from that session, as well as programs that use IPX to do PC-to-PC communications. The disadvantage of a private session is the loss of some memory to the TSR NETX.COM program.

Using the OS/2 NetWare Commands and Utilities

You can use the OS/2 versions of the NetWare utilities in the \PUBLIC\OS2 directory from an OS/2 full-screen or windowed session. In an OS/2 session, you have full access to the network's resources and don't need to distinguish between global and private sessions. If you prefer using a command-line interface, you can run NetWare utilities such as USERLIST or WHOAMI in OS/2 sessions. Figure 24.9 is the

NetWare utility SYSCON, running in a windowed OS/2 session on the desktop. Alternatively, you can use the PM interface provided by the NetWare Tools. Figure 24.10 shows the User List, NetWare Tools' equivalent of the USERLIST display.

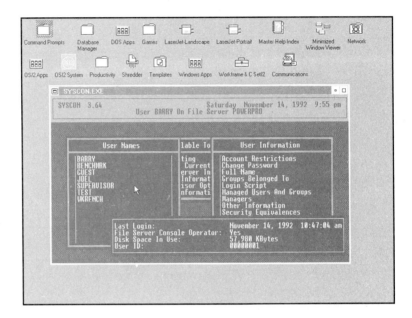

Fig. 24.9

The NetWare utility SYSCON in an OS/2 windowed session.

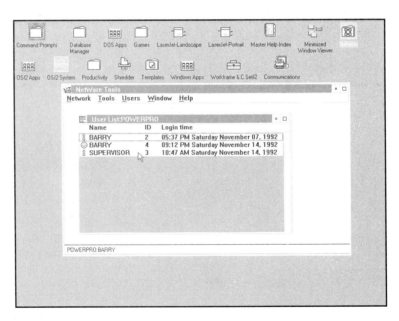

Fig. 24.10

Using the NetWare Tools User List.

Using NetWare for OS/2

Until recently, when you used NetWare, you had to set up a separate PC on the LAN to act as file server. In this configuration, the other PCs take the role of workstations. The file server PC is dedicated to acting just as a file server. A new Novell product, *NetWare for OS/2*, now enables you to install the NetWare file server software on a computer running OS/2 2.1. You can choose to set this computer aside as a file server, but you have the option of using OS/2 sessions on such a computer if you need OS/2 command-line access at the server. NetWare for OS/2 is based on Novell's "Portable NetWare" concept.

To the workstations on the LAN, NetWare for OS/2 is no different than any other NetWare server. The file-server PC, however, can do other tasks besides serve files. You can run a database manager product (such as Oracle or IBM's Extended Services DB Manager), for example, on the same computer that acts as file server. Such an environment is *client/server* computing.

For Related Information

◀◀ "Using CONFIG.SYS and AUTOEXEC.BAT," p. 159.

◀◀ "Understanding DOS Sessions," p. 386.

FROM HERE...

OS/2 LAN Server and LAN Manager LANs

Both LAN Manager (LM) and LAN Server (LS) run on top of OS/2 versions 1.21 and higher. Workstations can run DOS versions 3.3 and higher or OS/2 versions 1.21 and higher. You can use an OS/2 LM or LS file server as a workstation and a server—in a peer-to-peer arrangement—but you have the option of keeping the OS/2 file server isolated for security reasons. As a rule, no one uses LM/LS as the basis for a peer LAN.

Understanding LAN Server and LAN Manager Basics

You install LAN Manager and LAN Server after you first install OS/2 on the file server computer. Microsoft bundles MS-OS/2 version 1.3 with

LAN Manager 2.1; IBM's LAN Server 2.0 requires you to purchase OS/2 separately. IBM now also offers the new 32-bit version 3.0 of LAN Server, which runs only on OS/2 version 2.0 or OS/2 version 2.1.

Because LAN Manager and LAN Server consist of pure OS/2 software, you need to disable OS/2's capability to emulate DOS when you install OS/2 on a file-server computer. A DOS session on a file server merely consumes memory. You give the network operating system more memory by disabling DOS emulation. The installation documentation for LAN Manager or LAN Server describes other configuration changes that help the OS/2 computer provide a better file-server environment.

On the OS/2 computer, LAN Manager or LAN Server run in an OS/2 session. You have the option of running multiple OS/2 sessions on the file server. The LM or LS network operating system software does most of its work in the background. The file server shares files, disk space, and perhaps a LAN printer, across the network. The network operating system also performs administrative tasks such as recognizing workstations when LAN users log in and ceasing to recognize the workstations of users who have logged out.

You can use command-line entries or menus to perform administrative tasks on the network, including logging in and setting up your shared drive letters and printers.

When you set up a DOS-based personal computer to be a workstation on a LAN Manager or LAN Server network, you designate the workstation as having basic or enhanced capabilities. A *basic* workstation can use fewer commands, does not need to perform a log-in sequence to use the LAN, and cannot use menus. Although you do not have to log in from a basic workstation, you must provide a password to use each shared resource. An *enhanced* workstation offers menus and requires a log-in sequence that includes an account name and a password. OS/2 workstations on a LAN Server or LAN Manager network always use account names and passwords; an OS/2 workstation always operates in enhanced mode.

Taking Advantage of Client/Server Computing

LAN Server and LAN Manager are good environments for client/server computing. Programmability is the biggest reason that people talk about client/server in connection with these two OS/2-based network operating systems. OS/2 is easy to program, perhaps even more so than DOS.

Both LAN Manager and LAN Server can share the network adapter with other OS/2 application software running on the file server computer. Under the control of OS/2's multitasking, one computer program—the network operating system—responds to file requests from workstations. Another computer program may be a database server application. Your programming staff also may program the workstations to send and receive special requests and responses to and from the file server (or from a separate computer, for that matter). These custom-programmed requests and responses may carry, for example, SQL statements and relational database records.

OS/2 provides *named pipes* to programmers. The programmer treats a named pipe as if it were a file, but the named pipe actually contains message records. These message records travel from the workstation to the file server. On the file server, a custom-written application may do some record handling and other processing before returning a response to the workstation through the named pipe.

SQL Server is a Microsoft product that enables programmers to create client/server applications. SQL Server provides a relational database "engine" that you install on an OS/2 computer on the network. Programmers write workstation software that sends SQL statements to SQL Server. SQL Server honors each request by sending back the appropriate records from within its database.

Database Manager, a component of IBM's Extended Services (which you learned about in Chapter 23, "Understanding Extended Services"), provides functions similar to those of SQL Server.

Lotus Notes is yet another client/server application. Notes offers intelligent, group-oriented electronic mail services. Notes enables the sophisticated storage and retrieval of messages; an index contains the subject, recipients, and other key data items related to the messages. Notes is particularly useful for large, geographically dispersed organizations in which people need to exchange information frequently, but work in different time zones or have conflicting schedules or work styles. Notes stores its data at a centrally located OS/2-based personal computer on a LAN. Workstations on the LAN or on a remotely attached LAN, through a wide area network, can interact with the central OS/2 Notes computer.

Using LAN Manager or LAN Server

In the next few sections, you learn how to operate LAN Manager and LAN Server. You also see what these network operating systems look like on-screen. You first cover the menu interface these products offer, followed by the command-line interface. You learn about logging in on a LAN Manager or LAN Server network. You discover how to map drive letters, use files and directories, and print on the LAN. You learn how a computer operates when it becomes a workstation on a LAN Manager or LAN Server network, and you find out about the security features of these products.

Using Menus

The LAN Manager or LAN Server menu interface appears when you use the NET command with no arguments. If you type characters following the word NET, the network operating system assumes that you want to use the command-line interface. Figure 24.11 shows the initial menu screen you see when you run the NET program.

NOTE   On DOS basic (not enhanced) workstations, menus are not available.

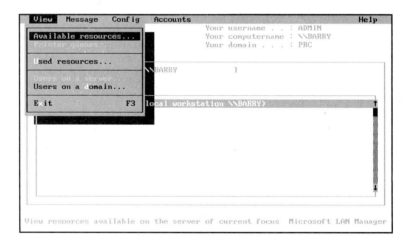

Fig. 24.11

The initial LAN Manager menu.

The LM/LS menu screens operate in text mode, not graphics mode. The menu screens are CUA-compliant, however. The LAN Manager and LAN Server menu interface enables you to do anything with menus that you can do by typing commands at a DOS prompt. You can log in to the LAN, log out, map drive letters, and redirect your printer port to the LAN printer. You can change your password, send short messages to other logged-in network users, and see lists of the file servers, disk drives, and printers on the LAN.

Using the Command-Line Interface

After you have gained some experience with LAN Manager or LAN Server, you may feel more comfortable issuing network commands at a command-line prompt. You invoke the network commands by running the NET command, but you avoid the menu screens by typing parameters after the word NET. The following table describes the most important and most frequently used NET command parameters and their functions.

Command	Function
NET CONTINUE	Continues a paused service
NET HELP	Gets help for a command
NET NAME	Assigns a computer name
NET PAUSE	Pauses a connection to a network service
NET PRINT	Displays the print queue or prints a file
NET USE	Displays shared resources or assigns a drive letter or device name to a new shared resource
NET COPY	Copies network files
NET LOGON	Logs on to the network
NET LOGOFF	Logs off the network
NET PASSWORD	Changes your password
NET START	Starts a workstation or learns what workstation connections exist
NET TIME	Synchronizes the workstation's clock with the server's clock
NET WHO	Lists who is logged on

Using Utilities

The NET command performs most of the administrative duties you accomplish on a LAN Manager or LAN Server network. The network operating system comes with additional utility programs you may find helpful for accomplishing certain tasks. These computer programs enable you to schedule commands or programs to run at a specified date and time, make backup copies of the network's administrative (passwords and permissions) files, restore these files, verify a physical connection to a remote computer, and do other odd jobs on the LAN.

Logging In

You use the NET LOGON command to log on to the network. This command establishes the user ID, password, and domain for a workstation (you learn more about domains in the section of this chapter entitled "Ensuring Security"). The user ID and password identify you in a particular domain and grant you access to shared resources. You can use shared resources in other domains after you have logged on to the network. You need to perform the logon sequence on OS/2 workstations and on an enhanced workstation running DOS. On a basic DOS workstation, you supply a password to use a shared resource. You do not need to identify yourself on a basic workstation running DOS.

If you forget your password, your account may be locked out of the network. If you make repeated unsuccessful attempts at entering your password, the system disables your account. When this situation occurs, only the network administrator can re-enable your account. This security feature helps keep intruders from gaining access to the LAN.

Mapping Drives

You use NET USE or the NET program's menus to map drive letters. Depending on how the network administrator has set up the file server's shared resources, your workstation's drive letter may refer to an entire server disk drive or to a single directory. The administrator decides the extent to which the workstations share the file server's resources. The system does not indicate at the workstations whether the drive letter refers to an entire disk drive or to a single directory.

The following is an example of a NET USE command that sets up drive F. The network administrator has published the shared resource with the name NORTHEAST on the server named \\SALES.

NET USE F: \\SALES\NORTHEAST

You also issue a form of the NET USE command to cancel the use of a drive letter. The same NET USE command that sets up your network drive letters also can redirect your printed output to the LAN printer, as you learn in a later section of this chapter.

After you establish the network drive letters your workstation can use, you work with your applications in the usual manner. Files on the LAN now are available to the computer programs you run, provided that you have permission to use those files.

If you do not have permission to read a particular file, you cannot access that file at all. Further, you may have read permission but not write permission on some files. You cannot save new data in files to which you do not have write permission. If you encounter strange error messages from the applications you run, you may want to talk to your network administrator to make sure that your permissions are correct and appropriate.

Printing with LAN Manager and LAN Server

In addition to providing network drive letters, the NET USE command redirects your printed output to the shared LAN printer. The network administrator assigns a name to the LAN printer in the same way that he or she assigns names to the file servers and to the shared resources that become drive letters at your workstation. The administrator may set up a printer named HP_LASER on the SALES file server, for example. In this example, the NET USE statement for your printed output is the following:

NET USE LPT1: \\SALES\HP_LASER

When you copy a file to the LPT1 device or when you tell one of your applications to print, the network operating system creates a print job. The print job goes into the server's print queue to be printed when the printer becomes available.

You can configure the network operating system to notify you when the print job is completed. If you want to see your job's position in the queue, you can view a list of the items in the print queue. You can hold, release, and delete your own print jobs in the queue.

Ensuring Security

You organize file servers and workstations into *domains*. A domain is a group of file servers and workstations with similar security needs. You can set up several domains on a large LAN Manager or LAN Server network. Domains enable you to control user access to the network and the network's resources. A network user can have accounts in multiple domains, but he or she can log on in only one domain at a time.

User-level security on a LAN Manager or LAN Server network consists of log-on security and permissions. Each user specifies a user ID and the password to gain access to the network through a domain. A network administrator can limit a user's access to certain times of the day or limit the workstation(s) from which the user can log on. Permissions limit the extent to which a user can use shared resources. The network administrator can create a COMMON directory that everyone can use, for example, and an UPDATE directory with files only certain users can modify but everyone can read.

The following table shows the permissions for files and directories that you can assign, and what actions the permission allows.

Permission	Allows
Change Attributes	Flag a file as read-only or read/write
Change Permissions	Grant or revoke access to other users
Create	Create files and directories
Delete	Delete files and remove directories
Execute	Execute a program file (EXE, BAT, or COM file) but allow reading or copying of that file
Read	Read and copy files, run programs, change from one directory to another, and make use of OS/2's extended attributes for files
Write	Write to a file

The OS/2-based network operating systems LAN Server and LAN Manager enable you to control access to the file server's keyboard and computer screen. In a special unattended mode, the file server enables users to view and manage print queues but not to modify user accounts or other administrative data. You must specify a password to use other screens.

FROM HERE...

For Related Information

◀◀ "Using CONFIG.SYS and AUTOEXEC.BAT," p. 159.

◀◀ "Using Communications Manager," p. 598.

Chapter Summary

This chapter helped you understand how to use OS/2-based PCs on a local area network. The chapter discussed PCs used as workstations or file servers. You learned about Novell's NetWare Requester for OS/2 and NetWare for OS/2 products, and you explored IBM's and Microsoft's LAN Server and LAN Manager products.

Using the Command Reference

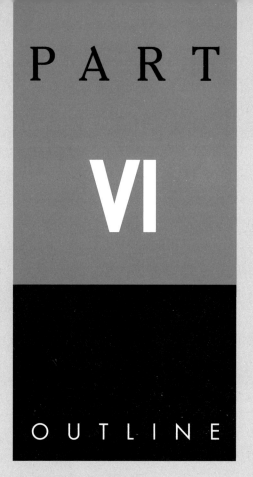

Command Reference

OS/2 2.1 includes more than 100 commands you can use at a command line prompt in DOS or OS/2 sessions, full-screen or windowed. This section explains how to use the commands. First you find the commands summarized in logically related groups, and then you see each command discussed in detail. This section can be used in conjunction with Chapter 12, which is a tutorial for the commands you use most often. Chapter 12 also contains a discussion of the on-line Command Reference that you may find helpful when you want to look up an OS/2 or DOS command.

Organization

The commands appear in alphabetical order. Most of them can be used in either OS/2 or DOS sessions; those that cannot are labeled *OS/2 Only* or *DOS Only*. Configuration commands, which you use only when you are fine-tuning your CONFIG.SYS file, are listed alphabetically at the end of this chapter.

Layout

Commands are a language you use to give instructions to OS/2 and DOS. A brief description follows the name of each command. Then you see up to four headings: syntax, switches, examples, and notes.

Syntax

Think of syntax as the grammar rules that tell how you can use each command. This book uses some simple conventions to make the syntax of each command clear and understandable.

For a command that operates on a file, the syntax for the command shows the following:

COMMAND *d:path***filename.ext**

This syntax tells you that *d:* represents a drive letter, *path* represents a single directory or a path of directories separated by backslashes (\\). The portion in italics, *d:path*, is optional. The portion shown in boldface, **filename.ext**, is required.

> **NOTE**   When OS/2 cannot find the command you typed, the following message appears:
>
> ```
> The name specified is not recognized as an
> internal or external command, operable
> program, or batch file
> ```
>
> The problem in this example is that OS/2 needs a path to the command.
>
> You can tell OS/2 where to find the command by modifying your path, as explained later in this section. You also can explicitly tell OS/2 where to find the command by prefixing the command with the drive letter and path (directory) containing that command. Type the following command, for example:
>
> C:\BIN\CHKDSK
>
> This command directs OS/2 to look in the BIN directory on drive C for the CHKDSK command. OS/2 automatically sets up your PATH statement in the CONFIG.SYS file, however, to point to all the directories containing

your OS/2 and DOS commands. If OS/2 informs you that it cannot find a command, the first thing to check is your spelling of the command. You rarely, if ever, need to prefix a command with the drive letter and directory containing that command.

This command reference shows literal text that you type in uppercase letters. Any variable text you replace with text of your choosing appears in lowercase letters. As an example, look at syntax of the following entry:

FORMAT d:

This command means that you must type the word FORMAT if you want to format a disk. You replace d: with the drive letter of the disk you want to format.

Switches

Many commands have optional parameters that modify how they work. Switches start with a slash. If you erase a group of files by typing **DEL *.* /P**, for example, the /P switch tells the delete command to pause before erasing each file. At each pause, you can continue the process or cancel the operation.

Examples

Theory is fine, but concrete examples are often the fastest, simplest way to see how a command works. You will find many examples in this section.

Notes

You will find hints, background information, and—when appropriate—cautions in the Notes for a command.

Commands that Help You Work with Your Files

ATTRIB	Shows or changes a file's read-only, archive, hidden, and system attributes.
BACKUP	Backs up a hard disk to floppy disks or other media.
COMP	Compares files.
COPY	Copies or combines files.
DEL	Erases files.
ERASE	Erases files.
FIND	Searches for text in files.
MORE	Displays a file or directory one screen at a time.
MOVE	Moves files from one directory to another on the same drive.
PRINT	Prints files, or cancels printing.
RECOVER	Salvages files from a disk with bad sectors.
REN or RENAME	Changes a file's name.
REPLACE	Selectively replaces files.
RESTORE	Retrieves files from a backup.
TYPE	Displays a file on-screen or to a printer with redirection.
VERIFY	Checks that data is correctly written to a disk.
XCOPY	Copies directories or groups of files.

Commands that Help You Work with Your Directories

APPEND	Tells the system where to find data files.
CD or CHDIR	Shows or changes the current directory of a disk drive.
DIR	Lists the files in a directory.

MD or MKDIR	Creates a directory.
RD or RMDIR	Removes a directory.
TREE	Displays all directories on a disk and optionally lists files.

Commands that Help You Prepare and Maintain Disks and Floppy Disks

CACHE	Controls the disk cache on HPFS drives.
CHKDSK	Analyzes a disk and gives you a report; fixes disk problems.
DISKCOMP	Determines whether one floppy disk is an exact copy of another.
DISKCOPY	Duplicates a floppy disk.
FDISK/FDISKPM	Manages hard disk partitions.
FORMAT	Prepares a disk for use in OS/2, and reports any defects.
LABEL	Gives a name to a disk.
MEM	Displays the amount of used and free memory in DOS sessions.
VOL	Displays a disk's label and serial number.

Commands that Support National Languages

These commands work with the CONFIG.SYS commands CODEPAGE, COUNTRY, and DEVINFO.

CHCP	Switches between national alphabets.
GRAFTABL	Enables DOS programs to display line-drawing and national language characters on a CGA monitor in graphics mode.
KEYB	Tells the keyboard which national alphabet you want to use.

Commands that Give You Information about Your System, or Let You Change How It Works

ANSI	Enables you to run OS/2 programs that require special support for the screen or keyboard.
ASSIGN	Redirects requests for disk operations on one drive to a different drive.
CLS	Clears the screen.
CMD	Starts a new copy of the OS/2 command processor.
COMMAND	Starts a new copy of the DOS command processor.
DATE	Displays or sets the date.
DETACH	Runs a noninteractive program in the background.
DDINSTALL	Enables you to install new device drivers after OS/2 has been installed.
EXIT	Terminates the current command processor.
HELP	Explains how to use a command, or what an error message means.
JOIN	Tells DOS to join a disk drive to a directory on another drive.
KEYS	Controls command recall and editing.
MODE	Controls the communications port, screen mode, or parallel printer.
PROMPT	Sets the string of characters that is displayed at the command line.
SPOOL	Redirects a file that you send to one printer so that it prints on a different printer.
START	Runs another OS/2 program in another session.
SUBST	Establishes an alias consisting of a drive letter for a path.
TIME	Displays or sets the time.
VER	Displays the version of OS/2 you are using.

Configuration Commands

These commands can be placed in the CONFIG.SYS file OS/2 reads each time it starts. CONFIG.SYS statements give information that OS/2 needs to control the computer and run programs. With the exception of the ANSI, PROMPT, SET, and PATH statements, you don't type CONFIG.SYS statements at a command line prompt. Because you don't type these commands at a command prompt, they are listed separately at the end of the chapter.

ANSI	Enables you to run DOS programs that require special support for the screen or keyboard.
AUTOFAIL	Gives you a choice in dealing with certain hardware errors.
BASEDEV	Enables you to install a base device driver.
BREAK	Controls how quickly DOS programs stop when you interrupt them by pressing Ctrl-Break.
BUFFERS	Sets aside a part of memory for moving data to and from disks.
CODEPAGE	Enables the computer to use, display, and print non-English language characters.
COUNTRY	Customizes your system for the country you specify.
DEVICE	Installs a device driver (a program that adds a function to the operating system) that is not on the device support diskette.
DEVICE (ANSI.SYS)	In DOS sessions, allows you to use extended keyboard and display support.
DEVICE (COM.SYS)	In OS/2 sessions, allows applications or system programs to use serial devices.
DEVICE (EGA.SYS)	Enables you to run DOS programs that control the Enhanced Graphics Adapter directly.
DEVICE (EXTDSKDD.SYS)	Enables you access a disk that uses a logical drive letter.

DEVICE (MOUSE)	Enables you to use a mouse or trackball, but this command must be used with the POINTDD.SYS device driver.
DEVICE (PMDD.SYS)	In OS/2 sessions, provides pointer draw support.
DEVICE (POINTDD.SYS)	In OS/2 sessions, provides mouse support.
DEVICE (VDISK.SYS)	Installs a virtual disk.
DEVICE (VEMM.SYS)	In DOS sessions, provides Expanded Memory Manager.
DEVICE (VXMS.SYS)	In DOS sessions, provides Extended Memory Specification.
DEVICEHIGH	Loads a DOS device driver into upper memory, leaving more low memory available to run programs in DOS sessions.
DEVINFO	Sets the keyboard, printer, and screen for the country you specify.
DISKCACHE	Makes your hard disk seem faster by keeping the data you use most frequently in memory.
DOS	Runs DOS sessions and enables you to control how they use memory.
DPATH	Tells OS/2 programs where to look for data files.
FCBS	Supports File Control Blocks, a method of using files that was common in older DOS programs.
IFS	Enables you to use the High Performance File System (HPFS).
IOPL	Enables you to run programs that need to bypass OS/2 and work directly with hardware devices.
LASTDRIVE	Specifies the maximum number of logical drives your system can access in DOS.
LIBPATH	Tells OS/2 programs where to look for Dynamic Link Libraries.
LOADHIGH	Enables you to load DOS memory-resident programs into upper memory.

MAXWAIT	Makes sure that no program thread is put on hold forever, even when the system is busy running other programs.
MEMMAN	Enables you to run time-critical processes more reliably by turning off virtual memory.
PATH	Tells OS/2 or DOS where to find programs.
PAUSEONERROR	Tells OS/2 to stop for a moment if it cannot process a line in CONFIG.SYS correctly.
PRINTMONBUFSIZE	Enables you to increase the size of the parallel port device-driver buffer.
PRIORITY	Tells OS/2 whether it should juggle the priority of different threads that are running at the same time.
PRIORITY_DISK_IO	Tells OS/2 the input/output priority for applications in the foreground.
PROTECTONLY	Tells OS/2 whether you want to run DOS programs.
PROTSHELL	Loads OS/2's built-in command processor CMD.EXE or enables you to run a different one that you have purchased.
RMSIZE	Sets the amount of memory DOS can use.
SET	Assigns values to variables in the environment.
SHELL	Loads OS/2's built-in DOS command processor COMMAND.COM or enables you to run a different one that you have purchased.
SWAPPATH	Tells OS/2 where to create a swap file, which uses free disk space to let you run more programs than can fit in memory.
THREADS	Sets the number of tasks OS/2 can do at the same time; the maximum is 4,096.
TIMESLICE	Sets upper and lower limits on the amount of time the computer spends on each thread.

VCOM   Enables you to use the communica-
                        tions ports for DOS sessions.

VMOUSE   Enables you to use a mouse or
                        trackball in DOS sessions.

Other Commands

Two groups of commands are not discussed in this chapter. Because entire chapters are devoted to REXX and batch file programming, the following commands are not included here:

CALL	PAUSE
ECHO	PMREXX
ENDLOCAL	REM
EXTPROC	SET
FOR	SETLOCAL
GOTO	SHIFT
IF	

The following commands are used only by technical service personnel:

CREATEDD	TRACE
LOG	TRACEBUF
SYSLOG	TRACEFMT

ANSI   OS/2 Only

Enables you to run those OS/2 programs that require special support for the screen or keyboard. Most OS/2 programs don't require ANSI support.

Syntax

ANSI

or

ANSI ON

ANSI OFF

Examples

To find out whether ANSI support is available:

ANSI

or

ANSI ON

To turn off ANSI support:

ANSI OFF

Notes

This command affects only OS/2 sessions. The special support it provides is available in OS/2 sessions by default, but you can turn it off; very few programs require ANSI support. Similar support is available in DOS sessions only if you load the ANSI.SYS driver in CONFIG.SYS with a DEVICE statement.

APPEND   DOS Only

Tells DOS programs where to find data files.

Syntax

APPEND *dir1;dir2;...*

dir1 is a directory, such as C:\MEMOS.

dir2 is another directory.

The ellipsis (...) means that you can specify more directories. Use semicolons to separate the directories from each other.

Switches

/E restricts APPEND to DOS.

/PATH:ON searches appended paths even if you have specified a path.

/PATH:OFF searches appended paths, or all if you have not specified a path (default).

Examples

To tell DOS programs to look for data files in the directories C:\ and D:\DATA:

APPEND C:\;D:\DATA

To find out where the current APPEND statement tells DOS to look for data files:

APPEND

To cancel the APPEND command:

APPEND

Notes

Data files that are in the current directory are always available to a program, even if you do not include the current directory in the APPEND statement. APPEND enables DOS programs to access files in other directories you name, as though they were in the current directory. They will not search other directories if they find the files they need in the current directory.

You normally use APPEND in AUTOEXEC.BAT, but you also can type it in a DOS window. The list of directories you specify with APPEND cannot be more than 128 characters long.

APPEND works only in DOS sessions. The DPATH command performs the same function in OS/2 sessions.

ASSIGN   DOS Only

Redirects requests for disk operations on one drive to a different drive.

Syntax

ASSIGN *d1=d2*

d1 is the drive you specify.

d2 is the drive that DOS uses instead.

Do not type a colon after the drive letters.

Examples

To make DOS use drive C when it gets a command for drive A:

ASSIGN A=C

To cancel all previous drive assignments or to show assigned drives:

ASSIGN

Notes

ASSIGN hides the true device type from some command; the following commands do not work in DOS sessions on drives that have ASSIGN in effect: CHKDSK, DISKCOMP, DISKCOPY, FORMAT, JOIN, LABEL, PRINT, RECOVER, RESTORE SUBST.

For the same result as ASSIGN, you can use SUBST:

SUBST A: C:

ATTRIB

Shows or changes a file's read-only and archive attributes.

Syntax

ATTRIB +A -A -H +R -R +S -S **file** /S

file specifies the name of the file for which you want to display or change the attributes.

+A sets the archive flag, which means that the file has not been backed up.

-A turns off the archive flag.

+H hides the file.

-H no longer hides the file.

+R sets the read-only flag, which prevents the file from being changed or deleted.

-R turns off the read-only flag.

+S turns the system file attribute on.

-S turns the system file attribute off.

Switch

/S shows or changes attributes of files in all subdirectories.

Examples

To make sure that your CONFIG.SYS file cannot be accidentally erased or changed:

ATTRIB +R CONFIG.SYS

To turn off the archive flag on a temporary database file so that an incremental backup will skip the file as if it were already backed up:

ATTRIB -A MYDATA.DBF

To find out which files in your \OS2 directory, and all its subdirectories, have not been backed up:

ATTRIB \OS2*.* /S

This command lists every file, placing the letter A next to each one that has not been backed up.

To list every program on a disk and its attributes:

ATTRIB *.* /S

Notes

Every file has several *attributes* (flags that store information about the file). OS/2 reserves most of them for its own use but allows you to change the backup and read-only flags. Avoid turning off the read-only flag on OS/2's system files.

When you make an archival copy of a file with the BACKUP command, the archive flag is turned off. When you make an incremental backup later on, it includes only files whose archive flag is not set.

If you remember a file name but cannot recall its location on a disk, use ATTRIB with the /S switch to find it.

ATTRIB issues a return code of 0 for normal completion.

BACKUP   OS/2 Only

Backs up a hard disk to floppy disks or other media.

Syntax

BACKUP d1:dir\files d2: */A /M /S /D:mm-dd-yy /T:hh:mm:ss*
/L:logfile /F:size

d1: is the hard disk you are backing up, such as C.

dir is the directory you want to back up. The default is the root directory.

files specifies the files you want to back up. You can omit it if you want to back up all files in a directory.

You must specify at least one of **d1:**, **dir**, or **files**.

d2: is the letter of the floppy disk drive or other media to which you are backing up, such as A.

Switches

/A adds files to an existing backup disk, leaving old backup files intact.

/M backs up only files that you created or changed since your last backup.

/S backs up files in subdirectories of the directory you want to back up (dir).

/D:mm-dd-yy limits BACKUP to files created or changed since a given date.

/T:hh:mm:ss limits BACKUP to files created or changed since a given time. Use this switch only with the /D switch.

/L:logfile creates a log that lists the name of every file that is backed up. The log file tells which floppy disk contains each file so that you can restore a single file without rummaging through all the floppy disks. The default log file is d1:\BACKUP.LOG.

/F:size formats floppy disks to the size you specify. Use this switch only if the floppy disks are not the default size for your drive. The following table shows the sizes you can choose.

Size	Description	Capacity
360	5 1/4-inch double-density	360K
1200	5 1/4-inch high-density	1.2M
720	3 1/2-inch double-density	720K
1440	3 1/2-inch high-density	1.44M
2880	3 1/2-inch ultra-density	2.88M

Examples

To back up every file in every subdirectory on hard drive C to floppy disks in drive A and create a log file:

BACKUP C: A: /S /L

To update a previous complete backup, adding only files that you have created or modified since the last complete backup:

BACKUP C: A: /A /M /S

To back up every file in C:\MEMOS that you have changed since noon on March 20, 1991:

BACKUP C:\MEMOS A: /D:3-20-91 /T:12:00

Notes

BACKUP may require a large number of floppy disks. You should format them first and discard any that have bad sectors. BACKUP formats them if you do not; it assumes that they are the same default size as the drive, unless you specify a different size with the /F switch. Write a number on each floppy disk because you must insert them in order when you restore the backup.

The files that BACKUP writes onto floppy disks are not immediately usable. You must use the RESTORE command to put the files back onto your hard disk.

You cannot back up OS/2's system files. If you restore a complete backup made with an earlier version of OS/2, you will not crash the system by writing over these critical files with obsolete versions.

The COUNTRY statement in CONFIG.SYS governs the national date and time format that the /D and /T switches use.

The following tables lists the return codes for BACKUP.

Return code	Meaning
0	Normal completion
1	No files were found to back up
2	Some files or directories were not processed because of file errors
3	Ended by user
4	Ended because of error
5	Not defined
6	BACKUP was unable to process the FORMAT command

CD or CHDIR

Shows or changes the current directory of a disk drive.

Syntax

CD *d1:*

CD *d1:dir*

d1: is the disk whose current directory you want to show or change. The default is the current disk.

dir is the directory to which you want to change.

Examples

To find out the current drive and directory:

CD

To find out the current directory of drive D:

CD D:

To move to the \OS2\MDOS directory on the current drive:

CD \OS2\MDOS

To move to the same directory as in the last example, if the current directory is C:\OS2:

CD MDOS

To move back to C:\OS2, if the current directory is C:\OS2\MDOS:

CD ..

The double period is convenient shorthand for the parent directory, one level back from the current one.

To move from C:\OS2\MDOS to C:\OS2\INSTALL:

CD ..\INSTALL

Notes

CD and CHDIR are different names for the same command.

When you specify a drive d1:, you show or change its current directory, but this does not make d1: the current drive. To make d1: current, type **d1: <ENTER>**.

CHCP

Switches between national alphabets.

Syntax

CHCP *page*

page is the number of the code page for the alphabet you want to use.

Examples

To find out the number of the current code page:

CHCP

To switch to the multilingual code page, assuming that you loaded it in CODEPAGE and DEVINFO statements in your CONFIG.SYS file:

CHCP 850

Notes

OS/2 stores many different national alphabets in *code pages*. You can load up to two pages through the CODEPAGE statement in CONFIG.SYS; only one national alphabet is active at a time. CHCP, Change Code Page, enables you to choose either one. You can find the number for each alphabet in the on-line command reference, under the COUNTRY command.

If you work with people in other countries, they can read your files more easily if you use the multinational alphabet, codepage 850. It includes most of the accented letters used in European languages. Stick to the letters A-Z and numerals 0-9 for file and directory names to prevent file access problems.

CHDIR

See CD.

CHKDSK

Analyzes a disk and gives you a report. This command also fixes disk problems. If OS/2 is open, CHKDSK conflicts with open files and cannot fix the boot drive.

Syntax

CHKDSK *d1:files /F /V*

d1: is the disk you want to analyze. The default is the current drive.

files specifies the files you want to analyze. CHKDSK checks whether each named file is stored all in one piece. The default CHKDSK checks all files but does not produce a report. Use *.* to get the report when checking all files.

Switches

The */C* and */F:n* parameters are only operable with the High Performance File System.

/C tells CHKDSK which files will be recovered if the file system was in an inconsistent state when the computer was started.

/F tells CHKDSK to fix any problems it finds.

/F:0 tells CHKDSK to analyze and display information about the disk but prevents the program from performing repairs.

/F:1 tells CHKDSK to resolve inconsistent file system structures.

/F:2 is the same as /F:1, but it also checks the disk space not allocated by the file system and recovers file and directory structures when found. This is the default if you specify no recovery level.

/F:3 is the same as /F:2, but it also scans the entire partition.

/V displays the name and path of each file as it is checked.

Examples

To analyze your drive C:

CHKDSK C:

To analyze C and report any fragmented files:

CHKDSK C:*.*

To analyze C and repair any problems found:

CHKDSK C: /F

Notes

The files and directories on your hard disk can get scrambled if the power goes off while you are using your computer or if you turn it off without ending all applications first. Run CHKDSK from time to time to check for problems. You cannot use CHKDSK on a network drive.

CHKDSK reports useful statistics such as the number of files on a disk and the amount of free space. In DOS mode, CHKDSK also gives a summary of memory usage. If CHKDSK reports bad sectors, the sectors were marked as unusable when you formatted the disk so that they cannot be used to store files. The sectors are physically defective and cannot be repaired.

Ideally, a file's contents should all be kept together in one place. Over a period of time, however, the disk space becomes fragmented, and some files are spread over separate blocks. CHKDSK *.* tells you which files are fragmented. OS/2 can still work with them, but it will work more slowly.

CHKDSK may tell you it has found chains of lost clusters. These chains may be pieces of files that were improperly saved, for example, because of a bug in the program that created them. They also can be files that a background program was writing when you ran CHKDSK. You can rule out that possibility by running CHKDSK all alone with no background sessions.

If the problem persists, run CHKDSK with the /F switch and answer Yes when it asks your permission to fix the problem. CHKDSK collects every piece of stray data that looks like it belongs to a file and puts each piece in a separate file in the root directory. This comand creates distinctive file names; in FAT, CHKDSK uses names like FILE0000.CHK and FILE0001.CHK; and in HPFS, names like FOUND.*xxx* (where *xxx* is the number of the file).

If you run CHKDSK with the /F switch and answer N (No), CHKDSK deletes these file parts without warning.

The following table lists the return codes for CHKDSK.

Return codes	Meaning
0	Normal completion
1	Not defined
2	Not defined
3	Ended by user
4	Ended due to error
5	Not defined
6	CHKDSK was unable to execute file system's CHKDSK program.

CLS

Clears the screen.

Syntax

CLS

Notes

OS/2 clears the screen and displays the prompt.

CMD   OS/2 Only

Starts a new copy of the OS/2 command processor, CMD.EXE.

Syntax

CMD */C/K/Q/S command-line*

command-line is a program you want the command processor to run—an OS/2 command or a program with either a CMD or EXE extension, plus any optional parameters.

Switches

/C terminates the new copy of CMD.EXE after it executes *command-line*.

/K keeps the new copy of CMD.EXE active after it executes command-line.

/Q prevents commands from echoing to the screen.

/S prevents installation of a signal handler (such as Ctrl-C).

Example

To start a new copy of the OS/2 command processor, use CMD to run the CHKDSK program:

CMD /C CHKDSK

Notes

Terminate the additional copy of CMD.EXE with the EXIT command.

COMMAND   DOS Only

Starts a new copy of the DOS command processor,
COMMAND.COM.

Syntax

COMMAND */C /E:size /K /P command-line*

command-line is the program you want the command processor to
run—a DOS command or a program with either a BAT, COM, or
EXE extension, plus any optional parameters. If you specify a command-line, you must also use the /C switch.

Switches

/C passes *command-line* to COMMAND.COM. The new DOS command processor terminates after executing the command.

/E:size sets the size of the DOS environment in bytes. The default
is 160 bytes, but you can set *size* to any higher value up to 32768.
The size is rounded up to the next multiple of 16.

/K does not return to calling command processor.

/P makes the new copy of COMMAND.COM permanent so that you
cannot terminate it with the EXIT command. Use this switch only
in the SHELL statement in your CONFIG.SYS file.

Examples

To start a new copy of the DOS command processor, use COM-
MAND to run the CHKDSK program:

COMMAND /C CHKDSK

To start a copy of the DOS command processor, with an 800-byte environment, from a DOS or OS/2 window:

COMMAND /E:800

Use the EXIT command to close this new DOS session.

Notes

You can use COMMAND /C inside a DOS batch file to run another batch file, but the DOS batch command CALL uses less memory to accomplish the same task.

COMP

Compares files.

Syntax

COMP file1 file2

file1 and **file2** specify the two files, or sets of files, you want to compare.

Examples

To determine whether CONFIG.SYS and CONFIG.OLD are identical:

COMP CONFIG.SYS CONFIG.OLD

To determine whether C:\MYFILE and A:\MYFILE are identical:

COMP C:\MYFILE A:

To determine whether all the files on A exactly match files of the same names on C:

COMP A: C:

Notes

COMP reads the contents of two files and tells you whether they are identical. If they are not identical, COMP reports the first 10 characters that do not match. This report uses a hexadecimal format. After ten mismatches, COMP stops comparing.

Two files can be identical only if they are the same size. If they are not, COMP tells you if they are not the same size and gives you the option to proceed anyway, up to the length of the shorter file.

If you do not specify either of the files to compare, COMP prompts you for their names.

COPY (Combining Files)

Combines files together.

Syntax

COPY file1+file2... *target*

file1 and **file2** are the first two files you want to combine.

The ellipsis (...) means that you can specify more files. Use plus signs to separate them from each other.

target is the name of the file that combines the contents of all source files.

Examples

To combine the contents of FILE1, FILE2, and FILE3 into a file called COMBINED:

COPY FILE1+FILE2+FILE3 COMBINED

To append the contents of FILE2 and FILE3 to FILE1:

COPY FILE1+FILE2+FILE3

Notes

If you do not specify *target*, the contents of all the files are combined into **file1**.

COPY (Duplicating Files)

Copies files between disks or directories, optionally changing each file's name.

Syntax

COPY files */A /B* **target** */A /B /V /F*

files specifies the files you want to duplicate.

target is the name or location of the duplicates you create.

Switches

When used with a source file name:

/A treats file as ASCII. Data is copied to the first end-of-file character in the file.

/B treats file as binary and copies the entire file.

When used with the target file(s):

/A adds an end-of-file character as the last character.

/B does not add end-of-file character.

/V verifies that target file(s) were written correctly.

/F aborts the copy operation if the source files contain extended attributes and the destination file system does not support them.

Examples

To make a duplicate of MYFILE.TXT and name it MYCOPY.TXT:

COPY MYFILE.TXT MYCOPY.TXT

To put a duplicate of MYFILE.TXT with the same name in the \DOCUMENT directory:

COPY MYFILE.TXT \DOCUMENT

To copy all files with the extension TXT from the current directory to \DOCUMENT and change each file's extension to DOC:

COPY *.TXT \DOCUMENT*.DOC

To copy every file in \MEMOS to a floppy disk in drive A:

COPY \MEMOS*.* A:

To copy MYFILE.TXT to the printer:

COPY MYFILE.TXT PRN

Notes

If you want to copy files to a different directory, first make sure that the directory exists. If a file that you tell COPY to create already exists, the old file is deleted first.

This command does not copy a file that is zero bytes long; you must use the XCOPY command.

DATE

Displays or sets the date.

Syntax

DATE *mm-dd-yy*

mm is the month (1-12).

dd is the day (1-31).

yy is the year (0-99, or 1900-1999).

Examples

To set the date to November 15, 1991:

DATE 11-15-91

To display and change (optional) the current date:

DATE

Notes

The computer remembers the date you set after you turn the power off. The COUNTRY command in CONFIG.SYS controls the way the date is formatted.

DDINSTALL   OS/2 Only

Enables you to install new device drivers after OS/2 has been installed.

Syntax

DDINSTALL

Enter the command (without a parameter) to begin the procedure to install device-driver files.

Example

To begin the procedure to install device drivers:

DDINSTALL

You are prompted to insert the Device Support disk into drive A. After files are copied, you are prompted to insert the Installation disk and restart the system. DDINSTALL automatically continues the installation procedure. When DDINSTALL is finished, press Ctrl-Alt-Del to restart the system.

Notes

The DDINSTALL program automatically adds necessary statements to the CONFIG.SYS and copies all necessary files to the appropriate directory on the hard disk.

DEL or ERASE

Erases files.

Syntax

DEL files *P* */N*

files specifies the files you want to erase.

Switches

/P asks your permission before deleting each file.

/N suppresses the Are you sure (Y/N) message displayed when OS/2 is deleting all files in a directory.

Examples

To erase the file PAYROLL.WK1 in the current directory:

DEL PAYROLL.WK1

To erase every file with the extension DOC in the \WORDPROC directory:

DEL \WORDPROC*.DOC

To modify the preceding example so that DEL displays each file name and asks your permission before erasing it:

DEL \WORDPROC*.DOC /P

Notes

DEL does not erase the OS/2 system files or any files that you have protected by setting their read-only attribute with the ATTRIB command. DEL also does not erase directories; use the RD command to do that.

Using DEL with wild cards can be dangerous. If you use DEL to erase every file in a directory, OS/2 asks you to confirm the command first. If you want to see which files are to be deleted before OS/2 deletes them, use DIR, not DEL, with the same wild cards. If you accidentally delete files, use UNDELETE to recover them before you do anything else.

DETACH   OS/2 Only

Runs a program in the background while the command processor runs in the foreground.

Syntax

DETACH command-line

command-line is the command you want to run in the background—an OS/2 command or a program with either a CMD or EXE extension, plus any optional parameters.

Example

To format a single floppy disk in the background:

DETACH FORMAT A: /ONCE

Notes

The command must not require any input from the keyboard or mouse. You will not see anything the command tries to write to the screen. Because the command runs in the background, you can type another command without waiting for the first one to finish.

DIR

Lists the files in a directory.

Syntax

DIR */F /N /P /W /A /B /O:sort-order /R /S /L files*

files specifies the directory or files you want to list.

Switches

/F lists files with full drive and path information, omitting date, time, and size.

/N lists files on a FAT drive in the format used for an HPFS drive.

/P lists files one screen at a time.

/W omits date, time, and size information, and lists five file names across the screen so that you can see more file names.

/A lists only files with specified attributes (-H, H, S, -S, D, -D, A, -A, R, -R).

/B lists directories and files without heading and summary information.

/O sort-order lists directory in sort order. The following table lists the sort order options.

Sort order options	Type of order
N	Alphabetic
E	Alpha by Extension
D	Date and Time oldest first
S	Size smallest first
G	Directories shown first

To reverse the order of a switch, place a minus sign in front of the switch.

/S searches all directories.

/R displays long file names in file systems that do not support them; in FAT, the /R switch shows FAT file names and the long file name to the right of the directory listing.

/L lists all file and directory menus in lowercase.

Examples

To list all files in the current directory of the current drive, showing each file's name, size in bytes, and date and time last modified:

DIR

To see the size, date, and time of \SALES\REGION1.WK1:

DIR \SALES\REGION1.WK1

To list only the names of all files with the extension SYS in the \OS2 directory across the screen and one screen at a time:

DIR /P /W \OS2*.SYS

Notes

DIR displays the volume label, directory name, number of files, and amount of space available on the drive, unless you use the /F switch. The /F and /W switches do not work together.

You can send the directory listing to your printer by typing:

DIR >PRN

DISKCOMP

Determines whether one floppy disk is an exact copy of another.

Syntax

DISKCOMP d1: d2:

d1: and **d2:** are the drives that hold the floppy disk to be compared. The command copies from d1: to d2:. The drives can be the same.

Examples

To compare a floppy disk in drive A to one in drive B:

DISKCOMP A: B:

To compare floppy disks by using only one drive:

DISKCOMP A: A:

Notes

DISKCOMP verifies the result of the DISKCOPY command. The command reports that two floppy disks are the same only if one is an exact clone of the other, with identical files in identical disk sectors. DISKCOMP ignores floppy disk serial numbers, however, because those numbers are always supposed to be different. To compare floppy disks that were not copied with DISKCOPY, use the COMP command.

DISKCOMP will not compare two floppy disks of different sizes. You cannot use the command to compare hard disks, even if they are the same size.

High capacity floppy disks can be compared in several passes if your computer does not have enough memory available to hold their contents all at once. If you are using a single drive, DISKCOMP prompts you to swap the floppy disk when necessary.

DISKCOMP issues a return code of 0 for normal completion or displays an error message if there was a problem.

DISKCOPY

Duplicates a floppy disk.

Syntax

DISKCOPY d1: d2:

d1: is the drive that holds the floppy disk to be copied from.

d2: is the drive that holds the floppy disk to be copied to. d2: can be the same as d1:.

Examples

To copy a floppy disk in drive A to a disk in drive B:

DISKCOPY A: B:

To copy a floppy disk using only one drive:

DISKCOPY A: A:

Notes

DISKCOPY makes an exact duplicate of a floppy disk. If you have not formatted the floppy disk to which you are copying, DISKCOPY formats the floppy disk you are copying to. If DISKCOPY finds defects while it is formatting, it reports the problem but continues copying anyway. To verify that the copy is accurate, use the DISKCOMP command.

Because DISKCOPY makes an exact clone, it will not copy between two floppy disks of different sizes. You cannot use it to copy hard disks, even if they are the same size.

High capacity floppy disks are duplicated in several passes because your computer may not have enough memory available to hold their contents all at once. If you are using a single drive, DISKCOPY prompts you to swap the floppy disk when necessary.

Use DISKCOPY if you want to make a backup copy of your original OS/2 floppy disk.

DISKCOPY issues a return code of 0 for normal completion or displays an error message if there was a problem.

DOSKEY   DOS Only

Controls command recall and editing and creates macros.

Syntax

> *dc:pathc***DOSKEY** */REINSTALL /BUFSIZE=N /M /H /*
> *OVERSTRIKE /INSERT macroname=macrotext*

dc:pathc refers to the disk drive and directory that hold DOSKEY.

macroname is the name of the macro to create.

macrotext is the command(s) contained by the macro name
macroname.

Switches

/REINSTALL installs DOSKEY and clears the buffer.

/BUFSIZE=N specifies size of buffer in bytes.

/M lists all DOSKEY macro commands.

/H lists commands stored in memory.

/OVERSTRIKE turns Overstrike on.

/INSERT turns Insert on.

Examples

To experiment with command recall, first type:

> **DOSKEY**

Next, list the contents of C:\OS2\MDOS:

> **DIR C:\OS2\MDOS**

Then press the up-arrow key once. You see the command again. Edit it by pressing Backspace three times:

DIR C:

Now press Enter to execute the modified command, which now lists files in the root directory.

Notes

After you have run DOSKEY (by typing DOSKEY and pressing Enter) you can press the up- and down-arrow keys to scroll through commands you have previously typed. You can edit a recalled command and then execute it by pressing Enter. You can use the previously mentioned switches and activate DOSKEY at the same time to complete an action.

DOSKEY works only in DOS sessions, but you can get the same effect in OS/2 sessions by using the KEYS command.

ERASE

See DEL.

EXIT

Terminates the current command processor.

Syntax

EXIT

Notes

If you loaded the current command processor from another one, you return to the program you shelled out of; otherwise, you return to Presentation Manager.

FDISK   OS/2 Only

Manages hard disk partitions.

Syntax

FDISK

Notes

This command sets up partitions on your hard disk. Be careful when you use it because any changes you make to existing partitions will wipe out all your data.

Before you can use a hard disk, you must partition it. Each partition looks like a separate drive. If you have one physical hard disk divided into two partitions, for example, your system probably shows two hard drives—C and D.

FDISKPM is a Presentation Manager version of FDISK. Except for the appearance of the interface, the two programs are identical. The on-line menus give complete instructions. See more on this utility in Chapter 19, "Using OS/2 Utilities."

FIND

Searches for text in files.

Syntax

FIND /C /N /V /I **"text" file1** *file2...*

text is the string of characters you want to search for.

file1 is a file you want to search for text.

file2 is another file you want to search.

The ellipsis (...) means that you can specify more files to search. Separate the files from each other by using blank spaces. Alternatively, you can use wild cards (*.*) in your search.

Switches

/C tells you how many lines contain the string of characters you want to search for (**text**), but does not display them.

/N displays each line that contains **text**, along with its line number.

/V displays all lines that do not contain **text**.

/I ignores uppercase or lowercase.

Examples

To show every line in CONFIG.SYS that contains the word "DEVICE":

FIND "DEVICE" CONFIG.SYS

To show every line in CONFIG.SYS that contains the word "DEVICE" along with the number of each line:

> **FIND /N "DEVICE" CONFIG.SYS**

To count how many lines in CONFIG.SYS contain the word "DEVICE" without showing each line:

> **FIND /C "DEVICE" CONFIG.SYS**

To show all lines in the files \BOOK\CHAPTER1.TXT and \BOOK\CHAPTER2.TXT that do not contain the lowercase letter *e*:

> **FIND /V "e" \BOOK\CHAPTER1.TXT**
> **\BOOK\CHAPTER2.TXT**

Notes

The text for which you are searching must be surrounded by double quotation marks. FIND detects only exact matches unless your use /I. Uppercase and lowercase are different ("This" and "this" do not match.) You cannot find a phrase that is split between two lines.

You have to list the full name of each file you want to search. Wild cards do not work with FIND.

You can combine the /V switch with either the /C or /N switch, but you cannot use /C and /N together.

FIND issues a return code of 0 for normal completion.

FORMAT

Prepares a disk for use and reports any defects.

Syntax

FORMAT d1: */ONCE /FS:file-system /L /V:label /F:size /4*

d1: is the disk you want to format, such as A.

Switches

/ONCE formats a single floppy disk. If you format a floppy disk without this switch, FORMAT assumes that you will want to format another when you are finished. You can always just answer No when the command asks you to insert another.

/FS:file-system tells what file system you want to use. /FS:HPFS means the High Performance File System. The default, /FS:FAT, means the DOS-compatible File Allocation Table format.

/L formats an IBM read-write optical disk.

/V:label specifies a volume label. If you do not use the /V switch, FORMAT asks you to type a label anyway.

/F:size reports the capacity of the floppy disk you are formatting. If the capacity is the default for your drive, you do not need this switch; otherwise, you must specify a value from the following table.

Size	Description	Capacity
360	5 1/4-inch double-density	360K
1200	5 1/4-inch high-density	1.2M
720	3 1/2-inch double-density	720K
1440	3 1/2-inch high-density	1.44M
2880	3 1/2-inch ultra-density	2.88M

/4 means the same thing as /F:360—that you want to format a double density, 360K, 5 1/2-inch floppy disk in a 1.2M drive. Floppy disks formatted this way will not work reliably in lower-capacity drives.

Examples

To format a 1.44M floppy disk in a 1.44M drive A:

FORMAT A:

To format just one 720K floppy disk in a 1.44M drive A:

FORMAT A: /F:720 /ONCE

To format a 360K floppy disk in a 1.2M drive B:

FORMAT B: /4

or

FORMAT B: /F:360

To format hard drive D for the High Performance File System and give it the label HPFSDRIVE:

FORMAT D: /FS:HPFS /V:HPFSDRIVE

Notes

FORMAT installs a file system on a disk and checks the surface for physical defects. If FORMAT finds defects, it locks the unusable sectors so that OS/2 will not place your data in them. You cannot use a disk until you have formatted it. If you reformat a disk that you have used before, all the data it holds is wiped out. You must partition a hard disk with FDISK before you can format it. You cannot format a network drive.

Most computers that can run OS/2 2.x have high-capacity floppy disk drives. For best results, use high-density floppy disks in these drives. Never format a floppy disk to a higher capacity than it was designed for. Even if it appears to work fine today, it may fail six months down the road, or prove to be unreadable on someone else's computer.

If you format a 360K floppy disk in a 1.2M drive, you should use the disk only in 1.2M drives; it will not work reliably in a 360K drive. But 720K floppy disks formatted in a 1.44M drive with /F:720 work reliably in either 1.44M or 720K drives.

GRAFTABL·   DOS Only

Enables DOS programs to display line-drawing and national language characters on a CGA monitor in graphics mode.

Syntax

GRAFTABL ? */STA nnn*

nnn is the national language code page you want to use.

? lists the number of graphic code pages in use and lists code page options.

Switch

/STA lists the number of code pages in use.

Examples

To enable DOS programs to display line-drawing characters in graphics mode, according to the U.S. code page:

GRAFTABL 437

To see what other code pages you can specify with this command:

GRAFTABL ?

Notes

Use this command only if you have a CGA monitor.

HELP

Explains how to use a command or what an error message means.

Syntax

HELP ON

· **HELP OFF**

HELP *command-name*

HELP *message-number*

command-name is the name of a DOS or OS/2 command.

message-number is the number of an error message.

Examples

To see which keys you can press to switch between tasks and how to use HELP:

HELP

To tell OS/2 or DOS to display at the top of the screen the keys you press to switch tasks:

HELP ON

To tell OS/2 or DOS not to show this information:

HELP OFF

To find out how to use the COPY command:

HELP COPY

To see an explanation of the OS/2 error message SYS0002:

HELP 2

Notes

Help on a command or an error message is available only for OS/2—not for DOS.

When you ask for help on an OS/2 error message, you do not have to type the letters SYS or the leading zeroes.

JOIN   DOS Only

Tells DOS to join a disk drive to a directory on another drive.

Syntax

JOIN d1: d2:*dir*

JOIN d1: /*D*

d1: is the drive you specify.

d2:*dir* is the drive and directory that DOS uses instead. The drives d1: and d2: must be different.

Switch

/*D* cancels any previous JOIN command for d1:.

Examples

To show all current JOINs:

JOIN

To tell DOS to treat drive A as the subdirectory \\DATA on drive C:

JOIN A: C:\\DATA

To cancel the effect of the above JOIN command:

JOIN A: /D

Notes

If the directory already exists, it must be empty. If it does not exist, it is created. It must be a subdirectory of the root directory—not of any other directory.

You may need JOIN to make old programs that run from a floppy drive run from a hard drive. Otherwise, avoid using this command. JOIN is dangerous to use with many commands, such as CHKDSK, DISKCOMP, DISKCOPY, FORMAT, LABEL, and RECOVER.

KEYB   OS/2 Only

Tells the keyboard which national alphabet you want to use.

Syntax

KEYB nation *alternate*

nation is the country whose alphabet you want to use.

alternate is a number that selects an optional "enhanced" keyboard layout. It is available only if **nation** is Czechoslovakia, France, Italy, or the United Kingdom.

Examples

To switch to the Hungarian keyboard:

KEYB HU

To use the "alternate" Czechoslovakian keyboard:

KEYB CS 245

Notes

Run this command only in a full-screen OS/2 session. It affects DOS full-screen sessions and all OS/2 sessions—windowed and full screen.

KEYB enables you to switch quickly to another national alphabet. It works only if you have a DEVINFO statement in CONFIG.SYS. To change the default keyboard layout permanently, modify the DEVINFO statement. The number for each alphabet is in the on-line command reference, under the COUNTRY command.

KEYS　　　　　OS/2 Only

Controls command recall and editing.

Syntax

KEYS ON

KEYS OFF

KEYS LIST

Examples

To turn off command recall:

KEYS OFF

To turn command recall on:

KEYS ON

To find out whether command recall is on:

KEYS

To see which commands are available for recall:

KEYS LIST

To experiment with command recall, first list the contents of
C:\OS2:

DIR C:\OS2

Now press the up-arrow key once. You see the command again.
Edit it by pressing Backspace three times:

DIR C:

Now press Enter to execute the modified command, which lists
files in the root directory.

Notes

When KEYS is ON, you can scroll through commands you have previously typed by pressing the up- and down-arrow keys. You can edit a recalled command and then execute it by pressing Enter.

DOSKEY works only in DOS sessions, but you can get the same effect in OS/2 sessions by using the KEYS command.

LABEL

Gives a name to a disk.

Syntax

LABEL *d1:name*

d1: is the disk whose label you want to see or change, such as C. The default is the current drive.

name is what you want to call the disk—any combination of up to 11 letters and numerals.

Examples

To display and change (optional) the current drive's label:

LABEL

To display and change (optional) the label of drive D:

LABEL D:

To set the label of drive C to HARDDISK:

LABEL C:HARDDISK

Notes

If you run the FORMAT command on a hard disk that has a label, it prompts you for the label and will not continue if you do not type it. This command provides extra protection against formatting the hard disk by accident, which destroys your data. You should always LABEL your hard disk.

MD or MKDIR

Creates a directory.

Syntax

MD *d1:path*\ **dir**

d1: is the disk where you want to create the new directory. The default is the current disk.

path is the parent of the new directory. The default is the current directory.

dir is the name of the new directory you want to create.

Examples

To make a directory \WORDPROC in the root directory:

MD \WORDPROC

To make a directory \MEMOS as a subdirectory of an existing directory \WORDPROC on drive D:

MD D:\WORDPROC\MEMOS

To make a directory \STUFF as a subdirectory of the current directory:

MD STUFF

Notes

You cannot create a directory with the same name as a file that already exists in the same location.

MEM   DOS Only

Displays the amount of memory DOS can use and the amount of memory already in use.

Syntax

MEM

Notes

This command tells how much conventional, expanded (EMS), and extended (XMS) memory is available for DOS programs. Chapter 16, "Running DOS and Windows under OS/2," explains how to use these different kinds of memory.

MODE (Communications)

Controls the communications port.

Syntax

MODE COMx:*rate,parity,databits,stopbits,P*

COMx is a communications port, such as COM1 or COM2.

rate is bits per second. The default is 1200. You do not have to type the last two zeros of rate; 12 is the same as 1200, for example.

parity is a single character that tells how to verify that data is sent correctly. Use N for none, O for odd, E for even, M for mark, or S for space parity. E is the default.

databits is the number of bits used to represent one character. It can be 5, 6, 7, or 8. The default is 7.

stopbits is the number of bits added to mark the end of each character. It can be 1, 1.5, or 2. The default is generally 1.

P tells DOS to wait up to 30 seconds for the port to respond. *P* is available in DOS sessions only.

Examples

To see the current settings for the second communications port:

MODE COM2

To set up the first communications port for 2400 bits per second, even parity, seven databits, and one stopbit:

MODE COM1:2400,E,7,1

Notes

You must load support for communications ports by including COM.SYS in your CONFIG.SYS file before you use MODE to configure the ports.

You can leave out any item you do not want to change, but you must include the comma that would have followed that item unless it is the last one that you do want to change. To change to eight databits while leaving all previous settings alone, for example:

MODE COM1:,,8

The *P* option, available only in a DOS session, tells the system to wait up to 30 seconds for the port to respond. This option is useful if you have a serial printer that may be busy.

MODE (Display)   OS/2 Only

Controls the screen mode.

Syntax

MODE *CONx* **mode,lines**

CONx tells which monitor to control. If your computer has two monitors, the first is CON1 and the second is CON2. You do not need to use this parameter if you have only one monitor.

mode tells what kind of monitor you have.

lines is the number of lines to display on-screen. Choose 25, 43, or 50. The default is 25.

Examples

To show 50 lines on-screen on a monochrome monitor:

MODE MONO,50

To show 43 lines on your second monochrome monitor:

MODE CON2 MONO,43

Notes

This command works only for full-screen OS/2 sessions.

MODE (LPT#)   OS/2 Only

Controls a parallel printer.

Syntax

MODE LPT*x char,lines,P*

LPT*x* tells which printer to set up. It can be LPT1, LPT2, or LPT3. You can use PRN as another name for LPT1.

char tells how many characters can be printed on one line. The number of characters can be 80 or 132.

lines tells how many lines to print per inch. The number of lines can be 6 or 8.

P tells OS/2 to keep trying to send each line until the printer responds. If you do not specify *P* and the printer is busy, OS/2 displays an error message.

Examples

To tell the first parallel printer to put 132 characters on a line and print 8 lines per inch:

MODE LPT1 132,8,,

You can leave out any item you do not want to change, but you must include the comma that would have followed that item unless it is the last one you do want to change. To tell the third parallel printer to keep trying to send each line until the printer responds without changing the width or spacing, for example:

MODE LPT3 ,,P

Notes

This command works only on parallel printers.

MORE

Displays a file one screen at a time.

Syntax

MORE< file

command file ¦ MORE

file is the file you want to view.

Example

To see \CONFIG.SYS one screen at a time:

MORE< \CONFIG.SYS

To get the same results by using the command and the pipe (split vertical bar):

TYPE CONFIG.SYS ¦ MORE

Notes

Think of the less-than sign as part of the command's name. You need to include it because MORE is a special type of program known as a *filter*. Filters are an advanced topic that this book does not cover.

MORE displays the file's contents one screen at a time. Press Enter when you want to go on to the next screen. If you do not want to see the rest of the file, press Ctrl-C.

MOVE   OS/2 Only

Moves files from one directory to another on the same drive.

Syntax

MOVE files target

files specifies the files you want move.

target is the new location for the files.

Examples

To remove all files with the extension DOC from the root directory and put them in \DOCUMENT:

MOVE *.DOC \DOCUMENT

To modify the last example so that the extension of each file is changed to TXT:

MOVE *.DOC \DOCUMENT*.TXT

To transfer OLDFILE.A from the current directory to \DATA, rename it as NEWFILE.B, and delete the original:

MOVE OLDFILE.A \DATA\NEWFILE.B

To remove the \DOCUMENT directory (and any subdirectories and files it contains) and re-create it as a subdirectory of an existing directory \WORDPROC:

MOVE \DOCUMENT \WORDPROC

To rename the \DOCUMENT directory as \DOC, assuming that no \DOC directory already exists:

MOVE \DOCUMENT \DOC

Notes

MOVE combines the functions of the COPY, RENAME, RD, MD, and DEL commands. MOVE removes files from one directory and adds the files to another directory.

PRINT

Prints files.

Syntax

PRINT *file1 file2... /D:LPTx*

PRINT */C*

PRINT */T*

PRINT */B*

file1 and *file2* are files you want to print.

The ellipsis (...) means that you can specify more files to print. Separate them from each other by using blank spaces. You also can use wild cards.

Switches

/D:LPTx tells which printer to use. The first three printers are LPT1, LPT2, and LPT3; network printers can have higher numbers. The default is LPT1.

/C cancels whichever file is currently printing. Any other files you have sent to the printer still are printed.

/T cancels all files you have sent to the printer.

/B ignores <CTRL-Z> characters and does not interpret them as end-of-file markers so that the entire file prints.

Examples

To send the file \MAIL\LETTER1.TXT to the second printer:

PRINT \MAIL\LETTER1.TXT /D:LPT2

To print the files LETTER1.TXT and LETTER2.TXT in your \MAIL directory:

PRINT \MAIL\LETTER1.TXT \MAIL\LETTER2.TXT

To print all TXT files in the \MAIL directory whose names begin with LETTER:

PRINT \MAIL\LETTER*.TXT

Notes

PRINT works only with plain text files. If you PRINT a word processing document, you probably will not get what you want because most word processors use special formats. If you tell your word processor to save a file as plain text, however, you can PRINT the document.

You cannot use the /C or /T switch with a file name.

PROMPT

Sets the string of characters that is displayed at the command line.

Syntax

PROMPT *string*

string is a series of characters to display. You can use most characters that you can type from the keyboard and any of the following special codes:

Code	Meaning
$$	$
$_	New line
$a	&
$b	|
$c	(
$d	Current date
$e	"Escape" character
$f	)
$g	>
$h	Backspace symbol
$i	Help information
$l	<
$n	Current drive
$p	Current drive and directory
$q	=
$r	Return code of last executed program
$s	Space
$t	Current time
$v	Version of the operating system

Examples

To set the prompt to show the current date and time on one line and the current drive and directory on the next:

PROMPT Date=date Time=time$_$p>

To restore the default prompt:

PROMPT

Notes

The default prompt in an OS/2 session is the DOS default prompt (current drive and directory). In a DOS session, $p>. The system stores the prompt as a string of characters in the environment. You can display it with the SET command.

RD or RMDIR

Removes a directory.

Syntax

RD *d1:path***dir**

d1: is the disk from which you want to remove a directory. The default is the current disk.

path is the parent of the directory to remove. The default is the current directory.

dir is the name of the directory you want to remove.

Examples

To remove the directory \\WORDPROC\\LETTERS from drive D:

RD D:\\WORDPROC\\LETTERS

To remove the directory \\WORDPROC\\LETTERS, if \\WORDPROC is the current directory:

RD LETTERS

Notes

You can remove only an empty directory (a directory that contains no files and no subdirectories). You cannot remove the current directory or the root directory. If a directory appears empty but it will not allow you to remove it, use ATTRIB to check for Hidden files.

RECOVER

Partially salvages files from a disk with bad sectors.

Syntax

RECOVER *files*

files tells which files you want to salvage. You cannot use wild cards.

Examples

To salvage A:\MYFILE.TXT, placing whatever can be saved in the root directory with a name like FILE0000.REC, and then to delete the original file:

RECOVER A:\MYFILE.TXT

To wipe out the entire directory structure of a floppy disk in drive A:

RECOVER A:

Notes

As you probably gathered from the second example, RECOVER is a dangerous command. It attempts to read all the data in a file and puts it into a new file in the root directory with a name like FILE0000.REC or FILE0001.REC. If RECOVER cannot read the data in a particular sector, it substitutes zeros. It then deletes the original file. If the file is a program, it probably will not work because part of the code was replaced by zeros.

Use RECOVER as a last resort and only on files that you know are unreadable. Always specify a file; if you specify a disk or directory, the command recovers all the files the disk or directory contains. The root directory can hold only a limited number of files, and if you try to RECOVER too many files at once, some may be lost. If you RECOVER a good file, it moves the file to the root directory and gives it an unrecognizable name. For safety, RECOVER does not work on a network drive.

REN or RENAME

Changes a file name.

Syntax

REN oldname newname

oldname is the original file name.

newname is the name you want to give the file.

Examples

To change the name of a file in the \PLANS directory on drive C from NEWPLAN.DOC to OLDPLAN.DOC:

REN C:\PLANS\NEWPLAN.DOC OLDPLAN.DOC

To change the name of JULIET1.DAT, JULIET2.DAT, and so on, to ROMEO1.TXT, ROMEO2.TXT, and so on:

REN JULIET*.DAT ROMEO*.TXT

Notes

You can specify a drive and path only for **oldname**. REN uses the same drive and path for **newname**, and it will not work if a file called **newname** already exists there. REM cannot change a subdirectory's name.

REPLACE

Selectively replaces files.

Syntax

REPLACE files target */A /F /P /R /S /U /W*

files specifies the files you want to copy.

target tells the location to which you want to copy the files. The default is the current drive and path.

Switches

/A restricts the command to files that do not exist on **target**.

/F makes the command fail if you try to copy a file with OS/2 extended attributes to a drive that does not support them.

/P asks your permission before adding or replacing each file.

/R enables REPLACE to write over read-only files.

/S replaces files in all subdirectories of target.

/U replaces files only with newer versions.

/W waits for you to insert a floppy disk. Use this when you need to swap floppy disks.

Examples

To copy all files from C that do not already exist on A:

REPLACE A:*.* C: /A

To replace files in every directory of drive C with files of the same name from drive A:

REPLACE A:*.* C: /S

To replace every file on drive C named FINAL.TXT with the one in
your \ULTIMATE directory:

REPLACE C:\ULTIMATE\FINAL.TXT C: /S

Notes

You cannot use the /A switch with the /S or /U switch. You cannot
REPLACE OS/2's critical system files or any hidden files.

RESTORE   OS/2 Only

Retrieves files from a backup.

Syntax

RESTORE d1: d2:files */F /D /S /N /M /P /A:yy-mm-dd*
/L:hh:mm:ss /B:yy-mm-dd /E:hh:mm:ss

d1: is the drive that holds the backup floppy disk you want to restore.

d2: is the hard drive to which you want to restore the backed up files.

files specifies the directory and files you want to restore. To do a complete restore, omit *files* and use the /S switch.

Switches

/F causes RESTORE to fail if the file contains extended attributes and destination file system cannot support them.

/D lists the files on the backup that also exist of the target but does not restore them.

/S restores files in all subdirectories. If you do not use the /S switch, only files in the directory you specify are restored.

/N restores only files that do not exist on the hard drive (if you deleted them since making the backup, for example).

/M ignores files that you have not modified since you made the backup. Only files that you have deleted or changed since then are restored. Use the /M switch if you made accidental changes to your files and want to restore them to the way they were before you changed them.

/P asks your permission before replacing any file that you have changed since you backed it up. This protects against accidentally wiping out the changes you have made since the backup.

/A:yy-mm-dd and */L:hh:mm:ss* tell RESTORE to undo changes you made after a given date and time. Use the /L switch only with /A.

/B:yy-mm-dd and */E:hh:mm:ss* tell RESTORE to undo changes you made before a given date and time. Use the /E switch only with /B.

Examples

To restore all the files from the backup floppy disk in drive A to drive C:

RESTORE A: C: /S

To restore all backed up files you have modified since 6:00 p.m. on March 1, 1991:

RESTORE A: C: /S /A:3-1-91 /L:18:00

To restore all Lotus worksheets in C:\123G:

RESTORE A: C:\123G*.WK*

Notes

This command restores files from a floppy disk backup you made with the BACKUP command. Because BACKUP wrote these files in a special format, commands like COPY cannot work with them; only BACKUP and RESTORE can work with these files. If the backup contains more than one floppy disk, RESTORE prompts you to insert the floppy disk in the right order.

You only can restore files to the same directory they were in when you backed them up. If the directory no longer exists, RESTORE creates it. You cannot restore files that OS/2 has locked because they are in use—for example, files used by programs that are running in the background. Because BACKUP will not copy OS/2's most critical system files at all, you cannot use RESTORE to create a bootable disk.

The COUNTRY statement in CONFIG.SYS governs the national date and time format that the /A, /B, /E, and /L switches use.

You cannot restore a backup made with any DOS version earlier than 3.3.

RMDIR

See RD.

SPOOL

Redirects a file that you send to one printer so that it prints on a different printer.

Syntax

SPOOL */D:printer1 /O:printer2 /Q*

Switches

/D:printer1 is the printer to which you say you are sending a file. The printer can be any parallel printer such as PRN or LPT1 but not a serial printer such as COM1.

/O:printer2 is the printer to which the file really goes. It can be any parallel printer such as PRN or LPT1, or any serial printer such as COM1.

/Q queries existing device redirections.

Examples

To make any file you send to PRN come out on a serial printer on COM1:

SPOOL /D:PRN /O:COM1

To cancel any SPOOL command that redirects LPT2 to another printer:

SPOOL /D:LPT2 /O:LPT2

Notes

You must install COM.SYS in your CONFIG.SYS file before using the SPOOL command to direct files to a serial printer.

START   OS/2 Only

Runs a program automatically.

Syntax

START "title" */C /K /N /B /F /PGM /FS /PM /WIN /DOS
/MAX /MIN /I* **command-line**

"title" is the name that appears at the top of the program's window. It can be up to sixty characters and must be in double quotation marks.

command-line is the program's name plus any necessary parameters.

Switches

/C closes the window after the program terminates.

/K keeps the window open after the program terminates.

/N runs the program directly, without loading the OS/2 command processor CMD.EXE. The program must have an EXE extension.

/B runs the program in a background window.

/F runs the program in a foreground window.

/PGM indicates that command-line is enclosed in double quotation marks.

/FS runs the program in a full-screen session.

/PM runs the program in a Presentation Manager window.

/WIN runs the program in a window.

/DOS runs a *bound* program—one that can run under DOS or OS/2—in a DOS window.

/MAX maximizes the window.

/MIN minimizes the window (makes it an icon).

/I allows the program to use the global environment rather than giving the program its own environment.

Examples

To open a windowed DOS session:

START /WIN /DOS

To copy all the files from a floppy disk to your hard disk in a background window:

START "Copy files" /B COPY A:UL C:

To run the OS/2 program C:\WP\WORDPROC.EXE and load the file MEMO.TXT in a maximized, foreground Presentation Manager window named WP that closes when you exit the program:

START "WP" /C /F /PM /MAX C:\WP\WORDPROC
MEMO.TXT

Notes

You normally use START in the STARTUP.CMD file that runs every time you turn on the computer. You can use the command to load the programs you run every time you use your computer.

SUBST   DOS Only

Establishes an alias consisting of a drive letter for a path. You
then can use the drive letter to refer to a long path instead of
typing the path.

Syntax

SUBST d1: *d2:\dir*

SUBST d1: */D*

d1: is the drive you specify in a DOS command.

d2:\dir is the drive and subdirectory that DOS uses rather than **d1**.

Switch

/D cancels any previous SUBST command for d1:.

Examples

To show all current drive substitutions:

SUBST

To tell DOS to treat the directory \DATA on drive C as though it
were a separate drive Z:

SUBST Z: C:\DATA

To cancel the effect of the preceding SUBST command:

SUBST Z: /D

Notes

If you already have a physical drive d1:, it becomes unavailable while the SUBST command is in effect.

You may need SUBST to make old programs that run from a floppy drive run from a hard drive. Otherwise, avoid using SUBST. It is dangerous to use with many commands, such as CHKDSK, DISKCOMP, DISKCOPY, FORMAT, LABEL, and RECOVER.

TIME

Displays or sets the time.

Syntax

TIME *hh:mm:ss.cc*

hh is hours (0-23).

mm is minutes (0-59).

ss is seconds (0-59).

cc is hundredths of a second (0-99).

Examples

To set the time to 5.98 seconds after 8:21 p.m.:

TIME 20:21:5.98

To set the time to midnight:

TIME 0

To display and change (optional) the current time:

TIME

Notes

You must use the 24-hour clock. The computer remembers the time you set after you turn off the power. The COUNTRY command in CONFIG.SYS governs the way you format the time. You can omit the hundredths of a second (*cc*) when you change your system time.

TREE

Displays and lists (optional) all directories on a disk.

Syntax

TREE *d1: /F*

d1: is the drive whose directory structure you want to see. The default is the current drive.

Switch

/F lists the name of every file in each directory.

Examples

To list all the directories on the default drive:

TREE C:

To list all the directories on drive C and all the files in each directory:

TREE C: /F

TYPE

Displays a file on-screen.

Syntax

TYPE file

file specifies the file you want to display.

Example

To show the contents of \CONFIG.SYS on-screen:

TYPE \CONFIG.SYS

Notes

If the file is too long to fit on one screen, the file scrolls by too rapidly to read. To overcome this problem, use the MORE command.

UNDELETE

Restores a file you recently erased.

Syntax

UNDELETE *dir***files** */A /F /S /L*

dir is the directory that you want to back up.

files specifies the files that you want to back up.

If you don't specify dir or files, UNDELETE looks for all deleted files in the current directory.

Switches

/A restores every deleted file in the directory.

/F tells UNDELETE to erase files completely so that no one can recover them.

/L lists the files that can be restored but does not actually restore them.

/S restores every deleted file in *dir* and in all its subdirectories.

Examples

To display the names of the current directory's deleted files that can be restored:

UNDELETE /L

To erase your performance evaluation in C:\PERSONAL\REVIEW.DOC so that no one can ever recover it:

UNDELETE C:\PERSONAL\REVIEW.DOC /F

Notes

When you delete a file, OS/2 moves that file to a hidden area on your hard disk. UNDELETE enables you to restore the deleted file if you act quickly. The area for deleted files is limited in size. When this area fills up, the oldest files are discarded to make room for new ones.

Use the DELDIR environment available in CONFIG.SYS to define the path and maximum size of directories used to store deleted files, as follows:

SET DELDIR= drive:\path, maxsize; drive 2:\path, maxsize

UNPACK

Restores compressed files on the OS/2 distribution floppy disk to a form you can use.

Syntax

UNPACK packed-file target */N:filename*

UNPACK packed-file /SHOW

packed-file is the name of the compressed file.

target is the drive and directory to which you want to copy the unpacked file.

Switches

/N:filename specifies the name of a single file that you want to extract from a bundle that contains more than one file.

/SHOW displays the names of the files that are combined in a packed bundle.

/V enables you to verify a compressed file while you unpack it.

/F enables you to unpack a file without discarding extended attributes.

Examples

To extract XCOPY.EXE from the file XCOPY.EX@ on a floppy disk in drive A and write it to the \OS2 directory on drive C:

UNPACK A:XCOPY.EX@ C:\OS2

To display the names of the files that are packed into the bundle GROUP.DA@ on drive A:

UNPACK A:GROUP.DA@ /SHOW

To extract FORMAT.COM from the floppy disk file BUNDLE.DA@ that contains it and put the extracted file in C:\OS2:

UNPACK A:BUNDLE.DA@ C:\OS2 /N:FORMAT.COM

Notes

Many of the files on the OS/2 distribution floppy disk are compressed so that they take up less room and fewer floppy disks are needed. The installation program automatically unpacks the files. However, if you accidentally lose one of OS/2's files and you know which disk contains it, you can unpack it yourself. Unpacking one file is easier than reinstalling OS/2.

On the OS/2 floppy disk, if the last character in a file's extension is @, then it is a packed file. Some disks contain only one file, but others are bundles of several files. You can tell what files a bundle contains by running UNPACK with the /SHOW option.

VER

Displays the version of OS/2 you are using.

Syntax

VER

Example

To see what OS/2 version is running:

VER

If you are using OS/2 2.1, the system responds:

```
The Operating System/2 Version is 2.10
```

VERIFY

Checks that data is written to a disk.

Syntax

VERIFY ON

VERIFY OFF

Notes

Although verifying disk writes sounds like a good idea, you should leave VERIFY OFF. If it is ON, OS/2 checks to make sure that something was written to the disk, but it does not guarantee that the right data was written. The slight benefit provided by VERIFY ON is not worth the extra time OS/2 takes to make the confirmation.

VOL

Displays a disk's label and serial number.

Syntax

VOL *d1:*

d1: is the drive whose label you want to examine. The default is the current drive.

Examples

To see the label of the current drive:

VOL

To see the label of drive C:

VOL C:

Notes

Every disk and floppy disk formatted with OS/2 has a serial number assigned by the system. You also should give it a label, which is any combination of up to 11 letters and numbers you choose. The VOL command displays both the serial number and the label.

If you run the FORMAT command on a hard disk that has a label, FORMAT prompts you for the label and will not continue if you do not type it, which provides extra protection against formatting the hard disk by accident.

OS/2 uses the serial number to keep track of your floppy disk. If a program is writing to a floppy disk and you change the floppy disk before the program finishes, the system can detect the change by comparing the serial numbers.

XCOPY

Copies directories, including all the files they contain.

Syntax

XCOPY dir *target* */S /E /D:mm-dd-yy*

dir specifies the directory you want to duplicate.

target is the location of the duplicate you create. If you do not specify it, XCOPY uses the current drive and directory.

Switches

/S copies files in **dir** and all its subdirectories as well.

/E can be used along with the /S switch to copy subdirectories even if they contain no files.

/D:mm-dd-yy copies only files created or changed since a given date.

/P prompts before copying.

/V verifies copying.

/A copies only archived files but does not clear the archive flag.

/M copies only archived files but also clears the archive flag.

/F halts copying if you are attempting to copy source files with extended attributes to a target that cannot support them.

Examples

To copy every file in the \MEMOS directory of drive C to a floppy disk in drive A:

XCOPY C:\MEMOS A:

To copy the drive C \MEMOS directory and each subdirectory of \MEMOS (whether or not it contains any files) to floppy drive A:

XCOPY C:\MEMOS A: /S

Configuration
Commands

The following commands can be added to your CONFIG.SYS
file so that OS/2 reads and acts on the command. Do not
type these commands at a command line prompt.

AUTOFAIL   OS/2 Only

Gives you a choice in dealing with certain hardware errors.

Syntax

AUTOFAIL=YES

AUTOFAIL=NO

Notes

Suppose that you run a program that uses a file on a disk, but you forget to insert the disk. If you put AUTOFAIL=YES in your CONFIG.SYS file, OS/2 displays a dialog box describing the problem and asks you to choose a response. In this case, insert the disk and then tell OS/2 to try reading it again.

If you set AUTOFAIL=NO, then OS/2 will just tell your word processor that it was unable to read the file. The recommended setting is YES.

BASEDEV

Loads base drivers through the CONFIG.SYS file.

Syntax

BASEDEV=driver <arguments>

driver is the name of the device driver file containing the code that the operating system needs to recognize the device and process information received from or sent to the device.

<arguments> specifies parameters of the base device driver.

Examples

To provide device support for a local printer (non-Micro Channel workstation):

BASEDEV=PRIN01.SYS

To provide device support for Micro Channel SCSI adapters:

BASEDEV=IBM2SCSI.ADD

Notes

The BASEDEV statement must not contain drive or path information; OS/2 cannot process this information during the startup sequence. OS/2 generates an error when the drive or path information is included in the statement.

BREAK   DOS Only

Controls how quickly DOS programs stop when you interrupt
them by pressing Ctrl-Break.

Syntax

BREAK=ON

BREAK=OFF

Notes

You can stop many DOS programs by holding down Ctrl and
pressing Break. With the default value, BREAK=OFF, DOS stops the
program the next time it tries to read a character from the keyboard or to write to the screen or a printer. When you set
BREAK=ON in your CONFIG.SYS file, DOS checks for Ctrl-Break
more frequently but runs your programs more slowly.

BREAK is OFF by default. You should leave this setting OFF unless
you are having problems when you use Ctrl-Break to interrupt
programs.

BUFFERS

Sets aside a part of memory for moving data to and from disks.

Syntax

BUFFERS=n

n is a number from 1 to 100 that tells how many disk buffers you want to use. Each buffer takes up 512 bytes.

Notes

When data moves to or from a disk drive, the data flows through a special area of memory called a buffer. If you use many different files at once, your system runs faster if each file has its own buffer. Each buffer takes up a small amount of memory, however, leaving a little less memory to run your programs.

The default, BUFFERS=30, usually works well. If you have plenty of memory and want to use some of it to speed up disk operations, increase the size of your disk cache (using the CACHE and DISKCACHE commands) instead of setting more BUFFERS.

CODEPAGE

Enables the computer to use, display, and print non-English language characters.

Syntax

CODEPAGE=primary,_secondary_

primary is a number that specifies your main national alphabet.

secondary is the number of another alphabet that you also want to use.

You can find the number for each alphabet in the on-line command reference, under the COUNTRY command.

Examples

To use the U.S. English alphabet and also have the multinational alphabet available:

CODEPAGE=437,850

To use the Icelandic alphabet only:

CODEPAGE=861

Notes

OS/2 stores many different national character sets in _code pages._ You can load up to two pages through the CODEPAGE statement in CONFIG.SYS; only the first page is active, unless you switch to the other page with the CHCP command. For a listing of the code pages supported by OS/2, see the OS/2 command reference on-line documentation.

If you do not put a CODEPAGE statement in CONFIG.SYS, your keyboard uses an alphabet based on the COUNTRY statement, but your screen and printer use their built-in defaults.

The multinational alphabet, CODEPAGE=850, includes most of the accented letters used in European languages. Stick to the letters A-Z and numerals 0-9 for file and directory names so that people in other countries can use them.

COUNTRY

Customizes your computer system for the country you specify.

Syntax

COUNTRY=nnn,file

nnn is a three-digit number that indicates which country's number-formatting conventions you want OS/2 to use. The number is usually the same as the telephone system's international dialing prefix for your country. You can find these numbers in the on-line command reference, under the COUNTRY command.

file is the file that contains information for the country you specify. **file** is usually C:\OS2\SYSTEM\COUNTRY.SYS.

Example

To customize your system for the United Kingdom:

COUNTRY=044,C:\OS2\SYSTEM\COUNTRY.SYS

Notes

Dates, times, and numbers are formatted according to the custom of your country. In France, one tenth of a second before February 1, 1995, looks like this:

31/01/1995 23:59:59,90

The SORT command works according to the order of the letters in your national alphabet.

DEVICE

Install a device driver (a program that adds a function to the operating system) that is not on the device support disks.

Syntax

DEVICE=path\driver

path is the location of **driver**.

driver is the device driver file.

Example

To load the DOS ANSI driver:

DEVICE=C:\OS2\MDOS\ANSI.SYS

Notes

Device drivers are special programs that actually become part of OS/2 when you load them. Think of them as optional parts of OS/2. You need to load DOS.SYS, for example, if you want to run DOS. If you do not need DOS support, you do not need to load DOS.SYS. You can save space by loading only the device drivers that you need.

Mouse support is another example. OS/2 includes device drivers for six different types of mice, but you probably have only one mouse. You waste memory if you build in support for the other five types.

DEVICE (ANSI.SYS)   DOS Only

Enables you to run the rare DOS program that requires special support for the screen or keyboard.

Syntax

DEVICE=path\ANSI.SYS */X /L /K*

path is the location of the file ANSI.SYS. By default, it is C:\OS2\MDOS.

/X Enables you to redefine keys with extended key values.

/L prevents applications from overriding the number of rows you have set on-screen.

/K prevents ANSI.SYS from using the extended keyboard functions.

Examples

To load special screen and keyboard support and allow applications to set the number of rows on-screen, type the following in CONFIG.SYS:

DEVICE=\OS2\MDOS\ANSI.SYS

To be able to redefine the extended key values, type the following in CONFIG.SYS:

DEVICE=C:\OS2\MDOS\ANSI.SYS /X

Notes

This command affects only DOS sessions. The special support it provides is available in OS/2 sessions by default, although you can turn it off with the OS/2 ANSI command. Very few programs require this setting.

DEVICE (COM.SYS)

Enables you to use the communications ports for mice, modems, and serial printers.

Syntax

DEVICE=path\COM.SYS

path is the location of the file COM.SYS. By default, it is C:\OS2.

Examples

To make the communications ports available, type the following in CONFIG.SYS:

DEVICE=C:\OS2\COM.SYS

You must list COM.SYS *after* any driver that uses the communications ports. Printer drivers must come before COM.SYS in CONFIG.SYS, for example.

DEVICE=C:\OS2\printer1.SYS

DEVICE=C:\OS2\printer2.SYS

DEVICE=C:\OS2\COM.SYS

Notes

Use COMDMA.SYS for IBM PS/2 Models 90 and 95 instead of COM.SYS. COM.SYS works for all other PS/2 models.

Both the COM.SYS and COMDMA.SYS support ports COM1, COM2, COM3, and COM4. COM.SYS do not provide support for devices that are attached to the COM port; application programs and system programs must provide the support. COM.SYS supports the asynchronous communications interface itself.

DEVICE (EGA.SYS)   DOS Only

Enables you to run DOS programs that control the Enhanced
Graphics Adapter directly.

Syntax

DEVICE=path\EGA.SYS

path is the location of the file EGA.SYS. By default, it is C:\OS2.

Examples

To load special EGA support, type the following in CONFIG.SYS:

DEVICE=C:\OS2\EGA.SYS

Notes

EGA.SYS must be installed for any application program that uses
the EGA register interface.

If the mouse cursor leaves a trail on-screen or you see strange
characters in a DOS window, try installing this device driver.
Some DOS programs, such as games, control the EGA directly; the
programs work better if you load EGA.SYS. In some cases, you
may need EGA.SYS even if you have a VGA monitor because some
programs treat EGA and VGA alike. Don't load EGA.SYS unless you
have a problem, however, because the file takes up memory that
your programs could use.

DEVICE (EXTDSKDD)

Enables you to use an external disk drive or specify the type of disks used in an internal drive.

Syntax

DEVICE=path\EXTDSKDD.SYS /D:n */T /S /H /F:type*

path is the location of the file EXTDSKDD.SYS. By default, it is C:\OS2.

/D specifies the physical drive number (0 to 255).

n is the number of the disk drive. The first internal drive, number zero, is the drive you normally call A, and the second drive (number one) is normally B. The first external drive is number two (D or E).

/T specifies number of tracks per side (from 1 to 999); the default is 80.

/S specifies number of sectors per track (from 1 to 99); the default is 9.

/H specifies the maximum number of heads (from 1 to 99); the default is 2.

/F:type specifies the device type (from 0 to 9); the default is 2.

Type	Description	Capacity
0	5 1/4-inch double-density	360K
1	5 1/4-inch high-density	1.2M
2	3 1/2-inch double-density	720K
3	8-inch	not used
4	8-inch	not used
5	hard disks	not used
6	tape drives	not used
7	3 1/2-inch high-density	1.44M
8	RW Optical	not used
9	3-1/2-inch ultra-density	2.88M

Examples

To tell OS/2 that you have an external 5 1/4-inch high density disk drive:

DEVICE=C:\OS2\EXTDSKDD.SYS /D:2 /F:1

To tell OS/2 to use an internal 1.44M A drive for 720K disks:

DEVICE=C:\OS2\EXTDSKDD.SYS /D:0 /F:2

Now the same drive is a 1.44M drive when you call it A but a 720K drive when you call it B. If you have two internal disk drives, the 720K drive gets a higher letter, such as D.

Notes

You can use EXTDSKDD to tell an internal drive to use disks of a different density. Be careful because not every drive will work this way. Even if the command seems to work, the disks you write on may not be readable on a different computer. The value of *F:type* should be 0 or 1 for 5 1/4-inch drives, and 2, 3, or 4 for 3 1/2-inch drives.

The internal drive is still available as A or as B if you have two internal drives.

EXTDSKDD creates a new drive letter. It uses the first letter that was not already claimed. If you have two internal disk drives A and B, and hard drives C and D, for example, the new drive is normally E.

DEVICE (MOUSE)

Enables you to use a mouse or trackball.

Syntax

DEVICE=path\MOUSE.SYS TYPE=t *QSIZE=n*

path is the location of the file MOUSE.SYS. By default, it is C:\OS2.

t is the type of mouse. Choose one from the table later in this section.

n is a number from 1 to 100 that tells how many mouse actions to save when you do things faster than the system can respond. Clicking a menu item counts as one action as does dragging a file to the Print Manager. The default, 10, is usually enough actions.

Examples

To tell OS/2 you have an IBM Personal System/2 Mouse:

DEVICE=C:\OS2\POINTDD.SYS

DEVICE=C:\OS2\MOUSE.SYS

To tell OS/2 that you have a Visi-On mouse:

DEVICE=C:\OS2\MOUSE.SYS TYPE=VISION$

Notes

The following table lists different mouse types and their special drivers:

Manufacturer/model	Mouse type *t*	Special driver
Microsoft Bus	MSBUS$	(not needed)
Microsoft Inport	MSINP$	(not needed)
Logitec Pointing Devices	PCLOGIC$	PCLOGIC.SYS
PC Mouse Systems	PCLOGIC$	PCLOGIC.SYS
Visi-On	VISION$	VISION$.SYS

If you do not see your mouse or trackball listed here, a driver may be available from the manufacturer. If the manufacturer does not offer one, try installing your device as one of the types listed in the table.

To use a mouse in OS/2, you need to load several device drivers in CONFIG.SYS. OS/2 installation takes care of this for you, but the following steps are listed in case you want to make modifications yourself:

1. Load POINTDD.SYS.

2. Load the special driver shown in the table unless it indicates that you do not need one.

3. Load MOUSE.SYS.

4. If you have a serial mouse, load COM.SYS.

To install a PC Mouse System serial mouse on the second communications port, for example,:

DEVICE=C:\OS2\POINTDD.SYS

DEVICE=C:\OS2\PCLOGIC.SYS SERIAL=COM2

DEVICE=C:\OS2\MOUSE.SYS TYPE=PCLOGIC$

DEVICE=C:\OS2\COM.SYS

For IBM PS/2 Models 90 and 95, be sure the final DEVICE= statement is:

DEVICE=C:\OS2\COMDMA.SYS

DEVICE (PMDD.SYS)   OS/2 Only

Provides pointer draw support for OS/2 sessions. If the PMDD.SYS device statement is removed from your CONFIG.SYS, your system will not restart.

Syntax

DEVICE=path\PMDD.SYS

path is the location of the file PMDD.SYS. By default, it is C:\OS2.

Example

To load PM:

DEVICE=C:\OS2\PMDD.SYS

Note

If your system does not start, insert the OS/2 Installation Program diskette and proceed to the Welcome screen. Press Esc and then copy the file CONFIG.BAK into your root directory. You then can rename the CONFIG.BAK file to CONFIG.SYS. The PMDD.SYS statement is:

DEVICE=C:\OS2\PMDD.SYS

DEVICE (POINTDD.SYS)

Draws the mouse pointer on-screen.

Syntax

DEVICE=path\POINTDD.SYS

path is the location of the file POINTDD.SYS. By default, it is C:\OS2.

Example

To load mouse pointer support:

DEVICE=C:\OS2\POINTDD.SYS

Notes

Installing a mouse requires other drivers as well. See the explanation under the MOUSE command.

POINTDD.SYS provides draw support in all text modes (0, 1, 2, 3, and 7).

DEVICE (VDISK.SYS)

Makes a part of memory act like a fast electronic disk.

Syntax

DEVICE=path\VDISK.SYS *disk-size sector-size directories*

path is the location of the file VDISK.SYS. By default, it is C:\OS2.

disk-size (bytes) is a number from 16 to 4096 that gives the size of the virtual disk in kilobytes. The default is 64.

sector-size is the number of bytes in a sector. Just like a real disk, a virtual disk is divided into sectors. The value must be 128, 256, 512, or 1024. The default is 128 bytes.

directories is a number from 2 to 1024 that tells how many directories you can put in the virtual disk's root directory. The default is 64.

Example

To create a 400K virtual disk with 256-byte sectors and a limit of 100 directories:

DEVICE=C:\OS2\VDISK.SYS 400 256 100

If you want to use the default value of any parameter, use commas where the values should be:

DEVICE=C:\OS2\VDISK.SYS 400 , ,

Notes

Virtual disks, also called RAM disks, act like real disk drives. Because virtual disks are part of the computer's memory, they are very fast. But virtual disks vanish when you turn the power off, and the memory they take up cannot be used for other purposes, such as running programs. You probably will not want a virtual disk unless you have over 4M of memory.

Try using a virtual disk to store files you read frequently, such as databases. You have to copy the database file to the RAM disk and then tell your database program to use the copy. This is safe if you only read the database to create reports. If you make any updates, however, you must copy the database back to your hard disk when you are finished. If you turn off the computer first or the power goes off, you lose your updates.

VDISK creates a new drive letter. It uses the first letter that was not claimed already. If you have two hard drives C and D, for example, the virtual disk usually is E.

Add up the space required for all the directories you want to put on the RAM disk, and set *disk-size* a little larger in case the files need more space.

If you use the virtual disk for large files, a *sector-size* of 1024 gives the best performance; your options are 128, 256, 512, and 1024. Because each file uses a whole number of sectors, a 100-byte file wastes 924 bytes. Use 128 for *sector-size* if you put dozens of very small files on the RAM disk.

Set *directories* (2 to 1024) according to the number of files you want to use on the virtual disk. Add a few extra directories just in case. OS/2 usually rounds *directories* up to an even multiple of sixteen.

DEVICE=(VEMM.SYS)   DOS Only

Allows DOS applications to use expanded memory.

Syntax

DEVICE=path\VEMM.SYS *n*

path is the location of the file VEMM.SYS. By default, it is C:\OS2.

n is the number of kilobytes of expanded memory available to each DOS session. It can range from 0 to 32768. The default is 4096, or 4M.

Example

To give each DOS session up to one megabyte of expanded memory:

DEVICE=C:\OS2\VEMM.SYS 1024

Notes

Expanded memory, also called EMS or LIM 4.0, is a method for letting DOS applications use more than the usual 640K of memory. Most DOS spreadsheet programs use EMS to enable you to work with large amounts of data.

You can override the amount of EMS available to each DOS application when you add it to a group by changing the value of EMS Memory Size under DOS Options.

To load expanded memory support without giving any to DOS (unless you override it for a particular DOS session):

DEVICE=C:\OS2\VEMM.SYS 0

Place VEMM and VXMS at the end of CONFIG.SYS. They need to know which areas in memory other device drivers have claimed so that they can make sure they do not try to use those same areas.

DEVICE (VXMS.SYS)   DOS Only

Provides extended memory emulation for DOS sessions.

Syntax

DEVICE=path\VXMS.SYS

path specifies the drive and directory that contain VXMS.SYS. By default, it is C:\OS2.

Example

To provide XMS (Extended Memory Specification) emulation and to allow DOS applications to access more than 1MB memory:

DEVICE=C:\OS2\MDOS\VXMS.SYS

Notes

Other parameters are available, such as system-wide maximum memory usage and setting the number of available handles in each DOS session. Consult the OS/2 command reference help file.

DEVICEHIGH   DOS Only

Loads a DOS device driver into upper memory, leaving more low memory available to run programs.

Syntax

DEVICEHIGH=path\driver

path is the location of **driver**.

driver is the device driver file.

Example

To load the ANSI driver into upper memory:

DEVICEHIGH=C:\OS2\MDOS\ANSI.SYS

Notes

DOS programs run in low memory, which is the first 640K. DOS device drivers normally load in low memory, leaving less space to run programs. When you load device drivers in upper memory (from 640K to 1024K), you keep more low memory free and give DOS programs more space.

If the computer does not have enough upper memory to load the driver, it is loaded in low memory.

DEVINFO (Keyboard)

Sets the keyboard layout for the country you specify.

Syntax

DEVINFO=KBD,layout,path\KEYBOARD.DCP

layout is an abbreviation for your country, such as US for United States. You can find these abbreviations in the on-line command reference.

path is the location of the file KEYBOARD.DCP, which tells what each key means. By default, it is C:\OS2.

Example

To use the US keyboard:

DEVINFO=KBD,US,C:\OS2\KEYBOARD.DCP

DEVINFO (Printer)

Tells the printer object the country whose national characters it should use.

Syntax

DEVINFO=printer,model,*ROM=(font,0)*

printer is LPT1, LPT2, or LPT3.

model is 4201 for the IBM Proprinter or 5202 for the IBM Quietwriter.

font is a three-digit number you use to specify a national alphabet. You can find these numbers in the on-line command reference, under the COUNTRY command.

Example

To set up an IBM Proprinter, attached to the second printer port, for the United States:

DEVINFO=LPT2,4201,C:\OS2\4201.DCP,ROM=(437,0)

DEVINFO (Screen)

Tells OS/2 what kind of screen you have.

Syntax

DEVINFO=SCR,type,path\VIOTBL.DCP

type is CGA, EGA, VGA, or BGA, depending on what kind of screen you have. BGA is the IBM 8514/A with memory expansion.

path is the location of the file VIOTBL.DCP, which tells what each character looks like. By default, it is C:\OS2.

Example

To tell OS/2 that you have a VGA monitor:

DEVINFO=SCR,VGA,C:\OS2\VIOTBL.DCP

Notes

To configure OS/2 to work with your monitor, you also must set a couple of environment variables. OS/2's Install program performs this complicated task automatically. If you change your monitor, run Install to update the settings.

DISKCACHE

Makes your hard disk seem faster by keeping the data you use
most frequently in memory.

Syntax

DISKCACHE=n,*LW,t,AC:x*

n is a number from 64 to 14400 that tells how many kilobytes of
memory to set aside for saving disk data.

LW (lazy write) tells the cache to delay writing data to the disk
until the system is not quite so busy. *LW* is the default.

t is a number from 4 to 128 that limits the number of disk sectors
OS/2 reads or writes at one time. A sector is usually 512 bytes.
The default value of *t* is 4.

AC stands for AutoCheck, and *x* is a drive letter. This option
causes OS/2 to run CHKDSK/F at boot time.

Examples

To set up a 256K cache:

DISKCACHE=256

To get even better performance with the same settings:

DISKCACHE=256,LW,32

Notes

You probably use just a few programs and files at a time, which
means that you are often reading the same parts of your hard disk
over and over. A disk cache saves whatever you have most recently read in memory and reads it directly from memory when
you need it again. A disk cache can make your hard disk seem

much faster because retrieving data from memory is faster than retrieving it from disks.

When the cache becomes full, data that you have not used for some time is discarded. If you work with files that are larger than the disk cache, data can be discarded before you need to use it again.

To prevent this problem, you can limit the amount of data that is saved any particular time you read the disk by giving a value for *max*.

LW, or Lazy Writing, means that when a program needs to write data to the disk, the cache holds the data and actually puts it on the disk when the system is not busy. The system seems faster because programs do not have to wait for data to be written onto the disk. If you use *LW*, you must run the Shutdown procedure before turning off the computer or data that has not yet been written onto the disk is lost.

DISKCACHE works only on drives formatted with the FAT file system. For High Performance File System drives, use the CACHE command.

If your computer has less than 6M of memory, use a 6K disk cache. If you have more than 6M, use a cache size of 256K.

DOS (Control memory) DOS Only

Enables you to control where DOS is loaded in memory.

Syntax

DOS=where,upper

where tells whether DOS is loaded in high or low memory. It can be HIGH or LOW.

upper can be UMB or NOUMB. UMB allows DOS to run memory-resident programs in upper memory. NOUMB prevents this.

Example

To load DOS in high memory and let it run memory-resident programs in upper memory:

DOS=HIGH,UMB

Notes

DOS recognizes three different areas of memory. Low memory, from 0 to 640K, is where DOS programs, and DOS, usually run. With OS/2's special support, DOS programs also can run in upper memory, from 640K to 1024K. High memory is the area from 1024K to 1088K. OS/2 can move DOS to high memory.

The DOS operating system is really just a program that runs under OS/2. If you run DOS in low memory, you have less room to run DOS programs there. To avoid this problem, run DOS in high memory.

If you specify UMB, you can run DOS memory-resident programs in upper memory, using the LOADHIGH command. **DOS=HIGH,UMB** leaves the most lower memory free for applications.

DOS (Load DOS support) DOS Only

Enables DOS sessions to work.

Syntax

DEVICE=path\DOS.SYS

path is the location of the file DOS.SYS. By default, it is
C:\OS2\MDOS.

Example

To load DOS support:

DEVICE=C:\OS2\MDOS\DOS.SYS

Notes

DOS sessions will not start unless you have this command in
CONFIG.SYS.

DPATH   OS/2 Only

Tells OS/2 programs where to look for data files.

Syntax

SET DPATH=dir1;*dir2;...*

dir1 is a directory, such as C:\MEMOS.

dir2 is another directory.

The ellipsis (...) means that you can specify more directories. Separate the directories from each other by using semicolons.

Example

To tell OS/2 programs to look for data files in the directories C:\ and D:\DATA:

SET DPATH=C:\;D:\DATA

Notes

Data files that are in the current directory are always available to a program, even if you do not include the current directory in the DPATH statement.

The DOS APPEND command is similar to OS/2's DPATH. Unlike APPEND, DPATH works only with programs designed to use it, such as most commercial applications. Suppose that you have a file MEMO.TXT in the directory C:\MEMOS and that directory is on your DPATH. A word processing program in the C:\WORDPROC directory may be able to find the memo, but the OS/2 System Editor cannot find the memo unless you start it from the directory where the file is saved or type in the full path name.

You normally set DPATH in CONFIG.SYS, although you also can set it in an OS/2 window. When you set a new DPATH, it replaces the old one.

FCBS   DOS Only

Supports File Control Blocks (FCBs), a method of using files that was common in older DOS programs.

Syntax

FCBS=max,*protected*

max is the number of files, from 0 to 255, that can be used at a time with the FCB method.

protected is the number of FCBs that will not be closed automatically when a program needs more FCBs than are available. The number cannot be greater than **max**. The default is 16.

Examples

To give DOS ten FCBs and to protect three from being closed:

FCBS=10,3

To give DOS 255 FCBs and to tell DOS not to automatically recycle any of them if it runs out:

FCBS=255,255

Notes

You probably will not need to change the default, which is FCBS=16,16. Increase it to FCBS=255,255 if you have problems running DOS applications from the early 1980s.

If a program tries to open a file with an FCB, but all FCBs are already being used, the least recently used FCB is closed and given to the program. The file that was previously using the FCB is closed automatically, and any attempt to use it later will cause an error. If all FCBs are protected and they are all in use, a program that tries to open a file with an FCB will fail.

IFS

Enables you to use the High Performance File System (HPFS).

Syntax

IFS=path\HPFS.IFS */C:cache-size /AUTOCHECK:drives /CRECL:x*

path is the location of the file HPFS.IFS. By default, it is C:\OS2.

cache-size is the number of kilobytes of memory used as a disk cache. The default is 20 percent of total memory.

drives is a list of disks that automatically is checked for problems when you turn the computer on. Just give the letter of each drive; do not type a colon after the letter.

/CRECL:x specifies the maximum record size for caching (from 2K to 64K in multiples of 2K).

Example

To start the High Performance File System with a 128K cache, a maximum record size of 4K, and to check drives D and E for problems:

IFS=C:\OS2\HPFS.IFS */C:128 /AUTOCHECK:DE /CRECL:x*

Notes

If you formatted one or more of your drives with HPFS when you installed OS/2, the setup program placed an IFS statement in your CONFIG.SYS file. You need this statement to use a HPFS drive.

HPFS has a disk cache to improve performance. You probably use just a few programs and files at a time, which means that you are often reading the same parts of your hard disk over and over.

A disk cache saves whatever you have most recently read in memory and reads it directly from memory when you need it again. A disk cache can make your hard disk seem much faster because memory is faster than disks. To use the HPFS cache, you need to use the /C switch and run the CACHE command.

The cache for HPFS drives, which you specify with the /C switch, is different from the cache for FAT drives, which you set up with the DISKCACHE command. Setting the cache too large can slow down your system because the memory the cache uses is not available for running programs. If you do not have enough room to run your programs, OS/2 swaps them to and from the disk, which negates the benefit of caching. A 128K cache is usually large enough.

The /AUTOCHECK switch tells OS/2 to run the CHKDSK command when you turn the system on. This switch detects and tries to fix problems with the file system. Always use this switch with all HPFS drives: the safety CHKDSK provides is well worth the extra time it will take to start the system.

IOPL   OS/2 Only

Enables you to run programs that need to bypass OS/2 and work directly with hardware devices.

Syntax

IOPL=YES

IOPL=NO

IOPL=list

YES means that all programs can access the hardware directly.

NO means that no program can access the hardware directly (the default).

list gives the names of specific programs that are allowed to work directly with the hardware. Programs not listed do not have this permission. Separate the names in the list with commas.

Examples

To prevent any program from working directly with the hardware:

IOPL=NO

To prevent any program except PROGRAM1 and PROGRAM2 from working directly with the hardware:

IOPL=PROGRAM1,PROGRAM2

Notes

OS/2 normally prevents programs from dealing directly with hardware such as the disk drive; one faulty program cannot crash the whole system. Setting **IOPL=YES** offers the best protection against crashing the system.

Some programs have to work directly with the hardware, in order to do things that OS/2 cannot do for them. If you have to run such a program, specify its name in the list.

LASTDRIVE   DOS Only

Specifies the maximum number of drives that are accessible.

Syntax

LASTDRIVE=x

x is the number of the last valid drive that is recognized.

Example

To give your system access to 13 logical disks:

LASTDRIVE=M

Note

This statement has no effect in OS/2 sessions.

LIBPATH   OS/2 Only

Tells OS/2 programs where to look for Dynamic Link Libraries (DLLs).

Syntax

LIBPATH=dir1;*dir2*;...

dir1 is a directory, such as C:\LIBRARY. Use a period to indicate the current directory.

dir2 is another directory.

The ellipsis (...) means that you can specify more directories. Separate the directories from each other by using semicolons.

Example

To tell OS/2 to look for DLLs first in the current directory, then in the directories C:\OS2\DLL and D:\DLL:

LIBPATH=.;C:\OS2\DLL;D:\DLL

The period following the equal sign means the current directory.

Notes

Many OS/2 applications put part of their program code in DLLs, which are program files with the extension DLL. To run these applications, OS/2 must know where to find their DLLs. Most applications come with an installation program that automatically adds the necessary LIBPATH to your CONFIG.SYS. Others may ask you to change the CONFIG.SYS manually.

LIBPATH is much like DPATH and PATH, but you can use LIBPATH only in CONFIG.SYS. You do not use the word SET when specifying LIBPATH. You should start LIBPATH with a period as in the example because OS/2 does not search the current directory for DLLs unless you include it.

LOADHIGH   DOS Only

Loads DOS memory-resident programs into upper memory.

Syntax

LOADHIGH path\program

path is the location of the memory-resident program.

program is the name of the memory-resident program. Follow **program** with any arguments you would use if you typed it at the command line.

Example

To load APPEND into upper memory with C:\OS2 and C:\OS2\SYSTEM as arguments:

LOADHIGH APPEND C:\OS2;C:\OS2\SYSTEM

Notes

Memory-resident programs, also known as TSRs, are DOS commands and applications that run in the background. Loading TSRs in upper memory leaves more lower memory free for other programs if the following statement is listed in your CONFIG.SYS:

DOS=HIGH,UMB

MAXWAIT   OS/2 Only

Makes sure that no program thread is put on hold forever, even when the system is busy running other programs.

Syntax

MAXWAIT=n

n is the maximum number of seconds that a thread can be put on hold. The default is three seconds.

Example

To keep any thread from waiting on hold more than one second:

MAXWAIT=1

Notes

If you run several programs at once and a few of them grab most of the computer's attention, you still may want to be sure that even low-priority background programs make some progress. If a program has not gotten any attention for the number of seconds you set with MAXWAIT, OS/2 temporarily increases that program's priority.

The default, three seconds, is usually a good place to start. Try decreasing it to one if background programs run too slowly.

MEMMAN   OS/2 Only

Enables you to run time-critical processes more reliably by turning off virtual memory.

Syntax

MEMMAN=*s,m,PROTECT*

s is SWAP or NOSWAP.

m is MOVE or NOMOVE.

PROTECT allows memory to be compacted by using protected dynamic link libraries.

Example

To turn off virtual memory:

MEMMAN=NOSWAP,NOMOVE

Notes

OS/2 can run more programs and use more data than can actually be stored in memory at once. OS/2 does this by swapping chunks of memory to disk when they are not being used and by reading them back in when they are needed. This swapping is called *virtual memory*. Turn virtual memory on with SWAP or off with NOSWAP.

When programs run, they grab chunks of memory and then release them when they are no longer needed. After a while, memory gets fragmented into little pieces, slowing down the system. OS/2 can overcome this problem by combining these pieces. You can turn this feature on by using MOVE or off by using NOMOVE.

The default, **MEMMAN=MOVE,SWAP,PROTECT**, is usually best. For some time-critical applications like controlling complex machinery in a factory, you cannot afford to let the computer divert its attention to moving or swapping for even a fraction of a second. In this case, specify NOMOVE and NOSWAP. These settings will increase the amount of memory needed to run the system because OS/2 won't be able to use the Swap File to overcommit memory. If you don't use the COMMIT setting and your Swap File grows enough that you only have MINFREE disk space left, OS/2 displays a message informing you that disk space is low and advising you to close applications and delete unneeded files to free some available disk space. If you ignore the message or if the PC runs in unattended mode, OS/2 may run out of disk space despite your MINFREE setting. Use COMMIT to cause OS/2 to refuse to allocate memory to applications in such low-disk-space conditions.

PATH

Tells OS/2 or DOS where to find programs.

Syntax

SET PATH=dir1;*dir2*;...

dir1 is a directory, such as C:\PROGRAMS.

dir2 is another directory.

The ellipsis (...) means that you can specify more directories. Separate the directories from each other by using semicolons.

Examples

To tell OS/2 to look for program files in the directories C:\ and D:\UTILITY, place this line in CONFIG.SYS or type it in an OS/2 window:

SET PATH=C:\;D:\UTILITY

To tell DOS to look for program files in the directories C:\ and D:\UTILITY, place this line in AUTOEXEC.BAT or type it in a DOS window:

SET PATH=C:\;D:\UTILITY

Notes

You can always run a program if you first use the CD command to change to the directory where you keep it. If that directory is on the PATH, however, you can always run the program from any directory without worrying about where you put it on the disk.

You normally set the OS/2 PATH in CONFIG.SYS, and the DOS PATH in AUTOEXEC.BAT. You also can use these commands in a DOS or OS/2 window. When you set a new PATH, it replaces the old one.

PAUSEONERROR   OS/2 Only

Tells OS/2 to stop for a moment if it cannot process a line in
CONFIG.SYS correctly.

Syntax

PAUSEONERROR=YES

PAUSEONERROR=NO

Notes

The default, YES, is generally the better choice. If OS/2 has a problem running a line in CONFIG.SYS, it displays an error message
and waits until you press Enter. If the setting is NO, the error message appears, but scrolls off the screen so quickly that you may
not have a chance to read it.

PRINTMONBUFSIZE

Sets the buffer size for the parallel port device driver.

Syntax

PRINTMONBUFSIZE=x

x is the size of the buffer.

Example

To set the parallel port device driver buffer size for the LPT1 as 2048 bytes:

PRINTMONBUFSIZE=2048

Note

You can set a value for the LPT1, LPT2, and LPT3 by separating the *x* value with a comma.

PRIORITY

Tells OS/2 whether it should juggle the priority of different threads that are running at the same time.

Syntax

PRIORITY= DYNAMIC

PRIORITY=ABSOLUTE

Notes

You should normally use **DYNAMIC** priority. This setting allows OS/2 to vary the priority of threads, depending on how active they are. A thread running in the foreground has a higher priority so that the program you are currently working with runs faster than a program running in the background.

In the rare case that you need to run a program that sets its own thread priorities, use **ABSOLUTE**.

PRIORITY_DISK_IO

Specifies disk input/output priority for foreground applications.

Syntax

PRIORITY_DISK_IO=YES

PRIORITY_DISK_IO=NO

YES allows an application running in the foreground to receive disk input/output priority.

NO allows background applications to receive disk input/output priority.

Example

To give the foreground application the disk input/output priority:

PRIORITY_DISK_IO=YES

Note

If PRIORITY_DISK_IO is turned on, the foreground application has a better response time than the background applications.

PROTECTONLY   OS/2 Only

Tells OS/2 whether you want to be able to run DOS programs.

Syntax

PROTECTONLY=YES
PROTECTONLY=NO

Note

YES means you want to run only OS/2 programs.

NO means you want to run DOS and OS/2 programs.

PROTSHELL   OS/2 Only

Loads OS/2's built-in command processor CMD.EXE or enables
you to run a different command processor.

Syntax

PROTSHELL=startup

startup is the statement used to start the command processor. It
includes the full path, the file's full name including its extension,
and various other parameters.

Example

To use the built-in OS/2 command processor:

PROTSHELL=C:\OS2\PMSHELL.EXE C:\OS2\OS2.INI
C:\OS2\OS2SYS.INI C:\OS2\CMD.EXE

To use Hamilton Laboratories' C Shell:

PROTSHELL=C:\OS2\PMSHELL.EXE C:\OS2\OS2.INI
C:\OS2\OS2SYS.INI C:\OS2\BIN\CSH.EXE -L

Type these commands all on one line in CONFIG.SYS.

Notes

The OS/2 command processor, also known as a shell, is the program that makes OS/2 full-screen and window sessions work. You
may want to buy a different command processor to replace the
shell that comes with OS/2. If you choose to use a different shell,
you can use the PROTSHELL command listed in the documentation for the new command processor.

PSTAT

Shows system information for current processes, threads, semaphores, shared memory, and dynamic-link libraries.

Syntax

PSTAT /C /S /L /M /P:processid

Switches

/C displays the current process and other system thread information.

/S displays system semaphore information.

/L displays dynamic-link library information.

/M displays shared memory information.

/P:processid displays process-related information for the process number you specify—for example, /P:4 displays information for process number 4.

Notes

PSTAT provides information about active processes in your system. By using this command without switches, you receive general information about current processes and threads, semaphores, shared memory, and dynamic-link libraries. By using the switches with PSTAT, you receive specific system information.

RMSIZE   DOS Only

Sets the amount of memory DOS can use.

Syntax

RMSIZE=n

n is the number of kilobytes of memory DOS can use, up to 640.

Example

To limit DOS to 512 kilobytes:

RMSIZE=512

Notes

DOS normally can use up to 640K of memory. You usually should use **RMSIZE=640**, which is the default, because many programs require this amount. A smaller value keeps you from running some programs but makes more memory available to OS/2.

SET

Assigns values to variables in the environment.

Syntax

SET

SET var=value

var is the name of a variable in the environment.

value is what the name stands for.

Examples

To see the values of all environment variables, type the following at the command line:

SET

To tell OS/2's on-line command reference that its files are stored in C:\OS2\BOOK:

SET BOOKSHELF=C:\OS2\BOOK

To tell OS/2 to look for its help messages in C:\OS2\HELP:

SET HELP=C:\OS2\HELP

To tell OS/2 to remember the commands you have typed and allow you to reuse them:

SET KEYS=ON

Notes

The environment is a part of memory where values are assigned to certain names. The command processor and your applications use these names for various purposes. The PATH variable tells OS/2 where to find programs, for example. DPATH, KEYS, and PROMPT also are environment variables. You can string paths together by using a semicolon between them.

SHELL   DOS Only

Loads OS/2's built-in DOS command processor COMMAND.COM or enables you to run a different command processor.

Syntax

SHELL=startup

startup is the statement used to start the DOS command processor. The statement includes the full path, the file's full name including its extension, and any optional parameters.

Examples

To use the built-in DOS command processor:

SHELL=C:\OS2\MDOS\COMMAND.COM C:\OS2\MDOS /P

To use JP Software's 4DOS shell, assuming that you have installed it in the D:\4DOS directory:

SHELL=D:\4DOS\4DOS.COM /P

Notes

The DOS command processor, also known as a shell, is the program that makes DOS sessions work. You may want to buy a different command processor to replace the shell that comes with OS/2. If you choose to use a different shell, you can use the PROTSHELL command listed in the documentation for the new command processor.

If you use a different shell, you must add a line to CONFIG.SYS that sets the COMSPEC variable. This line gives the full path and file name of the new shell. For the 4DOS example in the preceding section, add the line to CONFIG.SYS:

SET COMSPEC=D:\4DOS\4DOS.COM

SWAPPATH   OS/2 Only

Tells OS/2 where to create a swap file, which uses free disk space so that you can run more programs than can fit in memory.

Syntax

SWAPPATH=swapdir *minfree initial*

swapdir is a directory, such as C:\. The default is C:\OS2\SYSTEM.

minfree is a number from 512 to 32767. It specifies the number of kilobytes of disk space that the swap file leaves free for other purposes. If 2600K are free when you start OS/2 and *minfree* is 600, then the swap file cannot use more than 2000K. The default for *minfree* is 512.

initial specifies the size of the swap file initially allocated by the operating system.

Example

To put the swap file in the \SWAP directory on drive D and allow it to use all available space on D except for 1000K:

SWAPPATH=D:\SWAP 1000

Notes

For swapping to be active, MEMMAN must be in your CONFIG.SYS:

MEMMAN-SWAP

If possible, put the swap file on a drive that has several (10 to 15) megabytes of free space. A large swap file enables you to run many programs at once.

THREADS   OS/2 Only

Sets the number of tasks OS/2 can perform at the same time.

Syntax

THREADS=n

n is the maximum number of threads, from 32 to 4095.

Example

To allow up to 512 threads:

THREADS=512

Notes

A thread is a part of a program that runs on its own, independently from the other parts. A spreadsheet might create a thread when you tell it to save a file. This thread runs like a program in the background so that you can continue entering numbers in the spreadsheet without waiting for the file to be saved. The default is 64, but you can try setting THREADS to 256 if you run several programs at once.

TIMESLICE   OS/2 Only

Sets upper and lower limits on the amount of time the computer spends on each thread.

Syntax

TIMESLICE *min,max*

min is a number between 32 and 65536. A thread gets the computer's attention and keeps it for at least *min* thousandths of a second. The default is 32.

max is a number between 32 and 65535. A thread gets the computer's attention and keeps it for no longer than *max* thousandths of a second. The default is the value of *min*.

Examples

To set the minimum and maximum time slice to 32 and 500 thousandths of a second, respectively:

TIMESLICE=32,500

To set the maximum time slice to one second and use the default minimum value:

TIMESLICE=,1000

Notes

You should use 32 as the minimum value because OS/2 uses it for some special situations.

VCOM   DOS Only

Enables you to use the communications ports for DOS sessions.

Syntax

DEVICE=path\VCOM.SYS

path is the location of the file VCOM.SYS. By default, it is
C:\OS2\MDOS.

Example

To make the communications ports available to DOS, type this in
CONFIG.SYS:

DEVICE=C:\OS2\MDOS\VCOM.SYS

Notes

List VCOM.SYS *after* COM.SYS in CONFIG.SYS. Older versions of
OS/2 used a program called SETCOM40 to provide communications support to DOS sessions, but you should not use SETCOM40
with OS/2 2.x.

VMOUSE   DOS Only

Enables you to use a mouse or trackball in DOS sessions.

Syntax

DEVICE=path\VMOUSE.SYS

path is the location of the file VMOUSE.SYS. By default, it is
C:\OS2\MDOS.

Note

Installing a mouse requires other drivers as well. See the explanation under the MOUSE command.

The History of OS/2

O S/2 began as a combined effort of IBM and Microsoft in 1985. In August of that year, the two companies signed a Joint Development Agreement that let them design and build a new operating system, to be named OS/2.

The agreement no longer exists; IBM and Microsoft no longer work together on OS/2. IBM has shouldered that work load itself. The companies still have a top-secret Cross-Licensing Agreement, however, that lets one company use the other's software. The Cross-Licensing Agreement covers DOS, Windows, OS/2, and even some future operating system designs, such as Microsoft's Win-NT. (Microsoft's development of Win-NT, sometimes referred to as Win-32 and other similar acronyms, was still underway as this book went to press. The expected production date for Win-NT is sometime in the fall of 1993.)

IBM and Microsoft intended OS/2 to be a replacement for DOS. Software developers and end users alike had voiced their complaints about DOS. Specifically, people said they did not have enough memory in which to run their applications (the infamous 640K limitation), DOS did not support multiple concurrent applications, DOS was too fragile, DOS was too simple and rudimentary, and DOS was too slow when applications accessed large files. In short, DOS was not industrial strength. People's biggest complaint about DOS, however, was that each DOS application had its own user interface and required too much training to make the DOS environment truly productive.

The new operating system addressed almost all these concerns. A consistent user interface (Presentation Manager) did not appear in the very first version of OS/2.

OS/2 1.0 shipped in December of 1987. The first implementation of OS/2 had a single, small "DOS Compatibility Box" for running DOS applications. This first version of OS/2 did not contain or support a graphical user interface. That version did offer up to 16M of memory, however, to applications rewritten to run under OS/2 instead of DOS.

Version 1.1 of OS/2, essentially the 1.0 product with the addition of Presentation Manager, appeared in the last quarter of 1988. Still saddled with a small DOS Compatibility Box, OS/2 1.1 was nonetheless a technical marvel. OS/2 1.1 allowed software developers to transcend the limitations of DOS if they would rewrite their software. Unfortunately, few did.

At the same time that IBM and Microsoft released a Presentation Manager version of OS/2, IBM published a set of guidelines and standards, called *Systems Application Architecture* (SAA), to help the computer industry achieve some measure of consistency and coherence. IBM mentions its own products in the guidelines, but otherwise freely offers the guidelines as a set of suggested methods, interfaces, computer languages, and design techniques that software developers can follow. IBM reasons that consistency and coherence among software applications will encourage more people to use computers in more ways, more productively, and thus indirectly help IBM sell more hardware and software.

Microsoft and IBM also began offering an Extended Edition of OS/2. Called OS/2 EE 1.1, this special version contained a Communications Manager for computer-to-computer data transfer, a Database Manager based on IBM's *Structured Query Language* (SQL) standard for record keeping, and special support for local area networks. The regular version of OS/2 was called OS/2 Standard Edition (SE).

IBM and Microsoft enhanced OS/2 considerably and released version 1.2 in October 1989. Version 1.2 added features that addressed many of the concerns that people expressed regarding version 1.1, including the capability to switch between DOS and OS/2 (Dual Boot), an Installable File System (High Performance File System, or HPFS), and hardware compatibility with more kinds of personal computers. Unfortunately, IBM and Microsoft "broke" the print drivers in version 1.2, and many people had problems with their printouts with this version.

In December 1990, IBM and Microsoft released OS/2 1.3. Slimmed down considerably from earlier versions, OS/2 1.3 got the nickname "OS/2 Lite." You could run OS/2 1.3 on a computer with as little as 2M or 3M of memory. Version 1.3 did many things well for applications rewritten for OS/2, but it still had only a single, small DOS Compatibility Box. IBM did most of the development work for version 1.3. Version 1.3 was small, fast, reliable, and it printed. Its only drawback was its small DOS Box.

Late in 1991, IBM and Microsoft stopped working together on OS/2, which became purely an IBM product as Microsoft went off on its own to develop other operating systems. With the Cross-Licensing Agreement still in effect, both companies still have access to each other's work. This situation is unusual, to say the least. The picture is further complicated because IBM and former rival Apple Computer have jointly agreed to develop enhancements to OS/2 and OS/2-like operating systems in the future. IBM and Apple started the Taligent company to produce the enhanced operating system, code-named "Pink". It will be several years before Taligent releases the follow-on to OS/2.

March of 1992 saw the release of OS/2 2.0, the first version of OS/2 to support multiple DOS Boxes. The key features of OS/2 2.0 are the following:

■ Simple, graphical-user-interface installation

■ System integrity protection

■ Virtual memory

■ Preemptive multitasking and task scheduling

■ Fast, 32-bit architecture

■ Overlapped, fast disk file access

■ DOS compatibility

■ More available memory for DOS applications (typically about 620K of conventional memory)

■ Capability to run OS/2, DOS, and Windows software concurrently

■ Multiple concurrent DOS sessions

■ High Performance File System (HPFS)

■ Presentation Manager (PM) graphical user interface

■ The object-oriented Work Place Shell (WPS)

■ National Language Support (NLS)

■ Multiple Operating System Tool (MOST)

■ Configuration tool for tailoring OS/2 to your preferences

- Small, easy-to-use applications (Applets) bundled with OS/2, such as notepad, diary, spreadsheet, presentation graphics software, and other productivity tools

- Interactive on-line documentation and help screens

- Capability to run OS/2 on both IBM and IBM-compatible hardware

OS/2 2.0 can run the more than 2,500 OS/2 applications, 20,000 DOS applications, and 1,200 Windows applications. This makes OS/2 2.0 a versatile and flexible operating environment. By the end of 1992, IBM had sold approximately 3 million copies of OS/2 2.0.

A year after version 2.0 first became available, in March of 1993, IBM released version 2.1 of OS/2—the version that this book discusses. Version 2.1 adds the following features to the already capable version 2.0:

- Support for Microsoft Windows version 3.1

- Support for popular Super VGA video adapters, in a variety of resolutions, in both Presentation Manager and Windows sessions

- Support for more brands of printers

- Support for additional SCSI-based CD-ROM drives

- A CD-ROM installation capability

- A fax send/receive applet

- Support for the Advanced Power Management (APM) specification (intended for notebook computers)

- Support for the Personal Computer Memory Card International Association (PCMCIA) specification

- Support for pen-based computers

- Multimedia support

Workplace Shell Tasks and Keyboard Shortcuts

M any people find the Workplace Shell easy to use and intuitive. You don't use every task every day, however. The information in this appendix tells you how to correctly perform all the Workplace Shell tasks, especially the ones you use infrequently.

Workplace Shell task	Do these steps
Close a window	Double-click the Menu button in the upper left corner of the window.
Close a window or notebook	Point to (move the mouse cursor to) an object and click mouse button 2. Click the Close option.

continues

Workplace Shell task	Do these steps
Copy an object	Point to the object to be copied. Hold down the Ctrl key while you use mouse button 2 to drag the object to a new location.
Create a shadow of an object	Point to the object to be copied. Hold down the Shift key while you use mouse button 2 to drag the object to a new location.
Delete an object	Use mouse button 2 to drag-and-drop the object on the Shredder.
Display object's System menu	Point to the object and click mouse button 2 or press and release the Alt key.
Display the window list	Point to an empty area on the desktop. Press both mouse buttons at the same time.
Drag-and-drop	Point to the object. Grab the object and move it by pressing and holding down mouse button 2 while you move the mouse. Release the mouse button when you have moved the object to its new location.
Dual-boot DOS	Double-click the OS/2 System folder, double-click the Command Prompts folder, and then double-click the Dual-Boot icon.
Find an object	Display a folder's popup menu. Choose the Find option.
Maximize a window	Using mouse button 1, double-click the clock's title bar or click the Maximize button (the button with a large square) in the upper right corner of the window.
Minimize a window	Point to the Minimize button (the button with a small square) to the left of the Maximize button and click mouse button 1.
Move a window	Point to the window's title bar. Click and hold down either mouse button. Release the mouse button when you have moved the window to its new location.

Workplace Shell task	Do these steps
Open an object	Point to the object and press mouse button 1 twice in rapid succession (a double-click).
Open settings notebook	Point to an object and press mouse button 2 once. Then click the Open menu option. Click the Settings option.
Open Workplace Shell's system menu	Click mouse button 2 on any blank area of the desktop. Opening this menu is a little more difficult with the keyboard.
Print an object	Drag and drop the object on the appropriate printer object.
Resize a window	Move the mouse cursor to any edge or corner of the window. When the cursor changes to a double arrow, hold down either mouse button and move the mouse to resize the window. Release the button.
Restore a window to its original size	Double-click the title bar or click the Restore button (a medium-size square between two vertical lines).
See an object's popup menu	Point to an object and click mouse button 2.
See the desktop's popup menu	Point to an empty area on the desktop and click mouse button 2.
Select an object	Point to an object and click mouse button 1.
Shut down	Point to an empty area on the desktop and click mouse button 2. Then click the Shutdown option. Confirm the operation and then wait for OS/2 to indicate that you can reboot or turn off your computer.
Start a program object	Point to the object and double-click mouse button 1.

Workplace Shell Keyboard Shortcuts

Keystroke	Function
Alt-Esc	Switch to the next open window or full-screen session
Alt-Home	Switch a DOS program between window and full screen
Ctrl-Alt-Del	Restart the operating system
Ctrl-Esc	Display the Window List
Alt-PgDn	In a notebook, move cursor to the next page
Alt-PgUp	In a notebook, move cursor to the previous page
F1	Display help for the active window
F5	Refresh contents of the active window
F6	Move cursor from one window pane to another in a split window
F10	Move the cursor to or from the menu bar
Alt-F4	Close the active window
Alt-F5	Restore the window to previous size
Alt-F6	Move cursor between associated windows
Alt-F7	Move the active window or selected object
Alt-F8	Size the active window or selected object
Alt-F9	Minimize the window
Alt-F10	Maximize the window
Shift-Esc or Alt-Spacebar	Switch to or from the title-bar icon
Shift-F8	Start or stop selecting more than one object
Shift-F10	Display pop-up menu for the active object

Enhanced Editor Keystroke Guide

A fter listing the function key assignments for the Enhanced Editor, this appendix lists the other defined keystrokes by function and then by menu.

The following tables are included in this appendix:

- Function Key Keystroke Reference
- Basic Editing Keystroke Reference
- Cursor Key Keystroke Reference
- Mouse Cursor Reference
- Editing Keystrokes
    - Basic editing and reformatting
    - Selecting text (advanced mode)
    - Altering selected text (advanced mode)
    - Adding special characters
    - Menu shortcut keys
- File Menu Keystroke Reference
- Edit Menu Keystroke Reference

■ Search Menu Keystroke Reference

■ Options Menu Keystroke Reference

■ Command Menu Keystroke Reference

For further information, see Chapter 14, "Using the OS/2 Text Editors."

Function Key Keystroke Reference

Key	Function	Function with Shift
F1	Help	Scroll left
F2	Save	Scroll right
F3	Quit (no save)	Scroll up
F4	Quit (with save)	Scroll down
F5	Open Dialog	Make current cursor position center line in window
F6	Select line draw command	None
F7	Rename file	None
F8	Edit additional line	None
F9	Undo last action	None
F10	Go to menu bar	None
F11	Previous file	None
F12	Next file	None

Key	Function with Alt	Function with Ctrl
F1	Draw sample box characters	Make word uppercase
F2	None	Make word lowercase
F3	None	Make selection uppercase
F4	Close window	Make selection lowercase
F5	Reopen window	Move cursor to beginning of word

Key	Function with Alt	Function with Ctrl
F6	None	Move cursor to end of word
F7	Move window	Move selected area to left
F8	Size window	Move selected area to right
F9	Minimize window	None
F10	Maximize window	None
F11	None	None
F12	None	None

Basic Editing Keystroke Reference

Cursor Key Keystroke Reference

Keystroke	Action
Left arrow	Left one letter
Ctrl-Left	Left one word
Right arrow	Right one letter
Ctrl-Right	Right one word
Tab	Right one tab stop
Shift-Tab	Left one tab stop
Up arrow	Up one line
Down arrow	Down one line
PgUp	Up one page
Ctrl-PgUp	Top of page
PgDn	Down one page
Ctrl-PgDn	Bottom of page

continues

Keystroke	Action
Home	Beginning of line
Ctrl-Home	Beginning of file
End	End of line
Ctrl-End	End of file

Mouse Cursor Reference

Mouse button and action	Result
Click with button 1	Moves cursor to mouse position
Drag with button 1	Selects the block
Drag with button 2	Selects the lines; if in a selected area, moves the selected text
Ctrl key and drag with button 1	Selects the characters
Ctrl key and drag with button 2	If in selected area, copies the selected text
Double-click with button 1	Unmarks text
Double-click with button 2	Moves cursor to mouse position and selects the word

Editing Keystrokes

Key	Action
Basic Editing and Reformatting	
Backspace	Deletes character to left of cursor
Ctrl-Backspace	Deletes line
Del	Deletes character to right of cursor
Enter	Ends line
Ins	Toggles between insert and overwrite modes
Alt-J	Joins with following line

Key	Action
Alt-P	Reformats next paragraph
Alt-R	Reformats selected area
Alt-S	Splits line at cursor
Ctrl-D	Deletes word
Ctrl-E	Erases to end of line
Ctrl-K	Duplicates line
Ctrl-M	Inserts blank line
Ctrl-Tab	Adds tab character

Selecting Text (Advanced Mode)

Alt-B	Marks start or end of rectangular block
Alt-L	Marks start or end of lines
Alt-U	Unmarks selected text
Alt-W	Marks word
Alt-Z	Marks start or end of characters

Altering Selected Text (Advanced Mode)

Alt-A	Moves marked text, leaving blank characters in the former location
Alt-C	Copies marked text
Alt-D	Deletes marked text
Alt-E	Moves cursor to end of marked text
Alt-M	Moves marked text
Alt-O	Moves marked text overwriting
Alt-T	Centers marked text
Alt-Y	Moves the cursor to the beginning of the marked text

Adding Special Characters

Alt-F	Fills marked text area with selected fill character
Alt-N	Adds current filename to text
Alt-1	Edits file named on current line

continues

Key	Action
Alt-0	Executes current line or selected area as commands
Alt-=	Same as Alt-0
Alt--	Highlights cursor
Ctrl-Enter	Enter with no new line
Ctrl-2	Adds NULL character
Ctrl-6	Adds logical NOT character (ASCII 170)
Ctrl-9	Adds left brace character ({)
Ctrl-0	Adds right brace character (})

Menu Shortcut and Command Keys

Key	Action
Shift-Del	Cuts marked text to Clipboard
Shift-Ins	Pastes block from Clipboard
Alt-Backspace	Undoes the last action
Ctrl-B	Lists the bookmarks
Ctrl-C	Searches and replaces next occurrence of search text
Ctrl-F	Finds next occurrence of search text
Ctrl-I	Opens command dialog box
Ctrl-L	Copies the current line to command line
Ctrl-N	Goes to next file in ring
Ctrl-O	Opens existing file
Ctrl-P	Goes to previous file in ring
Ctrl-Q	Swaps to or from ALL file
Ctrl-R	Starts or ends recording keystrokes
Ctrl-S	Searches for text
Ctrl-T	Plays back keystrokes into editor
Ctrl-X	Forces syntax expansion
Ctrl-Y	Chooses style (font and color) for file
Ctrl-Ins	Copies marked text to Clipboard

File Menu Keystroke Reference

Use after opening File menu by pressing F10, then F.

Key	Action
A	Saves current file with new name
I	Imports text file
N	Opens new file
O	Opens existing file
P	Prints file
Q	Closes window without saving file
R	Renames current file
S	Saves current file
U	Opens untitled file
V	Saves current file and closes window

Edit Menu Keystroke Reference

Use after opening Edit menu by pressing F10, then E.

Key	Action
A	Moves marked text, leaving its former location blank
B	Pastes block from Clipboard
C	Copies marked text
D	Deletes marked text
E	Chooses style (font and color) for file
I	Prints marked text
L	Undoes last action
M	Moves marked text
N	Unmarks marked text
O	Moves marked text, overwriting any existing text

continues

Key	Action
P	Pastes lines from Clipboard
S	Pastes from Clipboard
T	Cuts marked text to Clipboard
U	Undoes multiple actions
Y	Copy marked text to Clipboard

Search Menu Keystroke Reference

Use after opening Search menu by pressing F10 and then S.

Key	Action
B	Opens bookmark menu
C	Finds and replaces next occurrence of search text
F	Finds next occurrence of search text
S	Searches for text
From Bookmark menu	
L	Lists bookmarks
N	Goes to next bookmark
P	Goes to previous bookmark
S	Sets a bookmark

Options Menu Keystroke Reference

Use after opening Options menu by pressing F10, then O.

Key	Action
A	Alters autosave settings
M	Displays program messages
N	Alters window appearance, such as menus and scroll bars
O	Saves current option settings
R	Alters settings, such as tabs and margins, advanced marking, or enable ring

Command Menu Keystroke Reference

Use after opening Command menu by pressing F10 and then C.

Key	Action
C	Opens command dialog box
H	Halts command

OS/2 Games

After installation, OS/2 places games in a template within the OS/2 System window. (Refer to Chapter 6, "Installing OS/2," for installation instructions.) You can open the games template by double-clicking the OS/2 games icon. The following games are included:

- Cat and Mouse
- Jigsaw
- OS/2 Chess
- Reversi
- Scramble
- Solitaire—Klondike

To start a game, double-click its icon. The following sections summarize the available games.

Cat and Mouse

The Cat and Mouse game called PMSeek helps you learn to use the mouse. The game is also handy for checking your mouse. When you start the game, a cat appears on the background and "chases" your mouse cursor. As you move the mouse cursor around, the cat follows. If it reaches the mouse cursor, the cat sits down, washes, yawns, and then goes to sleep until you move the mouse again. The cat only appears in the background area and does not intrude into the open windows.

Settings and Options

When you first start the game, your screen looks like figure D.1. The open window displays a control panel where you can adjust the play time, speed, and step.

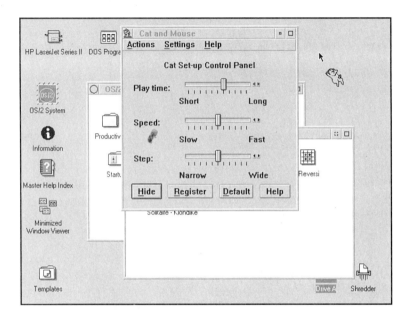

Cat and Mouse
Control Panel.

When you increase the play time, you lengthen the time the cat moves before resting. With a short play time, the cat follows the mouse without pausing.

The speed adjustment alters how fast the cat moves, and the step adjustment alters the size of the cat's step size.

To save new settings you select, choose Register from the Control Panel or Settings menu. To restore the default settings, choose Default from the Control Panel or Settings menu.

You disable or enable the cat without ending the program by using the Actions menu. You also can remove all the windows from the screen by using this menu, making the cat run away from the mouse. When you choose Actions and Hide or type F10 and I, the icons and windows disappear and you see a dialog box explaining that you can press Alt to redisplay your windows or click the cat. In this mode, the cat runs away from the mouse. You can chase the cat around the screen.

Jigsaw

The Jigsaw game displays a picture as a jigsaw puzzle. You assemble the pieces by dragging them with your mouse. Although OS/2 has only one bitmap sample image—the OS/2 logo screen, you can choose any OS/2 bitmap file as your puzzle's picture.

NOTE You need a mouse to move the pieces around the screen. You cannot use a keyboard to assemble the puzzle.

Settings and Options

After starting Jigsaw, load a bitmap into the window by choosing the File menu Open or by pressing F10 and then pressing O. Choose your image from the dialog box in the same way as you load files in most applications.

After loading the bitmap, choose the Options Menu Jumble to mix up the pieces or press F10 and then J. If you maximize the window, your screen may look like the screen in figure D.2.

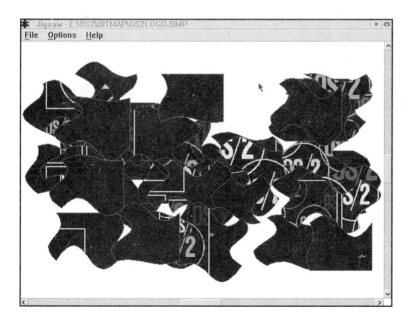

Fig. D.2

Jigsaw game.

You assemble the puzzle by pointing to a puzzle piece, pressing mouse button 1, and then dragging the piece to the desired position. You do not have to rotate the pieces. When you join pieces correctly, OS/2 beeps to show they are joined. You then can manipulate the joined pieces as a single piece.

 Listen for the beep that indicates that you have actually joined the pieces. Positioning the pieces exactly right on-screen is sometimes hard.

In addition to changing the picture by loading different bitmap images, you can change the size of the puzzle. Choose Options menu Size and then choose from small, medium, large, or full size. This option does not change the number of pieces in the puzzle but alters the size of the displayed image.

OS/2 Chess

OS/2 Chess is a chess game for one or two players. If you are on a network, you can even play against someone at another workstation. When playing against the computer, you can choose the computer's experience level.

Settings and Options

When you start a chess game, OS/2 prompts you for the name of each player. You can choose between playing the game on your computer (against a human or your computer), or, if your computer is connected to a network, you can link with another user.

When you choose the computer as your opponent, you can choose among five skill levels, ranging from beginner to advanced. You also can select the book opening the computer uses. OS/2 offers nearly 50 openings.

Choose the options for each player and press OK. Figure D.3 shows the screen that appears.

The rules for this chess game are the same as conventional chess. You move pieces by dragging them across the board or by keyboard entry using algebraic chess notation. The help file includes rules and some elementary strategies. You can load save or delete games in progress, and you can print the current position from the File menu.

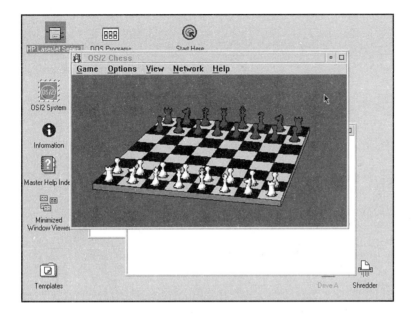

Fig. D.3

Chess Game.

The Options menu includes many selections for altering your screen's appearance and sounds. You can change the colors, turn the sound on and off, and enter moves from the keyboard. You can set up a game position, see the time taken for moves, and take back a move.

The View menu also includes selections that affect your screen's appearance, but these options are normally made during a game. You can rotate the board, see the possible valid moves, as well as get an analysis of these—your position, record of the moves made in the game, and captured pieces.

Network users can send a message indicating their move by using the Network menu. They also can disconnect from their opponent or get a list of users by means of this menu.

Reversi

Reversi, a game that you play against the computer, follows the rules of the board game Reversi. The object of the game is to place more red dots on an eight-by-eight square board than your opponent, the computer, places blue dots.

The rules for Reversi are simple, but the game is difficult to win. You place a dot in a square beside a blue dot. Try to choose a position so that a red dot at the other end traps the blue dot or dots. Trapped blue dots change to red. After you take your turn, the computer places a blue dot on the board.

If a horizontal row has a red dot and then two blue dots (moving from left to right), for example, you can place a red dot beside the right blue dot. The two blue dots then change to red.

Settings and Options

When you move the mouse around the board, the cursor changes from the shape of a pointer to a cross to show the valid moves. If you cannot make a valid move, you must pass. Figure D.4 shows a typical game in progress.

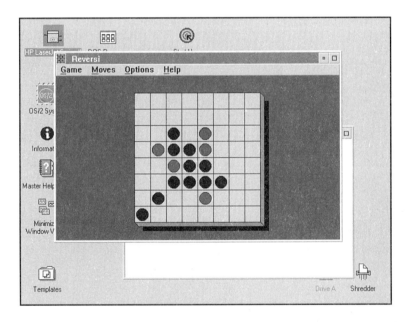

Fig. D.4

Reversi Game.

Options for playing the game include altering the computer's skill level between beginner, intermediate, advanced, or master and changing between two different starting positions. You can get a hint on the next appropriate move from the Moves menu.

Scramble

Scramble is a tile-arranging game similar to games that have a series of numbered tiles or tiles with a portion of a picture. The tiles are in a frame, and you rearrange them in different sequences. Scramble has a four-by-four tile frame with 15 tiles (see fig. D.5).

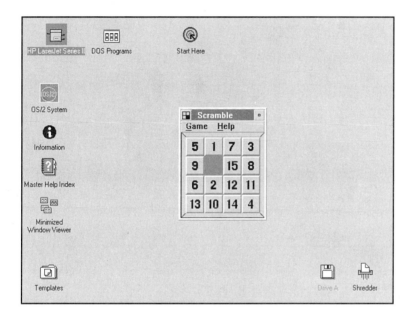

Fig. D.5

Scramble.

Options and Settings

The Open Game option offers three sets of tiles. One set numbers the tiles, another is a picture of cats (similar to the cat in the Cat and Mouse game), and the other is the OS/2 logo image.

You choose Scramble from the Game menu to mix the tiles. You point to the tile you want to slide into the vacant tile position and then click button 1 to make the move.

Klondike Solitaire

OS/2 includes a version of the solitaire card game called Klondike. The object of the game is to place the cards in numerical order according to suits along the right edge of the window. You can build on the central stacks by alternating red and black cards in descending numerical order. Figure D.6 shows a game in progress.

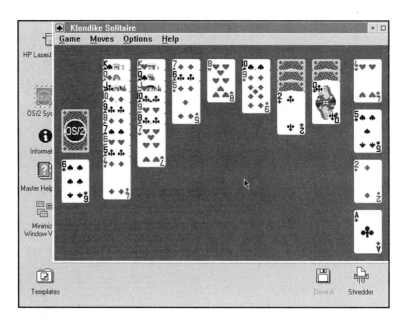

Fig. D.6

Klondike.

Settings and Options

You can make the computer play on its own by choosing the Autoplay option in the Game menu. Other options include turning the sound effects on and off, changing the cards' pictures, and altering the animation speed when the computer moves the cards. You can save and re-store your preferred settings and turn the scoring on and off. When you play the game, you can take back a move, replay a move, or cheat.

OS/2 Files by Function

File	Directory	Function
STARTMRI.DLL	\OS2\DLL	"Start here information," dynamic link library
STHR.EXE	\OS2	"Start here information," executable
8514.DLL	\OS2\DLL	8514 display dynamic link library
8514SYS.FON	\OS2\MDOS\WINOS2\SYSTEM	8514 font for WIN-OS2
8514OEM.FON	\OS2\MDOS\WINOS2\SYSTEM	8514 font for WIN-OS2
F80404.BIO	\OS2	Abios Patch File
F80403.BIO	\OS2	Abios Patch File
F80402.BIO	\OS2	Abios Patch File
F80700.BIO	\OS2	Abios Patch File
W050100.BIO	\OS2	Abios Patch File
F80600.BIO	\OS2	Abios Patch File
F80701.BIO	\OS2	Abios Patch File
W050101.BIO	\OS2	Abios Patch File
W020100.BIO	\OS2	Abios Patch File
W0F0000.BIO	\OS2	Abios Patch File

continues

File	Directory	Function
W060100.BIO	\OS2	Abios Patch File
W050000.BIO	\OS2	Abios Patch File
F80000.BIO	\OS2	Abios Patch File
000000.BIO	\OS2	Abios Patch File
W020101.BIO	\OS2	Abios Patch File
F80100.BIO	\OS2	Abios Patch File
F80702.BIO	\OS2	Abios Patch File
F80200.BIO	\OS2	Abios Patch File
F81000.BIO	\OS2	Abios Patch File
F80D00.BIO	\OS2	Abios Patch File
F80D01.BIO	\OS2	Abios Patch File
F81B00.BIO	\OS2	Abios Patch File
FC0403.BIO	\OS2	Abios Patch File
FC0500.BIO	\OS2	Abios Patch File
F88000.BIO	\OS2	Abios Patch File
FC0400.BIO	\OS2	Abios Patch File
F80903.BIO	\OS2	Abios Patch File
F80902.BIO	\OS2	Abios Patch File
F80A00.BIO	\OS2	Abios Patch File
F80904.BIO	\OS2	Abios Patch File
F80A01.BIO	\OS2	Abios Patch File
F80A02.BIO	\OS2	Abios Patch File
F80C00.BIO	\OS2	Abios Patch File
F80704.BIO	\OS2	Abios Patch File
F80703.BIO	\OS2	Abios Patch File
TOUMOU.BIO	\OS2	Abios patch file for touch devices
EXTDSKDD.SYS	\OS2	Access to an external drive
AHA164X.ADD	\OS2\DRIVERS	Adapter device driver (Adaptec)
AHA174X.ADD	\OS2\DRIVERS	Adapter device driver (Adaptec)

File	Directory	Function
AHA154X.ADD	\OS2\DRIVERS	Adapter device driver (Adaptec)
AHA152X.ADD	\OS2\DRIVERS	Adapter device driver (Adaptec)
FD16-700.ADD	\OS2	Adapter device driver (Future Domain)
FD850IBM.ADD	\OS2	Adapter device driver (Future Domain)
FD8XX.ADD	\OS2	Adapter device driver (Future Domain)
PMATM.DLL	\OS2\DLL	Adobe Type Manager dynamic link library
ATM.INI	\OS2\MDOS\WINOS2	Adobe Type Manager font support
README.ATM	\OS2\MDOS\WINOS2	Adobe Type Manager information
BASICA.COM	\OS2\MDOS	Advanced BASIC language interpreter
PMCHKDSK.EXE	\OS2	Analyze hard disk
PMCHKDSK.DLL	\OS2\DLL	Analyze hard disk dynamic link library
PATCH.EXE	\OS2	Applies fixes/patches to files
FIXWP.EXE	\OS2\MDOS\WINOS2	Apply WordPerfect patch
ASSIGN.COM	\OS2\MDOS	Assigns a drive letter to a different drive
BACKUP.EXE	\OS2	Backup files on hard disk
BKSCALLS.DLL	\OS2\DLL	Base keyboard calls
BMSCALLS.DLL	\OS2\DLL	Base monitor calls
VIOCALLS.DLL	\OS2\DLL	Base video calls dynamic link library
BVH8514A.DLL	\OS2\DLL	Base Video Handler dynamic link library (8514A)
BVHCGA.DLL	\OS2\DLL	Base Video Handler dynamic link library (CGA)

continues

File	Directory	Function
BVHEGA.DLL	\OS2\DLL	Base Video Handler dynamic link library (EGA)
BVHMGA.DLL	\OS2\DLL	Base Video Handler dynamic link library (MGA)
BVHSVGA.DLL	\OS2\DLL	Base Video Handler dynamic link library (SVGA)
BVHVGA.DLL	\OS2\DLL	Base Video Handler dynamic link library (VGA)
BVHXGA.DLL	\OS2\DLL	Base Video Handler dynamic link library (XGA)
BVHINIT.DLL	\OS2\DLL	Base Video Handler Initialization dynamic link library
BVHWNDW.DLL	\OS2\DLL	Base Video Handler window dynamic link library
BVSCALLS.DLL	\OS2\DLL	Base Video System dynamic link library
BASIC.COM	\OS2\MDOS	BASIC language interpreter
KBDBE.DLL	\OS2\MDOS\WINOS2\SYSTEM	Belgian keyboard dynamic link library
BDCALLS.DLL	\OS2\DLL	Bidirectional support dynamic link library
BDBVH.DLL	\OS2\DLL	Bidirectional support dynamic link library
BDKBDM.EXE	\OS2\SYSTEM	Bidirectional support for keyboard
BDPRTM.EXE	\OS2\SYSTEM	Bidirectional support for printing
SWAN.BGA	\OS2\BITMAP	Bitmap of a swan for 8514 displays
SETBOOT.EXE	\OS2	Boot Manager for a hard disks
KBDUK.DLL	\OS2\MDOS\WINOS2\SYSTEM	British keyboard dynamic link library
CACHE.EXE	\OS2	Caching program for HPFS file systems

File	Directory	Function
MORTGAGE.BAS	\OS2\MDOS	Calculates mortgages
CALIBRAT.DAT	\OS2	Calibrate touch screens data
CALIBRAT.EXE	\OS2	Calibration program for touchscreens
CALIBRAT.TXT	\OS2	Information displayed while calibrating
KBDCA.DLL	\OS2\MDOS\WINOS2\SYSTEM	Canadian keyboard dynamic link library
NEKO.EXE	\OS2\APPS	Cat and Mouse applet
NEKO.DLL	\OS2\APPS\DLL	Cat and Mouse applet dynamic link library
NEKO.HLP	\OS2\HELP	Cat and Mouse applet help
CDROM.SYS	\OS2	CD-ROM device driver
CDFS.IFS	\OS2	CD-ROM installable file system
UCDFS.DLL	\OS2\DLL	CD-ROM utilities dynamic link library
UCDFS.MSG	\OS2\SYSTEM	CD-ROM utilities message file
CGA.DLL	\OS2\DLL	CGA display dynamic link library
CGA.RC	\OS2	CGA resource file used to create OS2.INI
FSACCESS.EXE	\OS2\MDOS	Change access to the OS/2 file system from specific-version DOS sessions
OS2CHESS.BIN	\OS2\APPS	Chess applet
OS2CHESS.EXE	\OS2\APPS	Chess applet
CHESSAI.DLL	\OS2\APPS\DLL	Chess applet dynamic link library
OS2CHESS.HLP	\OS2\HELP	Chess applet help
CLIPVIEW.HLP	\OS2\HELP	Clipboard help file
CLIPOS2.EXE	\OS2\APPS	Clipboard program executable

continues

File	Directory	Function
CLOCK01.SYS	\OS2	Clock device driver for family 1 machines (NON-MCA)
CLOCK02.SYS	\OS2	Clock device driver for family 2 machines
XLAT850.BIN	\OS2\MDOS\WINOS2\SYSTEM	Code page 850 for WIN-OS2
XLAT860.BIN	\OS2\MDOS\WINOS2\SYSTEM	Code page 860 for WIN-OS2
XLAT861.BIN	\OS2\MDOS\WINOS2\SYSTEM	Code page 861 for WIN-OS2
XLAT863.BIN	\OS2\MDOS\WINOS2\SYSTEM	Code page 863 for WIN-OS2
XLAT865.BIN	\OS2\MDOS\WINOS2\SYSTEM	Code page 865 for WIN-OS2
CMDREF.INF	\OS2\BOOK	Command reference help file
DISKCOMP.COM	\OS2	Compare contents of two disks
TESTCFG.SYS	\OS2	Configuration device driver
4202L.CFG	\OS2\SYSTEM	Configuration file for bidirectional support
4201.CFG	\OS2\SYSTEM	Configuration file for bidirectional support
4019.CFG	\OS2\SYSTEM	Configuration file for bidirectional support
5204.CFG	\OS2\SYSTEM	Configuration file for bidirectional support
4019L.CFG	\OS2\SYSTEM	Configuration file for bidirectional support
5204L.CFG	\OS2\SYSTEM	Configuration file for bidirectional support
4216L.CFG	\OS2\SYSTEM	Configuration file for bidirectional support
4207.CFG	\OS2\SYSTEM	Configuration file for bidirectional support
5202-QL.CFG	\OS2\SYSTEM	Configuration file for bidirectional support
5201L.CFG	\OS2\SYSTEM	Configuration file for bidirectional support
5201.CFG	\OS2\SYSTEM	Configuration file for bidirectional support

File	Directory	Function
4216.CFG	\OS2\SYSTEM	Configuration file for bidirectional support
5202-Q.CFG	\OS2\SYSTEM	Configuration file for bidirectional support
4208.CFG	\OS2\SYSTEM	Configuration file for bidirectional support
4208L.CFG	\OS2\SYSTEM	Configuration file for bidirectional support
5202.CFG	\OS2\SYSTEM	Configuration file for bidirectional support
4202.CFG	\OS2\SYSTEM	Configuration file for bidirectional support
5202L.CFG	\OS2\SYSTEM	Configuration file for bidirectional support
README	\	Contains latest release information about OS/2
VIOTBL.DCP	\OS2	Contains video mappings for all characters
CONVERT.EXE	\OS2	Convert OS/2 1.x applications to 2.0
MOVESPL.EXE	\OS2	Converts OS/2 1.0 apps to 2.x apps
DISKCOPY.COM	\OS2	Copies contents of one disk to another
XCOPY.EXE	\OS2	Copies groups of files including subdirectories
COURIER.EGA	\OS2\DLL	Courier bitmap font
COURIER.PSF	\OS2\DLL	Courier postscript font
CREATEDD.EXE	\OS2	Create a dump disk for use with the Stand-alone Dump procedure
LABEL.COM	\OS2	Creates or changes a volume label
KBDDA.DLL	\OS2\MDOS\WINOS2\SYSTEM	Danish keyboard dynamic link library
DATABASE.DAT	\OS2\INSTALL	Database data file used in migrating applications to 2.1

continues

File	Directory	Function
DBTAGS.DAT	\OS2\INSTALL	Database data file used in migrating applications to 2.1
DATABASE.TXT	\OS2\INSTALL	Database text file used in migrating applications to 2.1
UNPACK.EXE	\OS2	Decompression program
CLEANUP.EXE	\OS2\INSTALL	Deletes extraneous files after installation
VTBL850.DCP	\OS2	Description profile table for code page 850
NOMOUSE.DRV	\OS2\MDOS\WINOS2\SYSTEM	Device driver for WIN-OS2 indicating no mouse is attached to the system
DDINSTAL.EXE	\OS2\INSTALL	Device Driver Installation program executable
DDINSTAL.HLP	\OS2\HELP	Device Driver Installation program help
FSFILTER.SYS	\OS2\MDOS	Device driver that provides access to OS/2 disk partitions when running a specific version of DOS
VXMS.SYS	\OS2\MDOS	Device driver that provides extended memory specification from DOS sessions
HIMEM.SYS	\OS2\MDOS	Device driver that provides high memory support in DOS
DOS.SYS	\OS2\DLL	Device driver used to bring up DOS sessions
IBM2ADSK.ADD	\OS2	Device support for non-SCSI disk drives on MCA machines
DIGITAL.FON	\OS2\MDOS\WINOS2	Digital font for WIN-OS2
DISPLAY.DLL	\OS2\DLL	Display dynamic link library
TREE.COM	\OS2	Displays all the directory paths found on specified drive

File	Directory	Function
TRACEFMT.EXE	\OS2	Displays formatted trace records
TRACEFMT.HLP	\OS2\HELP	Displays formatted trace records help
HARDERR.EXE	\OS2	Displays hard error messages
VIEW.EXE	\OS2	Displays on-line documents created with IPF
VIEWDOC.EXE	\OS2	Displays on-line documents created with IPF
SYSLEVEL.EXE	\OS2	Displays operating system service level
SYSLEVEL.GRE	\OS2\INSTALL	Displays operating system service level for graphics engine
SYSLEVEL.OS2	\OS2\INSTALL	Displays operating system service level for OS/2
MORE.COM	\OS2	Displays output one screen at a time
PICVIEW.EXE	\OS2\APPS	Displays picture files
PICVIEW.HLP	\OS2\HELP	Displays picture files—help
PSTAT.EXE	\OS2	Displays process, thread, system semaphore, shared memory, and dynamic link library information
MEM.EXE	\OS2\MDOS	Displays the amount of used and free memory in DOS sessions
DOSCALL1.DLL	\OS2\DLL	DLL that contains entry points for base operating system
DOSRFICO.DLL	\OS2\DLL	DLL to refresh icons used during install
DRAG.DLL	\OS2\DLL	DLL used by Presentation Manager to allow drag/drop
DOSKRNL	\OS2\MDOS	DOS

continues

File	Directory	Function
GRAFTABL.COM	\OS2\MDOS	DOS command to load a table of characters into memory for graphics mode
EDLIN.COM	\OS2\MDOS	DOS line editor
COMDD.SYS	\OS2\MDOS	DOS serial port device driver
DEBUG.EXE	\OS2\MDOS	DOS system debugger
KBDNE.DLL	\OS2\MDOS\WINOS2\SYSTEM	Dutch keyboard dynamic link library
EGA.DLL	\OS2\DLL	EGA display dynamic link library
EGA40WOA.FON	\OS2\MDOS\WINOS2\SYSTEM	EGA font for WIN-OS2
EGAFIX.FON	\OS2\MDOS\WINOS2\SYSTEM	EGA font for WIN-OS2
EGAOEM.FON	\OS2\MDOS\WINOS2\SYSTEM	EGA font for WIN-OS2
EGA80WOA.FON	\OS2\MDOS\WINOS2\SYSTEM	EGA font for WIN-OS2
EGASYS.FON	\OS2\MDOS\WINOS2\SYSTEM	EGA font for WIN-OS2
EGA.RC	\OS2	EGA resource file used to create OS2.INI
EMM386.SYS	\OS2\MDOS	Enables extended memory support in DOS
EGA.SYS	\OS2\MDOS	Enhanced graphics support
DRAW.EX	\OS2\APPS	Enhanced PM Editor
EPMHELP.QHL	\OS2\APPS	Enhanced PM Editor
EPM.EX	\OS2\APPS	Enhanced PM Editor
E3EMUL.EX	\OS2\APPS	Enhanced PM Editor
GET.EX	\OS2\APPS	Enhanced PM Editor applet
BOX.EX	\OS2\APPS	Enhanced PM Editor applet
EXTRA.EX	\OS2\APPS	Enhanced PM Editor applet
PUT.EX	\OS2\APPS	Enhanced PM Editor applet

File	Directory	Function
ETKE550.DLL	\OS2\APPS\DLL	Enhanced PM Editor dynamic link library
ETKR550.DLL	\OS2\APPS\DLL	Enhanced PM Editor dynamic link library
ETKTHNK.DLL	\OS2\APPS\DLL	Enhanced PM Editor dynamic link library
EPM.EXE	\OS2\APPS	Enhanced PM Editor executable
EPMLEX.EX	\OS2\APPS	Enhanced PM Editor executable
EPM.HLP	\OS2\HELP	Enhanced PM Editor help
HELPMGR.DLL	\OS2\DLL	Entry points into the help manager
NPXEMLTR.DLL	\OS2\DLL	Entry points to convert floating point values
EAUTIL.EXE	\OS2	Extended attributes
ANSICALL.DLL	\OS2\DLL	Extended display and keyboard support dynamic link library
ANSI.SYS	\OS2\MDOS	Extended display and keyboard support in the DOS environment
ANSI.EXE	\OS2	Extended display and keyboard support in the OS/2 environment
FDISKPM.EXE	\OS2	FDISK program
FDISKPM.DLL	\OS2\DLL	FDISK program dynamic link library
FDISKPMH.HLP	\OS2\HELP	FDISK program help
COMP.COM	\OS2	File compare program
COUNTRY.SYS	\OS2	File containing specific country information
MISC.FON	\OS2\DLL	File that contains system fonts
EA DATA.SF	\	File that holds all extended attributes in system

continues

File	Directory	Function
DRVMAP.INF	\OS2\MDOS\WINOS2\SYSTEM	File that maps WIN-OS2 printer drivers to OS/2 printer drivers
FIND.EXE	\OS2	Find a string of text in file(s)
KBDFI.DLL	\OS2\MDOS\WINOS2\SYSTEM	Finish keyboard dynamic link library
FFIX.EXE	\OS2\MDOS	Fix for DOS touch and find first APIs
SQ4FIX.COM	\OS2\MDOS	Fix for Space Quest 4 game by Sierra
SYSFONT.DLL	\OS2\DLL	Font dynamic link library
8514FIX.FON	\OS2\MDOS\WINOS2\SYSTEM	Font file for 8514 displays
CARDSYM.FON	\OS2\APPS	Font file for Solitaire Application
SCRIPT.FON	\OS2\MDOS\WINOS2\SYSTEM	Font for WIN-OS2
FORMAT.COM	\OS2	Format a disk
PMFORMAT.EXE	\OS2	Format a disk
PMFORMAT.DLL	\OS2\DLL	Format a disk dynamic link library
KBDFR.DLL	\OS2\MDOS\WINOS2\SYSTEM	French keyboard dynamic link library
FDISK.COM	\OS2	Full-screen FDISK
FKA.DLL	\OS2\DLL	Function key area dynamic link library
OS2DASD.DMD	\OS2	General purpose device support for disk drives
OS2SCSI.DMD	\OS2	General purpose device support for non-SCSI disk devices
IBM1FLPY.ADD	\OS2	Generic disk device driver for family 1 machines (NON-MCA)
IBM2FLPY.ADD	\OS2	Generic disk device driver for family 2 machines
IBM2SCSI.ADD	\OS2	Generic SCSI device driver for family 2 machines

File	Directory	Function
IBM1S506.ADD	\OS2	Generic support for non-SCSI disk drives on non-MCA machines
KBDGR.DLL	\OS2\MDOS\WINOS2\SYSTEM	German keyboard dynamic link library
CHKDSK.COM	\OS2	Gives you information about your disk
GDI.EXE	\OS2\MDOS\WINOS2\SYSTEM	Graphics device interface for WIN-OS2
HELP.BAT	\OS2\MDOS	Help batch file for DOS
HELP.CMD	\OS2	Help batch file for OS/2
HELP.EX	\OS2\APPS	Help for Enhanced PM Editor
VIEWH.HLP	\OS2\HELP	Help for viewing on-line documentation
HPMGRMRI.DLL	\OS2\DLL	Help manager—"translatable strings" dynamic link library
HMHELP.HLP	\OS2\HELP	Help manager help file
HELV.BMP	\OS2\DLL	Helvetica font
HELVETIC.PSF	\OS2\DLL	Helvetica postscript font
HPFS.IFS	\OS2	High performance installable file system
UHPFS.DLL	\OS2\DLL	HPFS utilities dynamic link library
IBMINT13.I13	\OS2\	IBM generic interrupt 13 device driver
KBDIC.DLL	\OS2\MDOS\WINOS2\SYSTEM	Icelandic keyboard dynamic link library
ICONEDIT.EXE	\OS2\APPS	Icon Editor
ICONEDIT.HLP	\OS2\HELP	Icon Editor help
IMP.DLL	\OS2\DLL	Imports dynamic link library
INSTAID.CNF	\OS2\INSTALL	Installation Aid configuration file

continues

File	Directory	Function
INACALL.DLL	\OS2\DLL	Installation Aid dynamic link library
STXTDMPC.DLL	\OS2\DLL	Installation Aid dynamic link library
CPISPFPC.DLL	\OS2\DLL	Installation Aid dynamic link library
DTM.DLL	\OS2\DLL	Installation Aid dynamic link library
DMPC.EXE	\OS2\INSTALL	Installation Aid file used to create EZVU panels
INSTAID.LIB	\OS2\INSTALL	Installation Aid librbary
ISPD.MSG	\OS2\INSTALL	Installation Aid message file
ISPM.MSG	\OS2\INSTALL	Installation Aid message file
INSTAID.PRO	\OS2\INSTALL	Installation Aid profile file
INSTAIDE.EXE	\OS2\INSTALL	Installation Aid program executable
INSTAID.EXE	\OS2\INSTALL	Installation Aid program executable
INSTALL.INI	\OS2\INSTALL	Installation program configuration file
INSTALL.EXE	\OS2\INSTALL	Installation program executable
INSTALL.HLP	\OS2\HELP	Installation program's help
INSTSHEL.EXE	\OS2\INSTALL	Installation program's shell
KBDIT.DLL	\OS2\MDOS\WINOS2\SYSTEM	Italian keyboard dynamic link library
JIGSAW.EXE	\OS2\APPS	Jigsaw applet (Puzzle)
JIGSAW.HLP	\OS2\HELP	Jigsaw applet (Puzzle) help
KBD01.SYS	\OS2	Keyboard device driver for family 1 machines (Non Microchannel)
KBD02.SYS	\OS2	Keyboard device driver for family 2 machines
KEYBOARD.DRV	\OS2\MDOS\WINOS2\SYSTEM	Keyboard device driver for WIN-OS2

File	Directory	Function
KEYBOARD.DCP	\OS2	Keyboard layout table for translating keystrokes into characters of each code page supported by the system
KBDCALLS.DLL	\OS2\DLL	Keyboards calls dynamic link library
KBDLA.DLL	\OS2\MDOS\WINOS2\SYSTEM	Latin keyboard dynamic link library
STARTLW.DLL	\OS2\DLL	Lazy writer dynamic link library
DOSCALLS.LIB	\OS2	Library containing entry points for 1.x programs
LIGHTHOU.VGA	\OS2\BITMAP	Lighthouse bitmap for VGA displays
ABIOS.SYS	\OS2	List of all applicable abios patch files
AAAAA.EXE	\OS2\BITMAP	Lists OS/2 developers' names
JOIN.EXE	\OS2\MDOS	Logically connects a drive to a directory
MINXOBJ.DLL	\OS2\DLL	Master help index dynamic link library
MINXMRI.DLL	\OS2\DLL	Master help index dynamic link library
MSG.DLL	\OS2\DLL	Message dynamic link library
HELPMSG.EXE	\OS2	Message file to obtain help on system messages
DEV002.MSG	\OS2\SYSTEM	Message file used by CD-ROM file system
AAAAA.MET	\OS2\BITMAP	Metafile that has the background picture
MSNET.DRV	\OS2\MDOS\WINOS2\SYSTEM	Microsoft network device driver for WIN-OS2
MIGRATE.EXE	\OS2\INSTALL	Migrates applications to OS/2 2.1
MIGRATE.HLP	\OS2\HELP	Migrates applications to OS/2 2.1 help

continues

File	Directory	Function
PARSEDB.EXE	\OS2\INSTALL	Migration database
OS2BOOT	\	Mini-operating system for booting other operating systems
MONCALLS.DLL	\OS2\DLL	Monitor calls dynamic link library
SYSMONO.FON	\OS2\DLL	Monochrome bitmap font
MOUCALLS.DLL	\OS2\DLL	Mouse calls dynamic link library
MOUSE.COM	\OS2\MDOS	Mouse device driver for DOS
PDITOU01.SYS	\OS2	Mouse device driver for family 1 machines (Non Microchannel)
PDITOU02.SYS	\OS2	Mouse device driver for family 2 machines
PCLOGIC.SYS	\OS2	Mouse device driver for PCLogic type pointing devices
MOUSE.DRV	\OS2\MDOS\WINOS2\SYSTEM	Mouse device driver for WIN-OS2
POINTDD.SYS	\OS2	Mouse pointer draw support
NAMPIPES.DLL	\OS2\DLL	Named Pipes dynamic link library
NLS.DLL	\OS2\DLL	National language support dynamic link library
NWIAPI.DLL	\OS2\DLL	Network API's dynamic link library
KBDNO.DLL	\OS2\MDOS\WINOS2\SYSTEM	Norwegian keyboard dynamic link library
KBDOLI.DRV	\OS2\MDOS\WINOS2\SYSTEM	Olivetti keyboard dynamic link library
SETCOM40.EXE	\OS2\MDOS	OS/2 1.1, 1.2, 1.3 compatibility file
LINK386.EXE	\OS2	OS/2 386 linker
OS2CHAR.DLL	\OS2\DLL	OS/2 character dynamic link library

File	Directory	Function
CMD.EXE	\OS2	OS/2 command interpreter
CONFIG.SYS	\	OS/2 configuration file
OS2KRNLI	\	OS/2 kernel
LINK.EXE	\OS2	OS/2 linker
OS2LDR	\	OS/2 loader
OS2LDR.MSG	\	OS/2 loader message file
LOGDAEM.EXE	\OS2\SYSTEM	OS/2 logging facility
OS2LOGO.BMP	\OS2\BITMAP	OS/2 logo bitmap
OS2SM.DLL	\OS2\DLL	OS/2 session manager dynamic link library
LPTDD.SYS	\OS2\MDOS	Parallel port device driver for DOS
PMPIC.DLL	\OS2\DLL	Picture dynamic link library
PICVIEW.DLL	\OS2\APPS\DLL	Picture viewer dynamic link library
PICV.DLL	\OS2\DLL	Picture viewer dynamic link library
PLASMA.DRV	\OS2\MDOS\WINOS2\SYSTEM	Plasma display device driver for WIN-OS2
BUTTON.DLL	\OS2\DLL	PM button control dynamic link library
PMCTLS.DLL	\OS2\DLL	PM controls dynamic link library
PMSDMRI.DLL	\OS2\DLL	PM CUA control dynamic link library
PMDRAG.DLL	\OS2\DLL	PM drag/drop dynamic link library
PMWIN.DLL	\OS2\DLL	PM dynamic link library
PMGRE.DLL	\OS2\DLL	PM graphics engine dynamic link library
PMGPI.DLL	\OS2\DLL	PM graphics programming interface dynamic link library
PMBIND.DLL	\OS2\DLL	PM Language Binding dynamic link library

continues

File	Directory	Function
PMMLE.DLL	\OS2\DLL	PM Multiline Edit dynamic link library
SELECT.DLL	\OS2\DLL	PM Selection Control dynamic link library
PMSETUP.INF	\OS2	PM setup information used for installing printer drivers
PMSHELL.EXE	\OS2	PM Shell
PMSHAPIM.DLL	\OS2\DLL	PM Shell dynamic link library
PMSHAPI.DLL	\OS2\DLL	PM Shell dynamic link library
PMTKT.DLL	\OS2\DLL	PM Shell dynamic link library
PMSHLTKT.DLL	\OS2\DLL	PM Shell dynamic link library
PMSHELL.DLL	\OS2\DLL	PM Shell dynamic link library
PMVIOP.DLL	\OS2\DLL	PM dynamic link library
PMVDMP.DLL	\OS2\DLL	PM virtual DOS machine private dynamic link library
FASHION.GRF	\OS2\APPS	PM Chart applet
MGXLIB.DLL	\OS2\APPS\DLL	PM Chart applet
GREEN.GRF	\OS2\APPS	PM Chart applet
FASHION.DAT	\OS2\APPS	PM Chart applet
MGXVBM.DLL	\OS2\APPS\DLL	PM Chart applet
PMFID.DLL	\OS2\APPS\DLL	PM Chart applet
INVEST.GRF	\OS2\APPS	PM Chart applet
PMCHART.EXE	\OS2\APPS	PM Chart applet
PMCHART.HLP	\OS2\HELP	PM Chart applet
INVEST.DAT	\OS2\APPS	PM Chart applet
GREEN.DAT	\OS2\APPS	PM Chart applet
PMDMONTH.EXE	\OS2\APPS	PM Diary applet
PMDNOTE.EXE	\OS2\APPS	PM Diary applet

File	Directory	Function
PMSTICKY.EXE	\OS2\APPS	PM Diary applet
PMSTICKD.DLL	\OS2\APPS\DLL	PM Diary applet
PMDALARM.EXE	\OS2\APPS	PM Diary applet
PMDDARC.EXE	\OS2\APPS	PM Diary applet
PMDIARYF.DLL	\OS2\APPS\DLL	PM Diary applet
PMDIARY.DLL	\OS2\APPS\DLL	PM Diary applet
PMDCALEN.EXE	\OS2\APPS	PM Diary applet
PMDIARY.HLP	\OS2\HELP	PM Diary applet
PMDCALC.EXE	\OS2\APPS	PM Diary applet
PMMBASE.EXE	\OS2\APPS	PM Diary applet
PMDTODO.EXE	\OS2\APPS	PM Diary applet
PMDDIARY.EXE	\OS2\APPS	PM Diary applet
PMDLIST.EXE	\OS2\APPS	PM Diary applet
PMDTARC.EXE	\OS2\APPS	PM Diary applet
PMDIARY.$$A	\OS2\APPS	PM Diary applet
PMSPREAD.EXE	\OS2\APPS	PM Diary applet (Spread-sheet)
PMDCTLS.DLL	\OS2\APPS\DLL	PM Diary Controls dynamic link library
PMDD.SYS	\OS2	Pointer draw support for OS/2 sessions
MOUSE.SYS	\OS2	Pointing device
KBDPO.DLL	\OS2\MDOS\WINOS2\SYSTEM	Polish keyboard dynamic link library
PARALLEL.PDR	\OS2\DLL	Port driver for parallel port (LPT)
SERIAL.PDR	\OS2\DLL	Port driver for serial ports (COM)
PSCRIPT.SEP	\OS2	PostScript separator file
PMPRINT.QPR	\OS2\DLL	Print queue processor
PRINT01.SYS	\OS2	Printer device driver from family 1 machines (NON-MCA)

continues

File	Directory	Function
PRINT02.SYS	\OS2	Printer device driver from family 2 machines
PRINT.COM	\OS2	Prints files to default printer
QBASIC.EXE	\OS2\MDOS	QuickBasic program
QBASIC.HLP	\OS2\MDOS	QuickBasic program help
DOSKEY.COM	\OS2\MDOS	Recalls DOS commands, edits command lines, and creates macros
MAKEINI.EXE	\OS2	Recover user and SYSTEM.INI files
RECOVER.COM	\OS2	Recovers files from a disk that contains defective sectors
SPOOL.EXE	\OS2	Redirects printer output from one device to another
RIPLINST.EXE	\OS2\INSTALL	Remote IPL installation program
RIPLINST.HLP	\OS2\HELP	Remote IPL installation program help
UNFIXWP.EXE	\OS2\MDOS\WINOS2	Remove WordPerfect patch for FIXWP.EXE
REPLACE.EXE	\OS2	Replaces files from one drive to another drive
KEYB.COM	\OS2	Replaces the current keyboard layout
RCPP.EXE	\OS2	Resource compiler
RCPP.ERR	\OS2	Resource compiler
RC.EXE	\OS2	Resource compiler
OS2_13.RC	\OS2	Resource file used to create the 1.3 "look/feel"
OS2_20.RC	\OS2	Resource file used to create the 2.0 "look/feel"
8514M.RC	\OS2	Resource file used in creating OS2.INI file for monochrome 8514 display

File	Directory	Function
VGA.RC	\OS2	Resource file used in creating OS2.INI for VGA displays
8514.RC	\OS2	Resource file used in the creation of the OS2.INI file
UPINI.RC	\OS2	Resource file used in updating 1.0 programs to 2.x
INI.RC	\OS2	Resource file used to create OS2.INI
XGA.RC	\OS2	Resource file used to create OS2.INI file for XGA displays
PLASMA.RC	\OS2	Resource file used to create OS2.INI for plasma displays
INISYS.RC	\OS2	Resource file used to create OS2SYS.INI
WIN_30.RC	\OS2	Resource file used to create the Windows 3.0 "look/feel"
RSPDDI.EXE	\OS2\INSTALL	Response file device driver installation program
SAMPLE.RSP	\OS2\INSTALL	Response file for response file installations
RSPINST.EXE	\OS2\INSTALL	Response file installation program
RSPMIG.EXE	\OS2\INSTALL	Response file migration program
RESTORE.EXE	\OS2	Restores backed-up files from one disk to another
REVERSI.EXE	\OS2\APPS	Reversi applet
REVERSI.HLP	\OS2\HELP	Reversi applet help
REXXAPI.DLL	\OS2\DLL	REXX API dynamic link library
REXXTRY.CMD	\OS2	REXX command file
REXX.INF	\OS2\BOOK	REXX documentation

continues

File	Directory	Function
REXX.DLL	\OS2\DLL	REXX dynamic link library
REXH.MSG	\OS2\SYSTEM	REXX help message file
REXXINIT.DLL	\OS2\DLL	REXX initialization dynamic link library
RXSUBCOM.EXE	\OS2	REXX language executable
RXQUEUE.EXE	\OS2	REXX language executable
PMREXX.EXE	\OS2	REXX language interpreter
PMREXX.DLL	\OS2\DLL	REXX language interpreter DLL
PMREXX.HLP	\OS2\HELP	REXX language interpreter help
REX.MSG	\OS2\SYSTEM	REXX message file
REXXUTIL.DLL	\OS2\DLL	REXX utilities dynamic link library
SVGA.EXE	\OS2	Run Super VGA in DOS mode
SCRAMBLE.EXE	\OS2\APPS	Scramble applet
SCRCATS.DLL	\OS2\APPS\DLL	Scramble applet dynamic link library
SCRLOGO.DLL	\OS2\APPS\DLL	Scramble applet dynamic link library
SCRAMBLE.DLL	\OS2\APPS\DLL	Scramble applet dynamic link library
SCRAMBLE.HLP	\OS2\HELP	Scramble applet help
SCREEN01.SYS	\OS2	Screen device driver for family 1 machines
SCREEN02.SYS	\OS2	Screen device driver for family 2 machines
PMSEEK.EXE	\OS2\APPS	Searches one or more disks for files or text
PMSEEK.DLL	\OS2\APPS\DLL	Searches one or more disks for files or text (DLL)
PMSEEK.HLP	\OS2\HELP	Searches one or more disks for files or text help
TRACE.EXE	\OS2	Selects or sets the system trace
SAMPLE.SEP	\OS2	Separator file

File	Directory	Function
COM.SYS	\OS2	Serial port device driver
SESMGR.DLL	\OS2\DLL	Session manager dynamic link library
APPEND.EXE	\OS2\MDOS	Sets a search path for data files that are outside the current directory
MODE.COM	\OS2	Sets the operation modes for devices
SHPIINST.DLL	\OS2\DLL	Shell installation file
PULSE.EXE	\OS2\APPS	Show CPU usage
PULSE.HLP	\OS2\HELP	Show CPU usage (help)
KLONDIKE.EXE	\OS2\APPS	Solitaire applet
KLONBGA.DLL	\OS2\APPS\DLL	Solitaire applet dynamic link library
KLONDIKE.HLP	\OS2\HELP	Solitaire applet help
SORT.EXE	\OS2	Sorts files
SOUND.DRV	\OS2\MDOS\WINOS2\SYSTEM	Sound device driver for WIN-OS2
KBDSP.DLL	\OS2\MDOS\WINOS2\SYSTEM	Spanish keyboard dynamic link library
SPL1B.DLL	\OS2\DLL	Spooler dynamic link library
PMSPL.DLL	\OS2\DLL	Spooler dynamic link library
SPOOLCP.DLL	\OS2\DLL	Spooler dynamic link library
SPLH.MSG	\OS2\SYSTEM	Spooler help message file
SPL.MSG	\OS2\SYSTEM	Spooler message file
START.HLP	\OS2\HELP	Start programs automatically help
SUBST.EXE	\OS2\MDOS	Substitutes a drive letter for another drive and path
KBDSW.DLL	\OS2\MDOS\WINOS2\SYSTEM	Swedish keyboard dynamic link library
KBDSF.DLL	\OS2\MDOS\WINOS2\SYSTEM	Swiss French keyboard dynamic link library

continues

File	Directory	Function
KBDSG.DLL	\OS2\MDOS\WINOS2\SYSTEM	Swiss German keyboard dynamic link library
BOOT.COM	\OS2	Switch between DOS and OS/2 operating systems that are on the same hard disk (drive C)
E.EXE	\OS2	System Editor
EHXHP.HLP	\OS2\HELP	System Editor dynamic link library
EHXDLMRI.DLL	\OS2\DLL	System Editor dynamic link library
SYSLOGH.HLP	\OS2\HELP	System error log help
LOG.SYS	\OS2	System error logging using the SYSLOG utility program
SYSLOG.DLL	\OS2\DLL	System error-log dynamic link library
SYSLOGPM.EXE	\OS2	System error-log viewer
SYSLOG.EXE	\OS2	System error-log viewer
OSO001.MSG	\OS2\SYSTEM	System message file
OSO001H.MSG	\OS2\SYSTEM	System message help file
SOM.DLL	\OS2\DLL	System Object Module dynamic link library
QUECALLS.DLL	\OS2\DLL	System queue calls dynamic link library
VTTERM.HLP	\OS2\HELP	Terminal emulation applet
SACDI.DLL	\OS2\APPS\DLL	Terminal emulation applet
SASYNCDA.SYS	\OS2\APPS	Terminal emulation applet
SACDI.MSG	\OS2\SYSTEM	Terminal emulation applet
SOFTERM.EXE	\OS2\APPS	Terminal emulation applet
SOFTERM.HLP	\OS2\HELP	Terminal emulation applet
OCSHELL.DLL	\OS2\APPS\DLL	Terminal emulation applet
OVM.DLL	\OS2\APPS\DLL	Terminal emulation applet
OTTY.DLL	\OS2\APPS\DLL	Terminal emulation applet

File	Directory	Function
OVT.DLL	\OS2\APPS\DLL	Terminal emulation applet
SASYNCDB.SYS	\OS2\APPS	Terminal emulation applet
XRM.HLP	\OS2\HELP	Terminal emulation applet
TTY.HLP	\OS2\HELP	Terminal emulation applet
OFMTC.DLL	\OS2\APPS\DLL	Terminal emulation applet
OCHAR.DLL	\OS2\APPS\DLL	Terminal emulation applet
OKERMIT.DLL	\OS2\APPS\DLL	Terminal emulation applet
OCOLOR.DLL	\OS2\APPS\DLL	Terminal emulation applet
OIBM1X.DLL	\OS2\APPS\DLL	Terminal emulation applet
OCM.DLL	\OS2\APPS\DLL	Terminal emulation applet
OKB.DLL	\OS2\APPS\DLL	Terminal emulation applet
OMCT.DLL	\OS2\APPS\DLL	Terminal emulation applet
ODBM.DLL	\OS2\APPS\DLL	Terminal emulation applet
SAREXEC.DLL	\OS2\APPS\DLL	Terminal emulation applet
OKBC.DLL	\OS2\APPS\DLL	Terminal emulation applet
OIBM2X.DLL	\OS2\APPS\DLL	Terminal emulation applet
OLPTIO.DLL	\OS2\APPS\DLL	Terminal emulation applet
CTLSACDI.DLL	\OS2\APPS\DLL	Terminal emulation applet
ACDISIO.HLP	\OS2\HELP	Terminal emulation applet
IBM31012.HLP	\OS2\HELP	Terminal emulation applet
CUSTOM.MDB	\OS2\APPS	Terminal emulation applet
ACSACDI.DAT	\OS2\APPS	Terminal emulation applet
CTLSACDI.EXE	\OS2\APPS	Terminal emulation applet
OANSI.DLL	\OS2\APPS\DLL	Terminal emulation applet
OACDISIO.DLL	\OS2\APPS\DLL	Terminal emulation applet
OANSI364.DLL	\OS2\APPS\DLL	Terminal emulation applet
IBMSIO.HLP	\OS2\HELP	Terminal emulation applet
OSOFT.DLL	\OS2\APPS\DLL	Terminal emulation applet
IBM31011.HLP	\OS2\HELP	Terminal emulation applet
ANSI364.HLP	\OS2\HELP	Terminal emulation applet

continues

File	Directory	Function
OSIO.DLL	\OS2\APPS\DLL	Terminal emulation applet
OPM.DLL	\OS2\APPS\DLL	Terminal emulation applet
OPCF.DLL	\OS2\APPS\DLL	Terminal emulation applet
OVIO.DLL	\OS2\APPS\DLL	Terminal emulation applet
OTEK.DLL	\OS2\APPS\DLL	Terminal emulation applet
OSCH.DLL	\OS2\APPS\DLL	Terminal emulation applet
OMRKCPY.DLL	\OS2\APPS\DLL	Terminal emulation applet
OXMODEM.DLL	\OS2\APPS\DLL	Terminal emulation applet
ANSIIBM.HLP	\OS2\HELP	Terminal emulation applet
OPROFILE.DLL	\OS2\APPS\DLL	Terminal emulation applet
OXRM.DLL	\OS2\APPS\DLL	Terminal emulation applet
ORSHELL.DLL	\OS2\APPS\DLL	Terminal emulation applet
TIMES.BMP	\OS2\DLL	Times/Roman bitmap font
TIMESNRM.PSF	\OS2\DLL	Times/Roman postscript font
FSGRAPH.DLL	\OS2\DLL	Touch device dynamic link library
TCP.DLL	\OS2\DLL	Touch device dynamic link library
TOUCO21D.BIN	\OS2	Touch device file
TCP.HLP	\OS2\HELP	Touch device help
TDD.MSG	\OS2\SYSTEM	Touch device message file
TDDH.MSG	\OS2\SYSTEM	Touch device message file
TDIH.MSG	\OS2\SYSTEM	Touch device message file
TDI.MSG	\OS2\SYSTEM	Touch device message file
TOUCH.SYS	\OS2	Touch devices—device driver
TOUCALLS.DLL	\OS2\DLL	Touch devices dynamic link library
TOUCH.INI	\OS2	Touch devices ini file
SYSTEM.TFF	\OS2\SYSTEM\TRACE	Trace file
SYSTEM.TDF	\OS2\SYSTEM\TRACE	Trace file

File	Directory	Function
TRACEFMT.DLL	\OS2\DLL	Trace formatter dynamic link library
PMDTUNE.EXE	\OS2\APPS	Tune editor applet
TUTORIAL.EXE	\OS2	Tutorial
ANMT.DLL	\OS2\DLL	Tutorial animation dynamic link library
ANIMAT.AMT	\OS2\HELP	Tutorial animation file
TUT.DLL	\OS2\DLL	Tutorial dynamic link library
TUTMRI.DLL	\OS2\DLL	Tutorial dynamic link library
TUTDLL.DLL	\OS2\DLL	Tutorial dynamic link library
TUTORIAL.HLP	\OS2\HELP\TUTORIAL	Tutorial help
UNDELETE.COM	\OS2	Undeletes files
KBDUS.DLL	\OS2\MDOS\WINOS2\SYSTEM	United States keyboard dynamic link library
KBDDV.DLL	\OS2\MDOS\WINOS2\SYSTEM	US-Dvorak keyboard dynamic link library
KBDUSX.DLL	\OS2\MDOS\WINOS2\SYSTEM	US-International dynamic link library
WINVER.EXE	\OS2\MDOS\WINOS2	Version of WIN-OS2 you are running
SWINVGA.DRV	\OS2\MDOS\WINOS2\SYSTEM	VGA device driver for WIN-OS2
V7VGA.DRV	\OS2\MDOS\WINOS2\SYSTEM	VGA device driver for WIN-OS2
VGA.DRV	\OS2\MDOS\WINOS2\SYSTEM	VGA device driver for WIN-OS2
VGAMONO.DRV	\OS2\MDOS\WINOS2\SYSTEM	VGA device driver for WIN-OS2
VGA.DLL	\OS2\DLL	VGA display dynamic link library
VGA865.FON	\OS2\MDOS\WINOS2\SYSTEM	VGA font for WIN-OS2
VGAFIX.FON	\OS2\MDOS\WINOS2\SYSTEM	VGA font for WIN-OS2
VGA861.FON	\OS2\MDOS\WINOS2\SYSTEM	VGA font for WIN-OS2

continues

File	Directory	Function
VGA863.FON	\OS2\MDOS\WINOS2\SYSTEM	VGA font for WIN-OS2
VGA860.FON	\OS2\MDOS\WINOS2\SYSTEM	VGA font for WIN-OS2
VGAOEM.FON	\OS2\MDOS\WINOS2\SYSTEM	VGA font for WIN-OS2
VGASYS.FON	\OS2\MDOS\WINOS2\SYSTEM	VGA font for WIN-OS2
VGA850.FON	\OS2\MDOS\WINOS2\SYSTEM	VGA font for WIN-OS2
VGAM.RC	\OS2	VGA monochrome resource file
ATTRIB.EXE	\OS2	View/Change attributes of a file
V8514A.SYS	\OS2\MDOS	Virtual 8514A device driver
VBIOS.SYS	\OS2\MDOS	Virtual BIOS device driver
VCDROM.SYS	\OS2\MDOS	Virtual CD-ROM device drive
VCGA.SYS	\OS2\MDOS	Virtual CGA device driver
VCMOS.SYS	\OS2\MDOS	Virtual CMOS device driver
VDMA.SYS	\OS2\MDOS	Virtual direct memory access support device driver
VDSK.SYS	\OS2\MDOS	Virtual disk device driver
VDISK.SYS	\OS2	Virtual disk device driver (Simulated disk)
VDPX.SYS	\OS2\MDOS	Virtual DOS extender for DPMI applications driver
VDMSRVR.EXE	\OS2\MDOS\WINOS2	Virtual DOS machine server for WIN-OS2
VDPMI.SYS	\OS2\MDOS	Virtual DOS protect mode interface device driver
VEGA.SYS	\OS2\MDOS	Virtual EGA device driver
VEMM.SYS	\OS2\MDOS	Virtual expanded memory manager device driver
VFLPY.SYS	\OS2\MDOS	Virtual floppy device driver
VKBD.SYS	\OS2\MDOS	Virtual keyboard device driver

File	Directory	Function
VMDISK.EXE	\OS2\MDOS	Virtual memory disk
VMONO.SYS	\OS2\MDOS	Virtual monochrome device driver
VMOUSE.SYS	\OS2\MDOS	Virtual mouse device driver
VNPX.SYS	\OS2\MDOS	Virtual NPX exulator device driver
VLPT.SYS	\OS2\MDOS	Virtual parallel port device driver
VPIC.SYS	\OS2\MDOS	Virtual picture device driver
VCOM.SYS	\OS2\MDOS	Virtual serial port device driver
VSVGA.SYS	\OS2\MDOS	Virtual SVGA device driver
VTIMER.SYS	\OS2\MDOS	Virtual timer device driver
VTOUCH.SYS	\OS2\MDOS	Virtual touch device driver
VTOUCH.COM	\OS2\MDOS	Virtual touch program (touch screen applications
VVGA.SYS	\OS2\MDOS	Virtual VGA device driver
VXGA.SYS	\OS2\MDOS	Virtual XGA device driver
SF4019.EXE	\OS2\MDOS\WINOS2\SYSTEM	WIN-OS2 4019 printer file
WIN87EM.DLL	\OS2\MDOS\WINOS2\SYSTEM	WIN-OS2 80X87 emulator dynamic link library
8514.DRV	\OS2\MDOS\WINOS2\SYSTEM	WIN-OS2 8514 display device driver
WOS2ACCE.GRP	\OS2\MDOS\WINOS2	WIN-OS2 accessories group
ATM16.DLL	\OS2\MDOS\WINOS2\SYSTEM	WIN-OS2 Adobe type manager 16-bit dynamic link library
ATMCNTRL.EXE	\OS2\MDOS\WINOS2	WIN-OS2 Adobe type manager control file
ATMSYS.DRV	\OS2\MDOS\WINOS2\SYSTEM	WIN-OS2 Adobe type manager device driver
CGA.DRV	\OS2\MDOS\WINOS2\SYSTEM	WIN-OS2 CGA device driver

continues

File	Directory	Function
CGASYS.FON	\OS2\MDOS\WINOS2\SYSTEM	WIN-OS2 CGA font
CGA40WOA.FON	\OS2\MDOS\WINOS2\SYSTEM	WIN-OS2 CGA font
CGAOEM.FON	\OS2\MDOS\WINOS2\SYSTEM	WIN-OS2 CGA font
CGAFIX.FON	\OS2\MDOS\WINOS2\SYSTEM	WIN-OS2 CGA font
CGA80WOA.FON	\OS2\MDOS\WINOS2\SYSTEM	WIN-OS2 CGA font
CLIPBRD.HLP	\OS2\MDOS\WINOS2	WIN-OS2 Clipboard help file
CLIPWOS2.EXE	\OS2\MDOS\WINOS2	WIN-OS2 Clipboard program executable
CLOCK.EXE	\OS2\MDOS\WINOS2	WIN-OS2 clock program executable
COMMAND.COM	\OS2\MDOS	WIN-OS2 command interpreter
CONTROL.EXE	\OS2\MDOS\WINOS2	WIN-OS2 control file
CONTROL.HLP	\OS2\MDOS\WINOS2	WIN-OS2 control program help
CONTROL.INI	\OS2\MDOS\WINOS2	WIN-OS2 control program initialization file
COURF.FON	\OS2\MDOS\WINOS2\SYSTEM	WIN-OS2 Courier font for 8514 displays
COURA.FON	\OS2\MDOS\WINOS2\SYSTEM	WIN-OS2 Courier font for CGA displays
COURB.FON	\OS2\MDOS\WINOS2\SYSTEM	WIN-OS2 Courier font for EGA displays
COURE.FON	\OS2\MDOS\WINOS2\SYSTEM	WIN-OS2 Courier font for VGA displays
COURG.FON	\OS2\MDOS\WINOS2\SYSTEM	WIN-OS2 Courier font for XGA displays
VWIN.SYS	\OS2\MDOS	WIN-OS2 device driver
LANGDUT.DLL	\OS2\MDOS\WINOS2\SYSTEM	WIN-OS2 Dutch language DLL
PMDDE.EXE	\OS2	WIN-OS2 dynamic data exchange program
DDEAGENT.EXE	\OS2\MDOS\WINOS2	WIN-OS2 dynamic data exchange program

File	Directory	Function
EGA.DRV	\OS2\MDOS\WINOS2\SYSTEM	WIN-OS2 EGA display device driver
EGAMONO.DRV	\OS2\MDOS\WINOS2\SYSTEM	WIN-OS2 EGA display device driver
EGAHIBW.DRV	\OS2\MDOS\WINOS2\SYSTEM	WIN-OS2 EGA display device driver
LANGENG.DLL	\OS2\MDOS\WINOS2\SYSTEM	WIN-OS2 English
WINOS2.COM	\OS2\MDOS\WINOS2	WIN-OS2 executable
WIN.COM	\OS2\MDOS\WINOS2	WIN-OS2 executable
LZEXPAND.DLL	\OS2\MDOS\WINOS2\SYSTEM	WIN-OS2 file decompression dynamic link library
LANGFRN.DLL	\OS2\MDOS\WINOS2\SYSTEM	WIN-OS2 French
LANGGER.DLL	\OS2\MDOS\WINOS2\SYSTEM	WIN-OS2 German
WINHELP.EXE	\OS2\MDOS\WINOS2	WIN-OS2 help
WINHELP.HLP	\OS2\MDOS\WINOS2	WIN-OS2 help
HELVF.FON	\OS2\MDOS\WINOS2\SYSTEM	WIN-OS2 Helvetica font for 8514
HELVA.FON	\OS2\MDOS\WINOS2\SYSTEM	WIN-OS2 Helvetica font for CGA
HELVB.FON	\OS2\MDOS\WINOS2\SYSTEM	WIN-OS2 Helvetica font for EGA
HELVE.FON	\OS2\MDOS\WINOS2\SYSTEM	WIN-OS2 Helvetica font for VGA
HELVG.FON	\OS2\MDOS\WINOS2\SYSTEM	WIN-OS2 Helvetica font for XGA
HERCULES.DRV	\OS2\MDOS\WINOS2\SYSTEM	WIN-OS2 Hercules card device driver
WINOS2.ICO	\OS2\MDOS\WINOS2	WIN-OS2 icon
WIN.INI	\OS2\MDOS\WINOS2	WIN-OS2 INI file
KERNEL.EXE	\OS2\MDOS\WINOS2\SYSTEM	WIN-OS2 Kernel
WOS2MAIN.GRP	\OS2\MDOS\WINOS2	WIN-OS2 main group
GOPM.EXE	\OS2\MDOS\WINOS2	WIN-OS2 mode to PM
MODERN.FON	\OS2\MDOS\WINOS2\SYSTEM	WIN-OS2 modern font
PRINTMAN.EXE	\OS2\MDOS\WINOS2	WIN-OS2 Print Manager

continues

File	Directory	Function
PRINTMAN.HLP	\OS2\MDOS\WINOS2	WIN-OS2 Print Manager help
PROGMAN.EXE	\OS2\MDOS\WINOS2	WIN-OS2 Program Manager
PROGMAN.HLP	\OS2\MDOS\WINOS2	WIN-OS2 Program Manager help
PROGMAN.INI	\OS2\MDOS\WINOS2	WIN-OS2 Program Manager initialization file
OS2K286.EXE	\OS2\MDOS\WINOS2\SYSTEM	WIN-OS2 real mode kernel
ROMAN.FON	\OS2\MDOS\WINOS2\SYSTEM	WIN-OS2 Roman fonts
LANGSCA.DLL	\OS2\MDOS\WINOS2\SYSTEM	WIN-OS2 Scandinavian
COMM.DRV	\OS2\MDOS\WINOS2\SYSTEM	WIN-OS2 serial port device driver
SETUP.EXE	\OS2\MDOS\WINOS2	WIN-OS2 setup file
SETUP.HLP	\OS2\MDOS\WINOS2	WIN-OS2 setup file help
SETUP.INF	\OS2\MDOS\WINOS2\SYSTEM	WIN-OS2 setup file information file
WINSHELD.EXE	\OS2\MDOS\WINOS2	WIN-OS2 shield for command prompts
LANGSPA.DLL	\OS2\MDOS\WINOS2\SYSTEM	WIN-OS2 Spanish
SYMBOLF.FON	\OS2\MDOS\WINOS2\SYSTEM	WIN-OS2 symbol font file for 8514 displays
SYMBOLA.FON	\OS2\MDOS\WINOS2\SYSTEM	WIN-OS2 symbol font file for CGA displays
SYMBOLB.FON	\OS2\MDOS\WINOS2\SYSTEM	WIN-OS2 symbol font file for EGA displays
SYMBOLE.FON	\OS2\MDOS\WINOS2\SYSTEM	WIN-OS2 symbol font file for VGA displays
SYMBOLG.FON	\OS2\MDOS\WINOS2\SYSTEM	WIN-OS2 symbol font file for XGA displays
SYSTEM.DRV	\OS2\MDOS\WINOS2\SYSTEM	WIN-OS2 system device driver
SYSTEM.INI	\OS2\MDOS\WINOS2	WIN-OS2 system ini file
WINSMSG.DLL	\OS2\MDOS\WINOS2\SYSTEM	WIN-OS2 system message dynamic link library

File	Directory	Function
TASKMAN.EXE	\OS2\MDOS\WINOS2	WIN-OS2 Task Manager
TMSRF.FON	\OS2\MDOS\WINOS2\SYSTEM	WIN-OS2 Times/Roman font for 8514 displays
TMSRA.FON	\OS2\MDOS\WINOS2\SYSTEM	WIN-OS2 Times/Roman font for CGA displays
TMSRB.FON	\OS2\MDOS\WINOS2\SYSTEM	WIN-OS2 Times/Roman font for EGA displays
TMSRE.FON	\OS2\MDOS\WINOS2\SYSTEM	WIN-OS2 Times/Roman font for VGA displays
TMSRG.FON	\OS2\MDOS\WINOS2\SYSTEM	WIN-OS2 Times/Roman font for XGA displays
TOUCH.DRV	\OS2\MDOS\WINOS2\SYSTEM	WIN-OS2 touch screen file
USER.EXE	\OS2\MDOS\WINOS2\SYSTEM	WIN-OS2 user interface code
OASIS.DLL	\OS2\DLL	Windows compatibility dynamic link library
MIRRORS.DLL	\OS2\DLL	Windows compatibility dynamic link library
WPCONMRI.DLL	\OS2\DLL	Workplace Shell configuration dynamic link library
WPCONFIG.DLL	\OS2\DLL	Workplace Shell configuration dynamic link library
PMWPMRI.DLL	\OS2\DLL	Workplace Shell dynamic link library
WPPWNDRV.DLL	\OS2\DLL	Workplace Shell dynamic link library
PMWP.DLL	\OS2\DLL	Workplace Shell dynamic link library
WPGLOSS.HLP	\OS2\HELP\GLOSS	Workplace Shell glossary help file
WPHELP.HLP	\OS2\HELP	Workplace Shell help file
WPINDEX.HLP	\OS2\HELP	Workplace Shell index help file
WPMSG.HLP	\OS2\HELP	Workplace Shell message help file
WPPRTMRI.DLL	\OS2\DLL	Workplace Shell printable translation support

continues

File	Directory	Function
WPPRINT.DLL	\OS2\DLL	Workplace Shell printing dynamic link library
XGARING0.SYS	\OS2	XGA device driver
XGA.DRV	\OS2\MDOS\WINOS2\SYSTEM	XGA device driver for WIN-OS2
XGA.DLL	\OS2\DLL	XGA display dynamic link library
XGAOEM.FON	\OS2\MDOS\WINOS2\SYSTEM	XGA font for WIN-OS2
XGASYS.FON	\OS2\MDOS\WINOS2\SYSTEM	XGA font for WIN-OS2
XGAFIX.FON	\OS2\MDOS\WINOS2\SYSTEM	XGA font for WIN-OS2

The Default CONFIG.SYS File

I f you use a text editor to make changes to your CONFIG.SYS file, you may make mistakes that will cause your system to no longer function. Chapter 8, "Troubleshooting OS/2," suggests that you make backup copies of your configuration files, including CONFIG.SYS. You may need the information in this appendix, however, to reconstruct a CONFIG.SYS file that you have made several changes to since you last backed up the file. Even if you don't get into trouble by editing your CONFIG.SYS file, you will find the following discussion of the default CONFIG.SYS file interesting. You can refer to this appendix whenever you want to know why a particular entry appears in the file.

The OS/2 installation process creates a CONFIG.SYS file on your computer similar to the file described in this appendix. You may find differences between the entries you see here and the ones in your new CONFIG.SYS file. Options you select during installation and OS/2's detection of the hardware components of your computer can cause OS/2 to create a slightly different CONFIG.SYS file for your PC. Use the information in this appendix as a guide, and compare your own CONFIG.SYS file with the following entries to see where differences exist. You may want to pencil a few notes into the margins of these pages to indicate these differences, for future reference.

```
IFS=C:\OS2\HPFS.IFS  /CACHE:64 /CRECL:4
```

In the preceding entry, *IFS* stands for Installable File System. OS/2 loads High Performance File System support by default each time you boot your PC, even if you didn't choose HPFS during OS/2 installation. OS/2 anticipates that you may want to work with HPFS in the future; you need this entry in your CONFIG.SYS if you want to format a disk partition with HPFS.

```
PROTSHELL=C:\OS2\PMSHELL.EXE
```

The preceding line identifies the main Workplace Shell executable.

```
SET USER_INI=C:\OS2\OS2.INI
SET SYSTEM_INI=C:\OS2\OS2SYS.INI
SET OS2_SHELL=C:\OS2\CMD.EXE
SET RUNWORKPLACE=C:\OS2\PMSHELL.EXE
```

These four SET statements tell the Workplace Shell where to find certain OS/2 components. These components are the initialization files for OS/2, the OS/2 command processor, and the Workplace Shell executable.

```
SET AUTOSTART=PROGRAMS,TASKLIST,FOLDERS
```

The Workplace Shell uses the AUTOSTART environment variable to determine how you want your desktop restored each time you start OS/2.

```
SET COMSPEC=C:\OS2\CMD.EXE
```

The COMSPEC environment variable specifies the location of the OS/2 command processor.

```
LIBPATH=.;C:\OS2\DLL;C:\OS2\MDOS;C:\;C:\OS2\APPS\DLL;
```

LIBPATH indicates to OS/2 where to find Dynamic Link Library (DLL) files. When you install an application comprised partly of DLLs, the application's installation procedure may modify this line of the CONFIG.SYS file. The default, which you see here, calls out the location of OS/2's DLL files.

```
SET PATH=C:\OS2;C:\OS2\SYSTEM;C:\OS2\MDOS\WINOS2; C:\OS2\INSTALL;
  C:\;C:\OS2\MDOS;C:\OS2\APPS;
```

The PATH environment variable names the directories that OS/2 searches to find OS/2 executable files. The PATH statement in your AUTOEXEC.BAT file does the same job for DOS executable files.

```
SET DPATH=C:\OS2;C:\OS2\SYSTEM;C:\OS2\MDOS\WINOS2;
    C:\OS2\INSTALL;C:\;C:\OS2\BITMAP;C:\OS2\MDOS;C:\OS2\APPS;
```

The DPATH environment variable indicates to OS/2 which directories to search for data files (rather than executable files). DPATH works like the DOS APPEND command.

```
SET PROMPT=$i[$p]
```

The default PROMPT for your OS/2 command line sessions indicates the current drive and directory, with the directory encased in brackets.

```
SET HELP=C:\OS2\HELP;C:\OS2\HELP\TUTORIAL;
SET GLOSSARY=C:\OS2\HELP\GLOSS;
```

The HELP and GLOSSARY environment variables tell OS/2 where to find on-line help files and the OS/2 glossary file.

```
PRIORITY_DISK_IO=YES
```

The default setting for PRIORITY_DISK_IO is YES, which means that foreground tasks receive speedier service from OS/2's disk access services.

```
FILES=20
```

The default maximum number of file handles in each DOS session is 20.

```
DEVICE=C:\OS2\TESTCFG.SYS
```

TESTCFG.SYS is a system configuration device driver.

```
DEVICE=C:\OS2\DOS.SYS
```

DOS.SYS is one of the OS/2 components that enables DOS sessions.

```
DEVICE=C:\OS2\PMDD.SYS
```

This device driver provides pointer drawing support in OS/2 sessions.

```
BUFFERS=30
```

The BUFFERS statement default is 30 sector buffers.

```
IOPL=YES
```

OS/2's default for allowing applications access to the PC's I/O port hardware is YES.

DISKCACHE=384,LW

The default disk cache is 384K, with Lazy Writing turned on.

MAXWAIT=3

The default value for MAXWAIT is 3.

MEMMAN=SWAP,PROTECT

OS/2 by default allows memory swapping to disk and provides protected memory to Dynamic Link Libraries.

SWAPPATH=C:\OS2\SYSTEM 2048 4096

OS/2 places the SWAPPER.DAT file in C:\OS2\SYSTEM. OS/2's default MINFREE value does not permit the SWAPPER.DAT file to leave less than 2048K (2M) of free disk space. Depending on the physical memory in your computer, OS/2 creates an initial 4096K (4M) SWAPPER.DAT file each time you boot OS/2.

BREAK=OFF

This DOS-related setting by default turns off the extra processing (in DOS sessions) for Ctrl-Break checking.

THREADS=256

The OS/2 default is 256 maximum threads.

PRINTMONBUFSIZE=134,134,134

OS/2's print buffers for LPT1, LPT2, and LPT3 is 134 characters each.

COUNTRY=001,C:\OS2\SYSTEM\COUNTRY.SYS

COUNTRY expresses the choice of country you made during installation.

SET KEYS=ON

The KEYS environment variable by default enables OS/2's command history recall feature in OS/2 command line sessions.

REM SET DELDIR=C:\DELETE,512;

OS/2 installation creates a DELDIR entry in the CONFIG.SYS file, but disables the entry by prefixing it with REM. You must remove the REM from the beginning of the line to enable undeletion of files.

```
BASEDEV=PRINT01.SYS
BASEDEV=IBM1FLPY.ADD
BASEDEV=IBM1S506.ADD
BASEDEV=OS2DASD.DMD
```

The preceding four device drivers manage OS/2 access to the printer ports, floppy disk drive, and hard disk drive.

```
SET BOOKSHELF=C:\OS2\BOOK
SET EPMPATH=C:\OS2\APPS
```

The BOOKSHELF and EPMPATH environment variables are OS/2's way of remembering where certain help files and Enhanced Editor files are located.

```
PROTECTONLY=NO
```

OS/2's default for PROTECTONLY allows DOS sessions.

```
SHELL=C:\OS2\MDOS\COMMAND.COM C:\OS2\MDOS /P
```

SHELL indicates the location of the DOS command processor.

```
FCBS=16,8
```

OS/2 provides by default 16 File Control Blocks in each DOS session. Eight of these FCBs are protected, which means OS/2 never closes and reuses FCBs in a way that leaves fewer than eight available. If you changed FCB values during installation, this setting reflects your choices.

```
RMSIZE=640
```

The default size of each DOS sessions is 640K.

```
DEVICE=C:\OS2\MDOS\VEMM.SYS
```

VEMM.SYS is a memory manager for DOS sessions.

```
DOS=LOW,NOUMB
```

OS/2 defaults to loading DOS into conventional (low) memory rather than upper (high) memory. OS/2 also defaults to not making DOS a provider of upper memory blocks.

```
DEVICE=C:\OS2\MDOS\VDPX.SYS
DEVICE=C:\OS2\MDOS\VXMS.SYS /UMB
DEVICE=C:\OS2\MDOS\VDPMI.SYS
```

These three device drivers are memory managers for DOS sessions. By default, VXMS is an upper memory block provider.

```
DEVICE=C:\OS2\MDOS\VWIN.SYS
```

The VWIN device driver helps manage WIN-OS2 sessions.

```
DEVICE=C:\OS2\MDOS\VCDROM.SYS
```

VCDROM.SYS provides CD-ROM support in DOS sessions.

```
DEVICE=C:\OS2\MDOS\VMOUSE.SYS
DEVICE=C:\OS2\POINTDD.SYS
DEVICE=C:\OS2\MOUSE.SYS
```

The preceding three device drivers provide mouse support. In particular, VMOUSE provides mouse support in DOS sessions.

```
DEVICE=C:\OS2\COM.SYS
DEVICE=C:\OS2\MDOS\VCOM.SYS
```

These two device drivers manage your serial (COM) ports.

```
CODEPAGE=437,850
DEVINFO=KBD,US,C:\OS2\KEYBOARD.DCP
```

The preceding two statements reflected your choice of country and national language.

```
DEVICE=C:\OS2\MDOS\VVGA.SYS
SET VIDEO_DEVICES=VIO_VGA
SET VIO_VGA=DEVICE(BVHVGA)
DEVINFO=SCR,VGA,C:\OS2\VIOTBL.DCP
```

These four statements provide display (video) management.

Programming with REXX

I n Chapter 18, "Batch File Programming with OS/2," you learned to create your own DOS and OS/2 commands by building on the operating system's existing commands. To write a batch file program, you create a text file with a text editor; each line of the text file runs a built-in command or computer program, just as if you had typed the command name or program name at a command line prompt. A batch file program is a named collection of commands and programs in a text file that has an extension of BAT or CMD. You run the collection of commands and programs by typing the name of the batch file at a DOS command line prompt (for BAT files) or at an OS/2 command line prompt (for CMD files). OS/2 (or the DOS within OS/2) then executes each of the lines in the batch file program. You also found in Chapter 18 how to turn a batch file program into a program object that you could store in a folder or leave on your desktop.

When you master writing batch file programs, you have much more control over your computer. You can use batch file programs to customize your use of operating system commands, application programs, and utility programs. Batch file programs don't offer a great deal of flexibility, however. Your batch file program can execute different commands or programs depending on whether a file exists, but a batch file program cannot prompt the person running the program for information. The batch file program also cannot perform calculations. The next logical step beyond simple batch file programs is REXX, which does provide these capabilities (and more). REXX allows you to embed programming language statements in your batch file programs, along with OS/2 commands and utilities. REXX programming is only slightly more complicated than batch file programming.

In this appendix, you learn how to extend the usefulness of your batch file programs with REXX. You first explore the basics of REXX programs. You learn how to use *variables* (data fields whose values you can modify), and you discover how to display information from within a REXX program. Next, this appendix discusses the several ways you can control the *flow of your program*—the order in which REXX executes the program statements you write. You learn how to compute results and how to manage *strings* (variables, such as a name or address, that contain textual information). You learn how to build REXX programs that accept parameters. This appendix concludes with a discussion of how you can exercise your REXX programs in a test environment to make sure that the programs behave exactly as they should. If you plan to try out some or all the example REXX programs in this appendix, you may want to read the last section, "Testing REXX Programs," before you type the examples into your computer.

Understanding REXX Basics

A REXX program is an OS/2 batch file with special capabilities. You write a REXX program by using a text editor to create a text file with an extension of CMD, and you make the first line a REXX comment line. A REXX comment starts with the two characters /* and ends with the two characters */.

 NOTE The first line of a REXX program *must* contain /*   */. If the REXX comment line is the second line of the text file (perhaps you left the first line blank), OS/2 will not treat the file as a REXX program.

You need to install REXX support before you can run your REXX programs. If you did not choose the REXX option during the installation process, you should now use Chapter 7, "Modifying Your OS/2 Configuration," to selectively install REXX support. You also should install the on-line documentation for REXX.

Mike Cowlishaw, who works for IBM, designed REXX. He had the help of over 300 other IBM people as he refined the REXX language. REXX is implemented in many types of IBM computing environments, from mainframes to PCs. Chapter 9, "Using Your Computer Screen as a Desktop," introduced you to IBM's System Application Architecture (SAA) standard. REXX is a part of the SAA standard.

T I P

If you would like more information about REXX than what this appendix provides, get Mike Cowlishaw's book *A Practical Approach to Programming REXX*, published by Prentice Hall. IBM also offers entire books and technical references on REXX. Two of the IBM books are the *OS/2 Procedures Language 2/REXX Reference* and the *REXX User's Guide*. Additionally, you can read the REXX on-line documentation that is part of OS/2. This appendix explains how to use the most popular features of REXX, but you will need a separate reference if you find yourself writing serious REXX programs. REXX is a full-featured, complete programming language.

Most REXX implementations, including the one in OS/2, interpret your REXX program statements immediately rather than compiling and linking the program statements into an executable file. The interpreted nature of REXX allows you to use a text editor to create a REXX program, save your file, and immediately run your program at an OS/2 command line prompt. You can conveniently develop, test, and run your REXX programs right on your desktop by opening a text editor window (perhaps the OS/2 System Editor or the OS/2 Enhanced Editor, both discussed in Chapter 14, "Using the OS/2 Text Editors") alongside an OS/2 windowed session. The OS/2 text editors are located in the Productivity folder, while the OS/2 windowed session is an icon in the Command Prompts folder. Figure G.1 shows one way you might configure your desktop to facilitate REXX program development.

REXX works by reading your text file, interpreting the lines of text, and performing whatever operations you specify. The OS/2 command line processor, CMD.EXE, knows to invoke the REXX interpreter because the first line of the text file is a REXX comment (the /*   */ discussed earlier). The OS/2 command line processor treats a text file with an extension of CMD as a normal batch file program unless the first line of the file is a REXX comment.

Your REXX program can execute REXX program statements, OS/2 commands, and OS/2 applications. This appendix explains the REXX program statements from which you can construct REXX programs. REXX program statements let you interactively get responses from the person who runs your REXX program, display information to that person, perform calculations, and do other information-processing steps.

Using the System Editor and a windowed OS/2 session to create REXX programs.

VREXX

Batch file programs and REXX programs operate through the OS/2 command line interface, which means that these programs cannot take advantage of Presentation Manager features such as windows, dialog boxes, and pushbuttons. However, IBM offers a companion product, called VREXX, that you can use to give your REXX programs a PM interface. VREXX—Visual REXX for OS/2 Presentation Manager—consists of a library of OS/2 2.1 REXX functions. You give your REXX programs a PM interface with VREXX, but you do not have to be an expert in Presentation Manager programming to use VREXX. You simply incorporate VREXX functions within the REXX programs you write.

VREXX includes functions for creating windows, drawing graphics, displaying text in multiple fonts, and displaying dialog boxes. The dialog boxes that VREXX supplies let you perform filename selection, font and color selection, string input, and message display. VREXX also gives you dialog boxes you can use to present and select options through list boxes, tables, radio buttons, and check boxes.

VREXX has on-line help and comes with sample REXX programs that show how easily you can add windows and dialog boxes to your REXX programs. You can find VREXX on many bulletin boards and information services as file VREXX2.ZIP.

Displaying Information with REXX

You use the REXX statement SAY to display information to someone running your REXX program. The following example is a REXX program that displays the prompt "Please enter the age of the computer: " on-screen.

```
/* This first line, a REXX comment, makes this a REXX program. */
SAY "Please enter the age of your computer: "
```

The preceding example displays a prompt and then exits back to the OS/2 command line. The next section explains how you can expand this example to obtain a response to the prompt from the person who runs your REXX program.

The SAY REXX command can display the value of a variable as well as the contents of a quoted text string. You learn about variables and other uses of the SAY command in upcoming sections of this appendix.

Using the PULL and PARSE PULL Commands

When you need the person running your program to type a response to a prompt so that your program can know and operate on the response, you use a PULL command. PULL gathers a line of typed characters, ending with a press of the Enter key, and stores the response in a variable. The following example asks the person running your REXX program to enter the age of his or her computer and then stores the response in a variable named *age*.

```
/* This first line, a REXX comment, makes this a REXX program. */
/* This example prompts for the age of the computer and stores */
/* the answer in a variable named age. */
SAY "Please enter the age of your computer: "
PULL age
```

The PULL command converts the person's keyboard response to uppercase. If you want PULL to store both upper- and lowercase strings in a variable, use PARSE PULL.

Defining Variables in REXX

A variable is a data field, or symbol, containing a piece of information. The information in the variable might be a number or a text string. You use variables in your REXX programs to hold numbers or text strings, and you refer to the number or the text string by using the name of the variable. You can PULL or PARSE PULL information into a variable, you can SAY the value of a variable, and you can store calculated results in a variable.

A variable can hold different numbers or different text strings at different times while your REXX program executes. The following example assigns the numeric value 0.06 to the variable *TaxRate* and the numeric value 4700.00 to the variable named *Price*. The example calculates the sales tax based on the price and stores the sales tax amount in a variable named *SalesTax*. The example then calculates the total price, re-using the *Price* variable, and displays the result as the number 4982.0000.

```
/* This first line, a REXX comment, makes this a REXX program. */
/* This example calculates a sales tax amount, using a tax rate */
/* of 6%. */
TaxRate = 0.06
Price = 4700.00
SalesTax = Price * TaxRate
Price = Price + SalesTax
SAY "Including tax, the price is " Price
```

When you name a variable, you should use names that suggest the meaning of the data contained in the variable. You can use names such as *A*, *B*, *X*, *Y*, and *Z*, but your program will be difficult to understand in the future. Someday you will find it necessary to add enhancements to your programs, and you will want the names you use in the program to immediately suggest what the program currently does. You will then be able to change the program with some confidence. Computer programming isn't easy, but you can give yourself significant help by using meaningful variable names.

When REXX interprets and processes your program statements, REXX (which is actually a computer program) tests each word in the program text file to know which words are your variable names. When REXX identifies your variables, it follows certain rules. The following rules dictate a variable name:

- The variable name should begin with a letter.

- The variable name cannot be the same as a REXX command (such as SAY).

■ The variable name can contain a mixture of letters and numbers.

■ The variable name can contain both upper- and lowercase letters.

■ The variable name can contain special characters (such as the underscore ("_") character) that have no meaning to OS/2.

■ The variable name can be up to 50 characters long.

These rules imply that names such as 123PROG, TEST<ONE, PROG&DATA, and PULL are invalid variable names. 123PROG begins with a number, TEST<ONE and PROG&DATA contain special characters that OS/2's command processor uses, and PULL is a verb in the REXX language. The variable names SalesTax, SALESTAX, AmountCalculatedSoFar, PointsPerGame, and Lotus123 are all valid variable names, however.

The value contained in a variable is distinct from the variable's name. It's certainly valid for a variable to contain the strings *123PROG*, *TEST<ONE*, *PROG&DATA*, or *PULL*. Also note that the value of a variable before you store anything in that variable is the name of the variable itself.

REXX has three pre-defined variables. They are RC, RESULT, and SIGL. The RC variable is similar to ERRORLEVEL, which you learned about in Chapter 18. RC contains the return code (exit code) of the most recently executed OS/2 command or computer program. RESULT contains a value set by a RETURN statement; you can use a RETURN statement to exit a REXX program that you have CALLed from another REXX program. (The REXX CALL statement works much like the batch file program CALL you learned about in Chapter 18.) The RETURN statement allows you to communicate a value from the subprogram to the main (calling) REXX program. The SIGL variable contains the line number of the REXX program statement that caused the most recent jump to a label when an error occurs and you have used a SIGNAL statement to handle the error. (Until you become more experienced at writing REXX programs, you may want to skip using SIGNAL and SIGL. The on-line documentation for REXX explains error handling and will help you determine if and when you might want to use SIGNAL and SIGL.)

Controlling Program Flow

REXX program statements execute sequentially, from the top of your REXX program to the bottom, unless you specify otherwise. You can control the flow of execution within your program with IF...THEN...ELSE statements, with SELECT statements, and with several forms of the DO statement.

You use an IF statement to determine whether the value of a variable or an expression has a certain relationship to another variable or expression. If the relationship (the test condition) you express is true, REXX executes the statement after THEN but before an ELSE. If the relationship is not true, REXX executes the statement after the ELSE. ELSE is optional, however; if you don't specify an ELSE statement and the relationship is not true, REXX resumes execution at the next statement following the IF.

As with many computer programming situations, the formal definition of what happens is more complicated than actually using an IF...THEN...ELSE. The following example, which shows how simple an IF...THEN...ELSE really is, sets the variable TaxRate to 0.08 if the variable named State contains the two-character string "NY" and sets TaxRate to 0.06 for any other State value:

```
/* This first line, a REXX comment, makes this a REXX program. */
IF State = 'NY' THEN
   TaxRate = 0.08
ELSE
   TaxRate = 0.06
```

Note that the ELSE clause is optional. The simplest form of the IF...THEN...ELSE statement is the following:

```
/* This first line, a REXX comment, makes this a REXX program. */
IF Computer = 'PC' THEN
   OperatingSystem = 'OS/2'
```

Perhaps the following syntax specifications for IF...THEN and IF...THEN...ELSE statements will help clarify what happens when REXX executes an IF:

> IF <condition> THEN <statement>

> IF <condition> THEN <statement> ELSE <statement>

As your REXX programs get more complex, you will want to perform two or more tests in the <condition> portion of the IF statement. You can express *and* and *or* relationships with the & and ¦ operators in REXX. The following example sets TaxRate to 0.06 for all states but New York, 0.08 for all parts of New York except New York City, and 0.09 for New York City:

```
/* This first line, a REXX comment, makes this a REXX program. */
IF State = 'NY' & City = 'New York City' THEN
   TaxRate = 0.09
ELSE
```

```
IF State = 'NY' THEN
    TaxRate = 0.08
ELSE
    TaxRate = 0.06
```

You will often want REXX to execute more than one statement as the result of your IF...THEN...ELSE test. You can encapsulate multiple statements with DO and END. REXX treats the statements between DO and END as a single statement. The following example uses DO and END to set the variable LongNames to the string "TRUE" and the variable Speed to "FAST", depending on a person's affirmative response to the question of whether a disk partition has been formatted with OS/2's High Performance File System:

```
/* This first line, a REXX comment, makes this a REXX program. */
SAY "Is the disk partition HPFS-based?"
PULL Answer
IF Answer = 'YES' ¦ ANSWER = 'Y' THEN
    DO
    LongNames = 'TRUE'
    Speed = 'FAST'
    END
```

Several IF statements can follow one another when you want to determine the particular value of a variable, as the next example shows:

```
/* This first line, a REXX comment, makes this a REXX program. */
SAY 'Program Run Menu: 1)Lotus 123      2)Excel/PM      3)Quattro Pro'
PULL Response
IF Response = '1' THEN
    DO
    SAY 'You picked menu option 1'
    123
    END
ELSE IF Response = '2' THEN
    DO
    SAY 'You picked menu option 2'
    EXCEL
    END
ELSE
    DO
    SAY 'You must have picked menu option 3'
    QPRO
    END
```

The preceding example displays a simple menu prompt with SAY, PULLs your typed answer into the Response variable, and then uses a series of IF statements to determine what you have typed. If the menu offers many choices, the series of IF statements becomes quite long. At your discretion, based on how understandable and readable you feel the IF statements are, you might want to instead use a SELECT statement. The following example is exactly equivalent to the preceding example:

```
/* This first line, a REXX comment, makes this a REXX program. */
SAY 'Program Run Menu: 1)Lotus 123      2)Excel/PM      3)Quattro Pro'
PULL Response
SELECT
  WHEN Response = '1' THEN
    DO
    SAY 'You picked menu option 1'
    123
    END
  WHEN Response = '2' THEN
    DO
    SAY 'You picked menu option 2'
    EXCEL
    END
  OTHERWISE
    SAY 'You must have picked menu option 3'
    QPRO
END
```

NOTE The menu prompt example REXX program reveals that you can execute OS/2 commands and run computer programs from within a REXX program. The menu prompt example runs 123.EXE, EXCEL.EXE, or QPRO.EXE depending on your response to the PULL statement. In fact, if you make a typing error in your program and ask REXX to do something it doesn't understand, REXX assumes that you mean to execute a command or program and gives your typing error to the OS/2 command processor CMD.EXE to handle. When CMD.EXE cannot understand what you want it to do, OS/2 displays the following error message:

```
"The name specified is not recognized as an internal
or external command, operable program or batch
file."
```

In addition to using IF statements to control the flow of execution of your program, you can use *repetitive* and *conditional* loops in REXX. A repetitive loop executes the statements within the loop a certain number of times (or forever, if you choose). A conditional loop executes the statements within the loop while or until a relationship is true.

To make one or more statements execute a certain number of times in REXX, you use DO <number>. The following example displays "ERROR!" on the screen five times:

```
/* This first line, a REXX comment, makes this a REXX program. */
DO 5
    SAY 'ERROR!'
    END
```

You can make a set of statements execute without stopping by using the word FOREVER in place of a number (DO FOREVER). Such a program is less than useful, however. To cause an infinite loop of statements in a DO FOREVER to stop, you can press Ctrl and Break on the keyboard (this halts the REXX program completely) or you can use a LEAVE statement at an appropriate point inside the loop. The following example shows how you might use DO FOREVER and LEAVE to ensure that a person has typed a correct response to a prompt; the example loops until the person enters a Y or an N:

```
/* This first line, a REXX comment, makes this a REXX program. */
DO FOREVER
    SAY 'Log on to the network? (Y/N)==> '
    PULL Response
    IF Response = 'Y' ¦ Response = 'N' THEN LEAVE
    SAY 'Invalid response! Try again.'
    END
```

You can use a variable in your REXX program to count the number of times through a loop. The variable's value increments for each iteration of the loop, starting with an initial value you specify. The syntax of this form of repetitive loop is as follows:

```
DO <variable> = <start value> TO <stop value>
<statements>
END
```

In a counted loop, REXX first sets the variable to <start value>. Then REXX evaluates the variable in the following manner:

1. If the variable's value is the same as the <stop value>, leave the loop.

2. Perform the statements within the counted loop.

3. Increment the variable and go back to step 1.

The following example illustrates a counted loop that creates five directories named TMP1 through TMP5. Note that there is no space (blank) between the string "TMP" and *DirectoryNumber* (the name of the variable).

```
/* A REXX program that creates five directories */
DO DirectoryNumber = 1 TO 5
MKDIR "TMP"DirectoryNumber
END
```

The REXX statements you use to perform conditional loops are DO <statements> WHILE <condition> and DO <statements> UNTIL <condition>. DO...WHILE and DO...UNTIL behave like the DO...FOREVER you explored earlier, but you can express the condition that you used to determine when to LEAVE the loop without having to use a separate IF statement and LEAVE statement. Use the DO...WHILE form of conditional loop when possible; in some cases, you do not need to execute the loop at all. Use the DO...UNTIL form to ensure that the statements within the loop execute at least once.

Computing Results with REXX

You can perform calculations inside your REXX programs. When you assign a value to a variable, you can express the value to be assigned as the result of a computation. You can use simple arithmetic operators, such as + (addition), − (subtraction), * (multiplication), and / (division), and you can use the math functions built into REXX. (The REXX on-line documentation lists the built-in math functions.) If you use a combination of the arithmetic operators, REXX evaluates the multiplication and division operations first, then the addition and subtraction. You also can use parentheses to make REXX calculate results in a particular order.

The following example calculates sales tax at the rate of 6%, applies a discount of 25%, and stores the total price in the variable named TotalPrice:

```
/* This first line, a REXX comment, makes this a REXX program. */
TaxRate = 0.06
Discount = 0.25
SAY 'Enter the price of the item==>'
PULL Price
/* calculate sales tax before applying any discounts */
TotalPrice = Price + (Price * TaxRate)
/* now apply the discount */
TotalPrice = TotalPrice - (TotalPrice * Discount)
SAY 'The total price is ' TotalPrice
```

Working with Strings in REXX

In REXX, a string is a group of characters contained within a variable, within single quotation marks ('), or within double quotation marks ("). When you need to use a single quotation mark inside a string, you can enclose the string with double quotation marks. To use a double quotation mark inside a string, enclose the string in single quotation marks. The following two examples show how to embed quotation marks inside a string:

```
SAY "The file couldn't be opened"

SAY 'The file "SCRIPT.DOC" has been processed'
```

REXX includes several built-in functions to help you manipulate text strings. You can make one big string from two smaller strings (a process known as *concatenation*); you can translate lowercase strings to uppercase, you can make a smaller string by extracting part of a big string (that is, obtain a substring); you can determine the number of characters in a string; you can find a substring within a larger string; and you can remove leading and trailing spaces from a string. The following examples clarify how these string manipulation functions work.

To combine two or more smaller strings to form one large string, type two string variable names one after the other. The same procedure applies if one or the other string is enclosed in quotation marks. REXX treats the *abutted* strings as one large string, and by default REXX inserts a blank between the string components. You can use the || string concatenation operator to eliminate the default blank that REXX would otherwise insert. The next example displays the string "Barry Nance" on-screen. Note the blank automatically inserted by REXX between the FirstName and LastName strings.

```
/* A sample REXX program */
FirstName = "Barry"
LastName = "Nance"
Name = FirstName LastName
SAY Name
```

Here is a second string-handling example to show how you can override REXX's default insertion of spaces during the concatenation of strings. The example also displays the string "Barry Nance" on-screen, but the program explicitly inserts the space by using a variable named Blank. The program uses the || operator to force REXX to use the strings exactly as specified, without inserting extra spaces.

```
/* A sample REXX program */
Blank = " "
FirstName = "Barry"
LastName = "Nance"
Name = FirstName ¦¦ Blank ¦¦ LastName
SAY Name
```

TRANSLATE is a REXX function which returns a string value. You use a function in REXX almost the same way you use a variable, but the function performs some processing as the function takes on a value. In the case of TRANSLATE, you give the TRANSLATE function a string as an argument and TRANSLATE returns a copy of the string with all the characters in the string converted to uppercase. The following example demonstrates how you can ensure that a string contains only uppercase characters. The example converts the string "New York" to "NEW YORK".

```
/* A sample REXX program */
StateName = 'New York'
StateName = TRANSLATE(StateName)
SAY 'After uppercase conversion, the StateName variable
     now contains ' StateName
```

SUBSTR is another useful REXX function. SUBSTR returns a portion of a string; you supply three arguments to SUBSTR to tell the function the string from which you want to extract a substring, the starting position of the substring, and the ending position of the substring. The following example extracts the substring "Barry" from the string "Barry Nance" and displays the substring.

```
/* A sample REXX program */
Name = 'Barry Nance'
StartPosition = 1
EndPosition = 5
FirstName = substr(Name, StartPosition, EndPosition)
SAY 'The substring is ' FirstName
```

If you omit the third argument to SUBSTR, the function returns a substring that begins at the starting position and extends through the end of the string.

The LEFT and RIGHT functions operate in a manner similar to SUBSTR. LEFT returns the leftmost portion of a string and RIGHT returns the rightmost portion. You specify the number of characters. The following example assigns "Barry" to the FirstName variable and "Nance" to the LastName variable:

```
/* A sample REXX program */
Name = 'Barry Nance'
FirstName = LEFT(Name, 5)
```

```
LastName = RIGHT(Name, 5)
SAY 'First Name is ' FirstName
SAY 'Last Name is ' LastName
```

You can use the LENGTH function when your program needs to know the number of characters in a string. LENGTH requires a single argument, the string whose length you want to determine. The REXX program statement `NumberOfChars = LENGTH('New York City')`, for example, sets the variable *NumberOfChars* to a value of 13. Note that spaces (blanks) count as characters.

When you want to know the number of discrete words in a string, use the WORDS function. WORDS requires a single string argument and returns a numeric value. The REXX program statement SAY `WORDS('11711 North College Avenue')` displays the number 4 on-screen. POS is another useful REXX function when you're dealing with string variables. You supply POS with two arguments, a substring to search for and a string that might contain the substring. If POS finds the substring within the second argument, POS returns the starting position of the substring. POS returns the value 0 (zero) if the string doesn't contain the substring you specify. For example, the REXX program statement SAY `POS('City', 'New York City')` displays the number 10 on-screen. The REXX function LASTPOS is similar to POS, except that LASTPOS returns the location in the string of the last occurrence of the specified substring.

The last string function this appendix discusses, but certainly not the last string function offered by REXX, is STRIP. When you want a copy of a string without leading or trailing spaces, you use the STRIP function. STRIP examines its single string argument and returns that argument with leading and trailing spaces removed. The REXX program statement SAY `STRIP('    This string begins and ends with spaces ')` displays `This string begins and ends with spaces` on-screen.

Reading and Writing Files in REXX

Your REXX programs can process information in text files on your hard disk in addition to strings you PULL from the keyboard. The LINEIN function requires a single argument consisting of the name of a disk file. LINEIN returns a string that is the next line of text from the file. Executing LINEIN repeatedly reads all the text lines in a file. Suppose that you have a file named PC.TXT whose contents are the following lines of text:

```
IBM PS/2 model 57
IBM PS/2 model 60
IBM PS/2 model 70
IBM PS/2 model 90
```

The first execution of LINEIN(PC.TXT) returns the string IBM PS/2 model 57. The second execution returns IBM PS/2 model 60. The third execution returns the third line of the file, IBM PS/2 model 70. The fourth execution of LINEIN(PC.TXT) returns the string IBM PS/2 model 90.

Your REXX programs can use the function LINES to know whether your program has more lines of text to read from a file. Like LINEIN, LINES requires a single argument consisting of the name of a disk file. LINES returns the numeric value 1 if more unread text lines exist in a file. LINES returns 0 if there are no more lines of text to be read. The following example uses the LINES and LINEIN functions to read every line of text in your CONFIG.SYS file and display the lines on-screen.

```
/* A sample REXX program */
FileName = 'C:\CONFIG.SYS'
DO WHILE LINES(FileName) <> 0
   Line = LINEIN(FileName)
   SAY Line
   END
```

The LINEOUT function writes string values to a text file you name. Each string value that LINEOUT places in the disk file becomes a line of text. LINEOUT requires two arguments, the name of the file and the string value to be written. If the file does not exist, LINEOUT creates a new file for you. If the file exists already, LINEOUT inserts your string values as lines of text at the end of the current file. LINEOUT returns the numeric value 0 if the write operation is successful. LINEOUT returns 1 if something went wrong. If LINEOUT returns a value of 1 as your program executes, it almost always means that the disk is full, or the first argument is not a valid OS/2 file name.

The following example copies the contents of your CONFIG.SYS file to a file named CONFIG.SAV:

```
/* A sample REXX program */
FileIn = 'C:\CONFIG.SYS'
FileOut = 'C:\CONFIG.SAV'
DO WHILE LINES(FileIn) <> 0
   Line = LINEIN(FileIn)
   Status = LINEOUT(FileOut, Line)
   IF Status = 1 THEN DO
```

```
      SAY 'Copy operation ended in error.'
      LEAVE
      END
  END
```

Passing Parameters to REXX Programs

Chapter 18, "Batch File Programming with OS/2," explained how you can use the variable markers %1 through %9 to retrieve and process individual command line parameters supplied by someone running your batch file program. REXX programs can similarly retrieve and process command line parameters with the ARG statement. You specify with the ARG statement the names of the variables to receive the individual command line parameters. Suppose that you have a REXX program named PARMTEST.CMD containing the statement ARG Parm1 Parm2 Parm3 and you run your REXX program by typing, at an OS/2 command line prompt, **PARMTEST IBM COMPAQ Compudyne**. The ARG statement stores the string 'IBM' in the Parm1 variable, 'COMPAQ' in the Parm2 variable, and 'COMPUDYNE' in the Parm3 variable. The following example REXX program simply displays any command line parameters supplied to the program:

```
/* A sample REXX program */
ARG CommandLine
SAY CommandLine
```

The ARG statement translates command line parameters to uppercase before storing the parameters in the variable you specify. You can use PARSE ARG when you want to retain the original lowercase or uppercase values of the command line parameters. When you need to know whether the person running your REXX program has supplied any parameters at all, you can use the ARG function (which is different and distinct from the ARG statement), as the following example illustrates by EXITing when run with no command line parameters:

```
/* A sample REXX program */
IF ARG() = 0 THEN DO
   SAY 'You forgot to enter the command line parameters.'
   EXIT
   END
ARG Parm1 Parm2
SAY 'The first parameter is ' Parm1
SAY 'The second parameter is ' Parm2
```

When you need to know the number of parameters supplied to a REXX program, you can use the following example REXX statements:

```
/* A sample REXX program */
ARG CommandLine
NumberOfParms = WORDS(CommandLine)
SAY 'You typed ' NumberofParms ' parameters.'
```

Testing REXX Programs

OS/2 gives you three tools to help you develop your REXX programs. Two of the tools are computer programs, PMREXX and REXXTRY, that you can use to help better understand REXX. The third tool is a trace facility you can use in your REXX programs.

PMREXX is a Presentation Manager program that runs REXX programs in a PM window on the OS/2 desktop. When you use PMREXX, the information displayed by the REXX program appears in a scrollable PM window. You can use the vertical scroll bar at the right side of the window to browse back through previously displayed output. PMREXX allows you to select a font in which the output appears, and you can perform Cut/Copy/Paste operations on the information displayed in the PMREXX window. You invoke PMREXX by opening an OS/2 full screen command line prompt and typing PMREXX followed by the name of your REXX program and any command line parameters your REXX program needs. The following example runs the REXX program REXXTEST.CMD in a PM window; REXXTEST.CMD has two command line parameters (Parm1 and Parm2) to process:

```
PMREXX REXXTEST.CMD Parm1 Parm2
```

Optionally, you can start PMREXX with a /TRACE parameter that turns on interactive tracing of your REXX program. An upcoming section of this appendix discusses tracing. To start PMREXX in TRACE mode, type **/T** before typing the name of the REXX program (for example, **PMREXX /T REXXTEST.CMD Parm1 Parm2**).

When you run your REXX program inside PMREXX, you can use PMREXX's menus to control the execution of your program. The following table shows the PMREXX menu options:

Menu choice	Description
File	Save, Save As, and Exit
Edit	Copy, Paste, Clear window display, and Select All lines

Menu choice	Description
Options	Restart the process, Interactive Trace, and Set font
Actions	Halt procedure, Trace next clause, Redo last clause, and Set Trace off
Help	Help index, General help, Keys help, and Using help

REXXTRY is actually a REXX program. As with other REXX programs, you can run REXXTRY in an OS/2 full-screen session, an OS/2 windowed session, or inside PMREXX. REXXTRY lets you try out different REXX statements and observe the results. You interactively enter REXX statements at the REXXTRY prompt and REXXTRY executes your statements, one by one. You can quickly experiment with REXX and become quite familiar with REXX by running REXXTRY inside the friendly PMREXX environment.

The REXX TRACE facility allows you to watch how REXX evaluates expressions. While your REXX program executes, TRACE displays information that explains how REXX is interpreting your program. You can insert TRACE statements in your program in one of three formats: TRACE ?, TRACE <number>, or TRACE <action>. Issuing a TRACE ? statement toggles tracing off or on. Using TRACE <number> (TRACE 5, for example) causes REXX to skip over the specified number of debugging pauses that TRACE would normally do. The TRACE <action> format of the TRACE statement lets you indicate what you want TRACE to monitor. The following table lists the actions you can use in the TRACE <action> statement.

Action	What REXX displays
All	All statements before execution
Commands	Each OS/2 command or utility before execution
Error	OS/2 commands with non-zero return codes
Failure	OS/2 commands that fail (same as the Normal option)
Intermediates	Intermediate results during evaluation of expressions
Labels	Labels encountered during execution
Normal	OS/2 commands that fail (default action)
Off	Nothing; tracing is turned off
Results	All statements before execution; REXX displays final results of each expression evaluation

Summary

Sometimes, when you want your computer to process information in
a way that your existing applications do not provide for, you can
use REXX to "do it yourself." REXX is simple to use, and a few REXX
program statements can do quite a bit of work. Computer programming
is generally tedious and error prone; you need to have patience if you
expect to write working, useful software. However, REXX lets you develop programs quickly and productively. This appendix has shown
you the REXX building blocks you can use to create your own software.

Symbols

A

M

P

T

W

X–Y–Z

Workplace Shell Keyboard Shortcuts*

Keystroke	Function
Alt-Esc	Switch to the next open window or full-screen session
Alt-Home	Switch a DOS program between window and full screen
Ctrl-Alt-Del	Restart the operating system (Shutdown is preferred)
Ctrl-Esc	Display the Window List
F1	Display help for active window
F5	Refresh contents of the active window
F6	Move cursor from one window pane to another in a split window
F10	Move the cursor to or from the menu bar
Alt-F4	Close the active window
Alt-F5	Restore window to previous size
Alt-F6	Move cursor between associated windows
Alt-F7	Move the active window or selected object
Alt-F8	Size the active window or selected object
Alt-F9	Minimize window
Alt-F10	Maximize window
Shift-Esc or Alt-Space bar	Switch to or from the title-bar icon
Shift-F8	Start or stop selecting more than one object
Shift-F10	Display pop-up menu for the active object

For complete coverage of the Workplace Shell refer to Chapters 9 and 10.

Quick Command Reference*

The following commands help you work with your files:

ATTRIB	Shows or changes a file's read-only and archive attributes
BACKUP	Backs up a hard disk to floppy disks
COMP	Compares files
COPY	Copies or combines files
DEL	Erases files
EAUTIL	Splits and joins extended file attributes
ERASE	Erases files
FIND	Searches for text in files
MORE	Displays a file one screen at a time
MOVE	Moves files from one directory to another on the same drive
PRINT	Prints files, or cancels printing
RECOVER	Partially salvages files from a disk with bad sectors
RENAME	Changes a file's name
REPLACE	Selectively copies files
RESTORE	Retrieves files from a backup
SORT	Sorts the lines in a text file, in alphabetical order
TYPE	Displays a file on-screen
UNPACK	Restores compressed files on the OS/2 distribution floppy disks to a form you can use
VERIFY	Checks that data is written to a disk
XCOPY	Copies directories or groups of files